THE
CAMBRIDGE
ECONOMIC HISTORY

GENERAL EDITORS: M. POSTAN, Professor of Economic History
in the University of Cambridge, and H. J. HABAKKUK, Chichele
Professor of Economic History in the University of Oxford

VOLUME II

THE
CAMBRIDGE
ECONOMIC HISTORY
OF EUROPE

PLANNED BY
THE LATE SIR JOHN CLAPHAM
AND THE LATE EILEEN POWER

VOLUME II
TRADE AND INDUSTRY
IN THE MIDDLE AGES

EDITED BY

M. POSTAN
Professor of Economic History in the
University of Cambridge

AND

E. E. RICH
Vere Harmsworth Professor of Imperial and Naval
History in the University of Cambridge

CAMBRIDGE
AT THE UNIVERSITY PRESS
1952

PUBLISHED BY
THE SYNDICS OF THE CAMBRIDGE UNIVERSITY PRESS

London Office: Bentley House, N.W.1
American Branch: New York

Agents for Canada, India, and Pakistan: Macmillan

Printed in Great Britain at the University Press, Cambridge
(Brooke Crutchley, University Printer)

PREFACE

The introduction to the first volume of the *Cambridge Economic History* carried only one set of initials, that of J. H. Clapham. The other editor, Eileen Power, died a few months previously, while at work on the page proofs of the volume. Sir John Clapham himself died in 1946. At the time of his death the second volume was still very young, but the list of post-war contributors and the table of contents had been definitely settled. The two men on whom it has fallen to launch this volume cannot therefore claim the main credit for its design. They have tried to adhere as faithfully as they can to the initial plans and dispositions. If nevertheless the volume is found to differ somewhat from its original conception, the differences must in the first place be put down to the special circumstances and contingencies of the war and post-war years. Here and there, the changes in the plan of the volume may also reflect the second thoughts of the editors. But the second thoughts are mostly those which had occurred to Eileen Power and J. H. Clapham themselves in the two or three years which followed the first blue-print of the series in 1938.

The circumstances and contingencies have been mostly unforeseeable and nearly all unfortunate. The five years of war not only interrupted the negotiations with possible contributors, but also depleted their ranks. Eileen Power herself was to have contributed one of the two general chapters, that on the trade of the Mediterranean South; Marc Bloch had promised to help in finding and guiding contributors on the continent, as he had helped in finding and guiding a group of contributors to the first volume. His last letter to the editors, sent through clandestine channels a few months before he was shot by the Gestapo, contained enquiries and suggestions about the volume. One of the authors, E. Sayous, died soon after he had submitted a first draft of a chapter on commercial technique; another, Gunnar Mickwitz, whom the editors had invited to write a chapter on the trade in Eastern Europe, died on active service in Finland before, or soon after, the invitation reached him. Only one of the foreign contributors originally invited, Professor van Werveke, was able to send in his contribution before Hitler occupied Western Europe; but the subsequent changes of plans compelled the editors to postpone to the third volume the publication of his chapter. All the other continental contributors were cut off from all contact in 1940 or soon after. British contributors were, without exception, compelled by the call of national duty to withdraw 'for the duration' from all active pursuit of economic history.

When, at the end of the war, Sir John Clapham and one of the present editors (M. Postan) took up again the broken threads, they had to reconsider the entire list of contributors and to issue invitations anew. Yet even then their plans proved too optimistic. The first two or three years of peace caused further gaps in the ranks of the contributors. The two British historians who had undertaken the chapters on land transport and shipping asked for leave to withdraw for reasons of health, but did it too late to be replaced by others. Contacts with scholars in Eastern Europe capable of replacing Mickwitz proved difficult to establish and impossible to maintain. In the end the only way of dealing with the casualties was to close the ranks, and this had to be done by asking the writers of the more general chapters to overlap into the fields which had now been made vacant. More especially, the authors of Chapters IV and V, dealing with the trade and industry of Southern and Northern Europe, had to be asked to cover, however briefly and superficially, the missing subjects of transport and shipping and the trade of the East.

The authors of these two chapters (and in the first place the author of Chapter IV mainly because he happened to be one of the editors) were also compelled to adapt themselves to some further changes in the original plans—changes which resulted not so much from post-war contingencies as from second thoughts of the editors.

It will be recalled that, according to the original plan, the series of medieval volumes was to open with a volume on agriculture, to be followed by a second volume which, to quote the editor's introduction to Volume I, was to be 'urban, industrial and commercial'. The third, to quote again, was 'to deal with credit and finance, public and private, coinage, prices, the economics of the late medieval nation-state and medieval economic theory'. This demarcation had the obvious advantage that it conformed to the manner in which the subject was commonly presented in University syllabuses and textbooks, and did not cut across the lines dividing the specialized fields of current research. At the same time it presented a number of serious editorial inconveniences.

In the first place, the plan for the second volume threatened to overwhelm it with matter not all of which was insolubly bound up with its main subject. Above all, the subjects which were in Clapham's phrase designated as 'urban', i.e. the development of towns, the economic policy of municipal governments, the history and policy of craft gilds, urban finance, etc., were on the whole equally well suited to Volume III, in which problems of economic policy and economic theory were to be discussed. In the end the editors decided to solve this problem by transferring the urban questions to Volume III and thus lightening the second volume and confining it to the narrow field of industry and trade.

Much more difficult to make good were the other shortcomings. If the historical outline of industry and trade was to be relevant to real economic problems it had to be drawn against the background of prices, population and the general trends of economic activity. Yet in the original plan the subject of prices was relegated to the third volume as a companion essay to that on coinage, while economic trends and population were not given an allocation at all. The omissions had already raised awkward problems in the preparations for the first volume; and by the time the preparations for the second were resumed in 1945, the editors were agreed that some provision for the 'background' topics would have to be made. The remedy they adopted was to ask the authors of the more general chapters to give full weight to prices, population and economic fluctuations. Above all, the author of Chapter IV, being himself an editor and to that extent a culprit, had to bear the main burden of the additional matter.

It is not for the editors to say whether the changes of plan have fully justified themselves. All lines of demarcation between epochs and aspects do violence to the unity of the historical process, but, assuming the necessity of a rational distribution of matter among the volumes, the present demarcation between Volumes II and III is probably more logical and convenient than the one originally adopted. The changes in the contents of individual chapters may not appear to be equally happy. The two general chapters in Volume II may now have grown to a size somewhat incommensurate with the other contributions and with the volume as a whole. On the other hand it had always been the intention of Eileen Power and J. H. Clapham to build the volumes around a few general essays, and to avoid as far as possible the fragmentation of the volumes into specialized essays dealing with short periods, small territories and circumscribed topics. The reluctance of would-be contributors prevented this intention from being fully carried out in the first volume, and a palliative was then found in entrusting Marc Bloch with the informal co-ordination of the chapters dealing with the agrarian economy of Western Europe at the height of the Middle Ages. The same palliative may still have to be adopted in the third volume. But in the present volume Dr Robert S. Lopez proved sufficiently self-sacrificing and the author of Chapter IV sufficiently reckless to attempt a general survey of medieval trade and industry as a whole, and in doing so to fill the most obvious gaps in the table of contents.

Apart from these changes the contents of the volume fall into obvious compartments. Chapters I and II are concerned with the antecedents of medieval trade, and the first of these chapters covers a period for which no separate provision was made in the first volume. In departing from that precedent, J. H. Clapham and Eileen Power were influenced by different habits of historians writing about agriculture and trade. Whereas in Volume I authors of the chapters dealing with Germanic agriculture, with agricultural technique and with settlement, could be expected to draw (as in fact they did) on prehistoric facts, the writers on medieval trade would not normally go back that far. And yet the editors knew that prehistoric evidence was indispensable for the understanding of certain fundamental problems of medieval trade, and especially of its function in economic life.

The chapter on Byzantium, like the projected but missing chapters on the trade and industry of Eastern Europe and Western Asia, is, so to speak, external to the main theme of the volume, which is, like the series as a whole, primarily concerned with Western Europe. The purpose of the 'external' chapters is to illuminate the economic conditions of the areas in constant trading relation with the West. The main subject of the volume—the trade and industry of Western Europe in the Middle Ages proper—is shared by two separate chapters. The alternative possibilities, that of dividing the subject into chapters dealing with separate periods, or of not dividing it at all, were considered and rejected. To have commissioned a single chapter on medieval trade would have meant delivering the central part of the volume, and nearly half of it in bulk, to the predilections and the point of view of a single writer. To have divided the topic into chapters arranged chronologically would have made it impossible to tell the story of medieval trade as one of continuous change and transformation. The last three chapters (and also the missing chapter on shipping and shipbuilding) are in a sense supplementary. Their purpose is to give greater weight to the principal medieval industries than could be given to them in the general chapters on trade.

This arrangement, like all such arrangements, could not avoid a certain amount of repetition. Although the periods preceding the Middle Ages proper are dealt with in Chapters I and II, none of the subsequent chapters could avoid altogether the pre-medieval beginnings. And although the cloth industry, mining and metallurgy, and building seemed to be sufficiently important to warrant separate chapters, their very importance made it difficult to avoid them altogether in Chapters IV and V. Other, and smaller, overlaps will be found elsewhere.

Where the same subjects happen to be dealt with, or even mentioned, by more than one contributor, the interpretations are bound to differ.

A careful reader will find no difficulty in spotting conflicts of opinion between contributors at more than one point. These differences the editors have made no attempt to reconcile or to conceal. The whole principle of the Cambridge Histories, made up as they are of separate contributions of reputable historians, must take differences of interpretation for granted. In a series devoted to economic history these differences are not only inevitable but also essential. Economic history is a new and a growing study. The facts and theories with which economic historians operate are even more provisional than the facts in the older and more stabilized branches of historical study. The authorised and established versions of economic history are therefore very few and will, let us hope, remain very few for many years to come. In their absence the study of economic history has done very well, for the striking advances in recent years have been greatly stimulated by the clash of opposing views. Is it too much to hope that the differences exhibited in the present volume will make their contribution to the stress and conflict of new discovery?

In the course of this volume's protracted gestation, the advice and the assistance of many persons was sought and received. The debt to Marc Bloch has already been mentioned; Professor Ganshof of Ghent has also placed at the disposal of the editors his unrivalled knowledge of medieval history in all its aspects; Professor Helen Cam has helped with question and suggestion on several occasions; Dr Grahame Clarke has helped with the preparation for the Press of the charts in the prehistoric chapter. The names of those whom Eileen Power consulted in the preliminary stages are too many to be enumerated, but they have had their reward in the pleasures of corresponding with her. Throughout the vicissitudes of this volume the Cambridge University Press has been as generous, as helpful and as efficient a patron as only it could be. The laborious work of proof reading fell upon Cynthia Postan.

M.P.

E.E.R.

CONTENTS

CHAPTER IV

The Trade of Medieval Europe: the North

By MICHAEL POSTAN, Professor in the University of Cambridge

CHAPTER V

The Trade of Medieval Europe: The South

By ROBERT S. LOPEZ, Associate Professor in Yale University

CHAPTER VI

The Woollen Industry

By ELEANORA CARUS-WILSON, Reader in the University of London

CHAPTER VII

Mining and Metallurgy in Medieval Civilisation

By JOHN U. NEF, Professor in the University of Chicago

CHAPTER VIII

Building in Stone in Medieval Western Europe

By GWILYM PEREDUR JONES, Professor in the
University of Sheffield

BIBLIOGRAPHIES

ILLUSTRATIONS

PLATES

Facing p. 143

I (a) A goods wagon

Woodcut from a Strasbourg edition of Vergil (1502)

(b) The operations of building

Woodcut from *Cronica van* der Hilligen Stat van Cöllen (1499)

Bound in between pp. 376–7

II (a) Combing, carding and spinning with distaff

From British Museum Royal MS. 16 G V f. 56 (Boccaccio, *De claris mulieribus*, in French, early fifteenth century)

(b) Spinning with spinning wheel

From British Museum Royal MS. 10 E IV f. 146 (Decretals of Gregory IX, *circa* 1320)

(c) Carding and spinning with wheel

Ibid. f. 147.

III (a) Weaving on single loom

From British Museum Egerton MS. 1894 f. 2 (Book of Genesis, early fourteenth century

(b) Fulling by foot

From M. I. Rostovtzeff, *Social and Economic History of the Roman Empire* (1926), Plate xxv, No. 7 (fuller's tomb at Sens; see also G. Julliot, *Musée Gallo-Romaine de Sens*, p. 85, and Plate IX)

(c) Tentering and mending

From L. Zanoni, *Gli Umiliati nei loro rapporti con l'eresia, l'industria della lana ed i comuni nei secoli XII e XIII*, Plate II (from chronicle Frà Giovanni di Brera, *circa* 1421)

(d) Dyeing in the piece

From British Museum Royal MS. 15 E III f. 269 (*Book of the Properties of Things*, written at Bruges in 1482, probably for Edward IV)

MAPS

CHAPTER I

Trade and Industry in Barbarian Europe
till Roman Times

THE exploitation of the natural wealth of Europe was initiated by illiterate barbarians, and the regular distribution of the products began thousands of years before written documents mention traders or merchandise. In other words our prehistoric ancestors laid the foundations of some at least of the industries considered in this volume and discovered the principal routes that have been followed by trade throughout historic times. Hence a brief account of the more reliable conclusions of archaeology is not irrelevant as an introduction.

I. *The Stone Stage*[1]

In the Stone Stage of course the words 'industry and trade' are applicable only in a somewhat restricted sense; for one definition of a Stone Age might be a period in which all people lived in self-sufficing communities with no more regular division of social labour than is imposed by age and sex differences. Hence this 'Age' or Stage can be dismissed in a few sentences although it occupies about 99 % of the span of sidereal time during which 'men' have been living in our continent. Yet, even in the latest phase of Old Stone (palaeolithic) Age that coincides with final spasms of the last Ice Age, substances were being transported by human agency—and presumably by some sort of intertribal barter—hundreds of miles from the regions where they occur in nature. So the mammoth-hunters on the middle Dnieper secured for ornaments shells from the Black Sea or the Mediterranean, and reindeer-hunters in the Dordogne too obtained Mediterranean shells, including cowries. In the so-called 'mesolithic age' during which the old economy, based exclusively on hunting, fishing and collecting, persisted in Europe after glacial conditions had passed, the same sort of evidence for trade continues; for instance shells of *Columbella rusticana* were brought from the Mediterranean to the Azilian inhabitants of the

---

[1] The archaeologists' Stone, Bronze, and Iron Ages are not periods of time, that coincide all over the world or even all over Europe, but Stages in technological and economic development that succeed one another in the same order everywhere. Here the term 'Stage' is generally used in place of 'Age', but where the emphasis is on the chronological aspect—for in any given region a Stage did endure for a period of time—the older expression is retained (Childe, *Journ. Roy. Anthropolog. Inst.* XLIV (1944), 1–17).

Falkenstein Cave in Hohenzollern.[1] Of course the same sporadic interchange of materials over wide areas was still practised by gathering
tribes that survived in the northern forests long after neolithic farmers
had begun to colonise their woodlands. Indeed a little evidence suggests
that such residual hunters helped in the transport of materials between
the more settled farming communities.[2]

But during the European neolothic age the evidence grows more abundant, and the 'trade' that it indicates appears more regular and intensive

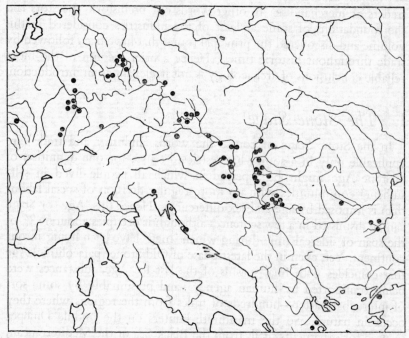

Map 1. Distribution of *Spondylus* shell in neolithic Europe (after Buttler).

as well as more extensive. For the criterion of the Neolithic Stage is
that subsistence farming—plot cultivation and stock breeding—supple-
ments the products of the chase and other gathering activities; and any
sort of farming, however rudimentary, makes possible, and indeed
requires, the production of a regular, if minute, social surplus. The
temperate zone of Europe was now occupied sparsely by a medley of
little communities, settled, but not very permanently, in tiny villages of
half-a-dozen to a score of households scattered about the all-pervading
forests. Despite the obstacles of forest, marsh and mountain that

[1] *Germania*, XVIII, 81–8.
[2] Childe, *Prehistoric Communities of the British Isles* (1940), 83–4.

separated each hamlet from its neighbours, archaeology yields evidence for an astonishing amount of transportation and interchange of substances and even of manufactured articles.[1]

Once more the most striking and convincing evidence is afforded by 'luxury articles'—shells and substances prized for ornaments, or rather, charms. In South-eastern and Central Europe shells of *Spondylus gaederopi* provide a particularly instructive example. Bracelets and other ornaments made from this Mediterranean mussel are found quite often in neolithic settlements not only in Thessaly, Macedonia and Istria, but also along the lower and middle Danube, in Moravia, Bohemia and Central Germany and even on the Rhine and as far west as the Marne.[2] Whether the *Spondylus* shells reached Central Europe from the Adriatic across the Julian Alps or, as is more likely, across the Balkans by the Vardar-Morava valleys, the distribution of the continental finds leaves no doubt of the use of waterways as means of communication. Rather later *Pectunculus* shells and coral were being transported across the Great St Bernard to Switzerland, and eventually the last-named Mediterranean shell reached Bohemia. By that time another magic substance, amber, was beginning to reach the same centre from the North, mainly from Jutland. In the sequel we shall see that the extension of this 'amber trade' to the Adriatic and Aegean played a leading role in Bronze Stage commerce.

But even in the Stone Stage trade was not limited entirely to what we term luxuries. Superior stones for the manufacture of implements were distributed far from their places of origin in a manner that foreshadows the genuine trade in industrial metal in the Bronze Stage. So obsidian from the Hegyalya near Tokay in North-east Hungary was transported to Moravia, Galicia and Upper Silesia on the one hand, to Pannonia, Serbia and perhaps even Macedonia on the other. Blades of the brownish flint of Grand Pressigny (Seine-et-Loire) were exported to Jersey in the West, to Switzerland and the Rhine valley in the East. The lava of Niedermendig near Mayen on the Moselle was used for querns round Liége on the Meuse—indeed a fragment of the same stone was apparently associated with neolithic pottery near Avebury in Wiltshire. Even manufactures were transported. Pots shown by petrographic analysis to have been made from the clays of the lower Main reached the neolithic village of Köln-Lindental, 50 miles down the Rhine. An isolated pottery rattle from a settlement at Gleinitz in

[1] For points not otherwise documented, see Childe, *Dawn of European Civilization* (1949).

[2] Buttler, in *Marburger Studien*, I (Darmstadt, 1938), 27–33, with map. Some authorities, however, maintain that the *Spondylus* shells found in Central Europe are fossils derived from local deposits. *Westpreussische Zeitsch.* XXIX (1942), 1–18.

Silesia must, judging by its style, have been brought from the middle Tisza in Hungary.

Under such circumstances there was room for intercommunal specialisation without sacrifice of economic self-sufficiency. In fact communities of, at least part-time, specialists undoubtedly existed in neolithic Europe. The best known are the flint miners of Sicily, Portugal, France, England, Belgium, Holland, Sweden and Galicia. In such renowned mines as Obourg and Spiennes[1] in Belgium, Grimes' Graves and Cissbury in England and many another the miners had elaborated a quite sophisticated technique for reaching the best seams of good flint nodules. With the simplest tools of bone, antler and stone, shafts were sunk up to 50 ft. deep from which galleries followed the seams. The operators were certainly no amateurs and just as certainly did not themselves consume the enormous quantities of flint won. If not full time specialists, they were at least adding to the proceeds of subsistence farming by bartering the products of their skilled labour with other communities.

The same inference can be drawn from numerous 'axe-factories'. At Graig Lwyd in North-west Wales, for instance, a small community was engaged in quarrying an outcrop of high grade rock and manufacturing therefrom axes that were occasionally used as far away as Wiltshire.[2] It may well be that the manufacture of querns at Niedermendig, attested for the Iron Age, began in neolithic times. While none of these workers need have been full time specialists, they were certainly producing commodities for sale or exchange.

Just as it was possible to add to one's livelihood by manufacturing axes or mining flint, so the same opportunity was offered by distributing the products. We have seen that the products of axe factories reached a wide market. In parts of Europe at least there is concrete evidence that such manufactures were distributed by professional hucksters, who need not of course have been full time specialists. This evidence consists of 'hoards'—collections of brand new implements dug up together. It is generally agreed that such a hoard represents the stock-in-trade of an itinerant vendor which he had hidden when overtaken by some danger on his journey with the intention of recovering it at some more auspicious moment. The survival of the hoard for modern archaeologists to study illustrates the perils of the road. In Central Europe most hoards of 'shoe-last celts'—adzes or hoe-blades characteristic of the Danubian neolithic province—are found significantly on the edge of

[1] Loe, *La Belgique ancienne*, I (1928), 186, cf. also Dechelette, *Manuel*, I, 355–8, and Hawkes, *Prehistoric Foundations* (1940), 138–40.

[2] Grimes, *Guide to the Collection illustrating the Prehistory of Wales* (Cardiff, 1939), 22–4.

that province, perhaps the frontier of tribal territory, and extend to North Germany and even Sweden.[1] In Western Germany hoards of axes that in form and material are suggestive of Brittany appear to mark a west to east route, directed to the salt deposits of the Saale valley. It may well be that neolithic 'merchants' dealt in salt and other desirable but perishable materials as well as in durable stone artefacts.

II. *The Early Aegean Period and the Early Bronze Stage*

The stage of neolithic barbarism north of the Alps is partly, and probably largely, contemporary with Bronze Stage civilisation in Egypt and Mesopotamia and is more or less infected by emanations of the new sort of economy established there. By 3000 B.C. the pharaonic monarchy in the Nile valley and the Sumerian temple states of the Tigris-Euphrates delta already disposed of a gigantic surplus, derived from the irrigation cultivation of the fertile alluvia and concentrated in the hands of a tiny minority of gods, divine kings, prelates and nobles. It supported a large variety of specialised craftsmen at home and helped to support the distant producers of raw materials not available in the river valleys. The insatiable demands of oriental rulers for magical substances, metal for armaments and a steadily expanding list of materials for ritual, pomp or luxury, gave barbarians who could supply those demands an assured market, an opportunity of sharing the surplus of Egypt and Mesopotamia. The process of satisfying these demands initiated barbarians into the techniques of civilisation, stimulated among them a desire for its luxuries, and compelled them in the end to imitate the new economy more or less.

Greece and the Aegean islands, including Crete and Cyprus, could supply copper, perhaps tin, silver, lead, marble, timber, emery, saffron, murex and other materials. Winds and currents were favourable to voyages between Egypt, Syria and the Aegean. Once 'sea-going ships' were available (and such existed from 3000 B.C. on East Mediterranean waters),[2] sea transport was easy and cheap. Very soon the peoples living round the Aegean began tapping the Egyptian market and, through Syria and Anatolia, the Mesopotamian. Villages of neolithic farmers, already tied to the soil by the cultivation of fruit trees and vines, grew into little townships comprising smiths and other specialised craftsmen and substantially supplementing the proceeds of farming and

[1] *Prähistorische Zeitsch.* VI, 40; *Altschlesien*, I, 67.
[2] On Egyptian ships see *Journ. Egypt. Arch.* XXVI (1941), 1–10 (Faulkner); on Aegean, *Bull. Corresp. héllenique.* LVII (1934), 170 ff. (Marinatos).

fishing by maritime trade. Once such trade was established, piracy offered an alternative means of extorting a share in the world surplus.

The share thus obtainable was in fact so great that it was possible and profitable to colonise minute islands, too small to support any population on the basis of subsistence agriculture; but offering safe and convenient anchorage for merchant ships or pirate galleys; there was nothing to recommend the island rock called Pseira off the north-east coast of Crete save a good harbour and a good spring.

Of course Pseira and Antiparos should not be taken as typical locations for Early Aegean townships. In the IIIrd millennium B.C., such normally appear as tiny agglomerations of farmers and fishers covering from $1\frac{1}{2}$ (Troy) to perhaps 6 (Phylakopi) acres and differentiated from a neolithic village by the inclusion of specialised craftsmen —coppersmiths, carpenters, and on some islands, lapidaries and others. Peasants had still to labour with wood and stone alone, but artisans used metal tools and exchanged their products not only with fellow townsmen but all over the Aegean world. Within it the intensity of trade is well illustrated by numerous vases and statuettes, made in the Cyclades from local marbles, but found also in Crete, the Peloponnese, Attica and the Troad. The regular use of metals—not only copper, but also lead, silver, gold and tin-bronze—in itself presupposes frequent trade though the supplies were still too small and too costly to allow copper to replace stone in harvesting or any sort of rough work. That any Aegean craftsmen were yet manufacturing for the oriental market is unproven. In any case hardly any Aegean manufactures have been identified in Egypt or Hither Asia before 2000 B.C.; a zoomorphic vase of Cycladic marble from protodynastic Egypt is among the exceptions.[1] Nor do many actual imports from the Orient survive to prove trade with the civilised States; an early cylinder seal of Mesopotamian style turned up in a Cycladic grave, and a not inconsiderable number of Egyptian stone vases, ranging from proto-dynastic on, found their way to Crete. On the other hand various Asiatic types of ornaments, like double-spiral headed pins imitated in the Cyclades and Greece, and Egyptian amulets, seals and vases copied in Crete and more rarely on other islands and the mainland, imply that the original manufactures did also reach the Aegean. But on the whole the foreign trade of the Aegean was occupied mainly with raw materials rather than manufactures. Cypriote copper was exported in large quantities to Asia in the IInd millennium and most probably also in the IIIrd, but no

---

[1] Frankfort, *Studies in the Early Pottery of the Near East*, I (1924), 112; metal vases from the 'Royal Tombs' of Alaca Höyük in central Anatolia reproduce forms familiar in pottery from the Cyclades, but the Cycladic pots may copy Anatolian metal vases rather than vice versa.

product of Cypriote metallurgy, though easily recognisable, has yet been identified outside the island. Schaeffer[1] concludes that Cypriote copper was exported as ore.

It must not be assumed that Aegean trade dealt only in local products; transit trade is also profitable, and the Aegean mariners were well qualified to annex its profits. In the IIIrd millennium Thiaki (Ithaka) was colonised from Corinthia, just as Corcyra (Corfu) was in the Ist, and presumably for the same sort of motives. From the Ionian Isles it is an easy sail to Apulia and thence coastwise to Sicily. Now in south-eastern Sicily, precisely in the area first colonised by the historical Greeks, some curious bossed bone plaques of Anatolian-Aegean origin have been found. They have been found moreover in tombs cut in the rock and used as collective sepulchres—a form of tomb and burial rite not previously current in the island, but familiar round the East Mediterranean and in the Greek islands during the Early Aegean Bronze Age.

Save for another bossed plaque from Malta and stray Early Aegean painted jugs from Marseilles harbour and the island of Ibiza,[2] no actual Aegean products have yet been identified west of Sicily in the IIIrd millennium. But on the strength of the architecture of 'megalithic' tombs and the ritual practised in them prehistorians have deduced an extension of maritime intercourse to Provence and the Iberian Peninsula, and thence along the Atlantic coasts of Brittany and the British Isles and across the North Sea to Denmark. Trade on this 'megalithic route,' both across the North Sea and along the Atlantic coasts, is in fact well documented in the Bronze Stage (pp. 16, 23) and earlier would afford the best explanation of the rise of metallurgy in Ireland.

Moreover, somewhere on the edge of this vast megalithic province there did arise a peculiar people, conventionally termed the 'Beaker folk'. They travelled about widely in small armed bands both in Western and Central Europe. Everywhere they used metal and collected gold and other precious substances. Whether or no their journeys were directed to obtaining the coveted materials, they had the result of diffusing the use of metal weapons and of opening up trade routes. In particular the Beaker folk seem to have been pioneers on the Brenner route between Upper Italy and the upper Danube basin and so in establishing a short cut for commerce between the half-civilised Mediterranean world and the barbarian tribes of Central Europe. At the same time they had begun to deal in amber and so prepared the way for a traffic that was vital in the Central European Bronze Age. If, as

[1] *Mission en Chypre*, p. 48.
[2] Bosch-Gimpera in *Il Convegno archeologico in Sardegna*, 1926 (Reggio, 1929), 98; *Cuadernios de Historia primitiva*, III (Madrid, 1948), 37–42.

I think, the main activity of the Beaker folk fell within the centuries 1900–1700 B.C., it would coincide with the Middle Aegean period in the east Mediterranean.

III. *The Full Bronze Stage*

To appreciate the sequel we must turn back to p. 6 where we left the Aegean about 2000 B.C. The first half of the IInd millennium witnessed the rise of Egypt to fresh heights of power and wealth under the Theban kings of the Middle Kingdom (XIIth Dynasty, 2000–1700 B.C.); the establishment in Mesopotamia of large and orderly empires under the IIIrd Dynasty of Ur (2150–2050 B.C.) and the Ist Dynasty of Babylon (Hammurabi, 1792–1750 B.C.)[1] which, while they lasted, gave opportunity for peaceful accumulation of wealth; the plantation in Central Anatolia of a colony of Assyrian merchants whose correspondence, the so-called 'Cappadocian tablets' dug up at Kül-tepe, describes regular trade in metals and other merchandise with Mesopotamia (1970–1870 B.C.); and the partial unification of Anatolia under the First Hittite Kingdom about 1900 B.C. These events enormously enlarged the effective demand of the civilised Orient while contemporary improvements in transport facilitated its satisfaction. Their repercussions affected the whole Aegean world but especially Minoan Crete.

During the Middle Minoan Age a high degree of cultural and some political unification of the island was achieved; economic and political power was concentrated in the hands of a few 'priest kings' who built themselves palaces at Knossos, close to Candia on the north, and at Phaistos on the Mesarà plain of the south, commanding the best road across the island's mountain spine. The Cretan palaces, like Sumerian temples, served also as economic establishments, comprising workshops and store rooms. At least on the royal estates, viticulture and orchard husbandry for the market may have replaced, or been combined with, subsistence farming; immense jars in the palace magazines would contain more wine and oil than should be needed for court consumption. New and more expert specialist craftsmen were attracted to the courts and eventually began to manufacture for a more than local market. In particular, master-potters, skilled in using the wheel, were induced to immigrate from Asia and then trained a native school of craftsmen whose products excelled both in technical perfection and aesthetic appeal any wares produced in the Bronze Age Orient. The egg-shell fine vases from the palace workshops found purchasers among

[1] I accept throughout the dates proposed by Sidney Smith, *Alalakh and Chronology* (London, 1940).

rich nobles on the Nile, at Ugarit on the Syrian coast and at Qatna further inland, as well as in barbarian townships on Cyprus, Thera, Melos, Aegina and in central Greece. By 1850 B.C. the world trade in Greek pottery that culminated in the Classical period, had begun. Tablets found at Mari on the Middle Euphrates mention vases, weapons and garments[1] of Cretan manufacture or at least style; the Minoan evidence itself illustrates the extraction of purple dye from the murex and yellow from the saffron plant.

On the Greek mainland, though it had been conquered by warlike tribes conventionally termed 'Minyans' and probably already speaking some sort of Greek, industry and trade maintained at least the level reached in the IIIrd millennium. Metal was common enough to be used for all sorts of craft tools including saws. Skilled potters brought their wheels from Crete to work on Aegina and the mainland so that this craft was industrialised.

Naturally the international trade of the whole Aegean world was maintained and extended. Goods, and perhaps even letters, sealed by the Assyrian merchants in Cappadocia, reached Gözlü Kale near Tarsus on the Cilician coast. Mesopotamian seals bearing the name of Sargon of Eshnunna (late nineteenth century) and of the time of Hammurabi (early eighteenth) reached Kythera and Crete. Commerce with the Hittites is reflected by the local reproduction of common types of metal vessels and ornaments at once in Cappadocia and the Aegean. There are hints that the Minoans imported silphium from Cyrenaica. Presumably they still drew on the resources of the barbarous West and North though concrete evidence is lacking till 1600 B.C.

Soon after that date, Minoan civilisation began to expand to peninsular Greece and reproduce there its industrial and commercial economy. The concentration of wealth to support industry and trade is symbolised by the erection of palaces and royal tombs. The latter contain an astonishing wealth of handsomely painted clay vases, ornate weapons, vessels of gold, silver and bronze, ornaments and ritual objects, all of Minoan style. Not all were imports. Some may well have been executed by Minoan craftsmen attracted to the court of the Helladic prince and working to his order. The palaces of Mycenae and Thebes were certainly decorated by fresco painters trained in Crete, but naturally working on the spot. Homer tells how a skilled craftsman,

---

[1] It should here be emphasised that the manufacture of, and trade in, textiles and other products of organic materials that, owing to their perishable nature, cannot normally figure in the archaeological record, must have gone on in prehistoric times, but cannot be considered at all here for lack of evidence. The silence of the succeeding pages does not mean the non-existence of industries and commerce handling organic materials that include also cosmetics, perfumes and foodstuffs.

like a minstrel and a healer, was welcomed everywhere and reports cases where a master craftsman was summoned from a distance to perform a specific job like making Ajax's shield in Locris.[1] That was apparently the normal procedure in Bronze Stage Europe and it would be a mistake to imagine anything like factories in Crete, turning out high class metal ware for sale on the market.

In any case the locations of the new dynastic seats bear witness to the importance of trade in enriching their lords. Mycenae, the oldest and richest, commands the sole land route from the Aegean to the Gulf of Corinth that avoids the notorious dangers of rounding the Argolid or the still worse promontories of Malea and Matapan. Others are planted at the heads of southward-facing gulfs, from Vapheio in Laconia to Dimini on the Gulf of Volo. Two rich settlements on the west coast—near Navarino and at Kakovatos in Elis—emphasise the importance of Adriatic trade. And just at this time, 1550 to 1450 B.C., amber beads, imported from the Baltic, begin to appear at Kakovatos, Mycenae and Knossos. The Aegean commercial system was now linked up with those that had been developed in Central Europe. To their rise we now turn.

There are many small copper lodes in the Balkans, the Transylvanian mountains, the Matra, the little Carpathians, the Eastern Alps, the Erzgebirge and elsewhere in Germany. Native copper may once have been found with the ores in many places; there is still a good deal in the Matra. There is gold in the Balkans and still more in Transylvania, and some can be obtained from many rivers including even the Rhine. Tin might be had in the Erzgebirge and Vögtland. How soon these resources were exploited for the benefit of the East Mediterranean market is not easily determined. Probably in the IIIrd millennium objects of gold and copper occur in tells (ruined villages) in eastern Bulgaria and Wallachia, simultaneously with local imitations of Asiatic ornaments. In the neolithic of the Danube valley we find, after the earliest *Spondylus* imports, imitations in clay of oriental or Minoan stone vases and what has been taken[2] for a representation of a Minoan double-axe appears scratched on a vase.

In any case, whether at the instigation of oriental prospectors or no, lodes of copper were exploited in the Balkans and Central Europe during the IIIrd millennium B.C. Most of the products may at first have been made of native metal and were most probably shaped by mere hammering. The commonest implements, 'flat axes', are really adzes, copying the local stone ones. In Transylvania a more truly metallic implement, the axe-adze (with a hole for the shaft), was produced probably still by the same process. As they are very common round the

---

[1] Glotz, *Ancient Greece at Work*, 43–4.
[2] Hawkes in *Brit. School at Athens*, xxxvii, 144 ff.

ore fields, Roska[1] has suggested they were used in 'mining'. From Transylvania axe-adzes spread sporadically up the Save and Drave, up the March to the valleys of the Oder, Elbe and Saale and eastward to the Dnieper.[2] Most of these may be regarded as traded from Transylvania, but considerable clusters in the Balkans may have been made on the spot from local metal. The trade in metal, thus attested in what is often termed the Copper Stage, was no more regular and no more vital to the consumers than the neolithic trade in obsidian and luxuries mentioned on p. 3.

With the Bronze Stage the whole set-up changes. Metal was won from its ores by smelting, and intelligently worked by casting. Copper was generally alloyed with tin, the products were systematically distributed and are actually found most often on the fertile, loess-clad slopes, far from the barren metalliferous mountains. In a word we are faced with a new industry and a new economy. Significantly enough the earliest products of intelligent metallurgy in Central Europe comprise a series of ornaments fashionable in Mesopotamia and Anatolia, but not in the Aegean. Hence it has been inferred that the new metallurgical techniques had been introduced by Asiatic prospectors who now began producing for a local market. On the other hand, the earliest dated piece of evidence for the technique of casting—a stone mould—comes from a Beaker grave in Moravia. Moreover, the Central European daggers of the Early Bronze Stage are provided with hilts of the same curious form as those of the western Beaker-folk, a form attested in Egypt before 3000 B.C. but never favoured in Asia. Hence the Beaker-folk may have contributed not only to opening up routes for the metal trade (p. 7) but also to the development of the industry itself.

They too may have played a part in producing the conditions for an effective demand. Having regard to the heavy costs in social labour of the extraction, transport and processing of metal, its regular use presupposes the availability of a quite substantial social surplus. Considering the low productivity of subsistence farming in the temperate zone, the requisite surplus could most easily be made available if the tiny surpluses produced by a number of households were concentrated in the hands of one or two chiefs. The migrations and conflicts of pastoral tribes in the late Neolithic Stage do in fact seem to have allowed of the rise of a class of petty chieftains who could accumulate the necessary surplus and would also appreciate the superiority of metal weapons. In

[1] *Dacia*, III–IV (1933), 355; he cites examples from the environs of the Balabanya copper mines (Ciuc), from the gold mines of Slatina (Serbia) and the salines of Targu-Ocna (Moldavia).

[2] Childe, *Danube in Prehistory*, 204.

Britain this result may have been achieved by the Beaker-folk themselves; in Northern and North-central Europe other warlike peoples at least shared the spoils with them.

So early in the IInd millennium B.C.[1] a native metallurgical industry in Central Europe began producing from local ores wares for a continental market. About the same time in the British Isles a parallel industry arose using Cornish tin and Irish copper to supply the island chieftains, but also exporting to the continent. Finally the copper ores of the Caucasus, previously exploited by prospectors for the benefit of Mesopotamia and Anatolia, supported a native industry producing for local consumption. It remained for a long time isolated from Central and Western Europe and will not further concern us here.

Of the extractive side of the metallurgical industries at this stage practically nothing is known. Copper was most probably won by open cuts from surface lodes, worked out long ago. There is as yet no evidence for the use of sulphide ores such as would be tapped by mining, and of course the techniques employed in mining flint in chalk would be useless for the hard rocks in which copper ores are embedded. In Central Europe the exploitation of deposits in the Austrian Alps is adequately attested. The metal was perhaps refined, certainly worked in, and probably shipped from pile villages on the Attersee and Mondsee conveniently situated at the head of navigation on the Traun whence the product could have been conveyed down tributaries to the Danube. No articles distinctive of continental metal work were demonstrably manufactured on the Austrian lakes, but neck-rings, that may have served as ingots, have been dredged up from them. An enthusiastic German, by many chemical analyses, has satisfied some of his countrymen and C. F. C. Hawkes that copper was smelted from the ores of the upper Saale valley and widely exported, while tin would have been drawn from Vögtland. In any case, throughout the Bronze Age in the temperate zone, as also in the Mediterranean and in the Ancient East, metal was normally smelted on the mine fields; at no time is refinery slag found in the villages or towns where the ultimate consumers congregated. In Central Europe the metal was transported in the form

---

[1] Since the Asiatic ornaments mentioned above cannot have been copied in Central Europe before they were current in the literate Orient, their first appearance there gives a *terminus post quem* for the start of the Central European Bronze Age. The finds from the Royal Tombs of Ur and contemporary Sumerian sites give 2400 B.C. as the requisite date. But the same types were commoner in Syria and Cyprus in the first quarter of the IInd millennium. So the author and many other authorities prefer a date of 1900 or even 1700 B.C. The first phase of the European Bronze Age had hardly ended before Egyptian fayence beads, fairly reliably dated to 1400 B.C., were reaching Hungary and England. Cf. Childe, *Amer. Journ. of Archaeol.* XLIII (1939), 16ff.; Hawkes, *Prehistoric Foundations of Europe*, 344, *et passim*; Schaeffer, *Ugaritica*, II, 56–120.

of neck-rings, termed 'ingot torques'. Hoards of such torques have been found at many points in Central Europe and Italy, including significantly the Mondsee itself. But from the Saale basin metal may have been exported as ingots, cast in the form of the Minoan double-axe, which, itself being a magic symbol, would be a suitable medium of exchange.[1] How tin was transported and alloyed with copper is still unknown.

With the rural economy prevailing in the early IInd millennium no single local group nor chieftain can normally have been rich enough to

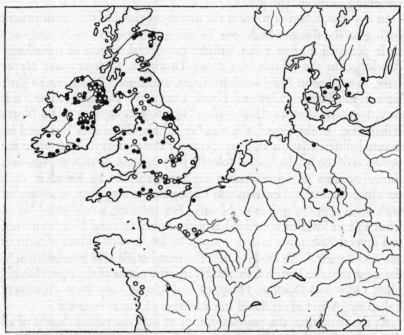

Map 2. Distribution of Irish (solid) and Britannico-Hibernian (open circles) decorated axes in the Early Bronze Stage (after Megaw and Hardy).

support a resident smith continuously and keep him regularly supplied with bronze; only in the prosperous villages of plough cultivators established now in the rich plains of Hungary and Upper Italy are so many moulds found as to suggest more than passing visits by itinerant craftsmen. For the most part metal ware would have been both distributed and worked by perambulating smiths who must have ranged over considerable areas and made, or at least finished off, weapons and ornaments to the order of individual patrons. Even if manufacture and distribution were more sharply separated than this account assumes, no

[1] Hawkes, *Brit. School at Athens*, XXXVII, 150 ff., who gives a map of the distribution of these 'ingot axes'.

workshops comparable to the neolithic axe factories have been identified in Europe during the Early Bronze Stage. Admittedly axes and halberd blades, of types represented in vast numbers in Ireland, were distributed quite widely in Great Britain,[1] though mainly on her western coasts and along routes leading thence, and reached even Scandinavia and North Germany by a traffic that crossed Scotland by well-defined tracks[2] to east coast ports near Aberdeen and on the Tay estuary. But moulds for the axes at least are found also in Britain as if transported by travelling artificers (Map 2).

In any case, whether to meet the divergent tastes of the consumers or owing to the distinct traditions inspiring the master smiths and even their personal idiosyncrasies, distinct provincial schools of metallurgy developed in the British Isles, Saxo-Thuringia, Hungary and Upper Italy, as well as in South-eastern Spain, and South Russia, and a little later in the Rhone valley and North Germany. Before 1500 B.C. it is easy, by inspection, to distinguish a British, a Bohemian and a North Italian axe. In the sequel, the number of schools steadily increased by internal differentiation and expansion of the industry. But while the products of the local school absolutely preponderate within its province, some products of other centres are invariably to be found in each province (save the Almerian and Caucasian), either stray or associated with local types in graves or hoards. For instance, a celebrated hoard from Pile in Sweden contained British, Bohemian and Northern axes, and several Bohemian hoards contain Italian, as well as local, forms of axe and dagger.[3] So by 1500 B.C. the metal trade was international in the sense that the British Isles, the North, the basins of the upper Rhine, Elbe, Oder and Danube, Hungary and Upper Italy were effectively linked up by not exceptional interchanges of metal products.

At the same time the populations, or at least the ruling classes, of all these regions had abandoned the neolithic economy of self-sufficiency in so far as they really depended for their personal safety, their self-respect and their political independence, on weapons and ornaments of imported bronze made by professional craftsmen—metal was not used in agriculture nor for any rough work and hardly, if at all, for craft tools save by metal-workers. On the other hand throughout the greater part of the boreal zone of coniferous forest and over most of France, save for an enclave in Brittany, a neolithic economy still

[1] See map, Fox, *Personality of Britain*, 1945, pl. VI.

[2] O Riordain, *Archaeologia*, LXXXVI, 195 ff.; the routes across Scotland marked by halberds have been made clearer by new finds listed in Childe, *Scotland before the Scots*, 1946.

[3] See also Forssander, 'Der ostskandinavische Norden während der ältesten Metall-zeit Europas' (*Skrifter av K. Humanistiska Vetenskapssamfundët i Lund*, XXII, 1936) with map of hoards on p. 19.

reigned scarcely relieved by occasional acquisitions of bronze or copper objects. Even in the Iberian peninsula it was only in Almeria that bronze was used at all regularly.

The routes of the merchant artificers who supplied this European market with bronze can be traced by stray products and still better by hoards that represent the stock-in-trade of the itinerants (cf. p. 4). The contents of the hoards show that these hucksters dealt not only in bronze ware but also in gold, jet, amber and other luxuries and probably too in salt and other materials that have left no trace in the archaeological record. In fact the frequent transportation and interchange of commodities is a phenomenon that distinguishes the Bronze Stage from a Stone Stage as much as the actual employment of bronze itself. For instance, in the British Isles elaborate crescentic collars of lignite (jet) beads are so widely distributed that many must have been traded though they may have been made at several places where the material crops out and worked only by part-time specialists. Irish gold counterparts of these collars occur also in Brittany, Belgium, Hanover and Denmark.[1] Lignite was doubtless valued in the first place for its electrical properties that would appear magical to any barbarian. Amber was still more highly valued for the same reason, and forms a constituent of many hoards. The amber traffic was indeed so important, and is so easily recognisable that some of the most important trade routes are termed amber routes by archaeologists.

The most important deposits are in Jutland and East Prussia.[2] The natives of Denmark began to barter the fossil resin for metal ware while they were still in the Stone Stage (i.e. while metal was so scarce that it was never deposited in graves which contain only stone weapons and only very few bronze pins and ornaments). It was sent to Britain in exchange for metal weapons and gold work mainly by sea, though van Giffen[3] has adduced some evidence for a land route across Holland. Its routes across Central Europe have been carefully studied by de Navarro[4] and coincide with the main highways of Bronze Age commerce. The main route followed the Elbe to the Praha basin, then turned west up the Vltava, crossed the Hercynian Forest and reached the Danube near Linz. Thence it followed a tributary to the Brenner Pass and so down the Adige and the Po to the head of the Adriatic. An early loop followed the Saale through Thuringia, descended the Main valley and thence reached the upper Danube over the Frankish Jura by

[1] Mapped by Fox, *Personality of Britain*, 1945, 48.

[2] But a little amber, transported southward by the ice, can be dug up from the moraines almost anywhere in the glaciated region of Northern Europe and some is obtainable on the North Sea coasts of Britain.

[3] *Die Bauart der Einzelgräber*, 1930, 120–2.   [4] *Geographical Journal*, 1925, 486 ff.

the same route as was followed by international expresses before 1939.
In Bohemia a spur branched off up the Elbe and down the March to the
Danube and Hungary. In return Transylvanian gold was received by
the Unĕtician population of Bohemia, and some of it was passed on by
them down stream to Denmark. The East Prussian deposits may have
been tapped but little later. Two series of hoards (that contain no amber,
however) converge upon the lower Vistula. One, leading across
Poznania and Silesia to the Glatz Pass, may have helped to swell the
stocks of the Unĕtician merchants; the other, across Pomerania and
Brandenburg and containing distinctive Saxo-Thuringian types, leads
to the Saale valley.

The crucial importance of the Central Amber routes is that they
linked the barbarians of Central Europe commercially with the
civilised Aegean and so formed a channel along which cultural advances
could be diffused. The amber ornaments from Kakovatos and Mycenae
(p. 10) in particular are obviously of Danish origin and probably
manufacture. They had been brought across Central Europe, over the
Brenner and down the Adriatic presumably by the same route as the
mysterious Hyperborean gifts mentioned by Herodotus reached Delphi
in the fifth century B.C. Of course this trade did not stop short in
mainland Greece but went on to Minoan Crete. Of the products of
higher civilisation received in exchange for amber, and inferentially
other products, only a few trinkets survive, appropriate payments to
barbarian chiefs as European traders in Africa and the Pacific know.
The most decisive are segmented beads of fayence, actually Egyptian
and fashionable there about 1400 B.C.;[1] quite a number have been
found in Early Bronze Age graves on the Tisza and the lower Maros in
Hungary.

But Britain too was in contact with Minoan-Mycenaean civilisation
about this time. Not only have a large number of segmented fayence
beads of the type just mentioned been found in Southern England, an
amber disc bound with, presumably Irish, gold and identical with two
from graves in Wiltshire, lay in a tomb near Knossos sealed about
1400 B.C. It is uncertain whether British trade with Crete traversed the
continent; four segmented fayence beads found together with beads
(also segmented) of Cornish tin and others of amber at Odoorn,
Drenthe (Holland), speak in favour of a connexion with the Central
Amber route through the metal trade between Britain and North
Central Europe, well attested by the distribution of bronze articles.
Alternatively the traffic may have followed the 'megalithic' sea route;
one of our segmented fayence beads was found in a tomb in Morbihan
and eight in a Bronze Stage grave in Almeria.

---

[1] *Archaeologia*, LXXXV (1936), 203-33.

THE LATE BRONZE STAGE 17

IV. *The Late Mycenaean Period and the Late Bronze Stage*[1]

In 1400 B.C. the palace of Knossos was sacked and the thalassocracy of Minos dissolved. In the previous century and a half Crete had enjoyed unprecedented prosperity. The island had held a virtual monopoly of Aegean trade with Egypt, always the most profitable market. And at this time Egypt was enriched by tribute from an Asiatic empire, acquired after the expulsion of the Hyksôs in 1580 B.C. by the New Kingdom Pharaohs. Moreover, in Central Anatolia the Hittite New Empire was recreating an old market without as yet threatening the peace of Hither Asia. In these two adjacent areas of enforced tranquillity trade and industry could develop undisturbed; metal became cheaper than ever before, not only in Egypt but in her Asiatic dependencies where bronze was now used even for sickles and heavy implements.

In two Egyptian tombs Cretan envoys are depicted bearing master-pieces of island handicraft, while a considerable number of Minoan or Mycenaean vases have been found along the Nile, offset by Egyptian alabastra at Mycenae. A colony of Minoan merchants was planted at Minet el-Beida, the port of Ugarit in Syria, and Minoan manufactures were purchased not only on the Levant coasts but as far east as Assur on the Tigris. The Anatolian shores of the Aegean from Cyprus to Troy received Minoan or Mycenaean manufactures—and Mycenaean Greece was an economic dependency of Crete; it may have been politically tributary too, though according to the grim Attic legend the tribute was not paid in merchandise or slaves, but in boys and girls to be devoured of the Minotaur.[2]

The economy of Minoan Crete had, since 2000 B.C., been achieving a growing degree of integration on which political unification was eventually imposed from Knossos during a brief imperial period from 1450 to 1400. The destruction of Knossos ended the empire of Minos and the economic supremacy of Crete in the Aegean. Minoan civilisation survived, but was henceforth rather provincial; the centre of gravity had shifted to the mainland with Mycenae as its capital. But the island's economic heir, more extensive and more diversified, never achieved the same high degree of integration. Homer's picture of the quarrelsome Olympians, intriguing against and thwarting one another

[1] No comprehensive treatment of Europe in the Late Bronze and Early Iron Stages has appeared since Dechelette's *Manuel d'Archéologie préhistorique et gallo-romaine*, 1910–14; N. Åberg's, *Bronzezeitliche und früheisenzeitliche Chronologie* (Stockholm, 1930–5) supplies some data on Italy, Central Europe and the North.
[2] Pendlebury, *The Archaeology of Crete*, 222–5.

CEH II 2

and their overlord, Zeus himself, and of Agamemnon's equally unruly 'vassals' is only confirmed by the archaeologists' descriptions of the multitude of Mycenaean citadels, each strongly fortified against attack by neighbours as much as foreigners.

Still the basic economic structure must have been much the same as the Minoan with perhaps more emphasis on subsistence agriculture as against specialised farming, and on piracy in lieu of legitimate trade. The same handicrafts were plied in all the rich Mycenaean burghs with the same degree of differentiation, but appreciably less refinement. Bronze was plentiful and used even for sickles; just at the close of the period we find for the first time metal hoe-blades and sledge-hammers. But perhaps it is only the growing insecurity of the times that has preserved for us this evidence for a use of bronze tools in rough work that may have begun earlier; Minoan metal-workers did use bronze sledge-hammers before 1600 B.C. The use of chariots in war (since 1550 B.C.) of course required the services of highly expert wainwrights and wheelwrights.

Foreign trade expanded. The best index to its scope is as usual pottery, but surely Mycenaean vases were not exported empty any more than the aryballoi and amphorae of classical times. The fall of Knossos had opened direct access to the Egyptian market; immense numbers of Mycenaean vases, mostly of Rhodian manufacture, have been dug up all along the Nile. Mycenaean wares are equally plentiful all along the Levant coasts and wherever Bronze Age levels are reached on the east shores of the Aegean, in Cilicia, at Colophon and at Troy. Trade in this direction may have been followed by colonists or at least settlements by merchants and artisans. Cyprus was certainly colonised in a force sufficient not only to enforce the domination of a local Mycenaean industry over the native, but also to impose a version of the Minoan-Mycenaean script and presumably a Greek dialect. Tombs of Mycenaean type were built at Colophon. Northward, Mycenaean pottery reached Macedonia where Mycenaean potters settled. Westward, vases have been found on the Apulian coast and in larger quantities in Eastern Sicily where Minoan weapons and jewelry had arrived even in the fifteenth century. Even in Sardinia a copper ingot of Minoan form *and inscribed* has come to light. Further afield, apart from a Mycenaean rapier in Bulgaria, we find copies rather than originals. Among the closest are rapiers with horned guards from Bavaria and Denmark,[1] and Irish chiselled versions of Cypro-Mycenaean earrings, made in the Aegean of gold ribbons soldered together.[2]

Mycenaean imports continued to reach Egypt till the time of

---

[1] Childe, *Danube in Prehistory*, p. 250.
[2] Childe, *Prehistoric Communities*, p. 167.

Rameses III (*c.* 1167 B.C.), but during the preceding two centuries Mycenaean culture seems to have been growing poorer and weaker through internal contradictions. About 1200, barbarian raids destroyed the Hittite empire, ruined Palestine and impoverished Egypt. Related events in the Balkans finished off the tottering fabric of the Mycenaean economy in Greece. The Aegean Bronze Age ended in a dark age during which most of the old techniques survived, but commerce was reduced to a low minimum; one reason was that iron, generally obtainable from local ore, replaced bronze as the material for essential tools and weapons.

But by this time the economy of the temperate zone of Europe and the Western Mediterranean too had undergone a development that was really gradual, but in its results revolutionary. We call the resultant the Late Bronze *Stage* advisedly since it begins and ends at different points in sidereal time in its several provinces, but preserves throughout its essential characteristics even, be it noted, in South Russia. The Late Bronze Stage is distinguished from the preceding Early and Middle Bronze Stages firstly by the universal adoption of mixed farming based on plough agriculture in place of stock breeding combined with plot cultivation. Hand in hand with this transformation of the rural economy went changes in the metallurgical industries that made bronze relatively cheap; the metal was common enough to be used for sickles for reaping and for axes for clearing the land as well as for a multiplication of craft tools. The latter presumably indicates a further separation of handicraft from agriculture. There must, for instance, have been specialists to manufacture the chariots that were now used in war. On the other hand the potter's craft was not industrialised; pots were nowhere made on the wheel, not even in Sicily as yet.

The various factors that combined to revolutionise the production and distribution of metal are only imperfectly known. One certainly was the development of deep mining involving further a technique for treating unoxidised sulphide ores that is fully documented only in the Austrian Alps. In the Tyrol the ore veins were followed by deep shafts and timbered galleries. Fire-setting was the approved method of splitting the hard rock while the ore was prized out with bronze-tipped gads, broken up with stone or bronze sledge-hammers and hand-picked at the bottom of the shaft. Windlasses were available for raising the winnings to the surface where they were further treated by washing and sedimentation. Finally the ore was roasted on an exposed hill-side

<hr>

[1] Andree, *Bergbau in der Vorzeit* (Leipzig, 1922); Zschocke and Preuschen, 'Das urzeitliche Bergbaugebiet von Mühlbach-Bischofshofen' (*Materialien z. Urgeschichte Österreichs*, VI (1934)); Preuschen and Pittioni, 'Untersuchungen in Bergbaugebiete Kelchalpe' (*Mitt. prähist. Komm. d. Akad. d. Wissensch.*, Wien, 1937).

near the pit mouth and then smelted. From the remains Zschocke and Preuschen, two mining engineers, estimate that 180 workers (perhaps partly slaves) must have been employed in the exploitation of the Mitterberg main lode for two and a half to three centuries; the smelters alone would have consumed as fuel wood equivalent to 19 acres of the local forest every year.

In processing, the perambulating smith did not entirely disappear in the Late Bronze Stage. But now, thanks to the improved rural economy, many villages were large enough and rich enough to support a resident smith. Smithies have been recognised in most Alpine lake villages, suitably placed on the edge of the settlement farthest from the prevailing wind to minimise the danger of fire. At least some metalworkers were now equipped with a fairly efficient kit of metal tools including hammers, rymers, saws, files, tongs (like enlarged tweezers without hinges) and embossing anvils in addition to instruments previously used. Bellows were available for producing a blast, and clay moulds and even the *cire perdue* process were employed in casting larger objects than formerly, and the hammer technique was everywhere highly developed.

Under such conditions a village smithy could easily grow into something like a factory producing for a distant market. A careful study of the distributions of several types on the Alpine lakes shows that each village smith tended to specialise in manufacturing one or two particular types of ornament that were purchased mainly by his fellow villagers, but sometimes also in other villages even on different lakes. Indeed the products of lacustrine bronze smiths found a market far beyond the present frontiers of Switzerland between 1100 and 800 B.C.; distinctive types of weapon, like the antennae sword, very common in Switzerland, are found in England, Denmark and Sweden, the Western Ukraine, Macedonia, Carinthia and Italy.[1] Conversely Northern, Hungarian and Italian types have been recognised in the lake villages. Still larger workshops are known, especially in Slovakia and Upper Italy. In the Carpathian basin, Aszod, Kis-Terenne and Pilin, round the metalliferous mountains, and Velem Szent Vid, where a deposit of antimony was worked, have yielded, even to very superficial examination, an imposing mass of moulds, crucibles, nozzles and slags. The celebrated *fondarie* of Bologna are even larger.

Now there are several classes of bronze vessels[2]—cups, buckets, cauldrons (and also helmets and girdle-plates)—distributed from the

[1] Sprockhoff, *Die germanische Vollgriffschwerter* (*Römisch-germanische Forschungen*, IX, 1934), 27–38 and 137. By no means all these swords were made in Switzerland.
[2] Sprockhoff, *Zur Handelsgeschichte der germanischen Bronzezeit*; Childe, *Proc. Preh. Soc.* XIV (1948), 177–95.

Dnieper to the Thames and from Upper Italy to Central Sweden, yet all examples of each class are so similar that one feels all must come from a single workshop or at least a single centre like the Capuan saucepans of the Roman period. But we simply do not know where they were made nor even whether the centre of production lay in Upper Italy, whence hammered bronze ware was admittedly exported in the Iron Age, or in Hungary where most specimens have actually been found.[1]

The trade in metal, best illustrated by the hammered articles just mentioned, was not only more intensive and more extensive than before, but exhibits novel features. Distinctive of the Late Bronze Stage are so-called founders' hoards that comprise many worn and broken articles. The distributors of bronze now took in part payment, and collected for resmelting, scrap metal. Some at least of this scrap found its way to the great workshops of Hungary and Upper Italy. One deposit at Prato di Francesco, Bologna, contained distinguishable pieces of 14,800 old tools, weapons and ornaments, shown by their forms to have been brought from all parts of Europe, including the British Isles. Secondly, more hoards than before consist of one kind of article only— axes, sickles, swords, vessels; some merchants, that is, travelled exclusively in one line of goods. Finally many hoards are enormous; one in Wallachia consisted of 244 objects or fragments, including 199 sickles.[2] Such could hardly have been handled by a single family of tinkers, but would require regular caravans. But of course some of these huge hoards may be just the treasuries of barbarian chiefs, for metal now surely represented 'wealth'.

To appreciate the extension of the metal trade and its operation it is necessary to turn back to see how the market for metal had expanded and new centres of production arisen since 1400 B.C. North Italy before that date had been an independent province of the Central European system into which the whole peninsula was being incorporated, presumably as a by-product of the 'amber trade' down its Adriatic coasts. After 1200 the peninsula became a major productive centre which perhaps received from the East Mediterranean and diffused northward the new technique of hammer-working and subsequently iron. Thereafter Sicily too, where native metal-workers had been adapting Aegean types from 1500, became more closely linked with the continent. Sardinia developed a very active but extremely insular metallurgical industry rooted in the local 'copper age' but stimulated by fresh contacts with the East Mediterranean (illustrated for instance by the Minoan ingot previously mentioned) and later by western influences. Copper was available locally, but tin, and some manufactured articles,

[1] Åberg, *Bronzezeitliche und früheisenzeitliche Chronologie*, v (1934), 87–95.
[2] Drajna de Jôs, *Dacia*, II, 349.

were brought from Galicia. In the Iberian peninsula the Argaric industry of Almeria long remained isolated and conservative, but at some undefined date the metallurgists in the West, who must have been exploiting Galician tin much earlier, began manufacturing distinctive products derived from British models. Their peculiar double-looped palstaves were exported to the British Isles, Sweden and Sardinia. Still later copper-smiths, trained in Alpine traditions, arrived to supply the local market.

France began to provide a market for British and Alpine metal work about 1200 B.C., but the establishment of local industries may be some centuries later. With the spread of iron working, these industries were generally short-lived, save in Brittany where the Bronze Stage survived late, as in Ireland, and produced a number of easily recognisable local types. In the North a local school of smiths had begun producing distinctive variants on imported British and Bohemian types in North Germany, while Denmark and Scandinavia were still in the Stone Stage (p. 15). In the thirteenth century their successors, established in Denmark and South Sweden, manufactured a splendid series of distinctively Nordic types of ornate swords, axes, spears and ornaments. While largely inspired by models of the Middle Bronze Age of Hungary, even the early phase of this Nordic Bronze Age is contemporary with the Late Bronze Age of Britain, as British imports associated in graves with its products show.[1] Finally, on the Pontic steppes and along the Volga, native or Asiatic traditions were fertilised by trade with the Aegean or Anatolia that brought glass beads and presumably the models for double-axes that were cast locally. The Pontic smiths used copper from the Dombas (Bakhmut) and the Urals as well as the Caucasus, but never alloyed it with tin. Their wares were exported up the Volga and eastward, but in the Ukraine competed unsuccessfully with products of the flourishing Hungarian province.

None of these new provinces, nor yet the new subdivisions of the old ones, were mutually isolated. As in the Early Bronze Stage, products distinctive of one province are always turning up in another, often very remote; indeed four socketed axes of the peculiar Armorican type somehow reached the Ukraine.[2] New routes were opened up for the metal trade to supplement those already established, and to reach the new markets. Conspicuous is the revival of maritime trade notably on the Atlantic that had begun with the megalithic culture and had presumably never been altogether suspended. On a large scale it is strikingly illustrated by the distribution of double-looped palstaves[3]

[1] Childe, *American Anthropologist*, XXXIX (1937), 12–15; cf. Cowen, *Proc. Preh. Soc.* XIV (1948), p. 243.

[2] *Swiatowit*, Warsaw, XVII (1936–7), 303.   [3] *Antiquaries' Journ.* XIX, 320.

from Galicia already mentioned and rather later by a 'hoard' dredged up from Huelva harbour and presumed to represent the cargo of a sunken merchant ship; it carried spearheads cast in the British Isles

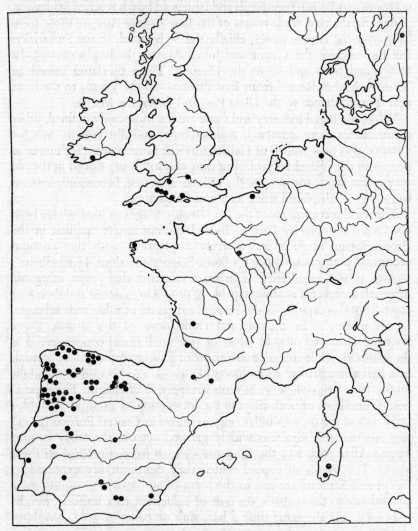

Map 3. Distribution of double-looped palstaves illustrating Atlantic trade in the Late Bronze Age.

and brooches manufactured in Sicily together with vaguely 'West European' swords and ornaments. In detail the same point can be brought home by the distribution of Irish types of weapons and ornaments round the west coasts of Scotland to Orkney and Shetland.

Incidentally a hoard from Lewis contained, besides Irish implements, beads of Irish gold, Baltic amber, and Mediterranean glass and a broken cup of Central European workmanship.[1] It was presumably by this sea route that British spearheads and Irish gold bowls reached Schleswig.

Among the new trade routes of the Late Bronze Age are those from Italy over the Alpine passes, chiefly the St Bernard, to the Swiss lakes and those across the Carnic and Julian Alps to the headwaters of the Drava and Sava and so to the Danube. There the latter joined an 'Eastern Amber Route' from East Prussia—up the Vistula to the bend near Torun, thence to the Glatz Pass and down the March.

While the metal industry and trade are the most easily defined, other commodities were extracted, manufactured and distributed. Salt for instance was now mined at Hallstatt by the same mature technique as copper in the adjacent Tyrol. But flint was still being mined in the old way in England; for, despite the reduction in cost, bronze implements had nowhere displaced stone axes and flint knives.

The regular commerce of the Late Bronze Stage can hardly have been conducted entirely by barter. Indeed the commerce implicit in the Bronze Stage as such was scarcely compatible with that 'natural economy' that was adequate for Stone Stage transactions. Heichelheim[2] regards it as a peculiarity of urban civilisation that 'even inorganic materials are treated as alive, capable of producing interest and therefore capital, but this capital can also serve as a measure of value and exchange, i.e. as money'. In the oriental civilisations of the Bronze Stage weighed quantities of gold, silver or (for small sums) copper served as the standard, while to barbarians an ox or a sheep seemed more natural. In a barbarian Bronze Age objects like rings, axes or cauldrons might on the same principle serve as units irrespective of weight. The deposition of hundreds of neck-rings in the foundation of a temple at Byblos in Syria and the use of similar rings as ingots in Central Europe (p. 13) suggests that this idea was widely grasped even in the Early Bronze Stage. After 1600 B.C. the Minoans seem to have combined all these ideas.[3] The ingots of copper which they demonstrably exported to Egypt and Sardinia are cast in the form of an ox hide to signify their equivalence to the barbaric ox unit of value, but to a uniform weight —25·5 kg. At the same time a bar, ring or pellet of gold, weighing about 8·5 gm. may also have been equivalent to an ox. The resultant equation of metal objects of fixed weight with the ox unit must have facilitated commerce with barbarian Europe and may even have been adopted by the barbarians themselves. Gold ring money has long been recognised in Late Bronze Age Ireland; 1200 bronze rings from an

[1] Childe, *Scotland before the Scots*, p. 71. [2] *Wirtschaftsgeschichte des Altertums*, p. 114. [3] Seltman, *Greek Coins* (1935), pp. 5–10.

Alpine lake village and 700 from a Silesian hoard might likewise represent currency.[1] At the same time lead weights from the lake dwellings demonstrate the use of the balance or steelyard (in Crete balances are depicted already in the sixteenth century) and the adoption in Europe of metric standards recognised in the oriental civilisations since the beginning of the IIIrd millennium. On the other hand scales and weights, so conspicuous in the graves of the Norse traders and pirates whom we term Vikings, have not yet been recognised in graves nor hoards of pre-Roman times.

V.   *The First Iron Stage*

The use of iron as an industrial metal, initiated in Asia Minor in the first half of the IInd millennium B.C.,[2] and reaching Greece just before its close, spread slowly across the Alps from Italy after 800 B.C., still more slowly from the Caucasus and the Greek colonies on the Black Sea and in the Iberian peninsula from Carthage and its colonies.

The significance of the new metal was its low cost as compared with bronze. Iron ore of some kind or another can be found almost anywhere. Most people therefore who possess the secret of smelting and forging and will take the trouble can provide themselves with efficient and durable tools without depending on the elaborate distributive machinery of the bronze industry or contributing to the support of specialist miners and a horde of middlemen. With these tools they could and did clear forest and drain land for cultivation. The result was a general increase in population and an enlargement of the local unit of settlement. On the other hand, weapons were cheapened too so that the growing population might be tempted to find *Lebensraum* at the expense of other communities rather than by laboriously bringing fresh virgin soil under cultivation. The multiplication of fortifications is just as conspicuous a feature of the Iron Stage as is the growth of villages. Incidentally, constant wars in which victory might depend on the manoeuvres of costly chariots guided by armoured knights soon counteracted the levelling tendency of cheap swords and spears.

North of the Alps and west of the Carpathians the Iron Age falls into two phases termed respectively Hallstatt and La Tène. Throughout both, the existence of Greek cities in Italy and soon also at Marseilles and farther west and of the civilised Etruscan and subsequently Roman states was a decisive factor in the development of barbarian economy. For trade with Italy remained as intensive as in the Late Bronze Stage and was soon supplemented by that with Massilia and Iberia on the one

---

[1] Ebert's *Reallexikon der Vorgeschichte*, IV, 214.   [2] *Antiquity*, 1936, 5–24.

hand, with the Pontic colonies on the other. For the Greek and Italic markets slaves must now have formed just as profitable an export as metals, amber and other raw materials and the trade therein just as potent a stimulus to wars in Europe as the American slave trade was to be in Africa.

The bronze industry was not abolished nor drastically curtailed by the substitution of iron tools and weapons. Bronze was still used by barbarians for ornaments, vessels and even armour, and was demanded in vast quantities by the Etruscans, Greeks, Phoenicians, Assyrians and other civilised peoples. Many of the old productive centres, like Velem Szt. Vid, flourished exceedingly during the Hallstatt period, and the commerce in bronze ware was as active as ever. Moreover, where the industry was well organised and raw material available near at hand, iron was slow in replacing bronze as the industrial metal—in Scotland not before 200 B.C., in Brittany and Northern Europe not till 500, in Transylvania only after 600; in the coniferous forests of the far North the industrial use of bronze only began in the first Iron Age of the centre !

Tin and gold naturally retained their commercial importance. The gold of Transylvania in particular found a ready market among the Scythians of the Pontic steppes; numerous Scythian objects in native graves along the Maros just confirm Herodotus' remarks about the Agathyrsi. Silver and lead were also extracted and traded.

As iron ores are so widespread, the new industrial metal was not traded to the same extent as bronze; moreover, it is much harder to determine by archaeological criteria the place of origin of iron work. Nevertheless superior ores like those of Noricum, Westfalia, Silesia, Lorraine, Burgundy and the Franche Comté must have been exploited for a wide market, especially when they were associated with other marketable materials, like salt as in Noricum, Lorraine and the Franche Comté.[1] Iron was exported from Lorraine in late Hallstatt times in the form of curiously shaped bars[2] about 0·25 m. long and weighing on an average 7 kg., as far west as the Somme, southward to Switzerland and westward to Saxony and Moravia. Ingots of precisely the same form were stored in the palace of Sargon (722–705 B.C.) at Khorsabad.

But even in such ferruginous regions the productive units seem to have been absurdly small; for iron could not be cast at the temperatures available but spongy masses had to be forged into a 'bloom' of pure metal by prolonged hammering by hand. The surviving hearths, of rather vague antiquity, were 0·60 to 1·60 m. in diameter; even if the principle of the blast furnace were applied in some places, the remains preserved nowhere exceed 1·20 m. in height and all seem to have relied

[1] Dechelette, *Manuel*, II, 2, 714.   [2] Ebert's *Reallexikon*, III, 63.

upon the wind unaided by any artificial blast.[1] At the same time and even much later iron was smelted in still smaller furnaces on lone steadings or in caves, for instance in Scotland.[2]

Salt was still extracted and traded more systematically than ever. The wealth of the Hallstatt cemetery in imported articles—Italic bronze ware, African ivory, Egyptian glass, Baltic amber—represents the profits on the traffic. At Hallstatt salt was no longer mined but extracted by evaporation in specially constructed apparatus, remains of which have been found in Noricum, Thuringia, Belgium, Lorraine and the Franche Comté too, near saline springs[3] and on the coasts, for instance in East Anglia.[4] But no new industries, apart from the manufacture of lignite bracelets, are archaeologically attested, though existing industries were doubtless further subdivided and specialised. Indeed what distinguishes the Hallstatt phase from the La Tène is that hardly any new industrial tools were invented or adopted. There were few refinements in daily life and these—flesh hooks, pot suspenders, spits—were confined to chieftains' courts.

The strongly fortified Hallstatt settlements must not be compared to an Aegean township of the Bronze Stage, still less to a Greek *polis*. Under their massive ramparts huddled the huts of peasant households who cultivated fields in the vicinity, made their own clothes and many utensils including very likely even pots. Though there were a smith and a carpenter such would not be producing for the market and displaying their wares in permanent booths. Periodical fairs may be perhaps assumed but with no more evidence than in the Bronze Stage. Itinerant hucksters are still attested, but, apart from iron and salt, trade was mainly in luxuries.

Trade in small articles of barbarian workmanship can often be detected as before; a few Hallstatt brooches, such as were not regularly worn nearer than the Alpine slopes, turn up in England and may rank as imports, like the glass beads and bronze cup from Lewis mentioned on p. 24. But now the trade in Italic and Mediterranean manufactures is the most easily defined and the best studied. Such reached the barbarians not only through Italy but also from Greek colonies on the Black Sea and at Marseilles. But most of the goods from the Pontic colonies were absorbed by the Scythians and the extent of Massiliote commerce with the interior is still disputed. The list of imports received this side of the Alps is swelled by fresh items. Glass beads from Italy or

[1] Weiershaufen, *Vorgeschichtliche Eisenhütten Deutschlands* (Mannus Bücherei, 65, 1939); W. Schmidt, *Norisches Eisen*, Vienna, 1932; *Zeitsch. f. Ethnologie*, 1909, p. 91.
[2] Childe, *Scotland before the Scots*, 1946, p. 80.
[3] *Zeitsch. f. Ethnologie*, 1903, p. 642.
[4] *Antiquaries' Journ.* XII (1932), 239; but cf. p. 30.

Greece are quite common; moulded glass vases of Egyptian manufacture and presumably filled with precious ointments must have been
rare luxuries though a few reached even Hallstatt in Upper Austria and
the Rhine valley. Ivory was slightly more widely distributed. Coral
was obtained first in the sixth century probably from Marseilles via the
Rhone and Saone.

Metal ware now includes armour—cuirasses almost certainly Italic
but mostly found in Gaul,[1] Corinthian greaves (Bosnia and Alpes Maritimes) and so on. Buckets, cauldrons, cups and urns of beaten bronze
and most probably of Italic workmanship are quite common round the
Alps, but reached even Brittany, Denmark and Transylvania before iron
had effectively replaced bronze in industry there—a distinct but parallel
series was manufactured in Bronze Stage Ireland and exported to
Britain and Denmark.

Only a limited number of actual Greek manufactures have survived.
An archaic hydria from Bene in Transylvania presumably came from
the Pontic colonies. Another from Grächwyl in Switzerland and a tripod
from La Garenne (Côtes-d'Or) might have been brought across the
Alps or from Massilia. The latter is the most likely source for sixth
century Rhodian flagons found in tombs in Vaucluse, Bavaria and the
Rhine valley, since such are missing in Italy.[2] They are symbolic of
another import that proved more potent than aught else to unlock
barbarian wealth; Greek wine among the Celts was as much coveted as
fire-water among the redskins.

Of European exports to the Mediterranean that actually figure in the
archaeological record amber remains the most conspicuous. Besides
the Late Bronze Stage routes defined on p. 24, a branch up the Bosna
and down the Narenta may be inferred from Greek and Italic imports
and amber beads found in the great Bosnian cemeteries. Another
northern commodity—furs—now figures in the list albeit only in
Scythia. Scythian trade and industry lie outside the scope of this survey;
suffice it to say that the Scythian chieftains, who had arisen like the
Celtic chieftains of La Tène, from a barbarian society penetrated by
Greek commerce, had concentrated enough wealth to provide an
effective market both for Greek manufactures and for raw materials
like Transylvanian gold and arctic furs.

Now the hunter-fisher tribes of the North Russian forests had
remained in a Stone Stage though they sometimes obtained some
products of Ural metallurgy, perhaps in exchange for East Prussian
amber that was occasionally traded south-eastward across White

[1] Fillinges (Haute Savoie), L. du Bourget (Savoie), Grenoble, S. Germain du Plain
(Saone–et–Loire), *Préhistoire*, III (1934), 93 ff.
[2] De Navarro, *Antiquity*, II, 425.

Russia[1] and eastwards along the Volga. But between 600 and 400 B.C. farmers established fortified settlements—the Ananino *gorodishche*—along the lower Kama and acted as middlemen in a trade in furs; for bones of fur-bearing arctic mammals are found in thousands in the *gorodishche*.[2] The furs must have gone to Scythia but stray bronze axes of Ananino type were diffused right through the coniferous zone to Finland, Norwegian Finnmark and Swedish Lappland[3]—even moulds for their manufacture have turned up in Finland and Finnmark. At the same time bronze axes and other products of the belated Bronze Stage of East Sweden found their way eastward along the upper Volga to its junction with the Kama and up to Molotov. Some come from graves of warriors, buried with iron weapons and Swedish ornaments; such were evidently combining 'trade' with military exploits like the later Varangs.

VI. *The Second Iron Age (La Tène)*

Before the end of the fifth century, thanks to the increased food supplies made available by iron tools the fecund Celtic populations living round the Alps had grown dense enough and rich enough to provide livelihoods for new classes of specialised resident craftsmen. At the same time constant wars allowed chieftains (p. 25) to concentrate sufficient wealth to support new industries. Master potters were attracted to many villages and began to manufacture vases on the wheel. Glass makers followed and, besides manufacturing beads, bracelets and other cheap trinkets (never vessels), developed the art of enamelling. A variety of new tools and machines, introduced from the Mediterranean— metal ploughshares, scythes, shears, hinged tongs, compasses, rotary querns—enormously increased production, encouraged further speciali- sation and demanded new industries for their supply.

The rich chieftains, like Homer's heroes, acted as patrons to artist craftsmen. Metal-workers happen to be the best known; wood carvers, leather workers and weavers of equal technical proficiency and artistic talent may safely be assumed. Both the equipment and the social standing of a Celtic craftsman in Gaul just before Caesar's conquest can be judged from the furniture of a burial under a large barrow at Celles, Cantal—a lance, a shield, a knife, a small sickle, two files, two saws, a hammer, a compass, a plane, chisels, gouges, a rotary quern, whorls, and twenty clay vases. The number and variety of handicraft products—

[1] A Hittite warrior statuette from Schernen, East Prussia, implies the use of this route even in the IInd millennium; *Swiatowit*, XIII (1929), 57.

[2] Schmidt, *Izvestiya GAIMK.* 106 (1935), 74ff. (Russian).

[3] Tallgren, *ESA.* XI, 1–44.

locks and keys, dice, mirrors, combs, etc.—found in graves or settlements are such that manufacture by specialists to order, if not for the
market, must be admitted.

Little can be said of the extractive industries, partly owing to the
difficulty of deciding whether a given bloomery or briquetage be
Hallstatt or La Tène, since many centres operated throughout both
phases. We happen to know that a small-scale industry was working
the Kimmeridge shale of Dorset[1] and that the ornaments it turned out
were exported all over South-western England.

Distribution kept pace with the expansion of the market. Trade was
both on a larger scale and safer. Merchants following regular routes
enjoyed the protection of powerful tribes, but had to pay customs dues
in kind for the privilege of transit. An immense accumulation of tools,
weapons, machines and ornaments found in a pile structure at La Tène
on Lake Neuchâtel represents, Déchelette believed, the share of the
customs on goods shipped from the lake, the transit dues having been
stored in a sort of customs warehouse. Dues from trade along the
Saône are represented by a similar collection dredged up from the
river at Châlon. These and similar collections emphasise the importance
of water-borne traffic and the variety of articles, often bulky and heavy,
that could profitably be transported.

The same point is driven home by the famous lake village of Glastonbury. Protected by marshes at the head of navigation on the Old Rhyne
it owed its prosperity and very existence to trade in lead, iron, shale
ornaments, etc., that could conveniently be brought along ridgeways
that converge here from the Mendips, Northamptonshire, Dorset and
other producing regions. Yet the villagers provided themselves with
food by farming, fishing and hunting, and plied the crafts of metallurgy,
carpentry, weaving, leather work and so on.

Of imports from the civilised Mediterranean cities, wine was perhaps
the most prized among the barbarian Celts. The evidence is at first of
the same kind as in late Hallstatt times—the burial of a luxury wine
service with a rich chieftain; three chieftains' tombs in Bohemia, one
on the Inn, twenty-three on the Rhine from Alsace to Hessen, including
ten round Birkenfeld on the Nahe, one in Belgium, four in Champagne
and two in Burgundy contained beaked wine flagons made in Etruria
on Greek models.[2] Similarly fifth-century Attic vases were buried in
three Rhenish tombs, in two on the Marne and in one in Switzerland.[3]
The actual wine would have been imported in skins though later
amphorae are common in Gaul. De Navarro[4] contends that most of

---

[1] *Archaeological Journal*, XCIII (1936), 200–19.
[2] Langsdorf and Jacobsthal, *Die Bronzeschnabelkannen*, Berlin, 1929.
[3] Jacobsthal in *Germania*, XVIII (1934), 17–18.   [4] *Antiquity*, II, 437.

this trade passed through Massilia, up the Rhone and Saône to the salt and iron producing area of Lorraine and thence to the Marne or the Rhine. Jacobsthal prefers a route from Italy, up the Ticino and across the St Bernard.

The principal exports to the Mediterranean civilisations would still have been metal, amber, furs and slaves. The last-named traffic is documented by slave chains found in Bohemia, Gaul and Britain. The trade in Cornish tin, as reported in literature from the third century,

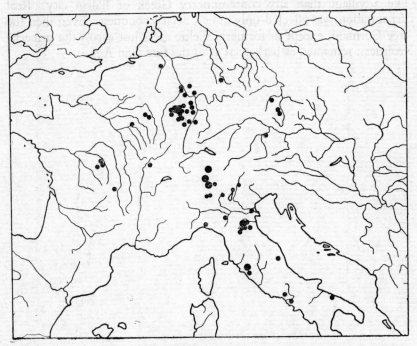

Map. 4. Distribution of beaked wine flagons illustrating trans-Alpine trade. Large dots denote concentrations of finds at adjacent sites.

followed land routes towards Marseilles after crossing the Channel to Brittany.[1] Archaeology justifies the belief that the Celtic occupation of South-western England was dictated by the desire to gain control of this lucrative traffic, but apart from a couple of Iberian bronze statuettes [2] fails to prove the receipt of Mediterranean manufactures in exchange.

The high differentiation of handicraft production and the intensity of trade so obvious in the La Tène culture were incompatible with the maintenance of a natural economy. The Celts of Southern England

[1] Hencken, *The Archaeology of Cornwall*, pp. 166–70.
[2] *Journ. Roy. Soc. of Antiquaries, Ireland*, XLVIII, 51–4.

used as currency iron bars, weighing multiples of 77·4 gm., down to
Caesar's day. But tribes living in the Danube basin and in Gaul began
to use Greek coins in the third century and eventually issued their own
coinages.

By this time farming technique had developed so far as to produce an
exportable surplus. It could support a population of artisans and
merchants. Nevertheless a normal Gaulish hillfort, save in the immediate proximity of the Mediterranean, remained economically more
like a village than any contemporary Greek or Italian city. Real
urbanisation was effected only after Caesar's conquest. Even then the
free Germani, except in formerly Celtic areas just across the imperial
frontiers, remained as barbarous as in the first Iron Age.

CHAPTER II

Trade and Industry under the Later Roman Empire in the West

IN the year of our Lord 301, 'aroused justly and rightfully by the abuse of immoderate prices and an uncurbed passion for gain, which is lessened neither by abundant supplies nor by fruitful years', the Emperor Diocletian issued an Edict in which, after analysing the evils of the times (in curiously pompous and tortuous Latin), he laid down for their improvement a tariff of maximum prices, to be observed on pain of death throughout the whole Empire. This Edict is significant not so much for its results (which were trivial), but as a symbol of the change that had come over the life of the Mediterranean world since the setting up of the principate by Augustus three hundred years earlier. A world of free, private economic activity had given place to one of rigid state control. Machinery had been devised for the organisation of production and trade. Forms of free association had been transmuted into organs of rigid regimentation. The imperial authorities, once content merely to provide facilities for the trader, to act as 'night-watchman for the business-man', now directed his whole life and his very movements from place to place.

The process of this transformation was involved. It had its ramifications in every branch of social and economic life; and it embraced the provinces no less than Italy, the original core of the Empire. Its beginnings can be traced in the earliest period of the principate; but unfortunately the critical time when the new outlines were solidifying is one of the most obscure in the whole history of Rome. In the absence of reliable literary sources, the economic history of the third century has largely to be reconstructed with the aid of archaeology, and by deductions made from such later evidence as the legal codes afford, and from a comparison of earlier conditions with the system set up by Diocletian and Constantine. Inevitably, therefore, a review of the trade and industry of the later Empire must begin with the principate.

I

The annexation of the old-established provinces of the eastern Mediterranean under the Republic had exercised a profound influence upon the economic life of the West. An influx of Greeks and Syrians, who came mostly as slaves, but rapidly and in large numbers achieved the status of freedmen, was responsible for a marked rise in the technical level of production. At the same time, new standards were set up, and the demand for more refined wares was stimulated by the actual import of eastern products. Nevertheless, the character of Italian industry was not fundamentally altered, but remained one of small businesses. Workers were engaged either in casual labour or in individual work-shops, *tabernae*, which frequently served as booths for the selling of the goods produced in them. Naturally this was a pattern which allowed of much variation. Sometimes the customer might bring his own materials, his cloth or his gold and silver, to be made up into garments or ornaments by the appropriate workman. But there is plenty of evidence for the craftsman himself providing the raw materials and in some cases making it up for the market. The existence of bazaars and the presence of pedlars on the streets and in the public baths presupposes a considerable amount of production of this kind.

Moreover, in some instances industry is known to have developed on a larger scale, and with the aid of slave labour to have approached something like a factory system; and despite the old Roman prejudice against trade, inscriptions reveal the presence of a class of rich business men, who were organised in companies, *societates*, and were prepared to contract for the provision of public and even private buildings, and occasionally to speculate in the buying up, repairing and reselling of damaged property. Usually the men engaged in this kind of lucrative activity were socially obscure. All the more remarkable therefore is the case of the Domitii, who between A.D. 50 and A.D. 150 established what was almost a monopoly in the brickyards of Italy, and so provided perhaps the only example in Roman history of political fame resting upon industrial wealth. The beginnings of the firm go back to the demand created by the great fire of Rome in A.D. 64; and judging by its stamped products, which reveal the existence of fifty-three slaves, twenty-two freedmen, and twenty-two others of uncertain status, the actual number employed must have been far in excess of this. By A.D. 155 the Domitian brickworks were employing no less than forty-six foremen; and the wealth of the Domitian family helped to lay the foundations of the Antonine dynasty, with which it had marriage connections. There are other examples of fairly large concerns, such as the pottery of C. Laekanius Bassus at Fasana near Pola, which produced *amphorae* for the marketing of Istrian oil, and employed at least fifteen slaves. The bronze industry of Capua, too, must have been highly organised; and we know the names of thirteen female slaves who worked in a weaving shed at Pompeii. In Rome itself there are records of two large factories during the early Empire, one for the reprocessing of papyrus, and another for handling Spanish red-lead. In general, however, these larger enterprises were exceptional. Thus the lead pipes provided under contract for the imperial authorities were mainly the product of small firms; and the predominant form of industrial organisation remained one of private individuals working for themselves, or small firms undertaking modest contracts.

The division of labour between free men, freedmen, and slaves varied from one industry to another; nor is it always easy to assess the value of the inscriptional evidence on which our knowledge rests. It has, however, been calculated that among the owners and entrepreneurs in business in Rome during the first two centuries of the Empire, there was a preponderance of freedmen over men of free origin in the proportion of two to one, and that a similar but much smaller preponderance also existed in the rest of Italy. The labourers, however, were mainly slaves, with some freedmen whose manumission had been qualified by a clause exacting continued duties of this kind; free wage earners were exceptional anywhere in Italy, though their occasional use is implied in a story of Vespasian, who is said to have rejected the adoption of a labour-saving hoisting machine with the significant words: 'I must feed my poor.' In the early Empire there was no kind of regulation of the conditions of labour in the various industries. Under a system of free contract, working hours normally stretched from sunrise to sunset, and child labour was used where it was profitable. Wages were paid sometimes by the day, sometimes by the piece.

What then were the main results of the setting up of the Augustan principate in the sphere of production and commerce? They are to be seen essentially in the quickening of economic activity, and the extension of the market which came with a higher standard of living. When Pliny says that every servant girl has her silver mirror, he is probably guilty of rhetorical overstatement. But the first period of the Empire undoubtedly saw the fruits of security, peace, and a good system of roads and safe sea communications, in the rise of a class of Italian business man, sometimes free and sometimes of freedman origin, who took the initiative in developing the western provinces. In particular this class extended the wholesale trade, which Roman sentiment had always regarded as almost respectable. 'Business on a small scale', writes Cicero (De officiis, 1, 150–1), 'is despicable; but if it is extensive and imports commodities in large quantities from all over the world, and distributes them honestly, it is not so very discreditable; nay, if the merchant satiated, or rather satisfied, with the fortune he has made, retires from the harbour and steps into an estate, as once he returned to harbour from the sea, he deserves, I think, the highest respect.' Earlier in the same passage Cicero expresses his contempt for manual work, which he describes as degrading. It is the typical attitude of the Republican nobility, of an aristocracy which was content to see its physical work done by slaves; and in so far as this attitude persisted under the Empire, its results were not happy. The capital accumulated by the *nouveaux riches* of the Augustan revolution tended to be invested in land rather than in manufacture or commerce; and these activities were left largely to freedmen and foreigners.

Thus Italy still preserved, if in a modified degree, the parasitical character which it had established under the Republic. Cicero's big business man, it will be observed, is one who imports and distributes; and this definition reflects the function of Italy in relation to the rest of the Mediterranean world. Strabo describes the Egyptian corn boats returning empty from Puteoli, which had once been a flourishing export harbour serving the rich districts of Campania; and Pliny asserts that India, China, and Arabia between them received annually the sum of a hundred million sesterces (nearly £800,000) from the Empire, a statement which is supported by the discovery of numerous Roman gold coins in India, and even in Ceylon and China. It may fairly be assumed that these coins represent payment for the luxuries—dancing girls, parrots, ebony, ivory, pearls and precious stones, spices, perfumes, silks, and drugs—which the far East sent to Rome. On the other hand, during the first century of the Empire Italy enjoyed a flourishing trade with the undeveloped provinces of the north and west. Africa, Spain, Gaul, Germany, the Danube areas and Britain were all markets for Italian bronze, glass and pottery, and this trade laid the foundations of the prosperity of Aquileia, through which much of it passed. From here the trading houses of the Barbii and the Statii despatched overseas goods, together with the products of Italy, northwards to the Danube and eastwards to Istria in exchange for slaves, cattle, hides, resin, pitch, wax, honey and cheese, and for the iron and wool of Noricum.

Other parts of Italy also flourished under the early principate. The bronzework and glassware of Campania, the pottery of Arretium, the textile industries of Apulia and Calabria in the south and of the Po valley in the north (where linen was also manufactured), all enjoyed a season of prosperity; and there was a considerable local trade and exchange of commodities throughout the peninsula. Gradually, however, this declined. Italy lacked the skill to compete with the East; and once the new western provinces were developed, they were able to exploit certain advantages of labour which quickly put them ahead of Italy. By the second century Italian overseas trade was reduced to a trickle and the parasitical character of the peninsula once more reasserted itself.

For this regression in the economic life of Italy the provinces of the north and west were in part at least responsible. Here the setting up of the Empire had been more than a mere stimulus. It was rather a creative act, which carried the benefits of Greco-Roman civilisation and town life to fresh areas, and extended the civilised way of life as far as the Roman legions went. The process had of course already begun. Under the late Republic, Provence and Languedoc had been for some time a second Italy, with rich olive groves and extensive vineyards. But now the consolidation after Caesar's conquests carried Roman civilisation to the English Channel and the Rhine, and northern Gaul began to take its place within the economy of the Empire. New towns, centres of Roman culture, and inhabited by craftsmen and merchants, began to spring up in all parts, not large indeed by modern standards, or even in comparison with an Alexandria or an Antioch—the populations of Nîmes, Toulouse, Autun and Trèves were never more than 50,000, nor their areas above 500–850 acres—but nevertheless important centres for the dissemination of civilised ways of thought and behaviour. In Spain too the cities grew in number and size. According to Strabo, there were more commercial entrepreneurs in Gades than in any other city of the Empire except Patavium in the Po valley.

The first stage in the Romanisation of a new province or frontier area usually came with the presence of the Roman army, which would supervise the building of forts, harbours, bridges and roads, and for this purpose frequently set up its own brickworks and opened up its own quarries. Thus the potteries of Xanten and Neuss, and the lamp factory at Weisenau near Mainz, which dates from the time of Augustus, were directly worked by the army. The next stage was the arrival in the new area of the Italian trader, with goods to serve the army and incidentally the native population. In the wake of the trader colonies and markets such as Cambodunum (Kempten in Allgäu) sprang up; and very soon, with the stimulus given to native industry, the third stage was reached, in which the colonial area developed its own economy. The net result was a decline in the demand for Italian products, and a shift in the location of industry outward from Italy to the provinces.

This tendency can be most easily traced in the history of the production of the fine red-ware pottery—*terra sigillata*—which is so typical of most important Roman sites, and fills so many of the display cabinets of local museums. About the end of the Republic we find *sigillata* produced at various centres in Italy, including Rome itself, Puteoli, and above all Arretium in Etruria; gradually, by the time of Augustus, Arretium has forged ahead, and captured the main markets. Its products appear in every province of the Empire, and especially in Spain, North Africa, North Gaul and Germany. The workshops seem to have been large, and organised on a basis of slave labour; thus we know of fifty-eight slaves in that of P. Cornelius. Sometimes, too, it is possible to trace the manumission of a slave and his subsequent appearance as an independent master. However, the centre of production soon began to shift. After a short period during which work from Modena, which lies nearer to the frontier, appears on Gallic sites, a brand of Gallic ware from la Graufesenque (Aveyron), and several minor centres such as Banassac (Lozère) and Montans (Tarn), makes its appearance and begins to supply Aquitania. By the beginning of Tiberius' principate pots from la Graufesenque were reaching the Rhine and the camp at Haltern on the Lippe. From its potteries, one square kilometre in extent, there poured forth thousands of vases, which by A.D. 40–70 had a complete control over the market. They are found all over Gaul and Roman Germany. The contemporary camp sites at Hofheim in Taunus and Aislingen in Württemberg contain virtually none but la Graufesenque ware. In the British Museum there are over a thousand sherds mainly from London; and under Domitian some even reached Scotland. From Narbonne they were exported to Spain, where they competed with the declining industry of Arretium, and even to Italy itself.

However, by Domitian's principate la Graufesenque too had passed its prime. The sites in southern Baden now begin to show sherds of a type which has been traced to Lezoux, the scene of a large collection of potteries with several hundred kilns seventeen miles east of Clermont Ferrand, and not far from the Allier, which served for purposes of transport. These potteries, which were pre-Roman in origin, reached the acme of their success from about A.D. 75 to A.D. 110. By this time Italy had completely lost its hold on the foreign market. Even under the Flavians the only Italian pots exported went to North Africa; and in the ruins of Pompeii there was discovered an unopened crate of pottery, largely from Gaul—so powerful had the competition of the new centres become. The main markets for Gallic ware were, however, in the military zones, along the Rhine and Danube and, to a lesser extent, in Britain. Very soon therefore the industry once more began to move eastward towards Germany.

Under ancient conditions land transport was always excessively slow and expensive. To bring an oil-crushing machine from Suessa twenty-five miles away to Cato's farm at Venafrum cost 72 *sesterces*, or 14·5% of its cost; but to bring it the 75 miles from Pompeii cost 280 *sesterces*, which is 73% of the cost. In Diocletian's time, to transport a wagon-load of hemp worth 4800 *denarii* 240 miles exactly doubled its price. So prohibitive was the cost of transporting cheap or heavy articles by land, and so little had the situation improved in nearly half a millennium. This fact explains not only the tremendous advantages enjoyed by a country with good river transport like Gaul, but also why the pottery industry migrated eastward into Germany. About A.D. 100, men from

Lezoux had established a flourishing centre at Heiligenberg in Alsace, and a little later the pots from Faulquemont-Chémeny, twelve and a half miles east of Metz, were reaching the Rhine, the Moselle, the Rhine-Danube *limes*, and other parts of Germany. In A.D. 83 civilian potters occupied the kilns at Rheinzabern between Mainz and Strasbourg, which had been abandoned by the army, when it moved forward to Heddernheim at the junction of the Nied and Main near Frankfort; in A.D. 125 they were joined by a group from Heiligenberg, and from this time onwards under Hadrian and the Antonines the pots of Rheinzabern dominated the markets of the whole Rhineland. Finally, in about A.D. 170, when M. Aurelius transferred the armies to the area of danger along the Danube, the Rheinzabern potters moved out to Werstendorf in Bavaria. The Rhenish factories survived until the invasions of the third century; and in Gaul, meanwhile, the process of decentralisation had taken on a secondary form in the appearance of a multiplicity of centres and zones producing local imitations of *sigillata*, and vaguely associated with the old sites. This new production served a small market and cannot compare in style, efficiency or organisation with Lezoux and la Graufesenque.

The movement towards the frontiers could be paralleled in other industries; and it was the result of several related causes. Some of these —the cost of transport, and the attraction of a market closely related to the frontier armies—have already been mentioned. In addition, as we saw, Gaul had a system of good waterways, and easy communications with both the Ocean and the Mediterranean. Technically too the Gallic products have the advantage over those of Arretium: they are harder baked, and have a brighter glaze. Yet another factor lay in the development of the internal Italian market, which was essential as a basis for the industry. During the first century of our era the upper classes in Italy turned more and more to rich metals for their table ware, and the poor of course could afford only the cheapest crockery. The few who still desired *sigillata* preferred the superior products of la Graufesenque and other Gallic sites.

Together these factors are no doubt sufficient to explain the migration of the pottery industry to newer lands. But in addition the organisation of production in Gaul was superior to that in Italy. Some forty *graffiti* discovered among the potsherds of la Graufesenque record the numbers of various kinds of vases included in a single firing, listed under the names of separate potters. These lists suggest that a common kiln was shared by a number of independent craftsmen, whose free status is clear from their signatures on their wares; yet there is evidence for an exchange of moulds between them, for we have copies of identical vessels turned out by different firms. The problem is to discover who ran the kiln. Was it some local *seigneur*, such as the Ti. Flavius Vetus, whom we find acting as *patronus* to a group of free iron-workers and stonemasons at Dijon? Or did the potters themselves own the kiln communally? The second view is the more likely, and it has been suggested that this form of cooperation between free labourers was the continuation of an old Celtic tradition. Traces of a similar system have been found in the later Gallo-Roman potteries of the Argonne.

Free labour working in this way within the framework of a coopera-tive society provided a very marked contrast to the conditions in Italy, where vase-signatures indicate that the potter was usually a slave. Indeed, out of one hundred and thirty-two workers at Arretium, whose names have survived from the period before A.D. 25, no less than one hundred and twenty-three are slaves. This contrast in itself affords a good reason why the pottery industry should have shifted outwards to Gaul and Roman Germany.

The history of Gallo-Roman pottery in Gaul is, however, no isolated phenomenon. On the contrary, the first two centuries of the Empire saw a similar expansion in all branches of economic life in these provinces. The application of classical techniques to the resources of a fertile land with an industrious and skilful population of free men brought quick returns. Primarily Gaul produced agricultural goods. Grain from the rich plains of Gascony was shipped from Narbonne to Ostia; and the freshwater boatmen of Lyons brought the corn harvested along the Loire and the Seine down the Saône and Rhone to the shippers of Arles. Alternatively the northern harvest went via the Escaut and the Meuse to help in the provisioning of the Rhine armies. Gaul played only a small part in the feeding of Rome; but the presence of a *procurator annonae* at Arles is not without its significance.

In addition to grain the province produced large quantities of timber, olive oil and wine. Much of the country was still under forest, and the lumbermen built their logs into rafts and floated them down the broad rivers for eventual export to Rome, where between 800 and 900 public baths consumed a vast amount of wood fuel. The vineyards of Provence were already famous under the Republic. By Pliny's time they stretched along the Rhone valley, and the wines of Vienne were highly rated. *Apéritifs* made from smoked Narbonese wine with aloes, or from the wine of Vienne with an infusion of resin, were both known at Rome, though it is unlikely that Gallic wines offered serious competition to those of Italy during the first two centuries of our era; indeed the *vinarii* of Lyons imported Italian wine for distribution in Gaul. Similarly, until about A.D. 150 merchants from the same town dealt in olive oil from Spain and Italy; after that date there is some evidence that Gaul itself began to export this important commodity.

The advent of the Romans also brought an impetus to industry. The manufacture of woollen cloth and linen is assigned by Pliny to the whole of Gaul. In the main it was a domestic industry, though Strabo mentions linen-workers among the Cadurci, who may have been employed in a factory. Textiles flourished especially in the North, with its abundance of wool, and in the East, where the export trade of Trèves was stimulated by the presence of the Rhine armies. There was also an increased exploitation of the mines; and the building of towns was directly responsible for the opening up of quarries. Many of these appear to have belonged to the state, and were organised under imperial procurators and exploited by contractors. This is true, not only of the Pyrenean marble quarries, which helped to civilise the valleys of the south-west and created the prosperity of Lugdunum Convenarum (St Bertrand de Comminges), their port on the Garonne, but also of the silver mines near Villefranche (Aveyron), and perhaps of the argentiferous lead mines of Melle in Deux-Sèvres. Others belonged to municipalities or to individuals like the *femina clarissima*, Memmia Sosandris, referred to as the owner of a group of *ferrariae* on an inscription of A.D. 226 from Lyons. Whether these *ferrariae* are iron mines or foundries is not clear: probably the term covered both, for it was customary to smelt iron near the mine and to bring it to the forge in long, lozenge-shaped ingots. The work of the smith was generally carried on locally, and in small independent smithies, though occasionally groups of iron workers are found, such as the clients of Ti. Flavius Vetus of Dijon. Nevertheless, the mineral wealth of Gaul proved disappointing, especially in the precious metals. In some fields great strides were made. The tin plating of bronze was a Gallic discovery, and silver-plating was practised in Alesia before the coming of the Romans; and though the bronze-ware of Capua maintained its pre-eminence in the markets of the West until about A.D. 100, after that it had to face the competition of both Gallic and German wares, which are found on sites along the lower Rhine, in Britain, Hungary, free Germany, and the Siebenbürgen. In particular the discovery of calamine (silica-zinc) at Gressenich, near Stolberg, on the north slopes of the Ardennes, led to the manufacture of brass objects which were both cheaper and in some respects technically superior to bronze; Gressenich was probably the origin of the famous Hemmoor pails, which are found on sites in free Germany dating from about A.D. 150 to the fourth century. Free Germany also absorbed bronze goods from Gaul; many of the *paterae* and sieves from German sites were probably manufactured at Eisenberg in the Rhenish Palatinate, and another workshop, that of L. Cusseius Ocellio, has been localised at Nyon in Switzerland.

In the production of glassware too Gaul soon became a rival to Italy. About A.D. 50, Pliny tells us, glass workers migrated from Italy to Gaul, and we find workshops at Arles and Lyons. But the movement did not stop here. As in the case of *sigillata*, the industry spread northwards and eastwards to the Rhine. By A.D. 100 works had been opened at Namur in Belgium, and at Trèves, Worms and Cologne. Very soon Cologne had become the main centre for glass-ware, supplying the whole of the western provinces except Italy. Finally, jewellers, goldsmiths and silver-smiths lived in all the large towns, especially at Narbonne and Lyons. They were mainly freedmen of eastern origin, like the Lydian *aurifex* whose name appears on an inscription from Avenches.

In all this development a primary part was played by the presence of the German frontier, with its armies of the Rhine and Danube and the vast plains and forests of free Germany beyond. The presence of the legions was a great stimulus to trade and also—as in the case of *sigillata* and glassware—it exercised a magnetic attraction upon industry itself. The wages of the army and the imperial administration made it easy for the frontier districts to import luxuries, and such necessities as could not be produced locally—special wines, oil and olives, papyrus— without corresponding exports. Thanks to these advantages Roman Germany became rich, and rapidly outgrew its early character as a colonial area. Settlements based on trade sprang up along the lines of communication in western Germany and Switzerland, where the lakes and rivers were exploited to the full, so that even after the legion abandoned its camp at Augst near Basel in A.D. 100 the prosperity of the district was maintained. Further east the direction of trade was mainly south to Aquileia, which took iron from Noricum in exchange for Italian manufactures; and from the Danube at Carnuntum in lower Austria the ancient amber route ran north to Samland, through the Moravian Gates, Kalisz, and Osielsk on the bend of the Vistula. This route was already known to Pliny, and continued to be used until the middle of the third century. But west of it in Pomerania, the markets were gradually captured by Gaul and the Rhineland; while in Bohemia, where first-century cemeteries show large quantities of Roman goods, native German products gradually grow more common in the graves of the second century, and finally predominate in those of the third.

The economic influence of a fortified frontier is also to be felt in Britain. Britain, however, was a distant province which had been late to enter the Empire—Claudius' invasion was in A.D. 43—and it long remained a colonial market for made-up goods, and a source of raw materials. Strabo lists its exports as wheat, cattle, iron, hides, slaves and hunting-dogs; and there were also oysters and (for a short time in the early second century) brooches. In return Britain imported the necessities of army life (there were three legions and their auxiliaries stationed in Britain) and considerable amounts of *sigillata*, most of which was brought up the Thames to London, as is clear both from the large amount found in the London district and from the discovery of the wreckage of a ship carrying *sigillata*, which ran aground on the Pudding Pan Rock near Whitstable in the late second century. *Sigillata*, however, never superseded the local wares from the native potteries, and these (which account for almost 96% of the sherds found in Britain) show a development from many different varieties to a smaller selection of successful types produced in a few large centres. A feature of British economic life, which can be paralleled in the early history of the occupation of the Rhine frontier, is the part played by the army in satisfying its own needs for manufactured products. There were for example several legionary potteries, that at Holt in Denbighshire turning out wares of a Roman type, and there were also legionary smithies. The one gold-mine, at Dolaucothy, and most of the lead-mines were state-owned, managed by imperial procurators, and probably worked by slave labour. Copper and tin were smelted to make bronze, and indeed bronze ornaments show local characteristics down to the early years of the second century. With the opening up of Cornwall in the third century, pewter begins to appear as a luxury for the owners of country villas who could not afford silver. But this takes us forward to the conditions of the later Empire, which in Britain coincided with the highest peak of prosperity.

In general, British economic life remained backward and retarded, though from the end of the first century the province became more or less self-sufficient in all but wine and oil. Four inscriptions illustrate the commercial links between Britain and the continent—with Bordeaux, Mainz and Zeeland; and inside Britain itself the dedication of an altar at Bowness-on-Solway, for success in his enterprise, by a trader just about to venture beyond Hadrian's Wall, is a vivid reminder of the traffic up both coasts of Scotland, which continued until the fourth century, taking glass, brooches and Rhenish pottery to exchange for slaves, cattle, leather, furs and the other commodities of the North. Trade with Ireland was desultory and insignificant: goods were carried in Irish ships, and the finds suggest that the Irish were most concerned to obtain Roman coins.

Gaul, wrote Pliny, was the equal of Spain for cereals, oil, wine, horses and metals; but Spain was superior in esparto grass (for ropes), vitreous rocks, and delicate dyes, and in the keenness and industriousness of its slaves, and the toughness and ardour of its people. This is on the whole a fair summary, if perhaps a little unjust to the character and enterprise of the Gallic people, and certainly inadequately appreciative of the superiority of the Spanish mines. Gold, silver, lead, tin, iron, copper, cinnabar, mercury, mineral dyes, marble and salt are all to be found in various degrees of profusion in the soil of Spain; and elsewhere Pliny (who probably overestimated the promise of Gaul rather than underestimated the achievement of Spain) pays a generous tribute to this abundance. Modern authorities have estimated that the annual gold yield of the mines of the north-west must have come to £10,000,000, and that the mines of New Carthage produced eight and a third tons of silver per annum. Both Pliny and Strabo have left detailed accounts of the technique of extracting metals which the Romans employed in Spain. In some cases gold could be obtained by surface washing, else-where deep shafts were driven into the mountain; and finally there were long tunnels 'outdoing the work of the Giants', which were excavated in the bowels of the earth and underpinned; then, when all was ready, the arches were removed and the whole mountain side would collapse. The soil thus laid bare was washed for gold with the aid of water often brought for many miles and precipitated from a height upon the debris. Within the shafts Diodorus mentions the use of Archimedes' screw for draining the flood water from the lower levels, and at least nine examples of this device have been found, each one capable of raising the water over a yard and a half. Ctesibius' pump and various types of drainage wheel were also employed.

From the time of Tiberius onwards most mines were in the hands of the imperial authority, which sometimes handed over the exploitation to a company under contract. Thus the large cinnabar mine at Sisapo was worked by *socii Sisaponenses*. More often, however, the emperor kept a closer control of extraction through his procurators. Mines near Hispalis in the Sierra Morena, for example, were under the management of a *procurator Montis Mariani*, who was responsible for sending the ingots to Ostia, where they were received by his opposite number, the *procurator Massae Marianae*. Such procurators might manage their mines directly, with the aid of slaves and convicts; alternatively, they too might pass on the work to large or small groups of contractors. Under Hadrian especially the authorities favoured a system reminiscent of that adopted about the same time in regulating the conditions under which *coloni* occupied parts of the large imperial estates of North Africa. The mines were handed over to the direct exploitation of small individual contractors; and two documents from Vipasca (Aljustrel) in Southern Portugal throw light on how this system worked out in practice. The first of these, usually known as the *Lex Metalli Vipascensis*, and probably dating to the Flavian era, contains some of the very detailed regulations which the procurator laid down for the mine and its adjoining village, which was independent of any municipality. The surviving sections of this inscription enumerate the conditions under which the various economic activities of the village are farmed out as monopolies to separate lessees: thus the auctioning of property (and the collecting of the sales tax associated with it), shoemaking, barbering, and fulling, are all concessions, leased out on monopoly terms and protected against any infringement of the monopoly by specified penalties. The local baths —important in a mining village—are also run on a lease, and the hours of opening (sunrise to noon for women, 1.0 p.m. to 8.0 p.m. for men), the prices of admission, and the other obligations of the lessee are all laid down. Among other items of interest the document records the exemption from the usual taxes of schoolmasters living in the village. A second document, dating from the time of Hadrian, contains part of the imperial regulations for the actual exploitation of the mines, and defines the obligations of the contractors (who as small men work their own sections). From this inscription it is clear that half the ore went to the *fiscus* and the other half to the contracting miners. However, there is evidence that, at some time subsequent to the principate of Hadrian, a change took place in imperial policy, whereby compulsion and the use of convict labour came to play an increasing part in the economy of the mines, and the small concessionaire lost his importance. We shall return to this development below.

Besides its metal ores (which mainly went abroad unworked) Spain exported a variety of products, agricultural and industrial, particularly from Baetica in the south. Fruit, wax, honey, pitch, drugs, and dye-stuffs were regularly sent abroad from all parts of the peninsula, and there was an export of wool to Italy from the districts of the Turdetani, from near Corduba, and from Salaecia in Lusitania. Most of this was sold in the raw state, but there was also a trade in Spanish cloaks from Baetica, where inscriptional evidence for weavers and dyers in several towns confirms the references in Martial and Juvenal; at Hispalis for instance there were *centonarii*, makers of patchwork quilts and felt coverings.

Another important and peculiar Spanish product was its fish-sauce. There were two main types, *muria* and the more highly prized *garum*. *Muria* seems to have been a liquid obtained from pickling tunny-fish in brine: *garum* was a juice distilled from the blood and entrails of the scomber or mackerel, and subsequently allowed to ferment in the sun for several months. Dealers from Malaca distributed the most famous brand of this delicacy, *garum sociorum*, in Rome; but despite the implications of this trade name, there is no evidence for a monopoly of either manufacture or distribution.

In general, Baetica was the richest and most prosperous part of the country. The valley of the Guadalquivir was the only district with a surplus of wheat for export; and it was Baetica too which furnished the two most important trading commodities—olive oil and wine. Samples of sherds taken from the so-called Monte Testaccio, a vast mound of broken pottery 140 feet high and 3,000 feet in circumference, which lies beside the Tiber emporium at Rome, have shown it to consist mainly of fragments of second-century *amphorae* from Spain. Marks similar to those inscribed upon these sherds are also to be found on fragments of pottery all over the Western provinces, for instance at Augsburg and Bregenz, along the whole Rhine valley from Switzerland to Holland, at York and London in Britain, in every part of Gaul, and· in North Africa. The *amphorae* of which these sherds formed part appear to have been in the main of two types, one with a long neck for wine, the other with a short broad neck for oil. Some may have held grain, but the majority were beyond doubt used for the transport of Spanish oil and wine. The chief centres of their manufacture are Astigi and Arva in Baetica, and it is estimated that Monte Testaccio contains the fragments of about forty million *amphorae*, each with a capacity of over eleven gallons. These figures indicate the success of the Spanish producers during the second century in capturing the Italian market (as well as the markets of the other western provinces of the Empire) through either the low price or the high quality of their wines and oils.

The sherds from Monte Testaccio also give information on the shippers; and these, somewhat strangely, seem not to have been Spaniards. Their three names show that they were free citizens, though many were clearly freedmen, and may have obtained full citizen rights by virtue of an edict of Claudius, which offered special concessions to such shippers, *navicularii*, as built a vessel of 10,000 *modii*,[1] and employed it in the grain trade on governmental call for six years. Shippers from all over the Mediterranean appear to have taken part in the Spanish trade, often working in partnerships; but there is evidence for a particular connection between the Baetican oil merchants and the shippers of Narbonese Gaul. A Roman knight, for example, who is described as an oil merchant from Baetica and a patron of oil merchants at Rome, appears on another inscription as a shipowner on the Saône and patron of the local shipowners' gild. On the whole, one has the impression of a greater degree of initiative in Gaul than in Spain; and this may be not wholly unconnected with the fact that Gaul was much less dependent on slave labour.

The remaining western provinces, Sicily and Africa, were both primarily granaries for Rome. The regular imports of foreign grain were a life-line without which the capital could not exist. Each year

---

[1] Such a vessel had a carrying capacity of 3083 cubic feet, which is approximately the equivalent of 31 registered tons (net registered tonnage).

Egypt sent five million, Africa ten million, and Sicily perhaps two million bushels of grain [1] to Ostia, where it amounted to six thousand loads of the ox-towed barges which conveyed it up the Tiber to Rome. This tremendous task of provisioning a city of perhaps a million inhabitants was the particular concern of the emperors from Augustus onward, and it was carried out by private shippers working on contract for the government. From time to time concessions were held out to those who would undertake this work. Claudius, for instance, was not content merely to regulate and subsidise the selling price like Augustus and Tiberius, but built a new harbour at Ostia linked by canal with the Tiber and issued his edict granting privileges to those who undertook to ship grain; thus corn merchants were indemnified for losses incurred in storms, and received bounties according to their social status. The importance of the corn trade to Ostia is illustrated for a slightly later period by a set of mosaics representing scenes connected with it, which are preserved in the so-called Piazzale delle Corporazioni, a large portico situated behind the theatre, and administered by the local authorities in Ostia. These mosaics, which date from after the reconstruction of the portico by Commodus in A.D. 196, are some indication of the occupation of many members of the audience which frequented it as a social centre during the intervals in the theatre. Surviving inscriptions from this building give us information concerning African, Sardinian, Gallic and Alexandrian shippers who foregathered here in lighter moments; but our records are incomplete, and there may have been others, including *navicularii* from Spain and Sicily.

In conjunction with its production of wheat Sicily was also famous for its stock raising; but notwithstanding some evidence for a flourishing internal trade in wines, mineral products, and woollen goods (Syracuse produced *trimitoi*, probably a kind of drill), and also for the conveying of grain to Ostia by Sicilian shippers from Messina, who took back pottery in return, Sicily never played a vital part in the commerce of the early Empire. Rather it remained a land of *latifundia*, large estates belonging to absent landlords of senatorial rank, which often attained the size of miniature principalities. Nevertheless, the towns remained prosperous down to the third century, and this implies an active local industry and retail trade. Catania, for example, which we know as a centre for fine woollens, and a town containing quarrymen and ship-builders, brought its water supply from Licodia, sixteen miles away, over a three-tier aqueduct, and possessed a theatre and a huge amphi-theatre holding fifteen thousand spectators, five or six public baths, and other large and impressive public buildings. Despite the paucity of

[1] For discussion of these figures, which are controversial, see T. Frank, *Economic Survey*, v, 218–20; V. Scramuzza, *ibid.* III, 338 ff.

records, these achievements point to a flourishing if somewhat parochial economic life.

African industry too makes little showing. The primary importance of the province lay, of course, in its export of grain and, as a secondary commodity from Caesar's time at least, of olive oil. Oil presses have been found in several areas of North Africa; and we have a second-century dedication at Rome in honour of the prefect of the imperial corn supply (*annona*) by the 'African grain and oil merchants'. It is curious, therefore, that there is not more evidence concerning the pottery industry. The evidence for the manufacture of earthenware lamps is plentiful, and allows one to trace the gradual ousting of Italian by local wares. But of the sample taken from Monte Testaccio only fifteen sherds showed markings identifying them with certainty as of African manufacture. Trade within the province was on a small local scale, with the town market as the main focus of distribution. Some records of industry have survived; inscriptions refer, for example, to silver workers from Caesarea, and to various kinds of textile operatives in Carthage and other towns. Cloth made from the wool of indigenous sheep was the only manufactured product from Africa which achieved anything like an international reputation; and the clothing workers alone appear to have been widely organised into gilds, the usual indication of a flourishing industry. Another trade of some importance —and a measure of the prosperity of the upper classes in the province— was the making of mosaics. Over two thousand have been discovered, many representing African scenes, and most of them of very mediocre workmanship. The absence of any references to gilds among the workers in the mosaic and pottery industries has been taken as evidence that the craftsmen concerned in them were mainly slaves. On the other hand Baetica too is singularly lacking in evidence for the existence of gilds. Both here and in Africa there may have been special local conditions or traditions working against the usual organisation of industry and trade.

Together, such details as these create a general picture of the Western and more recently developed provinces of the Empire, which fit into a whole, impressive in respect of both its size and its achievements. Within an area extending from the Scottish lowlands to the Euphrates, from the Black Sea to the Atlas Mountains, a single economic system was organised under one central authority. From the setting up of the principate in 31 B.C. the Empire enjoyed almost unbroken peace for nearly a quarter of a millennium. Freed from the threats of war and the burdens of military service, and protected by well-devised frontiers and a standing army several hundred thousand strong, its population could devote itself to the activities of peace, to agriculture, commerce, and industry.

The prosperity of the early Empire was a triumph for the principles of economic *laissez-faire*. Normally the Emperor left trade to the private individual, intervening rarely and guardedly. The state revenues, it is true, had a direct interest in commercial prosperity, in so far as taxes were imposed on sales and on commerce. The *portoria*, which embraced customs levied at certain frontier stations between provinces (for this purpose the Spanish, Gallic and Danubian provinces were each regarded as composite units), local *octrois*, and tolls exacted at fixed points along the main routes, were designed as a source of revenue, not as a bar to trade; the rate varied at different times, and in different places, but it was never a serious burden—though early in Nero's reign an abortive attempt was made to give an additional impetus to trade by the abolition of both the *portoria* and the 5% tax on sales. Both these taxes were farmed out to contractors, who were *equites* during the first century of our era, and subsequently, from Hadrian's principate onwards, freedmen acting under the control of imperial procurators.

Apart from these taxes, however, trade was left in private hands. In the course of romanisation, splendid roads had been built all over the West. Quick communications between the frontiers with their legionary camps, provincial centres like Lyons, and Rome itself, were essential to effective control; the goods of the traders followed the same roads, frequently in the same direction as the legions. Even the corn supply, on which the very existence of Rome depended, was left to private *navicularii*, who were merely encouraged by concessions to enrol on contract with the government. Thus the profits went to the individual entrepreneur, while the imperial authority patrolled the seas, protected the roads and trade routes, and guaranteed the peaceful conditions which would allow trade to develop. Moles, quays, lighthouses, and canals—such as those joining the Rhine and the North Sea, or the Red Sea and the Nile—were constructed at the public expense; inns were built by the government, water supplies charted. Indeed, in the whole economic field of the early Empire, the mines were almost the only exception to the general rule of free enterprise. Tiberius here initiated a policy of concentrating ownership in the hands of the Emperor. Even so, the exploitation was frequently carried out by contracting companies or, as at Vipasca, by groups of small contractors who worked their own concessions.

The apparent success of this economic system, and its impressive accomplishments, should not, however, be allowed to obscure the serious weaknesses which undermined it. Despite the phenomenal growth of cities in the West, it must be remembered that many of these were very small. The bulk of the population, even in the East, where cities were of ancient standing, and still more in Gaul, Spain,

Germany and Britain, lived on the land in only the most superficial contact with Roman civilisation or trade. Moreover, the cities themselves, with their elaborate public buildings, fora, baths, amphitheatres, circuses, statues, triumphal columns and arches, lawcourts, and temples, together with the festivals, the banquets, and all the tremendous outward paraphernalia of Roman life, tended to exaggerate the contrast between the comfortable townsman and the toiling peasants of the countryside. Yet his luxury could only be bought by their efforts; for the alternative—the multiplication of wealth through a decisive advance in technique—was at variance with the whole ethos of ancient civilisation. If we except a few devices such as the mill wheel, or the invention of valved bellows in the fourth century of our era, which for the first time made complete smelting possible, the level of technique under the Empire never surpassed that already reached in Hellenistic Egypt. Transport by land remained cumbersome, slow, and expensive; the Romans never learnt to use the horse-collar, which makes it possible for a draught-animal to drag a heavy wagon without choking. And though the discovery of the monsoons by a Greek sea-captain named Hippalus about 100 B.C. had immeasurably shortened the voyage to India—it was now possible to reach the Malabar coast sixteen weeks after leaving Puteoli and to complete the round trip within a year— nevertheless many of the ships were of low tonnage, and the captain normally crept along the shore, putting in frequently to take on board water and provisions, or to spend the night at anchor, as his Greek and Phoenician predecessors had done six hundred or a thousand years before. The adventures of St Paul, including a shipwreck and considerable discomfort, on board the three vessels which he employed to make the journey from Palestine to Rome, must have repeated an experience common to many whose business took them overseas.

Finally, the picture must be qualified by the reminder that it was not static. This very system of *laissez-faire*, with its freedom from control, its benevolent state apparatus, and its positive achievements in the new provinces of the West (as well as in the older Greek lands of the East) developed in a little over a hundred years into its direct opposite—the rigid caste state of the late Empire. How was this change effected? In particular, is it possible to detect the seeds of the new order germinating within the old?

II

The fifty years from Severus Alexander to Diocletian are shadowy and obscure. Assailed by Goths along the northern frontiers, and by Persians in the East, the Empire passed from crisis to crisis. Under Gallienus, the son and successor of the ill-fated Valerian, who died a captive in Persian hands, Gaul temporarily broke away from the Empire, and Italy was ravaged by the Alemanni and Greece by the Heruli. Only the superhuman efforts of a series of soldier-emperors like Claudius, the vanquisher of the Goths, Aurelian 'restitutor orbis' and victor over Zenobia, the queen of the desert-state of Palmyra, and Probus who restored the Rhine and Danube frontier, enabled the Empire to survive. Even so the cost was tremendous.

In the West the towns suffered severely, particularly in Gaul, where the ravages of barbarian enemies were exasperated by the rising of the *Bagaudae*, a native *jacquerie*, described by Paulinus of Pella as a 'servile faction with an intermixture of freeborn youths, raving mad, and armed for the especial murder of the nobility'. Here, for several centuries, open towns had grown and prospered behind the defences of the Rhine frontier; once these defences were down, the enemy could run riot through the provinces, burning and plundering. The commercial elements and small artisans virtually disappeared. From the time of Postumus' rising against Gallienus the towns, now too big for the remnants of their former populations, shrank into fortresses, and from Aurelian's reign (A.D. 270–5) onwards, these are rarely more than seventy acres in area, often less. Thus Bordeaux is exceptionally large with its perimeter of 2275 metres and an area of seventy-five acres; the new *castrum* at Strasbourg has forty-eight acres, Nantes, Rouen and Troyes have each forty, Beauvais, Tours and Rennes twenty-five, and Senlis a mere seventeen. A particularly noteworthy example is that of Autun (Augustodunum), which was 500 acres in area when it fell before the Gallic armies of Tetricus and the pillaging of the *Bagaudae*; Constantius rebuilt it with an area of twenty-five acres.

Such a reduction in size is incomprehensible without a considerable decline in the population. In some instances, such as Strasbourg, the civilians may still have lived outside the *castrum*, prepared to fall back on it in time of need. But Strasbourg was a military town, the headquarters of the *comes Argentoratensis* and the eighth legion down to the latest times, and therefore not typical of Gallic towns in general. There seems little doubt that by the middle of the third century most of the cities of Gaul had been sadly reduced in man-power as well as in area, partly as a result of the invasions and depredations, but also to some extent through a population trend common to all parts of the Empire. The existence of this trend is firmly established: the actual figures and the relative importance to be attributed to the various factors which may have given rise to it are less easily determined. Clearly invasions and massacres, and the toll of civil war, account for a good deal. Important too both as a cause and effect of the process are the growth of state pressure and the exactions of the *fiscus*: this aspect will be considered below. But already in the second century, under M. Aurelius, it had become expedient to fill up the empty lands of the Empire with barbarian prisoners; and Augustus' legislation, designed to encourage the birthrate, would not have remained in force for three centuries, had it not been felt to be both necessary and at least partially effective. It seems at least probable that the decline (which had already become acute in Greece during the second century B.C.) can be directly connected with the conditions of town life, in contrast to those on the land, especially where the town is an administrative rather than an industrial centre. Modern parallels are not without significance. The fertility rate for the whole of Sweden in 1933 was 0·73; for Stockholm it was only 0·36— a figure equivalent to a population decline from 1000 to 6 in six generations. Similar factors may have been operative in ancient times, accentuated by higher mortality figures.

The remedy was to continue M. Aurelius' practice of settling barbarians within the Empire. After the disasters of the third century we hear of groups of Chamavi and Frisii being established behind the frontiers, and Constantine similarly settled Franks. The restoration of Gaul was accomplished by the settlement, first of Gauls rescued from captivity, and then of barbarian prisoners. In the course of the fourth century this practice continued and increased. Barbarians were brought into the province in ever larger numbers and settled in veritable colonies under the control of prefects. Many a town or village in modern France, a Bourgogne, a Sermaize, an Alain, an Allemagne, betrays the original influx of some group of Burgundians, Sarmatians, Alans or Alemans. Thus one result of the third century crisis was a gradual barbarisation of the western provinces: and this has to be kept in mind in assessing the output and quality of its industry and commerce.

In particular, the conditions of uncertainty which prevailed during the greater part of the third century tended to break down the fabric of trade in distant commodities, and to reinforce the already existing tendency towards local production. A period of disorder imposed new strains on a credit system which had not always been equal to the demands made upon it, even in times of peace and expansion. There was no ancient equivalent of the joint-stock company with limited liability; hence risks were personal, interest rates were proportionately high, and it was impossible to amass the capital for large-scale enterprises. There was thus a constant temptation to reduce risk and expense, which takes its place along with the many other motives already discussed, which drove craftsmen out towards the market and the new centres of raw material. Moreover, as we saw, this movement was naturally accelerated when, as in Gaul, there was a free labour force with a vigorous tradition of cooperative organisation to take the place of the relatively inefficient slave labour of Italy.

The fact that so much ancient industry was based upon slavery was important for yet a further reason. Slavery as an institution had been adversely affected by the Augustan peace. From the first century onwards, but increasingly in the third and fourth, slavery was dying out. The Emperors had made it their concern to end war and wipe out piracy: and in both aims they met with considerable success. The great days of the Delian slave market were long since over. There had been a time, as Strabo records, perhaps with some exaggeration, when 'the island could admit and send away tens of thousands of slaves in the same day'. Now the source of foreign slaves was drying up; and even though the increasing humanity of the early Empire made it possible for many slaves to contract marriages and bring up families, the additional numbers thus gained were not sufficient to fill up the gap—especially since as early as the principate of Augustus, and even during the last decades of the Republic, this increase in humanitarian sentiment, coupled with the attractions of the free corn which was available for all citizens of the capital from the time of the *Lex Clodia frumentaria* of 58 B.C., also led slave-owners to manumit slaves on so grand a scale that the government was compelled to introduce limiting legislation. Clearly the economic basis of ancient industry was being undermined: and the immediate results were disastrous for the older industrial centres. In time, it is true, this decline in the quantity of available unfree labour might well have proved beneficial; for a new attitude towards trade and industry had already begun to appear. 'There is nothing noble about a workshop', wrote Cicero contemptuously. But by the time of Constantine, tradesmen are being granted exemption from public duties, in order that they may have the leisure to improve their skill. Unfortunately this change of heart came too late. The mental fetters which slavery had imposed were perhaps lifting: but as they lifted they were superseded by the harsher bonds of a system of economic and political compulsion. In the meantime there was nothing to be gained from maintaining a centralised and concentrated form of production. Concentration only brings an appreciable reduction in overhead expenses when much fixed capital is employed. As a positive incitement to migration there was the fact that ancient equipment was simple, a few tools and the skill of the individual; and for a potter of Arretium to open a new branch of the firm at la Graufesenque, where trade was booming, was a sound alternative to keeping all his eggs in a single basket.

The development of the Western provinces in the first hundred and fifty years of the Empire has thus a double aspect. In so far as it led to the release of new productive forces in hitherto primitive lands it was progressive. But at the same time it was accompanied by a reduction in the scope of inter-provincial commerce. From the time of Claudius it is possible to identify several large trading areas, not indeed wholly isolated from each other, but including within their frontiers (which might embrace several administrative provinces) the bulk of their trade. Thus Spain, Germany and to some extent Britain (though Britain is a special case) were grouped around Gaul; another block was formed by the African provinces from Mauretania to Cyrenaica; Italy, together with Sicily, Corsica and Sardinia, made a third grouping, which was increasingly driven back upon itself; and finally (to limit ourselves to the West) Rhaetia and Noricum were linked with the other Danube provinces of Pannonia and Dacia (and later with South Russia) in a block which remained anchored to Italy through the trade of Aquileia until the end of the second century. By this date the West as a whole had made itself self-sufficient for all its main needs, such as grain, wine, oil, salt, glass, textiles, brass-ware, and pottery. The converse of this independence was the decay of Italy. More and more the peninsula became parasitical upon the rest of the Empire, which supported it by subsidies in the form of taxes to maintain the civil service, and the vast income from the Emperor's private estates; and with the removal of the imperial court from Rome in the third century, even this prop was withdrawn. Gradually the economic links were being broken. From the middle of the third century onwards these large inter-provincial blocks fell yet further apart. For example, the latest dated Spanish *amphorae* from Monte Testaccio date from 257. It is a fair inference that the German invasions of Spain in Gallienus' reign had crippled the flourishing export trade of wine and oil to Ostia.

The strain and tension, and the general economic regression of the third century, are also reflected in the history of the coinage. But even earlier, in the first and second centuries, the burden on the treasury had led to repeated interference with the system originally set up by Augustus. Augustus had stabilised the relationship between the golden *aureus*, weighing c. $\frac{1}{40}$ of a pound, and the silver *denarius*, weighing $\frac{1}{84}$ of a pound, at 25:1. According to Pliny (*Nat. hist.* 33, 3, 47) these weights were reduced by Nero to $\frac{1}{45}$ and $\frac{1}{96}$ of a pound respectively; and the truth of this statement has been confirmed by weighing, which established an average weight of 7·29 gr. for the *aureus* and 3·41 gr. for the *denarius*. Subsequently Trajan reduced the silver content of the *denarius* from 90% to 85%; and further debasement brought it down to a figure variously estimated at 80% and 75% in the principate of M. Aurelius. The significance of this process is still the subject of controversy. It has been argued that down to the time of Antoninus Pius the change in the content of the *denarius* was not motivated by financial considerations, and the desire to subsidise the treasury, but was simply designed to compensate for a fall in the value of gold, and so to maintain the ratio between the two metals; and indeed it appears from Lucian that the ratio was still unchanged under Pius. But the reduction in size of both silver and gold coins by Nero is difficult to explain except as a concession to strained finances. M. Aurelius was undoubtedly attempting to replenish a depleted treasury, which had to meet the oppressive demands of war; and in reducing the silver content of the *denarius* to a mere 50% Septimius Severus was following the same policy.

The effect of this debasement on international trade is noteworthy. Coin hoards from Germany show that the northern peoples took for preference the pre-Neronian *denarii*; but they did not reject Trajan's issues, and it was apparently only the still further debased coins of M. Aurelius which encountered strong resistance. Those of Septimius Severus were refused outright, and from the end of the second century German hoards contain an increasingly large percentage of gold. The hoards of the Far East are less easy to interpret. Here there is a dearth of all post-Neronian silver, but there is no corresponding increase in gold; moreover, the fact that the break comes not in Nero's reign, but after that of Tiberius, leaves it uncertain whether Nero's change in the silver content of the *denarius* was in fact a decisive factor. Moreover, there is a decline in the number of post-Neronian *aurei* found in these areas.

All this time the size and content of the Neronian *aureus* remained constant, with the result that a growing disparity arose between the gold and silver coinage. This inflation of silver in terms of gold is recognised in a passage of the Digest, probably referring to the early third century, in which Ulpian and Modestinus reckon a sum which Gaius calls 10,000 *sesterces* (i.e. 2500 *denarii*) as fifty *aurei*. This calculation implies that the current ratio between *aureus* and *denarius* was 1:50, which would be appropriate to the *denarii* with a 50% silver content which are found in coinage from the time of Septimius Severus. From this time onward until the reign of Gallienus (A.D. 253–68) the metal ratio and purchasing power of the coinage remained steady, despite a gradual increase in the percentage of alloy in the silver; but after A.D. 256 the quality of the silver coins deteriorates at a catastrophic rate, until they are little more than silver-washed copper. Evidence from Egypt suggests that the main crash came in the early years of Diocletian's reign; and in his *Edict controlling prices*, published in A.D.301, the gold pound of forty Neronian *aurei* is reckoned as 50,000 *denarii*, which gives a ratio between the Neronian *aureus* and the *denarius* of 1:1250.[1]

However, the *aureus* itself had not come through the third century unscathed. After a period of fluctuation its weight had dropped to $\frac{1}{70}$ of a pound under Carus (A.D. 282–3), and in A.D. 286 Diocletian stabilised it at $\frac{1}{60}$ of a pound. To attempt an analysis of the new Diocletianic coinage, which was based partly on the reforms of Aurelian, would be irrelevant here. It is a subject on which dire confusion reigns among specialists, owing to the impossibility of equating with any degree of certainty the various names of coins, such as *radiatus* and *follis*, with actual specimens. It does, however, now appear to be established that the new silver piece (*argenteus*) coined by Diocletian, which weighed 3·41 gr. ($\frac{1}{96}$ of a pound), is the same as the *siliqua*, which is first mentioned in A.D. 323 as part of the new system introduced by Constantine. In A.D. 312 Constantine depreciated the *aureus* to $\frac{1}{72}$ of a pound (4.55 gr.) and gave it the new name of *solidus*. The *siliqua*, Diocletian's *argenteus*, was valued at $\frac{1}{25}$ of the *solidus*, a ratio which no doubt deliberately reproduced the traditional relationship between the Neronian *aureus* and *denarius*. From about A.D. 330 a silver coin weighing $\frac{1}{60}$ of a pound was introduced, named the *miliarense*, since it was reckoned as a thousandth part of a gold pound. This system, with minor modifications, which may have been designed to compensate for changes in the relative value of silver and gold, was maintained throughout the fourth century and beyond. Indeed the *solidus* persisted virtually unchanged until the eleventh century; and though it has been argued that the *solidus* was not a true coin, since it was weighed in commercial transactions, or upon being paid into the treasury, and credited only at its actual weight, and not at its nominal value, it has been pointed out[2] that the same was true of English sovereigns paid into the Bank of England between 1816 and 1889, a period when the sovereign was unquestionably a coin in the full sense of the word.

Meanwhile bronze or silvered bronze continued to be minted as small change. It was not treated as token-currency; consequently its value was liable to fluctuation, in response to variations in weight or silver content, as in the third century. It has been calculated that the *denarius*, which stood at 50,000 to the gold pound in A.D. 301, had dropped to 120,000 within four years. Some time before A.D. 324 it

[1] See however Mattingly, *Num. Chron.* 1946, 113, who questions the reading of the Elatea fragment of the *Edict*, which contains this equation, and makes the gold pound worth 10,000 *denarii* (giving a ratio of 1:250 between the *aureus* and the *denarius*).

[2] See G. Mickwitz, *Die Systeme des römischen Silbergeldes im vierten Jahrhundert*, 3.

reached 168,000, and was then stabilised by Constantine at 172,000. Later in the fourth century the figure reached 473,000, and in the middle of the fifth it stood at 504,000. The evidence for these figures is not free from ambiguity; but the general picture is clear. Moreover, the figures given represent a modest degree of inflation compared with the collapse in the exchanges of local Egyptian *drachmae* at the same period; here the *solidus*: *drachma* ratio dropped in the course of a hundred years from 1:4000 to 1:180,000,000.

What did such an inflation mean in the ordinary life of the population? Not so much as similar inflations in modern times. Prices of course tended to rise in terms of the currency that was being debased—in silver during the second and third centuries, and in the late third and fourth centuries in silver-washed bronze. Under both Septimius Severus and Caracalla, for instance, there were increases in the Legionaries' pay, which may have risen from 300 to as much as 675 *denarii* a year. Similarly at Ephesus the price of a loaf of 14 *unciae* rose from two to four obols between the time of Trajan and the years A.D. 220–30. In any inflation wages tend to lag behind prices, and this factor will have added to the general distress of the third century. On the other hand, in ancient times there were not the accumulations of savings to be wiped out overnight. Since the drop in the value of the *denarius* was the result of its decline in silver content, older and better specimens would maintain their previous exchange value; and indeed there is epigraphical evidence for a sharp distinction between 'old coins' and 'new'. Thus hoarded money—the commonest form of saving—maintained its value; and the only people to be badly hit were those who had lent large sums with an agreement for fixed repayments, and those who accepted the debased coins before the new rate became established. The inflation thus introduced an element of uncertainty into commercial life, which is reflected in an increase in the number of leases in which the rent is payable in kind rather than in money, and in a shortening of the periods stipulated for repayment of money loans. Our evidence is mainly from Egypt; but the effects of the same process must have been similar in other parts of the Empire, where the element of hazard thus introduced into trade will no doubt have contributed to the tendency to restrict and localise it.

The inflation arose out of the difficulties of financing the imperial machine. In the conditions of the third century in particular the cost of maintaining the structure of the civil service, and of buying the loyalty of an army increasingly recruited from barbarians, and with little fundamental loyalty to Rome or indeed anyone, was a burden which the depleted resources of the provinces were not strong enough to shoulder. In raising the legionaries' wages Septimius Severus and

Caracalla had added a crippling burden to the annual state expenditure. Yet the population was declining and technique remained stagnant. It is hard to see what other remedy than inflation the Emperors could have adopted to meet the difficulties with which they were faced. For though sooner or later the debased coins were bound to be retariffed in terms of gold, and their value to sink in terms of goods, the vast sums which were constantly being paid out to the civil service and the army could meanwhile be met in the new currency. Any measure which would relieve the tremendous strain on the treasury presented great attractions to any Emperor in times of crisis.

It is against such a background that Diocletian's *Edict* of A.D. 301 must be considered. The discovery of fragments of this remarkable document in Egypt, Crete, Greece, Asia Minor and Italy confirms the statement made in its introduction, that the maximum prices therein prescribed for all types of services and commodities and for freight charges, were applicable throughout the Empire. The introduction also gives a clear hint of the purpose behind the *Edict*, a subject on which there has been much disputation, when it complains that 'sometimes in a single purchase a soldier is deprived of his bonus and salary, and that the contribution of the whole world to support the armies falls to the abominable profit of thieves'. Primarily the Emperor was concerned to ensure that the soldiers' pay was adequate for their needs, and to prevent a repetition of the price increases of the last century, which could only be followed by further demands for increases in salaries. The decree is especially detailed in its enumeration of foods and types of clothing, male and female; for example it lists eighty-four different articles of wool and over two thousand of linen; and five linen centres are named for the eastern half of the Empire, each of which produces nine different qualities. The significance of this fact will be considered below. Here it may be observed that the prices for food are almost all higher than those calculated in terms of gold for similar commodities in Egyptian papyri of the second century. In short, Diocletian's *maxima* were high, and therefore not likely to interfere seriously with normal trade. They would, however, act as a check on any forcing up of prices in the vicinity of the armies or imperial courts.

The *Edict* was a failure. According to Lactantius (*De mort. pers.* 7, 6), goods were withdrawn from the market, thus forcing up the prices more than before, and there was 'great bloodshed on account of small and paltry details'—either through riots or the invocation of the death penalty. Whether the *Edict* could have succeeded inside a virtually closed economy of substantial size such as the Roman Empire is a subject for speculation. Its interest for us here is rather in the light which it throws on the more important developments of later Roman economic organisation. In particular it raises three questions: the growth of compulsion by the government as an essential feature of economic and political life; the extent to which the state was still based on a money economy; and the amount and character of inter-provincial trade still carried on under the later Empire.

III

Such an *Edict* as Diocletian's would have been completely at variance with the economic practice of the early Empire. But since the days of the principate a radical change had taken place in the organisation of labour. It was customary for free tradesmen, craftsmen and professional workers in the Hellenistic world to organise themselves in gilds, whose functions were partly religious and partly social. Through their contributions the gild members provided for their funeral expenses, and subsidised their periodic banquets; and the gild sometimes controlled and protected the professional status of its members, though it never played the part of a modern trade union in fixing wages. Similar gilds, with the name of *collegia*, sprang up at Rome, probably under Greek influence. During the Republic they were treated with suspicion and repeatedly banned as sources of political disturbance; but the Emperors realised their possibilities as machinery for the official control of the workers.

The growth of *collegia* is perhaps most easily to be traced in connection with the *navicularii*, the shippers responsible for the transportation of the grain with which the capital was provisioned. They were the object of special imperial solicitude. The concessions granted by Claudius were confirmed by later Emperors: but from Hadrian's time it was insisted that a shipper must employ the bulk of his capital on state duties to qualify for them. For some time these privileges were granted to the shippers as individuals. But an inscription from the time of Antoninus Pius, in which *navicularii marini* of Arles honour their 'excellent and most upright patron', the prefect of the corn supply, signifies the importance which the gilds were now acquiring. M. Aurelius laid it down that no one should belong to two *collegia*; and an item from the *Digest*, dating to the reign of Septimius Severus, which specifically asserts that concessions are to go to individuals for their services and not to gildsmen promiscuously, is a clear indication that the gilds were being drawn into the state apparatus. By the end of the second century there is evidence for the existence of various privileged gilds at Rome, including the shippers engaged in the corn trade, the smiths (who may have had public duties as a fire-brigade even under the late Republic), the oil merchants, the bakers, the 'cornmeasurers', and the swine merchants; and in A.D. 200 the five *collegia* of Arles shippers went on strike to enforce higher rates.

The further development of these gilds during the third century is unfortunately obscured by the paucity of the sources. The *Life of Severus Alexander* (33) in the *Historia Augusta* states that this Emperor (A.D. 193–211) established *collegia* 'of all the wine-merchants, dealers in lupins, makers of soldiers' shoes, and of all craftsmen', and that he granted these gilds legal advisers and assigned appropriate lawcourts to each. Unfortunately the *Historia Augusta* is wholly unreliable, and this extract may reflect fourth-century conditions. All that can be said with certainty is that by the time of Diocletian (A.D. 284–305) the *collegia* are no longer voluntary, privileged bodies, but controlled organisations, the members of which are tied to their trade and pass on their obligations to their heirs. The *collegia* were frequently treated with honour: they possessed *fundi dotales*, which might include estates, and premises, as well as technical equipment. They had patrons and a religious cult; their members were exempt from many taxes, and often their retired presidents were rewarded with honorific titles. But this show of esteem disguised a form of harsh tutelage. The gilds were increasingly integrated into a unified state system; more and more their members were compelled to work in the service of the state; and not only was it forbidden to the *collegiati* to leave their gilds and their work, but in some occupations—for instance in that of baker—marriages had to be endogamous within the families of fellow gildsmen.

The typical pattern can be illustrated from the *navicularii*. Claudius had given special concessions to anyone who would build a ship of 10,000 *modii* and employ it in the service of the *annona*. In the fourth century anyone owning a ship of this tonnage was obliged to put it at the disposal of the state, but was in return entitled to exemption from an appreciable amount of tax. In A.D. 326 Constantine gave such a ship-owner complete immunity from all fiscal charges in a rescript which somewhat grandiloquently asserted the privilege to apply to 'all shippers, throughout the whole world, throughout every age'. These privileges were reaffirmed in A.D. 334 and 337, and in 380 Gratian gave shippers the status of knights (*equites*). This, however, was only one side of the picture. For meanwhile the *navicularius* had been effectively tied to his occupation through the linking of this with the individual's property; thus the heir to the property also inherited the obligations of the occupation.

The shipper's duty was to assemble a crew and organise the voyage of his ship in the state service. During the time that it was thus in commission, he was compensated by the state at a rate which was defined by Constantine in A.D. 334, for the *navicularii* provisioning

Constantinople, as 4% of the value of a cargo of corn in kind, together with a grant of one thousandth of its value in gold, in order that they might carry out their duties with enthusiasm and 'scarcely any cost to themselves' (*Cod. Theod.* xiii. 5. 7). Whether this marked a deterioration or an improvement in the position of the *navicularii* since the publication of Diocletian's *Edict* in A.D. 301 cannot unfortunately be determined, for although newly discovered fragments prescribe a special tariff for fiscal goods, which appears to be lower than that for normal cargoes, the text does not allow us to determine by how much. But by the early fifth century, in A.D. 412 and 414, the percentage paid to the *navicularii* bringing corn to Rome from Africa was only 1%. A series of regulations hedged the shipper about, to ensure that he did not speculate with his cargo, delay in port, or attempt illicit trading, all of which were offences carrying the death penalty. Any shipwreck was food for imperial suspicion. An enquiry must be held and the crew examined under torture. If on the other hand all went well, the ship's captain must proceed by the shortest route to his destination, where he received a state *relatoria* or *securitas* (receipt) which absolved him from further state service for a period of two years, dating from the beginning of his present service; in what was left of this time he had to make his way back to his own port, but could undertake further trading voyages on his own account without fear of requisitioning. In conjunction with the *navicularii* we hear of a large group of subsidiary *collegia*, with special functions and all equally under state control—the small lightermen, dockyard workers, caulkers, ballast-loaders, divers, and stevedores. The duties of all are closely defined.

This special state concern with the *navicularii* sprang from their importance for the provisioning of Rome. A sum of 3,600,000 bushels of corn (14,400,000 *modii*) was required annually to meet the claims of the public service, and those entitled to free distributions; and in addition it was the duty of the *fiscus* to organise a supply of cheap corn for the rest of the population of the capital, so that the total annual imports may have been of the order of 17,000,000 bushels (see above, p. 47). Some time before the reign of Aurelian (A.D. 270–75) the distribution of bread was substituted for that of corn, and the gilds of bakers, which had been officially recognised under Trajan, now assumed special importance. By the fourth century they were completely organised in the state service; and because the work was hard and unpleasant, the regulations were harsh. As in the case of the shippers, their property was linked with the trade, which was inherited with it. If a man became heir to the estates of both a shipper and a baker, he was liable for both duties; moreover, anyone, of whatever status, who married a baker's daughter, must himself adopt the occupation. It was the baker's task to collect corn from the state granaries, grind it in his own cellar, bake it into bread, and distribute this at the appointed place in each quarter of Rome. After the widespread adoption of the water-mill during the fourth century, in place of that worked by human or animal power, we hear of the setting up of a separate gild of millers (*molendinarii*) at Rome, with headquarters at the foot of the Janiculum; this is but one example of the specialisation of function, and subdivision into subordinate gilds, which took place in this important industry.

However, the state did not confine its incursion into trade to corn. Free distribution of olive oil, which had been sporadic since the later Republic, became regular from Septimius Severus' time onwards. Two gilds of oil merchants dealt with Baetica and Africa respectively. Similarly the gild of pork merchants acquired official duties towards the end of the third century, when the regular distribution of pork was organised at Rome. These *suarii* had to receive the pigs from various Italian landowners who were liable to provide them as part of their tax, bring them to Rome, slaughter them there, and deliver the meat to those entitled to it. As we shall see below, there grew up a system by which the taxpayer was allowed to commute his liability by a payment in cash, which the *suarii* would use to buy the equivalent animals in the open market at or near Rome.

The same forms of gild organisation are to be found in most of the provinces of the West during the later Empire. Here the *collegiati* operated under the control of the municipality, represented by its *curia*, or town council. The *curiales*, who enjoyed a higher social status than the gildsmen, gave the latter their orders, and were responsible to Rome for their implementation. Although those gilds connected with the feeding of the people offer the earliest and most typical examples of state control, they are by no means the only ones. By the fourth century most trades and professions are organised in *collegia*, and there are records of gilds of innkeepers, fishmongers, potters and silversmiths, as well as the public employees in the state enterprises, which have still to be considered below.

The existence of these gilds is the background against which Diocletian could attempt the tremendous feat of regulating all prices throughout the Empire. Yet, even in the time of Diocletian it is plain that the economic system is not one of complete nationalisation: it is rather a hybrid form of controlled private enterprise, a logical development from the uncontrolled private enterprise of the early Empire. Most industrial and commercial property is still privately owned. But in place of the earlier relationship, by which the individual bound himself to the state for a prescribed period, with his property as a pledge, but emerged a free man at the end of the six years or so of his

contract, the state has now attached the property to the occupation, and
the gildsman is obliged to work for the benefit of the state in virtue of
his ownership. The state compensates him for his loss of income; but in
the fourth century this *solacium*, or 'consolation', as it was officially
termed, increasingly takes the form of payments in kind.

Why this form of semi-planned economy was evolved is a problem
on which there is no unanimity. No doubt special factors applied to
the various branches of production and distribution. But, in the main,
it appears that the state assumed the responsibility because the people
had to be fed, the goods had to be produced and distributed, and private
enterprise, left to itself, was proving unequal to the task. The same
phenomena are clearly apparent in political life, where the crises of the
third century, with its widespread destruction of wealth, brought with
them a dearth of citizens willing to shoulder the increasingly heavy
burdens of municipal office. From the time of Diocletian and Constantine onwards municipal office becomes the duty of a hereditary
caste of *curiales*, who have lost most of their initiative to imperial
officers, but remain responsible not only for financing the greater part
of the town's activities out of their own private fortunes, but also for
collecting the taxes and provisioning the town through the agency of
the local *collegia*.

Thus nationally and locally the feeding of the population of the
Empire became a public responsibility. It is of some importance to
determine to what extent this development was associated with a decline
in the use of money. For the fourth century in particular it has been
argued that over vast areas of the Empire a declining economy led both
the imperial authorities and individual citizens to abandon the use of
money, and to substitute a system of barter, by which all payments,
including wages and taxes, were made in the form of foodstuffs,
clothing, or any other articles of common use rather than in a now
worthless currency. It is suggested that under the stress of the upheavals
of the third century the Roman world reverted to 'domain-economy',
in which the large landowners maintained every class of workman on
their estates, which they sought to make economically self-sufficient.
This system, it is urged, is reflected in the taxation established by
Diocletian, in which payments in kind play a primary role.

This thesis is hard to reconcile with the evidence provided by
Diocletian's *Edict on Prices*. With its very full and precise list of prices
covering a wide range of commodities and services—commodities
moreover coming from every part of the Empire—this document gives
no indication of a decline from a money economy to one based on
barter. Moreover, it has already been shown that the crises and disturbances of the third century had not been sufficiently severe to drive

out money. Even the inflations had merely brought a slight increase in the number of contracts stipulating payments in *natura* in areas where this type of contract had always existed. On the other hand, from the time of Septimius Severus (A.D. 193–211) [1] the provisioning of the armies had been made the regular responsibility of the provinces through which their route lay. A special order (*indictio*), which tended to be of more and more frequent occurrence, laid down the details of the supplies to be furnished, and this impost in kind was known as *annona*. When Diocletian introduced his new fiscal system, based on double taxation units—the area of cultivable land (*iugum*) and the single unit of human labour required to work it (*caput*), combined in a twofold tax of *capitatio* and *iugatio* (see Volume I, pp. 106–7)—he made the annual payment of *annona* its central feature, thereby perpetuating and intensifying the far-reaching effects which had already been produced.

First, the payment of taxes in *natura* inevitably raised problems of transport. The large quantities of oil, grain, meat, wine, clothing, etc., which had to be paid annually into the *fiscus* required the setting up of vast numbers of public storehouses (*mansiones*) along the main routes of the Empire. Since, moreover, land transport was so difficult and expensive, this led to a progressive decentralisation of economic life. Outgoing payments in kind, for example allotments of food or the provision of uniforms for the army, were linked directly with the income from certain adjacent provinces, in order to avoid burdening the treasury with the cost of transport over long distances. Thus state employees received their wages in vouchers, which served as drafts on specified public storehouses in the vicinity. The recipient went to the *mansio* to draw his allowance of corn, wine or oil. His salary, varying according to his rank, was calculated in units (also known as *annonae*), which were equivalent each to sixty *modii* (fifteen bushels) of wheat per annum.

The payment of public employees, civil and military, in kind was very much in their favour during a period of inflation.[2] For clearly the debasing of the currency, carried out under the pressure of a succession of crises, would have defeated its own ends unless state employees, whose salaries were the main item in the bill of imperial expenses, could be paid in the new depreciated money. Naturally, this procedure aroused resentment; and it was an obvious advantage for soldiers and civil servants if they could enforce payment in goods rather than in debased silver. In order that wages might be paid in *natura*, however, the goods must first be in the hands of the government; and this could

---

[1] Cf. D. van Berchem, *Mém. de la soc. nat. des antiquaires de France*, 1936, 177 ff.

[2] See Mickwitz, *Geld und Wirtschaft im römischen Reich des vierten Jahrhunderts*, 176 ff.

best be effected by levying taxes in *natura* upon the agricultural population. Such were the considerations which seem to have led Septimius Severus to institute (and Diocletian to develop) a system which ensured the satisfactory provisioning, originally of the army, and later of the bureaucracy, on whom depended the existence of the whole imperial machine.

The payment of taxes in kind affected both the peasants and the *collegiati*. The institution of serfdom by the binding of the *colonus* to the soil soon followed the establishing of an annual tax in *natura*, which made the landlord personally responsible for the returns throughout his whole estate. But the gildsman equally found the new fiscal system tending to diminish his freedom. The collection of taxes in kind raised vast problems of transport: and the task was entrusted to the gilds. It is an example of the strong hold of tradition on the Emperors that they preferred to use the system of compulsorily requisitioning the services of the gilds rather than create new branches of the imperial administration. The hardships to which this policy gave rise can be illustrated from the system of land transport. Just as the *navicularii* had been pressed into government employment for the transport of the *annona* by sea, so the moving of fiscal products by land was carried out, first by the requisitioning of humble muleteers (*catabolenses*), and later by the adaptation of the public post. This too, despite its name (*cursus publicus*), was in fact worked by a system of requisitioning.

There were two speeds. The horses or light mule carriages employed by individual travellers would cover almost fifty and twenty-five miles a day respectively; whereas produce was conveyed slowly in ox-drawn wagons at an average speed of six to seven miles a day. The routes followed lay along the main imperial roads, and every six miles or so there were stables, and changes of horse for couriers. At longer intervals were built *mansiones*, where a traveller could stay, and associated with these, and often fortified against brigands, were the warehouses for the *annona*. In the fourth century the whole organisation was controlled by the *vir illustris magister officiorum*, who possessed the right to compel members of families associated with the municipal councils to undertake the task of supervising the *mansiones*, which included the responsibility for the prompt departure of postal services, the conserving of supplies, and the protection of the near-by population against arbitrary acts of requisitioning. Far the greater part of the service was carried out by this unpopular method. The stables were built by *corvées* of forced labour; and though the animals were public property, they were acquired, and a quarter of them renewed annually, by requisitioning. On the other hand the employees of the post, the grooms, muleteers and veterinary surgeons, were in receipt of state salaries.

It is clear that a system such as this was capable of inflicting great hardship and injustice. Moreover, in time of war, when armies moved rapidly from one front to another, the transport system was likely to suffer dislocation. On the one hand the ultimate destination of large stores of meat, oil, timber, clothing etc. might have to be changed at short notice; and in addition the kind of commodity required might itself change, and where building stone had been wanted in peace-time, the urgent need might now be for bricks, or timber to construct artillery. When these dislocations resulted in intolerable burdens being laid upon certain *collegia*, their members frequently abandoned their duties and took refuge in flight. It was primarily to prevent this that the practice grew up of binding a man to his occupation with the sanction of law. Henceforward *collegiati* must keep to the same profession and carry out duties for the state in return for a nominal *solacium*.

This evolution of the Roman Empire during the third century from a system of *laissez-faire* to one of controlled private enterprise, working within limits sharply defined by the state, removed a considerable body of the population outside the range of money economy for the bulk of its needs. But though the importance of money was thus partly reduced, the effects of this trend should not be exaggerated.

In the first place, money did not cease to play a vital part in imperial finances. The furnishing of *annona*, whether under the terms of the *iugatio-capitatio* tax, or of the modified form of it found in the Western provinces, was obligatory only for those living on the land. For other sections of the population there were taxes in gold and silver. Senators, for example, in addition to the *annona* payable on their estates, were liable to a super-tax (which persisted until A.D. 450), known as the *follis* or *collatio glebalis*, and also to the payment of a sum of gold (*aurum oblaticium*) on the occasion of an emperor's accession and each quinquennial anniversary of it. Similarly, the magistrates and council members of the various cities were obliged to contribute *aurum coronarium*, originally as a theoretically voluntary gift to celebrate special occasions, and later, by a rescript of A.D. 364, as a compulsory donation. Finally, there was a special tax, the *collatio lustralis*, which applied strictly to the trading classes, but was extended to include inn-keepers, brothel-keepers, and virtually everyone who followed an occupation for gain. This tax, which was levied every five years, was paid on the amount of capital involved in a business, with a minimum payment for those whose capital was negligible; and it had to be paid in gold and silver. The *chrysargyrum*, as it was therefore commonly called, went largely to pay for the shows given by the emperor, and for the donations which the army demanded and received on all important occasions. It was felt as a considerable hardship by the taxpayers, and Zosimus and

Libanius speak of fathers enslaving or prostituting their children in order to raise the required sum.

All these taxes, except the *annona*, were paid in silver and gold, and are reflected in the gold coinage instituted by Constantine. During the fourth century, moreover, following a practice which is found as early as A.D. 213 in Egypt, the *annona* itself gradually evolved into a tax paid in gold rather than in kind; and the substitution of gold for goods, *adaeratio*, also appears in the payment of government employees. In A.D. 325 Constantine specifically forbade the use of *adaeratio* in paying out the *annona* of tribunes; but in A.D. 364 and 365 it is permitted to certain categories of state employee, including the soldiers along the Danube, the *riparienses milites*, who are to receive nine months' wages in kind and three months' in gold. In A.D. 389 *adaeratio* is accepted as a general practice in Illyricum; and this decision is followed by various rescripts defining the rate at which the calculation shall be made. In the course of the fifth century the practice grows. In A.D. 423 a rescript of Honorius and Theodosius makes it compulsory in the payment of officials, and implies that it is already recommended for the army. An interesting example of its application comes from an edict of the same year, dealing with the payment of troops, which lays down that five sixths of the gold shall go to the first line troops in person, and one sixth to the weavers in the imperial factory, who in return are to provide uniforms for the *iuniores* and *gregarii milites*. In this way misuse of the money by the younger and less responsible troops was prevented. Finally, by A.D. 439, *adaeratio* was compulsory for army and officials alike.

The issue around which the main controversy concerning *adaeratio* centred was the rate of conversion. A calculation of the equivalent of any tax in gold might be made according to a fixed rate, or according to the market price current either in the district where the tax was levied, or at Rome. Thus in A.D. 324 the landowner who had to supply the *suarii* from Rome with swine was allowed to pay in gold at the local rate, which was fixed for the year. Later in the century, however, the *suarii* successfully appealed against this ruling, which might involve them in a loss, should the price of swine near Rome prove dearer than that in the local market; consequently in A.D. 367 the price at Rome was substituted for the local price as a basis for *adaeratio*, and such taxpayers as still preferred to pay in kind were allowed to do so, provided that they added $\frac{1}{20}$ of the value of the swine to cover the cost of transport to Rome. A similar clash of interest existed between the recipients of *annona*, the army, the civil service, and the employees in public concerns on the one hand, and the landowners who paid taxes on the other. The former were less likely to lose if their salaries were in kind; but if payment was made in money, they were concerned to ensure that its purchasing power should not fall through a rise in the price of goods. Consequently they preferred *adaeratio* to be carried out at the current market rate of the district where they lived or were stationed. The landowner on the other hand benefited from voluntary *adaeratio* at a fixed tariff. He could then decide on each occasion whether it paid him to meet his obligations in kind or in gold. The danger for the state was that of falling between the two parties, and shouldering the loss; and eventually a flexible system was devised, whereby the praetorian prefects laid down tariffs with fixed rates each season, and *adaeratio* became compulsory. This system, which was in full operation by the early decades of the fifth century, in effect brought with it the end of fiscal payments in *natura*, though *natura* remained the basis on which the obligation in gold was calculated.

Thus for upwards of two centuries taxation in kind removed from the workings of the market (though to a decreasing extent) vast quantities of commodities in everyday use; and accordingly it reduced the area and scope of the money economy. There is also evidence that many of the large landowners, who had been strengthened by the institution of the colonate, began to make their estates partially independent of the market, some even adding branches of industry to the normal activities of their domains. The *Theodosian Code* draws an important distinction between those merchants who buy in order to sell, who keep a shop, attend markets and fairs, and in general live from the fruits of their trade, and on the other hand those who merely sell the produce of their estates. The former are of course subject to the payment of *chrysargyrum*, whereas the latter are taxed only on their land and the number of their employees (*capitatio-iugatio*). Thus the landowner who mined iron or copper on his estate, set up workshops and smithies, producing tools, ornaments and household utensils even beyond the needs of his own establishment, still remained exempt from any further tax, such as his competitors in the town would have to pay.

That some degree of industrial activity was associated with country houses and estates has been proved by excavation. Britain is perhaps exceptional, for there the greatest prosperity came in the fourth century, and was based on the villas rather than on the already shrinking towns. There are remains of a fulling establishment in a villa at Darenth in Kent, which consisted of three separate buildings, of which two served as treading tanks, and the third provided drying rooms. The size of this *fullonica* suggests that it was capable of handling cloth woven at several weaving establishments, and these were probably situated in near-by villas. In a villa at Chedworth in Gloucestershire there is a similar *fullonica*, obviously operating on a commercial scale, a forerunner of the famous Cotswold woollen industry of the Middle Ages. Yet a third example has been found at Titsey in Surrey.

Gaul provides what are at first sight still more impressive examples of the same tendency. The most notable is the luxurious villa excavated at Anthée in the Belgian province of Namur. Here, within a walled enclosure 650 metres by 200 metres in extent, stood the villa itself, dating to the middle or perhaps the second half of the first century, and beyond it on the east some twenty separate buildings, of which at least half appear to have been used for industrial purposes; there are furnaces belonging to a forge, iron foundries, and shops for the making of bronze and enamelled articles, for brewing, and for pottery, harness, and leather work. Among the debris have been found large numbers of small objects, buttons, bells, hairpins, brooches, both plain and enamelled, rings, bracelets, keys and box-fittings, all on a scale far beyond what could be expected if this industry was merely to satisfy the needs of the villa. Even larger and more impressive, if less definitely industrial, is the establishment associated with a villa found at Chiragan in the plain of Martres-Tolosanes, a little to the south of Toulouse. The fortunes of this villa, which was frequently rebuilt between the time of Augustus and the fourth century, were at their greatest under the Antonines. Here, in close association with the villa itself, are some eighty smaller buildings, some of which at least show signs of having been used for domestic crafts: loom-weights and occasional tools have been found. Nevertheless the remains of Chiragan do not impose an assumption of industrial activity in a wider sense, as do those at Anthée. It is by no means impossible that the rich Gallic family of the Aconii, whose home this villa probably was, maintained an entourage of some four hundred persons simply to minister to their personal needs and those of the estate. Moreover, both Anthée and Chiragan appear to have been at the height of their activity from one to two hundred years before the date when the widespread reversion to domain economy is usually assumed to have taken place. In short, the evidence from Gaul is less decisive in this matter than has sometimes been supposed.

Literary evidence has also been adduced in support of the theory of industrialised domains. Palladius, in a much quoted passage (1, 6, 2), advises landowners to have iron-workers, carpenters, and makers of casks and barrels, available on the estate, lest it should be necessary to interrupt the agricultural tasks in order to send labourers into the town. This does not of course mean that the landowner should attempt to make himself independent of the town, but merely that there should be men on the estate able to do the simpler jobs and restrict the number of occasions on which the help of the town has to be called in. The presence of such craftsmen on an estate implies that they were regularly employed:

they will hardly have been kept idle in the expectation of emergencies. But the text is not to be pressed too far, the more as Palladius himself gives many indications of the dependence of the manor on the town market. In general, the estate which has developed specialised industrial activities, the fulling establishments in the British villas, the artisans employed at Anthée or the mining village of Vipasca, is to be regarded as exceptional. Normally the slaves on an estate of the late Empire would not be professionally trained workers. Carpenters and joiners, wicker workers and rope makers one would expect to find; and Palladius is evidence for iron smiths. But it seems clear that for anything more complicated the landowner fell back on the town, or called in the aid of travelling tinkers and other itinerant craftsmen. If the estate produced raw materials, these would usually be worked up in the towns; and from here too would come the bulk of the slaves' tunics, cloaks and felted woollen overalls, even though the domain would normally carry out some weaving and spinning. From the town too came pottery, metal ware, finer baskets and ropes, and farm wagons.

A far greater inroad into the realm of private economy was made by the state factories, which are mentioned in various rescripts in the *Codes* of Theodosius and Justinian, and in particular in the *Notitia Dignitatum*, a list of the dignitaries and departments of the imperial bureaucracy, especially in the western half of the Empire, which probably dates in its present form to the early decades of the fifth century, though the original on which our version is based was most likely compiled about A.D. 364. Already under the early Empire some of the needs of the army had been met by military factories for the production, for instance, of tiles and bricks. Examples are plentiful along the Rhine frontier, with its army potteries at Xanten and Neuss, and at Weisenau near Mainz. Now, under the directed economy of the later Empire, factories were employed to supplement the use of controlled private enterprise, and state arsenals, weaving mills, and dyeworks were set up in various places. The date of this new development cannot be exactly determined. The evidence of the *Historia Augusta*, which would bring them down to the reign of Severus Alexander, is unreliable; but although there is no certain proof of their existence before Diocletian, it seems at least likely that they developed in the latter part of the third century.

The supreme official responsible for the imperial factories of the West was the *vir illustris comes sacrarum largitionum* stationed in Rome; under him were the procurators of the individual factories, and the activities of these officials were closely controlled. The sanctions constantly laid down by the legal codes suggest that it was the practice of these officials to try both to cheat the state and to extort money from the provincials. Their appointment was for a limited period only, and was covered by the giving of surety beforehand and the rendering of accounts at the end of the term of office. Four kinds of factory are mentioned from the western part of the Empire, weaving mills (*gynaecia*), linen mills (*linyfia*), dye works (*bafia*), and the *barbaricaria* or *argentaria*, which were works carrying on embroidery in gold and silver thread; these embroidery workshops were under the control of *propositi*, who were probably subordinate to the *procuratores* of adjoining weaving establishments. In addition there were two *gynaecia* controlled separately by another official, the *vir illustris rerum privatarum*, and therefore perhaps regarded as being in some special sense the personal property of the emperor. Finally, there were various ordnance factories under the control of the *vir illustris magister officiorum*.

The weaving mills were at Bassiana, between Sirmium (Mitrovica) and Belgrade, at Sirmium itself, and at Split, in Illyria; at Aquileia and Milan; at Rome; at Canusium and Venusia, both of which were long famous for their fine undyed cloaks, and also for an inferior material dyed with cheap purple, and made up into tunics; at Carthage (where the 'slaves in our factory' are mentioned in a rescript of the *Theodosian Code* from the year A.D. 380); at Arles, Lyons, Reims, Tournai, Trèves, and Autun; and at Venta *in Britannis*, which is probably Winchester, near the sheep runs of Salisbury Plain and the Hampshire Downs. The two private factories are at Trèves and at another town, which may be Viviers. Only two linen mills are mentioned, at Vienne and at Ravenna. The dye works were at Tarentum, at Salona, on the island of Cissa (off Istria), at Syracuse, at Girba (in the Syrtes in North Africa), in the Balearic Islands, and at Toulon and Narbonne in South France; in addition there were several dye works in North Africa under the control of a single procurator, perhaps stationed in Carthage. The embroidery works were at Arles, Reims and Trèves, and were probably run in conjunction with the weaving mills in those towns.

The location of these factories seems to have been determined by two factors, their proximity to raw materials and their convenience as bases for equipping the armies. Transport difficulties made it essential to place them at a safe but not excessive distance from the frontier: Bassiana, Sirmium, Trèves and Tournai all fulfil these conditions. Moreover, where there are records of the moving of a factory, for instance from Salona to Bassiana or from Autun to Metz, the purpose seems to be to bring it nearer to the armies it supplied. It is significant that, despite the obvious facilities which South-west France and Spain afforded, there were no woollen factories in these provinces, and this is presumably due to their distance from the armies on the frontier. Similarly the imperial arms factories of the West were all situated in

Illyricum, Northern Italy or Gaul. In Illyricum shields were manufactured at Sirmium, Aquincum (Alt-Ofen), Lauriacum (Lorch) and
Carnuntum, and arms of various kinds at Sirmium and Salona; in Italy
shields came from Verona and Cremona, arrows from Concordia,
bows from Ticinum (Pavia), and broad-swords from Luca; and in Gaul
arms of every type were manufactured at Argenton (Argentomagum—
unless Argentoratum, Strasbourg, should be read), arrows at Mâcon,
broad-swords at Reims and Amiens, shields at Trèves and Amiens,
artillery (*ballistae*) at Trèves, and some unrecorded arms at Soissons.

In view, therefore, of both the precedents of army workshops of the
early Empire, and the situation of these late imperial factories, there can
be little doubt that they were designed to satisfy the needs of the army
and the bureaucracy; nor is there any evidence that they produced for
the market as well. As we saw, Diocletian's *Edict* is particularly comprehensive in its lists of articles of clothing, and in one place it lays down
prices for a soldier's *chlamys* and a tunic, which are described as '*indic-
tionalia*', which presumably means 'of the type specified in the imperial
indictio'. It has been argued that these articles of clothing were products
of the imperial factories, and that their procurators took an active part
in the fixing of the prices in the *Edict*. This is possible; on the other hand
the price fixed may simply be that at which an independent craftsman
was to sell certain articles of uniform to the taxpayer who was liable to
provide them in his *annona*. Nor can one draw analogies from the dye
works, which certainly sold to the public, for purple dyeing, unlike
weaving, was an imperial monopoly.

Doubts have been expressed whether these factories were all factories
in the modern sense, that is, concentrations of workers employed under a
single roof, or whether the terms *gynaeceum*, *linyfium*, etc., merely refer
to a collection of hand workers employed within their own homes on
conditions laid down by the authorities.[1] Evidence exists that weavers
and mint workers at Cyzicus in the fourth century worked on the cottage
system. But it would be obviously unsound to generalise from this one
instance; and in favour of the traditional view of these establishments
as genuine factories is the fact that the work in them, which was arduous
and unpopular, was increasingly carried out by forced labour, which
would require careful supervision. The dye works in particular, where
the raw materials included human urine and shell-fish which might
have been six months dead, were largely manned by slaves and convicts.
And frequently the law laid down labour in the woollen mills and
dye works as a penalty for Christians and other malefactors. In A.D. 336
the son of one Licinnianus, who had been apprehended after absconding,
was put in chains and assigned to the woollen mill at Carthage. More-

[1] A. W. Persson, *Staat und Manufaktur im römischen Reiche*, p. 91.

over, by an edict of A.D. 365, published at Milan, any freeborn woman who married a textile slave was herself compelled to become a weaver, unless she had already published particulars of her own status before marriage. One is reminded of the similar stipulation which forced the husband of a baker's daughter to become a baker; and indeed one can trace a tendency to make the status of both *collegiati* and employees of imperial factories unchangeable and hereditary. Thus an edict of A.D. 380 forbade the children of workers in the imperial mints to marry outside their class. As a safeguard against attempts at escape, mint workers were branded on the arm; and the Codes are full of penalties for the concealment of runaway textile workers.

As imperial employees, the workers in the textile mills, mints, dye works and arms factories will have received their wages in kind, like the troops. The labourers in the arms factories (*fabricenses*), whose status was higher than that of most other workers, were described as performing *militia*, military service; and the *bastagarii*, or baggage carriers, responsible for bringing up the armies' supplies, were also treated as a militarised ordnance corps. Thus, despite their free status, all these imperial workers were considerably less independent than the gildsmen, and Eusebius could describe textile hands, without any sense of incongruity, as 'slaves of the treasury'. They are a further example of a considerable section of the population which is withdrawn from the money economy.

Nevertheless this economy was never completely effaced, despite the system of tax collection and payment of imperial employees in kind. The *Edict* is evidence of this at the outset of the fourth century; and it is confirmed throughout the whole of the later Empire by the background of the writings of the Church Fathers, which consistently presuppose a world in which transactions are carried out with the aid of money. In this respect there is no appreciable difference between writings of the fourth century and those of the fifth. In both the rich man with money to spare lends it for interest, perhaps through the agency of a banker, to those who require it, sometimes to the poor, but also to business men. The landowner is more than once spoken of as profiting by scarcity and fearing a good harvest, a clear piece of evidence for the effect of the market on the price of his produce. His customers include both the city poor and also rich men without land, who buy their victuals and even their bread outside their own establishments. Further, there are craftsmen working either for themselves or as wage-earners for others; some work at home, others are itinerant. In the towns there is an active retail trade in foodstuffs and everyday articles, and for all this money is used. Other evidence tends to confirm the same picture. There is, for example, the case of Melania, a rich member of the Valerian family, with a palace on the Caelian hill at Rome and properties widely distributed throughout the western half of the Empire, bringing in 120,000 *solidi*; between A.D. 404 and 417 she succeeded in selling these, mainly for gold, and thereafter distributed the sum raised among the poor. Such a financial undertaking would have been quite impossible in an economy which had reverted predominantly to barter.

Indeed, during the fourth and fifth centuries, despite the state control of all large-scale undertakings, most provinces possessed a flourishing small industry in the hands of private craftsmen, organised of course in *collegia*. Even at this time state monopolies only applied to a very few commodities. From the time of Diocletian the provincial currencies disappeared (except in Egypt), and minting was completely restricted to the state mints. Otherwise the only true monopolies were purple dyeing with the finer products, which was reserved for the state by an edict of A.D. 369, and the making of purple and gold embroidered cloth, *paragaudas*. Neither of these monopolies is fiscal in origin, but they form part of a policy which ended by restricting the wearing of purple to the imperial house. Otherwise private competition was allowed in the most unlikely fields. We even hear of a certain Thalassius who owned an arms factory, perhaps at Antioch, towards the end of the fourth century. Small craftsmen, payers of *chrysargyrum*, existed widely in both halves of the Empire. The wages laid down in the *Edict on Prices*, and calculated on time rates, piece rates with keep, or piece rates without keep, most probably represent the maximum that an independent craftsman could ask from a casual employer (or customer), rather than the wages paid to the hands in a large-scale enterprise; and from the price of precious metals there recorded it may be assumed that, as in the early Empire, craftsmen such as goldsmiths and jewellers bought their own materials and produced to some extent for the market. However, when this independent activity is considered in relation to the compulsory duties exacted by the state from all these craftsmen as members of the *collegia*, and the obligation to pay burdensome taxes in gold, their hardships become apparent. Technically they are free men; but their prestige is indicated by the fact that the craftsman now usually carries only one name in place of the three on which the Roman had always prided himself.

In so far as craftsmen worked for themselves and sold their goods on the market they used money. But it was the debased silver and bronze of the inflations, and even the amount of this available varied from province to province. The government minted with an eye on the army and its military needs rather than on trade. This explains why Spain possessed no mint under the late Empire but had to rely on Southern

Gaul for currency, and why, except for a short-lived mint at Carthage from A.D. 296 to 311, Africa had to get its coinage from Italy. The virtual absence of a mint from the frontier province of Britain (there was one at London between A.D. 296 and 324) is less easily explained. Perhaps its distance led to a lack of interest in an unprofitable province. Even in those provinces well supplied with coinage, however, Constantine's *solidus* was too large a unit to finance small transactions, and these had to depend on the bronze currency. Throughout the fourth century the government made constant efforts to increase the supply of gold. For instance by an edict of Valentinian and Valens, dating to A.D. 365, anyone willing to go prospecting for gold might leave his present occupation, on condition that he subsequently remitted eight (later seven) scruples of gold annually to the treasury. Conditions cannot, however, have been very attractive, for in A.D. 376 measures had to be taken against Thracian miners who were seeking a refuge from their hardships with the Goths; and two years later a further edict laid down severe penalties for such miners of Gaul and Italy as might attempt to reach Sardinia. There are, moreover, repeated references to gold-miners who concealed themselves and were to be apprehended and brought back to their place of origin.

However, the fourth century saw what Symmachus describes as *enormitas auri crescens*; and by the time of Theodosius, the state had apparently sufficient gold and silver at its disposal to mint large quantities of small coins in these metals which served as a sound currency for small-scale trading. The source of this gold is not certain. But, though some of it no doubt came from prospectors, and some from the treasures of pagan temples or from Eastern campaigns, the bulk of it no doubt represented the fruits of a consistent policy of attracting all the silver and gold within the Empire to the imperial *fiscus*. The restoration of a full money economy (for the growth of *adaeratio* was gradually eliminating *natura* from fiscal transactions as well) was complete in the East by the fifth century. In the West, however, wars and political stresses were more acute. British fourth-century hoards show a unique preponderance of silver coins, which points to a shortage of gold in the province; and from A.D. 400 onwards there is a complete disappearance of small coinage from both Britain and the Danube areas. An occasional *solidus* is the only evidence for a money economy in these parts after that date. In the other western provinces too the restoration of a money economy was considerably hampered by the relative shortage of the precious metals, and by the absence of Spanish and African mints; moreover, the economy as a whole was much enfeebled, and the growth in the power of large landowners had weakened the central government. The truth about natural economy, in the western half of the Empire at least, appears to be this.[1] From the time of Diocletian onward two economies existed simultaneously. The needs of the general public were satisfied by a system of public distributions of the main necessities of life, supplemented by small purchases in the free market with the debased bronze currency. Simultaneously a sound gold and silver coinage circulated among the rich, enabling a land-owner like Ausonius, who wished to refurnish his household, to buy every kind of luxury from all parts of the known world.

This raises the third problem suggested by the *Edict on Prices*. To what extent was inter-provincial trade still maintained during the last two centuries of the Western Empire? This is a question not easily answered, largely because of the difficulty of deciding just how much weight is to be attached to the scattered evidence available. Where items of information are rare, the survival or disappearance of any one must be largely a matter of chance, and it is easy to exaggerate the importance of what evidence we happen to have. Recently, however, much new light has been thrown on this problem by the discovery of two new sets of fragments of the *Edict* of Diocletian. The first of these are fragments of a Greek version of the *Edict* and were found at Pettorano in the Abruzzi. This find finally confirms the view that, despite a certain stress on the products of the East, the *Edict* was in fact intended to apply to the whole Empire. The second fragments are those of a Latin version from Aphrodisias in Caria, and provide new and decisive evidence for widespread Mediterranean trade in everyday articles at the outset of the fourth century.

These Carian fragments for the first time give us the rates for the tariffing of sea transport. Hitherto the only transport charges known from the *Edict* were the rates for conveying various loads by wagon, ass or camel; and this worked out at $1\frac{1}{3}$ to $1\frac{3}{4}$ *denarii* per hundred pounds for every mile (without the driver's wages)—a rate which was prohibitive against the conveying of goods long distances by land. For example, a load of hay weighing 1200 pounds cost 600 *denarii*, but the prescribed rate for transporting it a mile by wagon was twenty *denarii*; thus a journey of only thirty miles was sufficient to double the cost. And since in fact 600 *denarii* was the prescribed maximum price for such a load, it is clear that the *Edict* virtually ruled out land transport outside the locality. The new rates for sea transport give a very different picture. They lay down the maximum prices to be charged per *castrensis modius* (which was double the ordinary *modius* of 17·51 litres) for some fifty-seven trips between five export regions in the eastern half of the Empire—Alexandria, Oriens (which probably includes such ports on the Orontes as Seleuceia-in-Pieria), Asia, Africa and Nicomedia

[1] See A. Piganiol, *Histoire romaine*, IV, 2: *L'empire chrétien*, p. 416.

(in Bithynia)—and every part of the Mediterranean; altogether thirty items preserve both the two terminals and the rate, but there is no reason to think that other journeys were not listed.

These fragments justify new and important conclusions. The fact that eastern ports are mentioned by name, but for the West only provinces, may be due to the fact that the *Edict* in many ways reflects conditions in the eastern rather than the western half of the Empire. It must not be regarded as evidence for a predominantly one-way traffic, for return rates from Rome to Asia would be the same as those from Asia to Rome. The rates themselves are a remarkable contrast to those for land transport. Thus the maximum price of wheat is 100 *denarii* per *castrensis modius*; but the cost of transport is only twenty-six *denarii* for the trip from 'Oriens' to Lusitania. To be able to ship a cargo the whole length of the Mediterranean for 26% of its maximum value made distant trade a feasible proposition; and the *Edict* presupposes a trade of more than local dimensions in objects of ordinary use. A few fragmentary items from the tariff for river transport serve to complete the picture of a fairly considerable inter-provincial trade, with products from Britain, Gaul and Africa going to all parts of the Mediterranean as late as the end of the third century. The same picture may appear at first sight to be confirmed by the *Expositio totius mundi*, the Latin translation of a description of the Empire compiled by a Greek of Alexandria or Antioch about A.D. 350. But the *Expositio* is more reliably informed about the eastern provinces than the west; and despite one probable reference to the imperial court at Trèves, much of the account of Gaul and Spain seems to reflect earlier sources. An assessment of the intensity of trade in the western half of the Empire during its last centuries must be based on the evidence surviving from the various provinces; and this considered *en bloc* points to a very marked economic regression from the position of the earlier Empire.

Gaul, despite the tremendous material damage done by the barbarians and the *Bagaudae* (see above, p. 51), still continued to produce textiles. Apart from the imperial factories, there is evidence for Gallic clothing in the *Edict* of Diocletian; cloaks came from the Treviri, the Ambiani and the Bituriges, and we hear too of wool from the Atrebates, and of a linen cloak from Aquitania as late as the fifth century. Moreover, in at least one industry, there was progress beyond anything achieved under the earlier emperors. The manufacture of glass, in imitation of that produced in Italy, was introduced into Gaul in the time of Pliny (see above, p. 42); but it began to make real headway only from the middle of the second century, when we hear of factories in Bourbonnais, Poitou, Vendée, Loire-Inférieure, Argonne, Eifel, and above all at Cologne. Technical improvements in the course of this century resulted in a fine transparent glass, which was frequently adorned with geometrical motifs, and even scenes of a mythological character, gladiatorial combats and the like. Various ordinances from the time of Constantine onwards gave special protection and concessions to the *vitriarii* (glass workers) and *diatretarii* (filigree workers), provided they taught their skill to their children. This policy, which was designed to repair the ravages of the third century among skilled workers, was tantamount to a subsidy of the glass trade, and throughout the fourth century it continued to flourish, especially in Gallia Belgica, where the proximity of the army and the court at Trèves acted as a strong stimulus to production. The merits of the great output of glass in this period are hard to assess. The shapes, based on those of gold and silver vessels, remained good; and new refinements of technique were evolved, such as gilding or painting between two layers of glass. On the other hand, there is a general decline in quality, and a yellow or greenish tinge begins to appear in the later specimens.

In its earlier stages the glass industry appears to have used foreign personnel. We have, for example, an inscription referring to a Carthaginian citizen, an African, named Julius Alexander, who practised as a maker of glass in Gaul. Later, for about a hundred years, from A.D. 275 to 380, the large factories of Frontinus seem to have operated with slave labour, producing a single type of monotonous barrel-shaped glass bottle. Frontinus' headquarters were probably Cologne, but his firm may have had branches near Boulogne and Beauvais, judging by the diffusion of specimens found. However, impressive though this industry may be, with its suggestion too of specialisation of types, it never reaches the scale of the earlier potteries. Glassware was used by the aristocracy, not by peasants or small artisans and traders, and though some of it was exported to Asia and Scandinavia, it remained a luxury. Nor is the revival of pottery in the Argonne, with a new type of decoration, imparted by the potter's wheel rather than the mould, evidence for a widespread commercial renaissance. The decline of the corporations is in itself against such an assumption. The shortage of inscriptions makes generalisation dangerous; but the badness of the lettering of those we have is symptomatic of the general regression. The vigorous Gallic shipping trade of earlier years now seems to have disappeared. Fourth-century texts mention *navicularii* from Africa, Spain and Egypt, but none from Gaul; and the new fragments of the *Edict on Prices*, which tariff the trade routes from the eastern ports, only confirm the impression that such emporia as Arles and Narbonne were frequented mainly by merchants from the East. Similarly there are no late references to the gilds responsible for Gallic river transport. How far the work formerly undertaken by these gilds had been transferred to the *bastagarii* (see above, p. 73) and the militarised flotillas of the lakes and rivers of France and Switzerland, remains a subject for speculation.

Further to the east, in Roman Germany, similar trends are apparent. The court at Trèves and the frontier armies provided a stimulus to Gaul and Germany alike, and Cologne glass circulated in both areas. On the Danube too, for similar reasons, the late Empire saw the flowering of an economy that had developed slowly. The *Edict on Prices* refers to clothing from Rhaetia and Noricum, and to 'cloaks from the Danube area'; and the state factories of Illyricum are likely to have been founded where the textile industry was already in existence. Trade over the frontier, however, was more and more restricted by imperial policy. References to *pelles*—especially beaver and marten furs—in Diocletian's *Edict* may point to the beginnings of a fur trade with the North. But the export of iron and bronze to the barbarians was forbidden from the early fourth century onwards; and an edict of A.D. 374 not only forbade the export of gold, but somewhat naïvely urged that 'wherever gold should be discovered in the hands of the barbarians, subtle guile should be employed to remove it'. About the same time the number of points at which trade with the barbarians was permitted was strictly limited; the Goths, for example, were allowed only two trading posts along the Danube. Shortly afterwards we find arms, wine, corn, oil and fish sauce also included in the list of articles which must not cross the frontier. These restrictions undoubtedly hampered the remnants of trade from the North; and the removal of the court from Trèves to Arles in A.D. 413 was a further blow. There is evidence that such rich men as could fled south about this time, leaving an impoverished area which rapidly deteriorated to something like the economic level of free Germany.

Britain on the contrary enjoyed an Indian summer in the fourth century. The towns had followed the general pattern of third-century decay, but this was succeeded by a period of prosperity—for the upper classes at any rate—based on the life of the villas. In contrast to Gaul, where in the early third century there was a recrudescence of indigenous decorative forms, especially in the art of enamelling and in the appearance of a native style which foreshadows that of the fourth century and later barbarian work, British craftsmanship during the third and fourth centuries shows a break with Celtic types, and instead we have a flood of standardised articles such as brooches, of which some may be importations from the continent, but others are certainly native imitations. It has, however, been pointed out [1] that the Romano-Celtic tradition eventually reappears, triumphant over this mass-produced ware, in the

[1] Cf. R. G. Collingwood, *Economic Survey*, III, 96.

hanging bowls found in Anglo-Saxon graves and in other late metal work, which proves that the Celtic traditions of art were not dead, but lived on somewhere in the work of third and fourth century British craftsmen.

The imports of *sigillata* from the continent ceased about A.D. 250, and were superseded—though on a much smaller scale—by glassware and pottery from the Rhineland. The army, as before, continued to make its own pots, though there was increasing specialisation; by the late fourth century most army sites in the north of England appear to have been supplied with a single type of ware, blackish grey and coarse in texture, which was probably manufactured at the Roman villa of Knapton in Yorkshire. Like the Danube provinces Britain also developed a textile industry. The imperial factory at Winchester was no doubt set up to provide uniforms for the army in Britain; but a reference to British cloaks in Diocletian's *Edict* points to some amount of export trade. There is also evidence for fourth-century exports of corn from Britain; but it is not clear whether this went in the ordinary way of trade or as a fiscal levy. Similarly the British workmen who helped in the rebuilding of Autun may have gone voluntarily to Gaul, but were more probably a *corvée*. In general the economic trend in Britain, as elsewhere, during the fourth century, was towards local self-sufficiency. Excavations have revealed few foreign products in the villas of this period; and the absence of a mint and the exceptional hoarding of silver coins have already been noted (above, p. 75). But largely for geographical reasons, it was an age of quiet prosperity, until the neglect of the imperial authorities and the withdrawal of the legions paved the way for the overrunning of the province, the destruction of the villas, and the coming of the Saxons.

Spain too continued to enjoy a modified prosperity. The large number of late milestones which have survived points to energetic work in maintaining the roads, and this in turn presupposes a degree of internal commerce, much of it, no doubt, as in Britain, carried out by hawkers and pedlars, such as can still be met with on the Spanish hills. The presence of a synagogue at Elche, however, and the canons of the Council of Elvira, which regulated the commercial as well as the social relations between Jews and Christians, point to a considerable body of Jewish traders in Spain by the end of the third century. Some export trade undoubtedly continued. Even in the fourth century, Ausonius in Gaul receives gifts of olive oil and fish sauce (*muria*) from Barcelona, and bears witness to the survival of the old trade name, *garum sociorum*. The *Expositio totius orbis*, too, though awarding pride of place to the learned men of Spain, *viri docti*, deigns also to notice its olive oil, fish sauce, lard, garments and esparto grass—'sufficient for the whole

world'. Its baggage animals too—if this document is to be trusted—
were still renowned; but there is no mention of race-horses, though
Julian presented one to Constantius, and both Symmachus and Vegetius
sing their praises. The *Edict* of Diocletian lists the hams of the Cerretani,
and Spanish wool; and though for reasons already considered there
were no state textile factories in Spain, the Balearic Islands contained
dye works. Both before and after the foundation of Constantinople, in
A.D. 324 and in 336, there is evidence from the *Theodosian Code* that
fiscal corn was being sent from Spain to Rome. However, a steep
decline in the amount of available evidence is clear proof of the decay
which the province suffered under the impact of civil war and invasion.
Spain had no mint, and the coins in the mining districts became rarer,
though some bear names as late as those of Theodosius (A.D. 378–95)
and Honorius (A.D. 395–423). Altogether we know little of the real
state of the country at this time, not even whether Avienus is to be
believed when he speaks of the once famous western port of Gades as
lying in ruins, or Ausonius, when he describes Hispalis, Corduba and
Tarraco as still flourishing.

Sicily, records the *Expositio*, is a land of unlimited wool, and baggage
animals; it abounds in rich and learned men, who speak both Greek and
Latin; it grows fine wines on the slopes of Etna; and both Syracuse and
Catania are famous for their circuses. In fact the province seems to have
remained a centre of primary production, and in the late fourth century
it was still sending corn to Rome, and breeding world-famous horses
for use in the gladiatorial games, the circus and the postal service. As
before, Sicily still imported pottery; fourth-century earthenware lamps
from Africa have been found both at Syracuse and at Camarina, and
there was some trade with Narbonese Gaul and the eastern provinces.
Tiles were manufactured locally and also imported from Africa.
Through its equable climate, its landscape, and its antiquities, the
island attracted tourists; but even though they were mainly drawn
from the richest classes, the senators, who were forbidden to visit other
provinces, they will hardly have constituted an important economic
factor. In general, Sicily was still a land of large estates and ranches, and
these with their *coloni* controlled the main pattern of life outside the
towns.

After the foundation of Constantinople, Rome was provisioned
mainly from Africa, and until its seizure by the Vandals a hundred years
later the province—together with Mauretania—remained primarily
a storehouse for the capital. Its people, says the *Expositio*, were crafty.
Their main passion was for gladiatorial games; there were few good
men among them, and they were unworthy of their rich country.
Those of Mauretania were, however, still worse, for their habits and

way of life were barbarous; Mauretania was significantly one of the few places which still furnished slaves. From the *Expositio* we also learn that Africa supplied olive oil 'sufficient for nearly the whole earth' (but the phrase, which has almost the character of a refrain in this work, should not be pressed too closely), and that it was rich in fruits and baggage animals. African woollens are not mentioned, though both Numidia and Mauretania are said to export clothing; however, the presence of a textile factory and several dye works under the control of a procurator stationed at Carthage is consistent with the independent references to African rugs, cloaks and linen tunics, in both the *Historia Augusta* and the *Edict on Prices*.

The important quarries of North Africa had apparently fallen into disuse during the third century, for in A.D. 320 Constantine issued a rescript authorising anyone who so wished to quarry there for marble —a policy subsequently extended to several eastern provinces. This shortage of quarrymen is an example of the growing failure of free labour to provide the necessities of life under the later Empire. At the quarries of Fruschka-Gora in Pannonia the workers consisted of convicts, mainly Christians *damnati ad metalla*, and some 620 slaves under the charge of five technical overseers with the somewhat inappropriate name of *philosophi*, and a troop of soldiers to give them moral support. No doubt the same system was also tried in North Africa, and similar conditions may well have existed in such a quarry town as Simitthus. The fact that even so attempts had to be made to encourage individuals to embrace the career is some indication of the decline in the population. Carthage, it is true, remained one of the great cities of the West even under the Vandals. Both St Augustine and the author of the *Expositio* mention the famous Street of the Silversmiths, the *vicus argentariorum*. But the province as a whole appears never to have recovered from the pillaging which followed the suppression of the revolt of A.D. 238, which set the Gordians on the imperial throne. This rising of the propertied classes was crushed by Capellianus, the *legatus* of Numidia, and his campaign was probably attended by a tremendous destruction of wealth. Later, in the fourth century, the supporters of the Donatist heresy formed themselves into wandering bands, whom their opponents dubbed *Circumcelliones*. If, as St Augustine says, they spoke only Punic, there were evidently elements of African nationalism in this curious movement, which displayed the violence of both a religious and social rising. The *Circumcelliones* remind us in many ways of the Gallic *Bagaudae*. The *Bagaudae*, so far as we know, had no religious aspect; but both movements represent the ineffective retaliation of a class oppressed beyond endurance. In Africa this rising of the countryside is one more index of the decay of the towns. Diocletian had attempted at the end of the third century to restore the municipalities to prosperity by direct governmental action and by orders to the *curiales*; but the shock and setback had been too great, and there is little evidence from Africa of even the modest degree of economic revival which the fourth century showed in many provinces of the West.

Of these, however, Italy was not one. The continued primacy of Rome is reflected in the new fragments of Diocletian's *Edict*, which place Rome first among the western destinations of ships leaving ports in the eastern half of the Empire; but its role had been established in the early Empire, and it continued to be provisioned out of the taxes. Under Diocletian Italy was divided into two *dioeceses*, of which the southern was exempt from the normal *annona*, but was specifically responsible for providing the capital with meat, wine, wood and lime. Northern Italy on the contrary was assessed for *annona* and its administrative centre was Milan. The general decline of the peninsula, already a feature of the early Empire, now shows itself in the fact that many previously prosperous towns such as Puteoli and Tarracina join the list of those provisioned from abroad. Much of the countryside had fallen out of cultivation, the roads had deteriorated, and by the middle of the fourth century brigandage was so serious that in A.D. 364 the use of horses was forbidden to shepherds and even landowners in seven provinces. By the end of the century half a million *iugera* in Campania, one of the richest regions, were lying fallow; and in A.D. 450 the legal codes speak of famine compelling men to sell their children into slavery. In these conditions trade could hardly flourish; and indeed Italy had long played a passive role in imperial commerce. In the early fourth century Italian wines had still some reputation. The *Edict* of Diocletian tariffs the prices of Picene, Tiburtine, Setine, Surrentine and Falernian vintages; but this does not necessarily imply that they were widely exported. In the same document there is evidence for trade in Marsian and Messapian hams, and for Lucanian pork sausage. This modest list may be reinforced from the *Expositio*; but the glowing picture which is given here of the cornlands of Calabria, and of Campania as the home of rich men and the pantry (*cellarium*) of Rome, induces justifiable suspicions that this description has little relation to the real conditions in the middle of the fourth century. The only evidence of Italian manufactures is in connection with the woollen industry. The old centres, it appears, are still active; we hear of woollens from Canusium and from Mutina (which is famous for its light cloaks), and the market contains both wool and woollens from Tarentum. Of these towns Canusium was the site of one of the imperial weaving mills; others were situated at Milan, Aquileia, Venusia and Rome; and the purple works of Tarentum lay in the second great area of Italian wool production. The north of Italy must also have enjoyed some prosperity from the imperial arms factories established there (see above, pp. 71–2). But there was little independent economic life. As the fourth century advances it is possible to trace the increasing power which the state exercises over the gilds; and with the Gothic invasion of the fifth century, the interruption of the corn supply from Africa, and its final cessation after the Vandal conquest, references become fewer and their significance more obscure. Whether the Italian *collegia* survived the fall of the western half of the Empire is debated. There were gilds in existence in Ravenna in the tenth century; but since Ravenna was under strong influence from the East, they are more probably revivals than survivals from the fifth century.

IV

These scanty records of trade and industry give some indication of the economic decline of the West during the last century and a half of the Empire. The large enterprises, the provisioning of the big centres, the army and the civil service, have been taken over by the state and they remain state responsibilities even after the growth of *adaeratio* has largely put an end to the experiment of taxation in kind; for though the taxes are now paid in gold and silver, it is the imperial authority which buys the goods and supervises their transport and distribution through the tied corporations. The pressure of taxation is now so great that no large-scale independent enterprise can survive. Yet it would be wrong to imagine the late imperial economy as one from which the independent man has vanished. Retail trade continues to flourish, especially of the type in which the craftsman makes and sells his own goods. Moreover, the wholesale trader does not die out, although his scope is reduced and his risk increased. The *Edict on Prices* shows a prosperous inter-provincial commerce for the beginning of the fourth century, including articles of common consumption as well as the luxuries which are the more obvious objects of later trade.

In the main, however, it is the rich man's market which trade in products from a distance seeks to satisfy; and not least, the large land-owners living on their estates, which are self-sufficient for many of the prime necessities of life, and rely on itinerant labour and the local market for the rest, expend their fortunes on rare goods brought from the ends of the Empire. The cleavage between these large landowners, who had gained increased power through the institution of the colonate (itself a secondary result of the introduction of annual taxes in *natura*) and the imperial administration on the other hand, was one of the factors which made for the break-up of the western part of the Empire. Less united and less vigorous than the

East, more torn by risings of native elements such as the *Bagaudae* and the *Circumcelliones*, poorer, and lacking the bulwark which Constantine's new capital had given to the East, the western half gradually weakened and dissolved into the successor states of the Franks, Goths, Vandals and Lombards.

With the collapse of the imperial state, that large section of the economy which depended on it simply disappeared. The residue—small artisans and traders in the towns, local markets, itinerant craftsmen, the villages around the manor or the monastery, and, for the rich, an irregular trade in luxuries from all parts of the Mediterranean—was left as the economic foundation of the new states of medieval Europe.

CHAPTER III

Byzantine Trade and Industry

I

BYZANTINE economic history shows a marked contrast to the economic history of other medieval states. Its evolution does not correspond with that of the peoples of Western Europe with their steady advance towards modern economy, nor does it resemble the story of the Arab Empire—the story of a vast loosely knit dominion, commanding natural resources of every sort but never fully developing them. Byzantium was a carefully administered state, dominating a large but not naturally very wealthy territory, and aiming at the greatest possible amount of centralisation in its capital, Constantinople, a city whose size and organised activity made it unique in the medieval world.

Byzantine history falls into clearly differentiated periods. The first, from the foundation of Constantinople till the Arab conquests in the seventh century, is a continuation of the history of the Roman Empire. The Emperor still possessed all the eastern provinces of the Empire, and his problems were similar to those of his predecessors. There follows the period when the Empire, reduced in size and at first hard hit, gradually readjusts its life to reach a high state of prosperity in the tenth and eleventh centuries. Then comes a period of new invasions from the East and military and economic aggression from the West. In the twelfth century Byzantium apparently recovers, then rapidly declines, till the capture of Constantinople by the Crusaders in 1204. The Empire of Nicaea and the recapture of Constantinople in 1261 again suggest recovery; but the last two centuries of the Empire tell a story of steady impoverishment and decay.

Throughout these periods the basic aims of the Byzantine government remained the same. The first was to provide and maintain a strong centralised administration. The Emperors, from Diocletian onwards, had diagnosed the main cause of the decline of Rome as being the lack of uniformity and control in her provincial government. At first the Empire had seemed too big to be ruled from one centre; Diocletian envisaged two or four centres. But the foundation of a new capital, at the same time easily accessible and easily defensible, and the barbarian invasions of the western provinces made further centralisation feasible, though it was resented by the rich provinces of Egypt and Syria, each with a great metropolis of its own, and it was not completed till the Arab conquest further reduced the size of the Empire. This centralisation went deep; not only were the market towns in closer connection

with the capital than in the West but the villages were in closer connection with the market towns on which they depended for most of their
supplies.[1] The connections were made possible by the good communications. The Byzantines maintained and improved the Roman road
system in their dominions and always possessed an adequate mercantile
marine. At the same time the administration was elastic. Local governors
enjoyed a large amount of autonomy and responsibility; but they were
liable to periodical inspection by officials from the central government,
which controlled them further by paying them their salaries.[2] The
whole system only began to collapse with the emergence, from the
late tenth century onwards, of a provincial nobility, rich enough to defy
the central government,[3] and with the destruction of communications
in the course of the Turkish wars in the late eleventh and the twelfth
centuries.

The second aim of the Byzantine government arose from the first.
It was to keep the population of Constantinople well fed and contented.
Disorder in the capital of so centralised a state might seriously damage
the whole administrative system. Consequently everything possible
was done to ensure a steady flow of cheap food and essential articles to
the city, to the welfare of which the provinces were often sacrificed.

Thirdly, the government aimed at obtaining a steady revenue through
taxation, to pay for the expenses of the administration and of the
mercenary army, and at building up and maintaining large stocks of
gold. In Byzantine eyes the good emperor was the emperor who left
behind him a well-stocked treasury. The gold was necessary as a reserve
against national emergencies and to provide a backing for the imperial
coinage. The government further understood the possibility of controlling prices by the regulation of the amount of gold in circulation.

In pursuit of these aims the Byzantine government issued a large
number of laws and ordinances that affected every aspect of the economic
life of its subjects. But this state control was potential rather than actual.
It did not represent an economic policy but was purely for administrative purposes; and if the administration did not seem to require the
enforcement of these regulations, they remained dormant. The attempt
at a caste system begun by Diocletian's legislation to make sons follow
their fathers' professions was officially kept up throughout Byzantine
history, but there is no evidence that it was enforced; nor does the
official ban on unrestricted travel round the Empire seem to have

[1] See *Cambridge Economic History*, I, 200.
[2] Governors of certain unruly provinces obtained all or part of their salaries from
the taxes that they collected. This gave them an incentive to collect the taxes efficiently.
Such provinces were liable to particularly frequent inspection from the capital.
[3] See *Cambridge Economic History*, I, 204 ff.

affected the movement of the average Byzantine. The Lives of the various Byzantine saints, which provide our best evidence for the habits of the average citizen under the Empire, give an impression of very little governmental control, except in times of crisis, of famine or of war. Even the *Book of the Prefect*,[1] the compilation made by Leo VI of the rules governing the gilds of Constantinople, probably shows an ideal rather than the actual state of affairs.

The Byzantine authorities were at no time concerned with the balance of trade. Exports from the Empire were of political rather than of economic interest to them. In fact, from Roman times onward, many more goods were imported than exported, and the balance was paid for in gold. This meant that the prosperity of the Empire largely depended upon the availability of gold. The Roman Empire had been able to support itself in the necessities of life but had imported luxuries, such as silk, precious stones and spices, from the East. In exchange, gold, and to a lesser extent silver, had been exported to the East. This gold came mainly from Nubia, to which the Romans had access, and, when the diplomatic situation permitted, from the Caucasus and the Urals. But at the same time the stocks of gold within the Empire were diminishing. Moreover, the gold exported to Persia went out of circulation, as the Persians used silver for their coinage and used gold either to make into ornaments or as stores of treasure. At the same time, with the un-reliability of the Roman coinage, private individuals and institutions within the Empire began to hoard precious metals. Constantine the Great's reform of the coinage, by restoring confidence, released some of these hoards, but this was countered by the desire of the newly established Christian ecclesiastical institutions to build up stores of treasure. At the same time barbarian migrations on the Russian steppes and in Africa, in the fourth and fifth centuries, and wars with Persia in the sixth, prevented easy access to the sources of gold. By the time of Justinian's reign (527–61) the position was beginning to alarm the authorities.

There was, however, still a certain amount of gold coming from the western half of the Empire. The establishment of barbarian kingdoms there had not much affected the trade of the Mediterranean, except for a period in the middle of the fifth century when the Vandals of Africa used their fleet for piratical purposes. The new rulers were as eager as their subjects to obtain the luxuries of the East, for which they paid mainly in gold as their own exports were small. But the trade was conducted by Egyptian and Syrian merchants in Egyptian and Syrian ships; and the gold went almost entirely to Egypt and Syria. Only a proportion of it reached Constantinople in the form of taxes. Some

[1] See below, p. 107.

was used for the imperial mints of Alexandria and Antioch, more went further east to pay for Asiatic goods. The rest went largely into the treasuries of Egyptian and Syrian churches and monasteries and so was withdrawn from circulation. Till the seventh century Egypt and Syria were both far richer than the provinces that centred on Constantinople. The new capital provided a market for local goods and for imported luxuries, but as yet its manufactures could not compete with those of Alexandria. It was Egypt that manufactured the glass, the high class pottery, the jewelry and the woven stuffs that were exported to the West; and Alexandria contained the chief ship-building yards of the time. The timber for the ships came from the Lebanon, and the Lebanese ports also, especially Berytus, built ships. Moreover, the eastern trade reached the Mediterranean through Syria and Egypt. Arabian spices, of which incense was the most important, came by caravan along South-west Arabia to the gulf of Akaba, where they either branched to the Mediterranean through southern Palestine, or went north through Transjordan, Damascus and the Orontes valley to Antioch. Spices from the Far East, such as pepper and cloves, and a certain amount of Chinese raw silk came by sea, conducted by Egyptian merchants in Abyssinian ships from Malaya or Ceylon across the Indian Ocean and up the Red Sea to Clysma on the Gulf of Suez and thence across to Alexandria. An imperial official stationed at Clysma superintended this trade and himself made yearly visits to the Indies. The Persian trade, consisting both of raw and of made-up silk, came chiefly to Antioch, though silk for the Constantinople market might travel through North Persia and Armenia to Trebizond. Gold, together with ivory and ostrich feathers, was obtained from East Africa, again by Abyssinian ships carrying Egyptian merchants.[1]

II

In spite of political problems caused by the religious and administrative grievances of Egypt and Syria against the central government at Constantinople, the fifth century was a period of growing prosperity. The Emperor Justinian on his accession found the treasury well enough filled for him to embark on an extravagant internal policy of public works and an ambitious foreign policy of expansion. Unfortunately a war with Persia had already broken out, caused largely by imperial resentment at the rising prices charged by the Persians for raw silk, and continued intermittently but with increasing severity for over a century. Syria in particular suffered from this war, not only from the interrup-

[1] The Abyssinian-Egyptian trade is described by Cosmas Indicopleustes in his *Christian Topography*, written in about 530 A.D.

tion to her commerce with Persia but also from the invasions of the Persians. Antioch was captured in 540; and the ensuing sack, following so soon after the great earthquakes of 526 and 529, dealt it a blow from which it never recovered. Justinian attempted to remedy matters by diplomatic activity with the Abyssinians, intended to keep open the Red Sea trade route and to maintain supplies of African gold. But before his reign was over the collapse of the Abyssinian dominion in Arabia and the Blemmyes' invasion of Nubia had made the fruits of his diplomacy barren. The establishment of a Turkish empire in Central Asia enabled him to open out a new route for raw silk from China that by-passed Persia to the north; but the collapse of the Turks before the close of the century closed it down again. It was, however, by this route that Nestorian monks travelled to Constantinople with the eggs of the silkworm hidden in their staffs, thus founding the silk-growing industry that later was to be the pride of Byzantium. Meanwhile the stocks of gold in the West were coming to an end with a consequent reduction in the trade across the Mediterranean. Justinian's wars further reduced the purchasing power of the West while they used up his own reserves of treasure.

The economic decline of the Empire, together with the political decline, continued under Justinian's successors. In the early seventh century the disastrous reign of the Emperor Phocas, in the course of which the administrative machinery of the Empire broke down and the Emperor himself deliberately sank in a shipwreck the contents of the imperial treasury, saw a renewal of the Persian war, which his successor Heraclius had to meet without resources. For fifteen years the Persians held Syria, making great inroads into the resources of the province and its stores of wealth; for ten years they held Egypt, though they seem to have interfered less with its economy. Heraclius could only finance the war on his side by taking over the treasuries of the Church in Constantinople and Anatolia. He was at last victorious; and a large part of the Persian royal treasure fell into his hands. But he used it to repay his loan from the Church, for which he further raised what money he could from the reconquered provinces of Syria and Egypt. Much wealth had been lost during the war, and now great stocks of gold again were collected to lie idle in ecclesiastical treasuries. In A.D. 630 there was about 20% less gold in circulation than there had been two centuries before.

The Arab conquest of Syria and Egypt followed swiftly and easily on the Persian war. The conquest had its economic causes. The Syrian merchant secured most of his goods from Persia and the East and sold them to the western peoples. His trade was naturally independent of Constantinople, and he resented its being heavily taxed in order to maintain a government at Constantinople which had done nothing for him except involve him in wars with Persia. The Egyptian merchant too was dependent on securing goods from the East, but his came for the most part up the Red Sea. When the Abyssinians were replaced by the Arabs as the dominant power on the Red Sea, the Egyptian merchant was inclined to make friends with the Arabs. Egypt also was a great corn-growing country. Shortage of gold forced prices down; and it seems that Constantinople, which once had bought its corn from Egypt, was now developing cornfields nearer home. The Egyptians were resentful of the loss of their main market, and they too suffered from the heavy taxation. To the Syrians and Egyptians the Arabs were from the outset attractive masters financially, for they demanded far lower taxes. When in very few years the Arabs owned an Empire stretching from the Atlantic to India, they offered their subjects sources and markets quite satisfactory to their needs, though transport in Mediterranean Arab lands tended to become land transport rather than sea transport. The Syrian merchant marine, the most vigorous on the Mediterranean since Phoenician days, declined, never to recover.

III

With the loss of Syria and Egypt, Byzantine economic history properly begins. The Empire was now a unit centralised in Constantinople. It is hard to imagine a better placed centre. Not only was Constantinople an almost impregnable fortress, surrounded on three sides by seas to which it was difficult for any enemy fleet to penetrate, but it lay upon the one easy land bridge from Europe into Asia and upon the one outlet from the Black Sea. It commanded therefore the junction of two of the great trade routes of the world. Moreover, it was always easy of access for peaceful voyagers and merchants. Consequently the victualling necessary for a great city could be managed without trouble. The population of Constantinople seems to have remained fairly constant till the eve of the Latin Conquest, and may be roughly estimated at 800,000. Probably there was a slight drop in numbers in the late seventh and eighth centuries and an increase again in the tenth. This population consisted of the Court, the vast civil service, the central Church organisation, a large number of monks, of lawyers and professional men, the small shop-keepers and retailers to be expected in so large a city, market-gardeners and small-holders whose plots lay within the city walls, and manufacturers and traders of all sorts and of many nationalities.

It was some time before Byzantine trade readjusted itself to the new circumstances. The Arab conquests and migrations in Asia cut the

Empire off from its supplies of gold, and it was only by a strict control of circulation that the Byzantine currency kept up its value. Early in the eighth century the Emperors' diplomacy with the nations of the steppes reopened access to the Urals. The kingdom of the Khazars, a commercially-minded Turkish race, had been established to the north of the Caspian during the seventh century. Byzantine craftsmen were employed by the Khazar Khan, for whom they constructed his one stone-built city, at Sarkel on the Sea of Azov; and in return Ural gold began to come through to Byzantium. About the same time contact was recovered with the Caucasian gold mines, whose output, however, seems to have been declining. In the later eighth century the anti-ecclesiastical policy of the iconoclast emperors brought a large proportion of church treasure into circulation. But the chief source of gold for the Empire was now provided by the Arabs themselves, whose trade with Western Europe, through Spain and the Western Mediterranean and with Northern Europe along the Volga route, brought to Western and Northern Europe sufficient gold to enable their merchants to buy once more the expensive luxuries of the Byzantine factories. By the ninth century the Empire had rebuilt large stocks of gold and could once more take imports from the East.

Owing to wars with the Arabs Far Eastern goods had begun to take a more northerly route across Turkestan to the north shores of the Black Sea or, a little later, to Northern Persia and Armenia. The former of these routes was only practicable if there was peace on the steppes of Central Asia and Eastern Europe. The Khazar kingdom guaranteed sufficient stability for this trade.

The Khazar capital at Itil on the lower Volga was from the eighth to the tenth century a market where merchants of all races could be found.[1] From Itil goods destined for Europe came to the Crimean port of Cherson, the northerly outpost of Byzantium, whence Greek ships conveyed them to Constantinople. This was the usual route for Chinese goods, which consisted, as far as Byzantium was concerned, almost exclusively of raw silk. Indian and Malayan goods, ivory, precious stones and all forms of spices, came rather through Afghanistan and Persia. In Persia, carpets and made-up silks would be added to the caravans. The Armenians made themselves the middlemen between the Persians and Greeks, and Armenian merchants would convey the goods to Trebizond, where the Greek ships would call for them. Direct trade between the Arabs and Byzantium at first was rare, though cotton from Egypt seems to have reached Constantinople, and later, before the end of the ninth century, woven goods from Syria and Baghdad which

[1] The Tibetan revolt of 663 was probably another cause of establishing the Turkestan trade route, as it interrupted the road from China to Northern India.

were exported from Seleucia, near Antioch, or travelled overland across Asia Minor.

The Greek Black Sea merchant fleets also brought to Constantinople the exports of Northern Europe, the slaves and furs and wax of the plains that are now Russia and amber and dried fish from the Baltic. For these too Cherson was the chief port till the Russians appeared in the late ninth century and began to conduct their trade themselves. Goods from the Balkan peninsula and Central Europe beyond it, such as Transylvanian salt and the minerals of Serbia, came usually by land to Thessalonica and thence by sea to Constantinople. From Western Europe there was imported a small quantity of slaves, weapons, timber, and, later, rough woollen cloth.

Goods coming to Constantinople from the Black Sea were stopped by the imperial customs officials at the entrance to the Bosporus, at Hieron, where a 10% *ad valorem* duty was imposed. Goods from the Mediterranean and the Aegean paid a similar duty at Abydos on the Hellespont. For the Asiatic land route there were customs houses at Trebizond, and at Thessalonica for the Balkan land route. Till the late sixth century the customs organisation was controlled by the Count of the Commerce at Constantinople. Afterwards it was decentralised and the local customs officers, the *commerciarii*, were allowed considerable autonomy. At the end of the eighth century the Empress Irene for a time allowed free imports, but the advantages to the city's trade were considered to be less than the loss to the imperial revenues, and her successor restored the duties and tightened them so that the importers of slaves from the South should no longer be able to evade them by landing their goods in some port to the west of Abydos. Henceforward such slaves, wherever they were sold, were liable to a special tariff of 2 *nomismata* (about 30 gold francs).

It is unfortunately quite impossible to estimate the volume or value of this import trade. We do not know what proportion of the imperial revenues was made up from the import duties, while estimates of the size of the whole imperial revenues vary from about 8,000,000 *nomismata* to six times that amount. Certainly the revenue from the duties was a considerable item in the imperial budget; but if Irene could contemplate carrying on her government without its help, its absence cannot have made a vital difference. On the other hand Irene may have hoped by lowering prices to secure more money in direct taxation and also to stimulate trade. There is reason to believe that the import trade was suffering something of a slump in her time. Of the commodities imported, Chinese raw silk was probably the most important. Even when the imperial silkworm farms were well established, the raw silk merchants and dressers bought the bulk of their material from abroad.

Made-up clothes of all sorts, particularly damasks and brocades, were similarly, despite the large home production, always imported in large quantities. Ivory and other precious materials were imported from Arab countries. The spice trade was also of considerable dimensions. The list of spices that the perfumers' gild was entitled to sell includes many items, such as pepper, cinnamon and musk, that all must have been imported from the East; and Byzantine medical treatises, such as that of Symeon Seth, assume that all manner of Indian spices, nutmeg, galingale or cloves, are easily obtainable in Constantinople. Furs from the North were probably a constant item, but furs seem to have been used only to clothe the rich.

The exports from the Byzantine Empire were less numerous. The East bought a few of the luxury products of Byzantium, such as glass *tesserae* for mosaic work, and a certain number of dyes and spices, such as mastic from the Aegean islands or Peloponnesian cochineal. The West and the North provided better customers, eager to buy Byzantine silks and enamels and carved ivories and jewels. Though this trade brought gold into the Empire, the imperial authorities did not care to encourage it too far. They preferred their products to have the value and mystery of comparative rarity. The finest silks might not even be exported for trade. They might occasionally leave the country as an imperial gift to some foreign potentate, but that was all. Silks of poorer quality were less restricted, but the supply for export seems never to have equalled the demand. Linens and cottons were exported in larger quantities; and from the tenth century onwards Peloponnesian carpets were popular in the West. Byzantine works of applied art, the enamels and ivories and steatites and so on, were equally sought after, but were too expensive to be exported in large quantities. Goods for export paid a duty similar to that on imported goods, at the same stations. The customs examination was very severe. Otto I's ambassador, Liudprand of Cremona, found that his diplomatic status was of no avail when he tried to smuggle out silk cloths whose export was prohibited.

A large number of the goods imported from the East were apparently re-exported to the West or the North without alteration.

The bulk of the carrying trade between eastern countries and Byzantium and all the coastal trade with the Empire was done in Greek ships. In the Black Sea they had a complete monopoly, conveying all goods from Cherson or Trebizond to the capital, till the Russians developed their own trade and the Khazar trade declined. Thenceforward, from the late ninth century onwards, goods from the steppes were taken in the yearly Russian expeditions which sailed down the river Dniepr and along the Bulgarian coast to the Bosporus. In the western trade the Greeks lost their monopoly about the same time. In the tenth century, Bari, the capital of Byzantine Italy, had a considerable merchant marine, while the vassal city of Amalfi was steadily increasing its connections, keeping up an establishment for its merchants in Constantinople. But the chief rival to Byzantine shipping came from Venice, itself also nominally a vassal city and as yet tactfully obliging in its attitude to its overlord. Venice by the end of the tenth century had already an expanding marine, and not only did all goods between Constantinople and the Western Empire travel in its ships, but they also provided the regular passenger and mail service. Nevertheless Greek ships still sailed to Italy. The merchantman that rescued the Western Emperor Otto II after his defeat at Stilo was by no means an isolated phenomenon.

Goods that came by land seem to have been escorted mostly by merchants of their own nationality. There were annually a number of Syrians in Constantinople who had brought Syrian stuffs by road across Asia Minor. In Constantinople and Thessalonica were also to be found men from the Balkans selling their local products to the gild organisations. Foreign merchants were by no means discouraged. It was considered only right that they, and not Byzantines, should pay the heavy import and export duties. On the other hand their lives during their visits to the capital were carefully circumscribed and superintended. On their arrival they had to report themselves to the city authorities who kept in touch with them. Special khans, called *Mitata*, were allotted to them, and three months was the maximum amount of time that any of them might remain. These rules applied to the ordinary Syrian or Italian trader. Later the chief Italian cities secured greater freedom for their merchants by maintaining what might best be called a consulate, whose officials took over the superintendence with the approval of the imperial government. Barbarous but regular merchants such as the Russians had special arrangements made for them. Their trade was so advantageous to the Empire that they were given free lodging and baths, but they were housed in a suburb and only allowed within the city walls under escort. Similarly Bulgarian traders had to register themselves and their goods. This took place first at Constantinople; and when in the late ninth century corruption at the imperial court caused the registration office to be moved to Thessalonica, Bulgarian trade was so badly dislocated that the Bulgarian king went to war about it.

Despite occasional interruptions due to wars Byzantine foreign trade increased in volume till the international convulsions of the eleventh century. It received very little encouragement from the imperial authorities, whose interference in it was only concerned with questions of revenue and of the acquisition of the raw materials needed by the imperial factories. They were ready to sacrifice it in the interests of diplomacy and of maintaining order in Constantinople.

Internal trade consisted primarily in the supplying of Constantinople with the necessities of life, and with a growing number of luxuries. The corn which fed the city grew for the most part in Asia Minor and was conveyed by sea from the port nearest to the corn-fields. If, however, the Asian crop failed corn could also be brought in from other provinces. In the famine of 1037 the government bought up 100,000 *modii* (650,000 kilograms) of corn in Hellas and the Peloponnese. Thrace, which later grew corn, mainly produced cattle and swine which were driven in herds to the city *abattoirs*. Sheep came for the most part from the highlands of Bithynia. Vegetables were grown locally and fruit along the sheltered shore of the Gulf of Nicomedia. Spices and flavourings came from all over the Empire, mastic from the islands, saffron from Cilicia, gum from Pisidia. Cloths of local manufacture were supplemented from Peloponnesian looms. Carpets were made both in the Peloponnese and in Anatolia. Raw silk would be sent from farms near Thebes or Corinth to be added to the Constantinopolitan stock. Linen and cotton would come to be finished and made up from flax grown in the West Peloponnese and along the Aegean coasts of Asia Minor, with the help of dyes from the Peloponnese and alum from Kerasount to fix them. All this provided opportunities for Greek merchants and filled the ships of the merchant marine. Even towns such as Thessalonica or Trebizond had to have their local products supplemented in order to maintain their considerable population.

The mercantile marine was carefully regulated. The rules that governed it were published in a code known as the Rhodian Law (apparently because in the days of the Early Roman Empire Rhodes was supposed to possess the best maritime regulations). This was re-issued at intervals without alteration from the eighth to the thirteenth century. From it we have some picture of the organisation of Byzantine shipping. Every ship had an owner or hirer who was distinct from the captain, though the captain might combine the functions. The captain, however, was in complete command, though he was tied by certain regulations. The ship-owner, if he was not a sailor, presumably seldom made the voyage. The wages of the sailors and the captain were fixed; the captain received twice the pay of the sailors. The petty officers, the mate, the chief carpenter and the helmsman, received one and a half times the sailors' pay. The cook received only one half of it. The captain was responsible in cases of theft and when the cargo was damaged by bilge water; he had also to see that suitable skins were provided to protect the cargo, according to its nature. Silk and linen goods required particular care. In a crisis the captain was empowered to raise a loan himself to obtain anything necessary for the ship. Merchants always accompanied their goods. Consequently passengers had the right to enter into any discussions about the jettisoning of cargo, though presumably the final decision was the captain's. They had, however, to deposit their gold and valuables with the captain, who would not otherwise accept any responsibility for their loss. When the cargo was lost by shipwreck or other cause the shipowner was liable to pay compensation according to its nature—one fifth of the value if it were silver, one tenth if it were gold, pearls or dry silk, less if the silk were wet. Cargoes of less valuable commodities, such as corn or oil, carried no such liability. Passengers were entitled to a space not exceeding three cubits by one; women had less. Their daily ration of water was regulated. Ships were valued at 50 gold pieces (roughly 75 gold francs) per 1000 *modius*, which was apparently a measure of capacity, based probably on the *modius* (6·5 kgm.) of corn, or at 30 gold pieces if they were old. Sea travel was full of peril. Against fire various precautions were taken. Passengers were specifically forbidden to fry fish on board. The galley fire was the only fire permitted. Shipwreck was avoided as far as possible by closing the seas from October to March, but both the Black Sea and the Aegean are liable at all seasons to sudden storms; the former has few snug anchorages, and the latter has many dangerous coasts and currents. Moreover wreckers existed in plenty. Pirates were a less constant danger. In the Black Sea they were comparatively rare, but the Aegean with its innumerable islands was admirably suited for them. From 824 to 961 Crete was the headquarters of Saracen pirates. Even the harbours contained land thieves who would cut cables and steal anchors. In view of these perils it was highly speculative to invest money in shipping. The authorities therefore permitted maritime loans to command a higher rate of interest than was allowed to ordinary loans. Throughout this period the rate was 16·66% *per annum*. It is doubtful if this rate was high enough for the ordinary investor. A removal of the limit would probably have greatly helped Byzantine shipping, particularly when the competition from the West became pressing.

The goods imported and exported changed hands for the most part in the markets and bazaars of Constantinople, where each trade had its own quarter, so arranged to facilitate supervision; and the conditions of sale were fixed in the regulations of the various gilds. The bazaars of Constantinople were busy at all seasons, though their activity was lessened in winter when the seas were closed and still more during the weeks when snow blocked the roads in Thrace and Asia Minor. Other towns had their particular annual fairs, one of which stood out pre-eminently, the fair of St Demetrius at Thessalonica, which opened on

October 20th and closed on the first Monday after St Demetrius's Day (October 26th). This was already an annual event in the eleventh century and was still flourishing on the eve of the Turkish conquest. During these centuries it was the greatest fair in the Near East. An early twelfth century satirist gives an account of it in its highest prosperity. It took place on the open plain outside the walls, in two long lines of tents, with side streets at right angles to them. It was here that the fine silken stuffs of Boeotia and Corinth were exposed for sale; it was here that the country produce of the Balkan peninsula found its market, together with skins and salt from the Carpathians. Moslem merchants brought Syrian damasks and Egyptian cotton. Italian merchants came chiefly to buy. All the trade of the Near East was reflected in St Demetrius's Fair. No other town within the Empire held a fair of such dimensions, though the bazaars of Trebizond were full of merchants of all nationalities during the summer months, and Antioch, after its reconquest in 969, was the chief meeting-place of Greek and Moslem traders.

IV

At the end of the eleventh century Byzantine trade began to undergo drastic changes from which it never was to recover. The Seljuk conquest of Asia Minor altered the whole of Byzantine economy by robbing Constantinople of the source of its corn supply and of numbers of the solid peasant population, which was one of the chief foundations of its strength. Moreover, the constant wars in Asia Minor upset its land and even its coastal trade. At the same time the presence of the Normans in Southern Italy meant piratical raids on the prosperous Greek peninsula and a very real danger to all the European provinces of the Empire. Meanwhile the Italian merchant cities were steadily increasing their fleets and enroaching more and more on eastern markets. Finally, arising out of the presence of the Seljuks on the pilgrim routes and the trade routes, Norman ambition and Italian commercial enterprise was to combine with a colonising instinct and a genuine burst of religious revivalism to produce a movement that we call the Crusades, a movement that soon revolutionised the trade of the Levant, to the eternal detriment of Byzantium.

In 1082 the Emperor Alexius I, already worn out by wars against the Turks in Asia and barbarian invaders of the Balkans, had to meet a Norman attack on Epirus. He was reduced to asking for the help of the fleet and the finances of Venice, whose Adriatic policy equally was endangered by the Norman advance. In 1092 Alexius issued a Golden Bull announcing the arrangements for the repayment of this loan. The Venetians were to be free to trade without any interference from the customs officials in a list of imperial cities, which named every important port except the Cretan and Cypriot ports and a few on the Black Sea. That is to say, whereas every other trader, Greek or foreign, had still to pay the 10% duty, Venetians could export and import duty free. At the same time they were to take over the Amalfitan factories and establishments within the Empire, Amalfi having by now been engulfed in the Norman Kingdom.

Alexius probably did not realise what he was doing. To excuse the Venetians their duty seemed to him the easiest way to pay off his debt out of his revenue, while the stimulus thus given to trade was undoubtedly useful to Byzantine manufacturers, especially as the Byzantine merchant navy had lost many ships during the Norman and Turkish wars. He failed to notice how damaging the concession would be to the rebuilding of his mercantile marine, perhaps because sufficient scope seemed to be offered by the Black Sea, where Russian fleets no longer sailed. But inevitably troubles followed. Alexius's son John II and grandson Manuel I each for a time withdrew the concession, but each had to restore it on hostile action on the part of Venice. Other Italian cities demanded privileges too. In 1111 Alexius reduced the tariff rate for Pisan merchants to 4% and gave them an establishmen in Constantinople. In 1155 the Genoese were allowed the same terms, and a little later their liability to the 4% duty was restricted to Constantinople alone. In other ports they could trade freely, with the exception of two ports on the north of the Black Sea, Rossia and Matracha, which seem to have been used for the dried-fish trade from the Don and the Caspian fisheries; the Emperor was unwilling to be dependent on foreigners for so important an article of his people's diet, to say nothing of his own caviare. The Pisan and Genoese concessions were periodically withdrawn and almost immediately restored.

As a result the carrying trade passed almost entirely into Italian hands. The Genoese successfully invaded even the Black Sea trade. A large Italian population grew up in Constantinople. In 1180 it was estimated at more than 60,000 souls. At first the Italians lived amongst the local inhabitants and intermarried with them, but as they grew more numerous, they brought out their own wives and families and began to enjoy a special position. They were known as *burgesii*, a graecised form of *bourgeois*, and formed a community, settled in definite quarters each with a quay and a church along the Golden Horn and with their own officials who administered the quarter. But the officials paid homage after the western fashion to the Emperor, and the whole community paid him large sums in taxation, often raised quite arbitrarily. Indeed the treasury was probably well compensated for its loss in tariff revenue by this direct taxation of foreign merchants.

7-2

The effect of the Crusades on the trade of Byzantium was vast but not immediate. Constantinople was at first on the Crusaders' main route, and their coming and going, though trying for the Byzantine police, brought new buyers to the city's markets. But the result of the movement was to open up again the ports of Syria that had been closed to European traders for five centuries, and so to provide a new route for oriental goods to reach Western Europe without passing through imperial territory. This at first did not make much difference. The Italians in the coastal cities might encourage the visits of caravans from the interior, but the crusading lords supported themselves in their Syrian castles by levying exorbitant tolls on these caravans. It was only with the decline of the secular military occupation of Syria and Palestine that the trade grew, and when the military orders themselves began to dabble in commerce. Moreover, events in Central Asia and the growth of the Kingdom of Georgia, which reached its climax under Queen Thamar at the end of the twelfth century, attracted much of the Far Eastern trade to the Black Sea route. The effect of the Crusades in embittering relations between eastern and western Christendom was less slow in appearing.

Despite it all, in the middle of the twelfth century Constantinople seemed still fantastically prosperous. The Jewish traveller, Benjamin of Tudela, was deeply impressed by its commercial activity and the merchants of many nationalities that he saw there—'from Babylon and Mesopotamia, Media and Persia, Egypt and Palestine, Russia and Hungary, Patzinacia and Bulgaria (the Black Bulgaria of the Upper Volga), Lombardy and Spain'. Only Baghdad was, he thought, in any way comparable. He added that the Emperor Manuel derived from Constantinople alone a revenue that we can translate as 106,000,000 gold francs. This sum may not be much exaggerated, and a large proportion of it must have come from the Italian settlers in the city.

At the end of the twelfth century, the decay in Byzantine commercial life became more obvious. The Emperor Manuel's splendid government had been costly, and the military disasters of its closing years had used up his resources. Rivalry between the various Italian communities caused endless rioting in the capital, in which many valuable goods would be damaged. Moreover the rivalry extended to the seas. Each Italian city would maintain a pirate fleet to prey on its neighbours' ships, and all would prey on Greek shipping. Nor could the Emperor afford to keep up a strong enough fleet to deal with them. After his death in 1180 a wave of anti-Italian feeling passed over the Empire. Eventually in 1182, under the Emperor Andronicus, there was a wholesale massacre of the Latins in Constantinople. Large numbers perished, and their quarters were destroyed by fire. The Italian cities revenged themselves in devastating the coasts of the Empire. Before the century was out their merchants were back in Constantinople enjoying all their old privileges, but too much hatred had been aroused by the massacre, and religious mistrust between Greek and Latin Christians was by now too acute for commerce to be carried on with any stability or confidence. The Italians, especially the Venetians who had most to lose, determined to undertake sterner action. They could not afford the periodical unfriendliness of the imperial government. Venice was particularly jealous of Genoa whose better relations with Byzantium enabled its merchants to secure the still rich Black Sea trade. Out of such feelings a desire to control the whole government of Byzantium was born; and an opportunity was provided by the Fourth Crusade.

The commercial history of the Latin Empire is part of the history of Venice. The Greek Succession States followed commercial policies suited to their respective positions. The Nicaean Emperors sought to be self-sufficient. In the interests of his national economy, the Emperor John Vatatzes for the bulk of his reign forbade all foreign imports and does not seem to have encouraged exports. His Empire did not lie across any of the great trade routes of the time, and it could supply itself with all its essential requirements. Luxuries were discouraged. The Emperors of Trebizond could afford to be luxurious. Their capital remained the port of the great Persian-Armenian trade route, a route that grew in importance as the Mongol Empire advanced. By charging low tariff dues on the caravans that entered his country and on the Genoese ships that met these caravans, the Grand Comnenus was able to keep himself in affluence and his people prosperous, despite the natural poverty of his territory, whose only asset was its silver mines. The Emperor of Thessalonica was equally dependent on foreign trade, on the merchants of many nationalities that came at all times to his capital, especially to the Fair of St Demetrius. But the central position of his Empire made its history tempestuous, like that of the short-lived Latin Kingdom that it succeeded.

The restored Empire under the Palaeologi Emperors can scarcely be said to have had any foreign trade. The restoration had been achieved with Genoese help, and the Genoese were the main beneficiaries. They were given free access again to all Byzantine ports. At Pera across the Golden Horn they maintained a station that soon attracted all the trade away from Constantinople itself. The northern and eastern trades were still highly prosperous in the late thirteenth and fourteenth centuries, but the Genoese carried the greater part of it, practically monopolising the Black Sea trade. At Kaffa and Tana on its northern shores they had their own colonies; at Trebizond they enjoyed preferential terms. Venice also was allowed to trade duty-free in all imperial ports and had a small colony in Constantinople itself, but these concessions were only given after the Genoese had had time to establish themselves, so that the Venetians were obliged to play a secondary part. They did so with a bad grace, and there were unending skirmishes and even wars between the two great Italian sea-ports, which were not conducive to peaceful trading. Pisa had fallen out of the running. Her merchants had to pay a 2% duty on all exports from and imports into the Empire, and the same duty was charged on merchants of all cities with which the Empire had a trade agreement, Florence, Ancona, Narbonne and the Sicilian towns. The Catalans paid 3%. Under the Emperor Andronicus III the rates seem to have been raised. The Narbonnais were charged 4%, which was at that time preferential treatment. Foreign ships trading between different parts of the Empire had to pay the duty at the port of delivery, as though they had been importing goods. These tariffs kept most foreign merchants out of the local eastern trade. Most of them bought the oriental goods that they required on the Bosporus, and shipped them home. Pera was now the entrepôt for such goods, though certain foreigners preferred to buy in Constantinople rather than in a Genoese colony. As the Genoese importer paid no duty, goods were no more expensive in Constantinople than in Pera.

It seems, however, from several oblique references, that there was still a considerable Greek merchant marine. The shipping corporation in Thessalonica in the fourteenth century was an important body, perhaps more important than the corresponding body in Constantinople. Most of the maritime trade within the Empire, except between the regular Genoese colonies, was still carried on Greek ships who paid no duty on it. The corn merchants by now usually bought their own ships in which to import corn, selling them at the end of the season. Greek traders were probably free from duties on their imports from abroad; but that would be of little use, owing to the Italian control of the ports of supply. This marine lasted on to the very extinction of the Empire. There were Greek merchant ships in the Golden Horn at the time of the Turkish capture of Constantinople. Minor Byzantine ports such as Mesemvria or Monemvasia each had their marine for local purposes, but the products of Thrace and the Peloponnese, such as the wine called Malmsey after Monemvasia, were exported in Italian ships. The Empire of Trebizond seems to have had practically no marine, largely, no doubt, because it lacked a harbour of any size that could withstand winter storms—Trebizond itself has only an anchorage exposed to the north. The semi-independent Despotate of Epirus, on the other hand, maintained a small merchant fleet.

The many regulations about tariffs obliged the Empire to keep up a large body of customs officials at every port, to discover the nationality of each ship that came in and to assess the value of her cargo. At Pera and probably also at Constantinople there was a further series of charges to be paid, taxes on measurage varying according to the quantity. The Byzantine customs-officials do not seem to have been particularly corrupt. Probably they were well supervised. But the elaborate regulations tempted smuggling on the part of nationalities that had to pay tariffs. The Narbonnais in particular had a bad name for it.

Before the fourteenth century was out the Ottoman Turks were established on both sides of the Hellespont. Early in the next century they reached the Asiatic shore of the Bosporus. Inevitably they used their position to levy their tolls on all shipping passing through the Straits, and even to close them entirely at times. The added burden became too heavy for the Genoese traders. So long, however, as Constantinople existed as a Christian city, foreign traders still came to the Golden Horn. The Ottoman Turks ended it all and for a time closed the Levant to commerce. It was fortunate that European enterprise so shortly afterwards discovered the ocean route to the Far East.

V

To medieval if not to modern eyes Constantinople had the air of an industrial city. Travellers were struck by the amount of industry carried on there, not only the building or the pottery or the furniture business, or other such necessary parts of a great city's life, but especially the manufacture of luxuries. Of these the silk industry was the most remarkable. Since the earliest days of the Empire vast quantities of raw silk had been imported into the Empire to be made up at Constantinople. From Justinian's day onward these had been supplemented by an increasing amount of home-grown silk, from worms farmed in or near the capital or in certain of the provinces, notably Greece itself. It seems, however, that the silk grown within the Empire was never sufficient for the demand.[1] Importation continued throughout Byzantine history. In Constantinople the silk was dressed, woven and dyed, and put on the market as finished cloth. Linen was also made up at Constantinople, though in this case it seems to have arrived from Macedonia or Pontus or the other flax fields, already woven, and only received the superior dyeing and finish at the capital that distinguished it from the provincial product. Cotton goods were also finished in Constantinople but apparently in much smaller quantities. The Byzantines of the capital never troubled much about fine woollen goods. Wool provided the

[1] Bury and Andreades consider that by the end of the sixth century Byzantium grew all its own silk. But both the *Book of the Prefect* (c. 900) and the Rhodian Code, as well as various casual references, indicate that silk was still imported in large quantities.

lower classes with their garments, but the rich Byzantine preferred other materials. Consequently, though large amounts of woollen cloth must have been made to clothe the numerous poor, such cloth remained rough. Probably each family made up its own woollen wear.

After the silk industry the metal industry was most renowned. This was an even more luxurious industry. Gold and silver plate were made in considerable but restricted quantities. More elaborate work, cloisonné enamel, Damascene, ivory-carving or the carving of semi-precious stones and all jewellers' work, was in great demand; but the supply was limited owing to the expense of the materials and the highly technical workmanship required. But the cash turnover of the industry must have been enormous. The third great industry of Constantinople was the manufacture of armaments. This was a state monopoly, for obvious reasons. In particular the secrets of Byzantine chemical warfare were very carefully guarded, though the manufacture of Greek Fire must have employed a certain number of workmen. The government also kept a close watch on the corn trade. It is obvious that these great governmental monopolies were for administrative rather than economic purposes.

Certain of the provinces had their own industries. In Cyprus gold was woven, and the product was much sought after in Constantinople. Samite was woven in the Greek Islands since the earliest times. Already in the ninth century the Peloponnese was exporting woollen and linen cloth and carpets to Constantinople, and from the tenth century onward Peloponnesian carpets were exported into Italy. By the middle of the eleventh century the silk-worm was farmed in Greece and Euboea, and Thebes and Corinth manufactured large quantities of silken cloth, which was not however quite as fine as that made up in the capital. Before the Seljuk conquest various towns in Asia Minor were manufacturing for export the pottery later known as Kutahya ware. Thessalonica manufactured all forms of cloth, and in the latter days of the Empire its carpets were famous.

These industries were organised in two main groups, industries run by the state or by individual magnates and industries run by the gilds. Throughout Byzantine history the Emperor was the greatest merchant in the Empire. Certain individual Emperors might resent this for snobbish reasons. Theophilus, for example, when he discovered that a certain richly laden merchant ship belonged to his wife, Theodora—a good business-woman, as her subsequent regency proved—ordered it to be burnt, on the ground that the Empress should not be engaged in commerce. But his disdain was illogical, and other Emperors were less haughty. Nicephorus II made vast sums by cornering the wheat supply of the Empire and retailing it at a profit to the bakers' gild. Rather more honestly, the Nicaean Emperor John Vatatzes made enough out of his poultry-keeping to buy his Empress a new crown. The chief silk factory of the Empire was situated within the imperial palace. Silk-worms fed on the Emperor's mulberry trees, and their silk, probably added to imported raw silk, was taken through the various stages of dressing and weaving in different buildings of the palace. Women attached to the court attended to the primary stages, though men provided the finishing touches. Certain dyes were restricted to the use of this factory—it was only here that the purple murex could be used full strength—and it seems that only here was it permitted to mix gold and silver thread in with the silk. The finished goods were mostly patterned brocades, over the designs of which great trouble was taken. Some of these brocades were sent out to be sold in the silk market, but the better grades were kept for the use of the court. The best entered the Emperor's and Empress's ceremonial wardrobes, or might be sent as presents to foreign courts. The others included the court uniforms for the upper grades in the court hierachy or the civil service. Uniforms for the lower grades were apparently bought by the government in the city cloth market. Whether officials had to pay the Emperor for their uniforms or received them free, is uncertain. Probably they were gifts, for the silk factory in the *gynaeceum* does not seem to have been primarily a profit-making concern. On the contrary, the imperial intention seems rather to have been to prevent the finest products of Byzantium from being launched on the market. By keeping them rare, the Emperor raised their value to an enormous height, and so enhanced the efficacy of his gifts. The palace factories had been founded in the early days of Constantinople when the Emperors aimed at bringing the whole silk industry under their immediate control. Despite popular opposition, this control was completely established in Justinian's time, when the high price of raw materials drove private dealers out of business. But within a century it had been abandoned as unworkable; and only the highest classes of silk remained an imperial monopoly. The workers in these factories were organised into three imperial or 'public' gilds,[1] the clothiers' gild, the dyers' and the gold embroiderers'. There was a Prefect[2] at the head of each, and general supervision was maintained by an office dependent on the Prefect of the city.

Armaments, as we have seen, were also a monopoly of the Emperor's, and were manufactured in the arsenal, next to the imperial palace. His object here was the interests of the state, not profit. No armaments were put on to the market. The same applies to the minting of money, another imperial monopoly. Mines throughout the Empire were also the Emperor's property. This was advisable to supply both his

---

[1] Δημόσια σώματα.   [2] Πραιπόσιτος or μειзότερος.

armaments and his mint; but they also brought in a certain profit. The highest class of jewelry seems, like the best brocades, to have been another imperial monopoly. But here the regulations were less strict. If the Emperor was the chief manufacturer of jewelled work, it was because he alone had sufficient capital to indulge in such a costly industry.

Labour in the imperial enterprises was servile or semi-servile. The mines were worked by prisoners of war or their descendants or by non-Christian slaves bought in wholesale quantities from the North. The women that worked in the *gynaeceum* were probably also wholly servile. More specialised labour was mostly in the hands of freedmen, though here and there an able slave would be found in such a position, and even the freedmen had in many cases succeeded hereditarily to their occupation and might be forbidden to break away to another.

The Emperor was probably the only big manufacturer in Constantinople. For political reasons the authorities were unwilling to allow any private man to manufacture there on a large scale. In the provinces, however, though we have very little evidence, industry seems to have been carried on by the magnates employing servile labour. Members of the nobility could receive authorisation to make up and sell silk. The widow Danelis, who manufactured cloth and carpets in the Peloponnese in the late ninth century and who employed over 3000 slaves, was considered a remarkably rich woman; but in those more remote districts, where markets were distant and free labour hard to obtain, it needed some one with a large amount of capital to get such a business going. In the previous century the parents of St Theophanes of Sigriana employed large numbers of slaves in industries on their properties in the Aegean islands. It was probably this dependence of Byzantine provincial industry on individual rich capitalists that made it so spasmodic. The later silk industry of Corinth and Thebes seems, however, to have been on a more cooperative basis and not to have employed slave labour. The great monasteries had their own industrial enterprises, producing wax and oil and, in the case of the monasteries of Mt Athos and Bithynian Olympus, timber. The monasteries, from Christian sentiment, did not employ slave labour, but each monastery had a population of lay servants, who worked for very exiguous wages.

It was slave labour that made the chief difference between the industrial magnate and the industrial gild. All the smaller manufacturers in Constantinople were organised into gilds—'private' gilds, as opposed to the 'public' gilds of workers in the imperial factories. These gilds were different from those of the West; they were not primarily associations created for the mutual self-interest and self-preservation of the industry. On the contrary, though they probably descended from similar Roman organisations, their chief use in Byzantine times was to enable the imperial authorities to keep a certain control, especially for fiscal purposes, over every industry in the city. The official in whose department the control of the gilds lay was the Prefect of the city. Fortunately we possess the book of regulations issued by the Emperor Leo VI about the year A.D. 900 for the instruction of his Prefect. This book did not contain new orders but was, rather, a summary of existing orders, and gives the clearest picture that we possess of Constantinopolitan industrial life, though it is unlikely that all the controls that it mentions were put continuously into effect.[1]

Of the industries mentioned in the *Book of the Prefect* the silk industry occupies most space. It was extraordinarily specialised. The raw silk when it was imported from abroad or collected from the local farms was bought by the raw silk merchants, who might not go outside of the city to buy it. Raw silk sold in the market was bought up by the raw-silk merchants acting together; each contributed to the fund and received silk in proportion to his contribution; but apparently it was permissible to buy raw silk privately from itinerant importers. The raw-silk merchant retailed his raw silk to authorised buyers, either private persons who made it up at home, or the raw silk dressers. He seems to have been an unnecessary middleman, but his value to the government was that he paid a small tax on all the silk that he handled, a tax collected through the masters of the gilds.[2] The silk dressers, whose business was to clean, twist, double and wind the silk and probably in most cases to weave it, either bought raw silk collectively, as a gild, at the same time as the raw-silk merchants, both gilds agreeing on the price, or bought individually from raw-silk merchants, who might not charge a profit of more than one *miliaresion* per *nomisma*—8·33 %. They could not buy raw silk just whenever they pleased. The amount required had to be registered at the Prefect's office. Above all no silk dresser could retail any raw silk that he had bought.

There is no mention of a specific gild of silk weavers nor of tailors. The dressers must have been weavers too, and probably a large amount of weaving was done privately. Tailoring and making up of cloth was done either by the silk dyers or by the silk stuff merchants, who each had their gild. There were restrictions on the dyes that could be used

---

[1] The tendency of modern economic historians, e.g. Andreades, Mickwitz and Lopez, is to minimise the strictness of the imperial control of industry. Not only were the gild regulations almost identical with those of the autonomous gilds of the West, but the government did not insist on all tradesmen becoming members of the appropriate gild. But the government's powers of supervision were on a scale unparalleled in the West, and gild regulations were a matter for imperial legislation.

[2] The text is too corrupt for us to decipher the rate of taxation.

and on the cut of the garments, though the Emperor Leo VI withdrew most of them on the ground that it was unsuitable for an Emperor to be an arbiter of fashion; but sufficient safeguards were left to prevent the gilds' products in any way competing with the products of the imperial factory. The merchants of silk stuffs simply retailed the finished article. It was, however, part of their business to see that foreigners or unauthorised persons did not buy for export silks on the list of goods that were forbidden to leave the country. There was also a gild of *prandiopratae*, merchants who bought imported finished silk goods, chiefly from Saracen countries, dealing as a gild with the Syrian importers. Syrian residents of ten years' standing, though not members of the gild, shared in its purchases.

Despite the careful regulations it seems that the relative functions of the various gilds were never clearly defined. For example a silk dyer could buy raw silk from the raw silk merchant, and he could apparently retail the finished article, though he was not allowed to be a member of the gild of merchants of silk stuffs. In most cases entrance to the gild cost 10 *nomismata*, though the entrance fee to the dyers was only 3 *nomismata*, and the applicant had to find five members of the gild to testify to his suitability; and the usual punishment for contravening the laws of the gild was flogging, shaving and the confiscation of property. Each craft had to expose its wares in a fixed place and had to permit thorough inspection by the authorities. It was possible for a slave to become a member of a gild (though not, it seems, of the gild of silk-dressers) if his master approved, stood surety for him and provided him with the capital required. Or apparently a master could delegate his authority to his slave who then was responsible for seeing that the regulations were obeyed. It was assumed that the gildsman usually employed free labour. The workman had a monthly contract and could be paid a month in advance. It was strictly forbidden to try to induce a workman to break his contract. There were a few private dealers in silk, the *metaxarii*, who were not enrolled in the gilds. The state gave them special protection, probably in return for special taxes.

The linen merchants' gild, the only other cloth gild mentioned, had similar regulations; but the linen merchants were retailers rather than manufacturers. Of the other gilds mentioned in the *Book of the Prefect* the most important in the eyes of the authorities were those of the dealers in bullion and the bankers. The first of these included jewellers and goldsmiths and money-lenders. They not only were obliged to give small change for *nomismata* on market days but they also made valuations. It was their business to see that precious metals were not sold to foreigners for export; nor were they themselves allowed to buy for any purpose more than one pound of gold at a time. The rates for lending money were strictly fixed; the dealers in bullion were allowed to charge an interest fixed in Justinian's day at 8%, while the private money-lender could only charge 6%. But by the tenth century 6% had changed to 6 *nomismata* per lb. of gold, that is to say 8·33%, and the gildsmen's 8% rose correspondingly to 8 *nomismata* per lb., 11·11%. The position of the bankers' gild is not clear. In Justinian's day the name (*trapezitae*) was given to the official cashiers in the public service; and the *Book of the Prefect* assigns to the dealers in bullion the duties that one would expect bankers to perform, and allots them no specific functions.

The other gilds, with the exception of the notaries', whose position is a question for legal rather than economic history—though we may notice in passing that they had to pay their clerks as salary a fixed proportion, one twelfth, of their earnings—were concerned with the daily necessities of life. The perfumers sold, as well as scents and dyes, the spices which were an essential part of medieval life. It was specially laid down that they might only sell goods bought by scale as opposed to goods bought by steelyard, which were the grocers' business. Their functions had been shared by the apothecaries' gild, but they had absorbed it before the tenth century. Most of their wares were bought from importers, but the transactions could only take place on certain fixed days, to facilitate supervision. The wax chandlers and soap chandlers formed two gilds. The former bought their raw material mostly from abroad, but also, it seems from Church organisations, and made it up into candles. They also dealt in lamp oil. The soap chandlers, whose business was purely the making of soap, seem to have had the highest entrance fee of any of the gilds, six *nomismata* payable to the imperial treasury and six more to the imperial *vestiarius*. The leather trade had three gilds, the pelters', who prepared the raw skins, the tanners', and the saddlers' who sold the finished leather. The leather gilds could be called upon to work for the Emperor if necessary for whatever remuneration he might choose to bestow upon them. This was owing to the value of leather in making the armaments of the time.

Of the gilds dealing with foodstuffs the grocers' gild was the largest. The goods that they were empowered to sell included, besides regular groceries, greengrocery, poultry, salt fish, earthenware, nails and bottles —all articles that were sold by steelyards and not by scales. Grocery was a paying business; the grocers were allowed to make a profit of two *miliaresia* per *nomisma*, that is to say, of 16·66%. The butchers and the pork butchers each had their gilds. The former dealt in beef and mutton. They were urged to go and meet the herds of sheep driven in from Asia Minor beyond the river Sangarius, so as to buy them cheaper, rather than to wait for them at towns on the road like Nicomedia. Sheep owners who brought their sheep themselves to the capital had to sell

them at fixed times in fixed places, sheep and lambs separately, and pay
a tax on each,[1] or to sell to certain authorised butchers. Government
officials had to be present at the slaughter of cattle, one beast in each lot
being cut up before their eyes. Pork butchers on the other hand had to
buy their swine in the market square of the Bull in Constantinople. The
fishmongers, who were apparently more numerous—the city's maritime position made fish a regular article of diet in season—sold their fish
at several markets. They could buy it from the fishermen only at the
quays or from fishing boats at anchor. They were forbidden to deal in
salt fish. The bakers' gild had special rights. So important was it to the
welfare of the city that no member could be called upon to perform any
public service. They bought corn and ground it themselves. They were
allowed to make a profit of one *keration* and two *miliaresia* per *nomisma*,
the two *miliaresia* being calculated to be the cost of labour, and the one
keration the net profit—just over 4%. Bakeries had to be built of stone,
so as to lessen the danger of fire. The innkeepers also had a gild. They
were the only accredited wine merchants, but the wine did not
apparently have to be consumed on the premises. Closing time was at
8 p.m. In all the gilds dealing with comestibles there were strict
penalties for any one convicted of hoarding against times of scarcity.
On the other hand, nonperishable foodstuffs, like salt fish, might not
be sold to persons leaving the city.

There was also a gild of *bothri*, agents who disposed of remainders of
all sorts of livestock. Very often there would be more beasts in the
markets than the butchers required, in which case the *bothri* acted as
agents for their sale to private individuals. The *Book of the Prefect* also
provides regulations for the building contractors and specialised members of the building industry, including carpenters, masons, lock-
smiths, house painters and so on, though they do not seem to have
formed a gild. The contractor was usually but not invariably a master
builder himself. Builders were not allowed to take on another job if
they were already engaged on one. Contracts could not be altered
except after a valuation conducted by the Prefect's officials. Stone
houses that fell within ten years had to be rebuilt at the contractor's
expense, unless the cause was an act of God. If the house was built of
mud, the contractor's liability lasted for six years.

Most of the gilds occupied specific quarters in the city, mainly in the
great Middle Street that ran from the palace to the church of the Holy
Apostles. The butchers and the fishmongers had their particular
markets. The grocers however were, for the convenience of the public,
scattered throughout the city and the same was presumably true of the
bakers. The perfumers' gild was stationed close to the Bronze Gate of

[1] The text of the *Book of the Prefect* is not quite clear as regards this tax.

the Palace, so that the pleasant scent should be wafted up to the great icon of our Lord that was carved over the gate. The concentration of each trade, whenever possible, in a particular place was a convenience for the officials of the Prefect, in facilitating their supervision. This supervision was minute. Where prices and profits were not specified in the articles of the gild the Prefect fixed them according to the circumstances of the moment. All weights and measures had to bear the Prefect's seal and were periodically tested. All cases of broken contract or complaints of bad behaviour between employer and employee came, not before any courts of the gild, but before the Prefect's bureau, as did also disputes between vendor and customer. The Prefect also had to see that regulations of a religious nature affecting the gilds were carried out. Sunday closing was enforced, but, to judge from the frequency with which the order was repeated, the rule must often have been broken. Even in the early fourteenth century we find the Emperor Andronicus II trying to reinforce it. Business was to stop on major feast days also. On Sundays and feast days taverns might not open before 8 a.m. The soap chandlers were forbidden to use animal fats during Lent or on other fast days. The dealers in bullion had to report the sale of any sacred object, in an attempt to prevent the dispersal of holy relics out of the Empire. Relic smuggling was a very profitable business, as Western European churches and potentates would pay enormous prices for the relic of any early Christian saint.

We are left in ignorance about the officials of the gilds. The head of the notaries, the *Primicerius*, was a personage high in the imperial hierarchy. It seems that there was an official at the head of all the silk gilds, but casual references to him confuse him with the superintendent of the imperial silk factory. The *prandiopratae* had an *exarch* at their head, who was nominated by the Prefect. The raw silk merchants had more than one *exarch*, probably owing to their greater numbers. The pelters, tanners and saddlers, each had a *prostates*, at the head of the fishmongers were several *prostatae*, one in charge of each fish market, at the head of the pork butchers *protostatae* and at the head of the innkeepers *proestotes*—these last terms being probably variants of *prostatae*. No mention is made of heads of any other gild, but that is no reason for assuming their non-existence. The *exarchs* enjoyed a higher rank than the *prostatae*, and their gilds were considered more reputable. Probably all the silk gilds had *exarchs* and the provision gilds had *prostatae*. These officials were clearly appointed by the Prefect, possibly from recommendations by the gildsmen, but such salaries as they had were obtained from the gild. The Prefect himself employed two ranks of superior inspectors, the *episceptetae* and the *epoptae*, and slightly lower officials, the *bullotae*, whose business was to stamp the weights and measures. In official tables of precedence the first two ranked above the *exarchs* and the *bullotae* between the *exarchs* and the *prostatae*. At the head of the Prefect's commercial bureau was the *symponus* or assessor, sometimes called the *legatarius*. He kept the registers of all imports and exports and was in charge of the customs. It was for him also to see that no foreign merchant or provincial merchant stayed for more than three months in Constantinople. Each gild seems also to have had its *symponus*, who may have been the representative of the chief *symponus*.

It is uncertain whether there were any definite regulations about apprenticeship. Apprentices certainly existed, as we know from casual references, but there is no mention of fixed rules or time limit for their services. The tendency throughout Byzantine history was for the various professions to remain hereditary. Circumstances had necessitated a relaxation of Diocletian's law forcing a son to follow his father's trade, but in fact this seems to have been the usual practice, which provided in most cases an automatic solution of the apprentice problem. The question of labour in the various crafts is equally obscure. As we have seen, in the silk trade it is assumed that the merchant or dealer employs one or more free workmen on a monthly contract. The bakers also are assumed to employ labour. The ordinary shopkeeper probably ran his business as a family concern. But the whole question is cut across by the question of slavery. Throughout Byzantine history there was a growing sentiment, fostered by the Church, for the lessening and even abolition of slavery. But slaves in private households existed to the last in Byzantium, though by the twelfth century they were rare and were almost exclusively prisoners of war. They ranked higher than the state-owned slaves; and a usual punishment for a privately-owned slave was to send him to join the latter. A merchant or manufacturer with slaves presumably employed them in his business without hindrance. But, as we have seen, a slave could, at least as regards the cloth trade, have an establishment of his own and be the member of a gild. In this case he was financed by his master, to whom he paid a regular proportion of his profits; and he might in the end purchase his freedom from his savings. The process represented one of the few ways in which a rich Byzantine was able usefully to invest surplus capital. A large number of the artisans in Constantinople were women, a circumstance that particularly impressed foreign travellers. At first, most of these women, including those employed in the imperial workshops, were in a semi-servile condition, bound to their occupation, with no hope of escape from it. Moreover, a man that married any of them was himself reduced to the same position, and any children of the marriage followed their mother's profession. This rule which dates from Justinian's time was probably later relaxed. Indeed, by the ninth century, work-people sought admission into the imperial factories.

Of the other trades that flourished in Constantinople, such as that of ship-chandler (the Emperor Michael V was a ship-chandler's son) or fisherman or of undertaker, our knowledge is too scanty for any description of their organisation. Fishermen and all shipowners might be called upon to perform public duties in an emergency.

There was no unemployment. The demand for goods remained more or less constant and most trades only catered for the local market, and consequently were not subject to fluctuations. If any able-bodied men were found out of work they were put by the Prefect under the *Quaestor*, who gave them employment in the state bakeries or market gardens that supplied the charitable institutions of the city. 'Idleness', said the Emperor Leo III in the *Ecloga*, 'leads to crime, and any superfluity resulting from the labour of others should be given to the weak, not the strong.' Occasionally bad harvests might cause a shortage of corn and hence distress among the poor. At such times, except in the notorious case of Nicephorus II, the Prefect intervened to keep the price down, and supplies were supplemented out of the stores that the government kept against emergencies. The infirm poor were cared for at great charitable institutions, almshouses and hospitals, either founded by great personages who provided them with ample endowments and issued strict regulations for their governance, or organised under the monasteries. The monasteries with their growing hoards of wealth have won a bad name amongst the economic historians of Byzantium, but they performed a very useful function both as charitable trusts, which could see to the needs of the deserving poor, and as refuges for retired and decayed gentlemen and gentlewomen. The Byzantine official or the business man might draw a good income, but there was nowhere that he could easily invest his savings; and so he, when he retired, or his widow when he died, might find him or herself a drag on the community. The monasteries provided homes for such people, where they had leisure if they wished for intellectual study or for useful open-air pursuits such as gardening. Monastic institutions played thus a very valuable part in Byzantine social economy. An alternative form of insurance against old age was provided by the opportunity of purchasing a title. The price varied according to the rank, but each title commanded a salary averaging $2\frac{1}{2}\%$ of the original cost.

Owing chiefly to governmental regulations about rates of interest, no one seems to have made a fortune out of any form of trade in the capital, though there was nothing to prevent the enterprising trader from making a comfortable living. The father of Michael Psellus, who was a merchant probably engaged in the silk trade, kept one or two domestic servants and could afford to give his son a first class education, and there was no official pressure made to induce Michael, who was an only son, to follow his father's profession.

In the provincial cities the supervision was less exact. In ports, such as Thessalonica, the local prefect carefully saw to customs business and registered exports and imports and there was probably an attempt to keep prices fixed. But there was no organised gild system as in the capital. When, later, trade corporations appear they are bodies founded by the tradesmen themselves in self-defence against the magnates. We find in consequence that by the thirteenth century society is more complicated in Thessalonica than in Constantinople. Besides the old nobility there is a rich bourgeois nobility of the greater merchants and shipowners at permanent enmity with the small shopkeepers and the artisans and eventually provoking them into the strange democratic movement known as the Revolt of the Zealots, which can better be paralleled by movements in Western Europe than by anything in Constantinople. This distinction was enhanced by the general trend in favour of municipal self-government which is noticeable in all the provincial cities of the later Byzantine Empire. The details of this movement are obscure. Most provincial cities seem to have fallen into the hands of the local nobility, who provided some constituted authority which supervised prices and local taxation.

The great fortunes of Byzantium were made in the provinces, or in the government service, many posts of which were very highly paid. The Melisseni, the first great family to arise and the last to disappear, probably derived their fortune from property in Constantinople and for that reason they retained their important position for some six centuries. But they were exceptional. Till the ninth century there was no portion of the imperial countryside free from the periodical devastation of foreign armies. But once land became a safe investment enterprising landowners, like the Peloponnesian widow Danelis, founded industries on their estates, or like the Cappadocian Philaretes indulged personally in farming on a large scale. In troubled times land could be bought cheap and far-sighted investors were rewarded. Most of the wealthy families of tenth or eleventh century Byzantium were descended from some successful soldier or government official, who had either been given a grant of land by the grateful emperor or had invested part of his salary in land.[1] Rents and local industries would soon enhance its value under careful management. Less scrupulous government officials had further opportunities for increasing their

---

[1] The annual salary of the chief provincial governors, the Strategi of the Anatolic, the Armeniac and the Thracesian themes, was 40 lb. of gold (about 43,200 gold francs).

incomes. But as a result of the restrictions on profit-making they all sought to buy land rather than trust their money to commercial under-takings. Land, however, was not always procurable and this land hunger on the part of the magnates was one of the problems that most worried the imperial government. The failure to solve it was disastrous to the Empire. A solution by means of providing better facilities for investment was, however, unthinkable at the time. In consequence few fortunes, except for those invested in land, survived more than one generation. Even in cases where a rich man owned servile shop-keepers, his piety usually made him manumit them on his death. The fluidity of private capital was reflected in the social organisation of the Empire. In direct contrast to Western Europe the aristocracy remained open to any wealthy newcomer, and the connection between the nobility and commerce was never broken, though in the later days of the Empire, in towns like Thessalonica and Trebizond, the land-owning nobility with a tradition of culture behind it began to despise the *nouveau riche* bourgeoisie.

VI

The merchant Cosmas Indicopleustes, writing in the sixth century, declared that the prosperity of the Empire was due to two causes, Christianity and the coinage. It is to be hoped that Christianity brings its reward on earth, but there is no doubt of the value of a good coinage. Constantine the Great had established the lb. of gold as the basis of the coinage. The *nomisma*, or gold piece, which was originally called the *solidus* and after the thirteenth century the *hyperpyron*, was fixed at the rate of 72 to the lb. The silver and bronze coinage had at first been variable, but about the year 500 Anastasius divided the *nomisma* into 12 *miliaresia* or 24 *keratia*, and the *miliaresium* was divided into 12 *pholles*. The *nomisma* contained its proper quantity of gold to the value roughly of 15 gold francs.[1] Silver coins were related in a fixed ratio to the gold, a ratio which there was no need to alter till the later Middle Ages, the silver lb. being valued at 5 *nomismata*. The government tried to main-tain a reserve of gold, largely in order to control prices by regulating the amount of currency that it issued. The Byzantines were well conscious of the value of their currency. Any Emperor whose reputa-tion historians wished to blacken was accused of trying to debase it. Nicephorus Phocas was said to have issued a defective coinage in which he paid out salaries, but no such coins have survived. The first Emperor

[1] The metallic value of the Byzantine gold *solidus* or *nomisma* (later called the *hyperpyron*) was 15·43 gold francs, and its theoretic weight 4·48 grammes. In fact all the examples that have survived weigh between 4·30 and 4·42 grammes. It was 24 carats.

seriously to debase the coinage was the usurper Nicephorus Boteniates, who, being in need of money and finding the treasury reserve empty, issued in 1078, *nomismata* that were under weight. His successor Alexius Comnenus attempted to restore the position and to call in the debased coinage but was driven by financial needs to issue *nomismata*, partly of brass, of two thirds of the value of the gold *nomismata*. He insisted on all taxes being paid in gold *nomismata* while he paid governmental expenses in the debased coin. He succeeded in rebuilding the gold reserve, but insufficiently to enable him to restore the coinage. Meanwhile his debased coins had passed into general circulation. Fiscal calculations continued to be made on the assumption that the *nomisma* was still worth 72 to the lb. of gold; but in fact it never recovered its old value. Foreign creditors often insisted in being paid in μιχαήλατα, the coins of Michael VII, the last that contained their proper amount of gold.

The *nomisma* fell slowly at first. At the time of the First Crusade it could be exchanged for 15 silver sous of the Franks. In 1156 the Genoese valued it at 10 of their silver sous (or 14·25 gold francs) and at 9½ in 1157. In 1204 it could be exchanged for 3 English sous—or roughly 14·60 gold francs—but the English sou was not easily exchangeable in the East and therefore cheaper than its metallic value. In 1228 the Venetians gave the *hyperpyron* of the Nicaean emperors the value of 11·81 gold francs, but in 1250 it was rated considerably higher in relation to the currency of the French monarchy. The Nicaean emperors had sold agricultural produce to the Turks in return for gold. Actually at this time it had 16 carats, and was therefore worth roughly 10·10 gold francs. In 1261 it had fallen to 15 carats, 14 in 1282. By 1310 it had 12 carats and 12 alloy, and was losing its international credit. Henceforward, even in Constantinople itself, traders preferred to use Venetian or Genoese ducats.

Of the purchasing power of money in Byzantine times and the general level of prices it is difficult to speak with confidence. The price of wheat in 960, just before Nicephorus II speculated in the corn market, was the same as that in Greece in July 1914 (3 *keratia* per *modius*), but all other foodstuffs were probably five or six times less expensive. A pair of oxen cost 8 *nomismata* (90 gold francs) in Constantinople in about 950 A.D. and 600 gold francs in Greece in 1914. Horses were about 4·5 times cheaper in 950. Silk on the other hand was costly; it was considered to be literally worth its weight in gold. Prices had probably been lower up till the late seventh century. In the eighth century, under the Isaurian emperors, there was an increase in monetary stock, which raised the price level. Nicephorus I in the early ninth century checked this by reducing the amount of money in circulation.

Prices began to rise again at the end of the eleventh century, and were steadily rising throughout the rest of Byzantine history. Corn, indeed, in the fourteenth century was about twice its tenth-century price. This was because of the difficulty of procuring sufficient corn for the capital ever since the Seljuk Turks had annexed the great cornfields of Asia Minor. Other factors were the devaluation of the coinage and the impact of Italian currencies.

The cost of living in Byzantium was enhanced by the heavy taxation, far heavier there than in any other contemporary country. Country communities had to pay the *epibole*. For the town dwellers there was a hearth-tax, the *kapnikon*, which was rated at 2 *miliaresia* per head in the early ninth century, but seems to have been increased later. There was a capitation tax, the *kephaletion*, but probably it was only applied to non-Christians and foreigners. There was a tax called the *aërikon*, introduced by Justinian and still existing in the ninth century, which was probably a tax on town property.[1] Augustus had introduced a system of death duties for property inherited from a collateral or a friend. Justinian seems to have repealed it, but it was reintroduced later to include direct inheritance also. Nicephorus I evolved a tax on unearned increment on the ground that it ranked as treasure trove and therefore the state was entitled to a share. But it proved difficult to assess and to collect and was abandoned. Indirect taxation consisted of the various tolls, import and export duties, market dues and harbour dues, and for a while a stamp duty on receipts. Tax collecting was efficiently done; evasion was almost impossible. The tax collectors were reputable government officials who were carefully supervised so as to prevent corruption. They were not unnaturally an unpopular class but as far as we can tell seldom corruptible, though they were occasionally accused of raising taxes to enlarge their commissions. There was, however, a tendency in the later Empire to introduce an increasing amount of tax farming and to reduce the employment of tax collectors directly dependent on the state. By the twelfth century, after the disorganisation caused by the Turkish invasions, this was general in the provinces. Already the customs dues on certain trades had been farmed out from time to time to imperial officials or favourites. There seems to have been no objection to this, unless farmers sacrificed the welfare of the trade to their own interests, as when Leo VI's favourites who were farming the customs dues on the Bulgarian trade attempted for their own convenience to divert it from Constantinople to Thessalonica.[2] In times of crisis the Emperor might charge a super-tax such as the

[1] The interpretation of the *aërikon* is a highly controversial subject, to which each article on Byzantine taxation cited in the bibliography to this chapter gives a different solution.   [2] See above, p. 95.

dikeraton, an extra $\frac{1}{12}$ on the *kapnikon* raised by Leo III to pay for the repair of the city walls; or he might add to his revenue by exacting forced loans from his subjects; and the usual punishment meted out to disgraced officials included the confiscation of their property. On the other hand, the Emperors freely disbursed large sums of gold as well as estates from imperial lands to favoured officials, and gold was constantly sent out as subsidies to foreign or vassal potentates.

There are many aspects of Byzantine economy that we cannot hope to envisage accurately, owing to the inadequacy of our sources. Published laws and administrative manuals give us some details. Lives of the saints and a few funeral orations, taking the form of biographical sketches, tell us something of social life under the Emperor. But Byzantine historians took very little interest in economic affairs in comparison with ecclesiastical affairs and personal politics. Moreover, especially from the late tenth century onwards, they were all conscious stylists who disliked to have to use technical terms for which they could not find some elegant classical equivalent. Their descriptions of economic affairs are therefore vague and often misleading. This objection was purely intellectual. There was never any feeling that it was disgraceful for a Byzantine gentleman to take part in trade or industry, except in certain circles in the later Empire where Frankish social influence was strong. Aristocracy was never exclusively dependent on the ownership of landed property. Money-making was always a permissible pre-occupation.

The general picture of Byzantine economic life shows a paternalist state with no idea of a planned economy but with the right, often but by no means regularly exercised, to interfere in every detail of its subjects' lives. Its main faults were an arbitrary and often shortsighted readiness to sacrifice the interests of the Empire for immediate gains in revenue or for purely political ends, and the lack of any proper provision for the investment of capital. Its main assets were an outlook that was for its time enlightened and unprejudiced, a determination that lasted for seven centuries to maintain a sound currency, and the possession of a superbly placed administrative and commercial centre in Constantinople.

CHAPTER IV

The Trade of Medieval Europe: the North

I. *The Trade in General*

(I) COMMODITIES

1

The international and inter-regional trade of Northern Europe and its principal industries bear little resemblance to the conventional image of medieval economy. The traffic across the continent of Western Europe, or between the European mainland and the lands immediately to the North and to the North-east, evokes in a modern reader none of that romance which clings to the trade of Southern Europe. The latter brought to Western Europe exotic goods of every kind: pepper, ginger and other spices of the East Indies, silks, brocades and tapestries, sweet wines, oranges, raisins, figs and almonds. It enticed the merchant into the mysterious lands of the Near and Middle East, to Byzantium and Syria, often to Africa, and sometimes even to China. It was also the trade of the caravans, the galleys, the junks; and of the Venetian, Genoese and Florentine adventurers and merchant princes. This was the medieval trade as popular writers know it, and this is the trade which some serious writers have in mind when they insist on the luxury character of medieval commerce.

The trade of Northern Europe was quite different. It was not greatly concerned with oriental and Mediterranean commodities. At various times between the sixth century and the tenth, traders and warriors brought goods from the extreme North of Europe to Byzantium and re-imported Byzantine goods into Northern Europe. Much more frequently the Italian merchants of the later centuries sailed into the harbours of England and Flanders, bringing with them all the infinite variety of Levantine and oriental products. Still more regularly —in fact throughout the Middle Ages—Italian merchants and the men of the North, Germans, Flemings, English and French, mingled in the great international marts of Central and Northern Europe: in Champagne during the twelfth and thirteenth centuries, in Bruges in the fourteenth and the early fifteenth centuries, in Geneva, Antwerp and Bergen-op-Zoom in the fifteenth; and there exchanged the Italian and the Italian-borne products for other goods.

Yet generally speaking, in the economic life of Northern Europe these contacts were of secondary importance. The main currents of trade across Northern Europe and between Northern Europe and other countries flowed with products of the northern hemisphere, cruder, bulkier and altogether more indispensable than the luxuries and the fineries of the text-book convention. This convention is not altogether true even of the South, for foodstuffs or raw materials also entered into the trade of the Mediterranean region. Nevertheless, what gave the southern trade its peculiar character was not the trade in the bulky essentials, but those luxury trades which we associate with it. By contrast, the trade of Northern Europe was almost exclusively devoted to the necessities of life.

Of the luxuries originating in the North and circulating in Northern Europe furs were probably the only one worth noting. Modest furs of local origin—the 'conies' of England, the Low Countries and France, the goatskins and the sheepskins of peasant wear, could perhaps be counted among the modest pre-requisites of humble existences. Not so the rare and rich furs of Scandinavian and Russian origins—fox, bear, beaver, sable, ermine. They were ceremonial wares, an insignia of wealth and standing; they rivalled the senatorial purple in the early Middle Ages, the Italian brocades and oriental silks in the later centuries, as marks of rank and worth. And so important did they become in European trade that by the end of the thirteenth century they formed one of the mainstays of Hanseatic commerce and wealth.

Furs, nevertheless, were something of an exception, for the main articles of northern trade were bulkier and cheaper necessities of life. Its main, and certainly the most permanent, branch was traffic in food. The very conditions of Germanic settlement in North-western Europe made it inevitable that some areas should early in their history have come to depend on food imports. Throughout the Middle Ages large portions of Scandinavia could not grow on the spot all the food they needed. Ever since the early days of the great migrations a relatively large population settled in the water-logged and sandy lands of the estuary of the Rhine—the Frisian country of the seventh-century nomenclature—which could not raise crops large enough to feed their population in normal years. Later in the Middle Ages, i.e. from the middle of the twelfth century onwards, the regions of the North-western litoral, Flanders, Brabant and Holland, maintained an industrial population which they could not feed out of their own agricultural production. In the words of a late fifteenth century description, the Dutch of that time still largely subsisted on dairy produce, birds and fishes. Further south and west, on the Atlantic coast of France, lay the rich lands of Gascony which specialised in wine and had to bring in some of their food from outside.[1]

---

[1] Quoted in J. E. Niermeyer, *De wording van onze volkshuishouding* (The Hague, 1946), 34.

What made it possible for these needs to be covered was that side by side with the regions deficient in foodstuffs there were to be found regions with exportable surpluses of food. It is doubtful whether the estuary of the Rhine before the ninth century and the flourishing areas of Flanders and the Netherlands in later centuries could ever have fed themselves had not rich grain-growing areas existed at their very backdoors. In the early Middle Ages grain came down the Rhine from the rich agricultural areas served by the upper reaches of the river. In the later centuries some grain came from the agricultural areas bordering on German Rhineland (Gelder, Gulik and Cleves), but the bulk came from Northern France. The valleys of the Somme and the Seine were the granaries of Northern Europe. The agricultural surpluses of the lower Seine went mainly to the South, to feed Paris. But the wheat of the rich loam lands of Santerre, Vermandois and Cambresis, went not only by the Oise to Paris, but along the Scheldt to Flanders and along the Somme to Rouen and overseas. Amiens, Abbeville and St Valéry became the *foci* of grain trade between France and the Low Countries, and the trade continued till the very end of the fifteenth century. Throughout the earlier Middle Ages, but more especially in the thirteenth century, England was an exporter of foodstuffs, including grain. Later still, another and much more important source of grain appeared. As a result of German colonisation of the Slavonic lands beyond the Elbe vast new agricultural resources were opened up, and from the end of the thirteenth century onwards East German and Polish rye flowed to the West. By the beginning of the fourteenth century Baltic grain began to contribute to the Flemish food supplies, and by that time also it ousted English grain from the Scandinavian markets.[1]

Grain, however, was only one of the essential foodstuffs carried across the continent and the seas of Northern Europe. The history of European dairy farming and milk trade is a somewhat neglected topic of economic history, but the importance of butter and cheese as articles of international commerce is now beyond doubt. There were apparently several regions of specialised butter production whence butter was exported to other countries: Holland, Scandinavia, Southern Poland, and to a smaller extent England. In historical records of the late thirteenth and fourteenth centuries butter appeared so suddenly as to suggest to some historians that there was a sudden change of diet among the inhabitants of Northern Europe as a result of which oil was displaced by butter. In England, however, the high-water mark of the dairying industry is in the earlier centuries—a time when the Earls of Lancaster

[1] W. S. Unger, 'De Hollandsche graanhandel en graanhandelspolitiek in de middeleeuwen', *De Economist* (1916). Also Z. W. Sneller in *Bijdragen tot de Vaterlands. Gesch.* VI, 2 (1925).

pastured vast herds of cows on their *vacaries* in Lancashire and Yorkshire, and when Ipswich, Boston and Lynn exported butter and cheese
by the ton.

Even more important was fish, for the consumption of fish in
the Middle Ages was high, and sea fisheries were many. Some fish
was caught in and off all the estuaries of Europe and along its sea
coasts. In the early Middle Ages the fishermen of Brittany and Normandy may even have brought in the flesh of whales and seals. But
great international fishing grounds were relatively few. One such
fishing ground was largely exploited by English fishermen: it was the
herring fisheries off the coasts of Norfolk and South Lincolnshire. Its
centres, and especially Yarmouth and its fishing suburb of Gorleston,
became famous as the home of England's herring, though it is doubtful
whether the red herring of Yarmouth, so important in the food supplies
of England, ever figured prominently in international commerce. More
international was the Scandinavian fishing industry, that of the white
herring and the stockfish. From Norway the art of 'white' curing or
salting spread to other countries, and it was very largely from Iceland
that the bulk of medieval supplies of stockfish came. Further south, the
estuary of the Rhine formed throughout the Middle Ages another
centre of the fishing industry. In the sixth and seventh centuries much
herring must have been fished by the Frisians in their estuary waters
and exported from there all over North-western Europe. But throughout the greater part of the Middle Ages, and certainly from the thirteenth century onwards, by far the most important of the fishing
grounds of Europe and also the busiest centre of the curing industry
and of the herring trade were the Baltic fisheries of Skania off the
south coast of what is now Sweden. It rose to prominence at the turn
of the thirteenth and fourteenth centuries, and as late as 1537 more than
90,000 tons were still salted there. By that time, however, the herring
fisheries off the coasts of the Northern Netherlands, modern Holland,
had risen to rival those of Skania as the main source of fish supplies.

It would not be difficult to catalogue a whole list of other staple
foodstuffs which entered the international trade of North European
countries. In the twelfth and thirteenth centuries England exported
bacon from her eastern counties, largely from Ipswich. Throughout
the later Middle Ages vegetables, especially very large quantities of
cabbages, garlic, onions and onion seed, regularly came from France
and the Low Countries, and apples—the pippins of Normandy—from
Norman ports. Towards the close of the Middle Ages hops and beer
began to come in from Holland and West Germany. Indeed so important had become the beer traffic that historians have sometimes ranked
it among the primary causes of Holland's rise in the fifteenth century.

Nevertheless, with the exception of grain and fish, no other comestible product was more indispensable to medieval diet, or was carried in larger quantities than wine. Large quantities of wine were apparently drunk in Northern Europe as well as in the growing areas of France and Germany. In the eleventh-century *Colloquium of Alfric*, Alfric did not drink wine because he was not rich enough to buy it. Four centuries later, on the morrow of the battle of Agincourt, Henry V would not allow his soldiers to celebrate on the heavy wines of Champagne, for they had been brought up on ale and beer and were not used to strong wines. But men of all stations above the lowest drank it in large and, as far as England goes, increasing quantities.

The significance of wine in international trade was not only in the quantities in which it was drunk, but also in the conditions under which it came to be produced. In the course of centuries the commercial production of wine, once widespread over the face of Europe, gradually concentrated in regions of highly specialised viticulture. There had once been vineyards in what would now be regarded as most unpropitious parts of England and the Low Countries. In France itself wine of some repute was grown everywhere. But by degrees the wines of three or four areas—Poitou, Gascony, Burgundy (Auxerrois) and the Moselle—all of them seats of flourishing viticulture since the days of Rome, rose to dominate the international demand. In a thirteenth-century *fabliau* narrating the combat of wines an English priest is made to pass in review some thirty or forty regional vintages. Having excommunicated a dozen or so of unworthy wines he leaves the field of battle to the northern vintages of Argenteuil, Meulent, Auxerre, Soissons, Épernay, the various wines of Guyenne and Limousin, and above all, the wines of Angoulême, Saintes, Bordeaux and Poitou. The prize goes to what were undeniably the most highly valued of medieval wines, the sweet wines of Cyprus, and the troubadour himself shows a true gift of prophecy in preferring the white wines of Chablis and Beaune. But the wine most generally drunk 'all over England, among Bretons, Flemings, Normans, Scots, Irish, Norwegians and Danes' and bringing in return good sterling is the wine of La Rochelle.

Had the *fabliau* been written a century or so later, it would not only have excluded from the list a number of local vintages, but would also have placed La Rochelle as a source of sterling-earning wine in a second place after Gascony. By the beginning of the fourteenth century these two regions had come to supply the bulk of wine entering into international trade. But whereas the products of Poitou and La Rochelle went mostly to other parts of France and to the Low Countries, the clarets of Gascony went mostly to England, forming a close and continuous link between the two countries.

As a result of the wine trade the two countries developed economic
systems which were mutually supplementary. Wine was Gascony's
chief product, and she was not self-supporting in either food or textiles,
while England was one of Europe's chief importers of wine (she
imported over four million gallons in 1415), and was also from time to
time able to supply Gascony with grain—with her own in years of good
harvests and with re-exported Baltic grain in other years.

Yet although the 'French' wines flowed between countries in
quantities far greater than any other, the wine of other nations also
contributed their quota. There was a regular flow of sweet wines from
Spain and the Eastern Mediterranean to the countries of Northern
Europe: the 'Malmsey', the 'vin muscadet', and a few others. Above
all, there were the wines of the Rhine valley. They were one of the
staple commodities of Frisian trade in the sixth and seventh centuries;
they were also one of the principal commodities imported into this
country by the merchants of Cologne when they began to come here
in large numbers at the end of the eleventh and twelfth centuries.
And it was Rhenish wine that German merchants sold in Scandinavia
before they had large surpluses of Eastern grain to dispose of.

2

So much for trade in food. It was large and, being food, was
indispensable, but both in value and in bulk it was rivalled by the trade
in basic raw materials. Of these, one of the most important and
certainly the bulkiest was timber. Timber resources were unevenly
distributed over the face of Europe, and were all but lacking in the
areas where the population was at its thickest: in Flanders, in the
Netherlands, and eventually in Southern England. As a rule, timber
was becoming scarcer as the countries of Western Europe were getting
settled and as forest was giving place to fields and pastures. But even
in those regions of Northern Europe which were still well wooded, as
in parts of this country, hardwoods predominated, and 'tall timber'
suitable for shipbuilding and for standard domestic structures had to be
brought in by water. In this trade water transport was even more
important than the ecology of native forests. For timber growing
away from navigable rivers and seaports, like much of the timber in
the forests of West and North Midlands of England, was often more
difficult to transport to other places within the country and much
costlier than timber imported from abroad by sea.

Timber was therefore an important article of water-borne trade. In
the earlier centuries, from the eleventh to the thirteenth, the chief
exporters of timber were Scandinavia and the wooded regions of South

Germany; but in the fourteenth century, with the opening of the Baltic, this trade, like the grain trade, changed in direction and volume. The vast coniferous forests of Eastern Europe including Russia, Poland and Livonia now became available, and from the middle of the fourteenth century onwards eastern timber shipped from the Baltic and more especially from Danzig all but ousted from the western markets the other types of 'white' timber. Pine, yew and fir of Baltic origin and occasionally some birch, both in logs and in sawn boards—'wainscot' and *klapholz*—became one of the main articles of Hanseatic imports into this country and also one of the chief magnets which drew English merchants to the Baltic regions. At one time in the fifteenth century hulls of boats and whole ships came to be imported from Prussia in lieu of shipbuilding material. Some wood shipped from Baltic ports may have come from countries even further afield. The bowstaves which won the battles of Crécy and Agincourt probably came from the Carpathian mountains and were shipped to England through Hungary and Prussia.[1]

The forest resources of Eastern Europe and Scandinavia were not exploited for timber alone. Russia was by far the most important source of medieval pitch and tar, and pitch used in this country in the later Middle Ages was nearly all of Baltic origin, though a little came also from Bordeaux and Bayonne. From Russian and Polish woodlands also came potash, obtained by the burning of wood.

The industrial raw material *par excellence* was wool. The cloth industry was the first, and for a long time the only, medieval handicraft to grow into a *grande industrie*. It was also the first industrial occupation to transform whole parts of Europe into specialised manufacturing regions. In Southern Europe specialised industrial centres of this kind sprang up in Florence, and centres of cloth industry were also to be found in Champagne and the South of France. But it was mainly in Northern Europe, at its north-western corner, that an industrial society wholly based on the cloth industry came into existence.

Industrial societies, in the plural, would perhaps be a better term. Several contiguous regions of Northern Europe became successively industrialised as the Middle Ages drew to their close, and all this industrial activity—ever shifting but never broken—grew up on imported wool. Some of the wool came from Central France, and the original prosperity of the Artois cloth industry was largely based on the wool of Auvergne and the Cevennes. But by far the most

[1] Th. Hirsch, *Danzigs Handels- und Gewerbgeschichte unter der Herrschaft des deutschen Ordens* (Leipzig, 1858). For a comprehensive, though possibly exaggerated, survey of Norwegian timber exports, see A. Bugge, *Den Norske Traelasthandels Historie*, 1 (Skien, 1925).

important centre of wool, a source which at the turn of the thirteenth and fourteenth centuries overshadowed all others, was Britain. By the second half of the thirteenth century the average annual exports of wool from England averaged more than 30,000 sacks, or about seven million pounds. Some of it went to Italy, but most was worked into cloth in the North—in the Low Countries and later, to an ever increasing extent, in England herself.

Cloth, thus made, was in itself a very valuable and by far the most important example of a 'wholly manufactured' export. In the seventh century we hear of English cloth exported to Carolingian Francia, and throughout that and subsequent centuries we find in the records stray references to traffic in Frisian cloth, which may have been cloth made in the Frisian lands and in their immediate vicinity or English cloth distributed on the continent by the Frisians. Various other regional varieties of cloth entered into the international trade of the ninth, tenth and eleventh centuries. But from the end of the eleventh century onwards, Flemish cloth began to overshadow all other cloths of Europe, and by the end of the thirteenth century we find it exported to the remotest corners of the then known world. In the later centuries it became the chief commercial *quid pro quo* for the grain, furs and timber products which the Baltic countries yielded up to the West, and therefore one of the pillars of German strength in Novgorod, Riga and Reval. When in the late fourteenth century English and Dutch cloth began to appear in large quantities on the continent it naturally flowed in the wake of the Flemish exports, gradually replacing them in all their ancient channels. Like the Flemish cloths they were soon to be found all over the civilised world—in Hungary, Russia and the Asiatic East as well as in countries nearer home.

Compared to cloth, the other textiles, though worn by men of all ranks, were not of very great importance in the inter-regional trade of Northern Europe. Silks and other luxury fabrics of Byzantine, Italian and oriental origin came in from the South throughout the Middle Ages. More important were linen and flax of northern growth. The damp and cool flax-growing areas of Europe were as clearly defined as its sheep-farming regions. They were as a rule to be found on land ill-suited to the growing of good quality wool, just as the chalk uplands and the salt marshes of Europe, which carried the largest and the best flocks of sheep, were ill suited to the cultivation of flax. Hence the broad geographic demarcation between the flax areas of the Low Countries, North-West France, Poland and Russia and the wool-growing areas of England, Central France and Spain. Yet in some areas the two textiles were mutually competitive, if not mutually exclusive, and in no other country were they more so than in Flanders. Parts of the Low Countries were well suited to the growing of flax and in fact grew and worked it throughout the Middle Ages. From the end of the eleventh century, however, the making as well as the wearing of woollen cloth spread so rapidly that to an observer the change might well appear as a combat between flax and wool. In a rhymed pamphlet of the eleventh century an anonymous pamphleteer defined the problem as *conflictus ovis et linis*. In the end, linen became one of Flanders' secondary exports. Some linen goods were still imported from there into England in the fourteenth and fifteenth centuries, but by that time the bulk of linen imports came from other sources; mostly from Northern France and from regions of Central and Eastern Europe controlled by the German Hanse. From Brittany and Baltic regions came also most of the canvas for sails and much of the hemp for ropes and cordage.

Wool and flax, however, were not the sole raw materials needed for the manufacture of northern textiles. Other subsidiary clothmakers' materials entered into northern commerce, and chief among them were woad and madder, the two commonest dyes of the Middle Ages. Both were to some extent grown in Northern Europe. Some woad came from Italy and was in the late fourteenth and the fifteenth centuries carried in Venetian galleys. A great deal of woad for English use came also from the region of Toulouse via Bordeaux. But before the fourteenth century Picardy was the chief northern home of the woad industry, and it was on woad that the economic prosperity of Amiens and Corby and the fame of their merchants were based. More exotic dyes especially the much valued and highly priced *granum*, came from Portugal, the still more precious ultramarine came from the East. Of the other materials used in the making of cloth, alum, black soap, mostly Spanish, and potash, mostly Eastern European, were the most important.

3

Potash, though a product of the Baltic timber industry and a raw material of the clothmakers, should perhaps be classified with the next important group of commodities in northern trade—the minerals. The basic mineral of modern times, coal, was worked in Northumberland throughout the Middle Ages—certainly in the thirteenth century—and was carried from there by sea to London and to the Low Countries. From the thirteenth century onwards coal was also mined in Hainault and, perhaps, Westphalia and elsewhere.

By far the most important of the mineral products was salt—one of the essential ingredients of medieval food, the indispensable preserver of meat, and the mainstay of the great fish-curing trades. Salt was both mined and obtained by evaporation from salt pans, and local centres of both kinds of salt industry were to be found all over Europe. The economic rise of Venice in the ninth century may well have begun with the development of local salt supplies. Further north the salt deposits of the Eastern Alps, already exploited in pre-historic times, revived in the closing stages of the Middle Ages. In this country the salt deposits of Worcestershire were also worked throughout the Middle Ages. But for the purposes of North European trade the most important salt-producing areas were the Lower Saxon region of Lüneburg and, still more, the Bay of Bourgneuf on the Atlantic coast of France. The Lüneburg salt deposits were conveniently situated for export to the Baltic as well as to the Netherlands. But in the course of the late fourteenth and the fifteenth centuries Lüneburg deposits, like most other important salt industries of Europe, shrank in importance by comparison with those of Western France. The shallow waters and flooded areas between the mouth of the Gironde and the Isle of Oleron —mainly in the Bay of Bourgneuf—formed natural salt pans of great extent and remarkable productivity. They were worked from early times, but it was not until the later centuries of the Middle Ages that they began to attract buyers from all over the world. In the first half of the fifteenth century, when our documentary evidence about Bourgneuf becomes most abundant, we find it frequented by great salt fleets of all the northern nations. Hanseatic 'Bay fleets' sailed there several times a year, and Dutch and English ships and merchants also resorted there in large numbers. By that time Bay salt also entered northern politics as well as northern trade. The lawless and riotous life of this salt 'Klondyke' generated international conflicts and quarrels, and the safety of the 'Bay route' preoccupied the Hanseatics throughout the fifteenth century, and gave rise to at least one war— that between England and the Hanse in the middle of the fifteenth century.[1]

Relatively less prominent in the annals of northern trade and in the records of its shipping were the exports and imports of metal. The mining of precious metals, especially of silver, was a great industry, and its products played a part in economic development of Europe so crucial that they should not perhaps be treated as mere items in a list of commodities. But bullion was not the only metal worked. Some ironstone was mined in most places, and some iron was smelted in almost every great country in the Middle Ages. But of important centres there were only three or four; one was Westphalia, others were in Saxony, in the Basque country in the Pyrenees, and above all in Sweden. It is doubtful whether there ever was a period since the

[1] A. Agats, Der Hansische Baienhandel (Heidelberg, 1904). About the importance of salt from Zeeland, see H. J. Smit in Bijdragen etc., VI (1930).

twelfth century when the high-quality iron of Swedish origin, the 'osmund' of medieval records, was not exported from that country to other parts of Northern Europe. We find it in the documents referring to Swedish trade in the twelfth century, in the records of Westphalian trade to Sweden in the thirteenth and fourteenth, in the English customs accounts of the fourteenth and fifteenth centuries. It was the most highly priced and internationally the best known of medieval irons.

Of other metals and metal wares, copper, mostly of Swedish and Hungarian origin, and lead and tin, mostly of English and German origin, were distributed all over Northern and Western Europe by Hanseatic merchants. So were also other miscellaneous metal goods, mostly produced in the area of Liège, Dinant and Cologne, and pewter goods of English make—altogether a current of trade not very abundant in comparison with grain, wool or timber, yet sufficiently important to attract the attention of the makers of commercial treaties and of legislators.

This catalogue of goods entering the commerce of Northern Europe could be continued almost indefinitely. Miscellaneous commodities of European origin crossed and recrossed the frontiers of northern countries and passed its tolls. Bricks from the Low Countries, swords and helmets from Cologne, tapestries and painted images from Flanders, books from France and the Low Countries, amber 'paternosters' from Prussia, wax and honey from Russia, thread and lace from Cologne and Brabant, hawks from Bruges and Calais, feathers for pillows from all over Germany. But it is not from these commodities, whether luxuries or playthings, that the commerce of Northern Europe took its colour. Its essential feature was trade in bulk, its characteristic commodities were the necessities of life and industry, its economic function was to bind the peoples of Northern Europe by real economic ties—ties without which life in many places would have been difficult if not altogether impossible.

(II) QUANTITIES

1

The catalogue of commodities cannot be complete, and as long as it is confined to the main branches of trade it cannot be even wholly representative. Above all, it cannot do full justice to the complexity of medieval commerce. The regions of Europe depended on each other's products or, to use the jargon of the economists, benefited from the geographical division of labour, to a far greater extent than a mere list of commodities would suggest. In spite of all the difficulties of long-distance trade the network of commercial exchanges had in the course of the Middle Ages come to be woven into a tight and complicated mesh. That whole industrial societies, like those of Flanders and Italy and later also that of Holland, should have come into existence even though the essential raw materials, as well as food, had to be imported, is an instance familiar enough. Less familiar, but equally characteristic, is the example of the export of beer from North-western Germany and later from Holland where it was brewed from grain imported from abroad. But nothing illustrates better the complexity of multi-lateral exchanges than the various secondary currents of trade which crossed and recrossed the main lines of commercial traffic. In the same years in the fifteenth century we find England exporting grain through Chester and Bristol to Ireland; importing grain through the eastern ports from the Baltic; exporting red herring from Yarmouth (to Holland of all countries!) and importing white herring through every port; exporting malt and ale and importing beer; exporting faggots and stakes and importing every other kind of timber; exporting figures made of alabaster and importing saints carved in wood; importing wax and exporting tallow; exporting pewter and importing Dutch pottery. And although these subsidiary currents were all small, they went far to give the economic geography of Europe the shape it has borne ever since.

Eloquent as these facts are, they cannot provide a full substitute for the missing statistics. They might, however, be sufficient to demonstrate how wide was the range of needs which inhabitants of Northern Europe covered by purchases from outside, and they might even support the surmise that the volume of the trade must have been high. For bulky goods would not be worth exporting or importing except in bulk, and a regular trade in essentials over long distances presupposed exporters relying on regular and substantial deficiencies in the importing countries as well as importers relying on a regular and substantial flow of supplies from abroad.

Here and there this general argument can be illustrated by numbers drawn from an occasional *cache* of figures. Thus the English trade returns, which are more abundant than those of any other country— they will be discussed later—make it clear that in the first half of the fourteenth century the value of British exports was at times not less than £250,000, or the equivalent of about 1½ million quarters of wheat or 2½ million quarters of oats at prices prevailing in the last decade of the fourteenth century. The evidence of the Hanseatic *Pfundzoll*—a war tax on sea-borne imports—suggests that in the seventies of the fourteenth century the annual value of the taxable sea-borne trade of the principal Hanseatic ports for which evidence is available was in excess of three million Lübeck marks or about 600,000 of contemporary pounds sterling.[1]

Even more concrete, though not necessarily more precise or relevant, may be the few surviving figures of individual commodities imported and exported. We are told that the total amount of herring salted on the fishing grounds of Skania in a good year could be as high as 120,000 tuns and that some 24,000 tuns of salt were imported in a curing season. In some years at the beginning of the fifteenth century Dutch grain imports by the Somme route may have been as high as 230,000 quarters. At the beginning of the fourteenth century wine exports from Bordeaux reached 100,000 tuns (some 25 million gallons)[2] per annum. In 1334 a few English merchants received royal licences to export to Bordeaux more than 50,000 quarters of grain. The English records show that in the late thirteenth and early fourteenth centuries this country at times exported as much as 35,000–40,000 sacks, the equivalent of about 15 million lb. of wool. In the good years of the fourteenth and fifteenth centuries this country exported more than 50,000 pieces of cloth of 28 yards per piece, and it is possible that at the height of their prosperity the Flemish cloth towns turned out a number of cloths at least three times as great.[2]

2

Similar estimates could be cited for a number of other places and other commodities, but however varied, they cannot and perhaps need not be turned into true measurements. The show of precision which they may impart to the history of trade is largely deceptive. Some of the figures are, to say the least, ambiguous; but even those which are not, have survived more or less in isolation and cannot be fitted into reliable estimates of total trade and still less into measurements of social income. It may be significant that in a fourteenth-century parliament it was confidently asserted that the wool of England represented half the total produce of the land; but what was the total produce of the land? It might also be important to know that the value of English exports in the thirteenth century was probably equivalent to the annual earnings of approximately 100,000 agricultural labourers. But even this figure, large as it is and close as it comes to a real measurement, does not mean very much unless related to the total size of English population or to the distribution of income between the various classes of the English people: a subject still shrouded in darkness.

[1] The value of seaborne exports of the four Hanseatic ports listed by Stieda approached 1·5 million marks in 1370. W. Stieda, *Revaler Zollbücher*, lvii ff. The other German figures in this and preceding paragraphs come from G. Lechner, *Die Hansische Pfundzollisten des Jahres 1368*, 57–8.

[2] Below Table III; also M. Gouron, *L'Amirauté de Guienne*, 47.

The most that these figures can do is to build up in a cumulative and circumstantial fashion the general impression that the volume of medieval trade was considerable; the least they can do is to make it unnecessary to disparage the part trade played in medieval life. No doubt, in comparison with the nineteenth and twentieth centuries, medieval trade at its highest would appear very small. But why compare with the nineteenth century, and indeed why compare at all? For all we know, the record of international trade in the nineteenth century may well turn out to have been a mere aberration in the economic development of the world. It has been argued that in the course of that century factors of production—land, labour, capital—were distributed more unequally over the face of the globe than in any other period of world history. As a result, inter-regional trade may have been greater in relation to total income than it would have been had the movable resources and especially capital been more evenly spread. By the same argument the international flow of resources has been slowly reducing the relative importance of trade, even though it may have raised its total volume and value. But even if the argument with all its implications were not accepted, it would still remain true that in the nineteenth century foreign trade was so great that, by comparison, the trade of all other centuries, the seventeenth and eighteenth as well as the thirteenth, would appear insignificant. And if historians and economists insist on matching century against century, they would be less open to accusation of irrelevance if they compared the Middle Ages with the earlier centuries of the modern era, the sixteenth, the seventeenth, the eighteenth. Thus compared, medieval trade of European countries would appear (and the argument is one of appearances and not of measurements) both smaller and greater than that of, say, the seventeenth century: smaller in the fifteenth century, greater in the thirteenth.

All such comparisons, however, are highly questionable. Not only must the magnitudes of commercial exchanges always be matters of vague surmise, but they must remain mutually incomparable even if they were capable of exact estimate. From this point of view more relevant than any attempt at a measurement of foreign trade are the simple historical facts indicating the place of trade in medieval life —the existence of specialised economies, the number and relative wealth of towns, the attention paid by kings and parliaments to trade and navigation, the readiness to engage in political and military conflicts on behalf of trade. The geographical and political implications of medieval trade will be discussed separately, but they must also be borne in mind in considering the problem of quantity. Did not the wool trade supply a link between Flanders and this country stronger than political, dynastic or cultural ties with France? Did not Gascon wine trade to England forge a link of political loyalty stronger than affinities of race, language and distance? In the twelfth century interruption in English imports could produce famine in Western Norway. In the early fourteenth century disturbances in Northern France could produce famine in the Low Countries. In the fourteenth century conflicts with England could result in unemployment all over the Low Countries. And in the fifteenth century the seizure of the salt fleet homeward bound from the Bay of Bourgneuf could produce a major crisis all over Northern Europe.

The economic interdependence of distant regions and the essential character of certain branches of trade may appear out of scale with the small quantities of goods in fact exchanged. In the middle of the sixteenth century, Thomas Barnaby, an enthusiastic sponsor of the coal trade, could argue that 'the thing that France can live no more without than the fish without water; that is to say the Newcastle coals, without which they can neither make steel work nor metal work nor wire work nor goldsmith work nor guns nor no manner of things that passes the fire'. In the Middle Ages coal exports were probably smaller than in the sixteenth century. The French were as yet rare visitors to the coal wharves of Newcastle: their calls there did not become at all frequent until about 1500. And before the advent of the French, the Flemings and the Zealanders did not apparently take out of this country more than about 10,000 tons in a good year. Yet, even then, coal was, as in the nineteenth century, a bulky return cargo without which the voyages might not have paid and would not have been undertaken.

It is therefore not surprising that in time of war some countries appeared to be even more vulnerable to blockade than in more recent times. The readiness with which embargoes and economic boycotts were used as political weapons is in itself evidence of the store men laid by foreign trade: indeed, of foreign trade in its most specialised manifestations.

(III) IMPEDIMENTS AND FACILITIES

1

The scope of medieval trade is all the more remarkable for the various obstacles which beset the merchant. It is perhaps true that medieval commerce could not have functioned as it did, had the obstacles in its way been quite as formidable as their history might suggest. Yet formidable they doubtless were, and none more so than the innumerable payments on the frontiers, along the rivers and roads, on town markets and in sea ports: payments which must have burdened commerce nearly as much as similar payments were to burden the trade of France on the eve of Colbert's and Calonne's reforms or the trade of Germany on the eve of Napoleon's conquest.

England was perhaps the largest area of Northern Europe in which trade was free from any but small tolls. If tolls were paid at all, they were usually in the nature of a *pontage* or a *viage*. Like the turnpike tolls of a later age they were levied to defray the cost of constructing or of maintaining a road or a bridge. As a rule the king's government seldom granted the right to impose a toll except in exchange for a true equivalent in road service; and grants were frequently preceded or followed by inquisitions into the revenue of tolls and their employments.

By comparison with these service tolls, or 'tolls-thorough' as they were known to a later age, the 'tolls-traverse'—payments based on ancient right and functioning as a customary source of revenue irrespective of the road service rendered—were not many. They were remarkably few in comparison with similar tolls in medieval and post-medieval France and Germany. There, at the best of times, no major trade route was entirely duty free. Thus even the much frequented international land routes from Flanders to France in the thirteenth century had to pass numerous toll stations, of which several, those of Bapaume on the French border and those of Péronne, Nesle, Compiègne, and Crépy-en-Valois on the roads of Northern France, were more or less inescapable. There were also provincial tolls all over the internal roads beyond Paris, and there were payments at the frontier stations on the South and the East leading to the upper Rhine and the main Alpine passes. Above all, there were innumerable tolls on the Loire, the Somme, the Oise, the Rhone, and the Garonne. The allegation that towards the end of the fourteenth century there were 130 toll stations along the Loire is probably far-fetched. But it is known that the tolls on the Loire, such as there were, grew as much in the following 25 or 30 years as they had grown in the preceding fifty. The Garonne and the Rhone were no freer than the Loire, and even on the Seine the toll charges on grain shipped in the late fifteenth century over a distance of 200 miles equalled more than half of its selling price.

The German picture was less uniform, for the country contained the relatively free arteries, like the great Hanseatic routes to the East, as well as the much taxed and restricted roads which connected the route with the interior. The surviving lists of tolls along the main German rivers may exaggerate the actual weight of impositions, but however much discounted they make formidable reading. At the turn of the thirteenth and fourteenth centuries there were said to have been more than 30 toll stations along the Weser and at least 35 along the Elbe. In the middle of the thirteenth century there were more than fourscore tolls along the Austrian stretch of the upper Danube and a score of tolls on the river Main. But the most advertised, the most bitterly resented and, from the point of view of trade, the most damaging, were the tolls on the Rhine. According to a recent account there were about 19 toll stations along the Rhine at the end of the twelfth century, about 35 or more at the end of the thirteenth century, nearly 50 at the end of the fourteenth, and more than 60 at the end of the fifteenth century; mostly belonging to the great ecclesiastical princes of Western Germany. Writing in the middle of the thirteenth century, an English chronicler, Thomas Wykes, could find no other way of describing the system on the Rhine than 'the raving madness of the Teutons' (*furiosa Teutonicorum insania*).[1]

The total weight of the internal tolls was thus heavy and growing, and may in part account for the gradual clogging of internal trade in the closing centuries of the Middle Ages. At the same time it is important not to misunderstand their incidence and their effect on commerce. The system as a whole may have been sufficiently exorbitant and sufficiently anarchical to impose here and there a weight of charges greater than the traffic could bear. Yet the yield of the main toll stations on the Rhine, the Main, and the Elbe remained to the end sufficiently valuable to justify their owners, and especially the great ecclesiastical princes, in fighting for their retention to the bitter end. The presumption, therefore, is that, generally speaking, they did not choke trade altogether. Extortionate as were the lords of the Rhine tolls, the trade of certain towns, and Cologne in the first instance, remained relatively free over long stretches of the river. And although in the later Middle Ages grain from upper Germany was eventually forced out of the river and took to the land route, timber could still be floated downstream to Holland. The same is broadly true of the Elbe, for the merchants of the Wendish towns never ceased to use the river for the bulkier goods originating beyond Magdeburg and for shipments of fish and salt up the river.

The general impression is that the main weight of the toll taxes fell upon local traffic, thereby reinforcing the particularism and self-sufficiency of local economies. Their chief effect on long-distance trade was to raise local prices for imports and to reduce local prices of exportable surpluses. This in turn may have reduced production for exports and narrowed down the markets for imports. But how great the reduction in fact was in different fields of trade will not be known until local prices have been studied in greater detail than has so far proved possible. The general impression is that among the factors, which at times held back the output of industry and agriculture, high

---

[1] *Annales Monastici* (Rolls Series), IV, 222.

tolls *en route* to distant markets were of relatively little importance. The ability of medieval agriculture to yield surpluses for export, or its failure to do so, depended much less on differences in costs of distribution (including tolls) than on variations of climate, of soil, of seasons, and above all, of social structure. The same argument may not apply to products of industry and mining. The supply of most industrial products was greatly affected by costs, and the demand for textiles, metal articles and luxuries was apparently quite elastic. Everything that helped to raise their final costs was therefore bound to restrict the volume of production and sales. But for reasons to be expounded later, long-distance trade was not as a rule greatly affected by local taxes, from some of which it was exempted and most of which it could avoid.

From the point of view of inter-regional and international trade, more effective because more unavoidable, were the national or princely taxes at the frontiers or the great international toll-stations, like those of Bapaume. But in the nature of things these taxes were not as a rule so high as to be crippling. Among the highest was the English export duty on wool in the late fourteenth and fifteenth centuries. The taxes, i.e. customs and subsidy, at times rose to about £2 to £2. 13s. 4d. per sack, to which about 1s. should perhaps be added for various local dues in English ports and 6s. 8d. for customs charged in Calais and sometimes levied as a special excise on wool shipped to Italy. The total customs payments thus computed were equal to about 20% of the value of good quality wool in Calais. The tax in the end penalised British wool exports and greatly stimulated production of cloth at home, but it never stopped the wool exports altogether; and had it threatened to do so it would almost certainly have been moderated. Tax on cloth exports at a rate which varied from 1s. to 2s. 9d. or from about 1·5 to 4% *ad valorem* was not much higher than stamp duties and registration fees were to be in the free-trade decades of the nineteenth century. Miscellaneous imports paid a tax of 3d. in the pound, to which frequently the poundage of 1s. in the pound was added. The additional duties levied on imports and exports were on the whole very small. Local dues such as 'anchorage' on boats or tolls on merchandise brought into ports varied from place to place and, on the whole, fell less heavily on distant trade than it might appear from the toll lists. In the Cinque Ports in the thirteenth century the tolls on wine, their main imports, varied from 2d. to 4d. per cask. The charges in Southampton averaged about 2d. per pound worth of merchandise; in Winchester they were at the rate of 1d. per cwt. of wool. But in all these ports most merchants and merchandise coming from other English towns were exempt from local tolls by royal charter or else paid reduced tolls by inter-urban agreements. In a port like Yarmouth where remission was not so general, local dues might vary from about 2d. per cloth to 4d. per pipe of wine or a last of herring: by no means an exorbitant charge. No doubt in a number of foreign ports where local taxation was employed as a means of enforcing the monopoly of the residents the taxes could at times be much higher than they were in English ports. The various dues which were levied on strangers along the roads leading from the vineyards to the port of Bordeaux were sufficiently high to deter them from buying wine directly from the growers. But customs in Bordeaux itself were not such as to impede the flow of wine exports.

2

There was indeed every reason why most taxes and tolls actually borne by long-distance trade should not have been as heavy as those which weighed on local trade. Where princely authorities were so many and so ill-coordinated, as on the Rhine, the total weight of dues might in fact pass the limit of what the international traffic would bear. Yet even at times and in places where this limit was passed, trade was merely forced into alternative routes.

For alternative routes there always were. In considering the much misunderstood history of medieval trade routes, it is important to remember that what made a route was not the physical attributes of a road—a stretch of tarmac or an immovable railway track—but a combination of conveniences, mostly of political and social character: residential and trading facilities en route, guarantees of safety and security, and above all, comparative freedom from imposts and taxes. Geographical and physical conditions were of course essential; mountains could only be crossed by passes, rivers by fords and bridgeable places. In general the medieval carrier stuck as long as he could to navigable rivers and to the greater ancient highways, many of which were Roman in origin and construction, and most of which contained sections made and maintained by the work of men. But, within limits set by geography, the man-made conveniences—even such conveniences as bridges—could be duplicated and multiplied, and their sites could be shifted. In a famous capitulary Charlemagne had to lay down that if the twelve bridges over the Seine were to be reconstructed they should be placed ubi antiquitus fuerant and not moved to new sites. The same motif recurs more than once in the history of European bridges, as in the clause of the Magna Carta providing that no man should be distrained to work on bridges on sites where they had not been ab antiquo. When in the later judicial proceedings we find the parties pleading that the bridges in question still were in locis quibus esse consueverant tempore Ioannis regis the main object was to prove that the bridges still had to be maintained, but the presumption was that the permanence of a bridge site could not be taken for granted.

What is true of bridges is even truer of the social and institutional components of a trade route. These could be combined and re-combined into linked chains stretching across the face of Europe in double, treble, and multiple strands. Thus between England and Flanders on the one hand and the Mediterranean on the other there were during the Middle Ages at least a dozen of geographically feasible lines of communication from which merchants could take their choice. There was, in the first place, the major alternative of land routes and sea routes. The latter did not become important until the closing of the Champagne routes by the action of the French kings in the late thirteenth and the fourteenth centuries; but eventually they rose to great prominence. In the last hundred years of the Middle Ages the bulk of English wool exports to Italy went that way, and whereas in the early fourteenth century the Genoese wool importers paid toll on wool in Milan, in the fifteenth century the merchants of Milan paid toll on their wool in Genoa. Among land routes, the Italians and the other merchants trading to the south rang the changes over a wide scale of trade routes across Flanders and France. There were in the first place the main lines of the Flemish rivers, and there were routes which were wholly or largely land-bound. In the thirteenth century, in addition to a number of secondary routes, there were two main arteries—that of Arras and that of Douai—which crossed Flanders to the South; and there were also at least several routes from Brabant to France which grew in importance in the later Middle Ages: a network of routes across Northern France, most of them converging on Compiègne and Troyes, and spreading out from there to Paris or to Saulieu, Dijon and the other places *en route* for the South-east. Marc Bloch has drawn attention to the several routes between Paris and Orléans, but a cursory study of French internal trade would reveal the several variants forming the routes between Paris and Brest, Paris and Lille, Paris and Rouen, Paris and La Rochelle, some following the main rivers of France, others mainly land routes.[1]

The same variety of routes traversed the continent from the West to the East. The time when the *Hellweg*, which bisected Northern Germany from Dortmund in Westphalia to Magdeburg or Bardowiek on the Elbe, was the sole line of communication to the Slavonic East passed away (if such time ever was) with the twelfth century. In the thirteenth and later centuries there were at least four trans-continental routes

---

[1] H. Laurent, *La Draperie des Pays-Bas en France*, 48 ff., 246–53; Armand Deroisy in *Revue du Nord* (1939), 40 ff.; F. Imbertin in *Les Annales* (1939); and M. Bloch's postscript, *ibid.* 416.

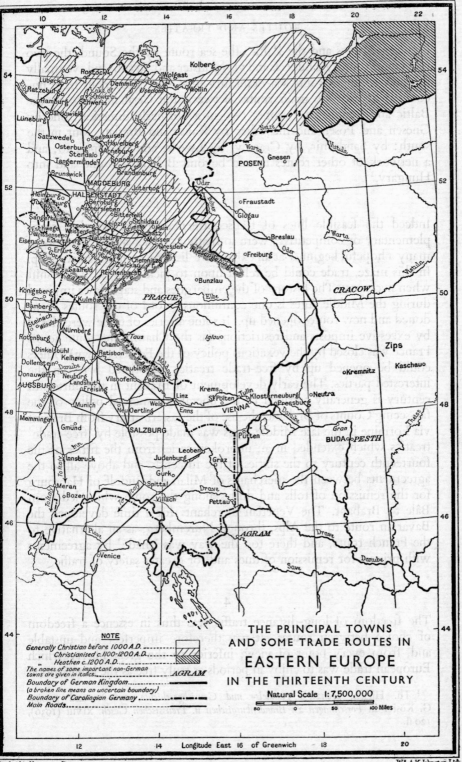

THE PRINCIPAL TOWNS
AND SOME TRADE ROUTES IN

EASTERN EUROPE

IN THE THIRTEENTH CENTURY

Natural Scale 1:7,500,000

NOTE
Generally Christian before 1000 A.D. ----------
  "   Christianised c.1100-1200 A.D. ----------
  "   Heathen c.1200 A.D. ----------
The names of some important non-German
towns are given in italics.   AGRAM
Boundary of German Kingdom ----------
(a broken line means an uncertain boundary)
Boundary of Carolingian Germany ----------
Main Roads ----------

Map 6.

between Bruges and the Baltic: the sea route by the Sound, the two older land routes via Lübeck and via Münster and Stettin, and eventually the new southern route via Frankfurt-am-Oder. Historians have uncovered at least six main routes between the German ports on the Baltic and South-east Europe; two in a northerly direction: one by Gnesen and Posen and the other by Kalisz and Breslau; four in the south: by Sandomir, by Cracow, by Lwow, and by Oposzno; and a network of other routes to and beyond Bohemia, round and into Hungary.[1]

3

Indeed the feasible lines of transcontinental traffic, whether complementary or competitive, were so many as to defeat the attempts of many a hopeful beginner at an exhaustive list or a comprehensive map. In this maze, trade could be relied upon to pick its way and to shift when necessary. The history of the embargoes and staple laws imposed during the Middle Ages is one continuous record of old routes abandoned and new routes opened up. If some arteries of trade were closed by excessive imposts and restrictions (as the Champagne route across France was closed by the vexatious policy of the French crown), others could be opened up by free-trade treaties negotiated between the interested parties. The early development of Brabant in the thirteenth century is generally ascribed to the liberal commercial policy of the far-seeing Counts of Brabant; the use of the eastern artery from Brabant via Lorraine in the late Middle Ages was made possible by 'free-trade' treaties which extended in an unbroken series from the fifties of the fourteenth century to the sixties of the fifteenth, and above all to the agreements between the merchants of Milan and Rudolf of Hapsburg for the remission of tolls and duties along the route which led from Bâle to Brabant. The Venetian merchants for a time developed the Bavarian route to the Alps, through Nuremberg, as an alternative to the French route, and there too the way was 'made' by agreements with princes for remission of dues and for greater safety of traffic.

4

The freedom of long-distance traffic was thus in essence a freedom of choice between routes. It was therefore imperfect and unstable and, from every point of view, inferior to the great liberty which European trade was to enjoy in periods as truly free as the honeymoon

[1] Th. Hirsch, *Danzig's Handels- und Gewerbgeschichte*, 178–80 and *passim*. G. Köster in *Forschungen zu Brandenburgischen u. Preussischen Gesch.* XLVIII (1936), 120 ff.

decades of the Victorian *laissez-passer*. For not only were routes newly chosen sometimes more expensive than the routes which had to be abandoned, but the whole system of communications suffered from lack of permanence and stability. In addition it was often insecure. Political conditions on which it depended changed frequently; princely whims and aims were often unaccountable; and above all wars were apt to break out at all times. And the crippling effect of war on trade must not be underestimated. Here and there war demands might inject a stimulating dose of inflationary expenditure into certain branches of trade; but on the whole war meant taxation, forced loans, monetary disturbance and physical hazards. Contrary to all the current notions, medieval conflicts could approach very closely the recent models of total war, for medieval princes did not as a rule hesitate to sacrifice their long-term economic prospects to the strategic or fiscal necessities of war. It was not so much the mere fact of annexation by France as the exposure to the demands of Philip le Bel's war strategy and war finance that ruined the cloth industry of Artois, the transit trade of France and the prosperity of the fairs of Champagne. It was Edward III's war finance that brought havoc into the English wool-growing and wool trade and into the Italian investment in this country. It was the Hanseatic war policy and its accidents that all but ruined in the fifteenth century the German position in Eastern Flanders.

Above all, in time of war and within the range of its operations, pillage and piracy reigned. Piracy and robbery along roads and rivers could at times develop into a major disaster, and it is therefore no wonder that it has now become one of the major themes of medieval history. The records are full of the complaints, petitions and counter-petitions arising from the seizure of ships and goods on the high seas, and it is doubtful whether there was any major act of piracy which remained unrecorded in the surviving medieval evidence. It is therefore not surprising that in modern accounts of medieval trade piracy figures very conspicuously.

It may even be that piracy has received more attention than it deserves. For if on some continental land routes ambushes and attacks on convoys were endemic, piracy on the high seas was not. Generally speaking it was much less a permanent feature of the medieval scene than an accident of war. In some parts of Europe, on the south-west coast of England, on the west coast of Brittany, and along the creeks of Normandy, and no doubt elsewhere, there was to be found a sea-faring population who at all times engaged in occasional piracy. But most of the piratical acts in medieval records were committed not by professional pirates practising their occupation in all seasons, but by merchants who turned pirate and sometimes acted as privateers under official letters of mark. They either were pressed into service by their princes or turned to privateering while trade was at a standstill, or were trying to recoup themselves for acts of piracy they or their compatriots had suffered at the enemy's hands. Pirates and privateers preyed on the French and English shipping in the Channel every time war between France and England broke out; with the result that during the Hundred Years War, i.e. for nearly 150 years, the sea-borne trade between Brittany and Normandy on the one hand and the English south coast on the other was reduced to a small and fitful trickle. The North Sea was thrown into a chaos of universal and promiscuous privateering of this kind in the fifties and sixties of the fifteenth century, and there were occasional outbursts of wholesale piracy in the disturbed periods in Anglo-Flemish relations in the early fourteenth century. But in the times when wars were not raging and in areas outside the range of privateering bases, the main channels of sea-borne trade were maintained more or less open.

On land the only true remedy was the enforcement of the king's peace. When and where the princes were strong enough to keep the roads safe—as in Flanders and Champagne in the eleventh, twelfth, and thirteenth centuries, in Burgundy in the fifteenth century, in Prussia and Livonia in the fourteenth and early fifteenth centuries—merchant traffic flowed unmolested both in peace and in war, and the wealth o their countries grew at the expense of lands and routes not so blessed. In Germany the safety of the routes was sometimes enforced by the action of the towns. In the later Middle Ages the great Hanseatic routes to the East were almost wholly free from the dangers of piracy and robbery. Somewhat more restricted and on the whole less successful were the activities of the inter-urban police unions (*Landfriedensverbände*) of the thirteenth and fourteenth centuries, which, with the occasional assistance of local princes, waged battle against the robber barons and their nests along the West German rivers.

On the high seas however the security of traffic was almost entirely the concern of the merchants and shippers themselves. Where shipments were valuable and regular and followed established sea lanes, they were as a rule made in convoy. The English wool was shipped in two great bi-annual convoys elaborately organised and controlled. The German and Dutch ships carrying salt from the Bay also as a rule sailed together, and so did often the English cloth boats sailing to the Baltic and the Prussian and Dutch boats plying between Danzig and the West. The system must have been effective, for very few of the great convoys were ever seized or disturbed. There was hardly an instance of the Venetian galleys being seized or plundered in northern waters on their annual visits to England and the Low Countries; not one of the great wool

PLATE I

(*a*) A goods waggon. (*See pp.* 143 *sq.*)

(*b*) The operations of building. (*See pp.* 501, 510–11.)

fleets which sailed from the main wool ports of England was ever seized; and of all the great Bay fleets, which regularly passed through the Narrow Seas on their way from the Atlantic coast to the Baltic, the first ever to be attacked was the great Bay fleet which was seized by Warwick in 1449. In short, piracy even more than the other disturbances of trade was a characteristic feature of the Middle Ages only in so far as the Middle Ages were specially prone to war. When and where peace prevailed trade flowed unhindered.

(IV) TRANSPORT

1

In times of war and on routes which happened to be no more than ordinarily insecure the dangers of the routes must have added to the cost of trade. But in most years and especially in the years of peace they were by no means the main constituent of costs and could not be blamed for the high expenses of distribution. Commercial distribution was bound to be a costly service, but—tolls apart—the main element of cost was undoubtedly transport. It is not that transport was as primitive as it is sometimes represented, but like all transport of the pre-railway age it was wasteful of time, equipment and manpower.

On land routes goods were carried by horse and ox, but not necessarily by pack. Carrying services on medieval estates in this country and abroad consisted of both summage, i.e. carriage by horseback (indeed sometimes on human backs), and cartage; but English manorial accounts make it quite clear that, for bulky goods or for carriage over distances, carts and, where suitable, boats were used. On some stretches, e.g. across mountain passes, pack animals might be the only feasible means of transport, and the *vectuarii* of Genoa and Asti who ran the traffic across the Alps to Champagne at the end of the thirteenth century apparently employed horses for the purpose. But carts of varying sizes as a rule made up the bulk of medieval trade caravans. A thirteenth-century tariff of Péronne suggests that the purposes of local traffic were served by the *colliers*—the medieval coolies—who drew barrows and other small vehicles *ad collum*; and that some local traffic also went by pack-horses. But the bulk of the traffic was apparently borne by the *bronnette*, a cart on two wheels, which according to a text of 1327 was capable of carrying a fardel of thirteen cloths; and more still by *car* or the *carrette* on four wheels capable of carrying a cargo two or three times that of the *bronnette*. (See Plate I*a*.)

The Péronne cart was not substantially different from the vehicle commonly used by peasants in the daily routine of their agriculture, and peasant carts therefore provided the main reserve of medieval transport. Wherever the accounts of local bulky traffic have survived, more especially of stone, brick, wood, or charcoal, we find it carried by horse and cart or ox and cart hired or requisitioned from nearby villages. Peasant carting was, however, in the nature of things seasonal and could not supply the needs of trade all the year round. It is therefore not surprising that regular traffic along the main lines of communication was in the hands of men who specialised in the business of transport and acted as common carriers. English records have preserved evidence of common carriers traversing the country in the thirteenth, fourteenth and fifteenth centuries from Southampton to Winchester and Oxford, from the Cotswolds by road and river to London, from the midland counties to the Stourbridge Fair near Cambridge, from Westminster and Oxford to York and Newcastle-on-Tyne. In towns like London there was a recognised profession of 'brokers of carts' who acted as intermediaries between carters and owners of cargo. Sometimes whole rural areas specialised in carting services. In the middle of the fourteenth century the carriers who transported wool from Flanders to Bâle were mostly Alsatians and Saarois; the Brabant route to the South was used mainly by carters from Lorraine, and the overland routes from Toulouse to the Atlantic seaports mainly by the wagoners of Béarn.

2

Wheeled traffic could not have been so general had roads been as impassable as some of the roads which Arthur Young depicted in the eighteenth century. Judged by modern standards they were certainly bad beyond all comparison, and most local roads were no more than mud tracks barely useable in bad weather. To conclude, however, that every King's road 'made and maintained itself', or to argue, as so well-informed a historian as Marc Bloch did, that medieval roads in general were no more than *l'endroit où on passe*, barely differentiated from fields and field tracks, is perhaps too disparaging a generalisation.[1] It may be true of the very early local example Bloch quotes: the village road which, in Flodoard's story, St Theodulph prevented from being ploughed up. On the other hand it could not possibly have applied to at least one local road in thirteenth-century Cheshire. For when the Cistercian abbey of Vale Royal in Cheshire was erecting its buildings, peasant carts transported stone from the quarry at Eddisbury about eight miles away, and made thousands of journeys, most carters managing to make two complete journeys—a distance of about 30 miles—per day for months at a time: and winter months at that.

The generalisation applies even less to main roads. Main roads

[1] C. T. Flower, *Public Works in Medieval Law*, II, xvi, Selden Soc. Publications, Vol. XL for 1923.

artificially levelled and drained were not universal; roads with artificial
metal or paved surfaces must have been very uncommon. Yet road
approaches to a number of towns were frequently paved, and artificial
road beds were also to be found in the open country. In origin they were

DIAGRAM OF GOUGH MAP SHOWING 14TH CENTURY ROADS.

—— Roman & probable Roman.

········ Non-Roman

(Settlements not connected by roads on Gough Map have been omitted.)

Reproduced from *Historical Geography of England*, ed. H. C. Darby, Cambridge, 1936

Map 7.

mostly Roman, for in spite of all the shifts and changes in medieval
routes, Roman roads were used whenever possible. In England ancient
Roman ways dominated the medieval road system, and the main
roads on a surviving fourteenth-century map were little different

from what they had been ten centuries earlier. Nor were they in this respect much different from what they were to be four centuries later, and it is also doubtful whether their surfaces were much worse. Their foundations were that many centuries 'newer' than in the eighteenth century, and in addition the average medieval cart was probably lighter than the later wagon. It was seldom furnished with metal tyres, which the Elizabethan legislators found so destructive of road surfaces.[1]

It is also probable that in England, parts of France and the Low Countries, surfaces and drainage were kept up to a standard well above that of a mere track. In most European countries the law of the road and the surveyance of roads were lax and rudimentary. Yet to assume, as Marc Bloch did, that roads were not subject to special legislation and control is not altogether true, even of France. For the legal notion of *strata publica* was part of the legal doctrine of thirteenth-century France, even if it may not have been greatly respected in practice. In this country, where documents have survived in greater abundance, they contain numerous indictments of people guilty of obstructing public roads, encroaching on them, or neglecting their duties of maintenance. And the indictments are evidence not only of the disrepair and neglect of roads but also of the legal and administrative provisions for their upkeep. For in Common Law, as defined by Bracton and enforced by royal courts, the definition of the King's highway included not only military roads but all roads leading to ports and markets, and their destruction or obstruction was an offence against the King. In addition, law and custom charged landlords and vills with the maintenance of the *via communis* in good passable order.

That the law was not always enforced may be taken for granted; and at certain periods the gap between law and practice was bound to be wide. In England the work of maintenance was as a rule confined to the upkeep of drains and ditches, and the road was not deemed impassable except when flooded or barricaded. Moreover, in the late fourteenth and fifteenth centuries the system, linked as it was with feudal obligations and manorial dues, may have suffered from the commutation of services and from the general tendency on the part of the landlords to cut their capital investments. The Royal Commissions of walls and dykes to some extent succeeded in checking the deterioration of bridges as well as of the main sea walls and dykes, but could not and were not expected to establish an effective national control over roads.

[1] Lamprecht in his well-documented appendix on roads in Rhineland (*Deutsches Wirtschaftsleben im Mittelalter*, II, 236 ff.) emphasised the continued use of Roman roads in the early Middle Ages; but his evidence does not support his argument that as time went on waterways replaced the Roman roads.

Yet, if in some respects daily practice fell short of legal ideal, in one or two respects the ideal was sometimes outstripped by practical achievement. Thus substantial towns paved their roads and levied a special pavage tax for the purpose. Roads across moors and fens often included causeways and reinforced beds which cost much to build and to maintain. The causeway by the Holland bridge near Boston was made up of thirty bridges; a road across Sedgemoor near Glastonbury was built of stone on a foundation of brushwood and alder sleepers held together by oak balks.

Some of the road works were carried out by princes. The French kings may have neglected to enforce the law of roads, but English thirteenth-century records have preserved evidence of work on roads and bridges undertaken by the crown on its own initiative. In England the crown in preparation for its military expeditions often undertook works on a very great scale, as in 1277 when Roger Mortimer was appointed to enlarge and widen roads and passes into Wales, or in 1283 when Royal Commissioners were appointed to widen the passes into Wales to a bowshot in width. But not all road works were fruits of state initiative. Religious houses, municipalities, landlords and private benefactors, all made their contributions. The Holland causeway was built by a religious house; the Glastonbury causeway was in fact maintained by another religious house. The Stecknitz canal which in 1398 cut across the base of Jutland peninsula was a part of Lübeck's endeavour to support the land road in competition against the sea route by the Sound. Similarly, when in 1332 the town of Ghent busied itself with the repair of a distant stretch of road near Senlis in the neighbourhood of Paris, this was taken for what it was—an act of enlightened self-interest of a community dependent upon traffic across France. History has not preserved the names of the anonymous masons (some writers thought they might have been smiths) or donors who by 1237 opened up the pass of St Gotthard by constructing a road and a bridge across the gorges at Schöllenen, thus opening up a great new line of communication between Italy and Europe. But records of all European countries have preserved scores and hundreds of references of charitable gifts, by will and otherwise, for the building and improvement of communications: gifts which contributed as much as acts of municipal and princely governments to the main system of European communications.

In the main, private enterprise and private benefactions were primarily concerned with bridges and causeways: so much so as to suggest to one historian of public works the generalisation that, whereas the Romans were road-conscious but were quite prepared to cross rivers by fords, the men of the Middle Ages were essentially bridge-conscious. The writer has cited the part bridges played in the ancient feudal obligation of *trinoda necessitas*, as well as the frequent references to pontage, a local tax levied for the upkeep of bridges.[1] But he could also have cited, if he wished, the English evidence of the building and repairs of bridges and the more stringent enforcement of legal obligations for the upkeep and maintenance of bridges. And if there is anything in this generalisation, it may well be connected with what is now known about Roman inefficiency in the use of draught animals. Where the Romans moved themselves and their goods on horseback, medieval men used carts.

3

The main alternative to wheeled traffic, however, was not the pack-horse but the barge and the boat. Here and there records have preserved curious instances of short sea routes for a time becoming unaccountably dear, but generally, in the Middle Ages as in modern times, carriage by water was much cheaper than by land; and this was one of the reasons why river traffic was able to bear the heavy tolls which weighed on it in so many countries. Traffic in heavy goods, such as timber and coal, over long distances was only possible where cheap waterways were available. Mineral coal was known as 'sea coal', not because it was necessarily mined by the sea but because it came to the South by river and by sea. Water transport explains also why in the south and east of England it was cheaper to import timber from the Baltic and Norway than from the north-west midlands and why it paid to import building stone from Normandy for the erection of cathedrals and castles in southern England.

Sea transport was cheap in spite of the small size of the medieval boat and in spite of the costly methods of navigation. Medieval shipping was as a rule coastal. Whether because navigation was mainly by sounding, or whether because the high seas were thought dangerous, masters preferred to hug the coasts. Whenever possible they left the sea and sailed by internal waterways, and Holland owes much of its importance as a centre of entrepôt trade to the medieval seaman's liking for the shallow and sheltered waters of Dutch rivers and canals stretched along the east to west route. Further east and west along the same route ships plied when possible in the narrow waters between the islands and within sight of dry land. As long as these methods prevailed, sea transport was bound to be relatively expensive, for it involved constant reloading at points where the coastwise route was interrupted by land masses. Lübeck and Hamburg were two such reloading places half-way from Bruges to Danzig. Amsterdam and Rotterdam, the two terminal points

[1] C. T. Flower, *op cit.* xix.

of the Dutch waterways, were two other ports serving the same function. There was also a great deal of reloading into lighters in sea ports which, like Bruges, happened to be situated in silted-up river estuaries. Cranes—and they were to be found in a number of large ports—lightened the labour, but they could not do away with it altogether.

Both the size of the boats and the methods of navigation may have improved as the Middle Ages drew to their close. The history of the shipbuilding industry in the Middle Ages has not yet been written, and the technical history of medieval ships, though better known, is still incomplete. But in so far as it is possible to generalise from the present state of knowledge, it appears that in the later Middle Ages more merchant ships were carvel-built than in earlier centuries and that clinker-built boats were being ousted from the main trade routes across the north seas. The Genoese and Spanish carrack, a swifter though not necessarily a larger vessel, did not as a rule go much further east and north than the ports of Flanders and Southern England, but towards the end of the Middle Ages it dominated England's western approaches and the sea-borne trade to the Mediterranean. In addition, in the later Middle Ages once a year there came into Southampton and Bruges the great Venetian galleys. But the mainstay of the new merchant shipping in the northern seas were the slower and roomier boats of local origin. The typical ships of the English wool and wine fleets and of the Dutch and Hanseatic shipping in the North Sea and the Baltic were the cogs and hulks frequently displacing as much as 100 or 200 tons and sometimes approaching the 400 and 500 ton limit.

Whether as a result of these improvements or through the spreading use of the compass or through the growing knowledge of their element, the seamen of the later Middle Ages ventured more frequently than before into the open sea. Such voyages had, since times immemorial, been occasionally made by Irish, Scandinavian and English merchantmen trading to Iceland, but from the economic point of view the most important instance of navigation not wholly coastal was the *Umlandfahrt* —the route to the Baltic round the Sound which was probably opened by seamen of Zealand some time in the middle of the fourteenth century. The direct routes as well as the larger ships must have helped to reduce the freights, and it was on lower freights that the Dutch established their sea power in the course of the fifteenth century.

In addition there were the internal waterways. The classical country of river navigation was east of the Elbe and more especially east of the Oder—in Lithuania, Poland, Galicia. Among the Western Slavs there were whole societies—villages and regions—which lived on and by their broad and sluggish rivers. In the course of centuries the Lithuanian and Slavonic peasants and fishermen had developed a system of river navigation ideally adapted to the transportation of timber and other bulky cargoes. The usual transport was by a local variant of a raft—the Slavonic *dubassy*—large timber platforms capable of carrying temporary huts and a great deal of miscellaneous cargo as well as large quantities of timber. Hence the importance of eastern river ports like Thorn, Kovno and Brest-Litovsk. Hence also the prominence which rivers and weirs occupied in the records of Eastern European trade and in the trade treaties between the Germans and the Slavonic princes.

It is doubtful whether rivers were equally important in the West, but here and there they formed essential links in transcontinental routes. The Seine was a great trade artery of Northern France and one of its main grain conduits, served and largely dominated by the rival companies of riparian traders of Paris and Rouen. The part which the Somme and the Oise played in the grain traffic has already been mentioned; the Scheldt and the Meuse never ceased to serve the needs of Flemish traffic. At times most of the great rivers of Europe, the Rhine, the Main, the Weser, the Elbe in Germany; the Loire, the Rhone, the Garonne in France, carried much of the heavy long-distance traffic. If they did not always do so and if, in spite of the greater economy of water carriage, traffic was at times apt to desert the great waterways, the fault lay with the owners of tolls who preyed upon them. It has already been shown how the general tendency was for the river tolls to multiply and how at times some rivers, mainly German, came near to being deserted by the merchant and the barge-man. Yet even in the later Middle Ages they were not deserted altogether. Traffic was reduced but never stopped.

In England rivers were freer than in most other parts of Europe and formed an organic part of the English route system. The Thames, the Lea, the Stour, the Wye, the Severn, the Avon, the Humber, the Trent, the Yorkshire Ouse, the Witham and other rivers were busy trade arteries reaching far into the interior. The Thames was navigated well into Oxfordshire, although in the fifteenth century wool from the Cotswolds was as a rule loaded on barges no further west than Henley. Nottingham was connected with the sea through the Trent and the Humber. In conjunction with the Ouse and the Fossdyke the Trent formed a chain of waterways from York to Boston. The Humber was also a great waterway serving places as far inland as York and Beverley. Other and smaller rivers with their estuaries were linked to the main rivers and marked the points at which England's inland ports sprang up in the course of the Middle Ages.

In England, in Flanders, in the northernmost reaches of the North German rivers, the waterways were kept up more or less continually and more or less efficiently. We read of course of mills and fishing weirs obstructing the passage, of mudbanks allowed to form, but we also read of dredging operations, of repairs to banks and embankments, of prosecutions for neglecting and obstructing the care of the waterways. Indeed in this country the very frequency of complaints shows what medieval men expected from their waterways and bears indirect witness to the use men made of the transport facilities they found.

4

Viewed in retrospect, medieval trade seems abundantly provided with means of communications—roads, sea lanes, rivers. Drawn on the map the network may indeed appear more imposing than it in fact was, for the final test of a transport system is not its density on the map but its effects on costs; and the costs were doubtless higher than the plethora of routes and quasi-routes might suggest to the uninstructed. What the average costs in fact were, no historian could now so much as guess, and it is doubtful whether the guess would be worth making even if it could be made. The most salient feature of trading costs in the Middle Ages was their infinite variety—a variety which would distort and falsify any attempt to strike an average for the system as a whole. Even a cursory survey of freights and charges would reveal striking contrasts in costs at one and the same time along routes of equal length and of similar physical character. In times unfavourable to commerce and on routes least favoured by governments, the charges could be very high and indeed prohibitive. But it would of course be a truism to insist that being prohibitive they must not be taken to represent the average costs of trade along the main lines of communication. For on routes which were so heavily taxed, or were so badly served by transport, or were so profoundly disturbed by war and piracy as to be unsuited to active trade, traders were not in fact active. They frequented instead those routes on which transport was relatively free and cheap. In theory this may have raised the costs of trade higher than they might have been had the merchants' choice of routes been unrestricted and had all the potential trade routes been in service; but in practice merchants engaged in the main branches of medieval trade could in most times find routes which were reasonably cheap or at least not so costly as to justify excessive 'traders' margins' or greatly to restrict the demand for commodities and their supply.

Thus the few surviving figures of costs of cartage in and around the Hanseatic towns suggest that in the second half of the fourteenth century it was sufficiently low to make it possible to divert the grain trade to land routes at a time when the river traffic was being choked up by tolls and taxes. The same conclusion also emerges from the English evidence which is sufficiently abundant to justify an impression more nearly statistical. The manorial rolls and other surviving accounts suggest that the existence of the peasant reserve of carts kept the level of cartage costs low. In 1278 a long and expensive transport operation on the king's behalf from Rhuddlan via Chester to Macclesfield, a distance of about 70 miles, was carried out at an average cost of 6d. per day per cart with two horses. The average charge elsewhere appeared to be from 3d. to 4d. per carthorse per day. Thorold Rogers computed that where the service was carried out over long distances by common carriers, who bore the legal responsibility of bailees of the goods and had to undertake loading and unloading, the charge worked out at about 3½d. per ton per mile for the double journey. But the services of peasant carts were much cheaper. According to Thorold Rogers a peasant cart could be hired at any time of the Middle Ages at an average charge of 1d. per ton per mile when the journey there and back was made in a day, and the charge did not appreciably rise even after the price revolution of the sixteenth century. For Norfolk a local historian has assembled the local carting charges in the fifteenth century, and these often worked out if anything lower than Thorold Rogers' penny. At these rates the cost of transporting goods over 50 miles would in the middle of the fourteenth century be rather less than 1·5 % of the value of the cargo if it were wool, and about 15 % if it were grain.

Sea transport was even cheaper, so long as it followed the well established and regular sea lanes. The cost of shipping a tun of Gascon wine to Hull or Ireland at the end of the thirteenth century worked out at about 8s. per tun or rather less than 10 % of its f.o.b. price in Bordeaux. It appears that in the late fourteenth and fifteenth centuries the transport charges in relation to the f.o.b. prices were if anything lower than a century earlier. In the fifteenth century the transport costs of wool from London to Calais, including the costs of convoy, worked out at about 4s. per sack or rather less than 2 % of its f.o.b. price in London or Dover. A weigh (400 lb.) of coal cost about 2s. to transport from Newcastle to the South, presumably to the Low Countries, whereas transport charges of a certain shipload of about 200 tons of miscellaneous, mostly valuable, cargo from Bergen-op-Zoom to London in the middle of the fifteenth century worked out at £20, or 2s. per dead-weight ton.

These charges were not very high, and they may largely explain why it was that in such active and well-established branches of trade as English wool exports to the Low Countries or the Gascon wine exports to this country the distributors' margins were not exceptionally high even if judged by modern standards. The surviving evidence of the wool contracts and the figures given in a fifteenth-century treatise, the

Noumbre of Weyghtes, make it possible to estimate the average cost of handling wool on its way from the grower to the foreign buyer. The total cost of packing, transport from a midland county to London, custom and subsidy (the latter at the lower English rate), amounted to about £2. 13s. 4d. per sack. To this there has to be added the freight from London or another wool port to Calais, including the expenses of the convoy, which in the second half of the fifteenth century worked out at about 4s. per sack (6s. 8d. per sarpler of rather less than two sacks). The average price which an English exporter was expected to pay for a sack of high quality wool in the Cotswolds in the second half of the century averaged about £8, so that the total expenses would amount to about 40% of the inland price and would bring the total cost of a sack to a stapler in Calais to rather more than £11. The selling price of the fine Cotswold wool in Calais and Bruges fluctuated between £12 and £13, thus leaving a nominal profit of £1 to £2 per sack of fine wool. A certain amount of disguised profit was also made on various allowances and premiums for differences of weight, wastage, etc.[1]

It is also possible to estimate with some accuracy the cost of distribution of Gascon wine. We are told that the f.o.b. prices at Bordeaux in the second half of the fourteenth century established themselves somewhere in the neighbourhood of nine Bordeaux livres and were made up of 5 li. paid for grapes, for the making of wine and for brokerage, 1 li. 10 sous paid for transport to Bordeaux, and 2 li. 10 sous for Great Custom from which the merchants of Bordeaux and the privileged merchants were exempt. Sea transport to English ports of the south and east coast varied between 2 li. 10 sous and 5 li. per tun and about 1s. 6d. had to be paid for various dues in English ports. The costs in England therefore worked out somewhere in the neighbourhood of 14 livres or about £5, and the wholesale price for Gascon wine in London appeared to be not greatly in excess of that figure. Considering the length of the route and the many hands through which the wine had to pass on the way from the Gascon grower to the English vintner, the added charges were by no means out of proportion to the costs of transport and handling which were to prevail in the wine trade of later ages.[2]

A somewhat similar conclusion would probably emerge from the study of other 'regular' branches of northern commerce—Baltic timber, Skanian herring, Bay salt. In the first half of the fifteenth century the price of salt in Danzig immediately on arrival of the Bay fleet was

[1] 'The Noumbre of Weyghtes', Brit. Mus. Cotton, Vespasian E. ix; E. Power and M. Postan, *Studies in English Trade in the Fifteenth Century*, 70–2.

[2] R. Boutruche, *La Crise d'une Société*, 151, n. 1; Francisque Michel, *Histoire du Commerce et de Navigation à Bordeaux*, I, 123, 127.

barely twice that which, following Warwick's attack on the Bay fleet in 1449, the merchants claimed to be the cost of the salt at Bourgneuf. What is more, it competed in price with salt originating from Saxon and other nearby sources. Transport and expenses of handling were obviously not the main constituent of costs.

On the other hand, the trades which did not happen to enjoy the advantages of relatively free and cheap lines of communication could at times be weighed down with vast expenses *en route*. What is more, even in favoured trades, like the English wool exports or the Gascon wine trade, war and commercial conflict sometimes obstructed the normal channels and added greatly to costs. Whereas in normal years, e.g. in the first two decades of the fifteenth century, the wholesale prices of Baltic timber in English ports were barely twice those in its Polish places of origin, in the years of 1437 and 1438, when trade between England and Danzig was opened after an interval of embargoes, prices were exceptionally low in Poland, very high in England, and the distributive costs and profits were inordinately high. Wainscoting then cost little more than 2 marks per hundred in Poland and 5 marks in Danzig and fetched 24 marks in Yarmouth; bowstaves which cost 14 marks per great hundred in Danzig were 51 marks in England; planks (*klapholz*) about 10 marks in Danzig and 35 marks in England.[1] Similarly, in the middle and second half of the fifteenth century, when direct relations between England and Gascony were broken by war and French occupation, and Gascon wine had to find its way through neutral countries and neutral hands, the cost of transport and of handling was so high as greatly to reduce both the price in Bordeaux and the price in England and indeed to reduce the English wine trade to a mere shadow. Even in the English wool trade the costs were not elsewhere as low as they appeared to be along the route which led from the wool grower to the stapler in Calais. Thus, the Italian merchants and the Englishmen who sent wool to Italy in the fifteenth century must have found transport and other charges very high. To begin with, the Italian merchants in England had to pay what amounted to disguised bribes for licences to avoid the staple of Calais and they also had to pay higher export duty. The transport was also costlier. According to the record of expenses incurred in the shipment of the King's wool to Italy in the late seventies and early eighties of the fifteenth century, the freight of a sack carried by a galley to Venice amounted to £3. 3s. 4d.—which was much less than the costs by the land routes—and the total cost of a sack of wool to the exporter came to well over £14. The wool then sold in Venice at about £20 per sack, and the profit of £5 to £6 per sack was much higher than that earned by staplers on their shorter and safer route.

[1] Th. Hirsch, *Danzig's Handels- und Gewerbgeschichte*, VIII.

In short, medieval communications, like other trading activities, suffered much more from instability and uncertainty, political in origin, than from high costs of an inefficient transport service. Inefficient the service certainly was, wasteful of manpower and other resources; but so was also medieval industry and agriculture. Judged by modern standards the making and growing of goods for sale may well have been costlier than the carrying of the goods to the consumer. To put it more abstractly, the proportion of trading costs to total costs was probably less in the Middle Ages than it is now, which is merely another way of saying that far greater economies have resulted from industrial revolutions of the eighteenth and nineteenth centuries than from the corresponding improvements in transport and distribution. If so, this may be one of the reasons why men in the Middle Ages found it not only necessary but also possible to trade and why commerce played the part it did in the economic life of the Middle Ages. And if it can be shown —as it appears probable—that local taxation, war and piracy became more disturbing and more difficult to circumvent as the Middle Ages drew to their close, this may also help to account for some of the 'long-term' trends of medieval trade. These trends will form the subject of the remaining sections of this chapter.

II. *The Age of Expansion*

(1) THE ORIGINS

1

The goods entering northern trade were as a rule products of local agriculture and industry and were often sold and bought in small quantities out of current production. From this point of view the great inter-regional currents differed in little but magnitude from the operations on the local markets. The staple commodities of international trade were handled in bulk and travelled over longer distances, but there was no hard and fast line between local and international trade. Both depended upon the surpluses of local production, rural and urban, and both grew with the general expansion of population and production.

It should therefore be possible to account for the 'origin' of northern trade without invoking any special cause not inherent in the general economic development of north-western countries themselves. Inter-regional trade, like the local trade from which it developed, was more or less endemic in the history of European society. Its use was familiar to prehistoric man, and there is therefore no reason why at the beginning of the Middle Ages men should have had to learn anew the lesson of its necessity and convenience. It has already been suggested that in the very choice of their *habitat* the tribal groups of Northern Europe appeared to assume the existence of inter-regional exchanges. For otherwise it would be very difficult to account for their deliberate migration into the waterlogged plains of the Rhine litoral, the fiords and uplands of Norway and the fenlands of Britain; or for the emergence at the very dawn of the Middle Ages in most European countries of specialised communities of sheepfarmers, fishermen, charcoal burners, saltmakers, and miners. It could of course be argued that in the early stages of medieval settlement men were able to wring a balanced supply of necessities from lands which eventually supported specialised economies. But some regions—fishing areas like the estuary of the Rhine, wool growing areas of Northern England—were fully specialised very early in the Middle Ages; and regional specialisation implies inter-regional exchange.

This does not, however, mean that specialised societies were the only ones to engage in trade. Some trade must have been essential even to agricultural areas capable of highly variegated cultivation and of a highly self-sufficient economy. For, however self-sufficient the large estates or the villages in the continental interior of North-western Europe in the Dark Ages, they were never entirely independent of commercial supplies from outside or unaffected by division of labour within. Few agricultural villages themselves produced their salt, their iron or all their textiles. And however closed the economy of a village, not all households in it were equally self-sufficient. From the earliest centuries of the Middle Ages there were to be found in the medieval villages and estates craftsmen—smiths, potters, and sometimes even carpenters and weavers. Among the peasant cultivators themselves there always existed smallholders, who had to work for wages, and substantial peasants, who had surpluses to dispose of. Rents, reckoned and often paid in money, were older than the oldest manorial documents; while wages were seldom paid wholly or entirely in kind. In order to pay rents the peasants had to sell their produce; and whenever wages were paid in money the wage-earners presumably spent them at the market. Indeed an unbiased student of medieval agriculture cannot avoid the conclusion that social existence in medieval villages would have been impossible without some market and some trade.

This conclusion is in the nature of things hypothetical, but it is sufficiently obvious to shift the onus of proof from those who assume some trade at all historical times to those who wish to deny its existence at any period of the historical, as distinct from the pre-historical, past.

2

In this sense medieval trade never 'arose'; but it undoubtedly expanded and contracted. During the six or seven centuries of its documented history the quantities of goods entering European markets grew and declined; and so did the area in which they circulated. But whereas the territorial scope of medieval trade is on the whole easy to trace on the medieval map, the changes in the volume of northern trade are very largely a matter of guess. So scanty is the quantitative evidence of medieval trade that it is not surprising to find historians still differing about the scale as well as the chronology of economic growth. As late as the eve of the first Great War they were still able to assume a trend which closely corresponded to the distribution of the evidence. The paucity of records of trade in the early Middle Ages was taken to signify the scarcity of the trade itself, while the wealth of evidence in the fourteenth and fifteenth centuries was taken to mean that trade had grown in the intervening centuries. In dealing with individual regions historians may sometimes have been unable to fit them into the general curve, but when it came to the trade of Western Europe as a whole they invariably represented the course of commercial development as a line steadily rising from the Dark Ages, when trade virtually disappeared, to the sixteenth century when it flourished abundantly.

Most obvious of all appeared to be the starting point of the story. Historians could take it more or less for granted that the irruption of the barbarians meant a complete break with the economic civilisation of the Roman Empire. The trade of Rome died a violent death, and with its demise European economy sank into a 'natural' condition, innocent of all industry and exchanges. Under the late Merovingian kings the Germanic societies were supposed to have moved forward far enough to acquire some trade and the rudiments of a settled urban life, but the advance did not become really rapid until the so-called Carolingian Renaissance. Soon after, the trade may for a time have been held back by the Norman and Saracen invasions and by the feudal anarchy of the ninth and tenth centuries. By the eleventh century, however, the pressure at the frontiers eased, and economic development and commercial expansion could be resumed and continued without break till the age of the 'great discoveries'.

The line, thus drawn, is straight and continuous—too straight and continuous for the present generation of historians. It is no longer possible to believe in the continued expansion of trade throughout Europe in the closing centuries of the Middle Ages, and more will be said about this later. There are also reasons for being doubtful about the beginning of the story. The starting point of the old version has been assailed and, probably, destroyed by converging attacks from two co-belligerent, though not necessarily allied, historical schools: Dopsch's and Pirenne's. Alfons Dopsch and his followers, basing themselves on their own interpretation of the literary evidence (principally Tacitus) as well as on recent archaeological evidence (principally the excavations in the Roman *Limes*), have attacked both the notion of the primitive barbarism of the German invaders and that of the complete break with the material civilisation of Rome. Dopsch found no difficulty in showing that in the 150 years between Caesar and Tacitus the Germanic societies had acquired most of the attributes of a fully articulated economic civilisation, including the use of coinage and the dependence on trade. He also discounted the accounts of the total destruction wrought by the barbarians upon the material fabric of the Roman countries in which they settled. Urban life in the older Roman towns had declined but had not wholly disappeared. The Merovingian age, having thus inherited some of the commercial life of Rome, carried it on until it merged into the ascending movement of the Carolingian age.

But for this assumed continuity between the Carolingian and the Merovingian ages, Pirenne's view of Merovingian trade is not much different from Dopsch's. He also found it easy to show that the economic life of the Roman provinces in Western Europe continued uninterrupted, even if impoverished, throughout the Merovingian age. Commercial relations with the East persisted; Syrian merchants and their goods circulated throughout Europe; and Marseilles still remained Europe's doorway into the Mediterranean and the Levantine world. A break did occur in the end, but according to Pirenne it took place not at the outset of the Dark Ages, but in the Carolingian epoch. In the eighth and ninth centuries Saracen invasions and Muslim domination in the Mediterranean broke Europe's commercial links with the South, while in the North, economic life—including urban life in general—dwindled and declined under the stress of Viking raids and conquests.

The difference between the two points of view is thus largely focused on the exact role of the Carolingian age, and to that extent has not yet been fully resolved. The weight of the argument, however, appears to be against the theory of a violent break in the eighth and ninth centuries. The commercial links with the East and the traffic of costly luxuries may have suffered from the Muslim conquests and from the general insecurity of the times. But economic activity—settlement, colonisation, agricultural production—continued to expand; and in the history of European trade, economic activity within Europe mattered more than ease of communication with the outside world. For it has already been shown that northern trade was more dependent on the production of Northern Europe itself than it was on the conditions in the Eastern Mediterranean. The recurrent periods of disorder and anarchy during the Norman raids may have interfered with economic activities of every kind, but recent evidence from the North of France suggests that the ruin and devastation which the Norman invasions brought with them did not break the continuity of urban life in places like Arras. On the British side, the accumulating evidence points not only to the early development of trade across the Channel but to its continued functioning throughout the Dark Ages.

Yet, whatever is the final verdict on the Carolingian 'break', there can be little doubt about the continuity of development between the fourth and the seventh centuries. In Europe no violent break had intervened between the centuries officially Roman and those officially Barbaric, and there is equally little doubt that from the end of the tenth century onwards trade, like economic life in general, entered upon a period of rapid and general expansion.

(II) THE GROWTH

1

The course of medieval trade from the tenth century onwards can be traced both in its changing volume and in its expanding geography. From both points of view the trade grew until some time in the fourteenth century. The volumes of medieval production and of trade were on the increase, but expansion quantitatively considered was not its only significant feature. During this period northern economy was, so to speak, formed, for it was then that its separate regions, its trade routes and its commercial connections, composed themselves into a single trading area. In addition, throughout this period the trading area gradually spread eastwards and ended by absorbing the whole of Central and Eastern Europe.

The expanding volume of trade was a part of an economic process so general and so all-embracing that its story is easier to tell as an episode in the history of population and agriculture than as part of a narrower history of trade. For it was in agriculture and settlement that the signs of expansion were most obvious. In countries like England, where from the beginning of the thirteenth century onwards manorial documents can be made to yield something in the nature of statistical evidence, the growth of output can be traced for at least a century. But here and there, as on the estates of the bishopric of Winchester in 1209, production at the beginning of the thirteenth century already stood so high that the historian cannot fail to discern behind the later figures the dim outlines of an earlier increase stretching far back into the eleventh century and beyond.

The impression is greatly reinforced by what can be learned about settlement and population all over North-western Europe in the eleventh, twelfth and the thirteenth centuries. England and the continent west of the Elbe were rapidly filling up. In England the comparison of the population data in the Domesday Book with that of the manorial surveys of the twelfth century and the early thirteenth century, and of the latter with the Hundred Rolls of 1279 and the later manorial documents (rough and ready as such comparisons are bound to be), will show agricultural holdings multiplying manifold, and areas under cultivation growing apace. French evidence, mostly monastic, from Burgundy, Normandy and elsewhere in the tenth and eleventh centuries, German evidence from the Rhineland, Westphalia, Lower Saxony and Holstein; and, above all, the evidence from Flanders, tell the same story of growing population and expanding cultivation.

By the turn of the twelfth and thirteenth centuries the process had gone far enough for the surplus population to break out of the confines of what was now an old and relatively over-populated land and to spill over into new 'colonial' lands east of the Elbe. Here and there—as in Artois in the late eleventh and twelfth centuries, Flanders in the late twelfth and thirteenth, and possibly in parts of Champagne at the turn of the twelfth and thirteenth, and parts of westernmost Germany in the thirteenth—population was so abundant as to seek a solution to its economic problem in general industrialisation. It will be shown later that this period saw the rise of most of the great regional industries— that of cloth in Artois and Flanders, and probably Champagne; that of metal goods in Cologne, Liège and Dinant; that of iron and coal, lead and tin, in England, Hainault, Eastern France and South Germany. But even in those parts of Europe, which did not industrialise during this period, the towns were receiving great and ever-growing reinforcements from the surplus population of the countryside.

This was indeed the time when the whole of Western Europe became urbanised. Towns large and small sprang up all over the continent; most of them, whether old or new, grew fast throughout the period. In Flanders and in North Germany surviving topographical evidence, chiefly early maps, has enabled students to lay bare the main stages of urban expansion in the Middle Ages and to show how growing settlement added suburb to borough and repeatedly burst through successive girdles of urban fortifications. Elsewhere, and more especially in England and Central France, the evidence of urban growth is less direct, but is none the less convincing. In the rural records of the time, as well as in its literary sources, the town figures as the place of opportunity to which the villein might flee in search of freedom and wealth. That in most of the greater towns of the eleventh, twelfth and thirteenth centuries opportunities were more or less unlimited is indirectly borne out by the prevailing freedom of immigration—a freedom which was not to be regulated and restricted until much later in the Middle Ages.

2

Growing production, both agricultural and industrial, and increasing population were bound to lead to greater trade and are sufficient to account for its expanding volume. Other favourable developments, more purely commercial and more directly involved with the processes of trade, may also have made their contribution; and one of them—the influx of bullion—may have played an important and certainly a conspicuous part. Increasing supplies of precious metals and their expanding circulation, may at times have influenced the prices of commodities (and more about it will be said presently). Now and again they may also have influenced agricultural and industrial invest-ment, and may thereby have given a further stimulus to both prices and production.

Recently, historians have laid special emphasis on the part which gold played as a means for the settlement of international accounts. It was Marc Bloch who first drew attention to the part which gold played in commercial exchanges between East and West, and it was he who first connected the main phases in the early history of international trade with the redistribution of gold in the world. Other students have supplemented Bloch's thesis and showed how dependent was the foreign trade of the Roman Empire on Rome's ability to pay for Eastern sup-plies in gold. In the last two centuries of the Empire supplies of gold dwindled away and Rome's purchasing power in the East declined; yet in the early centuries of the Merovingian era enough Roman gold was still available in the West to make it possible for the Frankish society to make some use of the as yet open channels of travel and commerce with Byzantium and the Levant. With the Muslim conquests, however, the world supplies of gold were radically redistributed. The Muslim conquerors acquired both the accumulated stocks of precious metals and the monopoly of supplies of newly mined gold. Starved of gold, European commerce with the East languished, and its *malaise* continued until the tenth century. It was not until the turn of the millennium that Muslim countries began to import slaves, metal goods, timber, and other commodities of European origin in quantities large enough to change the direction of gold movements. Eastern gold entered again into circulation, trade between West and East was resumed, and through it the whole economic life of Europe revived.[1]

This thesis, however questionable in detail, is in the main supported by a certain amount of evidence and can be accepted as a working hypothesis. Yet, even if it were fully borne out by further researches, it would still be insufficient to account for the evolution of northern trade. The commercial currents directly dependent upon supplies of gold were those which flowed to and from the Eastern Mediterranean. They doubtless touched economic life in the North at many points. Northern and Western Europe as a whole may now have enjoyed (if 'enjoyed' is the right term) an active balance of trade, with the result that gold was now coming into many a country producing raw materials. Italian florins and ducats and perhaps Byzantine and Arabian gold coins now augmented the local resources of currency—mostly silver—and gold coinage began to be minted. But more important than the Italian supplies of Levantine and Byzantine gold was the real wealth which growing commerce generated. Much of it found its way into the hands of merchants all over Europe and could now be invested in industry and trade. Its chief beneficiary was doubtless Italy and, more especially, its great commercial cities, but from there radiating circles of investment and prosperity reached the outlying countries of medieval Europe, and it is doubtful whether any part of the continent escaped their effects altogether.

Yet, the effects on the trade of Northern Europe could only be indirect. The opening of the Levant added relatively little to the demand for raw materials and manufactured commodities of European origin (metal goods being the chief exception). Slaves were the commodity which was most in demand in Islamic lands in the early Middle Ages and which, if we are to trust some recent studies, was mostly responsible for starting and maintaining the flow of gold from the East. But the traffic in slaves touched the economy of Northern Europe at very few points, if at all. In the Dark Ages, i.e. between the seventh and eleventh centuries, the trade was largely in the hands of Jews and Syrians who took their 'cargoes' across Russia, Poland and Western Germany to Spain and countries further East. Here and there they may have formed commercial *nuclei* within Europe: we are told that Verdun was an entrepôt centre of the slave trade, and it is possible that merchants resident there took part in the traffic. But from the point of view of Western Europe generally, this was merely a transit

---

[1] M. Bloch, in *Annales d'Hist. Econ. et Sociale* (1933), 4 ff. M. Lombard, *ibid.* (1947), 143 ff. In England the issue of 1343 is generally regarded as the first effective gold coinage in the Middle Ages, even though gold coins had been minted some hundred years earlier by Henry III.

trade skirting the outer fringes of its territory and leaving behind very little oriental gold. Later, from the eleventh century onwards, other commodities of European origin, such as cloth (and furs!), found their way East, and raw materials imported from the North went into the making of the Italian goods exported to the Levant. Yet the total quantities of continental goods thus exported were as yet barely sufficient to redress the entire balance of Europe's trade with the Muslim world and to support the commercial prosperity of the North.

Did the crusades make much difference? The idea that the crusades were a turning point in the history of European economy is one of the most cherished notions of economic history; and so also is the belief that having conquered the Holy Land the northern world proceeded to help itself to the wealth of the Levant. How true it is and whether true at all is a problem which more properly belongs to the history of Mediterranean trade. The repercussions of the crusades must however be mentioned here, even if the mention can only be of the briefest and vaguest.

An economic history of the crusades has not yet been written, but until it has been written, and the economic balance of the crusades has been struck, it will be difficult to say whether their consequence was to augment the flow of gold from Italy and the Levant to the continent of Europe, or on the contrary to drain the continent of its precious metals. Most probably the trickle of gold frequently changed direction, and at times contrary movements cancelled each other out. The occupation of the Holy Land may, to begin with, have brought in booty and ransom, and so must also have done the sack of Constantinople in 1204. On the other hand, ransom sometimes had to be paid and booty yielded to the Muslims. We are told that Richard I's ransom alone was the equivalent in value to 50,000 woolsacks, or much more than a whole year's exports. Similarly, crusading expeditions more often than not set up a drain on the western means of payment. The countries which sent them out financed them with levies and taxes; crusading nobles raised funds at home in many and various ways, but mostly by loans on which they could draw abroad. These methods of financing must have helped to mobilise the hoarded reserves of gold and silver, and thus indirectly to quicken the circulation and to influence prices and economic activity in general. Yet they must also have depleted the total supplies of gold in Northern Europe, since they sent precious metals moving away from continental Europe towards Italy and the Levant. Ecclesiastical taxation in support of the Latin kingdoms, the voyages to the Holy Lands, the military and religious activities of the Templars and the Hospitallers, must all have acted in the same fashion and added to the continental debit balance with Italy and the East.

This does not of course mean that the crusades did not stimulate the economic development of Europe, but the stimulus, such as there was, must have come from factors more general than mere importation of bullion. If Northern Europe felt it at all, it must have received it in the course of ordinary trading activities of the Italian merchants and through their expanding commercial and financial operations. In this revival bullion played its part, but it did so not by virtue of its function in international accounts, but as a result of its internal circulation and investment. And here again the Levantine current was a mere tributary, and probably a small one, of a far more abundant flow. Although Italians brought into Champagne, Flanders and England a certain amount of gold, mainly of their own coining, the bullion most in circulation was not Levantine or Byzantine and not even predominantly Italian. What is more, it was not gold.

Throughout the Middle Ages, and more especially in their earlier centuries, the precious metal most commonly used in coinage and in everyday payments was silver. The coins of Northern Europe until the second half of the thirteenth century were all silver, and continued to be predominantly silver until the end of the Middle Ages. The evidence of mints, such as the accounts of the royal mints of England and the surviving registers of urban mints and exchanges, makes it quite clear that silver formed the bulk both of existing stocks of money and of the new accretion of metal. Gold and gold coins were relatively more common in international dealings presumably because gold was more convenient to transport and also somewhat more stable in value. In addition gold coins had the advantage of being as yet few—mostly Italian—and therefore free from the curse of variety and heterogeneity which afflicted the silver currencies of Europe. For these and other reasons, in clearing accounts of Italian merchants at the Champagne fairs of the thirteenth century as well as in commercial dealings of Italian merchants in other parts of Northern Europe, payments were apt to be reckoned in gold coins. Similarly, royal debts to Italian bankers in England and France were frequently reckoned in ducats and florins. Yet there is no evidence that the Italian bankers in fact delivered equivalent sums in gold cash, and there is unmistakable evidence that loans reckoned in gold coins, such as the Frescobaldi loans to Edward I and the Bardi loans to Edward III, were often made and repaid in silver and in goods. And in international payments between merchants of other nationalities active in Northern Europe silver pounds and marks, English and Flemish, were most commonly used both as units of account and of payment. So even if it remains true that gold figured prominently in international payments it did not wholly displace silver even there.

The bullion in circulation was thus predominantly silver, and it is very probable that the amount of silver circulating in the twelfth and thirteenth centuries increased. How large the increases were cannot be said with certainty, but it is obvious that the increases came from several sources. Some new silver doubtless originated from mines recently opened up. Although silver must have been mined in Europe throughout the Dark Ages, the main sources of European silver, in Hungary, in Saxony, in the Harz mountains and elsewhere, were not fully developed until the tenth, eleventh and twelfth centuries. Mines, however, were not the only and may not even have been the chief source of additional silver, for even in the earlier centuries of the Middle Ages the volume of currency depended not only on the additions of newly mined metal but also on the uses of accumulated stocks of bullion. For it appears highly probable that the economic changes of the twelfth century set into motion a great deal of wealth previously immobilised in hoards, plate or ornaments. And that the bulk of the bullion thus 'de-hoarded' must have consisted of silver is clearly brought out by the evidence of wills and mint accounts.

So whether any came in through the early medieval contacts with the Levant, or during the crusades, imported bullion could not be held responsible for the revival and growth of medieval trade. Some of the other monetary factors were more important, but even they were not and could not be decisive. Their influence on trade would normally be transmitted through changes in price levels; yet even changing prices had a limited effect.

3

The problem of prices is, in Italy at least, closely involved with that of monetary circulation. We know now that during the earlier centuries of the Middle Ages, i.e. before the thirteenth, some prices changed a great deal. From the very moment at which documentary references to them become at all frequent, i.e. from the middle of the twelfth century in England, and from the middle of the thirteenth century abroad, until the first quarter of the fourteenth century, food prices appeared to move steadily upwards. The English prices alone have so far been assembled for the earlier period. The work of collection and tabulation is as yet far from complete, but Thorold Rogers and later Lord Beveridge's team of archivists and historians have been able to analyse their data in a manner which enables a statistical trend to be traced.

Expressed in percentages the prices of 1150 were about 30% of those in the first quarter of the fourteenth century; in other words the price rise in the intervening period was about three-fold. The price rise did not, moreover, begin in 1150, and, as far as the scanty evidence suggests, it went beyond that date. In so far as the figures of South-western Germany collected by Lamprecht can be relied upon, they suggest a progressive rise in prices from the eighth and ninth centuries to the tenth and eleventh, continued, though not so violently as in England, to the early thirteenth. Yet even Lamprecht's figures show a rise of at least 50% between the second half of the twelfth century and the first half of the thirteenth.[1]

Table I. *English Wheat Prices, 1160–1339*[2]

(Twenty years' means)

Period	Wheat price in shillings (per qr.)	Wheat price in grains of silver (per qr.)
1160–79	1·89	534
1180–99	2·60	744
1200–19	4·33	1082
1220–39	4·19	1047
1240–59	4·58	1144
1260–79	5·62	1404
1280–99	5·97	1491
1300–19	7·01	1734
1320–39	6·27	1547

This was a veritable price revolution. Yet, in considering its economic effects, it is important not to argue by analogy with price revolutions of later centuries. For reasons which will have to be mentioned again more than once, the effect of price changes could not have been very general or widespread.

Agricultural output was bound to react to a secular rise in grain prices so steep and continuous, but its reactions may have differed from region to region. In the wine- and wool-growing areas of Europe, where the rural economy was one of cash crops, and even in certain areas predominantly arable, such as parts of Western and Northern France and above all Southern England, estates continued to be run as large units producing mainly for the market, and even peasants marketed a considerable proportion of their output. And where the proportions to be sold were high, rising prices must have favoured and stimulated both output and sales. Indeed, the social historian of English agriculture cannot escape the conclusion that the high prices of the late twelfth and thirteenth centuries and the commercial boom in agricul-

[1] K. Lamprecht, *Deutsches Wirtschaftsleben im Mittelalter*, II, 512 ff.; esp. tables, etc., on pp. 612–13.

[2] Cited by the courtesy of Lord Beveridge.

tural produce were to some extent responsible for the continued survival of the large-scale units of agriculture.

To this extent the agricultural boom left its impression on European trade. As cultivation of cash crops expanded, larger quantities of agricultural products came on the markets; as rural wealth grew, opportunities for miscellaneous trade widened. Thus far the effect of prices is clear enough. What is not so clear is whether regions where the bulk of agricultural production was in the hands of peasants were equally affected. And it is not known how far industrial commodities, industrial raw materials and industrial regions were directly involved in the price changes. Historians do not even know how the prices of non-agricultural commodities moved, if they moved at all. Evidence is very scanty and difficult to interpret. Such as there is suggests that prices for commodities like cloth and iron goods rose less steeply and less continuously than food prices. Prices for some commodities like coal and timber may even have fallen.

It is thus probable that price movements of the twelfth and thirteenth centuries were not 'general' in the sense in which the term is sometimes employed to indicate more or less simultaneous and synchronous shifts in the price levels in all the main groups of commodities. If so, the probability is that such changes as there were were not due to monetary causes. Not only the influx of foreign gold but even the far more important supplies of silver and the still more important changes in its employment and circulation, could not have been the prime movers in the great economic transformation of the period—a transformation of which the expansion of trade was merely a part.

There is no need, however, to end the discussion of prices on this agnostic note. For even if the price movements fail to establish bullion's responsibility for the commercial efflorescence of the age, they can still reveal the action of other and perhaps more effective causes. More especially, steep and continuous changes in food prices unaccompanied by similar changes in other prices make it more or less certain that the relative costs of agricultural production were rising, and this again indicates a growing pressure of population against land.

This is not the place to discuss general problems of medieval land and population; in so far as they are relevant to the history of trade they will be discussed again in a later section. Here it will suffice to note that all available evidence, especially for France and England, shows land rents, land prices, and entry fines rising on a scale fully consistent with the hypothesis of 'pressure of population'. In this way the discussion of prices merely brings the argument of this chapter to the point at which it digressed to gold and monetary causes. Trade grew because Europe expanded. The lands of continental Europe carried an ever-growing population; growing population, in its turn, meant that agricultural production increased, that industries developed and that whole regions became industrialised. And growing wealth of rural Europe and economic specialisation of its regions meant bigger and better trade.

(III) THE PROFESSIONAL MERCHANT

1

Growth quantitatively considered was by no means the only important change in the history of medieval trade in its age of expansion. It was accompanied by other phenomena, less material, and more obviously related to the condition and behaviour of men.

One of them was the extension of professional trade. In general, the part which full-time merchants played in economic life, very insignificant to begin with, was becoming more important as time went on. Doubtless, some professional trade there must always have been. We are told of the Syrian and Jewish merchants visiting Gaul at the dawn of the Merovingian age, and probably forming in the predominantly rural societies of Western Europe alien *nuclei* of resident merchants, not unlike the Jewish towns and townlets in the eastern states of nineteenth-century Europe. A travelling Jewish merchant of the eighth, ninth and tenth centuries arriving in Western Europe from the East counted on finding there his coreligionists with whom he could trade, live and pray. When we are told by Gregory of Tours that, on his entering into Orléans, King Guntram was welcomed in Syrian, Latin and Hebrew, the presumption is that in the sixth century these were the native tongues of the merchants of Orléans.

Yet be it noted that merchants whose tongue was Latin were not altogether absent from the rudimentary communities of merchants. Evidence of indigenous merchants is scanty but is not altogether absent. We may know little about Philo, the merchant, whom Ausonius knew, or about Euphron of Bordeaux or about Eusebius of Paris, both mentioned by Gregory of Tours—their names like their age still appear to belong to Rome. But from the seventh century onwards evidence of merchants wholly indigenous becomes more frequent and more certain. In the seventh century King Dagobert founded the Fair of St Denis which Franks, Frisians and Saxons (Anglo-Saxons?) frequented; in the same century we hear of Frankish merchants travelling into the lands of the Slavs and Avars.

Some of the indigenous merchants were doubtless men of substance, like Christophe of Tours, who, we are told, speculated in the wine of Orléans, but in the main they must have been small fry, travelling hucksters of foreign wares. Their stock in trade must have consisted almost entirely of the small luxuries required on the medieval estates and villages: spices, silks, and other exotic fineries. For when it came to the buying and selling of agricultural commodities or of industrial articles locally produced, the services of the merchant were not always necessary. In medieval Europe, as in agricultural areas of our own day, the average producer was able to dispose of the petty surpluses of his household (eggs, cheese, hens, vegetables, milk, cattle and even grain) without the assistance of a professional trader. Similarly, wherever an industry happened to be organised in small handicraft units and goods were made in small quantities or to order, producers and consumers could deal with each other without the intervention of a trader. Not only the village smith and potter, but the urban butcher, baker and candlestick-maker themselves disposed of their produce. Even in the later centuries of the Middle Ages the distinction between craftsman and trader remained a very nebulous one, and men commonly traded with goods they themselves produced.

Merchantless trade, moreover, was not confined to transactions which were purely local. Manorial produce often travelled over long distances, and manorial trade in the early Middle Ages was sometimes in the hands of manorial officers themselves. Some of the larger estates were sufficiently large, and the quantities of marketable commodities which they produced were sufficiently great, to enable them to do their own selling, though perhaps it would be rash to assume that they always did so. Historians have made great play of the monastic *negotiatores* of the early Middle Ages, who were trade representatives of monastic houses selling their output in distant markets and sometimes making there the necessary purchases for their communities. The term *negotiatores* must not however be taken too literally. Some of the *negotiatores* were monks and manorial officials, but some may well have been professional merchants acting in the name of monastic houses and under their protection, just as the 'king's merchants' of the English kings of the thirteenth century traded under the protection of king's letters, but in a manner and on a scale wholly professional.

Much more important were certain other forms of non-professional or not wholly professional commerce, and most important of all was the commercial activity of certain semi-rural communities. There was nothing to prevent the members of the fishing and seafaring communities of Zealand and the Rhine estuary from venturing far away from their homeland in pursuit of markets and goods. The sea could not by itself provide for all their needs, but it enabled them to go anywhere they pleased in search of customers and supplies. Similarly, the fiords of Norway could neither feed nor occupy all the population throughout the year, and there was nothing to prevent the free Norse peasants from roaming the seas and visiting foreign lands. In this way a great deal of trade could be conducted all over Europe by men who were, so to speak, part-time merchants.

There was thus a great deal of non-professionalised commerce: rather more in the early Middle Ages than later. Indeed, what historians sometimes describe as the period where medieval trade 'arose' may merely refer to the time when conditions favouring part-time trade disappeared and a professional merchant class spread.

Some such unprofessional commerce could of course be found even in the later Middle Ages. Monastic communities acted as traders whenever and wherever they happened to derive their income from large and regular production of marketable commodities. The English wool-growing monasteries of the twelfth, thirteenth and fourteenth centuries not only sold their wool clip regularly to foreign exporters but often undertook to supply them with *collecta*, i.e. wool they themselves bought up from the surrounding countryside. We can also find English landlords dabbling in wool trade in every century of the Middle Ages; squire and squireen of Gascony taking a hand in wine trade, landlords on both sides of the English channel—in Devon as well as in Brittany—maintaining ships for piracy and trade. Similarly, seafaring communities of Zealand, Holland, Normandy and Brittany continued to combine a little trade and occasional piracy with their main occupations of fishing and shipping.

Broadly speaking, however, conditions in the later centuries were less favourable to part-time commerce than they had been at the dawn of the Middle Ages. In a number of medieval towns production of some commodities soon outstripped the potentialities of the local market. Cloth of the principal cloth-making towns of Northern France and Flanders, metal goods of the towns of Western Germany—to name only two most obvious instances—came to be made in large quantities for the distant and unknown demand; and whenever this happened the petty producer could not market his output, and the services of a merchant intermediary became unavoidable.

Still more significant and less obvious were the similar developments in the countryside. Feudal society and feudal law soon made it impossible for the average members of a rural community to combine agriculture with trade, while the passing of the large-scale demesne economy removed the *raison d'être* for the manorial *negotiatores*. In England it is possible to lay bare in the records of the wool trade the process whereby the social changes in wool-growing areas called forth a new merchant class. As the numbers of small sheepfarmers grew, so professional wool merchants interposed themselves between wool growers and wool exporters. The history of the grain merchant and fishmonger has not been investigated as fully as that of the wool merchant; but it seems more than probable that a similar connection was also to be found there.

2

The development of trade as a whole-time occupation played its part in the rise of towns. The story of the towns, their appearance and growth, does not belong to this chapter. Growth of towns has so far been mentioned as evidence of the general expansion of medieval economy, and need not be mentioned again except in so far as it was linked with the social transformation of trading activities. For so linked it doubtless was. Most historians are now agreed that the towns multiplied and grew in the two centuries following the tenth, for the simple reason that trade grew. Yet the logical and historical connection between growing trade and emerging towns is by no means an inevitable one. The Norsemen proved capable of engaging in active trade without towns; it is not at all certain that Dorstad and some of the other places mentioned as centres of Frisian trade in the seventh and eighth centuries were towns in the medieval and modern sense of the term and not merely clusters of fishing and seafaring settlements. At the very close of the Middle Ages most of the English wool trade was in the hands of merchants living in the country, and the bulk of cloth industry was in the hands of men who combined spinning and weaving with some agricultural pursuits and lived in what still were essentially rural habitations.

Indeed as long as industry and trade could remain part-time oc-cupations and be in the hands of men who were also peasants, fishermen, landlords or monks, there was no need and little opportunity for com-mercial and industrial towns. The reason why at the height of the Middle Ages towns became necessary and indeed inevitable was not merely that trade expanded, but also that conditions of feudal society made it difficult for the expanding trade to remain in the hands of the rural classes and to be combined with other rural pursuits. At a time when life and all its vocations had become wholly professional, when war and government had become the exclusive occupation of the landlord and the freeholder, and when agriculture had become the whole-time occupation of the semi-servile peasant, trade had to become equally professionalised. Gone were the times when farmers from Norwegian fiords, fishermen of Frisia, and monk procurators of monastic estates or privileged officials of the Carolingian estates were able to run all the trade there was. Trade was becoming to an ever increasing degree the affair of whole-time merchants and artisans trading in a professional way.

The effect on towns was obvious. In order to be professional and to conduct trade all the year round merchants and artisans had to be exempt from the ties and liabilities which restricted the liberty of movement and freedom of contract of the lower orders of feudal society. Their houses and tenements with their shops had to be free from the obligations which burdened the rural tenures; their trans-actions had to be judged by a law better suited to dealings between merchant and merchant than were the feudal custumals and common law. Hence the essential function of the medieval towns, as non-feudal islands in feudal seas; and hence their appearance in large numbers in the eleventh century—the time when trade grew and feudal order matured. Hence also the crucial part which the charters of privilege (which were nothing else than guaranteed exemptions from feudal order) played in the origin and development of towns. Charters of this kind created boroughs out of villages, and cities out of castle suburbs; and charters of this kind punctuated the subsequent progress of urban communities on their way to full urban status. The rising town was thus essentially a political and legal phenomenon, even though it served an obvious economic function.[1]

3

The argument is obvious enough, yet it may at first sight appear to clash with what historians have recently discovered about the social history of the early medieval towns. The growing volume of historical studies of the so-called patrician families suggests that the upper layers of urban society in the Middle Ages sprang from the families which happened to own land in the towns in the early stages of their history, and got rich as the rents and land values of town property rose. In detail the process may have differed from region to region, but in general, towns as different as Arras in the eleventh century, Barcelona in the twelfth century, and Lübeck in the early thirteenth seem to con-form to the common pattern. In all of them political and economic power in the early phases of their history belonged wholly or in part to the urban landowners or their descendants. Indeed, so general and so obvious was the landed interest in medieval towns that a generalising sociologist like Sombart was able to base on it his entire theory of medieval capitalism and to find in rising land rents the chief source of the 'initial' capital of medieval industry and trade.

---

[1] This argument is not affected by the well-known fact that agriculture continued to play a part, often an important part, in the economic activities of smaller towns. However agricultural the small town was, what differentiated it from the regions purely rural was its nucleus of traders and artisans.

Stated in terms so general and so simple the theory may indeed be difficult to reconcile with the impression of the town as the seat of a professional merchant class. But was the history of the 'patriciate' in fact so uniform and so simple? In the first place not everywhere in Northern Europe was the citizen landowner a linear descendant of the original owner of town sites. Some towns in the early Middle Ages had grown up on land belonging to their feudal overlords, whether kings or great feudatories. In some towns feudal landlords proceeded to alienate the income from urban property by sub-infeudation, by sub-letting and by outright sale of full property rights (burgage tenures in England, allodial tenements in France). But in some places, especially in the *Villes Neuves* of Western Europe—artificial foundations of a somewhat later age—the feudal founders sometimes retained the superior title to property as well as its income. In the English boroughs and in some towns abroad, e.g. Bordeaux, the freehold and burgess tenures of urban sites were as a rule shared among a whole number of manorial landlords of the surrounding countryside: a fact which stimulated several German and English lawyers, and Maitland among them, to propound the famous garrison theory of borough origins.

Wherever the land was in feudal hands, and as long as it stayed there, the rising profits of urban landownerships largely by-passed the burgess inhabitants. Yet even in towns, where in the twelfth century the burgesses owned or otherwise held most of the land, they did so not so much by succession from the original landowners as through later investment. The famous history of the market of Lübeck, as expounded by Rörig, may indeed prove that the great Lübeck families had all sprung from a narrow circle of men who had taken part in the founding of Lübeck and owned the sites of the market place. But the same history also makes it clear that the urban landowners of Lübeck had come from merchant families of Westphalia and that their venture into landownership was merely an investment and part and parcel of their great commercial speculations beyond the Elbe.

Altogether the distinction between investment in trade and investment in land in the early medieval town can be drawn too rigidly. Not only did investments in land and urban rents come naturally to medieval merchants, but the reverse process—the investment into trade of wealth mainly derived from urban rents—was equally common and equally easy. Commercial partnership serving the purposes of investment had been known to European law since times pre-medieval. The sleeping partnerships of the *commenda* type were the general practice in Italian towns in the eleventh century; and the life of St Godric, which will be mentioned again presently, shows that the commercial partnerships were an established practice in eleventh-century England. And commercial partnerships, especially of the 'sleeping' kind, made it possible for urban wealth to be employed on a large scale in foreign trade, even if it happened to be derived from land.

Indeed this employment of wealth in speculative ventures to distant lands was more characteristic of the leading figures in medieval towns than their connection with land. If we are to trust Pirenne, the typical representatives of North European trade in the eleventh and twelfth centuries were the men he calls 'early capitalists', but who should be described more exactly as merchants trading abroad on a large scale. The trace they left in records is very faint, but here and there Pirenne was able to discern behind the fog and silence of early sources the fleeting shadows of the early capitalists. In one instance he was even able to draw a full-scale portrait of a merchant engaged in far-flung speculative trade. Godric, a trader of East Anglia at the turn of the eleventh and twelfth centuries, began as a beachcomber, became in the fullness of life a substantial merchant and a member of a partnership, and ended his life by becoming a saint and by inspiring a *Vita*.

In this the merchants of this age differed both from the class of small pedlars from which some of them must have originated and from the more sedate and less adventurous burgesses who were to dominate the trade in a later age. They were not primarily interested in the daily trade of the local market, and their indifference imprinted itself on the very economic character of the town. As long as they formed the governing group, the economic and social policy of the town itself was one of expansion, free immigration, and relatively free trade. Our direct evidence of free immigration and free trade is of course very scanty: perhaps because it is in the nature of free trade to leave behind scanty traces in documents. But had settlement and local trade been as restricted as they were to become later, towns and town population could not possibly have grown as we know that they did. For growth and expansion was the hallmark of the age.

(IV) THE MOVING FRONTIERS

1

The expanding and professionalised trade also had obvious geographical and political implications. Indeed, the economic geography of medieval trade and its involvement with international politics have been studied more fully and are understood better than almost any other aspect of the subject. For, unlike the other aspects of the history of trade, the story of moving frontiers and of emerging trade routes is compounded of war, politics and exploration, and has therefore been well illuminated by fully documented events. No wonder historians of trade have given them so much attention.

The attention, however, has been by no means unwarranted, for the political and geographical features of medieval commerce were not only conspicuous but also important. As trade increased and declined and as new regions were opened and old ones decayed, the whole balance of power in Northern Europe altered. Nothing indeed proves more the essential function of inter-regional commerce in medieval life than the part it played in the rise and fall of European principalities or in their political, military and naval power.

The purely political implications of economic geography are perhaps most obvious in the opening phase of medieval trade. The one geographical feature of North European trade in the Merovingian and early Carolingian period which historians take more or less for granted is its withdrawal from the world economy of the Roman Empire. The fall of Rome meant that in the sixth century Gaul, Brittany, and Rhineland no longer stood in the same relation to each other and to the rest of the world as three centuries previously. The economic links with Italy and the Mediterrranean were not altogether severed, but the trade was undoubtedly becoming more localised. At the height of imperial prosperity, i.e. in the second century, the Empire formed an economic system dominated by the needs and policy of metropolitan Italy. Needless to say, there were exchanges between the provinces and within each province taken separately, and it is a mistake to think that even at the height of the imperial era all roads led to Rome. Yet, broadly speaking, the main currents of Roman trade formed a co-ordinated system, to which each province made a distinct and sometimes a highly specialised contribution. This system began to disintegrate in the closing centuries of the Roman era and was all but gone in 473.[1] In the course of the fifth and sixth centuries, movements of inter-regional trade, such as there were, conformed ever more to the shifting needs and opportunities of the different northern regions and ceased to form part of an imperial network or to be dominated by imperial merchants.

Here are a few examples. In the third and fourth centuries Britain exported foodstuffs to feed the Roman legions on the Rhine. In the Merovingian age the exports to the lower Rhine did not cease—for all we know they may have grown—but they were dominated not by the needs of the Roman legions but by those of the population of the Rhineland and they now probably consisted of metals and cloth, both of which in the imperial times used to be taken elsewhere. Another example is the North Sea fisheries. At the height of the imperial era Roman merchants conducted from Utrecht an active fish trade between

[1] See above, pp. 76–85.

the delta of the Rhine and the more southerly provinces of the Empire.
In the Merovingian times fish continued to be exported, but it now
went in many other directions, including that of France and South
Germany, and was carried by local merchants. Similarly, Flemish, Frisian
and possibly English cloth, which may previously have been used to
clothe the Roman legions, was now carried, among other places, to
Scandinavia.[1]

2

This picture of northern trade, grown more local and directed away
from the centres of the Empire, is wholly compatible with what
we know of the activities of the Syrian merchants and the continued
imports of oriental goods into Marseilles. What Syrian merchants and
the port of Marseilles handled were probably the exotic goods of the
orient. The trade which was now becoming local and separate was the
trade in the bulky and essential goods which was the northern trade
par excellence; and such network of inter-regional exchanges as was now
emerging was woven, not by Syrian merchants, but by other and more
local groups of intermediaries.

Of these intermediaries, the earliest and the most prominent were the
Frisians. They owed their importance to the geographical opportunities
as well as to the geographical limitations of their land. Frisia stretched
along the coast of the North Sea from the estuary of the Sincfal (now
Zwin) to the estuary of the Weser. It was relatively infertile, but its
network of navigable rivers opening into the sea, and its well sheltered
channels between islands, fitted it well for fishing, navigation and
water-borne trade. Within it, the point which gathered to itself most
of the commerce was Dorstad on the old estuary of the Rhine: a place
of great renown, the 'city of forty churches'. Whether it in fact was
a great city or merely a conglomeration of fishing and trading villages
is a problem which archaeologists will have to decide, but it was already
important enough to stamp itself upon most of the earlier references to
Frisian trade. Later, especially in the ninth century, it rapidly lost its
importance, partly through its destruction by the Normans, but chiefly
through the change in the bed of the river from its old arm to the Waal.
When this happened, the town of Tiel on the Waal took Dorstad's
place, though in the process some of Dorstad's trade and much of its
political importance may have passed to Utrecht.

From these centres, and from the delta of the Rhine as a whole, an
entire network of routes radiated in every direction: to England, to
Gaul and Western Francia, to Scandinavia and the Baltic. When we

In Pirenne's view this orientation would not presumably take place until the
eighth century. Cf. F. Vercauteren, *Civitates de la Belgique Seconde*, 451–2.

read in a seventh-century sermon, such as Bede's, that London was an emporium of trade housing many foreign merchants, we have to think in the first instance of the Frisians, for Bede expressly mentions Frisian merchants in another place. In most references to foreign trade and foreign merchants in the eighth and ninth centuries the Frisians invariably figure. Liudger, a visiting Frankish ecclesiastic of the eighth century, mentions Frisian merchants in London, and so does Alcuin.

We know much more about their trade to the South. Their main point of entry into Western Francia was Quentovic (near modern Étaples), from which they visited Rouen, Amiens and the interior of Western France. Certain records of the first half of the eighth century show them active at the fair of St Denis, which was at that time the most important internal market in France. But most of their commerce to the South probably flowed along the Rhine. Down the Rhine they shipped corn and wine from Alsace; up the Rhine they took their cloth, fish and other goods to pay for the corn. They established settlements in the chief Rhenish towns, in Cologne, Duisberg, Xanten near Düsseldorf, Worms; but Mainz was probably their most important destination. The town was well placed at the junction of the Rhine route with the routes which came from the South and the South-east, and there the trade of the Danubian plain and the Black Sea region entered the commercial currents of Western Europe.

Even more ancient, if not more abundant, were their trade connections with Scandinavia. Archaeological and literary evidence points to the immemorial antiquity of Scandinavian trade. This trade was largely in the hands of Scandinavians themselves, but in one period some of it was in the hands of the Frisians. A ninth-century *Vita* of St Anscarius, a priest engaged in missionary work in Denmark and Sweden, reveals by a number of accidental details the commercial activities of the Frisians. Anscarius apparently travelled with Frisian merchants to Schleswig and from there to Birca, the Swedish trading centre in the Baltic.

Such was the territorial scope of Frisian trade. Yet the part the Frisians played in it must not be misunderstood. They were its chief intermediaries, but they did not dominate it. The commodities they exported did not all stay in Frisia and did not even necessarily pass through it. Nor were they alone to serve the trade routes on which we find them. Though very active in the Anglo-Saxon trade, they did not dominate it to the exclusion of English merchants. Similarly, Frisians seem to have traded very actively to Western Francia, but we know that there was also direct trade between the Franks and their neighbours, and that some of this trade was in the hands of native merchants.

3

Even more independent and more important was the part played
in the northern trade by the Scandinavians. In the economic history
of the ninth and tenth centuries the Norsemen left, if anything,
deeper trace than the Frisians had done in the preceding period. In
doing so they, like the Frisians, were largely impelled by the necessities of their geography. Like the Frisians, they had to seek their livelihood on the high seas and in foreign lands for the simple reason that
their own land was unable to feed them. Here and there, in Eastern
Denmark, in Southern Sweden, in parts of Southern Norway, men were
able all through the Middle Ages to lead lives little different from those
of agricultural communities in other parts of Western Europe. But
elsewhere in Scandinavia society was of necessity made up of part-time
peasants—men who lived on their farms part of the year and roamed
the seas or navigated distant rivers the rest of the year.

Some of them went to sea as fishermen, others as robbers, adventurers,
colonists and conquerors, still others went as traders; in fact, most of
them were fishermen, traders and conquerors in turn. It is very largely
as Vikings, i.e. as sea robbers and conquerors, that they appear in history
textbooks, but economic historians meet them as traders long before
their Viking expeditions began and long after they had ceased.

The Viking expeditions began in the first quarter of the eighth
century, but archaeological evidence shows that there had been some
trade between Scandinavian countries and the rest of Western Europe
since pre-historic times. Even in the worst period of the Viking wars
there was a great deal of purely commercial intercourse not only
between the Viking settlements, but between Scandinavia and non-
Scandinavian lands. The journey of St Anscarius, already mentioned,
took place shortly after the reputed burning of Dorstad by the Vikings.
Yet he travelled in a Frisian boat, and in Schleswig he met Danes who
were apparently in the habit of going to Dorstad with purely pacific
aims.

We must not therefore allow the tumult of the Viking era to obscure
the story of common trade done in the ordinary way. The fact that it
was both common and commonplace explains why so many of the
contemporary sources pass it in silence. Our chief evidence of the
raids are the sagas, and sagas were heroic stories about heroic men. Yet
even in the sagas we find references to trade in its peaceful and prosaic
forms. They sometimes refer to people who were merchants pure and
simple, and also mention expeditions undertaken without any predatory aims. We also know that the Scandinavians built and navigated
not only the swift assault boats in which they carried out their raids, but

also the slower and roomier cargo boats for commercial traffic. It is indeed probable that some parts of Scandinavia specialised in trade to the exclusion of raiding expeditions. Thus the Gotlanders who traded with all the countries of Northern Europe did not, as far as we know, send out a single identifiable Viking expedition, even though we find them occasionally engaged in Nordic wars.

Thus considered, Scandinavian trade formed part of that network of commercial connections which we saw taking shape in North-western Europe under the leadership of the Frisians. In some respects, however, its part in North-western commerce was different from that of the Frisians, the Anglo-Saxons or the Franks. In the first place, the Scandinavian trade reached its highest point after the Frisians had begun to decline. In the second place, it far transcended in its range the older limits of northern commerce. In their voyages the Norsemen penetrated to Greenland and the coast of North America in the West, to the Bosphorus in the East; and while their western expansion was not of very great importance to European commerce, their eastern voyages were to have the greatest political and economic consequences. They forged a link between North-western Europe and the Baltic, and in addition they established important land routes across the continent of Eastern Europe.

The Baltic and the lands round it were until the eleventh and twelfth centuries well outside the scope of western commerce, just as they were outside the range of Germano-Latin Christian civilisation. But they were well within the range of Scandinavian contacts. The Scandinavians crossed and recrossed the sea on their way to the Baltic islands and from there to the Baltic coasts of modern Mecklenburg, Pomerania, Prussia and Livonia, and apparently maintained an active commercial intercourse with the inhabitants of these shores, Slavonic and Ugro-Turkish.

We know very little about the trade and navigation of the Baltic before the tenth century. There is little doubt that the Slav tribes inhabiting the Baltic coast had navigated the sea routes and traded by them. Jumne, on the Isle of Wollin at the estuary of the Oder, was the site of a Slavonic centre, and legend has preserved the fame of an ancient Baltic seaport on the same or a nearby site, the Vineta of the Slavs, the 'nobilissima civitas' of the chronicles, the reputed residence of great merchants and the repository of fabulous riches. Like the other legendary seaports, Vineta is said to have been engulfed by the sea, and, like the other villes englouties, it was reputed to toll its submerged bells in times of ill omen. Whether Vineta was in fact a town in the western sense of the word we do not know. Other towns of the Western Slavs depicted in the chronicles—Oppeln or Heithabu—were, we are told, little more than haphazard huddles of cabins made of wattle and mud. Nor can it be said with any certainty that Vineta was ever egularly visited by Scandinavians. It is however certain that, on the very border of the Slavonic East, near Lübeck, the Scandinavians possessed a trading settlement known to the chronicles as Reric, and that another settlement, Truso, sprang up not far from modern Elbing in West Prussia. But of all the towns and settlements they established on the fringes of the Slavonic East, none were more famous or endured longer than Novgorod. Novgorod the Great, the ancient city on Lake Ilmen, guarding the western terminus of a trade route from the Baltic to the interior of Russia, had drawn Scandinavian traders to itself since very early times, possibly since the eighth century, and we know of a Scandinavian settlement there in the tenth century.[1]

Scandinavian penetration into Russia did not, however, end with Novgorod. Before the eighth century was out the Scandinavians under Rurik established themselves as rulers of the 'Russian' tribes. Both before and after their conquest of Russia they regularly crossed and recrossed the great Eurasian plain en route to the East. Starting from the Baltic they went up the Neva and the Great Lakes, recrossed the Central Russian watershed by dragging their boats after them, and then sailed south and south-east by the rivers flowing into the Black and Azov Seas. Byzantium was their goal, and there they served as mercenaries, traded as merchants, and at least once pillaged the great city itself. But Byzantium was probably not the only eastern land they touched. We do not know whether they themselves penetrated into the trans-Oxian region of Baktria or into the trans-Caspian provinces of Persia. But they must at least have touched upon the fringes of the Asiatic steppes and traded with the Khazars and the Bulgars of the middle and lower Volga.

In this way the Scandinavians provided an economic link between Northern Europe and the lands further east—a link which became more important after the direct maritime connections with the orient had been severed in the eighth century. And this part they continued to play for several centuries. They were still active in the Russian, Polish, and Livonian centres in the twelfth century, still visited Utrecht in the second half of the same century and the east coast ports of England in the thirteenth century. But by that time their trade had already been overshadowed by the commercial activity in other parts of Europe, and before long it disappeared altogether under the pressure of the rising German tide.

[1] N. Vogel in *Hansische Geschichtsblätter* (1935), 181; *idem* in *Festskrift* in honour of Professor Koht; cf. F. Rörig in *Hansische Geschichtsblätter* (1933), 22 ff.

4

The time when the Scandinavian fortunes began to sink and the German flood rose to engulf them coincides with the beginning of the most rapid phase in the expansion of European economy and trade. The story of the expansion between the eleventh century and the thirteenth has already been told. So has also been the role of the Italians in starting it and in maintaining its momentum. Yet in spite of the Italian stimulus and the part they were beginning to play in the internal trade and finance of most continental countries, the two trading areas—the northern and the southern—remained more or less distinct. The great and growing exchanges between them were sometimes in the hands of the Italian houses with branches in England and France and the Low Countries. But most were carried on, so to speak, on the frontiers of the two areas—the places where the Italians met the merchants of the North-west and where the goods of northern origin and the Italian imports changed hands.

One of these frontier regions, at which the two commercial spheres touched, were the regions of East-central France, and in the first place Champagne. The story of the great Champagne fairs will be told else-where. Here it will suffice to note that the reasons why Champagne emerged in the twelfth century as the point of junction were to a large extent political. Under the rule of the Counts of Champagne and Blois, their country was one of the earliest in Europe to benefit from the feudal peace which in the eleventh century replaced the feudal anarchy of the preceding epoch. Its population and production grew. As now appears probable, it acquired very early in the period a flourishing cloth industry. But what favoured most its development as an intermediary was its convenient position at the intersection of ancient land routes leading from the Mediterranean to the North German frontier, and from Flanders to Central and Eastern France. Its ancient towns, Troyes, Langres, Rheims and Laon were well placed at the focal points of the trans-continental traffic and therefore provided convenient meeting places for the merchants of Italy and Provence on the one hand and those of Germany and the Low Countries on the other. It was at these meeting points that the great Champagne fairs sprang up in the twelfth century and developed into veritable nerve centres of medieval trade in the course of the thirteenth century.

What made the confluence of trade in Champagne so important is that the commercial currents which flowed into it had in the meantime swollen into broad rivers. It will be impossible in this chapter to describe them all, and still less to follow in detail their manifold courses. Thus the southern stream—that which flowed from the Mediterranean countries—was the most important of all, but its story is outside the territorial scope of this chapter. The western current, which issued from the central and western regions of France, may be part of this chapter's subject, but it has been little studied and may at first sight appear to be hardly worth studying. For it may be argued that so well-provided were each of the main regions of Northern and Western France that they were able to cover their needs from their own production and were not dependent on foreign supplies or markets. This notion of international trade as an occupation in which only poor countries need engage must not, however, be taken too literally or indeed too seriously. The richer provinces of France, perhaps because they were rich, had important surpluses to dispose of. There was grain to spare in Picardy and Normandy, wine to sell in almost every province of Central and Western France, wool in the uplands of Auvergne and the Cevennes, flax in the North-west, and other specialised products of agriculture elsewhere. As medieval countries go, France was a thickly populated country, and early in her history cities of Roman pedigree as well as towns of more recent origin began to attract large numbers of migrants from the country. By the thirteenth century, Paris, with its 30,000 inhabitants, was one of Europe's most important cities, and between the tenth century and the thirteenth urban centres of more than local importance sprang up everywhere—some of them, like Amiens and Orléans, were commercial capitals of large provinces; others, like Rouen and Bordeaux, great river ports or sea ports; others still, like Lille, Chartres, and Bourges, were seats of textile and metallurgical industry; others, like Paris herself, were all these things together.

A country so furnished could not remain a mere *congérie* of self-sufficient arcadias. That it in fact did not, is shown by such evidence of French trade as we have. The documents show foreigners visiting the fairs of Northern France—St Denis, Boulogne, Chartres, Compiègne—long before the fairs of Champagne rose to their fame. The ports of Northern France, Etaples (Quentovic) in the seventh and eighth centuries, Havre, Rouen, Barfleur and others in the eleventh and twelfth centuries, and countless other ports of call in the later centuries, figure prominently in the surviving records. In the English records the merchants of Amiens and Corbie importing woad are to be found among the earliest foreign visitors to London.

If, nevertheless, in the records of the Champagne fairs, the French current appears to be relatively unimportant, the reason for that is that by the end of the thirteenth century, when documents became abundant, commodities of other more highly commercialised regions (English wool, Flemish cloth) dominated the scene while France's economic connections with the outside world were beginning to suffer from the territorial conquests of Capetian kings, and from the consequent industrial conflicts, war taxation and military operations.

By comparison, more abundant and better illustrated was the stream which issued from the North and the North-east. It was fed from a multitude of tributaries and, of the latter, one issued from a region which was itself destined to succeed Champagne as a meeting point of north and south.

This region was Flanders. Flanders, like Champagne, was unusually fortunate in its political beginnings. In the course of the Dark Ages different political fortunes befell the two halves of the Roman Belgica Secunda. The southern part, that of the lower Seine and the Marne, plunged into feudal anarchy early in the Carolingian era and was just emerging from it as it fell under the domination of the rising power of the French Capetians. The economic prosperity it enjoyed at the turn of the eleventh century under the French kings proved ephemeral, for as a border country on the very front line of the Capetian expansion, it was not too well suited for active industry or trade. Not so the northern part of Belgica Secunda. By a fortunate accident the feudal fiefs and baronies of the South-western Low Countries were early in the tenth century assembled into a strong principality of the Counts of Flanders. Under their rule a large portion of the Low Countries, from Arras to Ghent, came to enjoy peace and order in advance of most other parts of Europe. And in the shelter of the Count's peace, arts could flourish, trade could prosper, and towns could grow.

The geographical situation of the country was equally favourable. The country lay on the coast of the North Sea, open to sea-borne trade from almost every quarter; it was also cut across by navigable rivers, more especially the Scheldt, and was well provided with sheltered estuaries for harbours. Yet Flanders owes its industry as much to its geographical limitations as to its geographical facilities. While, under the shelter of Flemish peace, population grew, the yield of the land remained relatively small. The Flemings carried out a great work of internal colonisation, added polder to polder, erected dykes all along the coast and along the main water-courses. By the middle of the twelfth century they had acquired all over Europe a reputation as experts in land drainage, and their qualities—the Flemish system of reclamation, the Flemish freedom and the Flemish experience in organising new settlements—they carried with them at the invitation of German princes into the new lands beyond the Elbe. Yet neither internal colonisation nor emigration could solve their population problem, and the solution was found where such solutions normally lie, i.e. in industrialisation.

By the middle of the twelfth century Flanders became the foremost—and possibly the only—predominantly industrial country in Northern Europe. The chief centres of its cloth industry, Ypres, Ghent, Douai, came to rank among the most important towns of Northern Europe. Together with the commercial port of Bruges which served them, they formed by the end of the century the four members—the Four *Leden*—of Flanders, which began to rival the political power of the Counts in the thirteenth century and were to challenge it in the fourteenth.

Flanders also possessed certain other industries and trades. But until the end of the fourteenth century none of the other occupations compared in importance with cloth, and cloth was also the mainstay of Flemish commerce. Cloth was also the magnet which drew to Flanders the merchants of the world and gradually helped to develop in Bruges another international mart, rival and eventual successor to the fairs of Champagne. Bruges' greatness was probably rooted in the function it fulfilled at the turn of the twelfth and the thirteenth centuries as the point of entry of English wool and of English merchants. Before long the Italians came there in search of English wool and English custom, but by the end of the thirteenth century the Germans had established themselves in Bruges as the chief exporters of Flemish cloth, and the principal buyers of Italian imports and the chief providers of Eastern European foodstuffs and raw materials.

5

By that time the Germans had come to dominate the international economy of Northern Europe. The thirteenth was indeed their century, but their pre-eminence in the economy of continental Europe was beginning to reveal itself at least a whole century earlier.

Eventually the range of predominantly German trade, like the area of predominantly German speech and culture, stretched from the eastern borders of North Holland and Lorraine to the heart of Central—and later also Eastern—Europe. But its focus, especially at its beginning, was in the Rhineland and its capital. For in the course of the twelfth and the thirteenth centuries all the trade routes and all the cultural influences which radiated from the Rhineland—its architecture, its crafts and its mystic art—came to centre upon one town, and that town was Cologne.

The early history of Cologne is shrouded in a certain amount of controversy. There is no doubt that its urban nucleus had survived from the Roman era and that as an administrative centre and as an episcopal residence Cologne preserved some semblance of urban life throughout the Dark Ages. It may also have preserved its economic function, for it could boast of an annual fair in the tenth century and housed merchants and artisans much earlier. By the end of the eleventh century Cologne had already become an emporium of trade and industry. Its two fairs—one at Easter and the other in August—were already well established, and so also was its fame for wealth and power. Writing early in the twelfth century Otto of Freising could assert that there was not a town in contemporary Germany or Gaul as rich as Cologne; and Cesarius of Heisterbach, a Cistercian compiler of miraculous stories, spoke of Cologne in somewhat the same way in which New York used to be spoken of in European books. There was something in the very air of Cologne that made men rich.

Some of Cologne's wealth was derived from industrial products: textiles, mainly linen, cloth and thread, and especially metal goods. Its bells were famous in thirteenth-century Europe, and so were other products of its copper-beating crafts. One of Cologne's masters, Frederick of St Pantaleon, ranks among the greatest metal workers of all ages. Still, it is in commerce and not in industries that the mainsprings of Cologne's wealth will be found. Its main field was the Rhine valley itself. Owing mainly to the growth of the hinterland, the estuary, once the focus of European trade, now ceased to occupy this position. Most of the delta's trade now passed through Cologne and, in the end, came to be handled by Cologne merchants. At the beginning of the period the merchants of Utrecht appear to have traded along the Rhine on their own account, but eventually Cologne ousted its competitors and succeeded in appropriating to itself the bulk of the valley's trade. In the twelfth century we find its merchants active as far south as Austria and Carinthia and also in Augsburg and Regensburg—a town which at that time gathered into itself the economic threads of the Danubian region.

Needless to say, the lands along the Rhine valley itself were not the only region to which Cologne's commercial connections extended; just as the Rhineland with Cologne was not the only area to play its part in the commercial development of the continent. Another such area was Flanders itself. Much of Flemish trade was with England, France and Southern Europe, and in the early phase of their commercial expansion, and especially in the twelfth century, the Flemings appear to have frequented the markets of Cologne and also the upper Rhine and Saxony as far east as the Elbe. But in the course of the thirteenth century as the active trade of the Flemings died out, the Cologners gradually became the chief intermediaries between Flanders on the one hand and Central and Southern Germany on the other. For a time in the thirteenth century they even succeeded in penetrating into the Anglo-Flemish wool trade and interposing themselves between the English wool growers and the Flemish cloth makers.

Another similar area lay to the west of the Rhine, between the Rhine and the Maas. The trade of this region, which the Germans usually describe as Maasland, was founded on the industries of its towns: Huy, Namur, Liége and Dinant. Huy and Liége produced some cloth for export, but their chief industry was metals, and Dinant was especially famous for its metal goods.

Almost equally important was the activity and greater still the future potentialities of the regions to the East of the Rhine. The territory between the Rhine and the Weser, usually described as Westphalia, was a valuable source of agricultural exports and of metal ores mined in the South-east of the region. Yet it was not in the export of domestic produce and not in Western Germany that the historical destiny of Westphalia lay. Ever since Frankish times the region had served as a corridor to the lands further east. Several important east-to-west routes crossed it, and none were more important than the famous *Hellweg* which began at Duisburg, went between the Ruhr and Lippe and passed the towns of Dortmund and Soest before crossing the Weser into Saxony. On this route were to be found the Westphalian towns which were to lead in the commercial development of Eastern Europe: and it was thanks to the men of these towns that Eastern European trade before long fell into German hands.

The Eastern specialisation of Westphalia was largely Cologne's own fault. Faced in the West with the barrier of Cologne's power, the rising towns of Westphalia naturally turned to the as yet virgin fields further East. And although the merchants of Cologne were as active in the East as the men of any other German town, they could not claim there that position of overwhelming economic privilege which they enjoyed elsewhere. It is therefore no wonder to find the Westphalian towns taking a leading part in the exploratory period of eastern trade and forming the earliest trading stations in the East. We find them also acquiring a lion's share in the work as well as in the profits of urban colonisation and town-building all over North-eastern Europe from Lübeck to Riga.

Some of what has been said about Westphalia applies also to the region immediately to the East, i.e. Saxony. Saxony, as the documents reveal it in the twelfth century, had for more than four centuries been part of the Holy Roman Empire and was now an integral part of the German homeland. Like Westphalia, it owed its first entry into the commercial system of Europe to its mineral resources, for by the late twelfth and thirteenth centuries the Harz mountains were rapidly becoming the principal mining area of continental Europe, the main source of copper and lead, as well as of precious metals. The industry was centred round Goslar, and the fame of Goslar as the capital of the mining industry outlasted, even if it did not outshine, its fame as the residence of the Saxon and Hohenstaufen Emperors. Yet Goslar was not the principal commercial town of the country, for the simple reason that in Saxony, as in Westphalia, the most flourishing commercial activities were those which led its merchants to the East. To this activity Saxony and its towns were especially suited. In the early Middle Ages, i.e. before it was wholly assimilated to the Empire, it lay across the German route to the East like a barrier. Now the barrier had become a corridor. Whereas in the opening centuries of our period—eleventh and early twelfth—the regular overland traffic stopped at the Elbe crossings—chiefly at Bardowiek, but also at Magdeburg and at a few smaller places—at the end of the twelfth and all through the thirteenth century the frontiers of German trade moved eastwards, and men from the border towns of Saxony took part in the movement and greatly benefited from it.

6

The eastward spread was indeed the most characteristic trend of the epoch. Its beginning can be traced as far back as the Frankish era. From about the sixth century onwards the civilisation of the Latino-German West began to expand into the continental interior of Central Europe; and, in consequence, the entire economic balance of the continent gradually shifted to the East. In the early Merovingian times the focus of the Frankish state and society was in Gaul, but in the sixth and seventh centuries it moved from the left bank of the Rhine to the right. In the centuries between the fifth and the eleventh the lands between the Rhine and the Weser were being fast reclaimed and settled by the overflow of their own population, and by the time Charlemagne became Emperor, the eastern and more purely Germanic parts of his kingdom were able to supply him with the bulk of his power and of his armies. But no sooner was this transference completed than a still further move to the East began, and the Saxon lands beyond the Weser were laid open to Frankish conquest and assimilation. It has been argued that to the Franks the acquisition of Saxony was a military and a political necessity, for they had to subjugate the Saxons if they were themselves to be saved from being submerged by the next wave of Germanic invasions. Whether in fact Charlemagne's Saxon expeditions were nothing more than preventive wars we do not know, but we know that the Saxon lands had been an object of attraction long before they could possibly have become a source of danger. Their military conquest was well prepared by missionary activity and was itself preceded and followed by commercial ventures and trading settlements. Before long Saxony was wholly absorbed in the trading area of Western

Europe, and by the beginning of the eleventh century it had itself become the starting point for a further leap in the same direction. This time it was the turn of the Baltic and of the Wendish lands east of the Elbe.

This final phase of the process was also its most important one. It began with the conquest of Slavonic lands which was led largely by princes, and it continued as a great enterprise in settlement and colonisation. And long before the work of colonisation ended it brought fundamental change into European, and, more especially, German commerce. Urban colonisation by merchants and for commercial motives accompanied, and in some places even preceded, rural colonisation by knights and peasants. Not all the Westphalian merchants in search of Slavonic markets and sources of supply stopped at the line of the Elbe. As often as not they themselves ventured into the interior of the Wendish lands, and now and again penetrated into the Baltic region. With the permission of the Slavonic princes they began establishing trading stations all along the main routes leading to Novgorod and Smolensk, which were the two main points of entry into medieval Russia. In Schleswig, the starting point of the Scandinavian sea-route to the Eastern Baltic, Westphalian merchants possessed something in the nature of a factory in the early twelfth century. At the next stage of the same sea-route, at Wisby on the island of Gotland, they established themselves at about the same time. But from the point of view of subsequent history, the most significant of their trading factories was the one they apparently built up very early in the twelfth century, or even at the end of the eleventh century, at the Slavonic town of Lübeck. Profiting by the liberality of the Wendish prince, they formed there a permanent settlement at least as early as the twenties of the twelfth century. But in the late thirties Adolph of Holstein conquered the land and burned the city, and in 1143 the new Lübeck, this time a purely German town, was founded.

Lübeck was to be followed by other new towns. In the extreme North-east the German merchants founded at the very beginning of the thirteenth century the town of Riga, henceforth the centre of their trade in Livonia. By the end of the twelfth century the trading settlement in Wisby grew to turn the entire town into a German port and strong-point, and at the opening of the thirteenth century the town of Hamburg rose to match Lübeck at the eastern foot of the Jutland peninsula.

Of this first generation of new German towns none could rival Lübeck. It soon drew to itself the trade which had previously gone overland to Bardowiek, replaced Schleswig as the chief starting point for sea journeying across the Eastern Baltic, established itself in the

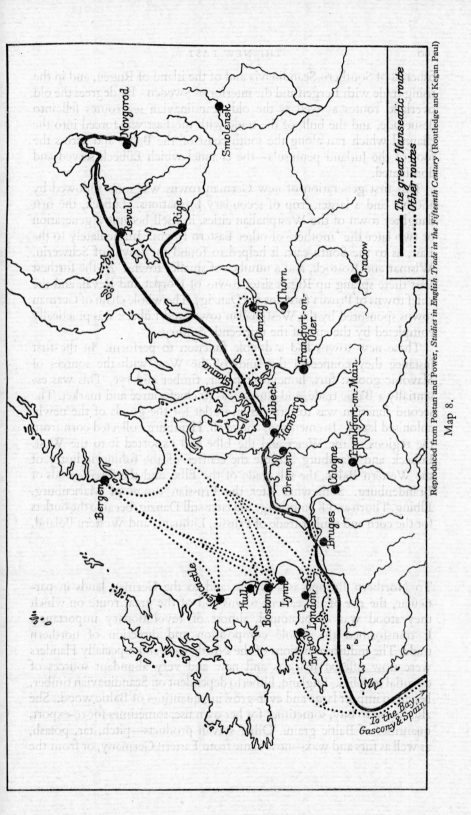

Map 8.

Reproduced from Postan and Power, *Studies in English Trade in the Fifteenth Century* (Routledge and Kegan Paul)

fisheries of Southern Scandinavia and of the island of Rugen, and in the rising trade with Bergen and the interior of Sweden. By degrees the old overland routes as well as the old Scandinavian sea routes fell into desuetude, and the bulk of the trade with the East was forced into the channel which ran along the south coast of the Baltic and across the foot of the Jutland peninsula—the channel which Lübeck served and dominated.

This first generation of new German towns was soon followed by another and a larger crop of secondary formations. Lübeck, the first daughter town of the Westphalian cities, in itself became a generation or two later the 'mother' of other Eastern towns. Immediately to the East, as to the South-east, it helped to found the towns of Schwerin, Wismar and Rostock, and a number of smaller towns. At the furthest East there sprang up Riga's sister towns of Dorpat and Reval, and the chief towns of Prussia (but not yet Danzig). The whole chain of German towns sponsored by the Westphalian towns and Lübeck was practically completed by the end of the thirteenth century.

These new towns had a double function to perform. In the first instance they connected the lands of the West with the sources of Slavonic goods: furs, honey, pitch, tar, timber and rye. This was essentially a Baltic trade, and Russia was its chief source and market. The second function was to serve as an outlet for the goods of the newly colonised lands. Bremen and, above all, Hamburg collected corn from the regions of the Weser and the Elbe and exported it to the West. Lübeck and Hamburg became the centres of the fishing industry of the Western Baltic, the salt trade of the Elbe, and the forest goods of Brandenburg. Somewhat later the Prussian towns of Marienburg, Elbing, Thorn and Königsberg, and later still Danzig, became the outlets for the corn and timber trade of Prussia, Lithuania and Western Poland.

7

To Northern Europe as a whole, and to the German lands in particular, the rise of the eastern towns and of the great route on which they stood was of profound, almost of revolutionary importance. It transformed the whole composition and direction of northern trade. The industrial nations of the North-west and especially Flanders were now offered markets and new and very abundant sources of essential supplies. England, hitherto dependent on Scandinavian timber, began to import large and ever-growing quantities of Baltic wood. She also began to buy, sometimes for her own use, sometimes for re-export, quantities of Baltic grain. Other sylvan products—pitch, tar, potash, as well as furs and wax—now came from Eastern Germany, or from the

Slavonic lands tapped by the Germans. Flanders, hitherto fed by the corn supplies from Northern France and Southern Germany, was now beginning to be supplied by Baltic grain. The Germans were also able to take food to Scandinavian countries previously dependent on imports from Britain.

All this brought wealth and power to the East German towns and marked the final stage in Germany's commercial rise. Their hold over East European markets, foodstuffs, and raw materials, also made them welcome and even indispensable all over Northern Europe. They won predominant power in Scandinavia, great economic influence in the Low Countries, important privileges in England. Before long, economic power was buttressed by a political organisation, and the German towns combined into the great naval, military and political union of the Hanse.

With the formal establishment of the Hanse the Eastern expansion of North European trade can be said to have been completed, and a new and a different chapter in its history began. For, paradoxically enough, the official founding of the Hanse in the sixties of the fourteenth century was not so much a further step in German expansion as a manifestation of an entirely new phase in the history of European trade and of German power. It marks the end of Eastward expansion—indeed of all expansion—and a new period in the economic history of Europe.

III. *The Age of Contraction*

(I) THE DEPRESSION

1

The great commercial expansion did not continue into the late Middle Ages and was not destined to merge without a break into the ascending economic movements of the sixteenth century. In some parts of Europe it slowed down; in others it ceased altogether. Historians will therefore be justified in regarding the two closing centuries of the Middle Ages, the fourteenth and the fifteenth, and more especially the second half of the former and the first half of the latter, as a period of arrested development, and even in speaking of a 'secular' depression succeeding the 'secular' expansion of the earlier centuries.

The contraction, like the expansion which preceded it, is easier to diagnose than to measure. Reliable figures capable of forming comprehensive statistical series are almost as rare in the records of the later Middle Ages as they are in the records of the twelfth and the thirteenth centuries. In England alone were national customs accounts kept in the later Middle Ages, and enough of them have survived to provide a broad statistical background to the history of English foreign trade. But even the English customs accounts are more complete and more reliable for some periods than for others. The figures for the fourteenth century are less comprehensive than those of the fifteenth and are not available in consecutive or comparable series except for wine, wool and cloth. The latter have been tabulated by Professor Gray in annual averages for two-yearly periods at intervals of about a decade. The fifteenth-century figures have been fully analysed elsewhere. The two series are in Tables II and III:

Table II. *Exports of Wool and Cloth from England in the second half of the fourteenth century (annual averages)*[1]

Years	Wool (sacks)	Broadcloths ‡
1353–55	—	3,040
1355–57	—	7,485
1357–60	35,840*	9,346
1366–68	26,634†	14,593
1377–80	21,627	15,449
1392–95	19,359	43,072

* 1357–59—2 years.

† 1367–69.

‡ The figures in this column slightly underestimate the total and slightly exaggerate the rate of increase, for they do not include worsteds and other cheap cloths of the same kind which were relatively more important in the early period.

The figures tell their own tale. The only exceptions to the record of decline were the short-lived boom in the value of miscellaneous exports and imports in the mid-thirties of the fifteenth century which probably reflected the high cost of imports during an acute economic conflict with the Hanseatic League; and above all the high level of cloth exports throughout the period. The latter were rising throughout the second half of the fourteenth century and mounted with exceptional rapidity between 1380 and 1395; but from the high point they then reached they soon descended to an average of about 30,000 broadcloths, round which they fluctuated for some 25 years. In the two decades of active trade with Central and Eastern Europe following the, so-called, Vorrath treaty with the Hanse in 1437, the exports of cloth rose well above the average and exceeded 50,000 cloths, but in 1448 they fell again to their pre-1437 level and remained there until the last quarter of the century.

[1] These figures have recently been corrected and supplemented in E. Carus Wilson, 'Trends in the Export of English Woollens in the Fourteenth Century', *Economic Hist. Rev.* III, No. 2, 1950, but the general trend they exhibit is the same.

Table III. *Exports and Imports of Dutiable Commodities in England, 1399–1482*

(Annual averages in 3-year periods)*

Years	Exports of wool (sacks)	Exports of broadcloth	Imports of wine (tuns)	Exports and imports of miscellaneous merchandise paying poundage (values in £)†
1399–1402	15,023	27,760	—	—
1402–05	10,864	24,502	6,237	60,887
1405–08	14,221	29,315	6,220	187,439
1408–11	14,393	30,718	13,696	150,368
1411–14	14,447	25,108	12,113	124,313
1414–17	14,131	29,488	17,063	136,683
1417–20	14,778	28,366	10,975	145,192
1420–23	13,893	36,359	5,168	135,994
1423–26	13,959	42,665	3,591	109,049
1426–29	15,437	38,417	6,821	129,420
1429–32	9,749	40,641	8,940	119,691
1432–35	8,294	39,693	9,950	146,754
1435–38	2,353	40,814	6,097	113,275
1438–41	9,101	56,097	10,509	127,221
1441–44	9,776	55,976	11,748	130,452
1444–46	9,279	52,482	12,275	106,168
1446–48	7,654	53,699	11,000	121,795
1448–50	8,412	35,078	9,432	91,456
1450–53	7,660	38,928	7,424	91,001
1453–56	9,290	37,738	6,826	82,533
1456–59	7,664	35,059	4,072	59,089
1459–62	4,976	31,933	4,190	65,503
1462–65	7,044	25,855	7,074	57,449
1465–69	9,316	39,664	5,942	93,942
1469–71	7,811	27,610	3,411	53,421
1471–76	9,091	43,129	4,729	115,475
1476–79	7,502	51,889	6,887	120,333
1479–82	9,784	62,586	6,927	179,340

* 1444–46, 1446–48, 1448–50, and 1469–71 are computed in 2-year periods; 1465–69 is a 4-year period, and 1471–76 a 5-year period.

† The figures do not include miscellaneous exports by Hansards.

For other parts of Europe there is little statistical evidence beyond a few figures of local imports and exports or occasional series of measurements reflecting the movements of the more important trades. The best known of the former are probably the returns of the Hanseatic *Pfundzoll*, a tax on sea-borne trade levied by the principal Hanseatic towns in the second half of the fourteenth and in the fifteenth centuries. Unfortunately, the returns have not survived in a series sufficiently consecutive to reveal a convincing trend; and with the exception of the Lübeck figures for 1368–69, they have not yet been presented to historians in a wholly usable form. The longest of the series so far available, that of Hamburg, suggests that the sea-borne exports and imports rose from 250,000 Lübeck marks in 1362 to 374,000 in 1371, and then dropped to 336,000 in 1400.[1] But the figures may well exaggerate the rise and underestimate the fall in Hamburg's trade, for the *Pfundzoll* was frequently imposed in times of strained international relations and sea war when a great deal of traffic, which would otherwise have gone through the Sound, sought the greater security of the overland route through Hamburg.

On the other hand, the evidence of individual trades covers a range of commodities and places so wide as to make up for the paucity of more general measurements. And though little of it is statistical in the narrow sense of the term it is sufficiently full and varied to reveal the main economic trend.

2

The trend and the facts from which it emerges may appear to be primarily concerned with agriculture and industrial production rather than with trade. But the distinction must not be pressed too hard. In an earlier section heavy emphasis was laid on the predominance in North European trade of products of European industry and agriculture. Where facts make it appear very probable that Europe's production declined, or at least ceased to grow, there is every justification for concluding that commercial exchanges must also have slowed down or stagnated.

Naturally enough, the evidence of agricultural production is most copious, though also most difficult to interpret. Superficial signs of agricultural crises abound in the records of the fourteenth and fifteenth centuries. Wars were more frequent and more continuous than at any other time since the tenth century; great pestilences visited Europe in 1348-49 and at least twice again in the second half of the century. Crops, buildings, equipment, as well as the agricultural calendar, were bound to suffer, and production was bound to decline. In addition, rural economy was undergoing a process of readjustment which helped to reduce the level of both agricultural production and of trade.

Arable cultivation contracted everywhere, but on large units, and especially on 'demesne' farms of great estates, the contraction was most rapid. Such demesnes as still functioned in the fourteenth century in various parts of France were wound up in the course of the late fourteenth and fifteenth centuries. In England, where the demesne farming

---

[1] W. Stieda, *Revaler Zollbeicher*, lvii ff.

had survived to a far greater extent than anywhere else in Europe, the transformation was most radical.

The contracting acreages of the demesnes must not of course be used as an accurate index of agricultural decline. Yet even if corrected and heavily discounted, they still bear witness to a general recession. By no means all the lands lost to the demesnes were acquired by tenants; and there is every sign of poorer lands, whether on the demesnes or on lands anciently in the possession of tenants, gradually going out of cultivation. Theoretically, the yield per acre or per man should have risen; but even if this happened in the fifteenth century (and there is no evidence to show that it did) the total output was bound to decline.

What is more, a smaller proportion of the output was now drawn into the main stream of inter-regional trade. The dwindling of demesne farming signified also the decline of commercial production. No doubt, in this country, some large-scale units continued to be run by substantial tenant farmers, but in general peasant tenancies increased and multiplied at the expense of large units of commercialised agriculture; and peasant landholders must have consumed a far greater proportion of their produce than the quasi-capitalist owners of the demesne farms.

Thus on the thirty-two manors of the bishopric of Winchester at the beginning of the thirteenth century some 1750 quarters of wheat were sold, nearly all outside the manors. This amounted to 48% of the gross output and 82% of the 'net' output (after deduction of seed). When a century later the yields, i.e. the 'net' output in relation to seed sown, had become considerably higher, the proportion of sales to gross output also rose to 70%. On the six Wiltshire manors of the Duchy of Lancaster at the very beginning of the fourteenth century, the 'net' output of grain of all kinds (including some 75 quarters bought but excluding some 525 quarters of seed) was about 1330 quarters, while the sales amounted to 1208 quarters: indeed the output was so large that it must have included a carry-over of old grain. On the Wiltshire estates of Lord Hungerford, on which demesnes functioned until the middle of the fifteenth century, sales of grain reached similar proportions. On the Hungerford estate of Winterbourne-Stoke in 1448, 97 quarters out of the 'net' output of 112 were sold.

No such sales could be expected from peasant units, however commercialised some of them were. A little calculation, indeed mere commonsense, will show that at a time when on the holdings of the peasants of the top rank—the virgaters—the area under corn in any year averaged about 15 acres per household (in Cambridgeshire at the time of the Hundred Rolls of 1273 the area sown annually by an average peasant above the rank of cottar was 7 acres) and when the yield of wheat, allowing for seed, was no more than six bushels per acre, the marketable surpluses of an average peasant household were small. So even if the extent of cultivated land had remained the same, the change-over to peasant agriculture would inevitably have reduced the amount of grain available for sale, and with it the total volume of grain trade.

Hence also the reduced scale of inter-regional traffic in grain. The evidence of urban food supplies leaves the impression of a trade shrinking in volume and sometimes restricted in its range. We are told that in the late Middle Ages London was drawing its supplies from a much smaller area than earlier and had become more or less dependent upon the agricultural surpluses in the Home Counties. There is also some evidence to suggest that the grain supplies of other important English towns were becoming not only smaller (this could also result from decline in the town population), but sometimes also more local. Hence the growing pre-occupation of towns with their food supplies and with the grain stocks: a pre-occupation which overshadows the urban policies of most of the greater towns on the continent.

At first sight, no such shrinkage could be observed in the grain trade of the Low Countries, where the sea-borne supplies from the distant Baltic appeared to assume an even greater importance. Yet a shrinkage there must have been. It is quite possible that Baltic imports into the Low Countries grew in importance merely because the French sources of corn supplies had been running dry. The exports from the valleys of the Somme and the lower Seine, though by no means exhausted, were not, and could not be, as abundant as they had been in the middle of the fourteenth century. Anglo-French war, the English occupation of Normandy and Picardy, the choking up of river traffic by tolls, were bound to interrupt the flow; and there were also other signs of a more general agricultural depression. It was not therefore an accident that in some years in the fifteenth century we find the Norman towns importing grain from the Baltic, and the records have preserved an accidental report of a whole Hanseatic grain fleet arriving in the estuary of the Seine in 1450.

In some of these examples Eastern Germany and the other Baltic regions figure as the only examples of unfailing bounty. Did then the grain production and the grain trade of Eastern Europe escape the depression that prevailed elsewhere? To some extent they probably did, since they still continued to yield marketable surpluses large enough to feed Holland and Norway and to keep the great east-to-west trade flowing. But even if the flow never ceased it was no longer as full as it had been in the middle of the fourteenth century. Comprehensive statistics of the Hanseatic grain trade do not exist; such figures as we have are largely confined to the evidence of the grain deals of the Prussian

Order, which are both incomplete and misleading. But all indirect evidence points to a slump in the fortunes of German agriculture throughout the greater part of the fifteenth century. An interval of at least a century separated the high-water mark of agricultural expansion in Eastern Germany in the fourteenth century from the outburst of large-scale commercial agriculture on the *Rittergüter* in the sixteenth century. During that interval, the map of Brandenburg, Pomerania, Mecklenburg and Prussia became covered with abandoned holdings, deserted households and depopulated villages, all pointing to the economic tribulations of peasant agriculture. But large-scale units of production were also going through a period of economic difficulty, for labour was getting scarce and dear, and grain was falling in price. Before the century was out landlords sought and found a remedy in *Bauernlegen*— a policy whereby peasants were deprived of land and forced to work on the estates. But the movement did not get under way until the very turn of the fifteenth and sixteenth centuries. From 1400 to 1475—these are approximate dates—the landlords found their old prosperity going and the new prosperity not yet arrived. Would it therefore be too fanciful to conclude that if in that century Baltic supplies in the West still appeared as abundant as ever it was not because supplies had grown but merely because the demand had shrunk?

For there is little doubt that the demand for grain in the main consuming areas was shrinking. On some of the main inter-regional markets, those of the greater towns and of the principal industrial areas of Northern Europe, the numbers of inhabitants declined. The process was of course more complex in detail than it may appear on a broader view. Yet for all its complexity, it leaves little room for doubt about its effect on the grain market. The demand for grain apparently receded in the main consuming areas, and it must also have receded on the innumerable local markets throughout the length and breadth of Europe.

The importance of the local demand must not be under-estimated. In chapters dealing with the earlier centuries attention was drawn to the large proportion of marketable foodstuffs which went to feed the villagers, manorial servants and artisans who did not possess enough land to cover their needs out of their own production. This class included agricultural labourers, rural artisans and smallholders of every type and size, and was always to be found in the countryside. It was, however, more numerous at some times than at others, and in most countries—certainly in Germany and England—this class contracted in the later Middle Ages. What with the steep decline of rural population and with the new opportunities for larger holdings on the lords' land and elsewhere, the numbers of landless or all but landless labourers in English villages fell out of proportion to the general decline of population. And as the numbers of wage-earners and smallholders sank, sales for local consumption must have dwindled.

It is because demand declined that the reduced production and smaller sales did not result in a chronic, still less a mounting, scarcity of food. Over the later Middle Ages as a whole, bread grains appeared more abundant than ever before. They were especially plentiful in the second quarter of the fourteenth century when prices fell more than 20% below their level in the first quarter. Soon afterwards came the succession of bad harvests and low yields following on the great mortality of 1348–49; but this again was followed in England and abroad by the 'good seventies'. According to several continental chronicles, the harvest of 1375 was the best for fourteen years, and was followed by four years so good that according to an Alsatian chronicle, people were 'fatigued by the abundance'. In 1377 the prices of bread in England touched their lowest point for thirty years, and in 1395 in Strasbourg grain became so plentiful and so cheap that bakers replaced the 'standard' penny loaf with a halfpenny one. Bread was never to be quite so plentiful again, but periods of relative abundance occurred in various parts of Europe throughout the fifteenth century at intervals frequent enough to justify historians in regarding the whole period as an age of low agricultural prices. Above all, the first and third quarters of the fifteenth century in Western Germany, in the Low Countries, and in some parts of France and England, were times when supplies, relative to demand, were near their peak.

The recurrent phases of plenty raise problems closely linked with those of prices and will therefore be discussed again later; but they should be mentioned here if only in order to record a warning against a possible *non sequitur*. The decline of the grain trade and of arable agriculture could be accompanied by signs of abundance and must not be judged by them. On the other hand, in other branches of agricultural production the declining or stagnating output was not always matched by the decline in demand, and signs of abundance may be absent. Thus, for reasons which have not been fully accounted for, the supplies of foodstuffs of animal origin, and especially butter, were smaller in relation to demand than were the supplies of grain; and their values fell more slowly or even rose. Therein, however, lies a tale which properly belongs to another section of this chapter.

3

The category of animal products here discussed does not of course include Europe's most important industrial material—wool. English customs figures make it clear beyond all doubt that trade in wool was on the wane. The tables II and III above will show that English exports, by far the most important in Western Europe and solely responsible for high quality wool imported into Flanders, Holland and Italy, declined from about 35,000 sacks per annum in the first half of the fourteenth century to about 8000 sacks in the second half of the fifteenth century. It would of course be wrong to ascribe the entire deficiency to falling production, for it is now well understood that in the meantime England had greatly increased her cloth industry and consumed a far greater proportion of her clip. Indeed so marked was the shift from foreign users to the English cloth-makers that until recently historians have used the figures of declining wool exports as evidence of England's rising cloth production. This argument, however, no longer holds good. H. L. Gray and others have shown that, at its highest, England's cloth production could not possibly have accounted for all the difference between the high level of wool exports in the middle of the fourteenth century and their low level in the late fifteenth.

Table IV. *Exports of Wine from Bordeaux in the Fourteenth Century*

(Annual averages)

Years	Tuns
1305–07	95,650
1308–09	102,724
1310–11	51,351
1328–30	81,366
1335–37	45,315
1348–50	9,675
1352–58	19,681 (five years only)
1363–70	22,111 (six years only)
1372–73	14,373
1374–79	13,297
1379–81	7,842

Declining supply, as well as other difficulties of trade, also accounts for the confused and broken pattern of the wine trade. We know little about the fortunes of the wine exports of the upper Rhineland or of the Moselle, and hardly more about those of La Rochelle, but much more is known about the conditions in the southern and by far the most important wine area, that of Gascony. The region experienced

[1] The figures of fourteenth-century wine imports have been derived from an article by Miss M. K. James, *Econ. Hist. Rev.*, n.s. IV (1951).

not only the general economic difficulties of the age, but also the direct effects of military operations of the Anglo-French wars. At times only Bordeaux and its immediate surroundings escaped wholesale devastation. The toll of the ruined vineyards has found faithful reflection in the statistics of fourteenth-century exports. The decline, interrupted for a while in the last decade of the fourteenth century, was resumed in the fifteenth. During the middle decades of the century, French occupation of Gascony led to a complete interruption of trade to England and all but deprived Gascony of its most important customer; and exports to England sank from the average of about 12,000 tuns in the thirties and forties (it was more than that at the beginning of the century) to less than 7000 in the fifties and sixties. It was not before the eighties of the fifteenth century that English merchants appeared again in force on the wine-market of Bordeaux and British imports of Gascon wine reached and passed their fourteenth-century volumes.

It is of course possible that the irregular and probably dwindling supplies of wine were in some parts of Europe compensated by increasing supplies of beer; for beer made with hops was the product of the Middle Ages in decline. From the middle of the fourteenth century onwards it was brewed in ever-increasing quantities in most of the North German towns, above all in Hamburg, and also in towns of the northern Netherlands. Historians do not, however, know enough about medieval consumption in different places and at different social levels to be able to judge to what extent wine and beer were true substitutes, and how far beer was merely ousting ales and other drinks of a humbler kind.

The light which the surviving records throw on the other branches of the victualling trade is equally uncertain and on the whole equally subdued. Enough is known about the salt trade of the Bay of Bourgneuf to suggest that here at least output and trade were growing in the fifteenth century. The documents, however, are not sufficiently continuous to report the effect of piracy and war in the forties and fifties, nor do we know enough about salt exports from other areas, e.g. Lüneburg, Zealand or South Germany, to be able to set the buoyancy of the Bay trade against the possible decline elsewhere. The evidence from the English salt areas suggests that there production was, to say the least, stagnating. The feudal farm of the main salt-making centres in Nantwich, Northwich and Middlewich, which was largely, though not wholly, made up of revenues of the salt-pans, fell from £168 in 1301 to £130 in 1347 and £90 in 1368. Indirect evidence—figures are lacking—suggests that production remained low for at least another century.[1]

A more general, even if an indirect, indication of a probable decline in international salt industry will be found in the vicissitudes of its chief

[1] H. J. Hewitt, *Medieval Cheshire*, 118–19.

customer—the herring trade. The great fishing industry of Skania was still active in the fifteenth century and was not to enter upon its final decline for another century or century and a half; but it was no longer expanding and was frequently depressed by war and by bad catches. In the good years at the turn of the fifteenth and sixteenth centuries as much was caught and salted as ever before. In Falsterbö, where most of the Skania fishing was then concentrated, at least 100,000 tuns (about 10,000 long tons) were salted in 1537, which was only about 20,000 tuns less than may have been salted in the same place in 1368. But in some years during the intervening period the catches and the trade fell to a mere fraction of the volumes of 1368 and 1537. The recurrent wars between the Hanseatic League and the Scandinavian kings, and political friction with Flanders and England, repeatedly interfered with both fishing and export. Possibly the fishing grounds themselves were beginning to show signs of wear, and there were complaints of bad catches in 1411, 1412, 1416, and 1425. In the late twenties, war, in interrupting both fishing and trade, proved to be a blessing in disguise, for with the return of peace yields recovered to reach their highest levels between 1432 and the mid-forties. In the middle of the century, however, complaints of poor catches became frequent again and continued at intervals throughout the period.[1]

This record of the fishing trade, if true, bears a striking resemblance to what was apparently happening in the great extracting industries of the time. More especially, the mining areas were now going through a phase which the old-fashioned economist would have described as one of rapidly diminishing returns. The symptoms were all local, and the complaint did not turn out to be permanent; but for the time being most branches of European mining were, so to speak, 'due' for a recession irrespective of what was happening at the same time in industry and trade in general. Sooner or later they were bound to pay the penalty for the rapid and cumulative expansion of the previous century and a half; and for most of them the fourteenth and fifteenth centuries were their time of reckoning. By then seams became exhausted, or else had to be worked under conditions which were raising technical problems beyond the powers of medieval technology to solve.

From this point of view the most characteristic is the history of European silver mining. Exhaustion appears to have come over all silver-mining regions, secondary as well as primary. Derbyshire and Devonshire in England, Poitou and the Massif Central in France, and probably Sardinia in Italy petered out in the later Middle Ages; but far more striking and much more important was the decline of silver mining in its main centres, in Central and South-eastern Europe. The

[1] D. Schäfer, *Das Buch des lübeckschen Vogts auf Schonen*, xxxix ff.

silver mines of Hungary had been exploited since the eighth century and reached full development in the twelfth and thirteenth centuries. The mining industry of Saxony and especially that of Rammelsberg by Goslar, which since the tenth century had been the principal source of European silver and copper, passed the peak of its output and prosperity by the thirteenth century. The highly important mining industry of Freiberg had risen in the twelfth century and reached the farthest limit of its development by the beginning of the fourteenth century; the development of the silver mines at Meissen, in Tyrol, in Carinthia, and especially of the rich Transylvanian deposits and of the Bohemian mines of Iglau and Altenberg was roughly contemporary; that of Silesia and perhaps Moravia somewhat later. But by the middle of the fourteenth century in nearly all these regions the mining industry was plunged into a depression from which it did not climb out until the second half of the fifteenth century. Water was the great enemy. The underground workings now reached the strata exposed to the danger of flooding, and in spite of all the experiments and abortive attempts to deal with the underground water it was not until about the late fifties that the experiments of Martin Claus of Gotha solved the problem, and Saxon mining could be resumed on a scale approaching that of the pre-crisis years.[1]

The vicissitudes of silver mining have been well recorded and well studied. On supplies of silver the entire currency of medieval Europe depended, and with them the price level was inextricably involved. Historians therefore know more about silver than about any other branch of medieval mining. It appears, however, probable that with the exception of iron most other medieval mining and metal trades went through the same experiences as silver. Copper was mined in Saxony and Hungary as a bye-product of silver and suffered a similar fate. The copper production of Sweden, which was of more recent origin and had developed relatively slowly, may have had a more even career. On the other hand, the tin industry of England—probably the most ancient of all the mining industries of Europe—contracted in the late fourteenth and fifteenth centuries. At least once before the industry had been faced with a similar prospect. In the early thirteenth century its ancient deposits in Devonshire had been showing signs of exhaustion and the industry had to move further west to Cornwall. In the fourteenth century it was the turn of the Cornish tin centres to suffer. The

---

[1] See below, VII, 457; Bernhard Neumann, *Die Metalle, Geschichte, Vorkommen,* etc. passim; E. Reyer, *Zinn,* 6 ff.; L. Lewis, *Stannaries,* 33 ff.; C. Neuburg, *Goslars Berghau bis 1552,* 55 ff., 78, 106; A. Weyhmann in *Jahrb. d. Gesellschaft für Lothringische Gesch. u. Altertumskunde* (1905), 3, 56 ff.; Ludwig Beck's *Geschichte des Eisens* is utterly unconcerned with quantities, but the medieval section of vol. I (pp. 643 ff.) strongly supports the impression of a general advance in the use of iron and steel in the later Middle Ages.

output fell from about 1328 thousand weights per annum in the thirties of the fourteenth century to under 500 thousand weights in the mid-fifties. It recovered for a while at the end of the century when it reached a very high peak of 1600 thousand weights per annum, but it soon slumped again and stayed low—mostly below 900 thousand weights—throughout the fifteenth century. The output was not to reach and pass the figures of the pre-Black Death decades until well into the sixteenth century. The decline was not so clearly marked and did not appear to continue for a period equally long in the other important tin area, that of Zinnwald and Altenberg in the Bohemian mountains, but there too the rising trend was interrupted in the first half of the fifteenth century (the Hussite wars were mainly responsible), and production could not wholly recover until the seventies.[1]

The iron industry alone appeared to have escaped the depression. For one thing, it was more dispersed and more dependent on local conditions than other branches of mining. And it is also possible that the very disorders and wars of the time, which did so much to disturb industrial development elsewhere, stimulated the making of guns, cannon and miscellaneous weapons, and created what appears to be a mild war boom in the main iron-making regions. For in at least two main European sources of high-quality iron—that of Sweden and that of Bayonne-Bilbao—output continued at a level which did not sufficiently differ from that of the previous centuries to attract the attention of contemporary commentators. In most of the other important centres of the iron industry on the continent—even on the Lorraine deposits of the low grade ore—the industry underwent in the second half of the fifteenth century a technical development—higher and better smelting ovens, greater use of water to work bellows and hammers—which suggests that the industry was expanding. How recent and how general this expansion was and how much it owed to war demand—all these are questions still awaiting an answer.

This catalogue of industries, sinking or just afloat, cannot be concluded without some reference to the most important of the medieval industries, that of cloth. This is not of course the right place in which to unravel its involved pattern in the later Middle Ages. If Europe is viewed as a whole, the later Middle Ages will appear as the time when cloth production both rose and fell. While it declined in Flanders and probably in France, it prospered in other places. In the fourteenth century the cloth industry of Brabant drew to itself some of the prosperity which seemed to be departing from Flanders. In the middle of the fourteenth century the English cloth industry made a sudden leap forward which brought it to its peak at the turn of the fourteenth and

[1] See below, VII, 456-458.

fifteenth centuries; in the fifteenth century the cloth industry of Holland, especially that of Leiden, got under way. We are told that a number of smaller centres of cloth production came to the fore at that time. However, nothing less than a statistical inquiry could show whether the industrial activity in the new areas was sufficient to match the declining production of Flanders; and comprehensive figures are lacking. But judging from the falling supplies of raw materials, the cloth industry, and more especially the output of the high quality cloth for export, must also have declined. In Flanders, Brabant and Holland, by far the most important source of high quality wool was England, and English wool exports were declining.

4

The story of the cloth industry epitomises the entire history of commerce and industry in the later Middle Ages. The contemporary record of most other trades was equally broken and confused by local and contradictory movements. Regarded as a whole, European economy had its irregular rises and falls—what the economists call short-term fluctuations—which broke the continuity of the falling trends. Above all, the last quarter of the fourteenth century and the second quarter of the fifteenth were marked both in this country and abroad by signs of economic revival, however sudden and short-lived. Yet, on a broad view, European trade passed in the later Middle Ages through a trough long enough—sometimes longer than a century—to justify the diagnosis of a 'secular' slump.

There is now a broad agreement about the facts of the slump, but there is still much uncertainty about its explanation. Was the depression sufficiently 'general', i.e. common to a range of occupations sufficiently wide, to justify the assumption of a common factor? Some of the causes were undoubtedly accidental and contingent: misfortunes, local and temporary, which will be found in the record of every major industry and trade. The Hussite wars had their effect on Bohemian mines; Gascon campaigns disturbed the wine trade; Scandinavian wars interrupted the fishing and the curing of Skania herring; the Wars of the Roses may have interfered with English exports; and urban revolutions had their obvious effect on the Flemish cloth trade. All these were, so to speak, 'events': fortuitous happenings which sometimes coincided but were not deeply related. Some historians might therefore be forgiven for their reluctance to treat them as anything more than a series of accidents and coincidences.

Accidents and coincidences they doubtless were. Yet some of them, even if regarded in isolation, might on second thoughts appear to be not wholly fortuitous. It will not be too far-fetched to believe that the

military and political conflict between the Hansé and the Danish kings
was in fact due to the remarkable expansion of the Hanseatic interests
in Skania fisheries and in Scandinavia in general during the previous
century, or that the social war in Flanders was prepared by the previous
century of industrial growth. Even less accidental and more obviously
rooted in the expansion of the previous age were the seemingly unrelated experiences of miners struggling in different parts of Europe
against the difficulties of deep workings and against the mounting
dangers of water. And in a field less purely economic, it is possible to
interpret the gradual clogging up of important trade routes, described
elsewhere, as a more or less inevitable consequence of the political
regime which had gradually evolved in the later Middle Ages in the
territories of France and the Holy Roman Empire: the solidifying of local
custom in the former, the withering of central authority in the latter.

It is not, however, on these considerations alone that the hypothesis
of a common cause rests. Much more important is the manifestation of
certain deep-seated factors similar to those which were responsible for
the ascending movement of the earlier centuries. In the first place, there
were prices. Just as the expansion of the twelfth and thirteenth centuries
was accompanied by steep price rises all over Europe, so was the decline
of the fourteenth and fifteenth centuries accompanied by price changes
no less continuous, though possibly less spectacular. Some of these
movements have already been mentioned; here they must be considered somewhat more closely. The series most easily available to the
historian and most generally studied, that of grain, shows prices expressed in terms of stable exchange medium either falling or stagnating
all over Europe. The 20-year means of English wheat prices collected
by Lord Beveridge and his team of price historians moved in the following manner:

Table V. *Price of Wheat in 20-year periods*

Years	Wheat prices in shillings (per qr.)	Wheat prices in grains of silver
1300–19	7·01	1734
1320–39	6·27	1547
1340–59	6·31	1372
1360–79	7·55	1508
1380–99	5·57	1113
1400–19	6·37	1188
1420–39	6·65	1107
1440–59	5·56	926
1460–79	6·02	812
1480–99	6·40	852
1500–19	6·91	920

Thus, apart from the high prices of 1360–79, which were influenced by a succession of bad harvests, the current prices sagged with a tendency to fall, while silver prices fell with hardly a break. Comparable foreign prices are not available for periods as early and in samples equally representative. The two collections most commonly used—Hanauer's for Alsace and d'Avenel's for France—do not lend themselves to close analysis and will not by themselves support any reliable historical conclusion. All that the two series can be made to yield is a vague and general impression.

Yet general impressions are not to be spurned, especially if they happen to agree with other and more reliable evidence; and the impression is that the continental prices, in terms of silver, exhibit the English trend to a greatly exaggerated degree. The exaggeration was obviously due to the currency troubles of the times, for whereas the English coinage remained comparatively stable (the silver content of the shilling stood at about 246 grains troy until 1344, and was thereafter reduced by slow steps till it fell to 133·20 grains troy in 1461) that of France and of most other continental countries was greatly debased throughout the fourteenth and fifteenth centuries. So fast and so continuous was the debasement that, however much the current prices rose, they never kept pace with it. According to recent authorities the Counts of Flanders at one time purposely manipulated their currency in the hope that the cost of living and wages would lag behind international prices.

Table VI. *Annual Wheat Prices in the Low Countries*[1]

(Index Number: 1375–99 = 100)

Years	Current prices
1375–99	100
1400–24	104
1425–49	138
1450–74	109

Yet, however exaggerated the trend of the French and Alsatian prices, they moved in the same direction as the trends of other and more reliable series. Among the latter should perhaps be included the price series for Flanders since 1375, which has also been assembled by the International Price Committee. It shows the 'current' wheat prices

---

[1] I owe the Flemish prices to Lord Beveridge's courtesy. They are derived from printed sources, mostly from H. Van Houtte's *Documents pour servir à l'Histoire des Prix*. The Königsberg prices (Table VII) come from an anonymous mid-nineteenth-century summary of grain prices in the records of the Prussian Order, quoted in W. Abel, *Agrarkrisen und Agrarkonjunktur*, 32–3.

fairly stable between 1375 and 1425 and then, after a brief and sharp rise in price in the first quarter of the fifteenth century, falling rather steeply for another twenty-five years. By the end of the third quarter of the fifteenth century they stood barely 9% above the price in 1375 and barely 5% above the price in 1400. In the same period prices measured in silver apparently declined.

The importance of the figures in Flanders lies in their relation to the world prices. The Low Countries were heavy importers of grain which they drew from more than one distant source and commonly from the Baltic. They were thus more sensitive to the general trends in European production and commerce than were the prices of such comparatively self-sufficient countries as England. From this point of view, also worth quoting is the little evidence we possess of the movement of prices in the principal source of grain exports in the same period, i.e. in the Eastern Baltic. In an anonymous mid-nineteenth century compilation based on the Koenigsberg records of the Prussian order, the price of rye expressed in units of silver is shown to behave in a manner strikingly similar to that of grain prices in the West. The prices for rye in Koenigsberg in the fifteenth century moved as follows:

Table VII. *Prices of Rye in Koenigsberg*

(Index Number: 1399 = 100)

Years	Prices (silver)
1399	100
1405	89·29
1432	85·32
1448	79·81
1494	49·84
1508	36·48

Owing to the heavy debasement of local currency in the fifteenth century 'current' prices may actually have risen, but the rise was probably gentle compared to the heavy depreciation of the mark.

A movement of prices so continuous must have had an obvious effect on economic life. The falling or sagging prices for agricultural products happened to be accompanied by steeply-rising costs of labour and must therefore have depressed the profits of demesne farming and discouraged commercial production for the market everywhere. In the absence of clear statistical evidence about trade in luxuries and semi-luxuries, it is difficult to say to what extent it was affected. Did the purchasing power of the upper classes and their demand for goods decline with the falling profits of industry and agriculture?

On general grounds some such correlation could be expected, but whether the effect of prices went further than that, whether it was also responsible for the slump in the major industries, depends on a number of other considerations. It depends, in the first place, on the extent to which price changes were general, i.e. common to the entire range of medieval commodities. It depends also on the susceptibility of medieval producers to price stimuli; above all on the susceptibility of those agricultural producers, who did not depend on 'cash' crops for their income.

On the whole the evidence on both points will not support the hypo-thesis of prices as the main, and still less as the sole, cause of the slump. Our knowledge of medieval prices is largely confined to grain, but in so far as other series are available they suggest that the fall in prices was highly departmentalised. Thus it does not appear that prices for cloth or those for iron, or indeed those for other commodities, fell at all or fell in the same proportion as prices for agricultural products. Hetero-geneous and difficult to collate as are the figures in Thorold Rogers' great collection, they nevertheless leave a strong impression that industrial prices did not in any way synchronise with those of grain. Prices for building materials were rising till the middle of the fourteenth century, were more or less stable from 1370 to 1425, and thereafter fell at a somewhat slower pace than grain. The prices of textiles (the least reliable in the collection) appear to fall from 1375 to 1440 and to rise thereafter. Prices for iron were rising fast in the second half of the fourteenth century and falling gently in the fifteenth, finishing in 1475 about 4% above their level in 1350. Expressed in bushels of wheat the index of iron prices in the second half of the century rose without a break from 100 in the first half of the century to 159 in the decade of 1351 to 1360, and to 352 in 1389 to 1400.

Thus the prices for separate commodities did not move together. Even the different agricultural products depreciated and appreciated at times and at rates somewhat different from those of wheat. As far as it is possible to judge from the variegated collection of prices for animals and animal products assembled by Thorold Rogers, the relation between their prices and those for wheat was not at all close.

The prices are here expressed in silver, and therefore somewhat exaggerate the fall in prices, but they reveal very clearly the difference between the two series. The prices for animal products in current coin-age actually rose and were considerably higher in the period of 1401 to 1425 than in that of 1351 to 1375 and were not much lower in 1451 to 1475 than they had been a century earlier. Indeed, expressed in current prices, the series after 1351 continues the rising trend of the previous two centuries for at least another 125 years. Hanauer's figures for Alsace, however exiguous, and d'Avenel's collection for France, however heterogeneous, are nevertheless sufficient to suggest that in other parts oɪ Western Europe the two series were at least as divergent as in England. Taking Hanauer's silver prices for 1351 to 1375 as 100, we find that in 1400–25 the grain prices fell to 64 while the prices for animal products stood at 87. Hanauer's silver prices, but not his current ones, broke thereafter, but while the index of his silver prices for grain fell between 1351 and 1450 from 100 to 71, that of his prices for animal products stayed at 100. In the subsequent collapse of silver prices, largely reflecting the debasement of French coinage, the index of grain prices sank by the end of the century to as low a level as 40, but prices for animal products still stood at some 40% higher at 54 to 56.

Table VIII. *English Prices of Animal Products and Wheat*
(Index number: 1351–75 = 100.)

Years	Wheat	Animal products and cattle
1351–75	100	100
1376–1400	71	88
1401–25	70	99
1426–50	70	89
1451–75	55	76
1476–1500	53	68

Similar—no more reliable but equally significant—evidence about most animal products could be quoted from almost every continental country, but none of these prices are more significant or have been better studied than those of butter. Trade in butter may appear to the uninitiated too slight a foundation for any argument, especially for an argument about medieval economy as a whole. Yet in spite of being cast on a small scale, it has turned out to be an important index of wider movements. For butter was a merchandise circulating over great distances and commanding an international price; and what is even more important is that it happened to be a semi-luxury entering into popular consumption. When we are told that in this period a Prussian labourer earned the equivalent of 30 kilogrammes of rye per day, it is not necessary to know what Alfred Marshall said about the elasticity of the demand for bread in order to conclude that agricultural labourers were now better able to indulge in a little butter, however expensive. The price of butter was therefore highly responsive to changes in demand and supply, and was more sensitive as a barometer of markets than prices of more indispensable foods. It is therefore very significant that the price of butter and the price of grain diverged more widely than the prices of any other commodities. In the fourteenth and fifteenth centuries the butter prices rose very steeply, in both current coinage and in silver, in all the main sources of supplies, with the possible exception of Holland—in Sweden, in Norway, in Western Poland. Steepest of all was the rise in Norway. There, after about seventy or eighty years of relatively stable prices, butter suddenly rose by about 10% in the sixties of the fourteenth century and by about 33% by 1400. In the course of the fifteenth century the prices continued to soar; and by 1457 reached a level 200% above that of 1400, dropping to about 100% above that of 1400 in the next decade. On the other hand, the prices for rye imported from the Baltic moved relatively little, and if anything sagged. A similar discrepancy between the prices of rye and butter developed in Sweden and in Prussia, and above all in the Polish hinterland from where Prussian seaports drew most of their butter. In Cracow the index of prices for rye between 1398 and 1450 sank from 33 to 10, but at the same time the prices of butter rose from 10 to 33 or more than threefold.[1]

From the present point of view, the precise cause underlying the behaviour of butter prices is less important than the fact that they behaved differently from grain prices, and that they bear out more fully than any other price series the danger of generalising from a price trend which was apparently confined to grain. Indeed, even in the grain trade the influence of prices is not very obviously related to changes in production and trade. While in most European countries prices expressed in silver were falling, current prices in local coinage were rising, and in regions as self-supporting as most provinces of France and Central Germany it was the current prices that mattered most, for it was in relation to current prices that the cost of living, the rate of wages, and the profits of agriculture fluctuated. In England the break in the prices in the second quarter of the fourteenth century was unmistakable, but the downward trend was neither continuous nor very marked—certainly less continuous and less marked than the earlier rise. The line representing the long-term trend of English prices and based, say, in moving 25-year averages, is all but horizontal; the prices of 1500 being actually 10% higher than those of the first quarter of the fourteenth century. The lowest prices of the period—those from 1450 to 1475—were only 20% below those of 1300 to 1325. Expressed in silver, the English prices fell rather more steeply; yet even they did not fall more than about 25%: from 1372 to 1107 grains of silver per quarter of wheat in the century between 1340 and 1440. And it was in that century that English agriculture contracted most and its organisation changed most profoundly.

[1] Julian Pelc, *Ceny w Krakowie w latach 1369–1600*, 127 ff.; for other butter prices see J. Schreiner, *Pest og Prisfall in Senmiddelalderen*, 82.

The economic and more especially the commercial trends of the time were thus out of scale with the movements of grain prices. Is that surprising? The only way in which changes in grain prices could influence production and trade was by calling forth greater or smaller supplies of marketable products. But earlier in this chapter it has already been emphasised that in agriculture prices were by no means the sole, or the main, conductor of economic stimuli. Peasant producers were far too self-sufficient to order their production and to regulate their marketable surpluses in direct response to commercial considerations; and in the later Middle Ages this element of self-sufficiency increased rather than diminished, or, what is the same thing, the proportion of agricultural producers sensitive to prices was smaller than before. There is thus even less reason for seeking in grain prices the main cause of the falling trends of the later Middle Ages than there is for seeking in them an explanation of the rising trends in the earlier centuries.

The doubts are reinforced by the uncertainty of the monetary factor. One of the reasons why prices offer such an obvious and tempting explanation is that at first sight they can easily be fitted into what is known of the contemporary changes in the supply of precious metals. The supplies of silver from the European silver mines gradually gave out, as silver mines entered upon their decline. The supplies from the Goslar region dwindled in the thirteenth century, those from the other mining areas of Central and Eastern Europe declined or ceased altogether in the fourteenth or early fifteenth centuries. There is also evidence of local scarcities of silver. Indeed, such re-minting as the English crown undertook in the fourteenth and fifteenth centuries, in 1344, 1346, 1351, 1412 and 1461, had for its object to bring the silver content of the English coins into line with the shorter supply and the higher price of silver.

This now appears to be the generally accepted view. Its relevance to the problem of falling prices, however, is not as clear as it might at first sight appear. In the first place, there is a purely historical difficulty of dates and places. The movements of prices cannot easily be synchronised with the dates at which the mining of silver is known to have declined, nor can they be put into geographical relation with areas in which silver was mined. Whereas the Goslar mining was already depressed in the thirteenth century, and silver mining elsewhere reached its lowest depths by the middle of the fourteenth century, the fall in prices did not begin till some time in the first half of the fourteenth century and did not become general till much later. Silver began to flow again from the Saxon mines in the fifties of the fifteenth century, yet, expressed in terms of silver, prices stayed low and, in England at least, continued to fall till 1480. Moreover, the price changes occurred no earlier and were no more spectacular in the regions nearest to the sources of new silver than they were elsewhere; and it is difficult to read into the regional differences between the price series in Cracow, Alsace, Holland and Norway the familiar sequence of concentric ripples by which falling investment and employment in the mining areas could normally be expected to transmit the effects of a mining slump over the entire face of Europe.

There are also the more general arguments some of which have already been mentioned in the discussion of the thirteenth-century rises. To begin with, the annual increments of new silver at their highest were not as great as other changes in silver supplies could be and, in fact, were. By 1300 or 1320, the dates at which supplies of silver from continental mines began markedly to fall off, the total stock of silver in Europe, in relation to annual output, must have been truly enormous, for it had been amassed in at least two centuries, and probably three, of large and steadily mounting output. And when the total stock was thus two hundred to five hundred times that of its annual accretions, the international price of silver was influenced more by the manner in which it was employed than by the current flow from the mines. The falling investment in industry and agriculture as a result of the low level of profits, the changing financial technique, the diversion of currency into the hands of the crown and its soldiers, the greater demand for silver for buckles and buttons: each of these phenomena could and should have had at least as great an effect on the value of silver as the changes in the supply of new bullion.

What makes the hypothesis of silver supplies all the more difficult to accept is that, even if the flow of new metal from the mines affected international supplies of silver, it did not in the same degree, or indeed in any degree, determine the supplies to individual countries. Individual countries received the bullion by means of international trade, and such was the structure of foreign trade in the later Middle Ages that while some countries earned vast balances, others did not; and that the changes in trade balances did not synchronise with the ups and downs of silver mining. On the roughest calculation, England's favourable balance on the visible trading account oscillated in the course of the fifteenth century between £50,000 and £150,000, and was on the average equal to about half the total value of English foreign trade and more than twice the value of coinage drawn in and out of the mint in the years of recoinage. And if, in the fourteenth and fifteenth centuries wool exports and grain exports declined, the deficiency was more than made up by the high taxes on wool, the development of English cloth exports, and the virtual cessation of Flemish cloth imports. There is thus every reason why silver should have continued to be imported, and there was nothing surprising or anachronistic in the verse of the fifteenth-century, *Libel of English Policy*, in which its well-informed author describes the Prussians as importing

> plate of silver of weighes good and sure
> in great plenty which they bring and buy
> out of the lands of Bohemia and Hungary.

In times of reviving trade, such as the last quarter of the fourteenth century and the thirties and forties of the fifteenth, when the *Libel* was composed, the balance of trade and the imports of bullion may well have risen not only in relation to the total value of trade of those years but also in comparison with the trade balance of earlier centuries. True, that visible balance was apt to be eaten into by papal taxation and often frittered away in payments for war and garrisons abroad, but all this means is that the flow of silver in and out of this country was due to war and payments abroad, and not changes in silver output alone.[1]

5

Thus price movements there were, and from most of them important consequences followed; but they could not be entirely ascribed to monetary causes, and moreover they were not general. And price changes which are not 'general' but are mainly confined to grain, point to a factor which has already been shown to have operated in the opposite direction in the early centuries of the Middle Ages, i.e. population. On broad, and largely theoretical, grounds a fall in population would be compatible with all the phenomena which our evidence exhibits, and should raise none of the objections to which other general explanations are open. When population fell, some marginal lands would in all probability be abandoned and food would be produced on better land. Relative to the amount of land and labour engaged in food production and relative to the demand for food, supplies would then be more plentiful and therefore cheaper. There would thus be every reason to expect both smaller production and lower prices accompanied

---

[1] The problem is further complicated by the use of gold. Most countries in Europe introduced gold coinage by the middle of the fourteenth century, and even before that happened, gold and gold coin of Italian and Byzantine origin was often used in settlement of international payments. The value of silver, or rather its local scarcities and superfluities, was therefore bound to be affected by the terms on which silver and gold coins were exchanged. And as commercial values of the two metals were often at variance with the 'official' or mint terms of exchange, flights to and from silver coinage were very frequent. When they happened they did at least as much to cause local scarcities and abundances of silver as any other changes in the supply of bullion.

214 DECLINE OF POPULATION

by the show of abundance which is so conspicuous in the late fourteenth and fifteenth centuries. A fall in population would also have, so to speak, a selective effect on prices, in that it would tend to lower the prices of agricultural products, which were previously being produced at high and ever rising cost—or, to use the economist's terminology, under steeply diminishing returns—but would have little effect on commodities not greatly subject to diminishing returns, i.e. most industrial products. By increasing the proportions of silver per head it would counteract the effects of falling supplies from the mines, and might even counterbalance what economists would describe as 'deflationary changes in liquidity', but what historians would classify as greater tendency to hoarding. It would help to increase the 'effective demand' of large masses of population, i.e. stimulate their outlay on food and other goods, and thus lead to higher prices and greater supplies of semi-luxuries especially sensitive to fluctuations of demand.

All this is theory, and like all theories it may at first sight appear too simple to fit the infinite variety of medieval experience. But it so happens that this particular argument has emerged from evidence purely descriptive and from arguments largely empirical, and has in fact been first announced as a matter of historical fact by medievalists as innocent of population theory as only medievalists can be. To make this clear it may be worth marshalling some of the evidence even if this will mean transgressing the strict limits of this chapter's subject.

The most familiar evidence is that derived from the topographical record of depopulation, and, above all, from the evidence of vacant holdings and uncultivated fields in the later Middle Ages. In England neither the story of colonisation in the earlier centuries nor that of the depopulation in the later ones has been studied sufficiently closely to yield statistical estimates, but the historians who handled evidence abroad happened to be more quantitatively minded; and, if their results are to be trusted, the abandoned fields and holdings represented throughout the late Middle Ages a very considerable proportion o land erstwhile occupied. In South-western Germany the *Wüstungen* at the turn of the fourteenth and fifteenth centuries were so high as to account in some places for more than half of the holdings. Recent computation puts the proportion of vacant holdings in Scandinavian countries almost equally high.[1]

Needless to say, the evidence of abandoned holdings is apt to magnify the depopulation process it reflects. But allowing for fields abandoned

<hr>

[1] Wilhelm Abel, *Die Wüstungen des Ausgehenden Mittelalters*, 1-13, 25-30; J. Schreiner, *Pest og Prisfall i Senmiddelalderen*, 58-63 and *passim*. For a detailed quantitative analysis of German *Wüstungen*, see Heinz Pohlendt, *Die Verbreitung der Mittelalterlichen Wüstungen in Deutschland*, ch. II and III, Göttingen, 1950.

for reasons other than shortage of population, allowing also for subsequent re-lets and re-occupation, there still remains a large balance of
lands unoccupied and depopulated through shortage of manpower.
Moreover the shortage was obviously general, i.e. not confined to
agriculture alone. Contrary to what is sometimes assumed, the fall of
population in the countryside was not the result of flight to towns, for
population in towns was also dwindling. In this country the old
corporate towns—Northampton, Lincoln—filled the air with protesta-
tions of poverty and with claims for reduction of royal taxes on
grounds of depopulation. A German historian has computed that the
population of North German cities declined in the course of the fourteenth and fifteenth centuries by at least 20%. No such computation
has been made for the towns of England or France, but those towns
where the urban evidence has been studied at all closely—Bordeaux,
Rouen, Arras—bear signs of contraction at least as great. The Flemish
decline has already been noted.

Depopulation, both urban and rural, was of course a complex process, mostly discontinuous and sometimes compensated by new growth;
and indeed some of the new growth was so boisterous that in the
absence of quantitative data it might well give the impression of a
balance successfully redressed. Thus, while the population of most
English towns fell after 1350, it may have remained more or less
stationary in London, Bristol and Southampton and two or three other
sea ports, and may for a time have grown in the cloth-making towns
and villages of East Anglia, Yorkshire and the West Country. Similarly
while the population in the towns of France, Flanders, Northern and
Central Germany declined, that in North Netherlands (Holland) and
in Southern and South-eastern Germany may have grown in the course
of the fifteenth century.

This was a redress in some measure, but the measure must not
be exaggerated. Judging from the amount of cloth produced—say
50,000 cloths per annum—the numbers engaged in English cloth
industry at its height could not have been greater than 25,000 persons,
if as great.[1] Abroad the cloth industry of Holland was not yet on
a scale sufficient to make up for the decline of the industry elsewhere,
just as her towns could not as yet have grown sufficiently to balance
the fall of urban population in Flanders and France. Similarly,
the development of Augsburg and Nuremberg was also too much
in its infancy to counter-balance the ebbing fortunes of Hanseatic
economy.

[1] There are several ways of computing the figures. The simplest is to compute
from the price of cloth and the costs of production. See M. Postan in *Economic
History Review*, II (1950), 232.

Further evidence of falling population will be found in the falling land values. In various parts of France payments for land continually fell, in spite of the rising wheat prices in current coinage. On the estates of St Germain-des-Prés near Paris rents fell without a break from 84*d.* per *arpent* in the second half of the fourteenth century to 55*d.* in the middle decades of the fifteenth century and to about 30*d.* in the seventies and eighties. In Sweden, Denmark and Norway land prices—both rents and capital values—were falling throughout the period, at a pace which appeared to outrun the fall in prices of grain.

Finally, there is the evidence of wages. For whereas prices of agricultural products fell, wages rose. Evidence of rising wages will be found all over Europe, but the most complete as well as the most reliable series of wages so far available is that of the wage rates on the manors of the bishopric of Winchester published by Lord Beveridge. That series reveals a twofold rise in real wages between 1300 and 1350: a rise strangely suggesting a scarcity of labour through falling population.

So unless and until new evidence to the contrary is produced, the commercial and industrial depression of the later Middle Ages must be accounted for by decline in numbers. There were fewer hands at work, and there were fewer mouths to feed. This need not have left individuals any worse off; indeed, there is every reason for believing that the working population of Northern Europe was now more prosperous than ever before. Yet collectively Europe became smaller and poorer, and the decline in her trade and industry was merely one manifestation of a contracting continent.

(II) THE REGULATED TRADE

1

A long period of contracting trade left its mark on the men engaged in it. The economic status of the merchants, indeed their very behaviour, changed; and no change was more typical, more in tune with the times, than the passing of the great men. If the characteristic figure in commercial and industrial development of the early centuries was the adventurer-merchant depicted by Pirenne, the typical representative of the later Middle Ages was the sedate *bourgeois* of middle rank. Rich men were of course to be found in many large towns. Above all, the Anglo-French wars brought forth small groups of war financiers and speculators. But careers and fortunes like those of Jacques Cœur in fifteenth-century France remain isolated and short-lived; for this was no longer the time of the great speculators moving about the western world, founding cities, forcing open new trade routes, founding new commercial empires. Their race had all but died out and was not to be reborn until the very threshold of the Renaissance, the time when the Welsers and the Fuggers rose in the South of Germany, and the new generation of speculators appeared on the bourses of Antwerp and Amsterdam.

The fifteenth-century merchant new-style was a composite type made up of several elements of different antiquity. One of its components was that of a merchant turned financier; and both the type itself and the process by which he appeared on the scene were of course much older than the later Middle Ages. Medieval merchants of all centuries were prone to retire from active trade as soon as they had made their fortunes. Having retired, the more substantial business men in England often abandoned their towns and their urban associations altogether and established themselves in the country as gentlemen. On the continent, they would more frequently choose to stay in the town as *rentiers*. They might participate as sleeping partners in the active trade of others; they might buy urban tenements and rents, take up municipal and other public bonds and sometimes advance private loans.

The propensity to retire into a life of *rentier* is not difficult to account for. The physical hazards of active trade abroad were not always matched by opportunites for enrichment, and the opportunity grew poorer as the foreign markets grew smaller. At the same time it is probable that capital was still sufficiently scarce to command a high rate of interest. As far as it is possible to judge (and the problem has not been investigated as fully as it deserves), the return expected on the investment of sleeping partners in fifteenth-century England was on the average well in excess of 10% per annum. The later Middle Ages also offered new and ever-growing opportunities for financing needy municipalities and kings at rates nearly as high.

There is therefore nothing incomprehensible or in any way mystical about that process of financial degeneration which seems to have come over a number of wealthy cities in the Middle Ages. When we find in the middle of the thirteenth century the ruling class of Arras made up largely of financiers advancing money to towns and princes all over Northern Europe, we cannot explain this otherwise than by concluding that many of the families, which in the late eleventh and twelfth centuries had pioneered in European cloth industry and in long-distance trade, had now 'made their pile' and sought in money-lending a quieter mode of life and a less adventurous occupation. Other cities might also, like Arras, pass out of the plane of active trade into mere money-lending. It so happens that the rise of Arras to the position of a banker city to the rest of Northern Europe occurred very early (for Arras's industrial career had also begun very early) and has been well studied; but a historian with a practised eye will find no difficulty in detecting in the later Middle Ages the same process in most of the towns of Northern Europe which had gone through a period of expansion and enrichment in the previous century or century and a half. Much of the mystery of the otherwise inexplicable withering away of the active trade of Flemish merchants might be found in the growth of the *rentier* class. The men, who would in an earlier age have acted as traders to foreign lands or even as employer-clothiers, were now tending to withdraw into quieter occupations: into brokerage and hostel-keeping in Bruges, into passive investment elsewhere.

In the later Middle Ages this process became more general, more, so to speak, disseminated, but it did not account for the entire change in mercantile society. It accounted only for one component of the new *bourgeoisie*, and there were other components as well. Above all, there were the men who looked for and found security not outside but within occupations still largely commercial. They did so by trading in a smaller way, within well organised and protected markets.

The typical figures of Northern European commerce in the late Middle Ages were on the whole a humbler lot of men than the merchants of some other times and places. Historians have always noticed the social differences which distinguished the commerce of the great Italian cities from that of the Hanseatic towns. Whereas the bulk of Italy's foreign commerce and finance in the later Middle Ages was in the hands of great commercial and banking houses, the Frescobaldi, the Bardi, the Peruzzi, the Medici, the Datini, the trade of the Hanseatic towns was in the hands of a greater number of smaller people. The difference, however, was not so much geographical as chronological. The records of the earlier centuries, the time when the great Hanseatic cities were being founded, are filled with the acts of great families attempting great things. In a few cities like Cologne it is still possible to find in the later Middle Ages great traders and speculators, like Tidman of Limbourg who financed Edward III, or Gerard von Wesel who tried in the middle of the fifteenth century to lead Cologne's break-away from the Hanse. Elsewhere in the German North, men of this stamp were no longer to be found. It is not that the great families wholly died out, for there were still Castorps and Warendorps all over Hanseatic regions. What happened was that they no longer occupied the position in the Hanseatic trade which had been theirs when they were blazing its trails in the newly opened lands beyond the Elbe.

The bulk of the trade was now in the hands of men of middling substance. And being middling they looked for safety and found it in co-operation, in combination, and more generally in numbers. It was for their benefit that the Hanseatic League maintained in most foreign

centres within its influence their great factories or *Kontors* with large
bodies of resident agents or factors. It was their cargoes that were
marshalled in convoys to the Bay of Bourgneuf, to the east coast of
England, to Bruges. And it was their trade that was looked after by
corporate organisations within the German towns—the *Bergenfahrers*
and *Schönenfahrers* of Lübeck, the *Englandfahrers* of Cologne.

The English development was even more remarkable in that the
dividing line was drawn more sharply. The early years of Edward III,
coinciding as they did with the opening phases of the Hundred Years
War and Edward's great fiscal operations, forced into bloom all the
capitalist or quasi-capitalist elements in English life. Men like the
brothers de la Pole, representing the upper rank of the English merchant
classes, now rose to great wealth gained in supplying the armies, in
arranging and transmitting payments abroad, in managing the king's
taxes and levies on wool. Their economic power as well as their
hold over the English wool trade reached their highest point in the
thirties and forties when, having formed several syndicates, they
were able to finance the crown and to monopolise the entire British
export trade in wool. But Edward's insolvency in the fifties brought
about their collapse; and their collapse meant also the demise of a
whole social order. When in the last quarter of the century the Staple
of Calais finally took shape it was made up of a larger number of
smaller men—men who in the fifteenth century were to be represented by the three generations of Cely's: respectable, prosperous
traders who, though in the highest rank of the wool trade, could not
claim more than one fiftieth or even a hundredth share of England's
wool exports. Needless to say, individuals of outstanding wealth did
not wholly disappear from English trade and finance. The wars of
Richard II call forth Brember and Lyon; the trade of Bristol could
boast of Robert Cheddar and William Canning. And in fifteenth-
century London, there was Dick Whittington. Yet in a curious way
none of these men were as typical of the fifteenth century as the great
London dynasties were of the thirteenth. They were probably not
quite so rich; they were certainly less numerous. Above all, they no
longer dominated the trade of the country. The economic and financial
power of the wool trade in its relations with the crown and with the
outside world now rested not on the wealth or influence of individuals
but on the power of the corporate organisation—the Company of the
Merchants of the Staple of Calais.

The Company of the Staple was not alone. The 'general' traders of
England, who specialised in importing and exporting miscellaneous
merchandise other than wool, now for the first time appeared in records
as the Company of Merchant Adventurers. By then the name was

out of date. The time when English general merchants adventured furthest into distant lands and seas was the turn of the fourteenth and fifteenth centuries and preceded by at least two or three generations the establishment of a company claiming the title of Merchant Adventurers. It was in the fifteenth century, when the expansion of English trade both in area and in quantity was long over, and when most opportunities for commercial adventure had fallen away, that the merchants arrogated to themselves the name to which they were no longer entitled. Their company was coming into an ever greater prominence as the century drew to its close, and made up in collective power and influence for the more modest substance of its members.

2

Corporate trade was indeed the typical feature of the later Middle Ages. Mediocre men combined to do what greater ones might have done in isolation. In later centuries, the late sixteenth and the seventeenth, corporate trade could be made to serve the ends of great speculative business. Similar corporations may also have existed in the earlier centuries of the Middle Ages. Did not the great Flemish capitalists of the thirteenth century operate in London through the Hanse of the Flemish towns, and did not the magnates of Cologne establish themselves in England at the same time through a similar Hanse? In the later Middle Ages, however, corporate action and corporate support became the mainstay of mediocre firms. With their support large numbers could share in the trade of Northern Europe, and without it no merchant from Northern Europe could successfully operate. For corporations both protected and circumscribed the trade they controlled; and they did not confer collective power on their members without acquiring collective authority over them. By virtue of this authority, they were now able to regulate the scale and the methods of individual enterprise and to lay down rigid rules for prices and credit, for terms of sales, for relations with agents, and for the latters' residence and conduct.

As the scope of individual enterprises contracted and their reliance upon corporate organisation grew, so their methods and organisation changed. This is not the place to deal with all the facts of medieval business technique. One fact, however, is strictly relevant here. The modest scope of individual enterprises, as well as their large numbers, forced upon them a method of trade which in at least one respect differed from the methods of the great houses of Italy and South Germany. They were less, so to speak, self-contained. An individual English firm trading abroad, or a Hanseatic firm trading in England, or a Dutch firm trading in Antwerp and Bruges, did not as a rule trade through channels entirely and exclusively its own. Whereas a great Italian firm might be served by bodies of servants and partners, a typical Hanseatic or English firm, being too small to maintain a large body of permanent servants, would try and avail itself of the services of more or less independent agents and brokers. The difference must not of course be driven too far. Most English firms trading in Flanders sent out for shorter or longer periods representatives of their own, and there were Italian merchants in Bergen, London and elsewhere ready to act for any client in Italy. But on the whole the North European machinery of factories and corporate companies as well as the smaller scale of individual enterprise favoured a far greater development of resident agencies and of a specialised profession of foreign factors.

The corporate tendency manifested itself, however, not only abroad and in dealings with foreign countries but also at home and in matters of local trade. The municipal governments at home began to take an ever greater interest in the commercial activities of their burgesses, and the age was one of mounting urban regulations and of accumulating urban legislation. The right to participate in the trade of the local markets and in the staple branches of foreign trade was being defined and circumscribed, the entry into them was being limited. Monopoly was indeed the prime object and the pre-requisite condition of urban regulations and became the guiding object of town policy. It was only the power of the king, as in England and France, or the political links with other towns, as in North Germany, that prevented the whole of Europe breaking up into a loose assembly of small but economically independent territories, each dominated by a monopolistic town. And even in England and France and the Hanseatic North, the monopolistic and corporate interests came to the fore in most towns.

Urban economy was indeed beginning to approximate to the textbook fiction of a medieval town: a diminutive region forming with its rural belt a self-sufficient unit, within which trade and industry were partitioned into equal shares and regulated by law. The reason why historians have so often been led to accept this fiction as a representative sample of medieval economy is that they know much more about regulated economy of the corporate town than they do about trade in its freer and less regulated aspects. For it is in the nature of regulation and control to breed documentary evidence and thus to perpetuate itself in history out of all proportion to its real importance in historical development.

The corporate and monopolistic features of fourteenth and fifteenth century towns have thus shielded from view the meagrely documented activities of freer trades and freer towns. There were 'open' towns, and 'open' trades within them, even in the later Middle Ages. For we know that the great fair towns of Northern Europe—Bruges, Antwerp, Bergen-op-Zoom—were free ports where strangers were allowed to enter and where trade with strangers was more or less unrestricted by any law, except perhaps the law of residence and brokerage. Greater or smaller elements of freer trade might also be found in great metropolitan centres like London, in seafaring communities like Middelburg. Yet, on the whole, it was not these towns that typified the new order, but Danzig, which ended by excluding even the other Hanseatics from its local trade; Bergen, where the German merchants who dominated it established a close and highly-regulated monopoly over its trade; Rouen and Paris, where local companies watched and fought jealously over their fields of operations; and countless other smaller towns in France and Germany, which now sank into that well-regulated stupor from which they were not to awake until the French revolution and Napoleon's conquests.

The monopolistic and regulated economy of medieval municipalities was of course related to the political as well as to the social changes within the towns. In the political struggles, which mark the history of the North European towns in the fourteenth century, the rising parties were the craft gilds, which voiced the interests of the smaller men rooted primarily in the local markets. In many German towns, in Wismar, in Rostock, in Bremen, indeed in Lübeck itself, craft gilds rose in the second half of the fourteenth century or the beginning of the fifteenth to sweep out of office the descendants of the patrician families entrenched in town government. Similar revolts took place elsewhere—the Flemish risings of the fourteenth century indeed belong to the mainstream of the politics and diplomacy of the age. Except in Flanders, most of the movements of revolt failed; in towns, in which the democratic governments established themselves, they were as a rule ousted from office after a few years and replaced again by representatives of the patrician families. Yet, even at times and in places at which the counter-revolutions succeeded what they re-established was the political ascendancy of illustrious families and not the conditions which had once upon a time helped them to acquire their lustre. As has already been said, the great families themselves were no longer the same. They were mainly landowners, *rentiers*, public servants, or else traders differing only in name and personal descent from the middling men around them. The time for capitalists was over or not yet.

(III) THE HANSE

1

The commercial depression, which for all its local variations, affected the whole of Northern Europe, and which, for all its discontinuity, lasted for a century and more, was bound to influence the political history of European trade. More especially it was bound to influence the economic policies in regions which happened to be most exposed to the action of commercial change.

North Germany was thus exposed to an extent greater than other parts of Europe. It would be natural to expect that, at the time when both population and commerce ceased to grow, the territorial scope of German trade should have ceased to expand and its outer frontiers should have ceased to move. Danzig was the last great foundation of the German town builders. After the beginning of the fourteenth century no other towns of importance and no new commercial positions were founded in the Slavonic East. The newest and easternmost Germanic settlements—beyond the Oder and the upper Danube—were destined to remain isolated oases amidst a culture which they failed to assimilate and within an economy which they never wholly subdued or integrated with their own.

It is therefore not as paradoxical as it may seem that the age which saw the end of German expansion should also have given birth to the most important political formation in German history of the late Middle Ages—the Hanseatic League. At first sight the League was a step so novel and so forward that it may be difficult to see in it signs of decline. Yet viewed from the point of view of economic and geographical facts, it represented in the field of transcontinental trade the all-prevailing trend towards collective protection. For in the second half of the fourteenth century German commerce had all but reached the limits of its territorial expansion. From now onwards the German towns were more anxious to keep the positions they possessed than able to acquire new positions further afield. This indeed became the purpose of the Hanseatic League, and from this point of view the League was little more than a federation which the German towns established among themselves to maintain by political action that place in European trade which they had won for themselves in the course of the economic changes of the preceding epoch.

The rise of the League was thus essentially a political event; and its early development was largely a constitutional process. Its starting points were the unions of German merchants abroad. The organisations of German merchants in Wisby and London were the earliest unions of this kind. Indeed it was in England that the very term 'Hansa' was used for the first time to designate the right of merchants to form trading associations, and by the beginning of the thirteenth century the word ceased to be applied to the burgesses of English towns and was confined to the organisations of foreign merchants in London.[1] Thus a number of Flemish towns headed by Bruges formed in the thirteenth century a London 'Hansa', which represented them before English authorities and acted on their behalf in defence of their interests and privileges. Another such organisation was the Cologne 'Hansa', which was eventually to grow into the Hanse of the Steelyard comprising all, or nearly all, the German merchants trading in London.[2] The Great Charter of 1303, which greatly extended the privileges of German merchants in England and which in later centuries came to be claimed by the Germans as the constitutional foundation of their privileged status in this country, dealt with the North German merchants as a single body. Since then the English merchants knew only of the *mercatores alemanniae*, and in this way the London Hanse of the Cologners became the London Hanse of the Germans. Under the Great Charter the Hanseatic merchants acquired valuable exemptions from customs, which put them in a more favourable position than other aliens, or indeed the native merchants of England. Their corporate organisation of the Steelyard received extensive powers of self-government and jurisdiction and a share in municipal authority in London. All in all, the Hanseatic rights in England established the Germans in a position of privilege and autonomy comparable to the 'capitulations' of a later age.

England, however, was not the only place where the merchants from North Germany came to have a corporate organisation and a privileged status. There was hardly an important commercial centre in Northern Europe, in which some German towns did not at one time or another receive grants of commercial liberties and did not organise into communal bodies of very much the same type as the German Hanse in London. Of these communal organisations the most important were the German 'factories' at the two termini of the great route: in Bruges and Novgorod.

The German factory, or *Kontor*, in Bruges was not as old as their London Hanse, but in the course of time it became their chief trading

[1] For a closely argued discussion of the evolution of the term, see R. Doehaerd, 'À propos du mot "hanse"', *Revue du Nord*, xxxiii, No. 129 (1951).

[2] It has been suggested, but not definitely proved, that there were originally two German *Hansae*, that of Cologne and that of the Easterlings, which later fused into one: see M. Weinbaum: 'Stalhof und Deutsche Gildhalle zu London' in *Hansische Geschichtsblatter*, Jahrgang 1928 (Lübeck, 1929).

station abroad. A the time when the *Kontor* was established, Bruges was about to enter upon the most illustrious stage of its history. With the rise of the *Kontor* the active commerce of the Flemings themselves gradually declined; but, strange as it may seem, the importance of Bruges grew as the active trade of its burgesses dwindled. At the height of Flemish industrial and commercial development in the thirteenth and the early fourteenth centuries Bruges had been one of the economic centres of Flanders, one of its four *Leden*, but unlike the other three it was from the very beginning more important commercially than industrially. Its cloth industry was far behind that of Ghent, Ypres and Douai; nor did it possess any other important industries. And even in commerce Bruges had at first fulfilled a highly specialised function. Its geographical situation was inconvenient for internal trade: off the main artery of the Scheldt and on the periphery of the main internal land routes. But it proved very convenient as a port for commercial traffic between the Low Countries and England, and its trade expanded as the cloth industry of Flanders became more and more dependent on English supplies of wool.

Apparently it was this connection with England that attracted the Germans to Bruges in the first instance. There has been a certain amount of argument among German historians on this point, but on the whole it appears that the Germans had been in the habit of going to England long before they established themselves in Flanders. It was because Bruges had been the centre of Anglo-Flemish trade that it also became the centre of German-Flemish trade. But with the Germans there it soon developed into something more than an Anglo-Flemish trade junction and before long acquired many features of an international emporium. Bruges, the sea port and the seat of a great fair where the Germans and the English had been in the habit of going, now became also the port and the fair where the Bretons, the Normans, the Spaniards and later the Italians came to do their buying and selling. And as Bruges rose in importance, the Hanseatic *Kontor* drew to itself an ever greater proportion of German trade. In the course of time its privileges, its federal organisation and its hold over the Hanseatic trade became the standing, not to say the burning, issue of the inter-urban politics of the German Hanse.

The third important centre of German foreign trade where the merchants from northern and eastern towns enjoyed important privileges and a communal organisation was the 'Petershof' of Novgorod. Novgorod was the eastern terminus of the great route and the chief centre of German trade in Russia. In the early Middle Ages the Scandinavians, and especially the Gotlanders, who were probably the first to establish a commercial factory in Novgorod, possessed there a 'Hof', i.e. a 'yard', with hostels and warehouses. But eventually the 'Hof' passed into the hands of the Germans and became the seat of a communal organisation of German merchants trading to Novgorod protected by treaties with Russian princes and enjoying liberties roughly of the same kind as those possessed by their factories elsewhere.

In addition to the three main corporations of Bruges, London and Novgorod, the merchants of the Hanseatic towns also possessed outposts in smaller places like the English 'treaty ports' of Lynn, Boston, Hull and Bristol, or the distant factory—'Fondacho dei Tedeschi'—in Venice, and a more permanent stake in the muncipal institutions of most Norwegian and Swedish towns, and more especially of Bergen. In addition, improvised corporate organisations were sometimes set up in the towns of the Low Countries to which German traders happened to transfer their activities in times of trouble. Thus a network of commercial stations enjoying exceptional treaty rights and valuable commercial privileges and often connected by routes completely dominated by German merchants, formed a commercial system as close and, by all appearances, as tightly knit as any Europe had ever seen.

This system in its main outlines was already in existence at the beginning of the fourteenth century, but at that time the system, like the 'informal' empires of a later age, owed its cohesion and unity to economic facts rather than to political ties. For, in theory, the corporate organisations in foreign places still led separate and independent existences and, so to speak, 'belonged' to the merchants trading in them. Viewed politically and juridically, the rise of the Hanseatic League in the closing decades of the thirteenth and the first half of the fourteenth centuries was nothing else than a gradual transformation of the informal system into a formal one, and of the separate corporations, *Hansae* of German merchants, into a single union of the towns themselves. How this transformation occurred is more or less clear and does not need much explaining. Equally clear is the process by which the union of the towns acquired a permanent organisation. Sporadic meetings of the 'home' towns to discuss matters raised by their merchants abroad could be, and were, held several times in the middle of the fourteenth century. All that was necessary to bring them together more or less permanently was a suitable occasion and a determined leadership. Both came in the second half of the century, at the time when trouble was brewing in Flanders and a growing tension in relations with Denmark led up to the first great Hanseatic war.

At the very outset of the conflict, in 1367, the towns met in Cologne to form a confederation which was this time to be provided with the rudiments of a permanent constitution and a common purse. The League survived the war, and the peace of Stralsund of 1370 which concluded the conflict is therefore regarded as the birthday of the Hanse. Furthermore, in both these conflicts, and particularly in the conflict with Denmark, Lübeck came forward as the leader of the towns and the spearhead of their attack. And from that time onwards it came to be regarded, both within the Hanse and outside it, as the guardian of Hanseatic unity and as the sponsor of its policies.

This concludes the political and constitutional story of the rise of the Hanseatic League. But the most significant part of the story was neither political nor constitutional. It was economic, and the economic processes behind the constitutional evolution of the League were not those of rising unity and strength. On the contrary, the necessity which drove the towns to unite sprang from the recent, and on the whole dangerous, deterioration in their commercial position.

2

The changes in the internal relations of the Hanse might conveniently be considered first. No sooner had the Hanse emerged fully fledged from the war with Denmark than fundamental disunity began to reveal itself in the affairs of the newly born League. In the past the economic basis of Hanseatic unity had been their common interests in the monopoly of the great route and in the common privileges which they had won for themselves in foreign markets. They exercised their monopoly and enjoyed their privileges as economic confederates rather than competitors, and in this non-competitive combination Lübeck was the cementing agent—a role for which it was well fitted both by its history and its geography. German urban colonisation owed much to Lübeck's enterprise, and many of the towns to the east of the Elbe had arisen more or less as Lübeck's colonies. Throughout that early period they continued to be bound to it by social and personal ties. Lübeck also exercised a strong economic influence by virtue of its peculiar position on the route from the Baltic to the North Sea. As long as navigation went along the sea coast and internal waterways, goods from and to Prussia had to be discharged for carriage by land across the Jutland Peninsula and thus had to pass through Lübeck. However rapidly the trade of the Prussian and Livonian towns grew, Lübeck stood to benefit by it; and as long as Lübeck continued to be indispensable, none of the other towns was likely to object to its exalted part in Eastern trade.

This position could not last for ever. By the second half of the fourteenth century Lübeck was losing, even if it had not yet wholly lost, most of its special advantages. In the first place its social ties with the other towns grew weaker. The colonisation movement had spent itself before the end of the fourteenth century, and, after that, Lübeck all but ceased to send out settlers to the newer towns. In Prussia alone the towns continued to grow, but they appear to have drawn their population from Prussia itself. So, while Lübeck still remembered that it was the mother of the Baltic towns, the other towns were beginning to forget that they were Lübeck's daughters. In the second place, Lübeck was ceasing to be an unavoidable *entrepôt* on the east-to-west route. In the second half of the fourteenth century, the men of Zuider-zee—of Campen, Deventer and Zwolle—popularised the direct sea route to the East round Jutland, the so-called *Umlandfahrt*; and their example was soon followed by the Prussians going west, and by the English and Dutch going east. Among the Prussian towns Danzig grew in the forties and fifties to become the chief city of Prussia; and the Danzigers from the very beginning preferred to trade to Flanders and to England by the direct sea route. Finally, Lübeck was losing its predominant share in the trade of Prussia and Livonia. By the second half of the fourteenth century the towns of Prussia and Livonia were not only learning to trade to the West without the assistance of Lübeck, but were also acquiring an ever-growing share in the exploitation of their own hinterlands. The time was not distant when they would begin to look upon their respective regions as fields exclusively their own. The towns of Prussia would then begin to claim a monopoly of the trade of the Vistula as against the other members of the Hanse; Riga and Reval would lay the same claims to the trade of the Dvina.

The economic exclusiveness of the Livonian and Prussian groups of towns was a symptom of a *malaise* the effects of which were to be felt by all the Hanseatic towns and not by Lübeck alone. The local policies of separate territorial groups asserted themselves with ever-growing vigour. Most vigorous of all were they in Prussia where they derived not only from the local economic interests of the towns but also from the peculiar position of the Teutonic Order. The Teutonic Knights were both the makers and the rulers of Prussia, for they had organised its conquest and ruled it as its sovereign princes. But unlike most other territorial rulers of Germany the Order was very efficient: its administration was highly centralised and well organised, and its towns never assumed the same degree of independence as they did in other parts of Germany. So when the Hanse emerged it had to accept as a participant not only the towns of Prussia, but the whole of the Prussian state, that is to say, the Teutonic Order and its High Master.

The affiliation of the Order was undoubtedly a source of political strength to the League, for the High Master possessed a standing in international politics which was not to be trifled with, and his membership gave the Hanse a formal position in the world of territorial states.

In the constitutional parlance of the time, the High Master was the *Beschermer*, the protector, of the League; something like a prince of the Hanseatic empire. At the same time the insistent particularism of the Order was a source of weakness. And nowhere did the particularism manifest itself more clearly than in the Order's commercial enterprises. It traded on a very large scale in corn, amber and other commodities. It possessed an elaborate commercial organisation with central offices (*Schäffereien*) in Marienburg and Königsberg, with a whole fleet of commercial boats and agents in Prussia and other large centres of Europe. In all this trade the Order acted very much as a competitor of the Hanseatic towns and even of its own towns. What is more, it made use of its political power to regulate internal trade in a way most suitable for its own commercial interests.

So much for the separate attitude of Prussia. The other group with very strong separate interests was the western wing of the Hanse, especially the Rhenish towns with Cologne. The latter continued to find their chief fields of activity in the Netherlands and in England. Whenever the Hanse had to undertake any measure against England and Holland, the merchants of Cologne disobeyed and circumvented it and were ready to give up the membership of the Hanse rather than suffer a loss in any of their own trade in the West.

The only towns whose interest and policy seemed to be directed all through the fifteenth century towards the maintenance of Hanseatic unity were those of the central groups of the Hanse, and especially the so-called Wendish towns with Lübeck at their head. But even here Lübeck's particular interests asserted themselves. It was determined to maintain its position as a barrier and an indispensable intermediary on the east-to-west route, and it strove for Hanseatic unity largely because that unity was the only means to maintain the *status quo*. Hence its constant attempts to prevent the direct connections between the Eastern Baltic and the North Sea. Hence also its bellicosity in all the conflicts with Holland and later also with England, the two countries which made the widest use of the direct sea route through the Sound. In other words, what Lübeck strove to maintain was not the Hanse *per se*, but the particular version of the Hanse which pivoted upon its port: an attitude which the other towns understood very well and frequently resisted.

3

In this way the close of the fourteenth and the fifteenth centuries witnessed the ever-widening divergencies of policy among the main constituent groups of towns within the Hanse. The divergencies were largely due to the differences of regional interests which have already been described. But, behind the regional particularism of urban groups like the Prussian, the Livonian or the Rhenish, it is also possible to discover signs of an economic contraction and reaction—the latter in the literal sense of a recoil from a new and unfavourable situation.

Some of the symptons of the recoil will be found in the growing urban exclusiveness. Its general spread in the fourteenth and fifteenth centuries has already been described, but nowhere was the change-over towards local protectionism more clearly marked than in Northern Germany. In the centuries of German growth and expansion there was relatively speaking very little of what might be called a protective or exclusive tendency in municipal policy. Germans were expanding their trade with great confidence and seemed to fear no competitors. In their early treaties with Russia and England the foreigners were given liberties of trade in German regions, and the Baltic was treated as an open sea. The internal government of the towns matched the liberal spirit of their trade. It was largely in the hands of patrician 'founder' families: an expansionist and adventurous race of men who cared comparatively little for the internal trade of their towns, and, as a rule, allowed foreigners to trade and to settle among them.

By the time of the Stralsund Peace of 1370 this liberal period was over. The gilds of artisans and traders were becoming very powerful. The democratic revolts in a number of towns have already been mentioned. When the epidemic of petty-bourgeois movements subsided, the municipal governments, even where they were in the hands of the old families, found it easy to meet the wishes of the local gilds and to exclude the foreigner from the town markets and the surrounding rural regions. And some towns began applying anti-alien laws even against the Hanseatics.

The social changes in Hanseatic towns were of course a local reflection of an ageing process through which the whole of Europe was then passing. But at the same time they also reflected a change which was more economic than social, and as such peculiar to the Hanse. The reason why the towns now turned to their own regional trade and tried to protect their local markets was that their opportunities elsewhere had either dwindled or were seriously threatened. For since the middle of the fourteenth century the international position in Northern Europe had been continually changing to the detriment of German trade.

4

It has already been said that the immediate occasion for the formation of a permanent Hanseatic League was a threat to the Hanseatic interests in Scandinavia. The threat was not economic in origin. It sprang from a political movement in the Scandinavian kingdoms and did not threaten to raise up a rival economic power. Yet it was sufficiently characteristic of the difficulties which the Hanseatics were henceforth to encounter all over Northern Europe, and above all in Scandinavia, to be worth looking at more closely.

In the late twelfth and the thirteenth centuries the Scandinavian countries were, so to speak, an economic vacuum. The native merchant class had either disappeared or had not yet risen, while the rulers were too anxious to attract whatever trade they could and, besides, were too weak to resist the outright exploitation of their countries by the Germans. The Hanseatics first appeared in Scandinavia quite early in the Middle Ages, and the merchants of Cologne traded there in the thirteenth and probably in the twelfth century. But it was only when the Germans began to import their corn surpluses that they were able to appropriate to themselves the entire commerce of the region and to acquire there a position of overwhelming power. Towards the middle of the fourteenth century the German merchants dominated the economic life of the three countries, supplanted the native commerce and shipping, and, with the single exception of the English, had no rivals or competitors to fear.

In Sweden they controlled the chief source of her riches—the mines. So great was their power in that country that by the beginning of the fifteenth century they appointed from among themselves one half of all the municipal governments. Equally deep was their penetration of Norway. The Norwegians were still actively engaged in commerce and navigation in the thirteenth century, but towards the end of the century the Germans made rapid inroads into their trade. We find them extending their hold over the towns of Oslo, Tunsberg, Trondjem, and especially Bergen. Bergen was the Norwegian staple town for the trade in the products of Iceland and other Norwegian islands and of the northern provinces, and it was from these regions that the most valuable products of Norwegian export came—stockfish and fish oil. And in Bergen, more than in any other Scandinavian town, the Germans were a kingdom within a kingdom, with their own laws and jurisdiction.

Their power in Denmark was somewhat more localised. Germans were settled in every Danish town, and German law replaced the Danish in national courts. But the chief point of their activity was the north shore of the Sound, the coastlands of Skania with its famous fishing grounds. For a time—a century and a half—Skania was a focal point of North European fish trade, and the periodic confluence of merchants at Skania made it also an important centre of exchange in other commodities. No wonder that the East Germans regarded Skania as an economic possession of great, not to say crucial, importance.

In the second half of the fourteenth century this position, so valuable, above all so powerful, suddenly deteriorated. Waldemar Atterdag, who rose to the throne of Denmark in 1340, not only set out to unify the Scandinavian kingdoms and thus to fill that political void in which the German towns had built their power, but, by his taxation, he also directly encroached on the Hanseatic privileges. The Germans were compelled to fight the immediate threat of taxation as well as the further danger of a united Scandinavia. The result of the struggle was a victory enshrined in the Peace of Stralsund of 1370, which was followed by the formal establishment of the Hanse.

The debut of the League was thus very successful. As a political weapon it proved itself equally successful in the struggles which it was to wage in the subsequent hundred or hundred and fifty years. The Treaty of Utrecht of 1474, which concluded a somewhat similar conflict with England a century later, still found the League in full possession of its foreign privileges and as triumphant over its enemies as it had been in 1370. Yet, successful as the League was in direct political action, it failed, as it was bound to fail, in its attempt to arrest the march of economic and political forces which continued to shape the evolution of trade in Northern Europe. It was unable to defend its position in Novgorod in the face of the rising power of the Tsars; unable to maintain its old position in Flanders in opposition to the new centres of northern trade which were rising under different auspices in Brabant and Holland; unable to maintain its monopoly of eastern routes; in fact unable to maintain the route itself, which came in the end to be rivalled and replaced by other routes crossing the continent further south. Above all it was incapable of preventing the rise of the two great rivals who were destined in the sixteenth and seventeenth centuries to supplant the Hanse in the economic leadership of Northern Europe—England and Holland.

(IV) THE ENGLISH CHALLENGE

1

The expansion of the Western Powers into regions hitherto monopolised by the Germans began to make headway in the second half of the fourteenth century, and at first it was with the English threat that the Hanseatics appeared to be concerned most. English commercial activity in the North had been gathering strength all through the fourteenth century, and came to a head in its closing years. Yet what requires an explanation is not that that challenge should have come so early but that it should not have come earlier still. For throughout the Middle Ages England formed an essential part of the north-western trading area, and throughout the Middle Ages English merchants were themselves active on the trade routes to and from their country.

England's economic geography fitted her well to play an important part in the trade of North-western Europe. The shores of England were easily accessible across the narrow seas, and it will be recalled that in the Middle Ages as in the modern era sea routes were on the whole more efficient and cheaper than land routes. What is more, the English coast was not only easy to reach but was also worth reaching. Throughout the greater part of the Middle Ages England supplied the more highly specialised regions of Europe with the food and raw materials which some of them lacked. In this sense England's economy in the Middle Ages could be represented, as it often has been, as 'colonial'.

Like the colonial countries of more recent times England may in some respects have lagged behind the neighbouring continental countries, but what justifies the appellation most is that the goods she exported were of the kind that would now be described as 'primary produce'. Some manufactured commodities were of course made in England and sold to foreigners throughout English history, and in the later Middle Ages wholly or partly manufactured cloth was to become the mainstay of English trade. But until the second half of the fourteenth century it was minerals, wool and foodstuffs that sustained England's trade and made the English connection so indispensable in the economic life of Europe. At the very dawn of European history England supplied the rest of Europe with rare minerals, mostly tin. There is also every reason for believing that until the very end of the thirteenth century England was an important source of foodstuffs, grain and animal products which made her valuable to the Low Countries and indispensable to Scandinavia. Above all, it was the wool of her grasslands that made it possible for the highly specialised cloth-producing economies of the Low Countries and Italy to develop. Not until the late fourteenth century did England's part in European trade cease to be mainly that of a supplier of raw materials. But as long as she played that part she was bound to attract foreign trade and foreign investment in a larger measure than many other regions of Europe and to figure prominently in the commercial fortunes of the western world.

It is thus not surprising that the history of commercial voyages to and from England should have reached to the very dawn of history. Phoenicians may or may not have paid regular visits to the West Country in search of tin, but it seems highly probable that in the

Bronze Age bronze articles, manufactured from indigenous metals in Ireland and England, were exported or perhaps re-exported to the continent.[1] Even before they occupied the country the Romans may have imported minerals mined in Britain: Strabo mentions gold, silver and iron. There is also a strong presumption that Southern England became a source of grain supplies to neighbouring provinces of Gaul. Strabo mentions wheat exported from Britain in pre-Roman times, and centuries later Roman writers speak of wheat shipped from Britain to Rhineland. And although one writer, Ammianus Marcellinus, describes the shipments as a wheat tax (*annona*), the probability is that England had a large exportable wheat surplus.[2]

What happened during the long interruption of the Anglo-Saxon invasions, indeed how long it lasted and how complete it was, we do not know. But no sooner does the darkness lift and the documentary evidence become available than references to England's commercial relations with the continent reappear. Miscellaneous Anglo-Saxon sources bear testimony to the wide range of Anglo-Saxon imports and exports and so do other surviving facts of Anglo-Saxon archaeology. King Æthelred's enactment about the tolls of London reveals that at the time of the tenth and eleventh centuries London was frequented by merchants of Flanders, Normandy and North Europe in general; men from Francia and the German Empire are explicitly mentioned.[3] England was then obviously within the trading area of Central and Northern Europe. From Britain came foodstuffs, raw materials, and, for a time, slaves, and the famous letter of Charlemagne to King Offa complaining of the deterioration in the quality of English cloths bears witness to the existence of a well-established cloth trade. Some historians have gone so far as to suggest that the so-called Frisian cloth, to which there are numerous references in continental sources, was nothing else than Anglo-Saxon cloth distributed by Frisian merchants.[4]

Whether this particular hypothesis is right or wrong there is no doubt that the Frisians played an important part in Anglo-Saxon trade of the time. Bede mentions Frisian merchants settled in York and London, and there are other, less indirect, indications of Frisian participation. But the Frisians were not alone. In the first place there were

[1] S. Pigott, 'The Early Bronze Age in Wessex', *Proc. Prehist. Soc.* (1938).

[2] In the view of R. G. Collingwood and J. N. L. Myres, *Roman Britain and the English Settlement* (Oxford, 1937), 243, the exports were *annona* on a large scale; but was large *annona* exported from provinces not normally producing exportable surpluses?

[3] Brit. Mus., Cotton, Titus A, fol. 140, cited here from text in *Hans. Urkundenbuch*, I, no. 2.

[4] C. J. Klumker, 'Der friesische Tuchhandel zur Zeit Karls des Grossen u. sein Verhältnis zur Weberei jener Zeit', *Jahrbuch d. Gesellschaft f. bildene Kunst etc. zu Emden*, XIII, 1899.

also the Scandinavians. In English political history contacts with the
Norsemen were mostly those of war, migration and conquest. There
is, however, little doubt that both before and during the age of the
Danish invasion Scandinavians were in the habit of trading to the
British Isles, and the Norsemen continued to trade even after they had
established their reputation as marauders and invaders. We find Danes
settled in London, in York and Exeter, and there is widely scattered
evidence of Scandinavians trading with Anglo-Saxon England not
only from Scandinavia proper but also from Scandinavian settlements
in Ireland and Iceland.[1]

The Norman conquest did not break the commercial ties with
Europe, but, if anything, added to them. The trade to Norway
apparently continued uninterrupted and was very active in the twelfth
century. In the Sverrir's Saga, King Sverrir is shown commending in
a speech the trade of the English who brought wheat and honey, fine
flour and cloth. The date of the speech in the Saga is 1186, but its
sentiments might with equal justice have applied to the English trade
a hundred years earlier or a hundred years later. There are continuous
references throughout the thirteenth and the early fourteenth centuries to commercial shipments from Norway to the harbours of East
Anglia, mostly to Lynn and the ports on the Humber,[2] laden with
typical products of the North: timber, fish and fish-oil. But in
addition connections with Flanders were now developing very fast
and the economic partnership between this country and the Low
Countries, so characteristic of the European economy in the Middle
Ages, was taking shape.[3]

That partnership was founded upon wool. English pastures with
their persistent moisture and permanent grass, with their chalk subsoil
or their salt-laden air, were ideally suited to the pastoral economy and
more especially to the grazing of sheep. Pastoral pursuits therefore
dominated the life on this island throughout the Celtic and the early
Saxon ages. Livestock was then the mainstay of agricultural wealth,
the standard unit of value and form of capital. Throughout the
Middle Ages pasture continued to play an indispensable part in the
processes of internal colonisation as well as in the routine of settled
agriculture. England's marginal lands were mainly used for grazing,

[1] A. Bugge, Die Wikinger, 130–1. Cf. also idem, Den Norske Traelasthandels Historie
(1925), 47–8.

[2] The Great Red Book of Lynn, passim; Diplomatarium Norwegicum, IX, nos. 102, 159,
201, etc.; cf. A. Bugge, Den Norske Traelasthandels Historie, 138–86.

[3] For a view that commercial connections between England and Flanders in the
Merovingian and Carolingian periods were negligible, see P. Grierson, 'The Re-
lations between England and Flanders before the Norman Conquest', Trans. Royal
Hist. Soc. 4th ser., XXIII (1941).

and even in the boulder clay valleys, mostly heavily wooded, herds of swine were pastured. As population grew in the twelfth and thirteenth centuries and more land was put under plough, some of England's natural pastures, such as the uplands in the Cotswolds, the high grounds of the South Downs, the Lincolnshire wolds, or the marshes of Somerset, might be put under plough and made to yield grain, mostly oats. But no sooner did population recede than the marginal 'outlands' were again turned into pasture whenever suitable. And there were also areas, such as the downlands of Hampshire and Wiltshire, the uplands of Yorkshire and Lancashire, the wet grasslands of Cheshire, the Welsh borders in Shropshire and Herefordshire, where pasture remained inviolate through the Middle Ages and where flocks and herds grew with expanding population and settlement. Cattle and more especially sheep were also to be found in the purely champion parts of England, where they played an essential part in the prevailing economy of mixed farming. They manured the soil and they supplemented the income from arable farming; indeed, the entire routine of the common field system was adjusted to suit the needs of village herds and flocks.

It is therefore natural that in spite of the inroads which the plough occasionally made into grassland, English wool production should have been growing throughout the earlier centuries of the Middle Ages. How much this growth owed to large-scale commercial investment and how much its quality improved by selective breeding, we do not know for certain. There is clear evidence that in the twelfth and thirteenth centuries Flemish and Italian financiers (and they were the only ones who happen to have left behind them written records) made long-term loans to wool-growers. But by then English wool production was already at a very high level and its pre-eminence in Europe was already well established. As for breeding, there is every evidence to show that sheep-farmers in the Middle Ages understood the hereditary factor. They took care to mate the better animals *pro stauro meliorando*; they imported rams of good breeds, such as the Lindsey.[1] Whether as a result of breeding the quality of English wool as a whole was improving throughout the early Middle Ages is more difficult to tell. By the beginning of the fourteenth century wools of certain areas established their reputation for quality. The highest prices were paid for the fine and short wool of the scanty pastures on the Welsh marches, the home of the Ryeland sheep; and for the fine long wools of the Cotswolds, and of the wold and marshland of Lindsey and of Kesteven in Lincolnshire, the home of the 'old Lincolns'.

Wool exports grew with wool production. Wool merchants from abroad figure in almost every early document in which commercial

[1] H. Hall (ed.). *The Pipe Roll of the Bishopric of Winchester* (1903), 8, 40, 76.

dealings are mentioned. At the turn of the twelfth and thirteenth centuries we find Flemings buying wool in large quantities, and involved on that account in complicated transactions with kings and landlords. One of them, William Cade, a Fleming active in the middle of the twelfth century, left a brief but very illuminating record of his commercial and financial transactions; but he was obviously not alone. It has already been mentioned that by the beginning of the thirteenth century the merchants of the Flemish towns formed in London something in the nature of a corporate organisation, the Flemish Hanse, which represented the Flemish merchants and presumably provided them with a common residence and essential commercial services. Some of the greater Flemish merchants of that age, Boinebroke, or Pied d'Argent, left almost as clear a mark in the English records as they did on the history of their native towns. They were capitalists of the purest water, speculators on a large scale, employers of large numbers of their countrymen, lenders of large sums to English monasteries and magnates, traders in cloth.[1]

Important as the Flemings were, they were not alone, and in the end they were not even the most important, among the foreign merchants drawn to England by her wool. In the second half of the thirteenth century the German merchants—the Cologners at first and later the Hanseatics—became active among the foreigners trading to England and exporting English wool, but the lion's share of the trade was eventually acquired by the Italians. How and why the Italian merchants first came to England is a somewhat controversial question. As the twelfth century was advancing to its close Italians appeared all over Western Europe, in France as well as in England, and there is no telling why individual adventurers from Lombardy and Central Italy should have decided to try their luck in England. But there is little doubt that some of them were drawn to England and above all to English wool by the financial business with which they happened to be charged. Many of the Italian merchants from Central Italy, who came to this country in the late twelfth and thirteenth centuries, were active in the first instance primarily as collectors of papal taxation, not as traders or as money-lenders. In the financial dealings between individuals and in the loans to the crown, it was still the Jews and not the Italians who were most active (indeed finance was the only occupation of the English Jews at that time). Such were, however, the economics of papal taxation that the Italian tax collectors were bound to be drawn into wool trade and into private and royal finance. The

[1] H. Pirenne, 'La Hanse Flamande de Londres', *Bulletins de l'Académie royale...de Belgique* (1899); Georges Espinas, *Sire Jehan Boinebroke* (Lille, 1933); G. Dept, 'Les Marchands flamand et le roi d'Angleterre, 1147–1216', *Revue de Nord*, XII (1926).

proceeds of taxes had to be remitted and wool was the most obvious form which the remittance could take. Some of the ecclesiastical taxpayers would indeed pay their tax in kind even though the transaction might be clothed in monetary form. And in the process of their wool business the Italian merchant bankers were bound to come very close—as it proved, too close—to the royal exchequer. Export licences, exemptions from duties and miscellaneous royal favours had to be negotiated and paid for. Above all, the sums of money and of goods which passed through the hands of the Italian bankers and tax-collectors were so large as to attract the greedy eye of the needy kings. Some of the papal taxes in Henry III's reign were in fact levied for the benefit of the English crown and found their way into the royal coffer not as loans but as outright gifts.[1]

In this way wool trade and royal finance became inextricably mixed, and the mixture proved sufficiently potent to raise the Italians at the end of the thirteenth century to a dominant position in the English wool trade. By the turn of the thirteenth and fourteenth centuries, the great Italian houses of the Ricardi, the Frescobaldi, the Bardi and the Peruzzi, were dominating the English wool exports and in some years exercised a total monopoly of exports and entire control of the royal Customs.

From this position the Italians were eventually ousted by syndicates of native merchants and finally by the English Company of the Staple. In the last century of English trade in the Middle Ages English merchants controlled the bulk of the wool trade as well as a large share of other exports and imports. To a historian anxious to record the evolution of national power this dénouement might indeed appear as an act of fulfilment, and it was represented as such by Archdeacon Cunningham and other writers of the same generation. They saw the English merchants slowly and continually graduating to a position of pre-eminence in English trade. The early initiative and leadership belonged to foreign merchants, to Flemings, Hanseatics and Italians, but the English were good, if slow, learners, and by the middle of the fourteenth century they had acquired all the arts of commerce. Now at last, the moor who had done his duty could be dismissed—it was Edward III who did the dismissing—and the English merchants were at last able to establish and enjoy the leadership for which they were now fully qualified.

[1] W. E. Rhodes, 'The Italian Bankers in England and their loans to Edward I and Edward II'. *Historical Essays of Owens College Manchester*, ed. T. F. Tout and J. Tait (Manchester, 1907). C. Johnson, 'An Italian Financial House in the XIV Century', *Trans. St Albans and Hertfordshire Archt. and Archaeolog. Soc.* n.s. 1 (St Albans, 1903). A. Sapori, 'La Compagnia dei Frescobaldi en Inghilterra', *Studi di Storia Economica Medievale* (Florence, 1949).

This story, however, no longer appears as credible as it did once upon a time. The very notion of trade as a social art acquired by men at the end of their progressive ascent through history may have come natural to a generation which not only believed in continuous progress, but valued the commerce of their own day as the highest manifestation and fulfilment of their culture. Present-day historians, rubbing shoulders as they do with anthropologists and sociologists, find it more difficult to treat trade as a characteristic attribute of a sophisticated civilisation. The processes of trade itself were sufficiently simple to be practised by medieval man at all stages of medieval development. What determined the exact place which trade was to occupy in their daily lives and in their development was the historical setting taken as a whole—their laws and customs, their distribution of wealth, their access to circulating capital, as well as the political circumstances of the time. And it so happened that neither the institutions nor the provision of capital in medieval England were so deficient as to prevent English merchants from taking an active part in English trade.

The first references to English or Anglo-Saxon merchants are probably as old as references to any merchants in England. We hear about Saxon, which is commonly taken to mean Anglo-Saxon, merchants visiting the Merovingian fair of Saint-Denis, the fairs of Rouen and Troyes in Charlemagne's time, and resident in Marseilles early in the eighth century. In his letter to King Offa Charlemagne promises protection to English merchants 'in accordance with ancient customs of trade'.[1] It is possible that the Saxons among the foreign merchants resident in Rome in the ninth century were also Anglo-Saxon, but, in general, references to English trade and English merchants in the ninth century are few, for this was a disturbed period both in England and on the continent. References to Englishmen abroad become more frequent in the tenth and the eleventh centuries, and one of them suggests that in 1050 Englishmen sailed to the Baltic. The evidence of Anglo-Saxon towns reveals the existence of native merchants throughout the last two or three centuries of the Anglo-Saxon era.

That the native merchants were not all hucksters serving the local market is perhaps indicated by the accidental survival of the life story of a merchant whose career bestrides the end of the Anglo-Saxon and the beginning of the Norman period, St Godric of Fincham, whose *vita* has been so tellingly exploited by Pirenne. The English merchants who visited Utrecht at the end of the twelfth century were probably wool traders. The Anglo-Norman documents repeatedly mention English

[1] Haddon and Stubbs, *Councils*, III, 496. Cf. also G. Jacob, *Der nordisch-baltische Handel der Araber* (1887), 112; A. Dopsch, *Die Wirtschafts-Entwicklung der Karolingerzeit*, Part II, 194-5.

wool merchants, and their numbers increase as the records of English trade accumulate. In 1273 the hostilities with Flanders led to a royal embargo on wool exports, and that in its turn led to the institution of licences for export; the surviving collection of licences reveals the existence of a very large body of native merchants engaged in wool trade.[1]

In general, the surviving evidence of English trade and finance of the thirteenth and fourteenth centuries abounds with names of great merchants who were either English born or permanently settled in England and who played a great part in every branch of English trade: acted as king's merchants, or on occasions helped to finance the king and to serve him in various financial and commercial capacities, administered his war chests, organised the remittance of funds abroad, purveyed goods for his household and armed forces, or merely supplied him with large quantities of imported commodities. In the twelfth century and the thirteenth there were de Waleys, de Haverhills, Finks, Fitz Alans, de Cornhills, Basings, Blands, Buckerels, de Rokesleys, Aswyks, de Ludlows: a small but powerful class which was fast acquiring the character of a hereditary caste, dominating the civic councils of London, active in every important branch of English trade, and holding large investments in landed property and mortgages (Gregory de Rokesley at one time held a mortgage over the lands of no less a person than the Bishop of Ely). The class merges imperceptibly into the financial oligarchy of the mid-fourteenth century—the de la Poles and their associates.

True enough, it was not until the middle of the fourteenth century that the English merchants succeeded in establishing themselves in full control of the wool trade and in a condition of predominance in English trade as a whole. This development however did not come about by a gradual process of apprenticeship and graduation, but through a series of political and economic events of a kind that would have given English merchants an equivalent position at any time in English history. The effective cause was the financial crisis in the affairs of the crown in the early phases of the Hundred Years' War.

That wool trade and wool traders should have become enmeshed in the tangled skein of fourteenth-century finance is not at all surprising. The annual wool crops may not have represented half of the nation's wealth as a petition in Parliament would have it; but they undoubtedly represented a very large proportion of the nation's marketable produce or of what now would be described as the country's main 'cash crop'. The wool trade therefore had an obvious attraction for kings on the look out for money or for goods capable of

[1] A. Schaube, 'Die Wollausfuhr Englands vom Jahre 1273', *Viertelj. f. Sozial u. Wirtschaftsg.* VI (1908).

yielding quick cash, and wool was bound to become an obvious object of royal finance. Taxes on wool grew throughout the fourteenth and fifteenth centuries. In addition to the 'old Custom' of 7s. 6d. per sack fixed in 1275, 'new custom' of 3s. 4d. was levied on foreigners since 1303. In the course of the fourteenth century the king repeatedly tried to force out of the reluctant Parliaments grants of high subsidies on wool. By the end of the century grants of wool subsidies became regular, and, with this addition total taxation on wool rose to 40s. per sack exported by Englishmen and 53s. 4d. per sack exported by foreigners. This new tax was not, however, established without a previous deal with the Commons over the control and the management of the wool trade.[1]

The wool trade was also involved with the royal debt. The wealth represented by the annual wool crop was frequently raided by the crown for short-term loans. Richard I's ransom had been paid out of a loan raised by the proceeds of English wool sales abroad, and loans raised in such fashion became common at the end of the thirteenth and the early fourteenth centuries. In 1297 Edward I financed his Flemish expedition by pre-empting in England and then selling abroad 8000 sacks of wool. This device was later employed by Edward III on a much larger scale and with less regard for the interests of the wool traders and the wool growers.

In this way the wool trade was inevitably drawn into the machinations which mark the history of Edward III's war finance. With each successive crisis the conduct of the wool trade had to be reorganised, and each reorganisation brought it a step nearer to the monopoly of the Staple. The first and most important crisis led to the destruction of the Italian interests. The Italian commitments in the wool trade and in royal finance reached the highest point under Edward III. For the first thirteen or fifteen years of his reign, and more especially in the years of hectic war finance between 1337 and 1340, the Florentine house of the Bardi and from 1336 onwards also the great Florentine house of Peruzzi lent the king vast sums generally on the security of taxes, most the wool customs. In the end, however, financial operations in England and elsewhere overstrained their resources. As long as they were still able to add loan to loan they remained in possession of their privileges in English wool trade. But as soon as their liquid resources began to give out, as they did in 1343, the king inevitably defaulted. By 1346, the whole of the English business of the two houses was reduced to a vanishing point, and for a time the Florentine bankers had to withdraw not only from the English wool trade but from the English scene altogether.

[1] E. Power, *The Wool Trade in English Medieval History* (Oxford, 1941), pp. 63–103.

The place of the Italians was at first taken by a consortium of the wealthier English wool traders and financiers. The consortia, made up of more or less the same group of commercial magnates and as a rule led by William de la Pole and his associates, were formed or re-formed on three of four occasions after 1345. They helped to finance the siege of Calais and the Crécy campaign by a series of large loans (up to £100,000) on the security of the wool customs. In return they received the virtual monopoly of the English wool exports. On several years all exports of wool were prohibited except under licence, and only the members of the consortia were allowed to export.

By 1349 the syndicates suffered the same fate as the Bardi and the Peruzzi, and the royal default led not only to the temporary eclipse of de la Pole's circle but also to a change of system. The king had now to turn to a larger body of wool merchants, and to do this at a time when he badly needed parliamentary consent for higher subsidies on wool. In the end he was able to obtain both the subsidies and the loans in exchange for important concessions. The parliament of 1351 granted the wool subsidies for three years in exchange for abolition of all monopolies, but in the end monopolies were not so much abolished as widened by being vested in the English Company of the Staple. That Company became the main source of regular loans on the security of wool and wool customs.

The device of the Staple was by no means new. A staple of sorts was already in existence in the last quarter of the thirteenth century when, in order to operate his forced loan on wool of 1294–97, Edward I directed his own wool and that of the wool merchants at first to Dordrecht and then to Antwerp: both towns situated near the places where he needed funds for his war. But this was not yet a full-fledged staple. It was permissive and not compulsory and it did not create a monopolistic Company of the Staple. An attempt to make it compulsory was made in 1313 when it was fixed at St Omer, but even then the system was as yet very fluid and experimental. Between 1316 and 1326 the Staple was moved from one foreign town to another; between 1326 and 1337 it twice crossed the Channel to selected English ports, and for a brief interval the trade was altogether free. But after 1337 and more especially after 1350 the organisation of the trade rapidly moved towards the monopoly of the English Company of the Staple.

The process began with a full swing away from monopolies of any kind. It has already been shown that in 1351 parliament stipulated, as a *quid pro quo* for the grant of wool subsidies, that all monopolies should be abolished. In accordance with this stipulation the Ordinances of the Staple enacted in 1353 left the aliens free to buy and export wool as much as they liked, and no Englishman was allowed to engage in exports. This arrangement could not last. It was profitable to wool growers, entrenched in Parliament, but too unfavourable to the English merchants and consequently also to their ability to lend money. The system began to break down in 1357. By 1361 the English Company of the Staple was in possession of a virtual monopoly of wool exports to Northern Europe; by 1399 it was safely and permanently launched in Calais. Even then Italians were able to export some wool under royal licence on condition that they took it to Italy and did not sell it in competition with the staplers on the wool markets of the Low Countries. But on the latter the English monopoly was now unchallenged.

The monopoly suited the bulk of the English wool merchants who now formed the Company of the Staple; it suited the rising interest of the clothmakers for it created wide discrepancies between wool prices at home and abroad. Above all, it suited the king. The custom and subsidy on the export of wool was the best possible security which he could offer, and a chartered company enjoying the monopoly of the trade was a much safer source of loans than the series of firms and syndicates which had, one by one, gone bankrupt in the early years of the Hundred Years' War. The link with the Crown was further reinforced by the Act of Retainer of 1446, by which the Company farmed the whole of the custom and the subsidy on wool, and undertook in return to pay the wages of the garrison at Calais and certain other fixed charges, repay itself for its past loans and deliver any surplus over and above a fixed sum into the exchequer. The only interest which suffered was that of the wool growers; and this may have been one of the reasons why the production of wool declined.

The English predominance in the wool trade was thus a product of political and fiscal causes. It was not a manifestation of English trade 'come of age', still less a stage in the economic growth of English trade and economy. It was brought about by successive acts of royal policy and as a result of a bargain between the king and merchants. Moreover it did not result in any increase in the volume of the wool trade handled by English merchants. If we are to trust the figures of the royal export licences of 1273 which have already been mentioned,[1] the English share in the wool exports of the time, though not more than one-third of the total, represented some 11,500 sacks, shared by some 280 exporters. By the middle of the fifteenth century about the same number of staplers exported eight to ten thousand sacks. The English predominance had grown, while the wool trade shrank.

[1] See above, p. 240.

2

More relevant to the story of English economic growth was the development of the cloth trade and the wine trade. English wine trade was in some respects one of the oldest branches of English commerce, and also one in which English merchants were predominant from the outset. Evidence of English imports of foreign wine—mostly French— go back to the early years of the Norman rule and beyond. Under the Angevins England found itself politically linked to Gascony, the main wine-producing area of Europe, and the connection thus established stimulated Gascon viticulture and also opened before English merchants a great and ever expanding field of enterprise. Large, and for a time growing, quantities of wine were imported from Gascony, and most of the imports came to be handled by English merchants, mainly those of Bristol. In return Gascony had to be supplied with foodstuffs, cloth and other miscellaneous goods, which came from England or via England, and were mostly brought by English merchants and English ships. The trade reached its highest point at the beginning of the fourteenth century, when in some years as much as 90,000 tuns of wine were imported into England.

The most spectacular event in the history of English trade in the late Middle Ages—an event which did more than anything else to conjure up the spectre of the English challenge in the Baltic—came as a result of English cloth exports. Manufacture of marketable cloth was indigenous in this country, and some cloth was always exported. Exports of cloth to France in the seventh and eighth centuries have already been mentioned. A Norwegian saga mentions English cloth among imports to Iceland at the end of the tenth century.[1] English cloths of various kinds, sometimes described by the parts of England from which they came, continue to be mentioned in the records of the twelfth and thirteenth centuries. But although active, the trade was rather small: very much smaller than the Flemish cloth trade and the wool and wine trades of England. In the second half of the fourteenth century, however, the industry suddenly grew to rival and finally to overshadow all other branches of English industry and trade.

The factors behind the growth have been described elsewhere. Cloth manufacture was establishing itself outside the bounds of corporate towns and was thus better able to keep its labour costs low and to employ mechanical devices, mostly water power. The disorder in Flanders and emigration of artisans from there brought an addition of skilled labour to the English industry. Some protection to more expensive brands of cloth resulted from the prohibition of Flemish

[1] A. Bugge, *Die Wikinger* (Halle, 1906), p. 132.

imports. But from the point of view of this essay most significant of all is the connection which undoubtedly existed between the growth of the cloth industry and the financial vicissitudes of the wool trade. Continuous interruptions and disorganisation of wool exports hit the rival cloth industries. Above all an export tax of some £2. 10s. per sack greatly lowered the costs of production at home by comparison with foreign cloth, and it is also possible that English wool monopoly also helped to raise the price of wool to the foreign clothmakers. Thus assisted, the English cloth manufacture forged ahead until by the 1490's the English exports at times exceeded the high figure of 50,000 cloths or an equivalent of some 10,000 to 12,000 sacks of wool and about twice that in value.

With English cloth exports so great, the whole character of English foreign trade and the behaviour of English foreign traders were bound to be transformed. As long as English exports consisted mainly of wool, there was no need for English merchants to go far afield in search for markets and customers. Wool was a raw material of industry; its customers were foreign cloth manufacturers; and the only important cloth manufacturing centres were not only highly localised but also situated near at hand, mainly in the Low Countries. On the other hand, finished cloth had to be sold to potential consumers, and in the main centres of potential consumption, or in other words, to men and women all over continental Europe and beyond. It is therefore no wonder that whereas the wool staplers were able to transact their business in Calais and had no need to venture beyond Bruges, English cloth exporters had to push out in every direction, and, in the first place, into East European markets where Flemish cloth had previously been sold. We find fleeting references to Englishmen in Stralsund and Danzig in the eighties of the fourteenth century. In Danzig they were well established by the nineties and possessed a settlement and a factory by the end of the first quarter of the fifteenth century. By that time there was also an English company in the Norwegian trading port of Bergen, where, in exchange for English cloth and other miscellaneous goods, goods of Norwegian and Icelandic origin, mostly fish, could be bought. It is quite possible that there was also an English component in the international mart at the fishing centres of Skania.[1]

[1] For these and most of the subsequent facts of Anglo-Hanseatic relations, see M. Postan, 'The Economic and Political Relations of England and the Hanse', E. Power and M. Postan (eds.), *Studies in English Trade in the Fifteenth Century* (London, 1933).

3

The English appearance in the Baltic brought home to the Hanseatics the dangers of the English challenge. Unfortunately for Anglo-Hanseatic relations and for peace in the Baltic, the English penetration into the northern markets began in earnest at a time when conditions for it were least propitious. The English merchants began to frequent the east-to-west route at the very moment when foreign competition appeared to threaten the foundations of Hanseatic prosperity and unity. They tried to establish themselves in Danzig at the very time when the protection of the local market and regional monopoly was becoming the fundamental purpose of municipal policy. Their appearance in the Hanseatic system would have produced a considerable conflict in any case but, in the conditions of the late fourteenth and early fifteenth centuries, it was bound to result in a bitter and desperate struggle.

To begin with, the struggle was developing in English favour: mainly because for the time being the English drive was well backed at home, whereas the German opposition was not. In the English towns the relatively small and specialised groups of men trading to the Baltic found support from the main body of urban opinion which was strongly anti-Hanseatic. Left to themselves the towns could always be relied upon to act against all foreigners, the Venetians, the Genoese, the Flemings as well as the Hanseatics; but the Hanseatics offered the best and the easiest targets. Their exceptional fiscal privileges and their proud position in the city of London—a city within a city—were bound to draw on them the greater share of urban xenophobia. The anti-Hanseatic movement combined the demands of merchants threatened with exclusion from the trade of Prussian towns with the appetites of merchants anxious to exclude the Hanseatics from the trade of English towns. The common enemy produced a sense of common interest and ranged the mass of English urban classes behind the agitation.

At first this movement also enjoyed the full support of the government. In the conditions of the early fifteenth century the government, and more especially the House of Commons, found it easy to respond to the pressure of anti-Hanseatic interests and to understand their motives and their language. The temper of the age, fed by accidents of the Hundred Years' War, was charged with nationalist pride; the social changes of the times were helping to draw together the official class in English government and the upper ranks of the merchant class. In addition the City of London had evolved in the fifteenth century an efficient 'lobby' in Parliament, and even the provincial towns sometimes elected special deputations 'to make suit in Parliament against Hanseatic privileges'. No wonder the Hanseatics came to regard Parliament as their chief adversary and never expected from it any favour or concession.

The policy of the Lords and of the King's Council was somewhat less definite, for individual lords and prelates sometimes shielded the merchants of the Hanse from enmity and vindictiveness of the Commons and were often referred to in Hanseatic correspondence as their only friends in England. Yet as long as the Council was capable of comprehending and obeying the *raison d'État*, the underlying assumptions of its policy towards the Hanse was little different from those of the merchant classes. On those occasions when personal and party interests of magnates were not much involved, and when conciliatory attitudes to the Hanse were not dictated by the military and political events in Flanders and France, the Council did its best to back the merchants over their demands in the Baltic.

Thus backed (and as long as it was thus backed) the English mercantile offensive appeared to be very formidable and was indeed scoring success after success. A conflict in the eighties of the fourteenth century ended somewhat to the advantage of the English merchants, and the treaty of 1388 which wound it up recognised for the English their 'old rights' and their freedom to come to the lands of the Hanse and Prussia and to settle there and to traffic freely and undisturbed. A similar conflict in the first decade of the fifteenth century ended by another treaty, in which the English were confirmed in their right to come to Prussia and there *mercari, ibidemque morari et exiende ad lares et domicilia propria redire*. Under the cover of this treaty the English merchants established a flourishing factory in Danzig with a communal organisation, a communal house and a governor with disciplinary powers over its members. When difficulties again arose in the thirties, mostly over the position and privileges of the English company in Danzig, the Treaty of 1437 conceded to the English merchants not only their old rights of entry, trade and residence, but also fiscal exemptions as exceptional as those the Hanseatics possessed in England. The English traders were to be free of all taxes imposed in the course of the previous hundred years or more.

On each of these occasions the English merchants benefited from the fundamental disunity in the ranks of the Hanseatic towns. Even though the Danzigers were bitterly opposed to the English merchants in their midst, the Prussian Order and even some interests within Danzig itself set great store by their trade to England and were among the first to seek an end to the successive conflicts. Similarly, the western wing of the Hanse, especially Cologne, had no part in the quarrel of the English position in the Baltic and was always willing to compromise. Even the position of Lübeck was not as yet very consistent and she could be found on occasions counselling moderation and concession to the English claims.

Thus aided, the English prospects appeared very bright indeed. To some Hanseatics the English danger appeared in a light curiously prophetic. Viewed in this light the English threat appeared greater than it actually was, more urgent and more threatening than that of the Dutch. This alone would be sufficient to explain why the strength of Hanseatic opposition stiffened in the middle of the century and why Lübeck swung in support of the anti-English policy. It was badly hit by English piracy, it had grown to fear the effect of great maritime links between Prussia and the West, and in general it was now adopting a belligerent attitude in defence of the Hanseatic hold of the Great Route. At the same time the English pressure was weakening. This was not altogether due to factors purely or mainly economic. The export of English cloth declined in the middle decades, but the decline was in itself due to failure of the English commercial offensive. The reason why the latter failed is more likely to be found in the political disorders of the middle decades of the century.

With the War of the Roses approaching, the Council became a mere instrument of the rival baronial parties and was no longer able to give support to the English claims against the Hanseatics. It is not that the economic policy of the late Lancastrian and the early Yorkist governments was inspired by any new and different principles. Its worst failing was that it ceased to be inspired by any principles whatsoever. The private interest of ruling magnates in and out of King's Council was allowed free licence, and matters of state policy were made to serve the predatory aims of powerful men. Not only were the merchants unable to rely on the latent power of English arms, but that power itself became a mere instrument of predatory sea-war and piracy. There were easy and substantial gains to be derived from attacks on Hanseatic shipping, and the Council not only did nothing to stop piracy on the high seas but itself directly and indirectly contributed to its extension. It was largely under the auspices of influential members of the Council that the first great attack on Hanseatic shipping in the Bay took place in 1449, and the second great attack in 1458 was led by no other person than Warwick. The outburst of piracy helped to consolidate Lübeck's anti-English policy and to cement the unity of the Hanseatic League and led to a naval war which threw the entire trade and navigation on the North Sea into chaos. At the same time, in spite of the raging naval war, the parties in the Council were not averse from making use of the Hanseatic assistance in their domestic struggles.

In the end a private deal between Edward IV and the Hanseatic League put an end to all English chances in the conflict with the Hanse. Under that deal the Hanseatics helped Edward to equip the expedition which brought him back to England, and in exchange they received back, in 1474, unaltered and unimpinged their old privileges without having to concede any rights to the Englishmen in the Baltic towns. They immediately stepped into the place they had occupied in English economic life in the first half of the century, and this place they were to preserve until well into the Tudor era. Their share in English foreign trade soon passed the highest point it had reached before. While they exported on the average about 6000 cloths annually between 1406 and 1427, and about 10,000 annually between 1438 and 1459, their exports rose to well above 13,500 between 1479 and 1482.

The English merchants derived whatever profit and comfort there was to be derived from the restoration of peace and the resumption of Hanseatic trade. But their attempts at direct relations with the markets of Central and Eastern Europe received a set-back from which they were not to recover until the age of Elizabeth. Their chances of establishing themselves there were further reduced by political changes in Prussia. Danzig, now under the sovereignty of Polish kings, enjoyed almost a complete *Landeshoheit*, involving full autonomy in matters of government and economic policy. In confirming the treaty with England it postulated that the English were to be treated as all other foreigners. The English merchants themselves ceased to press for parity in the old and full sense of the term, since by now the Baltic trade was no longer vitally important to them. Whether as a result of the continued friction with Denmark and consequent closing of the Sund, or as a result of the war-time rearrangements in the organisation of English trade, the direct trade of English merchants to Danzig was dwindling very fast. Whereas on several occasions in the first half of the century there were over thirty English boats anchored in the port of Danzig, only twelve boats arrived from England during the three years following the cessation of hostilities, and in 1497, when the registers of the Sund tolls begin, not a single English boat passed the Sund. As late as 1503 there were only twenty-one English boats passing the Sund and it was not until 1547 that the English shipping to the Baltic could again stand comparison with that of the Dutch.

4

The effects of the English defeat reached further than the mere failure to establish a factory in Danzig. Its net result was to interrupt for nearly two generations the expansion of English trade into the outlying European markets and to canalise all English commerce into the single current which led to the Low Countries. The traffic in Baltic goods was taken out of English hands; some of it proceeded indirectly by way of Brabantine fairs, some of it was carried on by the Dutch and the Hanseatics. And with the end of the Baltic trade there also came the end of the Baltic trader. Not until the rebirth of direct Baltic connections in the middle of the sixteenth century and the rise of the Eastland Company did the Baltic 'interest' establish itself again among English merchants.

The loss of the Prussian connection happened to coincide with the lopping off of most other outlying branches of the English trade. In Norway the Hanseatics had since the beginning of the fifteenth century tightened their hold over the trade of Bergen and defeated all the attempts of the English merchants to restore that position. The cessation of the Bergen trade at first sent the English merchants directly to Iceland, but this new enterprise, however important in itself, only completed the ruin of the English trade in Scandinavia. It plunged England into a state of chronic conflict with Denmark, and in the second half of the century it finally shut the Dano-Norwegian waters to English trade and navigation. Even more damaging, though less enduring, was the interruption of English trade to Gascony. This connection, so old and so important in the economic life of the country, was to be disturbed and finally broken during the concluding phases of the Hundred Years' War. The French reoccupation of Gascony put an end to the flourishing English exports of cloth and all but interrupted English imports of wine. For a time even the clarets of Gascony were not obtainable except through neutral markets in the Low Countries.

Thus, having lost the more distant markets on the periphery of their trading area, the English merchants were compelled to restrict their maritime and commercial ventures in Northern Europe to the Low Countries; and the 'Merchant Adventurers', a corporation of merchants trading to Flanders and Holland, absorbed the bulk of English trade and the mass of English traders.

The effects of this concentration reached even further than commerce. The historians of the English cloth industry may also find a connection between concentration of English trade to the Netherlands and concentration of English production on undyed and unfinished cloth. There is no doubt that the bulk of English cloth exports in the late fourteenth century and beginning of the fifteenth century consisted of fully dyed and fully finished cloth. But, when with the falling off of the outlying markets the English exporters lost direct contact with the main body of consumers, they had to adjust themselves to a trade on a market still largely dominated by local cloth industries.

A *modus vivendi* was found in increasing the exports of undyed and unfinished cloth and selling it to the dyers and finishers from Flanders and Holland. These were essentially the terms on which the great expansion of English cloth exports under the Tudors was made possible, and the old symbiosis in England and the Low Countries was re-established.

(v) THE RISE OF HOLLAND

1

Compared with the English challenge that of the Dutch matured relatively late, but its late inconspicuous beginnings turned out, from the Dutch point of view, to be a blessing in disguise. It was very largely because the English attack opened rapidly and successfully that the Hanseatics, and especially the Prussians, read into it the dangers which it did not in fact spell. It had received strong backing from the English government in the first half of the fifteenth century, and thus added further weight to the German alarm. For, after all, at the beginning of the fifteenth century England was a first-class military power with a long record of successful aggression, and in the estimation of the Prussians it had already revealed some of its congenital propensities for empire-building. Did not the Danzigers argue in 1410 that if the English were allowed to settle and to trade in Prussia they would soon annex the country as they had annexed Bordeaux and Gascony? It was because the English danger loomed so large that the Prussians at first and the whole of the Hanse in the end opposed it with remarkable vigour.

The strength of the Dutch position was that their rise owed little to political action, and that it was purely economic throughout its early history. They had insinuated themselves into the Baltic trade before the Hanse as a whole woke up to their menace; and so firmly was their power grounded in economic and geographical facts—and eventually in naval prowess—that it could not easily be countered by the political and naval measures at the disposal of the Hanse. Hence the paradox of their challenge: it turned out to be so strong in the end because it appeared so weak at the beginning.

One of the reasons why the so-called commercial rise of Holland in the later Middle Ages was so inconspicuous is that it was a product of local rather than of national development. The country which we know as the Netherlands consisted of at least four geographical regions, each with an economic history of its own: Zealand, Friesland, South Holland and North Holland. In the so-called Dark Ages the delta of the Rhine was the centre of northern commerce. Later, during the Middle Ages, the region of the delta, with Utrecht at its head, was still important as a centre of trade in corn, fish and wine. At the end of the same period, South Holland with Dordrecht was also showing signs of considerable commercial activity, and so did also the northernmost end of the Netherlands: Campen, Deventer, Zwolle, Gröningen. These towns stood in a loose connection with the Hanse which seems to have paid them very well. But in the fourteenth century important centres of commerce began to appear in parts of the Netherlands hitherto relatively backward, i.e. in Zealand and in North Holland. It is this development of North Holland that is usually meant when the rise of the Dutch is discussed, and it was this development that hit the Hanseatic trade most.

The exact circumstances of the development are somewhat obscure. Dutch historians sometimes connect the rise of Amsterdam, and with it of the rest of North Holland, with the German transit trade through the waterways of Holland *en route* to Flanders and England. According to this view the new dykes obstructed the northern entrance into the Dutch system of rivers and made it necessary to transfer the goods into smaller boats. Amsterdam sprang up at the northern entrance to the dyke system, and Rotterdam at the southern, but other Dutch towns also began to take a hand in this traffic, and by the end of the fourteenth century Holland could already stand on her own feet and was able to enter into a competition with the Hanse. On a somewhat broader view the trade of North Holland grew partly out of the internal trade of the country, and partly out of the sea-borne trade between some of its towns and other countries. Like the rest of the Netherlands, North Holland and South Zealand possessed ships and engaged in trade from time immemorial—they were forced to it both by the abundance of their waterways and by the one-sided economic development of the surrounding regions which necessitated a constant movement of food-stuffs. But, whereas in the earlier centuries the distant journeys of Hollanders were probably confined to England and Flanders, in the late fourteenth century they turned to the Baltic. One of the reasons why Hollanders went eastwards was probably the introduction of the *Umlandfahrt* round Jutland. But the chief cause was that the Dutch economy was expanding at the time when opportunities for sea-borne trade in other directions were limited.

Their economic expansion, though two or three centuries old, was gathering speed in the fifteenth century. The thirteenth century saw the Dutch completing the dyking system which protected them from the invasion of the sea. The following century saw a great development of agriculture and cattle breeding and industry, and the fifteenth was marked by a sudden efflorescence of the old cloth industry. When at the close of the fourteenth century events disorganised the Flemish manufacturers, Holland, together with England, rose to the leadership of the continental cloth production, and by the middle of the fifteenth century Leiden became one of the foremost cloth centres in the world. Simultaneously with the cloth manufacture there developed also other industries, and especially beer brewing and fishing. In the course of the fifteenth century Holland was also becoming an important source of herring for Western Europe, and its salted fish was carried as far south as Bâle. In addition, both the industry and the trade benefited by the unification of the Netherlands in the fifteenth century by Philip of Burgundy and by the long spell of peace under his rule.

It was largely because their economy grew so gradually that their appearance in the Baltic passed almost unnoticed by their contemporaries. Apparently they entered the Hanseatics' preserves chiefly as carriers, and until the very end of the Middle Ages they were active in the Baltic as sailors at least as much as traders. On some routes they carried Hanseatic goods and were therefore very useful to those towns which had large quantities of bulky goods to carry, such as Riga, Reval or Danzig. By the same token they were most unwelcome to Lübeck. Lübeck was consequently the first to rise in opposition to the Dutch, and throughout the fifteenth century Lübeck was at the back of all the anti-Dutch activities of the Hanse. And for exactly the same reasons Prussia was unwilling to quarrel with the Dutch and on several occasions did its best to thwart Lübeck's plans against Holland.

The story of the Dutch penetration and of their successful combat with the Hanse cannot be told here with all the detail it deserves. By the end of the second decade of the fifteenth century, Dutch progress in the East had grown far enough to have drawn to itself the alarmed attention of the Hanseatic politicians and to have produced the first serious conflict. The issue was raised in 1417 by Lübeck and the other Wendish towns which managed to get through a Hanseatic Diet some limitations of the Dutch trade, but were unable to carry with them the Prussian towns in further attempts to close the Baltic to the Dutch altogether. This, however, was only the first of the many Dutch-Wendish clashes to come. By degrees friction became chronic and, for many years, peace was with difficulty maintained by temporary truces. In 1437 the truce was not renewed and a formal state of war lasted from 1438 to 1441. It was during that war that the Dutch revealed to the outside world how much their economic power had grown in the preceding fifty years. In the end the Hanse had to give way in spite of a whole succession of what seemed to have been political triumphs and to conclude the peace treaty of 1441 recognising the freedom of the Dutch trade in the Baltic.

The strength of the Dutch resistance during the war was something of a revelation to the German towns. But the defeat of the Hanse was clinched not so much by the power of Holland as by that conflict of interests within the Hanse, which appeared every time the Wendish towns tried to do anything against the Dutch. Prussia would not support Lübeck against Holland, and in addition the western wing of the Hanse, and especially the towns of the Zuidersee, Campen, Zwolle and Deventer, vacillated between their loyalty to the Hanse and their commercial interests in Holland. In the end, some of them concluded separate agreements with the Dutch and thus broke the ring of the Hanseatic blockade. With slight variations the same story repeated itself each time the Wendish towns proposed action against Holland, and all the active measures of the Hanse against the Dutch remained ineffective.

2

What made the Dutch especially difficult to combat was that very often the Hanse could not help handicapping itself by the aggressive policy it adopted towards other foreign powers. In their endeavours to arrest the course of economic change the Hanseatics repeatedly took measures which, whatever their avowed object, in the end merely contributed to the increase of Dutch trade. There were several such measures in the fifteenth century. In the fifties the Dutch trade received a great stimulus from a Hanseatic blockade of Flanders, when a great deal of Hanseatic trade passed to the South Germans and the Dutch. In the sixties and the seventies the blundering Hanseatic politicians offered the Dutch the greatest of all their opportunities by their short-sighted and aggressive defence of their Bruges 'staple'. The circumstances of this staple policy are indeed sufficiently interesting in themselves to be worth describing in greater detail.

As a result of the process already explained, Bruges had become by the first half of the fifteenth century the most valuable of Hanseatic markets abroad. It was the centre of German cloth trade and the terminus of the great Hanseatic east-to-west route—the point where this route tapped the channels that led to the French, the Italian and the Iberian South. But in the course of the fifteenth century Bruges began to lose its advantageous position. There were political complications in Flanders itself and there were also economic causes. In the first instance the Zwin, the waterway connecting Bruges with the sea, was silting up and no amount of dredging and dyking could stop the process. Secondly, in the course of the fifteenth century the Flemish industries migrated in directions unfavourable to Bruges. Partly as a result of Brabantine policy, but partly as a result of decline in South-west

Flanders, economic leadership passed to the regions in the North-east, especially to Brabant. And, according as the trade and industry of Brabant grew, the old ports of Brabant, Antwerp, with its satellite market of Bergen-op-Zoom, began to rival Bruges as centres of cloth and wool trade. Before long they also began to rival it in other fields. In the same way as Bruges had grown to become the all-important western terminus of the great Hanseatic route to the Baltic, Antwerp now grew to become the terminus of more recent and rival routes: one to the South via Lorraine and one to Eastern Europe via the Rhine valley, Frankfurt-am-Main, and Frankfurt-am-Oder. The alternative routes appeared in response to a number of incentives, but it is probable that they owed much of their prosperity to the initiative of the Dutch and of the merchants of the South German towns seeking a way round the Hanseatic monopoly. And the tighter the Hanseatic hold over the northern trade, the more determined became the endeavours of the outsiders to develop the alternative routes.

To Lübeck the old route was of greater significance than to anybody else. Lübeck was the town of the Hanse most interested in maintaining the old Hanseatic lines of communication, but in addition it was also the town most closely linked with the Bruges *Kontor* by a network of interests woven together in the course of a hundred years. But the measures it adopted in defence of Bruges were doomed to failure. They were not supported by other parts of the Hanse and, what is more, they still further undermined the economic position of Bruges. This is especially true of the so-called 'staple' rules. In order to restore Bruges to its old position in the Hanseatic trade, the Hanse laid down in the middle of the fifteenth century a series of rules by which costly goods and goods which constituted the monopoly of the Hanse, i.e. wax, furs, metals, Skania herring, had to be imported to Bruges before they could be sold elsewhere in Flanders or the Low Countries. In addition, all cloth, whether it was produced in Flanders or in Holland, had to be brought to Bruges before it could be exported to the East. At one time an attempt was even made to exclude Dutch cloth altogether, and to force every German boat carrying staple goods to call at Bruges even if the goods were directed to England or to the towns of the western Hanse. Needless to say this staple policy defeated its own ends. Hanseatic trade could not at one and the same time maintain its volume and be tied down to a decaying place. What happened was that the rules of the staple were evaded in spite of their energetic enforcement; and that in so far as they were obeyed they depressed the Hanseatic trade and stimulated the trade of the South German and the Dutch towns. The Hanseatics themselves began to call in ever-increasing numbers at Antwerp and the towns of Holland—Amsterdam, Middelburg,

Haarlem, Delft and Vere—and to stay away from Bruges. Even the Flemings began to send their cloth to Bergen-op-Zoom and Antwerp, from whence the Dutch carried it to Amsterdam, which was now a very important centre of cloth trade.

In 1477 the Hanseatic Diet revoked the staple rules, but it was already too late, for they had done all the harm they could. By the end of the century Bruges was beginning to take on the aspect of 'Bruges le mort', Antwerp with Bergen became the chief mart of Northern Europe, and the Dutch were in an impregnable position. They now traded as far east as Breslau and Cracow, and the towns of Prussia themselves began to look with dismay at the Dutch entering Poland. For 1495 we possess the earliest returns of the toll-stations at the Sound, the famous *Sundtolls*, and in that year the Dutch vessels formed the bulk of all the shipping bound for the Baltic.

CHAPTER V

The Trade of Medieval Europe: the South

I. *The First Five Hundred Years*

(I) LIGHTS AND SHADOWS IN WESTERN TRADE

On the eve of the formal collapse of the Western Empire in 476 the European provinces were in desperate crisis. Large estates everywhere tended to become self-sufficient units surrounded by no man's land where roaming bands of brigands were the only challenge to the power of Roman or barbarian lords. In the ruined cities, bled white by Roman tax collector or barbarian invader, the merchants were rapidly losing contact with the neighbouring countryside. The Vandals, solidly entrenched in North Africa and in the islands, had a stranglehold on long-distance sea trade in the West. Greeks, Syrians and Jews were taking from the local merchants a large share of whatever business was left. Their ascendancy was the climax of centuries of growing predominance of the East over the West. The Roman provinces of Asia and Egypt, though seriously affected by the general depression, were the only regions where large cities, important industries, strongly organised workers, and affluent merchants and shippers could still be found.

Five hundred years later, around 975, Muslim and Byzantine fleets were powerful in the Western Mediterranean, and eastern wares and merchants still played an important role. But the commercial and military counter-offensive of Western Europe was already in progress. Old seaports such as Naples and Pisa, new centres of maritime trade such as Venice and Amalfi, and towns in the interior from Pavia to Mainz and from Cambrai to Prague indicated growing prosperity. Spain and Sicily, the outposts of the Muslims in Western Europe, were rivals of Egypt, Syria and the Byzantine Empire in their thriving economic activity. A revolution had begun, which eventually reversed the relations between East and West. Italians largely displaced easterners in the function of middlemen between the two worlds and were preparing to become predominant in the Eastern Mediterranean itself.

Between the dusk of the fifth century and the dawn of the tenth stretches half a millennium of history upon which the documents cast intermittent and dim light. Looking for a clue to the economic process of the entire period, scholars have endeavoured to evaluate the volume of trade in the early Middle Ages. Some historians have described this 'period of transition'—a long transition, indeed—as an epoch of deep, uninterrupted commercial decadence. Others have denied that trade ever sank lower than it had in the fifth century, and even have asserted that there were moderate revivals under the Merovingians, the Ostrogoths, or the Carolingians. One great historian has maintained that the centuries previous to the Arab conquests brought no change for the worse, but that the real depression set in after these conquests. The controversy has not been ended. It will never end, so long as the main point in discussion is the volume of trade. There are no records upon which any commercial statistics can be based. All we can say is that the quantity of early medieval trade cannot possibly have been great at any period.

Quantity, however, is only one element of judgment and not always the most important. The fact that Charlemagne's armies were smaller than Napoleon's, or that the readers of Paul the Deacon were fewer than those of Macaulay does not make Charlemagne and Paul the Deacon unimportant. Their resonance was perhaps amplified rather than muffled by the dull and rarefied atmosphere in which they operated. All we need to know in respect to quantity is whether or not trade and merchants continued to exist; for even this has been doubted. If they always existed, we may abandon the hopeless investigation of the volume of trade to focus our attention upon quality—and the test of quality is the variety of goods exchanged, the specialisation of the merchant class, and the complexity of business methods. By using what evidence we have, we can thus restore a picture in which the main lines of the design are clearly recognisable even though large portions of the canvas remain blank.

Coins are the only material evidence of which we have a continuous series throughout the early Middle Ages. They enable us to discard the extreme assumptions that all trade except for barter ever came to an end or that commerce completely recovered from the crisis of the fifth century. But this is all that they tell us with certainty. State or private moneyers throughout barbarian Europe issued both gold and silver coins, but the largest denomination, the gold *solidus*, soon became only a money of account. The gold coins issued in the Visigothic and Lombard kingdoms were worth but one third of the Roman *solidus*. The Merovingian coiners, after striking *solidi* of a reduced weight, gradually shifted to the silver standard, which was more familiar to the Germans than the gold standard. Finally, at various dates between 700 and 850, the coinage of gold was discontinued throughout Western Europe including Islamic Spain, where no economic decline is postulated. Silver pennies became the only western money in circulation and the silver *libra* took the place of the gold *solidus* as the principal money of account. At the same time, however, foreign gold coins equivalent to the *solidus*—the Byzantine *nomisma* and the Muslim *dīnār*—were currently used in Italy, Southern France and the Spanish March. Replicas of these coins were struck in some western mints to supplement the insufficient supply of foreign gold. Evidently the volume of business had not contracted so much that gold coins had become useless! The reasons for these changes, impossible to analyse here in detail, were *political rather than economic.*[1]

If the evidence of coins is indecisive, can we regard the increasing frequency of barter and the mounting heaps of hoarded objects of gold and silver as proofs that trade had declined to the vanishing point? No doubt these phenomena caused the tempo of commercial exchanges to slacken considerably. All references to unproductive investment or precious metals, however, concern lay and ecclesiastical lords. Noblemen seldom engaged in trade even in Roman times, and ecclesiastics were expected to abstain from trade. Precious objects were the best investment for a lord because they satisfied his desire for magnificence, and in case of need they were promptly melted down, sold or pawned to obtain cash. Despite this hoarding, the availability of large sums or money is proved by many contracts. In one instance (eighth century) a Lombard lady assumed an obligation to pay no less than 4770 gold *solidi* in cash. There are few records of large monetary payments in France after the early sixth century when King Thierry I lent to the Bishop or Verdun 7000 gold *solidi* for distribution to the impoverished merchants of the city. Small pieces of silver, however, had universal circulation even in France. In the ninth century, for instance, the abbey of Corbie used to give pennies to the poor wanderers who asked for alms. Evidently these coins could buy food along the road. Furthermore, ingots or gold dust served as money in the early Middle Ages as they did in later Roman times.

For information on barter we must depend almost exclusively upon private charters, of which the earliest notable series goes back to the eighth century. At that time barter was a common business practice between individuals, while today it survives as an exceptional method of clearing between nations. Then, as now, the underlying motive was not the lack of currency, but the preference of the seller for a means or

---

[1] The gold *solidus* or *aureus nummus* (Greek *nomisma*) in the later Roman Empire weighed 4·55 grams. It was 1/72 of the Roman *libra*, which was not a coin, but a uni of weight and of account. The Byzantine Empire continued to issue the *nomisma* or unaltered weight and alloy up to the mid-tenth century; then the *nomisma* began to be increasingly debased. The *dīnār* (Latin *denarius*) originally weighed 4·54 grams of pure gold, but after the ninth century it was recklessly debased by the Muslims. Charlemagne's silver *libra* (unit of weight and of account) was divided into 20 *solidi* (units or account) or into 240 *denarii* (coins). Otto I went back to the Roman *libra* of 327·45 grams. The *denarius* had already been seriously debased at his time.

payment other than money. Not *any* object was accepted in payment, but always specific essential wares such as horses, cattle, grain and textiles. In 768 a coiner of Lucca bought a piece of land for 28 *solidi*. Presumably a man in this trade would have been in a position to pay cash, but he gave only 15 *solidi* in coin. For the balance he delivered a horse, which he probably bought in the market. At any rate, barter is trade even if only commodities are exchanged.

Barter must be distinguished from unilateral payments in kind in discharge of tributes. If a man or an institution needing an article receives it directly from dependents who produce it, the merchant is eliminated. But the process was not always so simple. For instance, not all the Lorraine peasants who were required to give wine to their lord had vineyards in their fields. Moreover, a poor harvest might force a serf to purchase the goods he owed his lord or to redeem his obligation in cash. In turn, the lord usually did not himself consume all the products he received, but sold the surplus in the market. Furthermore, wares were a safer means of payment than coins whenever coins were debased. In conclusion, not all payments in kind are symptoms of natural economy, nor is natural economy incompatible with the existence of trade.

The key to the understanding of early medieval commerce does not lie in such broad formulae as 'natural economy' or, conversely, 'money economy', but in a patient investigation of specific branches of trade. Long-distance commerce commands the greatest attention because it requires the investment of considerable capital and it can be practised only by professional merchants. Evidence is very meagre, but sufficient for us to state that practically the same oriental wares which Western Europe had imported in the fifth century were still in use there throughout the 'period of transition'. The only important exception is papyrus. Parchment, cheaper than papyrus, had displaced it as a material for books long before the fifth century. Roman Law, however, still required papyrus to be employed exclusively in the drafting of certain public documents. This is why the Merovingian chancery continued to use this material up to the late seventh century, when the obsolescence of Roman Law in France removed the only obstacle to the adoption of parchment. Papyrus lost further ground when a quarrel between Caliph 'Abd al-Malik and the Byzantine Emperor led to a temporary embargo on the export of that material from Egypt (692).[1] Nevertheless, the Popes and many bishops, faithful to Roman tradition,

---

[1] Wilhelm Levison rightly pointed out my mistake in dating 692 instead of around 660–70 the last extant Frankish document on papyrus. But his suggestion that Frankish fears of a Byzantine offensive caused the shift to parchment is untenable. Papyrus did not come from the Byzantine Empire but from Muslim Egypt.

continued to use Egyptian papyrus, even if their exhortations and decrees were topped by an Arab inscription praising Allah! They shifted to parchment only in the tenth century, when the Egyptian papyrus mills, in the face of the competition with paper, closed down.

At no time between the fifth and the tenth century were oriental silk and purple textiles not available in the West. Moralists did not like their luxury and anti-Roman zealots preferred the national furs, but a poet of Liége in the ninth century branded a rich man who wore furs in preference to purple as a miser. The comparative abundance of references to silk and purple proves that at least on Sundays and formal occasions those who could afford it robed themselves in foreign cloth. For a prince and for the Church, purple and silk were more than super-fluities: they were regarded as prime requirements for ecclesiastical ceremonies and as indispensable symbols of political authority. Byzantine and Islamic rulers restricted the export of the most valuable textiles, but the trade continued. *Ersatz* purple manufactured in France would not satisfy the true aristocrat. Not even the collapse of the T'ang dynasty in China, which forced Muslim merchants for more than a century to go no further than Malaya, had any serious repercussions on the volume of imports to Western Europe.

As for imported foodstuffs, the victory of butter over olive oil in early medieval France—but not in Italy—probably was due to a change in taste: butter is still preferred by the French housewife. On the other hand, the French gourmet managed to procure the spices he wanted throughout the 'period of transition'. In the late seventh and early eighth century the monks of Corbie in North-western France took advantage of a toll exemption granted by the Merovingian kings to import considerable quantities of spices directly from far-away Marseilles. One or two centuries later, when French kings no longer controlled the tolls of Provence, the monks were able to buy even greater amounts of spices in the market of Cambrai, only thirty miles distant from their convent.

Western merchants, in turn, had in slaves at least one luxury article to export. Men were rather cheap in the West up to the seventh century, as large numbers of Anglo-Saxon, Lombard, Sardinian and Spanish slaves were sold in the Mediterranean region. As late as 725 a French boy was sold in Milan for 12 gold *solidi*; a good horse sold for one to three *solidi* more. But at that time an untrained slave brought as much as 100 *dinār* in the Umayyad Caliphate, and one well versed in poetry 600 *dinār*. In time, slaves became expensive even in the West, but the trade continued. Teuton warlords or Croatian pirates sold them to Venetian, Greek or Lorraine merchants who smuggled them to the

East and to Muslim Spain: between 912 and 961 the number of
Ṣaḳāliba (Slavonic?) slaves rose from 3750 to 13,750 in Cordoba alone.
Many slave dealers were Jewish; Agobard, an anti-Semitic bishop,
claimed that the Jews stole children in France. There were 'manu-
facturers' of eunuchs in Verdun and in the island of Favignana near
Sicily. The Swiss bishop of Chur as late as the eleventh century
collected the moderate duty of two pence per head for slaves sold in
Wallenstadt.

All this is not surprising. Luxury trade by its very nature is little
likely to suffer from a change of political regime or interruptions of
traffic. The upper classes in the early Middle Ages needed traders in
luxury goods, and were willing to compensate them for any risks they encountered in their long journeys. Rare commodities, however, were not
the only article in the international trade of Southern Europe: iron and
timber were exported to the Muslim countries, olive oil was imported
into Italy. Perhaps the list of bulky goods exchanged between East and
West would be longer if sources were not so desperately inadequate.
It would be absurd to assume that long-distance trade approached the
volume it was to attain in the twelfth or thirteenth century. There may
have been only a handful of merchants engaged in it; but if quality is
as important as quantity in economic phenomena, these merchants were
not insignificant. In the thinly populated early medieval world they
were representatives of a distinct economic and social class.

Nevertheless, no prosperous commerce can be built solely on long-
distance trade. What makes the difference between closed economy
and economy of exchange is chiefly local trade in cheap wares. Stronger
reasons than the understandable silence of sources have led many
scholars to assume that local trade declined much more than international
commerce. The larger estates were self-sufficient in regard to all but
the most extraordinary needs.

It is true that the merchant still supplied the townspeople and the
small landowners. But these prospective customers were few, and had
no easy communication with each other. All but the most important
roads used by lords or pilgrims had fallen into great disrepair. The
lodging-houses established at every stop of the Roman *cursus publicus*
also had disappeared. In Italy, at least, foreigners put up in private
houses along the main roads and in the maritime towns. The development of inns, however, would hardly be encouraged when a German
bishop, as late as 1014, complained with naïve arrogance that the
Italian 'hospites' often poisoned their guests and *always* presented a bill.
The *xenodochia* (guest-houses) supported by the Church were intended
chiefly for the use of pilgrims. It is true that pilgrims, who were
exempted from tolls, enjoyed a golden opportunity to engage in trade

illegally. But the only important case related by the extant sources is that of the Mercian pilgrims who smuggled cloth into the territories of Charlemagne. Another Englishman, St Willibald, in 726 smuggled balm in a pilgrim's stick through the Muslim custom office at Tyre, but cheating the Muslims was a very commendable deed.

At any rate, how much was the trade with the townsfolk worth? Most cities, unable to produce much for export and almost cut off from the countryside, endeavoured to become as self-sufficient as the large estates. Little food was imported, as we may judge from the existence of cultivated plots inside the walls and from the importance of *scholae* or gilds such as those of the market-gardeners and the fishermen in some of the larger Italian cities. Industrial goods for the town dwellers obviously were produced by the city's own craftsmen. There remained little for the professional merchant to do. As for the small landed proprietors, their purchasing power could not be great. Moreover it was dispersed in too many rural markets and weekly or yearly fairs of the cities.[1] The multiplication of these markets and fairs, even in times of commercial depression, has led one historian to assume that their function was mainly to enable the country folk to obtain simple objects of local manufacture in exchange for a few chickens and eggs. Small pedlars and retailers selling goods 'by the penny' could care for the needs of such markets. Real merchants—middle class business men —were not needed.

To these observations, however, many important qualifications must be added. Local trade was thin, but thinness does not necessarily mean simplicity. In 901 a *negotiator* rented a stall in the weekly market of Pavia for 6 pence a year; he certainly was not a pedlar. Nor were pedlars the *negotiatores* who in the eighth century owned shops in different sections of Milan, or the lady who in 950 owned the house in León where she had her residence and her shops (*tendae*). Rents were low, but they appear less low if one considers that in addition the merchant had to pay the *banchaticum* (a licence tax) and sales taxes usually not lower than 10 %.

The commercial decline caused by the downfall of the middle class may not have affected all western articles alike, but manifested itself mainly in household goods such as pottery, shoes and common clothing. Some wares probably were not even sold by merchants. Goatskins must have been prepared and sold by the peasants themselves. Even to-day one can see peasants carrying goatskins on their bicycles to the town markets in Provence. 'Frisian' cloth and Pisan or Sardinian 'sagi', however, had more than local reputation and must have been sold by

[1] In the Mediterranean world the sources do not always clearly distinguish between international 'fairs' and local 'markets'.

professional merchants. In the tenth century Naples produced linen which a Baghdad merchant saw there and judged the best he had ever seen. A piece of Neapolitan linen, he said, sold in the city for 38 gold *dīnār*.

More important than the commerce of manufactured goods was the heavy trade in grain and wine. Wholesalers in these commodities made the fortune of some fairs. The fair of St Denis, founded by King Dagobert I in 634 or 635, probably ranked with the great markets of the orient for the volume if not for the variety of goods. Certain Italian fairs seem to have developed even more rapidly than St Denis. Piacenza in 819 had only one fair lasting one day. Three fairs of eight days each were added in 872 and 873. A fifth fair held in the *xenodochium* of a monastery was granted in 896 and was to last 17 days. It is hard to believe that such a crescendo did not correspond to an expansion of trade, especially to the trade which flowed through the city, because it was located where the Po was crossed by the *via Francigena* from Rome to France. Yet Piacenza had to compete with two primary commercial centres only a few miles distant, Pavia and Milan.

Even the problem of communications was not quite as desperate as some historians have maintained. Sea and land robbers might infest some of the main commercial routes, but they seldom attacked large convoys and caravans. They were not attracted to the minor paths, nor did they molest the short-haul navigation along the coasts. It took centuries before the entire network of highways left by the Romans became impracticable, and towards the end of the 'period of transition' horses, mules and donkeys were able to manage rougher paths owing to the introduction of the horseshoe. Pack animals, who walked along the narrowest trails, were used much more than carts. Men also served as pack animals in this age of serfdom and slavery. Then we must notice that the breakdown of roads after the sixth or seventh century led to a gradual intensification of internal navigation to a degree which may seem almost unbelievable today. Even the small lake of Wallen in the Swiss mountains, the swampy waters of the Sile river in Eastern Venetia and the stony bed of the Scultenna in the Apennines were familiar routes of boatmen. Artificial waterways linked to the sea inland towns such as Maguelonne (Languedoc) and Torcello (Venetia) —tiny commercial centres whose ruins we may see today. The Po, the Arno, the Rhone, and later the Aude, with their tributaries, became main routes of trade, joined by road or canal to the Rhine, the Meuse, the Seine, the Loire, the Garonne, and other rivers flowing into the Atlantic.

It was chiefly through rivers, lakes and coastal waters, highways which required little or no upkeep, that the leisurely merchant of the early Middle Ages moved in many small boats considerable loads of inexpensive goods. Operating costs in river transportation are so low that today, even as in the time of King Liutprand, one can see barges loaded with salt towed by one or two men and moving slowly up the Po between Comacchio and Ferrara. Oar-propelled boats can go fast downstream. The famous Liutprand of Cremona casually reports that in 943 he went in three days from Pavia to Venice by river and coastal waters, a distance of at least 200 miles; if he really did, the performance of his oarsmen could not easily be beaten today. Boats laden with iron descended the streams of the central and eastern Alps with dangerous speed. Salt, grain, wine, oil and other wares were carried in bulk on water. Venice, Pisa and Marseilles owed their fortune not only to trade in eastern goods and western slaves, but also to the distribution of salt of the Laguna, the Maremma and the Provençal marshes.

It has been observed that local merchants and carriers, unlike the importers of oriental commodities, often were attached in some way to a lay or ecclesiastical lord, whom they served as supply agents and business managers. For instance, the monks of French and northern Italian abbeys entrusted what they called 'our merchants' to buy and sell what they defined as 'our necessities' throughout the Frankish or Lombard states. We must not be deceived by these expressions. Ecclesiastics were forbidden to engage in business by Canon Law, strengthened in 789 by a capitulary of Charlemagne. Their boats, their pack animals and their carts were exempted from tolls on explicit condition that they transported only goods for the personal use of the ecclesiastics and their dependents. Most monasteries, however, organised their production with a view to obtaining a surplus which was sold in the market. When the monastery of Santa Giulia (near Brescia) introduced the silkworm into one of its manors, it was not only a question of supplying ornaments for the local chapel. The tenants of the manor in the tenth century carried the silk to the royal market of Pavia, and paid the monastery a lump sum of 50 *solidi* for the ten pounds sold there.

The use of merchants as supply agents was not invented by the abbeys but adapted to their particular needs. Their employment went back to the later Roman Empire. Following Roman practices, Theodoric frequently ordered Italian merchants and shippers to effect *coemptiones*, that is, to purchase at ceiling prices and to transport for the use of the state the foodstuffs required by his administration and army. Less efficiently, Priscus and Solomon, Jewish merchants 'by appointment' to Merovingian kings, and their coreligionist Abraham of Saragossa, palace merchant of Louis the Pious, exercised the same functions: they supplied goods to the court and, in exchange, obtained fiscal privileges in their trade. Similarly privileged merchants were responsible for the supply of the Lombard court. As late as the tenth century the 'great, honourable and very rich *ministri* of the Pavian merchants' claimed special prerogatives as royal supply agents. The independent Venetians had to offer their spices and precious cloth to the Palatine Count before they could display the wares for sale to the public in Pavia. Within the limits of a less advanced economy, these merchants may have been almost as indispensable to the early medieval kings as the Bardi, the Fuggers and the Rothschilds were to the monarchs of their time.

We have thus been able to single out, if not to describe thoroughly, various types of business men: court merchants, abbey merchants, wholesalers in foodstuffs, retailers of manufactured goods, pedlars, slavers and importers of oriental commodities. Their number in all probability was very small, and specialisation was incomplete. Nevertheless, the very existence of so many branches of commerce is worthy of notice.

Furthermore, the thunderbolts that French, Spanish and less frequently Italian councils kept hurling at the *usurarii* prove that the activity of money-lenders continued. Who the 'usurers' were, however, we do not know. In the later Roman Empire silversmiths (*argentarii*) and, to a smaller extent, money-testers (*nummularii*) discharged many of the functions of bankers. But Gregory the Great was forced to intervene to save from bankruptcy the last *argentarius* doing business as a banker in Rome; after that time we still meet some *argentarii*, but they seem to be silversmiths only. It is very probable, however, that the early medieval *monetarii* or *nummularii* (coiners and money-changers) extended loans in coins and bullion. The meagre sources of the centuries between the sixth and the tenth do not mention credit operations by coiners, but they shew that these men steadily rose in economic power and in political prestige. In the eleventh century the Milanese coiners shared with the merchants the highest rank in the business world, and the Roman coiners according to the enemies of Hildebrand financed him in the investiture struggle. At the same period French documents mention loans by *trapezitai*, and use this term as a synonym of *monetarii*. In ancient Greece and apparently in medieval Constantinople the *trapezitai* were deposit bankers and they extended loans. Presumably the western coiners exercised similar functions. Their organisation in regional and national gilds (*sacramenta*) may have enabled them even to transfer credit from place to place. Ordinary merchants also may have discharged some of the functions of agents of credit in the early Middle Ages. The *bancherii* mentioned in the Genose sources of the twelfth century were engaged in general trade as well as in deposit banking.

While the Catholic clergy were unanimous in their condemnation of 'usury', the attitude of laymen was not equally unanimous. In Lombard Italy we find significant expressions in legal sources which seem to imply that interest-bearing loans were regarded as lawful. And whatever the doctrine, we observe that in those obscure centuries of the early Middle Ages the Italo-Byzantine cities slowly elaborated contracts which circumvented the prohibition of 'usury': the sea loan, the commission (rogadia) and the commenda. Only one of these contracts, the sea loan, was inherited from Roman and Greek Law. The others were medieval innovations of the utmost importance. The contracts cannot be described in this chapter, but we must watch their first traces as they emerge from the meagre sources of the 'period of transition'. Expressions later used in both the commenda and the rogadia appear in Venetian documents of the ninth century. In the later Middle Ages these contracts became common to the whole Catholic West as the revival of trade brought conditions that made them serviceable in a wide area. One can hardly imagine, however, that they could have been serviceable in Liguria, Provence, Languedoc or Catalonia before the eleventh century. In the writer's opinion the commenda contract developed first in the seaports of Byzantine Italy between the late eighth and the early tenth century under the direct influence of the oriental commercial contracts (the Byzantine χρεωκοινωνία and the Muslim mudhāraba) and not without some slight influence of agrarian location contracts of the Lombard hinterland (the soccida and the colonia partiaria). It was not wrought in one piece in the reviving schools of law, but was the ultimate result of everyday practice and the unconscious invention of hundreds of obscure men.

These men will for ever remain obscure. There are no biographies of business men of the early Middle Ages, and we cannot trace the formation and development of commercial fortunes. Venetian wills of the ninth century, however, show that some merchants owned land both on the tiny islands of the lagoon and in the Lombard hinterland. Lombard charters from the eighth century on also refer to negotiatores who owned not only houses in the city but also country estates. Farther inside Europe, a merchant of Ratisbon in 983 donated to an abbey three pieces of land in the country as well as real estate within the walls of his town. Even the French Jews bought or rented land, as we can see from the vehement protests of religious writers throughout the early Middle Ages; so did Catalan and Italian Jews. A modern historian, generalising on the basis of late evidence from a few cities, has maintained that the merchants of the later Middle Ages were mostly descendants of early medieval lords and landed proprietors who invested in business the increased rents of their estates. This assumption sharply contrasts with that of another historian, who has described the small pedlar and the adventurer of the early Middle Ages as the real ancestors of the late medieval business magnates. Yet both theories have a common ground: they are based on the notion of total disappearance of the mercantile middle class in the early Middle Ages. This notion is certainly exaggerated.

No progress can be made by substituting other generalisations for those already suggested. To state that all the merchants of the twelfth and thirteenth centuries were descendants of merchants of the ninth and tenth would be not only to minimise the 'rush to the cities' after the year 1000, but also to ignore the teaching of our own times. We still see sons of business men retiring to the country, and sons of farmers trying their lot in business. There may have been less social mobility in the early Middle Ages, but the diversity of origins among merchants is proved by the fact that some *negotiatores* or *mercatores* seem to have been less than full freemen, while others were *milites*, that is, members of the feudal hierarchy. In Italy a large number of minor noblemen engaged in trade after the tenth century, but at an earlier period we witness the opposite process of merchants acquiring land. The Lombard charters from the eighth to the tenth century show that apart from large seignorial holdings there were moderately sized pieces of land which changed owners with considerable rapidity as *negotiatores*, craftsmen and professional men sold, bought or exchanged them. In 742, for instance, a Tuscan merchant bought for 35 *solidi* a vineyard and a slave or serf from a northern Italian. Ten years later he purchased two other 'small pieces' of land for 3 *solidi*. One has the impression that he was a 'nouveau riche' seeking in real estate both a safe investment and a way to climb the social ladder. On the other hand, a law of King Ahistulf, issued in 750, indicates that even if some merchants were equals of the land-owners in wealth and rank, nevertheless they were still regarded as merchants. The king, who needed equipment for his army, divided the assessable population into *negotiatores* and *possessores* (landowners), and each of these classes into three parallel groups. The *negotiatores potentes*, like the proprietors holding at least seven country homesteads, were expected to supply corselets, shields, lances and horses in proportion to their means. Merchants and landowners of the third class furnished only the equipment of a bowman. The only difference between land-owners and merchants was that the latter were allowed to redeem their obligation in cash.

This completes our picture of early medieval trade. There are many blanks in it, and it is better to acknowledge their existence than to try to guess. The parts of the picture which can be restored are sufficient for us to see a great variety of nuances. The business world was certainly small, but it was a highly complex world.

(2) THE RISE OF ITALY

The complexity of the early medieval economy can be fully appreciated only if the static picture we have had under our eyes is transformed into a dynamic projection of the different developments taking place in each region of Western Europe. The legacy of the Roman Empire was a commercial economy centred in the Mediterranean and dominated by oriental merchants. Spain, France and Italy equally partook of this trade, no region being much ahead of the others; Germany was barely touched by the commercial currents coming from Africa and Asia. By the tenth century, however, Spain had become part of a different economic community, while Germany was included in what we may call Catholic Europe.[1] France no longer formed a commercial unity gravitating on the Mediterranean, but was divided into two areas, the larger of which opened on the Atlantic and communicated with the Mediterranean by the devious route of the Alps and Upper Italy. Italy, while losing her political independence, had risen to an economic primacy such as she had never known when her armies ruled the world. Let us now review briefly this development country by country.

There was no sudden change after the formal collapse of the Western Empire. The barbarians, far from continuing their destructive work after the conquest, endeavoured to preserve the old institutions, both good and bad. They had neither the desire nor the ability to cure with radical means the economic and social disease which had spelled death for Rome. They did not substantially change the oppressive taxation of trade, though they enforced it less efficiently, and they made no serious effort to break up the large estates. There was no parallel in the West to the abolition of the sales tax in the Byzantine Empire, or to the renaissance of free peasantry as indicated by the slightly later Byzantine Agrarian Law. Merchants from the Eastern Empire continued to tighten their grip on the commercial life of Western Europe and North-west Africa. Greek words—*cataplus*, *catabolus*—designated the dock areas and the incoming ships in all barbarian kingdoms. Since the Byzantine emperors were usually on good terms with the kings, oriental merchants found open doors everywhere.

---

[1] It would be highly desirable that the expression 'Christian Europe' be used only when the Byzantine Empire is included.

Soon after the Vandal conquest, Africa apparently resumed the usual shipments of oil to Constantinople and Rome. Carthaginian merchants continued to go to Spain and Byzantine merchants remained in Carthage. After the Byzantine restoration in Africa and Italy, in the time of Gregory the Great, several ships went every year from Carthage to Rome. Southern Spain also became a Byzantine protectorate in the late sixth century, and this made the resumption of direct communications between the Eastern Mediterranean and the Atlantic possible. There was a Greek colony in Cordoba; other Greek merchants, 'arrived by ship from the Orient', were found in Merida. Both cities, well inside Spain, were situated on rivers flowing into the Atlantic. In the seventh century there are indications that Byzantine ships may have reached England. The account of a Greek hagiographer, who speaks of a ship of the Alexandrian Church which carried grain to England and loaded tin there, was regarded until recently as historically worthless. But the unearthing of an Anglo-Saxon burial ship, containing Byzantine silver plate, in East Anglia has brought unexpected confirmation to the legendary account. Soon after, however, the Visigothic reconquest of Southern Spain must have brought the direct relations between the Atlantic and the Eastern Mediterranean to an end.

Law-books are almost the only source giving information on trade in Visigothic Spain. We catch glimpses of kings endeavouring to control the coiners and to maintain what was left of the Roman *cursus publicus*. We see *mercenarii* carrying on the roads and rivers of the kingdom the 'gold, silver, clothing and various ornaments' which the *transmarini negociatores* import into the sea towns. If we may judge from the story of a *mercenarius* of the late fifth century as related by Sidonius, men of this class were both carriers working for the oversea merchants and small merchants on their own account. It may be surmised that the *transmarini negociatores* were mostly Orientals and belonged to a higher class than the local merchants. The Visigothic kings heavily taxed these 'oversea merchants', but tried to remove obstacles from their path. The royal protection, however, did not cover the Jews, who were very numerous in all the larger cities. A series of laws restricting their activity reached a climax under King Egiza (687–702) when he forbade them to approach the docks or to trade with Christians. No wonder that a few years later the Jews welcomed the Arab invasion. The commercial history of Muslim Spain will be presented later. Before leaving the Iberian Peninsula, however, we must recall that Christian merchants from Urgel and Barcelona, in the Spanish March, maintained relations with Cordoba and other cities in the Spanish Caliphate. Slaves are the only item of trade specifically mentioned in the sources.

In Mediterranean France trade was much livelier, especially after the Frankish kings had wrested Provence from the hands of the Goths, making it the main outlet of the greatest barbarian state to the southern sea. Even Narbonne, which remained in Visigothic hands, benefited from its proximity to the Frankish border. In Provence not only Marseilles and Arles but also smaller centres such as Nice and Lérins maintained relations by sea with Italy, Spain, Africa and the Levant from the fifth to the early seventh century. They exported slaves, cloth and timber. They imported spices, wine of Gaza and Falerno, olive oil, rice, dates, figs, papyrus, leather goods and silk. Considerable quantities of these goods were forwarded from the coast to the most distant regions of Merovingian France by river and road. We still hear of *constituta evectio tam carralis quam navalis* (state transportation by both carts and boats) in 716. Many Roman bridges had collapsed, but they were replaced by pontoon bridges like that of Arles. Local fairs were organised in the smaller centres such as Rodez and the neighbouring towns. In the larger cities the merchants had permanent residences and shops, but they were quick to go wherever the trade opportunities were favourable. Orientals seem to have outnumbered native merchants in wholesale trade. The entrance of a Frankish king into Orléans, which is today the linguistic capital of France, was cheered in Latin, Syrian and Hebrew !

Mediterranean France, which increased its boundaries when Charles Martel annexed Languedoc and Charlemagne the Spanish March, did not lose all commercial importance after the beginning of the eighth century. Reliable sources mention more than once the Italian ships which called at Marseilles in the ninth century. Less reliable accounts, referring to the later years of the reign of Charlemagne, mention a variety of 'Arab' wares in Arles and speak of African, Jewish and even Breton (or British?) ships along the Narbonese coast as if they were a far from uncommon sight. A lost charter of Boso, the king of Provence (879–87), granted the church of Arles the tolls collected from the Greeks and other strangers in the *portus* of that city; the grant was confirmed by Boso's son in 921. In the ninth and tenth centuries the Rhone and perhaps a Provençal harbour may have been used by merchants of Verdun on their way to sell slaves in Spain. We only know with certitude that the route from Northern France to Spain branched off from the *via Francigena*—France to Rome—somewhere near Lyons; slavers and pilgrims went in the same caravan before having to part. Lyons itself was the home of many Jews, who owned synagogues and slaves, and who were well supplied with wine and other luxuries.

Nevertheless, it seems undeniable that Carolingian and early Capetian France gradually turned its back on its own Mediterranean coast.

Among probable causes of this slow change one must give due importance to the political anarchy, local warfare and foreign invasions
which grew steadily worse from the seventh to the late tenth century.
Similar disasters, however, also affected the trade of the Italo-Byzantine
cities with the Lombard hinterland without disrupting it. Probably
a more specific factor of decline was the lack of normal and continuous
diplomatic relations between France and the oriental powers. While no
war has ever eliminated contraband, reciprocal trade agreements and
favourable tariffs are essential for a full development of commerce.
Even in the 'Dark Ages' a passport (*sigillum*) was required to cross the
frontiers and to be admitted to the main markets of the Muslim states,
the Byzantine Empire, Lombard Italy and the Carolingian Empire. It is
significant that Muslim wares are mentioned in Arles when Charlemagne's relations with Cordoba and Baghdad were at their best, and
that Greeks appear in the same city when the kings of Provence were
negotiating for an alliance with Constantinople. As a rule, only the
Jews could freely go back and forth between France and non-Catholic
lands because they had no definite nationality and were politically
harmless. Their ascendancy was no less helped than hindered by dis-
crimination against them. In Carolingian France they became so
predominant in trade that the texts often divide traders into two
classes, 'the Jews and the other merchants'.

This does not mean that the commercial currents from the East
ceased to reach France, but only that they had to follow devious
channels. In the ninth and tenth century a new economic unit, Catholic
Europe, was slowly emerging in place of the older Mediterranean unit.
Contacts with the Byzantine and Muslim worlds were maintained
mostly through peoples who lived near the frontier and who were
admitted to the oriental markets: Slavs, Scandinavians and Italo-
Byzantines. (Already in the seventh century caravans of Frankish
neguciantes, mostly slave traders, went to Slavonic and Avar territory for
trade. Charlemagne established a series of frontier outposts across
Europe, from the Danube to the northern shore, where his subjects
could trade with the Slavs.) The frontier outposts shifted eastwards as
Catholic Europe expanded. In the tenth century, Polish, Russian,
Turkish, Muslim and Jewish merchants went to Prague to purchase
slaves, furs, tin and other European wares, and no doubt to sell oriental
commodities. This overland travel, however, was slow, expensive and
frequently interrupted by war. The Scandinavian river and sea route
via the Volga or the Dnieper and the Baltic was longer but cheaper. The
Italo-Byzantine route via the Mediterranean, the Po valley and the
steep Alpine passes was the shortest and probably the cheapest.

It would not be surprising if French trade with the East suffered from this change of routes. Germany, however, owed to the new routes unprecedented commercial importance and her cities along the great rivers of Western and Southern Germany benefited the most. Mainz is a good illustration. Local merchants carried grain down the Main to the city while traders from Magdeburg linked Mainz with Bardowiek near the mouth of the Elbe. Frisian merchants resided in the best houses of Mainz before 886. They brought with them not only the textiles of their country but also oriental wares purchased in Scandinavia or in Rome. Other wares were imported into the city by Slavonic merchants. Jewish traders obtained salt from central Germany, and boasted of bringing to Mainz some commodities imported directly from Palestine. A lone Muslim traveller from Spain who visited Mainz in 973 was surprised at the quantity of 'Indian' spices he found there. The spices might well have been bought by local traders in the Italo-Byzantine cities: one 'opulent merchant' from Mainz, Liutfred, appointed by Otto I as ambassador to Constantinople, went there via Venice. Certainly that was not his first journey by that route. His city, in the heart of Europe, could use equally well the Baltic, the overland and the Mediterranean supply routes from the orient. German and Swiss centres farther south, however, definitely gravitated towards the Italo-Byzantine cities. So did Southern France. Only the lack of statistical data makes us hesitate to affirm that trade between France, South Germany and the East via Italy was considerable. We know that a good number of transalpine references point to the Italians as the principal if not the only suppliers of eastern wares to the larger part of Europe.

Italy at last had begun to exploit the advantage of her central position in regard to both continental Europe and the Mediterranean basin. A fruitful transformation took place in Italy during the first five centuries of the Middle Ages, in spite of recurring political and military disasters. A nation of moderately successful peasants and farmers, who in Roman times were dependent upon easterners for their trade and who did not produce enough food for their overgrown capital, now was on its way to becoming the first commercial and industrial nation in the world. The first phase of this revolution was all but completed before the end of the 'period of transition'. Italo-Byzantine merchants almost entirely replaced the Greeks and the Syrians as middlemen between the Eastern and the Western Mediterranean.

The transformation was slow at first. Jews, Greeks and Syrians still dominated commerce in Italy under the Ostrogoths. The administration imported grain and other foodstuffs from the non-Italian provinces of the kingdom and from Africa in larger quantities than it exported its own commodities. One wonders whether the survival of Roman municipal administration, craft gilds and taxation system was really a boon, since this burdensome structure had speeded the collapse of the Western Empire. A more substantial advantage was the continued upkeep of the Roman highways, even though this delayed the utilisation of internal waterways. Sea trade was promoted by the fact that the Western Mediterranean for a few years became an Ostrogothic lake save for Africa, which was controlled by the friendly Vandals. However, we must not accept at face value the hyperboles of Cassiodorus, whose imagination placed in the harbour of Rome the traffic of bygone times and transformed the fishermen of the Venetian coast into shippers 'wont to cross infinite stretches of the sea'. Nor must we give much credence to a chronicler who spoke of *negotiantes* flocking in to enjoy Theodoric's perfect order; other sources of that allegedly fortunate period mention brigands in the country and armed bands in the cities.

At any rate, any recovery that may have occurred in the time of Theodoric was nullified by the frightful ravages of the Graeco-Gothic war (535–53) and of the Lombard invasion (568). The years of the lawless Lombard 'interregnum' (574–84) probably were the worst in Italian history. The Lombards, however, were unable to wrest from the Byzantines most of the coastal areas and the control of the sea. All along the hollow shell of the 'Roman' possessions, the inhabitants were gradually driven to rely upon sea trade for the means of subsistence they could no longer obtain from the lost hinterland. The letters of Gregory the Great point out the commercial importance of Ravenna and mention numerous ships leaving Naples and Rome practically every month from March to early October for the islands, Africa, Provence and the Levant.

Three centuries later (around 875), when Muslim and Norman raids were at their worst and the peninsula was in a state of anarchy, the sailing season in the Tyrrhenian had been contracted but slightly. Ships, usually grouped for security in large convoys, navigated in the period from April to September. Some of them succumbed to enemy attacks, but others attacked the enemy and reached friendly shores with their prizes. Naples and Rome were now less important than Amalfi and Gaeta. The tiny harbours of these seaports which were hemmed in by the mountains found this handicap a stimulus to commercial expansion by sea. Soon after, Salerno, a 'Lombard' city, forsook national ties and sought new fortunes by recognising Byzantine overlordship. Farther east, on the lower Adriatic, 'Roman' Bari hesitated to choose between agriculture and trade because it still had a wide hinterland. Eventually the proximity of the Balkan coast, where the *via Egnatia* from Constantinople reached Durazzo, tipped the balance on the side of trade. Ravenna, the old political and maritime capital, continued to thrive. Farther north, along the fringe of Venetian islets from Comacchio to

Grado, a people of fishermen had become a nation of merchants. A chronicler, referring in particular to Venice, pointed out that though 'these people do not plough, do not seed, do not gather vintage', nevertheless they are able to obtain grain and wine in Lombardy, where they go 'on business' (cum negocio).

The prosperity of these communities of merchants and shippers was built upon a series of delicate compromises with Byzantine overlords and with Lombard and Muslim neighbours. The Byzantine Empire never abandoned the later Roman practice of channelling most of the foreign trade through a number of outposts beyond which no alien could go without special permission and escort. In addition to these border markets local depots (ἀποθῆκαι) were established in the main harbours and road termini, while in the capital a system of state-controlled lodging-houses (μιτᾶτα) was placed at the disposal of authorised foreign merchants. In the West the chief Italo-Byzantine cities were naturally fitted to fulfil the function of border markets; moreover, their merchants as Byzantine citizens had free access to both the local depots and the lodging-houses in the capital. The Venetians as a reward for their services in lending ships for military transportation and state mail were granted a reduction of customs rates at the Dardanelles. The merchants of Amalfi were excluded from this privilege in the late tenth century, no doubt because their loyalty was questionable. Under the special tariff the incoming Venetian ships paid only 2 gold nomismata, while outgoing ships paid 15. This seems to indicate that the value of the wares imported into Constantinople was far smaller than that of the precious textiles, the spices, the perfumes and the other commodities exported to the West. In addition to the legitimate imports passing customs inspection, however, we must take into account the slaves whom the Italo-Byzantine merchants smuggled in despite imperial decrees forbidding that trade. There also were many restrictions in regard to exports: gold, war materials, basic foodstuffs and precious textiles worth more than 10 nomismata a piece were sometimes smuggled out, but they could not be legitimately exported. The legitimate trade, however, was enough to attract to Constantinople a large number of merchants from Venice, Amalfi, Gaeta, Salerno and even Rome. No permanent Italo-Byzantine colony was formed, because no one was permitted to dwell in the lodging-houses of the capital longer than three months.

Commercial relations of the Italo-Byzantine cities with the Muslim countries were no less close. The comparative abundance of Arab coins in Western Europe shows that exports and imports were in better balance than they were in the trade with the Byzantine Empire. The Italians imported from Muslim lands spices, perfumes, ivory, textiles, oil and, no doubt, other commodities not mentioned in the few extant sources. They exported slaves, timber, iron, wooden and iron objects. Slaves, timber and iron were vital supplies for the Muslim armies and navies. Hence the Byzantine emperors when at war with a Muslim power added to the usual prohibition of the slave trade specific decrees forbidding the export of timber or iron to enemy territory. Only the Venetian Doges, however, made any attempt to enforce the orders of their overlords, and even they could not prevent contraband. As for the South Tyrrhenian cities, they more often than not allied themselves with the Muslims in open warfare against their own neighbours. As early as 722, when the Byzantines, Franks and Lombards were locked in bitter struggle against the Caliphate, ships from Egypt were welcomed in the harbour of Naples. In the ninth century, the Bishop and Duke of Naples joined the rulers of Amalfi and Gaeta in an alliance with the Muslims against Pope John VIII. The economic advantages of this alliance were so great that the Pope was unable to win back the support of Amalfi either by the threat of excommunication or by an offer of total customs exemption in Rome and by the payment of the huge sum of 10,000 silver *mancusi*. Ironically enough, both the *mancusi* and the papyrus on which the Pope wrote his entreaties were of Muslim origin! The Muslims were no more bound by religious scruples than the Christians. In 813, ambassadors of the African Aghlabids aboard a Venetian convoy aided the crew in attacking a convoy of Spanish Muslims. The ambassadors then carried out their mission of inducing the Byzantine governor of Sicily to renew the agreement which had insured to the citizens of each country the right to journey and trade in the other. Several records tell how merchants of Venice and Amalfi undertook voyages to Africa, Egypt and Syria. The Muslims, like the Byzantines, did not allow aliens to reside permanently in their territory. This is the only reason which prevented the formation of Italo-Byzantine colonies.

Italo-Byzantine commercial relations with the Lombard kingdom were from the beginning an inescapable consequence of the fact that coastal towns without a hinterland and a hinterland without coastal towns were economically interdependent. The gradual conquest of wide stretches of the coast by the Lombards and the Franks did not alter these relations. The reason seems to be that the rulers of the Italian kingdom seldom were on speaking terms—if we may use this expression—with the Byzantine and Muslim rulers and hence made no commercial treaties with them. They concluded only local agreements with single Italo-Byzantine cities, profiting from the fact that these cities were semi-autonomous. In 715, representatives of King Liutprand granted special reductions from the usual 10% tax on foreign trade to the inhabitants of Byzantine Comacchio who carried salt, oil and pepper up the Po to Cremona. These homely comestibles bear witness to the three sources of wealth of the North Adriatic seaports: salt extracted in bulk from local marshes, oil obtained in substantial quantity from Africa, and pepper imported in smaller amounts from Constantinople or Alexandria. King Liutprand is also said to have concluded an agreement with Venice that permitted the Venetians to frequent the fairs of Pavia. Thus the Italo-Byzantine merchants stepped into the shoes of the easterners who had been predominant in earlier times, but who now could not enter the kingdom because there was no trade agreement. Nor could the Lombard merchants enter Byzantine territory except in those regions where the boundary line was not clearly defined. The loopholes must have been wide, but they did not lead to Constantinople; as late as the tenth century the merchants of the Lombard kingdom seem to have been excluded from the lodging-houses of the Byzantine capital.

The commercial monopoly of the Italo-Byzantine seaports was threatened for a time by the direct negotiations of the Carolingians with the courts of Constantinople, Cordoba and Baghdad. Perhaps the treaty of Charlemagne with Hārūn al-Rashīd, about which we have little positive information, was concerned only with the travel of pilgrims. These pilgrims, however, probably availed themselves of the market near the Christian *xenodochium* of Jerusalem, where anyone could exhibit his wares by paying two pieces of gold a year. Charlemagne's lost treaty of 813 with the Byzantine emperors apparently granted subjects of each empire access to all highways and waterways of the other as well as admission to the state-controlled markets of the respective capitals. This πάκτον, however, was abrogated almost immediately after ratification. Therefore the Carolingians, despairing of being able to patch up their differences with Constantinople, transferred to Venice the reciprocal facilities which the treaty of 813 would have insured to the entire Byzantine Empire. This seems to be the origin of the Franco-Venetian *pactum* of 840 which, through promulgation by Emperor Lothar and successive confirmations and improvements, laid the foundations for the absolute primacy of Venice over the other Italo-Byzantine seaports in western trade. In the same period the open collaboration of Amalfi, Naples and Gaeta with the Muslims eventually caused these cities to lose their privileged position in the Byzantine Empire. Other Italo-Byzantine cities—Comacchio, Ravenna and some Istrian seaports—were conquered by the Lombards or the Franks. The complaints of the Istrians to their Frankish governors show what this conquest meant: 'We are laughed at by our Venetian and Dalmatian neighbours and by the Greeks our former masters... (we cannot) give hospitality to foreigners.' At last, in order to retain some of their old trade, the Istrians begged the Venetians for a protectorate, while Comacchio was ruined and forced to submit to Venice. Even Ravenna began to decline, though her greater vitality is proved by the presence in the tenth century of a *schola* of merchants—probably a survival of Roman times and perhaps the earliest merchant 'gild' mentioned in western sources of the Middle Ages.

By the first years of the eleventh century Venice by force of arms and diplomatic cunning had won a position of decided predominance among the intermediaries in commerce between East and West. The city was virtually independent of Constantinople and yet still enjoyed the privileges of Byzantine citizenship. Venice maintained diplomatic relations with all Muslim powers and dealt as an equal with the kings of Italy and the western emperors. A series of agreements with local authorities in Upper Italy ensured low tariffs for Venetian trade moving up the main rivers flowing from the Alps. Beside the Istrian cities, several Dalmatian towns and islands, formerly included in the Byzantine Empire, had accepted Venetian suzerainty in order to escape Slavonic occupation. With the Dalmatian raw silk coming in as tribute and with state-controlled *xenodochia* where foreigners were admitted on the same terms as they were in the lodging-houses of the Byzantine capital, Venice was a little Constantinople in the West.

The future rival of Venice, Genoa, in the early eleventh century was just beginning to recover from more than three centuries of extreme decadence caused by the Lombard occupation and by the breakdown of the Roman highways across the Apennines and along the coast. There still are to-day a few Ligurian villages which can be reached only by small boats or through rugged mountain paths. The larger part of Liguria must have fallen into these conditions after the Lombards conquered it (around 642). In three hundred years we hear only once of a convoy stopping in Genoa on its way from Rome to Provence (878), and it was not a commercial convoy. The Muslim fleet which sacked the city in 934 (or 935) must have found very few merchants, but mainly a community of peasants and fishermen, besides a few noblemen. This raid, however, was important because it set in motion a vigorous reaction, the effects of which began to be felt after the year 1000.

The Lombards succeeded in maintaining in a position of international importance one of their seaports, Pisa. The town not only was the terminus of ships coming from Corsica, the only island in Lombard hands, but also it continued to receive Greek slavers, to send convoys to Byzantine Sardinia and, possibly, to be in direct communication with Constantinople. As far as one can judge from the extremely meagre sources, Pisa owed this exceptional position to the fact that the

Lombards granted an autonomy comparable to that enjoyed by the Italo-Byzantine cities. Many 'Lombards' went to live in the city, but a group of *waregangs*—aliens, who were most certainly 'Romans'— remained there under the special protection of the king. When this autonomy was revoked is unknown. The harbour, still active under the Carolingians, seems to have sharply declined in the late ninth and early tenth century. Overland trade, however, must not have entirely ceased, because Pisa was close to the *via Francigena* which, restored by the Lombards, was the most important highway in the kingdom throughout the Middle Ages. Coastal navigation to the salt marshes of southern Tuscany and to Rome also probably continued, as did navigation up the Arno and Serchio rivers to the larger centres of northern Tuscany.

Space forbids describing in detail the economic organisation of the Italian kingdom under the Lombards and their successors down to the Saxon dynasty. Historians still disagree on the interpretation of the fragmentary sources of the seventh, eighth and ninth centuries. These can be completed only by drawing from a fuller account which describes conditions of the tenth century, when the centralised organisation set up by the Lombards and preserved by their first successors had already begun to fall to pieces. What still remained, however, resembled more closely the solid administration of the Byzantine Empire than the loose structure of the Frankish state. In Pavia, the capital, and apparently in some other cities, the main crafts and professions, including those of the merchants and of the moneyers, were headed by *magistri* and controlled to some extent by the king's officers. The state claimed all gold found in the kingdom's rivers, presided over the mints and punished counterfeiters under a law introduced by King Rothar in imitation of a Byzantine law. Pavia, like Constantinople, was the terminus of all foreign ships, the Ticino river being a miniature Bosporus. Instead of lodging-houses, however, the merchants coming from the coast found only an empty square where they could pitch their tents and stay for a limited period. A Lombard official, similar to the Prefect of Constantinople, supervised the market and received the tribute of the Italo-Byzantine sellers of precious textiles, spices, mirrors, salt and oil. To control merchants coming overland, the Lombard kings had established *clusae* or customs stations, much like the Byzantine border outposts, in the last town of each route just before it reached the Alpine passes. There foreigners had to stop, pass inspection, and pay 10% on their horses, slaves, tin, swords and textiles of wool, linen and hemp. Pilgrims went free of customs. Anglo-Saxons, favoured by a special agreement, paid every third year a lump sum and a tribute in kind.

Feudalism doomed to early failure the attempts of the Carolingians to establish in the whole Empire an organisation similar to that of Lombard Italy. In Italy, however, traces of centralisation remained. The shops in the market of Pavia were in most cases granted to ecclesiastical institutions, which also built their own lodging-houses; but state officials continued to exercise some control. Against the new tolls imposed by the Bishop of Cremona the merchants of the city waged a long if not always successful struggle. The right to strike money was granted to or usurped by only a very small number of bishops, and bestowed upon no lay vassal. The Roman notion that coins are a public utility was never lost; in 945 the king forbade the Bishop of Mantua to alter the weight or the alloy without the agreement of the assembly of the citizens. Similar restrictions on feudal debasements do not appear in France until the twelfth century, and in Germany still later.

The rise of Italy to commercial primacy in Western Europe well before the end of the early Middle Ages was partly the result of the happy accidents which stopped the barbarians at the doors of Venice and Rome and the infidels at the gates of Naples and Amalfi, thus enabling the Italo-Byzantine seaports to develop their autonomy, their original business methods and their trade. But it was also due to the fact that behind the flexible structure of the maritime towns was the solid organisation of the kingdom, which sheltered the Lombard and Tuscan *negotiatores* as they accumulated their capital and elaborated their own business methods. Eventually the *compagnia* contract, rather than the maritime *commenda*, emerged as the main instrument to pool capitals in overland trade. Differences in method, however, did not prevent the Italian merchant of the interior from becoming a worthy collaborator of the Italo-Byzantine sea trader. One is led to assume that French and German merchants were willing to undertake the long and hard journey across the Alps because they found in Italy a commercial world less disorganised than their own was. Asti, a little inland town but one with a great future, in the tenth century attracted the attention of the Spanish traveller al-Ṭarṭūshi on account of its security and efficiency. 'When its inhabitants purchase an article (to resell it)', he said, 'they write on it the price and leave it in its wrapping. Whoever finds the price convenient takes the article and leaves its price in its place. Watchmen are in charge of the wares, and if something is lost, they refund the price.' The praise of the Muslim observer, who was accustomed to the endless bargaining in the oriental markets, has almost symbolic value. It foreshadows a period when Italian merchants, after gaining the first place in Catholic Europe, would extend their supremacy to the Greek and Muslim markets of Asia and Africa.

(3) THE MUSLIMS

Leaving the north-eastern corner of the Mediterranean for the immense regions controlled by the Muslims is much like departing from the grim halls of the Germanic epics for the enchanted palaces of the Arabian Nights. The traveller is dazzled by the glow of 'Egyptian' emeralds, turquoises from Nīshāpūr, rubies from Yemen, pearls from the Persian Gulf, coral from North-west Africa and Sicily, and marble from Syria and Azerbaijan. He is astonished at the great quantities of linen from Egypt, Yemen and South-western Persia, of cotton from Merv, Eastern Persia and Spain, of silk from Turkestan and the South Caspian area, of carpets from various regions of Persia, of leather work from Andalusia, of pottery from Khurāsān and other provinces, of glass ware from the Syrian coast, and of iron ware from Farghāna. He is enchanted by the scent of Irakian violet water, of Persian rose water, of Arabian incense and ambergris, while he delights in Maghrebine and Spanish figs, Irakian and African dates, Turkestanian melons, Tunisian olive oil, Persian, Yemenite and Palestinian sugar, saffron from North-western Persia, sturgeon from the lake of Van, 'edible earth' from Ḳūhistān, and—regardless of Mohammed's prohibition—excellent wine from Irak and Spain.

According to Muslim geographers, historians and poets of the early Middle Ages, these and many other wares formed the basis of a lively trade extending from the Atlantic coast to the borders of China. Wide differences in climate and civilisations within the economic empire of Islam favoured both local specialisation and the transmission of techniques and products. The primacy in the manufacture of arms, for instance, passed in the later Middle Ages from Irak, Oman and Yemen to Damascus and Toledo, while the superiority in production of leather reversed the direction by going from Andalusia to Persia. What could not be obtained or was rare in the land of the Believers was imported from abroad—iron, lumber, furs and honey from Christian Europe; ivory, tortoise shell, gold and various spices from Africa; spices, gems and tin from India and the East Indies; fine porcelain and silk from China; slaves from all parts of the world. Foreign plants were acclimatised and foreign techniques were adopted, sometimes with important improvements. The manufacture of paper, for instance, was introduced into Samarcand from China, but the method of making rag paper was perfected by the Muslims. Furthermore, the Muslims gained a large share of the profits of other peoples' trade by employing their own ships and caravans to link together the markets of Catholic Europe and the Sudan, East Africa and India, the East Indies and China.

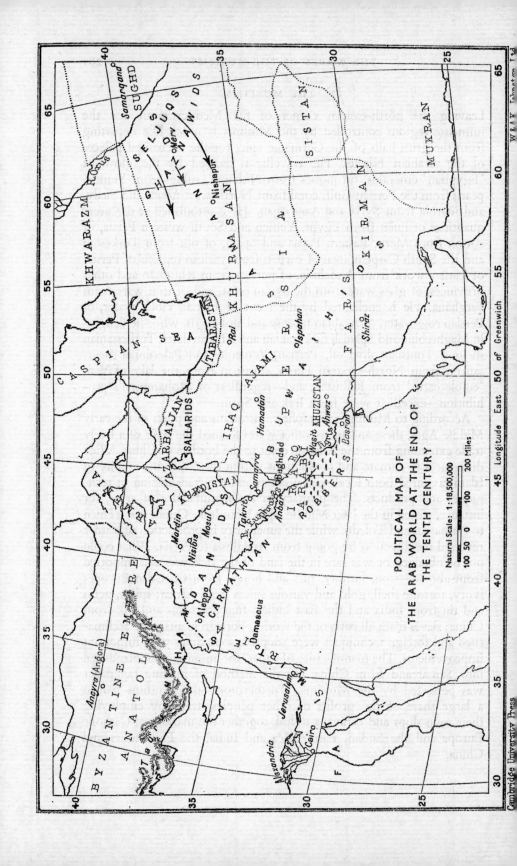

POLITICAL MAP OF
THE ARAB WORLD AT THE END OF
THE TENTH CENTURY

Natural Scale: 1:18,500,000

100 50   0   100   200 Miles

To be sure, much of this trade antedated the rise of Islam. Even in antiquity Arabs and Persians had acted as intermediaries between Europe, Africa and Asia. The followers of Mohammed, however, welded together East and West in a new unity based upon common religion, language, law and business practices. Thanks to this unity, which survived the collapse of the ecumenical Caliphate, Muslim merchants could travel from Spain to India without feeling that they were going to foreign lands. The Arab population grew rapidly owing to polygamy. This increased both the opportunities and the need for the production of consumers' goods and for commercial development. In Persia, Africa and Spain the old spirit of adventure of the town merchant was spurred by closer contact with the desert nomad, and stimulated by the religious precept of pilgrimage. Mohammed's own example emphasised the honourableness of commercial occupations.

No detailed description of the economic empire of the Muslims is possible here, but we can, at least, make the acquaintance of the more important types of merchants as portrayed in 'The Beauties of Commerce', a panorama of Muslim trade and business practices disclosed by the Syrian Abu al-Faḍl. The *staplers* bought up goods of ordinary consumption to resell locally when prices were soaring. The *travelling importers* made purchases wherever prices were low and competition was small in order to resell the goods elsewhere at a higher price. The sedentary *import and export merchants* sent goods to trusty correspondents who sold them and either sent back the proceeds in cash or invested them in other wares. The *sellers of textiles, spices and similar products* were also sedentary business men; they coupled commercial skill with a thorough knowledge of the materials they handled. Professional *brokers* and, apparently, specialised *transport agents* were indispensable auxiliaries of trade. To all merchants, Abu al-Faḍl addressed this advice: 'Do not invest in commodities for which there is little demand because the plain people do not need them', that is, cling to heavy trade for mass consumption. He specifically warned against commerce in jewels, purchased only by the rich, or scholarly books, bought by learned men 'who are mostly poor and few in numbers'. Similar suggestions were made by the famous Ibn Khaldūn in the fourteenth century, but 'The Beauties of Commerce' is much earlier. Internal evidence leads us to believe that it was composed in the late ninth or early tenth century.

Abu al-Faḍl's picture shows that there was considerable specialisation in trade, but fails to indicate which business men were more important than the others. We must turn to the literary sources of the same period, always keeping in mind that most numbers in Arabic literature are highly exaggerated. A writer of the tenth century reported that some

100,000 camels loaded with dates left the province of Karmān every year to distribute the fruit to the whole of Persia. Another writer, of the twelfth century, tells of two business men who in 800 had gained nearly 12 million *dirham* by speculating in the Irakian harvest, but who eventually lost 66 million *dirham* owing to a sudden decline of prices. Even if we cannot accept these figures at face value, we may infer that regional trade in cheap bulky goods was very important. The profits of trade in luxury goods, however, must have been much greater. The largest private fortune mentioned in Arabic sources probably is that of a Baghdad jeweller who, it is said, remained rich after Caliph al-Muḳtadir (908–32) had confiscated 16 million *dīnār* of his wealth. Dealers in linen and traders in spices were generally regarded as the aristocracy of business. Importers of spices often amassed particularly large fortunes. We hear of a merchant from Aden who left home with 1000 *dirham* and came back with 1000 *dīnār*, that is almost fifteen times as much.[1] Some of these men displayed a magnificence worthy of Sindbād the Sailor: al-Iṣṭakhri, a tenth century geographer, tells of a merchant from Sīrāf who had spent 30,000 *dīnār* to make his house beautiful. Sīrāf on the Persian Gulf was probably the most important terminus of India and China voyages.

While a general evaluation of Muslim trade is obviously impossible, some of the figures quoted by Arab writers inspire confidence because of their moderation or because they are drawn from official statistics. We can believe Ibn Ḥauḳal, a tenth century geographer and merchant, when he relates with astonishment that he saw in a Saharan oasis a letter of credit of 40,000 *dīnār*. The sum is huge, but still larger sums are quoted in western sources of the later Middle Ages. Reliable figures are available also in regard to the 10% tax on the sea trade of Sīrāf. During the reign of al-Muḳtadir the tax yielded 253,000 *dīnār* per year, and in the second half of the tenth century the yield rose to 316,000 *dīnār*. Although it is hard to compare data of different places and times, the latter figure seems to indicate for Sīrāf in its prime a sea trade almost equivalent to that of Genoa at its peak (£3,822,000 Gen. in 1293).

It is particularly remarkable that the trade of the Muslims reached these great proportions when we consider the material and moral obstacles which merchants faced. Similar obstacles, in the opinion of some scholars, had all but destroyed commerce in Catholic Europe. The word 'risk' comes from the Arabic word *rizk*, originally meaning

---

[1] The *dirham* (from Greek *drachmē*) was the main unit of silver coinage in the Muslim monetary system. Originally one gold *dīnār* was worth only 10 silver *dirham*, but the ratio underwent important fluctuations. It must be noted that in the tenth century most coins were debased.

'quotidian bread' or 'distribution'. To earn his daily bread and to distribute marketable goods, the Muslim merchant encountered the same risks as his Catholic colleagues in the early Middle Ages—foreign and civil wars, attacks of sea pirates and land brigands, assaults by wild beasts, and exactions by tax collectors which were often more redoubtable than all of the other dangers combined. Of course he could reduce hazards by travelling in large convoys and caravans, but this restricted his opportunities since he had to wait until these collective expeditions were organised; namely, he had to make his voyages during the 'safe' months, and his travel by land on occasions of weekly markets and fairs. He benefited from a circulation of metallic money and bills far greater than that of Catholic Europe, but he had also to contend with widespread barter, partly the result of unproductive hoarding of much gold and silver. He also often employed the silver rather than the gold standard, since the use of gold coinage was restricted in Spain, Persia and all provinces east of Persia. In the tenth century the gold standard won the day in these regions, but at this period a general debasement of coinage set in. Egypt, Syria and North-west Africa always remained faithful to the gold standard, but the *dīnār* soon became only a money of account, as did its equivalent, the *solidus*, in Catholic Europe. The circulation consisted mainly of coins worth one fourth of the *dīnār*.

The problem of communications was particularly acute owing to the immense distances. Internal navigation was not as important in the Muslim economic empire as it was in Catholic Europe because large rivers were few. The Guadalquivir, the Nile, the Euphrates, the Tigris, the Hilmend carried a heavy traffic in bulky goods, and even the smallest streams of Sicily and North-west Africa conveyed some merchandise. Nevertheless, it was necessary to transport most goods by camel and pack mule along tracks, at times marked only by posts driven into the soil. The network of postal routes which Ibn Khurdādhbih described in the ninth century was supplied with 930 relays. Yet if we examine its operation carefully, we see that it was nothing but a collection of beaten trails which were kept open mainly by the passage of pack animals and horses. The Roman and Sasanian highways had fallen into disrepair soon after the Muslim conquest; in the tenth century the last permanent bridges on the Tigris collapsed. Most rivers could be crossed only by pontoon bridges or ferries. Cordoba owed her fortune largely to the only stone bridge spanning the Guadalquivir, a legacy of Roman times. There were many pious hospices along the main roads, but there were few inns in the cities before the eleventh century: Egypt had none before the time of Saladin. Navigation was probably more important than long-distance overland travel, but it

was confined in four non-communicating seas—the Indian Ocean, the
Caspian, the Black Sea (barred at its western entrance by the Byzantine
Empire) and the Mediterranean. Some of the most frequented harbours
were so shallow that few ships could come close to shore. Large ships
were used only in the Mediterranean, and even there the shortage of
shipbuilding material hindered naval construction. The vessels of the
Indian Ocean were too small to face the frequent storms of these waters;
indeed, their planks instead of being solidly nailed were held together
by ropes. The sailors who by the tenth century reached Sofala (today
in Portuguese East Africa) must have had undaunted courage. Lucky
was the man who had sailed to China seven times and survived.
Intolerance, which drove many dissenters into the African wild, was
kinder to other heretics, who settled in 'golden' Korea. The real
Eldorado, however, was Wākwāk (Wakoku, Japan in Arabic); neither
the Muslims nor Marco Polo were able to reach it. Sailors often
boasted of sailing east of China or west of Lisbon into the 'Pitchy Sea'
which encompassed the world. But who can believe sailors' stories?

It is hard to determine to what extent the religious prohibition of
usury, which today still hinders Muslim business men, hampered
medieval trade. It certainly was ignored by a very large number of
merchants. A writer of the ninth century refers to trade in *shukūk*
(*cheques*, letters of credit; the word is of Persian origin) in the time of
Omar, the second Caliph (634-44). A convenient escape to legal and
moral objections was found in the eleventh century by a prominent
jurist, Abu Ishāk. He stated that it was not forbidden for a borrower to
pay more than he had received, provided he did so of his free will and
without making any promise in writing. Likewise, in Catholic Europe,
interest-bearing loans were currently cloaked under the formula of
mutuum gratis et amore, gratuitous and loving loan. There seems to have
been some similarity between the twelfth century Genoese *bancherius*
and the tenth century Muslim *jahbadh*, although the methods of the
latter probably were less advanced. Like the *bancherius*, the *jahbadh* was
not exclusively a money dealer or a deposit banker, but engaged in
general trade. As a banker he received deposits which could be drawn
by written order (*shakk* or *suftadja*), and no doubt he extended loans to
the depositors. He also discounted money orders, receiving a commission of one *dirham* per *dīnār*, which was about 6·66%. He often
farmed taxes and lent money to the government, not always spontaneously. In one instance he charged the government monthly
interest of 25%.

Nevertheless the objections against the taking of commercial interest
continued to embarrass the Muslim investor and money-lender or, at
least, to trouble his conscience when he felt the approach of death.

Indirectly, these objections paved the way for the ascendancy of the Jews and of the Syrian Christians, who, like the Byzantines, regarded interest as legitimate. While these Christians became prominent in money-lending, the Jews enlarged their share in certain industries and in commerce. Linguistic affinity with the Arabs and the higher sense of toleration of Islam afforded the Jews a far better lot in Muslim than in Christian lands.

In the ninth century Jewish merchants surpassed not only Christian but also Muslim merchants in the scope of their trade. The 'Rhadanite' (*Merchant*?) Jews, who spoke Arabic, Persian, Greek, Frankish, Spanish and Slavonic, spanned the whole known world. According to Muslim geographers, these international merchants went from the farthest west to the farthest east by three routes. One route went by sea from the 'Frankish' shore (Southern France or more probably Italy) to Egypt, Syria or the Byzantine Empire; thence it went by caravan to the Red Sea or the Persian Gulf, and finally by sea to India and China. The other routes went almost entirely overland from Spain, either via North Africa and Damascus to Baghdad, Persia and India, or via 'the route behind Rome' through the Slavonic and the Khazar land, Transoxiana, the Turkish state of the Ghuzz and the northern trails to China. Jewish merchants journeyed wherever profitable trade was to be found. Many visited the capitals of both the Eastern and the Western Empire; others went to Bulgaria to purchase slaves whom they later sold in Venice; still others went to Prague, the great city of stone where Arab coins circulated side by side with cloth which the Baltic peoples used as money. The Jews were thoroughly at home in the wooden houses of Itil, the capital of the Khazars on the banks of the Volga, since the majority of the Khazars had embraced Judaism before the end of the ninth century. They also had a stronghold in 'Samkarsh of the Jews' at the entrance of the Sea of Azov. In the tenth century even Sīrāf, the greatest Persian seaport, was at one time under a Jewish governor.

Gradually, however, the main interest of Jewish business men in the Muslim states shifted from commerce proper to finance. In the early tenth century the Jewish 'Court Bankers' Joseph ben-Pinḥas and Aaron ben-Amram played an important role in the Abbasid Caliphate. A few years later in the Fatimid Caliphate of Egypt and Syria most bankers and money changers were said to be Jewish; one of them, after adopting Islam, became vizier. At the same period in the Umayyad Caliphate of Spain the Jew Ḥasdāi ben-Shaprūṭ was director of customs and carried out important negotiations, sometimes in behalf of his coreligionists, with the greatest monarchs in Europe. This was the high tide of Jewish political and economic power, and it did not last long. Both in finance and in commerce, however, the Jews throughout the later Middle Ages continued to exert a much greater influence than their number warranted whenever they had the good fortune to live in Muslim lands.

In a very general way it may be stated that Muslim trade reached its peak in the period from the ninth to the twelfth century. The picture, however, varied greatly from place to place. In Egypt and to a smaller extent in Syria, the Muslim conquest resulted in a growing predominance of Persians and Irakians in business. While transit commerce with the East increased, traffic with Christian Europe probably remained below the level it had reached before Mohammed. Cyprus in the seventh and eighth centuries and Aleppo in the late tenth took advantage of their autonomy to act as intermediaries in trade between two hostile worlds, much as did the Italo-Byzantine cities. Around 912 the only survivor of the numerous Syrian colonies in Europe probably was that of Constantinople. Syrians had the unique privilege of being allowed to reside in the Byzantine capital and to purchase and sell goods by bargaining as a unit just as the local gilds did. At that time Syria seems to have thriven more than Egypt, which in the early tenth century was in a state of political and economic crisis. Both countries increased their production and commerce towards the end of the century under the vigorous rule of the Fatimids. A very large share of trade, however, was monopolised by the government, which owned textile manufactories, most of the ships, and all of the 20,000 shops or stalls said to exist in Cairo around 1050.

North-west Africa probably reached its economic zenith in the tenth century, when the rulers of the coastal area succeeded in checking the inroads of the camel-riding nomads of the desert. New cities were founded and old centres revived. Kairwan at that time competed with Baghdad and Constantinople; indeed, even Ajdābia, now an insignificant desert post, was one of many centres which manufactured and exported textiles to both Muslim and Christian countries. Far to the south, in the chain of oases, were communities which had grown prosperous from production of dates and from the rich traffic with the negro peoples of Senegal and Sudan. The pearl of the Sahara was Sijilmāsa, probably near modern Tafilelt. Today even its ruins have disappeared, but in the tenth century its independent dynasty struck the best *dīnār* in the world made from gold of the Senegalese rivers.

Spain and Sicily, judging from the meagre information available, were, as late as the tenth century, more important for their thriving agriculture than for their trade. Agricultural and mineral products, but no manufactured goods, were mentioned by a Muslim writer as staple exports from Spain. Onions were the only article of which another writer noticed and deplored the abundance in Sicily; we know, however, that the island had already recovered from centuries of Roman and Byzantine mismanagement. In the twelfth century the famous geographer al-Idrīsi spoke with enthusiasm of Spanish and Sicilian trade. This advance coincided with important political changes. During the eleventh century Spain had been split into many states, each of which, not unlike the Italian communes, was centred about one trading city. Commercial relations with Catholic Europe were as intensive as those with the Muslim countries, and not even the victories of the Almoravids had succeeded in turning the tide against the Christian military and economic *Reconquista*. The struggle was over in Sicily: the island, now in Norman hands, had ceased to be a province of the Muslim economic empire, and had become an outpost of the expanding Catholic world.

II. *The Golden Age*

(1) THE COMMERCIAL REVOLUTION

The startling surge of economic life in Europe in the 'high' Middle Ages is probably the greatest turning point in the history of our civilisation. All of the peoples directly affected registered gains, but these gains were in different directions. The new era created strong and compact national states in England, France and the Iberian peninsula, opened to German sword and plough the great plains east of the Elbe, and gave the Italians—and to a much smaller extent the other peoples of the Western Mediterranean—unchallenged supremacy in world trade. The gains of the Mediterranean peoples proved less stable, because a few merchants cannot root themselves as solidly in a foreign soil as can a mass of agricultural immigrants, and because control of trade is more precarious than the power of a self-sufficient national state. While it lasted, however, the Italian commercial and financial empire brought unequalled prosperity to its masters and on the whole advanced the lot of the people. By the twelfth century, Venice, Genoa and other mercantile cities had surpassed in wealth the greatest business centres of the classic world. In the late thirteenth and early fourteenth century, when the pinnacle was reached, the sphere of direct or indirect influence of Western Mediterranean business men stretched as far as England, South Russia, the oases of the Sahara Desert, India and China. It was the greatest economic empire that the world had ever known.

The commercial expansion of the Western Mediterranean peoples was accompanied by far-reaching changes in the volume of trade, in the methods of business and in the spirit of the merchants. It was instrumental in bringing about all the momentous changes which ushered in our contemporary civilisation much before the end of the

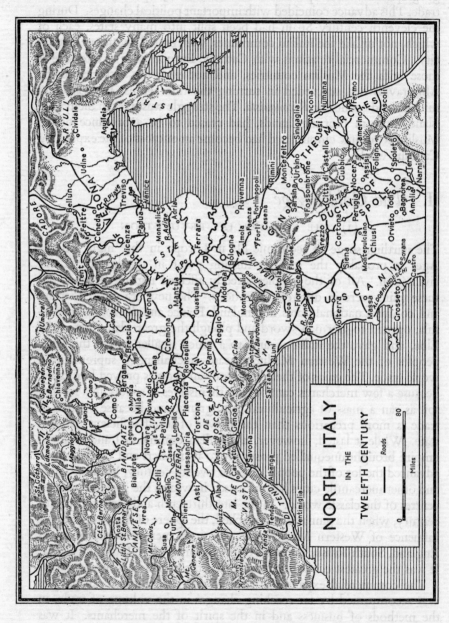

NORTH ITALY
IN THE
TWELFTH CENTURY

Roads ——

Miles

0   80

Map 10.

Middle Ages and was, in turn, influenced by all of these changes. It caused the old feudal system to crumble and the old religion to weaken; it gave liberty to the serfs over large areas and it created a new aristocracy of wealth. The blossoming of a new bourgeois literature and art, the revival of science and law, the beginning of political and religious individualism, the spread of education and of social consciousness to larger strata of the population were at least in part the result of the great Commercial Revolution of the later Middle Ages. No other economic upheaval has had such an impact upon the world, with the possible exception of the Industrial Revolution of the eighteenth century.

Italy was to the medieval economic process what England was to the modern. Even as the Industrial Revolution first transformed economy and society in some English areas and spread later to the rest of the world, the Commercial Revolution first affected a few Italian cities and then made its way slowly through the rest of Europe. If we consider that today, almost two centuries after Hargreaves and Arkwright, 'industrialisation' is far from having penetrated the entire world at a uniform depth, we ought not to be surprised if the march forward of 'commercialisation' in the rarefied and inert atmosphere of feudal Europe was neither rapid nor sweeping. Furthermore, while in the nineteenth century the industrial supremacy of England was successfully challenged by other countries after a few decades, in the Middle Ages even Flanders and the Hanseatic cities, which were autonomous centres of commercial expansion, never overtook the metropolitan business centres of Italy. A student of northern trade has pointed out that in 1500 there was a lag of perhaps two centuries between the commercial and financial methods of the Hanseatic merchants and those of the Italians. Even a Jakob Fugger left his Augsburg to learn business practice in Venice. Moreover, backward areas such as the larger part of Castile, the lands of Eastern Germany and of Western England, and even some remote areas in the heart of Italy were 'commercialised' only superficially. Finally, everywhere the country lagged behind the city, smaller towns did not develop as rapidly as key centres, and within any one city some business men still clung to old-fashioned methods while others inched forward. Indeed, the modern process of 'industrialisation' has followed the same chequered pattern.

Descriptions of modern economy usually follow the most highly industrialised countries, often disregarding entirely the persistence of the less advanced economy of the Shetlands, Tennessee, the Balkans or Afghanistan. They pay more attention to great industrial cartels than to small business and local workshops. This method of ignoring sluggish groups to focus attention upon economic pacemakers leads to some

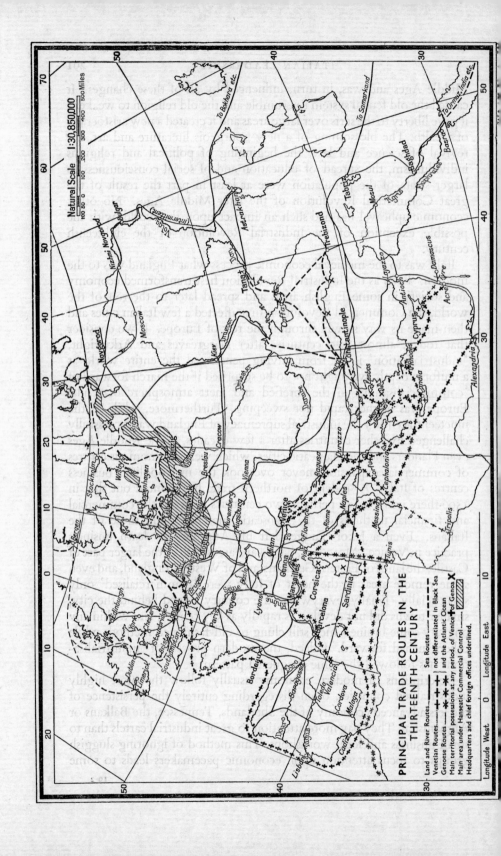

PRINCIPAL TRADE ROUTES IN THE
THIRTEENTH CENTURY

Land and River Routes. —————— Sea Routes. ——————
Venetian Routes. —+—+—+— not differentiated in Black Sea
Genoese Routes. —*—*—*— and the Atlantic Ocean ——————
Main territorial possession at any period, of Venice × or Genoa ×
Main area under Hanseatic Commercial Control. ——————
Headquarters and chief foreign offices underlined.

Natural Scale 1:30,850,000

100 50 0   100   200   300   400   500 Miles

distortion of the truth, but it has the advantage of pointing out clearly the dominant trend. We shall have to adopt the same projection, inasmuch as most of the extant documents come from a few prominent Italian cities, Genoa and Florence above all. Most of the limited space will be used to describe the development of Northern and Central Italy during the Commercial Revolution. Italy itself, then, was a cluster of independent city-states with disparate political, social and economic backgrounds. There were substantial differences between maritime and internal cities, largely inherited from the old political distinction between 'Lombard' and 'Byzantine' territory; the Po valley and Tuscany differed from each other and from mountainous regions; Venice and Rome had unique traditions; the relation of agriculture and industry to commerce was not the same everywhere: and each of these significant regional and local peculiarities reacted on the others, creating an incredible variety of nuances. We shall have to generalise, but let us remember that each Italian city-state was a microcosm with no exact parallel elsewhere.

A revolution is primarily the work of men, both famous and obscure, and of men's ideas: but it depends for success upon favourable circumstances. Leaving to others the discussion of personalities and cultures, let us explore the circumstances. Three factors seem to have been particularly important: the unprecedented growth of the population with the consequent spilling over of agriculturists into the channels of trade: the counter-offensive against infidels and schismatics, and the rise of the Papacy as an international power. The increase of the population must definitely be regarded as the initial thrust which set in motion the rest. The other two factors, however, determined the main direction of the process in Italy and, to a smaller extent, in other Mediterranean areas. It was largely because of them that the intensive growth of population oriented the overflowing energies of the Italians towards commercial expansion overseas and overland, whereas in other countries it precipitated the consolidation of national states or the settlement of frontier areas, and only partially led to an intensification of trade.

A. Expansion of the Home Market

Demographic history is still in its infancy. The documents are insufficient, their interpretation is difficult, and in many cases the inquiry has not even been attempted. But at least it seems well established that the increase of population in all classes alike was steady and considerable from the late tenth to the mid-fourteenth century. At first only a small minority of the population contributed in any way to the Commercial

Revolution, and even when the shift to trade reached its full tide most people remained engaged in agriculture. Yet the growth of the merchant class, no matter how small in absolute numbers, was sufficient to change the character of the entire society. Let us now trace those groups who engaged in commerce and see how they became involved in it.

Fathers of large noble families were forced either to disinherit all except their eldest sons or to split the ancestral holdings until the estate became 'pulverised'. From the great reservoir of landless, land-hungry knights which was thus formed came many of the fighters for the military enterprises which enlarged the commercial frontier of Catholic Europe. Most of them came from non-Mediterranean areas, although some were Italians, Southern French or Catalonians. These fighters, however, merely opened new ground for trade without taking a direct part in commercial enterprises. Our interest in them ceases when the campaign in which they were engaged ends.

Much more important were those prolific families of the lesser nobility who lived in a town or in its suburbs, and whose landed property became insufficient to support them in a manner befitting a feudal lord. In many 'Lombard' towns of Northern and Central Italy descendants of city viscounts and of episcopal *advocati*, and other small fry of the nobility joined the upper bourgeoisie in a struggle against German overlords, Muslim invaders and other common enemies. United they won political liberty and economic opportunities for the city in the eleventh and twelfth centuries. Engaging in commerce was a natural step for noblemen whose feudal resources were insufficient, and who found themselves at the helm of free commercial communities. At the same period the members of the nobility played a prominent role in the commerce of the 'Italo-Byzantine' cities, which had gained or were gaining independence under their leadership. But this was not a new fact, for commerce there had always been the occupation of the larger part of the population including the nobility. On the other hand, the farther one goes from Italy, the smaller is the participation of noblemen in the rise of trade. The viscounts of Marseilles, Montpellier and Barcelona remained feudal lords, interested in commerce only in so far as they could levy tolls upon it. It is true that many landed proprietors, who probably belonged to the lowest strata of the nobility, seem to have been included among the early 'merchants' of Southern France and Catalonia. But it is impossible to tell whether they had become traders because they owned land rents or whether they had become noblemen because they had accumulated money in trade. The second process can be followed easily in the documents of cities which developed in a later period. In fourteenth-century Lyons some ten non-noble families year after year supplied all of the consuls of the young commune. Eventually they made their entrance in the lower nobility, only one step below the feudal aristocrats whom they had fought for centuries.

In Italy the inclusion of many truly noble families among the commercial class quickened and strengthened the recovery of trade to a greater extent than elsewhere. Some of these families after a few generations of political and economic predominance sank into insignificance. Others preserved a leading position for centuries owing to many factors, two of which seem to have been decisive: their continued fertility and their undivided interest in trade. Two hundred and fifty members of the D'Oria family, which descended from the Genoese viscounts, were listed as present in a battle in 1284 (others had stayed at home), and another Genoese noble lineage, the Grimaldi, had 110 members living in 1333. These swarms of noblemen would have faced increasing poverty unless they had engaged in trade. Many prolific Provençal gentlemen, who had failed to open their eyes to the new opportunities in commerce, in the thirteenth century drove their own donkeys loaded with manure. Feudal land rents did not rise as fast as the general increase of the population would have warranted, because they usually were fixed for long terms in coins whose value was constantly undermined by debasement and inflation. Feudal tolls and taxes on markets, bakeries and butcheries rose rapidly as trade grew in volume, but not rapidly enough to keep step with the increase of the nobility who shared the proceeds. A shrewd nobleman would sell or pawn his estates and his portion in the tolls to invest the proceeds in trade; later, if he wished, he could buy back some land with part of the profits, as most merchants did to secure a safe investment. In 1268 the larger part of the estate of Raniero Zeno, the Venetian Doge, was invested in trade and government obligations. In 1240 a descendant of the Genoese viscounts left to his heirs an estate consisting entirely of commercial credits, except for a share in the property of the house where he had lived.

It was, however, ordinary merchants, commoners rather than noblemen, who filled the ranks of the business class in Italy as elsewhere. As early as 1068 the Milanese non-noble *ordo negotiatorum* played an important role by the side of the *ordo capitaneorum vassorum* (the class of noblemen living in the city). Non-noble merchants formed the rank and file of the private associations which set up the communes—in some places before the end of the eleventh century, in others in the twelfth or the thirteenth. Soon they ruled the cities almost as if the cities had been their own property, making communal policy an expression of their own mercantile interests. In Milan their hegemony was not challenged by the humbler classes until 1198; elsewhere they remained sole masters for a longer period, and in some cities they never had to share their power with other groups. Their individualistic tendencies were somewhat restrained by the powerful bonds of relationship. Families formed units whose numerous members usually were closely bound by common political and business interests. There were confederations of families—often rallying around some party label, Guelf or Ghibelline, 'White' or 'Black'—but merchant gilds, where they were created, only made their appearance long after the consolidation of the communes. In Siena, Bologna and elsewhere they were formed simultaneously with the gilds of money dealers. In most of the maritime cities and in some important centres of the interior (Asti for instance) there never was a merchant gild of any sort, probably because commerce directly or indirectly was the occupation of the overwhelming majority. For the same reason the 'consuls of the sea' in Pisa, Marseilles, Montpellier and other seaports were not heads of a special group, but municipal officers entrusted with harbour and navigation police. In one way or another nearly everybody drew his means of subsistence from the sea.

As commerce absorbed larger and larger strata of the population in the cities, wealth rather than birth became the main basis of class distinction. In many Italian cities some merchants at least were descended from a very long line of early medieval *negotiatores*, but others were upstarts and newcomers to trade. In neither case can we discover their actual ancestors, because family names were not in use for ordinary people until very late. At the beginning of the twelfth century a Genoese notary copying a number of obscure family names—they were often derived from ridiculous or obscene nicknames—gave up the task and simply added: 'and many others whose names are difficult to write'. Some nicknames were destined to be transmitted to generations of great Genoese business men. Venice itself, when it closed almost hermetically the rolls of the merchant 'nobility' (1297), listed as noble both old and new 'patrician' families (*case vecchie* and *case nuove*). The Malipieros, who claimed aristocratic origin of great age, actually descended from a maestro Piero, a master merchant or craftsman. In most of the other cities 'nobility' became merely a social distinction which could entail indirect economic advantages, but no legal privileges whatsoever. The Florentine Commune liberally knighted rich merchants and shop-keepers, and these often imitated the ways of the old aristocracy by buying country estates and building palaces in the city. At the same period (1293) enrolment in one of the commercial, industrial or professional gilds was made a pre-requisite for holding public offices. A time was to come when men of noble origin in some towns, in an endeavour to win the support of the lower class, would insist upon being regarded as commoners. Outside Northern and Central Italy the dividing line between noblemen and merchants was not erased, but it became thinner and thinner in the more 'commercialised' areas. In Majorca, for instance, noblemen and bourgeois were lumped together in one class, the *homens de honor* who lived in the capital and subjected the peasants to thorough exploitation.

Commerce also eventually opened new horizons to some branches of industry, which became major forces in the economic and political life of the city. To be sure, in many minor business centres the presence of craftsmen in the group which ruled the town merely meant that most of the merchants themselves were hardly richer than ordinary gild masters. This may have been the case even in Montpellier, where some representatives of the humblest crafts were commonly elected to the Consulate. But in cities such as Florence, Lucca, Bologna and Milan the only crafts which gained a place in the government usually were those capable of capitalistic development, that is, textile and metallurgical industries producing for export or trades working for mass consumption such as the butcher shops, whose number remained restricted by law while cities continued to grow. The master craftsmen who thus attained equality with the merchants and bankers were not plain artisans, but entrepreneurs who applied to industry some of the capital derived from commerce and finance. Their prosperity ultimately rested upon the increase in number of humbler gildsmen and industrial labourers who consumed or manufactured their goods, and this increase was a result of the general demographic growth. As we watch these masses struggling for better living conditions and for a share in what was called now, somewhat ironically, 'government of the people', we are led to wonder how far 'commercialisation' meant prosperity for all. It is true that salaries rose—between 1194 and 1228 those of the masons in Northern Italy apparently more than doubled—but the debasement of coins sometimes reduced real wages to a bare minimum. Yet there are definite indications in the sources of the late thirteenth century that the standard of living went up. The Commercial Revolution, not unlike the Industrial Revolution, increased the distance between the very rich and the very poor, but on the whole tended to improve the lot even of those who were unable to rise above their class.

Still, the greatest gift of the Commercial Revolution was the continuous creation of new opportunities for everyone to climb from one class to another. To be sure, there were sharp fluctuations and crises, which we probably would call business cycles if we could gather complete commercial statistics. But the increase of the population continued, and with it continued the expansion of the home market which

created the opportunities. Apprentices became masters, successful craftsmen became entrepreneurs, new men made fortunes in commerce
and money-lending, merchants and bankers enlarged their business.
The middle class waxed more and more prosperous in a seemingly
inexhaustible boom.

Expansion was also stimulated by a constant immigration from the
country, where the population was also increasing and becoming more
and more open to the influence of the city. A scholar has stated, perhaps
with some exaggeration, that family names of the inhabitants of Italian
cities in the twelfth and thirteenth centuries indicate a peasant origin for
two-thirds of the number. Entire villages gradually lost to nearby
towns all of their inhabitants, peasants and landowners. After a few
generations the newcomers might gain a place among the leading
families. The Cerchi who headed the White Guelfs in Dante's Florence
came from the Sieve valley; the Manduel who ranked with the greatest
merchants in Marseilles in the early thirteenth century, came from
a village near Nîmes. The larger part of the immigrants, however,
settled among the lower class, supplying cheap manpower to the leading
industries and manual work to harbours and agencies of transportation, or, at best, becoming shop-keepers and masters in the humbler
crafts.

Capacity to absorb further members in the already existing urban
business class rather than political advantages offered by towns determined the size of immigration. Although the Aragonese serf could
gain personal freedom and citizenship by residing one year in a town of
the kingdom, the growth of towns there was slow. In the fourteenth
century serfdom was still widespread at the very doors of Gerona and
even in the surroundings of Barcelona. In contrast to this, 'foul
smelling villeins' swarmed to the Italian towns, even though hospitable
Genoa granted citizenship only after three years and conservative
Venice only after twenty-five years. Unlike the bourgeois of Northern
Europe, who invited immigration to build up the strength of the city,
the Italian burgher usually felt strong enough to conquer the feudal
class unassisted, and regulated immigration according to the needs of
specific branches of trade. He destroyed the imperial palace within the
city walls and the country castle of the lord. Then he transformed the
serfs into free men—with no political rights—and told most of them to
stay where they were and produce cheap and plentiful food for the city.
His demands and often his personal interest in agriculture stimulated
economic activities in the country, both by introducing improved
methods to secure larger yields of staple foods and by intensifying the
production of raw materials for industry, such as flax in Romagna, silk
in the Lucchese territory, saffron in Eastern Tuscany, wool in Abruzzi,

metals in Sardinia, Elba and the Alpine region. The increased returns of the land in turn enabled the peasants to buy more products from the cities. Literary sources represent the Northern and Central Italian rustic as possessing few fineries, but sufficiently well provided with necessities. Money economy, which already in the early Middle Ages was not unknown in the Italian rural communities, by the fourteenth century was almost as prevalent in the country as in the cities. This minor 'agricultural revolution' also spread to Southern Italy, Provence and Catalonia, but only to a less degree.

The Commercial Revolution itself penetrated the smaller centres. Notwithstanding the inadequate documentation of country life, we catch glimpses of merchants, shop-keepers and artisans of the main crafts even in the smallest towns. In fact, the availability of water or the proximity of mines caused some industries to move away from the main towns. Smiths and armourers of the mining valleys north of Bergamo and Brescia wrought masterpieces which were sold by city wholesalers, the limpid streams around Fabriano enabled that tiny city to become the world's greatest centre for the production of paper, and artistic industries began to flourish in several townlets, some of which are still famous today. The fulling mills and almost all ship-yards were not located in the main cities. A third-rate Ligurian seaport, Noli, in the thirteenth century had local 'patricians', merchants, bankers, ship-owners, drapers, carders, weavers, fullers, dyers, furriers, farriers—all this notwithstanding the wretched conditions of the communications with the hinterland, which caused Dante to seek in the trail to Noli a term of comparison for the superhuman difficulties he met in climbing the mountain of Purgatory. Similar pictures can be drawn for many minor centres in Northern and Central Italy, Dalmatia and Provence, and for several in the other Mediterranean countries.

Inland in Languedoc and Gascony where old cities were few, some of the new agricultural settlements (*bastides*) assumed the functions of towns. In the early fourteenth century the Bonis brothers, merchants and bankers in the *bastide* of Montauban, carried on a trade worthy of many a large city business man and kept one of the best books of accounting that have come down to us from non-Italian areas before 1500. A number of new trading centres also sprouted up from the open fields and the rugged coastlines of Sardinia and Corsica, sometimes from an outgrowth of Genoese or Pisan *castelli*. But in the larger part of Italy, Provence and Catalonia, the old cities were too many and too strong to tolerate the growth of new rivals. In the Po valley Alessandria, founded by the Lombard League as a bulwark against Frederic Barbarossa, was the only notable addition to the galaxy of large towns of Roman origin.

The inevitable direction of the Commercial Revolution was through urban to metropolitan economy. The process, however, was far from complete even in Italy. As soon as they had demolished whatever unifying elements—mostly political but partly also economic—may have remained in the feudal monarchies, the Communes set out to construct states proportionate to their ambitions and resources. Then followed a protracted and costly struggle for primacy or one simply for breathing space, since chances for expansion were great but not unlimited. Weapons of the struggle included embargoes, piracy, destruction of harbours, discriminatory tariffs, and the construction of new routes to displace old highways and canals. Eventually some cities emerged on top and increased their lead by leaps and bounds, whereas others—including glorious towns such as Pavia, Ferrara, Ravenna, Siena and Pisa—had to resign themselves to second rank. Other towns hopelessly trailed. But even the smallest cities usually retained some degree of autonomy and served as markets for the surrounding countryside, as stations along ways of communication and as homes of some highly specialised industrial skill. Therefore they continued to grow absolutely, while steadily losing men and capital to the larger cities. We must not imagine the smaller centres as cut off from the main commercial currents. In medieval Italy international trade always remained comparatively more important than local trade. The very smallness of the territory of most communes made it impossible for them to live as self-sufficient units, even though they tried to maintain a well rounded economy by a series of measures which we may call 'pre-mercantilistic'.

When drawing a distinction between urban and metropolitan economy, we must consider the intensity rather than the extension of commerce. Not only the 'metropolitan towns' but also many minor cities drew their food from distant areas, exported their wares to all directions of the compass, played host to colonies of business men from other towns and sent colonies radiating through Europe and the Mediterranean. What especially singled out a 'metropolis' was the all-embracing influence of trade, so powerful that it dwarfed all other activities within the city. It was not the number of the inhabitants but their spirit that made the difference. While Paris, the largest city in Catholic Europe and the capital of a great kingdom, was not a business metropolis, one needs only to thumb through the cartularies (books of minutes) of the Genoese notaries of the thirteenth century to see how high ran the fever of commercial profit in that 'metropolis'. Men and women, widows and spinsters, adolescents and octogenarians, noblemen and servants, landed proprietors and artisans, laymen and priests all alike engaged directly or indirectly in business. Practically every citizen had a stake in the galleys, the trains of pack animals, the fairs or the colonies and had investments with the bankers, the craftsmen or in the market of government bonds—be it a matter of many thousand pounds or only a few pence. Those who had nothing to invest, contributed their labour and expected their reward from commercial operations.

Outside Northern and Central Italy, the picture was different. Cities grew more slowly and could not attain or maintain full independence. While all political energies of free communes were directed to the support of economic expansion, feudal lords and monarchs often neglected the best interests of the cities under their rule in order to pursue political ambitions or to increase their income. But there were some rulers who adopted vaguely 'pre-mercantilistic' policies and employed feudal forces and income drawn from the agricultural hinterland in behalf of trade. Robert Guiscard and Roger II were pioneers in this practice. Under their rule the Italo-Byzantine seaports of Southern Italy and the cities of Muslim Sicily underwent the difficult conversion from outposts of oriental trade to outlets of the new territorial kingdom. They managed fairly well. Agriculture flourished, industry was encouraged and there was a brilliant, if fleeting, beginning of oversea expansion. Before the end of the twelfth century, however, a series of invasions and internal disorders ushered in a decline, which also depended on the comparative poverty of the soil of Southern Italy. To establish their power and to wage megalomaniac wars the kings imposed heavier taxes and became increasingly dependent upon Genoese, Pisan and Florentine seamen, merchants and financiers. Little by little the native merchants were confined to local trade, while Northern and Central Italians gained the control of international commerce and took from Sicily, Apulia and Campania more grain than these regions could safely export. Desultory measures of Hohenstaufen and Angevin sovereigns aimed at restoring the economy of the realm were either too little or too late. Even Frederic II, whose economic policy was intelligently planned, dealt a serious blow to agriculture by encouraging the spread of trans-humance. Notwithstanding the splendour of the capital cities, Palermo and Naples, and the prosperity of such seaports as Messina and Trani, there were unmistakable marks of decline apparent by the middle thirteenth century. The war of the Vespers (1282–1302) split the kingdom into two and made the decadence of the South incurable. The population nevertheless continued to grow, but this growth was not accompanied by a proportional increase of production and it could only lead to pauperism.

At the same period, the larger part of Provence and Languedoc, having fallen under Capetian or Angevin rule, had come to the end of a period of boom which had lasted about a hundred years. During the twelfth century the small seaports of Southern France had slowly gained partial or total independence of their unbusinesslike feudal lords and had profited from the rivalry between Genoa and Pisa to creep into the lanes of international trade. Then, in a few decades, they had grown to considerable importance. Marseilles, which had the best harbour, surpassed all but the main Italian seaports during the first half of the thirteenth century and beamed with municipal pride. But Charles of Anjou subdued the city as well as other trade centres of Provence—Arles, Grasse, Nice—and ruined its trade by involving it in his unfortunate naval enterprises. At the same time the Capetian kings gained a foothold on the Mediterranean coast and endeavoured to channel all foreign commerce of the realm through Aigues-Mortes, a harbour built by order of St Louis in the delta of the Rhone. This only hindered the development of Narbonne and other Languedocian seaports and furthered the Italian penetration of France. Genoese and Tuscans, with their superior business technique, controlled the trade of Aigues-Mortes as well as that of Nîmes, an inland centre which Philip III had tried to build up. Furthermore, the Languedocian lagoons, like the lagoon of Venice, required continuous vigilance to keep open their entrances—and the Capetians were too engrossed in other affairs to be constantly on the alert. By 1320 the harbour of Narbonne was completely sanded, and Aigues-Mortes was threatened with the same disaster. Only Montpellier escaped the general decadence, largely because its lords were the kings of Aragon and Majorca.

The sudden rise of the Catalan star in the thirteenth and fourteenth centuries was in sharp contrast to the slow decline of Southern France and Southern Italy. Earlier the trade of Catalonia had been lively but mostly local. The sovereigns had shown some mild interest in textile workshops (operatoria) but very little in commerce. But under King Jayme I of Aragon (1243–1276) and his successors, the entire resources of the kingdom were mobilised for expansion overland and oversea. Catalan merchants were granted privileges throughout the new conquests, and royal ambassadors secured franchises for them far beyond the frontiers of the realm. Thus it was that Barcelona, latest of the Mediterranean harbours to come to prominence, 'every day must be enlarged because of the many ships coming to it', as King Jayme stated with pride. At the beginning of the fourteenth century the Catalans were the most formidable competitors of the Genoese and the Venetians and wrested from Pisa most of what Genoa had left to that unfortunate city after crushing its fleet at Meloria (1284).

Yet even Catalonia was far from approaching the commercial

importance of Northern and Central Italy. Perhaps the best indication of the incomplete development of a native business class in Spain, France and Southern Italy is the position which Jewish money-dealers and merchants continued to occupy in spite of severe legal restrictions and sometimes of pogroms. In Marseilles, for instance, no more than four Jewish merchants were allowed to embark in any one ship, and none at all were admitted to vessels bound for Alexandria. Yet notarial contracts of Marseilles prove that the Jews were successful in oversea trade and farmed out or purchased large shares of the taxes levied upon navigation and industry. In the Aragonese kingdom, where mob attacks were not infrequent, the Jews were still more numerous and influential. In contrast to this, in Northern and Central Italy they were almost unmolested, but their economic power was slight.

The difference of development between Italy and other countries can also be measured by comparing the sizes of their towns. The earliest reliable data upon which a comparison can be based are censuses of homesteads taken in the first half of the fourteenth century just before the Black Death suddenly interrupted the rising trend which had continued for some four hundred years. Different historians have variously interpreted the census figures by checking them against other contemporary documents, but even though there may be some doubt about the absolute figures the proportion between different towns can be accurately calculated. According to what seem to be the best estimates the population of Catalonia before the Black Death was roughly 600,000, or 42-43 inhabitants per square mile (Beloch; perhaps the figure is a little too low). The fertile kingdom of France had 16 to 17 million inhabitants in 1328, more than 100 per square mile (Lot, Marc Bloch). At the same period the mountainous kingdom of Naples had roughly the same density with a total of 3,300,000 inhabitants (Egidi, Beloch). The territory of Florence in 1328 had at least 330,000 inhabitants, or more than 200 per square mile (Barbagallo, Beloch). The density was still higher in Central Lombardy. The dominant fact, however, was the size of the cities—even though the proportion of citizens engaged in trade was not the same everywhere. Both Milan and Venice had close to 200,000 inhabitants (Barbagallo, Luzzatto); Florence, Genoa and perhaps Palermo and Naples had some 100,000 inhabitants (Luzzatto, Doren, Carli) and a number of minor Italian cities had several tens of thousands. These figures, while low in themselves, are impressive if we consider that outside Italy only Paris surpassed 100,000, Narbonne had about 30,000 (Port) and Arras, one of the major centres of northern trade, barely surpassed 20,000 (Lestocquoy).

B. *Expansion Overseas*

The Italian ascendancy in the Commercial Revolution was fore-shadowed by the many facts we have already noticed in the early Middle Ages—the rise of Italo-Byzantine merchants as middlemen between Catholic Europe and the Muslim and Byzantine world, the wealth of the Italo-Lombard landowning *negotiatores*, and the diffusion of *commenda* and commission contracts among the former, of interest-bearing loans among the latter. When the hour came, the men were ready. The numerical increase of both the producers and the consumers kept adding momentum to trade.

But this explanation is only part of the truth. Venice in the later Middle Ages reaped larger profits in the fields which she had harvested for centuries before, but the Italo-Byzantine cities of the South saw their prosperity wither away in the midst of the general boom. Pavia, the Lombard capital, became a centre of third rate, while Milan, her smaller rival, grew into a metropolis. Cities like Genoa and Florence, which had been almost insignificant in the early Middle Ages, later jumped to the forefront. We must regard the incessant increase of the Italian population as a strain as well as a stimulus. The French at home found ample territory in which to settle the overflow of their people; the Spaniards spread over land seized in the *Reconquista*; the Germans colonised the East. But in Italy, so far as one can tell from inadequate evidence, most of the marginal lands were taken up at an early period. Very few *castelli* were built after the twelfth century, and new tracts of land were reclaimed only through costly irrigation or reckless de-forestation. Agricultural methods improved, but climatic conditions limited the development of the three-field system. If some provinces of Southern Italy exported grain, it was because the peasants lived on chestnuts and fruit—as many of them still do to-day. With the possible exception of Milan all the larger cities in Northern and Central Italy had to import foodstuffs from distant countries. Apart from Corsica and Sardinia, there was no near frontier open to emigration. Yet on the whole Northern and Central Italy were not only the most densely populated but also the wealthiest regions in Europe. Commerce was the frontier of the Italians.

Italian participation in the Catholic counter-offensive extending from the late tenth to the early fourteenth century was a commercial frontier movement as well as a religious and military enterprise. Italy's mari-time towns won absolute mastery of the sea and permanent trading posts across the Mediterranean by fighting for 'God, glory and gold', alone or in conjunction with feudal armies. They accumulated capital by looting the enemy, while extending loans and supplying ships to the crusading powers. They added to their customers the former crusader who had learned to enjoy the luxuries of the orient and the crusader's friend who had heard his tales of wealth and wonder. War, however, was only one instrument of commercial expansion. The 'Iliad of the barons' was preceded, accompanied and overstepped by the Odyssey of the merchants. Often the individual initiative of daring unarmed pioneers accomplished more than much bloody fighting; so did diplomatic pressure and sometimes missionary work. Even where conquest opened the way, peace and collaboration with the former enemy were necessary to exploit the gains. A Muslim writer philosophically stated that 'the military men are busy in their wars, the peoples trade in peace, and the world belongs to whoever takes it'. A Catholic archbishop candidly declared that commerce with the Egyptians 'always yielded us advantages and honour'. Yet a vague feeling of uneasiness remained in the innermost conscience of the merchant who had dealings with the man of another faith, much as it persisted in the conscience of the business man who took 'usury', that is, commercial interest. In spite of the steady progress of toleration the religious and racial antagonism between Catholics and non-Catholics, kindled especially by zealots who had never been overseas, continued to the end a disturbing element in the conduct of international trade.

It was a series of military enterprises, harbingers of the general Catholic counter-offensive, that brought to commercial greatness two hitherto inconsiderable towns, Genoa and Pisa. Ever since the Lombard conquest, Genoa had little if any international commerce, and even Pisa in the tenth century was more an agricultural than a commercial centre. Their earliest raids can hardly have been aimed at 'opening the high sea' to Christian merchant ships, as some scholars have suggested, since Venetian, Amalfitan or Byzantine convoys never had ceased to sail the waters of the Mediterranean. At first the Pisans and the Genoese only intended to destroy nests of Muslim marauders who were laying waste their fields and occasionally attacking their cities. They had practically completed this task with the liquidation of the last Muslim forces in Corsica and Sardinia (1015–16), when they decided to continue their raids and rapidly extended them to the entire Western Mediterranean. They also expanded their trade and by 1065 we hear of Genoese commercial convoys in the Levant. In 1088, Pisans, Genoese and a few Southern Italians joined forces under Papal sponsorship in what may truly be called the dress rehearsal of the Crusades. They stormed Mahdīya, the strongest Muslim base in North Africa, and after offering the city to the Norman king (who refused it) they returned it to its ruler on condition that he pay an indemnity and exempt Christian merchants from every toll. Genoa and Pisa had come of age. Before the

middle of the twelfth century they outpaced all Italo-Byzantine seaports except Venice. By the end of that century Genoa had surpassed
Pisa and overtaken Venice itself.

This extraordinary transformation must have been the result of
successful commercial exploitation of the 'initial' capital, the origin of
which we shall discuss later. How rapidly investments could grow we
know from a few examples of the twelfth century. The accounts of
three contracts of *societas* and *commenda*, drawn up in 1156–58, show
that within three years a descendant of the Genoese viscounts trebled
his original investment of £205·4 Gen. even without leaving his city.
His travelling partner, a 'new man' who had started without capital,
earned almost £150 Gen. as his share of the profits. At the same
period a Venetian merchant and shipowner could amass a fortune even
when paying from 43 to 50% interest on his loans for oversea trade.
There were thousands of similar ventures. The earliest surviving
Genoese notarial book, including entries for part of the period 1154–64,
records investments of more than £10,000 Gen. for Syria alone, and
almost as much for Alexandria.

How was the 'initial' capital formed and why did the minds of the
Genoese and Pisans turn to trade in the crucial eleventh century? Only
later sources can help us to reconstruct tentatively a process of which all
contemporary evidence is lost. We know, for instance, that in 1101 the
Genoese helped the Crusaders to capture and sack Caesarea, a Palestinian seaport. They reserved rich prizes for their officers and re-
munerated the shipowners with 15% of the loot. They distributed the
remainder among 8000 sailors and soldiers, each receiving 48 *solidi* and
two pounds of pepper. Thus each of them was transformed into a petty
capitalist. An incentive to exploit this capital came three years later,
when the King of Jerusalem further rewarded his allies with the grant
of one third of Caesarea and full exemption from tolls. Probably
similar if smaller raids in the early eleventh century had given the
Genoese and the Pisans a strong gusto for adventure, a clear realisation
of the wealth of the Muslim world and the initial capital necessary to
build up their fleets and to engage in trade. Then, as commerce multiplied the original investments, they shifted their attention from mere
plundering to the acquisition of tariff reductions. Finally, they followed
the example of the Italo-Byzantines in founding autonomous and
permanent oversea settlements. This last step was a great turning point,
because it meant that there was a continuous flow of trade in the Mediterranean at a time when in so large a part of Europe commerce was
still carried out intermittently at the fairs.

The first Italian colonies were established in Constantinople, Antioch,
Jerusalem and perhaps in some African seaports in the eleventh century,

many years *before* the First Crusade. They probably became permanent settlements merely as the result of the gradual obsolescence of Byzantine and Muslim restrictions of residence of alien merchants, but autonomy and tariff exemptions must have been derived from formal grants. Some of them certainly were not obtained by war or threats of war, but by peaceful agreement. During the twelfth and thirteenth centuries Venice, Genoa and Pisa built up extensive networks of trading posts all along the Mediterranean shores. 'So many are the Genoese, so scattered world wide—that they build other Genoas wherever they reside', said a vernacular poet of the thirteenth century. Other maritime centres of Italy, Southern France, Catalonia and Dalmatia and even some inland cities of Lombardy and Tuscany also sent forth settlers oversea, but their commercial colonies were fewer and either too scattered or too localised to constitute a complete system. The process of colonisation reached its peak in the late thirteenth and early fourteenth centuries. By this time the Italian merchants had penetrated deeply into three continents, opened new routes and turned to colonial imperialism.

At first most settlements were small. They sometimes were crowded into one large building, the *fondaco* (from Arabic, *funduk*) or into a group of buildings where the merchants deposited their wares, paid their duties, transacted their business, prayed to their God, and lived according to their national law as administered by their own officers. They felt safer and freer, and the state which had granted the *fondaco* found it easier to supervise them. The same principles led Venice to establish a *fondaco* for the Germans; in turn, many Southern German towns kept lodging-houses for foreign merchants to prevent these visitors from taking part in local trade. In the Mediterranean, the *fondaco* system continued to prevail for a long time only in North-west Africa, Muslim Spain and Egypt. As late as the fifteenth century all Catholic merchants in Alexandria had to spend the night in their *fondaci*, which were locked from the outside. In the Crusaders' states, however, trading posts from the beginning constituted entire sections of cities including small orchards and cultivated plots. In the Byzantine Empire the Italian colonies also rapidly spread over large areas. By the late twelfth century there were some 10,000 Venetian residents in Constantinople, and their number greatly increased after the Fourth Crusade. In the thirteenth and fourteenth centuries Italian communes, individual Italian 'colony builders' (we cannot say 'empire builders' because the size of the colonies was never very large) or Catalan military adventurers conquered or were granted wide domains including fields and sometimes mines operated by local serf or hired labour.

Nevertheless, the importance of a colony was not necessarily proportional to its size. More often it depended upon the resources of the commercial hinterland and the privileges enjoyed by the settlers. In fact, true settlers were the exception in the early colonial 'settlements'. The trading post served as an advanced operational base rather than as a self-contained unit. Most of the inhabitants were young men who went to a colony to gain experience and capital and then returned home. Others were travelling merchants who lingered in the colony a few months or a few years, so long as their business required. Even later, when a large number of merchants took roots in the colonies and developed interests, aspirations and special characteristics of their own, they were as little sedentary as the merchants of their motherland. They collaborated with the latter not as commission agents but more frequently as independent business men who accepted short-term *commenda* partnerships, sea-loan contracts and letters of exchange.

It did not take long before the Italians and other Catholic Mediterranean merchants had reversed completely the relations between their country and the highly civilised, but weary Muslim and Byzantine worlds. The Italians controlled the sea and the largest fleets, and found in the Alps and the Apennines timber for countless new ships. In many of their colonies they had won total exemption from duties or at least considerable reductions, whereas local merchants still had to pay full tariffs. Their capital and commercial organisation, though still unimpressive at the beginning of the twelfth century, grew quickly in the hands of men who had intelligence, initiative and courage, the invisible and indispensable tools of every success. At the side of these business men were the free artisans and the seafaring freemen of the home territory. Back of them was a continent in full growth. No wonder that the Italians practically monopolised the freight and passenger traffic throughout the Mediterranean, and took from the Muslims and the Byzantines not only all the trans-Mediterranean trade but also an ever-increasing share of local business in North Africa and the Levant. Their expanding commercial, financial and shipping activity powerfully stimulated both the young European industries and the old industries of the Near East. The latter, however, often tended to decline after a first period of boom. Let us take a typical instance. In the twelfth and thirteenth centuries the Italians exported woollen cloth and some linen to Syria and Palestine, and imported silk fabrics of Syrian manufacture. At first this exchange seems to have favoured the orientals, whose products were perhaps less abundant but more expensive. Gradually the Italians with their growing demands induced the Syrians to shift to mass production, not without some sacrifice of quality and variety. At the same time they constantly increased their exports of French, Flemish and Lombard cloth to the Levant. Meanwhile Italian silk manufacturers so successfully imitated and improved oriental patterns, that they eventually became the main suppliers of Europe. Moreover, by the fourteenth or fifteenth century silk fabrics made in Italy even competed with oriental silks in the Levant itself.

Yet if we could reconstruct the trade balance of Europe with the rest of the world in the twelfth and early thirteenth centuries we would probably find that Europe was not in a creditor position. To be sure, the excess of exports over imports in trade with the immediate hinterland of the colonies continued to grow. So did the shipping and commercial profits which the Italians reaped when taking part in local business of the Muslim and Byzantine world. But these credits were hardly enough to balance the debts contracted by importing increasing quantities of spices, raw silk, furs and other products of farther Asia, Africa and North-eastern Europe. The land and sea routes leading from the colonies to these countries were open only to Muslim and Byzantine merchants. The Byzantine Emperors barred foreign traders from the Black Sea, the Sultans of Egypt claimed the monopoly of trade beyond the coastal zone, and the rulers of North-west Africa, by a conspiracy of silence, kept the Italians from learning the whereabouts of gold mines in Darkest Africa. The latter was not a serious handicap, since Northwest Africa's very unfavourable balance of payments forced the Muslim traders of the coast to deliver to the Italians substantial quantities of the Senegalese gold dust. This gold and that mined in Southern Germany helped the Venetians, the Genoese and the Pisans to strike a balance in their dealings with the Egyptian and Byzantine intermediaries who monopolised the long-distance trade extending beyond Constantinople and beyond Alexandria, Cairo and the Red Sea.[1]

In the twelfth century the Venetians, the Genoese and the Pisans did not resent too much being exploited by the oriental monopolists, because they themselves had the monopoly of the European end of this trade. The very high prices paid by the ultimate consumers inside Catholic Europe allowed large profits for both groups of monopolists.

[1] It would be interesting to carry the investigation one step further to discover in what way the Muslims settled their apparently unfavourable balance of trade with China, India and Africa. The fact seems to be that the balance was not really unfavourable. The Senegalese gold miners exchanged their precious dust for salt and copper, both of which were abundant in Muslim North Africa. India imported horses from Arabia and ivory from Muslim East Africa. China imported so many wares that it developed an increasingly unfavourable balance of trade which was settled by payment in cash. In the mid-eleventh century the annual import of ivory, pearls, aromatics etc. was paid by the Chinese with more than 53,000 'units of count', and it rose to more than 500,000 'units of count'—almost ten times as much!—in 1175.

But when the number of Italian buyers increased and when other Catholic merchants entered the competition, the first group of monopolists—the Muslims or the Byzantines—were able to raise their prices. Since the ultimate purchasers inside Europe could not absorb this rise, it was the Italians and, no doubt, their Provençal and Catalan competitors who had to absorb it by reducing their profits. In Genoa the price of pepper, which had been £4 to 5 Gen. in the mid-twelfth century, was raised only to slightly more than £6 Gen. a century later. Even this apparent increase was offset by the decline of the Genoese pound in metallic content and in purchasing power. The decline of the profits is indicated by a number of Genoese *commenda* contracts of the mid-thirteenth century. These contracts show net gains ranging from an exceptional 50%, which was high, but not excessive considering the risks, to less than 9%; some contracts even show a loss. Venetian documents indicate much the same trend. Expressions of resentment against the oriental monopolists grow more and more frequent in literary sources of that period.

Meanwhile the Muslim counter-offensive had rekindled the flickering fire of the Crusades. Saladin had united inner Syria and Egypt and had all but hurled the crusaders into the sea. Even in its best days the kingdom of Jerusalem had been a mere toe-hold in the Levant. Its trade depended on friendly relations with inner Syria, and Syria itself was not as good a commercial basis as was Egypt. The new 'kingdom of Jerusalem' which was rebuilt by the Third Crusade was only a narrow coastal strip. It depended wholly upon the Italian navy for defence and subsistence. To preserve that strip, which did not even include the Holy City, the Italians had frequently to engage in war against Egypt-Syria. Reluctantly they had to enforce the Papal decrees forbidding export of war materials to Egypt, even in peacetime—and hence had to export more gold to purchase spices. While the situation deteriorated in the Muslim Levant, in Constantinople the old friction between Byzantines and westerners also increased. In the numerous conflicts that ensued the Italians probably were wrong as often as the Byzantines. But the Byzantine Emperors went to the extreme of encouraging or tolerating mobs to plunder the quarters of the wealthy Italians in Constantinople and to kill some of the merchants. Maritime circles in Italy increasingly felt that only the conquest of both Egypt and the Byzantine Empire would solve at once the military and the commercial problem. Such conquests would furnish large supporting bases for the crusaders' states and would break the bottle-necks through which trickled the goods from the Black Sea and from the 'Indies'.

This grand strategy had a beginning of execution when the Pope, the Venetians and a number of feudal lords planned the Fourth Crusade as an expedition against the Byzantine Empire.[1] The Crusade was not fully successful because Asia Minor remained to the Greeks and hence no overland communication with Palestine was obtained. Victory in Europe, however, enriched the feudal armies with more land and more booty than had the First Crusade; it secured for Venice the most valuable islands in the Aegean and quarters in every important seaport, and it opened the Black Sea to the Latin merchants. The Greek upper class and whatever was left of the bourgeoisie were ruined; the lot of the humbler labourers and peasants probably underwent little change. Fifty-five years of Venetian commercial hegemony (1204–61) ended when the Genoese aided the Byzantine Emperor in recovering Constantinople, and thus followed the Venetians in being the privileged exploiters of the Empire. As a Byzantine historian sadly noted, 'the Latins incessantly increased their profits and their power on sea, while the Greeks were growing weaker and weaker'. In the early fourteenth century the Genoese suburb of Pera had a trade worth approximately fifteen times more than that of the Byzantine capital. Constantinople itself was thronged by merchants of the minor Catholic centres. Marseilles, Montpellier, Narbonne, Barcelona, Ancona, Florence and Ragusa (Dubrovnik) established colonies in the capital and some merchants even came from Spain, England and Germany. The shores of the Black Sea were studded with Genoese and Venetian colonies. The Genoese easily granted colonial citizenship to Latins, Greeks, Armenians, Turks and Jews, but the Venetians jealously excluded all outsiders.

In 1218, fourteen years after the conquest of Constantinople, the conquest of Egypt was the aim of another Crusade led by a Papal legate and manned largely by citizens of the three major Italian seaports. Damietta, the second best Egyptian harbour, fell. Western merchants at once deserted the seaports of the Holy Land to rush to Damietta. But the expedition proved a failure, and Damietta was lost. Later Frederic II tried to rebuild the kingdom of Jerusalem by making agreements with the Egyptians, but this attempt was sabotaged by the Pope. A second expedition against Egypt, led by St Louis, temporarily recaptured Damietta, but it finally ended in disaster. Since Egypt could neither be conquered nor be befriended, commercial and military common-sense advised evacuation of the Holy Land. Whatever defence was attempted in the following years was prompted chiefly by religious sentiments. As the final catastrophe approached, the traders gradually transferred their business to the island of Cyprus and the little Christian kingdom of Cilician Armenia. Therefore the fall of the last beach-heads in Syria in

[1] The legend of a last-minute 'diversion' of the Crusade from the Holy Land to the Byzantine Empire is no longer tenable in the light of decisive Greek and Latin evidence.

1291 caused no sudden crisis. The only disaster suffered was caused by the Pope, who prohibited all trade with Egypt. These 'economic sanctions' bore more heavily upon Venice and Genoa since the Catalans utterly disregarded the embargo and gained a predominant position in Alexandria. Other Catalans captured Athens in 1311. Sicily had become Aragonese in 1282. All this constituted a threat for the Italians, but not yet a vital challenge, because the Catalan merchant class was still small.

The importance of Egypt, however, was greatly reduced by the most momentous event of the thirteenth century—the Mongolian conquest and unification of the larger part of Asia and Southern Russia. The Muslim world never recovered completely from this terrible blow. Splendid cities were wiped out; their population was decimated. Yet to the western merchants, who had been spared the horrors of the Mongolian war, the subsequent Mongolian peace disclosed immense horizons. The heart of the eastern Muslim world; the depth of Russia and Turkestan; the lands of the Farther East where the largest cities, the widest rivers, the greatest plains and plateaus were found and where gun-powder, coal, paper money and printing were everyday objects— the fatherland of silk and the fountainhead of spices—all this lay open for everyone to reach.

As the immense empire of Chinghis Khan was transformed into a loose confederation of four wide Khanates, the friendly attitude of the western Khans of Persia and of Kipchak (South Russia) attracted to these countries large groups of Italian merchants. Laias, Trebizond, Caffa, Tana and other seaports of the Syrian and Cilician coast, of the Black Sea and of the Sea of Azov became the golden gates through which a hitherto barred continent was entered. Tabriz and Astrakhan became almost as familiar to the Genoese and the Venetians as was Constantinople in the twelfth century. Genoese pioneers sailed the Caspian Sea and the Persian Gulf on ships built in their colonies. Some merchants went much farther into the eastern Khanates of Turkestan and China. Between 1260 and 1269 the father and the uncle of Marco Polo reached Peking by land. In 1275 young Marco was received by Kublai Khan. Before he returned by sea to describe in an immortal book the wonders of the 'Indies', many others had left for the Farther East. In 1291 the Vivaldi brothers of Genoa endeavoured to reach the Indies by sea, sailing 'west' from the Strait of Gibraltar. One wonders what turn the history of the world would have taken if they had succeeded, two centuries before Columbus and Vasco da Gama. They never came back. Their fate seemed to spur other Italians to take the land routes to Central Asia, India and China. By the early fourteenth century Pegolotti, the Florentine merchant and writer, stated that the route from the Crimea to Peking was 'quite safe'. Chinese silk now reached the English market; its cost in Italy fell below that of silk from the Caspian region, though the latter was less than one half as distant. Genoese merchants established residences in Central Asia, in India and in China. Franciscan monks built a *fondaco* for Catholic merchants in Ts'üan-chóu (Zayton), the great seaport facing Formosa and the site of Muslim merchant colonies ever since the ninth century.

The wealth of Eastern and Far Eastern trade seemed to dwarf the commercial opportunities in the Western Mediterranean and beyond the Strait of Gibraltar. The precipitous decline of North African economy under the attacks of the nomads and of the desert transferred nearly all coastal trade to European merchants and shippers. These men brought industrial products from their continent and even oriental wares to Tunis, Bougie and Ceuta, and purchased wool, hides, wax, indigo, alum, coral and sometimes grain, but usually not oil, since Africa no longer had surpluses to sell. Both the investments and the returns were comparatively small. This tended to make Africa the refuge of declining merchant communities such as Pisa, Marseilles and Messina. To be sure, some Genoese and Venetians continued to come, but they would have been more interested in reaching the mysterious Palola, the medieval Eldorado, which, as we now know, was a Senegalese island between two rivers where negro gold washers exchanged their precious dust for a little salt, copper and other necessities. Palola could not be found, but the search for it led to considerable expansion. In the early fourteenth century we hear of a Genoese merchant living in Sijilmāsa, deep inside the Sahara, and of another Genoese discovering one of the Canaries and building a castle there. Italian ships now more frequently sailed along the Atlantic coast of Morocco. In the twelfth century their terminus usually was Saleh, but after 1250 it was displaced farther south to Safi.

The fact that the Mediterranean merchants hesitated much longer to sail along the Atlantic coast of Europe is rather surprising if we consider their lively trade with the Muslim seaports of Eastern Spain from Palma to Almeria and Malaga. Perhaps the main reason was that commercial opportunities in the western Iberian states were too modest to warrant carrying goods in galleys, which were the fastest but the most expensive means of conveyance. On the other hand, the risks of storms and piracy were too great to employ the rounded sailships which carried the cheap and bulky goods in the Mediterranean trade. An early attempt of a bishop of Santiago de Compostela to create a navy with the help of a Genoese shipwright was not followed up; Santiago itself, if we may believe a description of the twelfth century, could scarcely compare with the second-rate commercial centres of Italy and Provence. The complex, but meagre long-distance trade of Castile and Navarre fed many small seaports on the northern shore from Bayonne to La Coruña; iron mines and other local resources helped the Biscayan and Cantabrian towns to gain some prosperity. But the slow and destructive pace of the *reconquista* up to 1233 tended to stifle rather than to promote the economic development. The rapid conquest of Andalusia and Murcia, however, marked a turning point. Castile, through her new southern outlets, breathed more freely the air of the Mediterranean and of the Atlantic. Merchants from Genoa, Piacenza, Pisa, Lucca, Como and Marseilles flocked to Seville which had become Castilian in 1248, and met there Portuguese, English, French and German merchants. Special streets and a new *barrio* (suburb) were set apart for the privileged foreign traders. The export of Castilian wool, leather, alum and mercury mounted to new heights. The import of cloth and luxury goods also stepped up.

By 1277, if not earlier, a new advance was made. Genoese galleys began to sail via Cadiz and Seville to France, Flanders and England. Their lofty hulls dwarfed the northern ships in the ports of La Rochelle, Calais, Sluys, Sandwich, Southampton and London, much as modern transatlantics tower above minor steamships. Spices, alum, grain, wine and other wares from the Mediterranean area and the Farther East were exchanged for Flemish cloth, English wool and other wares. Some merchants made important remittances in cash to stimulate their promising business. Before the mid-fourteenth century England and Flanders had become regular destinations of one of the yearly convoys which both Genoa and Venice sent out with fixed schedules. No attempt was made by the Mediterranean merchants to extend their voyages to the Baltic, where they would have had to compete with the Hanseatic merchants. This competition might not have been a forbidding obstacle for the Italians, but neither the fish of the northern seas nor the grain of the Baltic attracted sailors who had access to the fish and the grain of South Russia. Newcastle and Sluys, the seaport of Bruges, were the farthest harbours where their galleys could profitably sail.

The returns of taxes derived from Genoese sea trade reflect the effect of oversea expansion in its latest and most sweeping phase. They indicate a more than fourfold increase from 1274 to 1293. In the latter year the incoming and outgoing wares subject to tax in the Genoese harbour were valued at £3,822,000 Gen. This figure, which does not include tax-free trade by sea or the important trade by land routes, is not very large in itself, even if we consider that at this period a bushel of grain cost in Genoa 3 to 5 *solidi*, a good ox £4 Gen., a piece of Flemish cloth from £6 to £14 Gen., and a Genoese sword with a carved handle 9 pence. But the sum indicated seems to be roughly seven times as high as the income of the French monarchy under Phillip Augustus, and almost ten times as high as the exports by sea from Lübeck in Lübeck's peak year 1368.[1] It must be noted that soon after 1293 Genoa's commercial progress was particularly hindered by civil wars. The tax returns of 1334 indicate only a trade of £1,806,000 Gen. In the same year, however, tax returns of Pera registered a movement of wares by sea valued at £1,648,000 Gen. Thirty years later similar documents place the sea trade of the Genoese colony in Alexandria at about one million pounds. The 'other Genoas' praised by the vernacular poet had grown to a size approaching that of the motherland itself.

C. *Expansion Overland*

The opening of a direct route to the North Sea crowned two centuries of northward expansion of the Italian merchants and financiers. Although this expansion took place mostly beyond the geographic limits of the present chapter, we must outline it briefly because of its impact on trade in the Mediterranean area.[2]

While the appearance of Italians in China and in the Sahara was in a way the outgrowth of a process begun in the early Middle Ages, their

[1] The comparison is based upon metallic contents according to the estimates of Desimoni (Genoese gold pound), Schaube (Parisian silver penny) and Grautoff (mark of Lübeck), and upon the assumption that a 10·1 ratio between gold and silver was prevalent during the thirteenth and fourteenth centuries. It does not take into account fluctuations in this ratio, differences caused by the simultaneous use in each place of various coins of different metals and alloys, variations in the purchasing power of the metals, and the other elements of error which make an accurate comparison impossible. It seemed useful to express roughly by figures the magnitude of Mediterranean trade as compared with other economic data. The writer, however, is fully aware of the basic inexactitude of comparisons between different times, places and moneys.

[2] Space limits force us to disregard the northward expansion of other southern merchants. With the exception of Gascon wine merchants in Northern France and England (who will be dealt with briefly in this and other sections) this expansion was not of great consequence. A good number of merchants from nearly all Southern European countries attended the fairs of Champagne; smaller groups of Spaniards went to the fairs of Beaucaire and Nîmes and established a consulate in Bruges; other Spaniards carried wine and iron to Atlantic France and England; a small Portuguese colony was established in Middelburg; merchants from Montpellier and other towns of Southern France were often seen in the northern provinces of the kingdom, including Flanders; money-lenders of Cahors seem to have preceded the 'Lombards' in England and their name remained a synonym of 'usurer' long after their star had set. Elsewhere we occasionally find isolated traders from southern countries other than Italy. None of them seems to have risen above mediocrity. As for northern traders in Southern Europe, perhaps the only group deserving special attention is that of the merchants from Arras who were prominent in Genoa in the late twelfth and early thirteenth centuries, but lost importance after that period.

penetration inside Europe was substantially a new trend. In the tenth century as a rule it was northern merchants who went to Italy or Southern France to exchange their wares with those of the Mediterranean world. In the later Middle Ages, however, Italians crossing the Alps gradually surpassed in numbers and importance the Northerners who visited the Mediterranean countries or who settled there. As early as 1034 we hear of merchants from Asti going to France through the Cenis. Forty years later, Pope Gregory VII assailed the King of France because the latter had seized 'infinite sums' from Italians visiting his fairs (St Denis?). In the twelfth century the fairs of Champagne, situated roughly two-thirds of the distance from the Mediterranean to the North Sea by the shortest land route, became the main meeting place between northern and southern merchants. The importance of these fairs continued to grow in the thirteenth century, and was not seriously threatened by the beginning of Italian voyages in the Atlantic, but it sharply declined after the first ten or twenty years of the fourteenth century. Long before that period, however, Italian business men had also established relations with other fairs and had settled in nearly every important city of France, Flanders and England. Smaller groups went to Germany, Hungary and Poland. Up to the late twelfth century Northern Italians, especially from Asti, Piacenza, Milan and Cremona, probably outnumbered the Tuscans and the Romans. In the thirteenth century the Tuscans took the lead. First Siena, then Florence, held the most prominent place, while Lucca maintained herself in the third place and Pistoia followed closely. Of maritime cities only Genoa contributed substantially to this emigration, but all of the major inland centres and even small towns such as San Gimignano witnessed the sorrow of the wives 'deserted in their couch because of France', as Dante bitterly complained. It is true that until the late thirteenth century this exodus, like that of the oversea colonies, had most frequently a purely temporary character.

The Italian diaspora of *Oltremonte* (beyond the Alps) was numerically smaller than that of *Oltremare* (across the sea), but its activities were so various that they defy summary description. Emigrants exercised one or several of the following professions: mercenary bowmen, sailors, shipwrights, captains of merchant ships and fleet admirals; textile manufacturers, mining entrepreneurs, lessees of mints; importers of Italian and oriental wares and exporters of cloth, linen and wool; staple traders in grain, wine and salt; pawnbrokers serving the lower class, money-lenders and supply agents serving the upper bourgeoisie, the great ecclesiastics and lay vassals and the monarchs; farmers of customs, tax collectors and bankers in the service of the Pope and the kings of France and England. Their status could be as high as that of the

Florentine Franzesi brothers ('Mouche' and 'Biche') who became the revenue agents and financial wizards of Phillip the Fair until the king sacrificed them to the wrath of the people who had been hit by an inflation. It could be as exalted as that of the Genoese Antonio Pessagno, who under Edward II was 'king's merchant', purveyor of the wardrobe, farmer of the Cornwall mines, seneschal of Gascony and founder of a *bastide* which he called Genoa, while his brother Leonard was Portugal's admiral-in-chief and obtained fiefs in that country. But it could also be as low as that of the money-lenders from Chieri, a little town near Turin, who competed with the Jews for the monopoly of petty usury in various towns of the North, where the legal rate of interest was higher than that allowed in their country. Again, an Italian in *Oltremonte* could be a member of a great *tavola* or *compagnia* of merchant-bankers, a great business man alternating trips to the Champagne fairs with voyages to the Levant, a transport agent (*vecturalis*) carrying goods for both Italian and northern international traders, a lone adventurer with little baggage of his own, or a prominent political emigré trying to make a living until his party regained control of his home city. Merchants from Gascony and Toulouse kept in their hands most of the export trade in French wines to Flanders and England, but in all other branches of international trade the Italians far surpassed the other southern groups in wealth, number and versatility.

Various as were the interests and the background of these Italians, their fortunes very frequently were allied directly or indirectly to the international influence of their most powerful fellow-citizen, the Pope. It probably was not an accident that the second earliest evidence concerning Italians at the French fairs comes from letters of the great Gregory VII in their behalf. Pontifical credentials opened many doors to the Italians, and other valuable connections resulted from each of the Crusades, often as a by-product of financial and shipping services rendered to crusading clergymen, knights and princes. Finally the Popes entrusted the great Tuscan companies with the transmission to Italy of ecclesiastical tithes collected throughout Europe. It was as Papal agents that the employees of the Lucchese Scorcialupi company went as far as Greenland, where the tribute was paid in 'sealskins, whalebone and sinews of whales'. The money that was collected could seldom be reinvested in trade, because the Curia needed the cash promptly. But the Italians took a commission and benefited from the ready cash available throughout Europe. They also carried out commercial operations in behalf of the Pope. On 10 April 1336 the Avignon branch of the Florentine Acciaioli company received an urgent order to ship grain to the poor Armenians. It transmitted the order to the branches in Naples and Bari. By the end of the month more than

7000 tons of grain had been purchased and the ships were ready to forward the relief to the Christian outpost in the orient. Thus, paradoxically enough, one of the greatest vehicles of the Papal charitable activities and of the moral and political supremacy of the Pope over the national monarchies was the experience of the Italian international business men and *campsores* who had flouted the canons against usury ever since the early Middle Ages. This 'sinful' activity placed at the disposal of the Pope, in the Pope's own country, the best organised group of financiers in the world. Similarly the old trade of Venice, Genoa and Pisa with the infidel and the schismatic had supplied the information, the ships and the money without which the Popes could never have planned the Crusades.

This association with the Roman Church was not an unmixed blessing for the Italians. It induced them to venture deep into the Catholic kingdoms where their navy could not protect them and where they enjoyed no self-government and often paid heavier duties than the local merchants. It also encouraged their natural tendency to couple extremely dangerous and hated lending activities with the healthier practice of international trade. The favours of temporal rulers had the same result. To be sure, many Italian companies did not succumb to the temptation of the high interest promised by loans and clung to strictly commercial activities. Even those companies most deeply committed to banking never abandoned the practice of trade, and indeed they constantly used loans to public authorities as a trump card to obtain commercial favours. Such favours met with no local opposition in regions economically strong. The great manufacturing communities of Flanders and Brabant and the wealthy merchants of the North who frequented the great fairs did not fear the Italian merchants, who bought from them much cloth and linen in exchange for spices, silk and useful dyestuffs. But in the larger part of France and England not only the sellers of oriental commodities, but also the Florentine and Milanese buyers of wool aroused the antagonism of the petty local craftsmen and wool merchants by outbidding them. King's officers and local authorities adopted all sorts of protectionistic measures to hinder the encroachment of the foreigner upon the citizen's preserve.

The benevolence of French and English kings often shielded the Italians, much as it had protected the Jews. But it was a precarious protection, which could at any moment be displaced by hostility and by decrees of confiscation or expulsion. Arbitrary seizures of wares already paid for, failures to pay ecclesiastical dues for which advances had been made to the Pope, and sometimes unilateral repudiations of debts rendered the risks of the Tuscan merchant-bankers in Catholic countries still greater than those of the Mediterranean traders voyaging on stormy seas and doing business with Muslims and Greeks. All the ponderous companies which sprang up in the thirteenth and early fourteenth centuries from fortunes made partly through interest-bearing loans ultimately went bankrupt. Their collapse involved in ruin partners and depositors alike. Yet the crash of a bank did not destroy all the wealth that had been created. Some partners had succeeded in hiding part of their profits. Moreover, the raw materials a *compagnia* had imported had given employment to hundreds of craftsmen at home. Finally, much credit had been created—and credit was precious at a time when gold was scarce and trade was booming.

Southern Germany was the only important producer of gold in Europe. Was it partly because of this that it was far less affected than France or England by the Italian penetration? Was it rather because of the smallness of commerce and exclusiveness of commercial legislation in the Southern German cities? Provisions to put foreign merchants at a disadvantage and to enforce equality among local merchants seem to have been stricter than anywhere else in Southern Europe. The results of this policy can be observed in the exceptionally small size of the towns up to the fourteenth century, and in the gradual shrinking of the commercial horizon. The old supply line from the Levant through the Danube or Bohemia lost its importance. Though in the twelfth century we still hear of Ratisbonians in Kiev and of Germans in the Levant, in the thirteenth even the merchants of Prague depended on the Venetians for the supply of spices. Furthermore, the Northern German city of Cologne expanded its trade into Southern Germany and took from Ratisbon part of the Danubian commerce.

Some progress, however, was made in local trade and in the textile and iron industries. Danubian trade, though no longer prominent in world economy, continued to grow absolutely: it has been estimated that about 15,000 tons of merchandise went through the customs office of Linz in 1295. Vienna, Passau, Ratisbon, Nuremberg, Ulm, Constance, Schaffhausen and other cities attained a modest prosperity. Their merchants kept in their hands most of the trade of Southern Germany with Italy; they went to Venice, Verona, Trento, Milan or Genoa to export their metals, timber and linen and to fetch Eastern goods and many other wares. Their activity, humble as it was, held a promise which was later to be fulfilled by the tremendous growth of Nuremberg and Augsburg. Up to the mid-fourteenth century, however, Southern Germany was rather a neglected corner than a rival economy within the immense Italian commercial empire.

(2) SOUTHERN MEDIEVAL COMMERCE AND CAPITALISM
AT ITS ZENITH

The golden age of medieval trade certainly knew many of the characteristics which we regard as typical of capitalism. When we scan the records from the late eleventh to the early fourteenth century we cannot fail to notice a steady accumulation of capital in money and in goods; a growing use of credit and a trend toward gradual separation of management from both ownership of the capital and manual labour; a constant endeavour to improve the methods of business and to compete with other business men in the same field; a planning of large-scale operations with a view to expanding the market; an elevation of trade interests to the importance of state affairs; and, above all, a desire for profits as a leading motive for commercial activity. On the other hand, these phenomena occurred on a far smaller scale, affected fewer persons, and were much less pronounced than they are in the modern world. Furthermore, the anti-capitalistic religious theories of the Middle Ages had probably more widespread acceptance than anti-capitalistic Marxist theories have today. It is also true that important features of modern capitalism such as the joint-stock corporation cannot be found in the Middle Ages.

These and other qualifications, however, should not force us to ban the term *capitalism* from a description of medieval trade. Those scholars who condemn the use of this word on the ground of the very profound differences in method and scope between medieval and modern economy are merely expressing a truism. We all know that economy never stands still, and that indeed no aspect of contemporary life has its exact parallel in any other period of history. Still what matters, in the writer's opinion, is the trend rather than the fulfilment. Even to-day, who can say that pure capitalism has reached its full development throughout the world, or even within any single state? Although the physiognomies of modern Great Britain and the United States are deeply etched by capitalism, living remnants of less advanced economies and striking deviations from the capitalistic path remind us of the past at every step and, perhaps, warn us of the impending future.

In the pages that follow, however, we are concerned rather with actual fulfilment than with trends. Other writers will discuss in detail the methods, the spirit and the technical background of medieval capitalism. Here we can only describe briefly the main aspects of trade in Southern Europe in the period of the greatest prosperity of medieval Europe, between the mid-thirteenth and the mid-fourteenth century. The positive achievements of the late medieval business man and the progress accomplished over less than four centuries since the beginning of economic expansion certainly claim our deep respect. Lest this feeling lead us to exaggerate the stature of commerce at that period, let us first stress the most important limitations in size, rhythm and organisation. If measured according to modern standards, these limitations appear extremely serious.

Late medieval trade of Mediterranean Europe seems gigantic only in comparison to early medieval or ancient commerce. True, the circulation of capital and goods increased in geometrical progression as money, credit and the economy of exchange decisively triumphed over economic isolation. Yet the absolute volume of trade in the early fourteenth century was still small, not only because the entire population of Europe was much nearer to 50 than to 100 millions, but also because large areas remained almost impermeable to the new commercial currents and because the purchasing power of the lower class developed too slowly to permit the demand of the common man to weigh very heavily. Outside Italy trade depended chiefly upon the demand of the upper class. Two-thirds of the 445 clients of the Holzschuher company of Nuremberg in 1304–7 belonged to the nobility or the clergy, and the amount of their purchases far outweighed the transactions of the bourgeoisie. In Italy the purchases of the growing middle class probably surpassed in quantity and value those of the upper class. But even the bourgeoisie was a small minority of the population, and it usually was more interested in quality and durability than in quantity and cheapness. Around 1338 the historian of Florence, Giovanni Villani, who was an employee of the great Peruzzi company, rejoiced when he noted that the cloth production of his city had doubled in value owing to the adoption of better wool. He saw no harm in the fact that the increased price had caused the output to fall from 100,000 to 70–80,000 pieces yearly.

There seems to be no sound reason to doubt Villani's figures, although they have been challenged. They definitely indicate mass production. Yet if we consider that the woollen industry was the greatest exporting trade of Catholic Europe, that Florence in the fourteenth century was one of its main centres and that according to Villani no less than 30,000 Florentines drew their livelihood from it, the figures appear low to a modern reader. Certainly the larger part of the population in Europe used homespun cloth except perhaps on Sundays. If we turn from industrial products to staple foods, we shall come to similar conclusions. A few large cities and densely populated areas imported grain from distant countries, but the larger part of the inhabitants of Southern Europe depended on local production except in years of famine.

The comparative smallness of trade was probably both the cause and the consequence of the inadequacy of the revolution in transport. To be sure, technical improvements continued to be made after the three epoch-making innovations—the horseshoe, the horse collar and the galley, all gifts of the eastern world to Catholic Europe—that had opened the way for the Commercial Revolution. In the later period the compass, astrolabe, *martelojo* and other nautical inventions facilitated long-distance navigation, while the French *pavé du Roi* with its rectangular slabs and the Lombard circular stones improved the surface of roads in muddy regions. But these and other improvements did little to add speed and power to the desperately slow and weak means of conveyance used ever since the eleventh or tenth century. There was nothing in the Commercial Revolution to parallel the successive injections of the railroad, the screw propeller, the internal combustion engine and the aeroplane into the arteries of the Industrial Revolution. Hence effort had to be concentrated on making the best use of the already existing means of conveyance, on multiplying and improving the ways of communication, and on organising a more efficient and intensive circulation. Great as was the progress in these directions, it could scarcely have revolutionary effect. Cheap bulky goods, in particular, seldom could stand the costs of transportation over a long distance, unless that distance was covered by water—preferably on the *naves*, slow sailing ships that cost one-third as much as the galleys while they carried four times as much freight, or on the canal barges towed by men or horses. With such means of conveyance little improvement could be made. As late as the sixteenth century the Milanese Chamber of Merchants decided that 18 days was still a reasonable time to cover the distance downstream from Milan to Venice, perhaps 200 miles, by its regular line of internal navigation. Let us recall that in 943, according to Liutprand of Cremona, a fast boat went in three days from Pavia to Venice, about the same distance.

The lack of good communications was not unconnected with the smallness of many states and the decentralisation of others, which in turn led to monetary chaos, to physical insecurity and to arbitrariness of the customs system. In these respects there was hardly any progress since the early Middle Ages. Some coins had wider circulation than others and were less debased, but no coin up to the mid-thirteenth century had a stable value or was accepted everywhere, except the Byzantine gold *hyperperon*. The resumption of independent gold coinage in the Italian Communes in the second half of the thirteenth century caused the *hyperperon* to be displaced by the florin and the ducat in the international market, but it did not eliminate disorder in local coinage. Furthermore, municipal and national wars in the later Middle Ages may have been perhaps slightly less frequent than the feudal wars of the earlier period, but they affected larger areas and were directed very frequently at the methodical destruction of the economic resources of the enemy. On sea, war between the major Italian seaports was almost continuous. If a merchant desired a minimum of safety, he usually had to join a convoy or a caravan as he did in the early Middle Ages. No matter where he went, he had to face vexatious restrictions. Most states, for instance, did not permit export of gold or basic foodstuffs except in special cases. Tolls were high except where a special agreement reduced or lifted them on behalf of the merchants of a given town. Their collection placed the merchant at the mercy of customs officers, who might sometimes be bribed into undervaluing his wares, but who might also extort much more than was due. A ship while at sea obviously had no tolls to pay, but it was subject to the menace of storms. Upon his arrival a merchant might be arrested because a war had broken out after his departure, or because the local authorities had issued a 'reprisal' order against all citizens of a state of which one citizen had defrauded one of their subjects. Reprisals were so harmful to trade that they were imposed only as a last resort, but they could not be eliminated so long as the fatherland of the offender neglected to force him to refund the damage. Only Genoa in 1296 set up a special tribunal to hear claims against its own citizens. Moreover, the inhuman custom of seizing the goods of shipwrecked vessels survived even after it had been outlawed in all civilised countries. Charles I of Anjou in 1270 enforced this custom against his own fellow-Crusaders. Finally, in the Mongolian states and in the Muslim principality of Ormuz the goods of a merchant who died when travelling were seized.

These and other risks prevented the original commercial partnerships from developing into more flexible and powerful instruments to pool capitals. Traders who sailed overseas continued for centuries to use chiefly the *commenda* contract, which brought together *for a short term* a resident party who supplied capital but no management and a travelling party who supplied management but no capital. In practice, if not in theory, liability toward third parties was limited to the amount of the investment. The short duration of the *commenda* contract may have depended originally upon the fact that in the early Middle Ages Catholic merchants were not allowed to reside in Byzantine or Muslim territory. But there were no long-term *commendae* even after colonies were founded, no doubt because the investors were afraid to entrust their money to a travelling merchant for more than one round trip. Consequently the travelling party could not plan a permanent business, but had to conclude his transactions as soon as possible and to return to his home city or send back the funds to the lender. On the other hand, traders who went overland used chiefly the *compagnia* partnership, which associated for many years a large number of partners, who supplied both capital and management and were alternatively travelling or resident. Each of the partners was *unlimitedly liable* toward third parties for the debts of the entire company. This collective responsibility may have been originally a legacy of the time when the *compagnia* really was, as the name indicates, a non-commercial association of members of the same family eating the same bread and working for the increase of the common patrimony. But liability remained unlimited when the 'table-companions' became merchants often unrelated by blood, no doubt because third parties were averse to deal with a member of a company unless all partners shared full responsibility with the latter. Consequently any partner could ruin completely the others by a poor speculation, and the risks increased with the number of new partners admitted to the company.[1]

The advantages which neither of the main commercial contracts combined—indeterminate duration and limited liability—existed in other forms of investment, especially in the public loans. A prudent investor would buy shares in one of the numerous loans floated by the greatest Communes. Shares could be kept as long as desired, or sold in the market, if possible when the quotation was high. Another conservative form of investment was real estate. Commerce could compete with the state and the estate only if it offered very large profits. But large profits could be obtained only by maintaining prices at a high level. High prices made it hard to sell to the common man and kept down the volume of trade. We have now apparently closed the vicious circle and we are back to the point from which we started.

The circle, however, was not really closed. All brakes to commercial development were loosened by the continuous thrust of the ever expanding market which we have previously described. This expansion made progress possible—a slow progress if measured in terms of nineteenth century dynamics, but a fast progress if considered from the point of its modest departure and geometric rate of increase. Our picture has been gloomy enough so far. It could have been still gloomier if we had had more space to go into details. But very dark pictures have also been given of modern capitalism by stressing only the negative aspects. Now let us review briefly the positive aspects of medieval capitalism at the time when the Commercial Revolution reached its zenith between the mid-thirteenth and the mid-fourteenth centuries. Small trade in the small towns probably is a better starting point for our survey than would-be big business in the metropolitan

[1] We cannot discuss here special clauses which improved some *commenda* and *compagnia* agreements, and other commercial contracts which had smaller importance or shorter popularity. Some of the latter had advantages which the more popular contracts lacked.

cities. We will recall that in the early Middle Ages local exchanges between village and village or trade between the town and its agricultural hinterland had been comparatively rarer than long-distance trade in luxury goods. Hence the progress of 'commercialisation' in rural or semi-rural areas was in a way a more revolutionary change than the growth of international commerce.

The fact that in the later centuries of the Middle Ages most peasants in Italy and many peasants elsewhere in Southern Europe were able to pay their rents in cash is by itself a significant indication of 'commercialisation'. Unfortunately, however, we lack a clear picture of commercial activities in the countryside, not only because the attention of most scholars has been almost monopolised by the glamorous long-distance trade, but also because the purchases and sales by the peasants usually were carried out orally and have left no trace in the records. Only occasional entries in the books of town notaries show that the country dweller in many parts of Italy was thoroughly familiarised not only with money economy, but also with the simpler commercial contracts. In the region of Nice at the border between Italy and France, however, traces of barter were still noticeable in the late thirteenth century; a Piacenzan merchant when dealing with the farmers had to insist that they should pay 'in hard cash and not in kind, without giving or offering goods in payment'. Significantly enough, the general store and the sedentary shopkeeper or trader had appeared in a number of Central and Northern Italian villages, whereas the itinerant merchant was still paramount in France. But he was no longer a humble pedlar. His business had grown large enough for him to become worried at the intrusion of outside competitors. In the fourteenth century we first hear of a general gild of mercers in Provence, headed by a man bearing no less a title than *Roi des Merciers*. Before the mid-fifteenth century similar gilds had been organised in nearly all regions of France, from Champagne and Ile-de-France to Blois and the Dauphiné. That the members as a rule were itinerant we may infer from their care to be sure of lodgings wherever they went.

A visit to Maître Ugo Teralh, notary and draper at Forcalquier, will take us one step higher in the commercial hierarchy. His town consisted of a cluster of houses built on the slopes of a mountain dominating a dead-end valley of Northern Provence. Neither the main trail from Avignon to Mount Genève nor the Durance, which was used by boats as far as Manosque, went through Forcalquier. The counts 'of Forcalquier' themselves, in fact, lived in Manosque. To-day Forcalquier has about 2500 inhabitants; how many did it have in the Middle Ages? Perhaps only a few hundred—no more than a manor's population. To these few and to the inhabitants of the nearby villages Maître Teralh sold cloth by the auln. He required those who bought on credit to enter their names in a primitive book of accounts he kept. In May 1331 there were 36 entries; some of them were in Hebrew, since many Jews traded and lent money in the smallest Provençal villages. The cloth came mostly from nearby Languedoc, but some had been manufactured in St Denis, Rouen and Provins. What could Forcalquier offer in exchange? Probably the cattle of its lean prairies, the wild rabbits whose preservation was so important that the hunt was open only every second year, and possibly some timber. Its trade, small as it was, is significant for a region where even the toll of Aix—a much larger city—often made no collection in one entire day.

Now let us move to a slightly larger town, Bonifacio—another new beneficiary of trade, since it was founded only in 1195 by Genoese subjects on a rock overlooking the strait between Corsica and Sardinia. Among the early settlers of Corsican Bonifacio was a Ligurian Bonaparte. But we are not interested in him. We shall stop at the store of the late Armanno the Currier, deceased in 1238. When an inventory of his goods was made, there were in stock 947 skins of goat, lamb, deer, stag, fox and marten, 14 whole pieces and two bundles of woollen cloth of unidentified provenance, 12 smaller cuts of woollen, $2\frac{1}{2}$ pieces of silk, 60 pieces of burlap, one of fustian from Pontremoli (a tiny city in the Northern Apennines), some wine, some pepper, and other wares. Armanno had bought houses and had received in partnership £1507 Gen. from 26 small investors. He had died too early to see his town develop into a lively commercial centre, which long before its first centenary maintained relations with every important harbour of the Western Mediterranean and with its own rugged hinterland on both sides of the strait. Since Bonifacio had practically no manufacturing of its own, its resources were chiefly salt, skins and cheese from the hinterland. Petty piracy offered a pleasant alternative to the routine of peaceful trade. In a regular commercial contract of 1287 we have an extreme example of the length to which the business spirit in Bonifacio sometimes went, when a 'lady' hired herself out as 'servant and mistress'.

Even without extending our inquiry to other secondary towns a little larger than Bonifacio and Forcalquier, we have been warned by these examples of the importance of small centres. Hundreds of Ugo Teralhs and Armannos perhaps purchased only a few thousand pieces of cloth, but they were the men that partly filled the gap left in medieval trade by the weakness of marketing organisation in the metropolis. The most enterprising provincial merchants some day would emigrate to the larger cities to become big business men. The others remained obscure but precious cogs in the exchange of cheap industrial products of the larger cities with the surplus agricultural production of the forgotten areas.

Other regions which were better provided with communications brought their surplus to the markets of middle-sized industrial cities. Of these markets we know very little—again, not only because sources are insufficient but also because few historians have regarded them worthy of attention. Many markets remained as unimportant as most of them were in the early Middle Ages, but others rapidly grew, and there were so many of them. One of the fairs of Parma, for instance, specialised in transactions in cloth and in cattle, two main articles of exchange between city and country, ever since 1126. Parma was comparatively unimportant in long-distance trade, but we know that it was a thriving city. Its rural market explains the origin of many of the resources that enabled the Parmans to buy expensive products in the commercial cities and to build their splendid cathedral. Nor was trade of this kind restricted to intermittent markets. It was carried on almost continuously in eight successive fairs of the secondary cities in the valley of the lower Po, where cheap bulky goods were shipped by river or canal. Throughout Italy, towns and their districts were commercially interdependent.

In Italy, Provence and Catalonia local trade underlay greater commercial currents, but in the larger part of Central and Western France—the core of the kingdom—it was paramount. There were many middle-sized towns and a densely settled free peasantry, but no business metropolitan cities and no great native merchants. Even in Paris two Italians, who in 1292 had a yearly taxable income of £5625 and £4700 Par. respectively, far outdistanced the wealthiest Parisian bourgeois, Pierre Marcel, who had a taxable income of £2900; then there were four Italians whose income was more than £2500 each. Yet France was a thriving country. In Castile, in Portugal and in Aragon proper the same phenomenon took place. Towns had not lost their rural characteristics; many of them, in fact, still look rural to-day. When they were not exclusively administrative and military communities, they were usually centres of local exchange of low-grade industrial products for slightly below average agricultural staples. Yet throughout the Iberian peninsula we witness the progress of fairs and markets, including the daily market (*azogue*), where foodstuffs and coarse cloth were the main articles of exchange. In Southern Germany the towns usually carried out some long-distance trade, but they lived mainly on production of fustian, cutlery and other products consumed chiefly in their agricultural districts. This may explain the large number of 'cities' under 1000 inhabitants and the comparative affluence of petty merchants (*kramer*) in the larger towns, very few of which surpassed 10,000 inhabitants.

Then we must consider that specialised merchant staplers lived in many seaports and road hubs from Barletta or Manfredonia in Apulia to Casablanca or Arsila in Morocco and to Libourne or Bordeaux in Gascony, to mention only a few such places. They offered the travelling merchant of the commercial cities and the sedentary agent (*fattore*) of the great companies considerable amounts of their staple commons in return for heavy consignments of cheap Lombard or Languedocian fustian or for a handful of spices. Their business was so organised that they could patiently wait until the products of the countryside reached their stores after a slow trip in barges, on mules, or on the backs of peasants. More often than not they had purchased in advance the harvest of the next year, in spite of the ecclesiastic prohibition of dealing in futures. They knew as well as did big business men how to handle the local officers whose duty it was to forbid the export of certain staples and to levy heavy tolls upon other commodities. 'Do remember', says Pegolotti, 'that if you treat the customs officers with respect and give them something...they will always reckon your wares for less than they are worth.' He spoke of Constantinople, a great market of grain as well as of precious goods, but he could have said the same for Messina, La Rochelle or Sandwich.

It was by these procedures that the metropolitan towns obtained the larger part of the raw materials of industry and basic foodstuffs which their immediate hinterland could not supply. Some grain, wool and wine and nearly all silk, cotton and best colour dyes came from the Levant and Africa, but the most important supply areas of food and raw materials were in Europe itself. The needs of the larger cities were far from negligible. Villani's figures, which seem to be substantially accurate, reckon Florence's daily consumption of grain at more than 1300 bushels. Almost two-thirds of it came from territories not subject to the city. The Florentines ate 4000 oxen and calves, 80,000 lambs and 30,000 pigs a year. They drank 25 million quarts of wine, or about a gallon a week per man, woman and child. Both Milan and Venice consumed much more. While Milan's territory was exceptionally fertile, that of Venice was far less productive than that of Florence. Marseilles exported wine produced in its district but had to import grain. So did Barcelona. The kitchens of pontifical Avignon swept almost clean of meat on the hoof the entire area between the Rhone and the Alps. Loftier appetites of the urban population were satisfied by increasing purchases of objects of industrial art, such as ivories of Paris, enamels of Limoges, glass ware and mosaics of Venice.

The consumption of the raw materials of industry was particularly important, not only in the metropolitan cities but also in secondary towns. All sources of iron and timber in Italy were exploited, but this was not enough. The smiths of Lombardy and the shipbuilders of the Italian maritime cities imported their basic raw materials partly from Germany and France. Cotton came mostly from the Levant. Lucca imported yearly some 165,000 pounds of silk (chiefly of Turkestanian and Chinese origin) in the period 1337-40. This may seem a very low figure for the greatest centre of silk industry in Europe, but we must consider that in 1317 a revolution had forced many craftsmen into exile. In the fourteenth century the Lucchese used water power to speed up the output of their throwing mills. This was the greatest technical invention in the textile industry since the introduction of the pedal loom, which was already in use in the twelfth century, both in the Byzantine Empire and in Western Europe. To feed these looms the manufacturing cities usually had to import wool from distant regions, except perhaps the minor centres of Languedoc and Central Spain which may have been supplied entirely by the production of wool of their immediate hinterland. In Italy nearly every region produced wool, but the Lombard towns, whose output of cloth was the largest though not the finest in Southern Europe, imported additional quantities from France, North Africa and Syria. Choice Spanish wool supplied the greater part of the needs of the Florentine manufacturers up to the last years of the thirteenth century, when it was displaced by English wool. Even in 1273, when the vogue of this wool had hardly begun, 44 Italian merchants in England exported 8000 sacks (about 1325 tons); but this amount was sufficient for the manufacture of only 24,000 pieces of cloth—a very small percentage of the total Italian production. In the following years the demand for English wool increased many fold, and imports from other countries also stepped up.

The expansion of the city market led to the development of groups of wealthy cloth sellers, spice sellers, mercers, grocers, butchers, bakers and other specialised merchants who bought wholesale and sold retail. Their permanent stores largely displaced the weekly market and the craftsman's workshops as channels for distribution to the public, at least in the larger Italian cities. In a smaller city, Pavia, benches in the four main squares continued to be more numerous than stores, but they also became a permanent feature of what we may call the shopping centre. In a commercial metropolis such as Genoa the store (*apotheca*, *bottega*) had eliminated the bench at least by the mid-twelfth century. No article was either too precious or too humble to be offered for sale in large lots. We come across a seller of glass who purchased a hundred chamber pots, and a jeweller who in one sale disposed of 111 precious rings, 169 sapphires and topazes, 348 hardstones, 59 pearls and 132 cameos, one of which contained a piece of the Holy Cross. Individual trademarks and mail orders were introduced in different fields. Credit sales and sales by instalment were commonplace. Banking accounts were used not only for commercial operations but in everyday life. In extant documents of a single month in 1253 we meet with lodgers who paid their rent into their landlord's account, with a city employee who intrusted a bank to cash his salary and with a farmer who deposited in a bank money to discharge a debt due in nine months. Add to all of this the innumerable transactions of oversea and overland trade, the speculations on the money exchange and in the shares of public loans, the purchases, sales and mortgages in real estate, the operations of the loan-sharks, the contracts of shipbuilding, building and other industries, and you will then have some idea of the swirling activity in a business metropolis of the thirteenth or early fourteenth century.

At the head of all traders, of course, were the big business men—import and export merchants, international bankers, industrial entrepreneurs and 'colony builders'. Perhaps as much as nine-tenths of them were Northern and Central Italians. The balance was mostly made up of Provençal, Languedocian and Catalonian sea merchants, of wine exporters from Gascony, Toulouse and La Rochelle, of grain exporters from Sicily and Apulia, of salt exporters of the Aunis and of the upper Danubian region, and of linen exporters from Switzerland and Southern Germany. The wealth of the Italian big business men can be estimated by such examples as that of Federico Corner, a Venetian merchant who *declared* a taxable estate of £60,000 Ven. (1379), or that of Salimbene Salimbeni, a Sienese merchant-banker who offered his city a loan of £236,000 Sien. to win a war (1260).[1] The splendid palaces of the Salimbeni and Corner families, still extant, testify to the humanism of these merchants, many of whom were close friends of literati and scholars. The medieval big business man most frequently was a very active politician and a dogged fighter in civil and external wars. But his love of fatherland, home and family did not prevent him from being always on the move, always ready, until old age prevented, to leave his comfortable home to wander *per diversas mundi partes*, wherever business opportunities might call him.

Unlike most big business men of our time, the great merchant of the later Middle Ages usually spread his activities into many different lines

---

[1] Obviously much larger capital than the entire fortune of any individual could be concentrated through *compagnia* or *commenda* contracts. One of the many notaries who drafted contracts for the Genoese merchant Filippo Magnavacca recorded *commenda* contracts to a combined amount of £25,352 Gen. in three consecutive days of September, 1227. The Florentine Bardi and Peruzzi companies lent King Edward III of England a total amount of 1,365,000 florins according to Villani's figures, the substantial accuracy of which has been proved by Armando Sapori. We lack data to evaluate the fortunes of non-Italian partnerships during the thirteenth and early fourteenth centuries, but it can be assumed that the figures were much lower.

of trade and coupled large-scale operations with small retail purchases and sales. Of course a modern tycoon might smile at the methods and at the comparative smallness of the capital and credit of his medieval predecessor. He would probably feel less inclined to implore the assistance of heaven in his work, since his rate of travel does not depend on wind filling the sails or sun baking mud-caked roads. But who can tell whether in another five hundred years future business magnates will not smile at the methods, the capital and the transport used by business men of our time? Quantity is only one element in the evaluation of economic development, and it has little meaning if it is not in the general background of the times. Restrictions of capital and speed existed not only for the big business man, but for his contemporaries as well. No doubt the courier of a Venetian trading house who covered in four days the distance to Florence—usually a 22 to 25-day trip for pack animals—astonished his contemporaries even more than does the modern business man who travels by aeroplane while most of the laymen travel by railroad or car. Furthermore, in the Middle Ages absolute specialisation would have been unwise in view of the great hazards attending each kind of trade, and retail operations could not be spurned since the opportunities for wholesale operations fast exhausted themselves.

But let us leave to others the discussion of business methods and techniques and turn instead to survey briefly the main objects of import and export trade. The main axis of commerce continued to run from the northwest to the southeast, from Western and Southern Europe to Muslim and Byzantine countries, as it did in the early Middle Ages. Western textiles and eastern 'spices' (chiefly seasonings, dyestuffs and medicinals) occupied the first place, at least by value, among the various articles which were exchanged in ever increasing quantity. Pegolotti in the early fourteenth century listed no less than 386 items under the heading 'spices'. He included also many commodities of western origin, and such wares as copper, glue and cotton, which we would hardly reckon as spices. Eastern 'spices', however, were usually more valuable and there was a greater variety of them. Pegolotti quoted 11 kinds of sugar (of which nine at least came from the Levant), 7 sorts of kermes dyes (from different parts of the Balkans, Provence and Spain) and 23 different types of raw silk (mostly from the Middle and the Far East). As for western textiles, every important centre of Northern France, Belgium and England, as well as Florence, gave its name to one or more expensive woollens. Cheaper woollen cloth and fabrics containing cotton came mostly from the Lombard cities, from Languedoc, from Pisa and Siena and from South Germany. Linen was obtained especially from Champagne, Switzerland and South Germany.

The finest linen was the only western article that could bear the cost of transportation as far as Peking. Bulky goods, however, were commonly shipped to any destination in the Mediterranean, the Black Sea and the Atlantic from Safi to Newcastle and Bruges. Venice, for instance, exported leather goods, furs, salt, grain, oil, iron, copper, tin, mercury, timber, fruit, soap, animals and slaughtering meat and slaves as well as expensive textiles and 'spices'. A secondary but not negligible source of income for the Mediterranean shipowners was passenger traffic. Pilgrims paid little but they were content with the poorest 'accommodation', and there were so many of them. Muslim pilgrims were almost as good customers as were the Christians. When it came to mass transportation of Crusaders, the larger seaports engaged in a cut-throat competition. Marseilles in 1268 tried to capture the market by reducing the fare to Palestine to 60, 40 and 35 *solidi* in first, second and third class respectively. If one was stoic enough to sleep in the stables aboard ship one paid only 25 *solidi*.

By the early fourteenth century the increased movement of goods and passengers had led to important changes in transport facilities both by sea and land. Different types of ships, ranging from the speedy but narrow war galley to the slow but roomy *navis*, were used for different wares. While in wartime even the strongest and fastest galley loaded with light expensive wares might be unable to go through the blockade, in 'normal' times (that is, when only minor wars and piracy threatened navigation) the regular convoys of heavy galleys, escorted by war galleys, were quite safe. In these larger galleys enough light precious wares were laden to cut the cost of transportation of the heavier goods. The value of the cargo of one of these ships could well surpass 200,000 ducats, and sometimes a single merchant supplied the cargo for as many as three of them. Convoys of *taride*, still heavier galleys which were almost as rounded as a *navis*, transported grain and fish from the Black Sea. Toward the end of the fourteenth century Venice sent convoys almost entirely composed of comparatively fast *naves* to take on cotton in bulk in the ports of Syria and Cyprus. The regular convoys were subventioned and supervised by the governments of Genoa and Venice, and were sent out every year on a fixed schedule to various destinations in the Mediterranean, the Black Sea and the North Atlantic. Usually they were open only from February or March to September or October, but the Genoese became the pioneers of winter navigation in the early thirteenth century, and the Venetians soon followed their example. The increased number of ships and voyages partly made up for the tonnage, which even in the heaviest *naves* was very small.

Overland traffic never completely overcame the handicaps which made it more expensive than oversea traffic, but it did become safer on the most frequented roads. Whereas merchants still had to travel in caravans (*caterve*) along certain trails infested by brigands, such as the route from Trebizond to Tabriz, elsewhere they went without escort or entrusted their goods to thriving organisations of transport agents. Competition between markets and toll stations led to substantial reductions of customs and to improvements of roads. As an instance we can recall the main episodes in the duel between Swiss mountaineers and French carters to capture the great commercial currents running across the Continent. In the eleventh century most of the traffic between the valleys of the Po and of the Upper Rhine went through the passes of the Central Alps—especially the Septimer—even though wares had to be transported on porters' backs or on wheelbarrows over the steepest stretch. In the twelfth century that traffic was gradually diverted to the route through Champagne, the Rhone valley (or the Rhone river itself) the Provençal seaports, the sea as far as Savona or Genoa and the Apennines. This itinerary was almost three times as long, but it avoided the Alps and exploited to the utmost the possibilities of cheap transportation by water. In the thirteenth century the construction of a bridge across the Schöllenen gorge opened the St Gotthard to pack mules and restored part of the traffic to the Alps. Then the carters and boatmen of France began to lower their prices. In 1318 the Florentine Del Bene company, which imported French cloth, paid less per mile on the overland stretch from Paris to Marseilles than on the maritime stretch from Marseilles to Pisa. Exceptional as this case may have been, it indicates a sweeping change from the mid-thirteenth century, when (as it has been calculated) it would have cost about 3 *solidi* to ship 100 pounds of merchandise by sea from Civitavecchia to Genoa, but 80 *solidi* to send the same amount by land from Marseilles to Provins, a distance only a little longer. Nevertheless the Swiss did not give up the struggle. After 1338, work was begun in the old Septimer Pass to construct a road passable for small carts—the first of its kind in the Alps.

All available data on transport, tolls, business practices and volume of trade in the early fourteenth century convey the impression that there was a sharp distinction between what we may call the 'inner' and the 'outer' area of long-distance commerce—omitting the 'forgotten' areas such as Navarre and the core of the Balkan peninsula where there was very little commerce. The 'outer' area was a field of large risks and large profits, a frontier where good luck was almost as important as good management. Travel in the depths of Asia, for instance, still required more than ordinary resistance and courage in spite of Pegolotti's reassuring words about the Tana-Peking route. In 1338, when the Venetian merchant Giovanni Loredano prepared to go to Delhi with his brother and four other partners, his family and his parish priest besought him to desist. He died en route, as did two of his companions. The venture at first suffered losses, but thanks to the fabulous lavishness of the Sultan of Delhi, it ended with a 100% profit. This, however, was hardly a consolation to Loredano's wife, who later retired to a convent.

In the 'inner' area of long-distance trade, however, commerce had now ceased to be an adventure. It was a highly competitive market, where success depended mainly on efficiency, quickness and almost meticulous weighing of transport charges, tolls and marketing conditions. Investments were comparatively safe and profits were usually moderate, even if judged according to modern standards. Distance was not always the dominant factor in drawing the border between 'outer' and 'inner' areas, since war could at any moment render trade extremely dangerous even at the gates of a commercial metropolis. Similarly, the financial and political vicissitudes of France under Phillip the Fair sometimes made Paris a less safe place for international merchants than Peking. Normally, however, the 'inner' area included the entire coastal zone of the Mediterranean, of the Black Sea and of the Atlantic from Ceuta to Safi and from Bayonne to London and Bruges, the thickly populated internal regions of Northern and Central Italy, Champagne, Île-de-France, Flanders and Brabant.

In some types of business, merchants endeavoured to reduce or to eliminate competition in the 'inner' area by forming monopolistic compacts and cartels. In 1255, a Genoese and a Venetian jointly controlled the production of alum in Seljuk Anatolia and were able to provoke an artificial rise of price. In 1283, the government of Venice ordered all Venetian merchants to form a cartel for the purpose of buying cotton and pepper in Alexandria. In 1331, the wine merchants of St Jean d'Angély, Bordeaux, Libourne and La Rochelle united to dictate their terms to the Count of Flanders. Craft gilds, of course, worked in many ways like cartels. Notwithstanding all this, the margin between cost of production and selling price continued to shrink. In the early fourteenth century the Del Bene company purchased cloth in Flanders, finished it in Florence and sold it there, in the Champagne fairs or in Southern Italy only 11·70 to 20·34% dearer than they had bought it. Only efficient management—and low salaries to the finishers—enabled this company to make a 7 to 15% profit. It would certainly be dangerous to generalise from the data furnished by this particular company alone. That this example is not exceptional, however, we may infer by noting that the interest rate for deposits in banks, government loans and real estate investments also had fallen to around 8 to 12% from the 20 or even 25% which had been the customary commercial interest rate *in Italy* in the early thirteenth century. Obviously profits from oversea commerce were subject to much greater fluctuations, but the average profit does not seem to have been very far from these figures.

The reduction of the margin of profit and the tremendous increase of the volume of traffic quickened the development of business techniques and slowly undermined the superiority of the travelling merchant over the sedentary business man. What we may call a process of rationalisation enabled traders not only to weather the serious crisis that came with growth, but also to reach new peaks of prosperity. Some scholars have considered these changes so important that they have spoken of a 'commercial revolution' in the late thirteenth and early fourteenth centuries. The revolution, however, had been on the march for at least three centuries and had caused a great number of transformations, not only in business techniques but also in many other fields. Improvements in management in the thirteenth and fourteenth centuries might be compared to the inventions of the railway, of the dynamo and of the Diesel motor in the Industrial Revolution. They added speed and power to an already feverish and mighty economic expansion. They saved the Commercial Revolution from being choked by its own magnitude.

Let us not assume, however, that the sedentary merchant of the fourteenth century had a better grasp of economic opportunities than had, for instance, the travelling merchant of the old *commenda*. Both were adapted to the specific conditions of their times. In a regime of little competition and huge profits the travelling merchant had all the advantages except that of personal comfort. It was he who managed the enterprise, and those who entrusted capital to him had to accept his decisions and his accounting almost blindly. He shared with no one the profits of his own investment, and was entitled to no less than 25% of the profits of the numerous investments he received in *commenda*. We know very well that more often than not he retained more than his legal share. Nevertheless people kept offering their money to him, much as men nowadays in times of boom rush to subscribe to new stock offerings, because they felt that even the most reckless and unscrupulous travelling merchant would earn enough to enrich them as well as himself. When, however, competition grew and many small profits were required to form a respectable capital, the cost of travelling became too heavy to bear. Then the sedentary merchant took over as well as he could the management of long-distance trade and carried out his business through branches manned by his employees and through oversea commission agents. He endeavoured to obtain more adequate accounting and to keep close track of his affairs by correspondence. Thus he saved the share which would have been paid to the travelling merchant, but he had to carry a heavy managerial structure which could be supported only on condition that business was continuous and intensive. The robust, but more inflexible, body of maturity had replaced the lean, but more pliable frame of youth.

Our survey must come to a close. We have begun it with a sketch of two very humble business men, Ugo Teralh and Armanno the Currier. Let us conclude it with the quick portrait of two very great business men, Benedetto Zaccaria and Francesco Datini. The former was a travelling merchant, a great nobleman, and a man of the sea. The latter was a sedentary business man, a self-made man, and a native of an inland town. Between the two, they summed up the best characteristics of the medieval merchant prince. They were utterly different, but two sentiments made them similar: a very medieval religiousness, and a very 'modern' eagerness for profit.

Benedetto Zaccaria, born some time before 1240, was one of ten Genoese brothers and sisters who claimed descent from the viscounts of the city. Most of his family was as actively engaged in business and politics as he was. His triumphs as an admiral and a diplomat alone would make him one of the outstanding men of his time. He was one of the commanders at Meloria where Genoa destroyed the Pisan navy, and he commanded the Castilian fleet at Marzamosa where the Moroccans were crushed; he wrote, in witty French, a plan for a 'continental blockade' of England and helped Phillip the Fair to execute it; he conquered Tripoli in Syria, witnessed its fall to overwhelming Egyptian forces, and later toyed with the idea of a crusade of women to recapture it; he engaged in both grand and petty piracy and carried out vital secret missions in various courts. Let us concentrate on his activities as a business man. With the typical eclecticism of his time he traded in spices, cutlery, cloth, linen, furs, salt, grain and other wares, and speculated in foreign exchange, in shares of the public loans and in real estate. What made him exceptional, however, was the way he exploited two fiefs he had obtained from the Byzantine Emperor. One of them, the island of Chios, yielded a crop of mastic worth about £16,000 Gen. a year. Chios was the only place in the world where this aromatic herb, much appreciated in the Levant, was produced. Later records indicate that excess production of mastic in any year was destroyed since a larger crop would have lowered the price without increasing substantially the quantity sold.

More important were the alum mines of Phocaea, in the other fief jointly held by Benedetto Zaccaria and one of his brothers. Alum was an indispensable material for the dyeing industry. Phocaea's alum was the second best in the world, while the best quality came from Koloneia in Northern Asia Minor. Zaccaria managed by political intrigue to keep all exports from Koloneia off the market while he was developing

Phocaea's mines, and then exported Koloneia's alum as well as his own. In a few years a new city of 3000 inhabitants, New Phocaea, sprang up near the mines, which yielded about 700 tons yearly. The ore was processed in the old town on the sea shore. In one recorded instance Zaccaria sold 33 tons of processed alum for £3000 Gen., carriage free in Bruges. He used his own ships to distribute the alum in different countries, and employed all his diplomatic and military skill to enlarge his markets. In Genoa, his home town, he owned a dyeing house and financed a Florentine clothmaker. Some of the by-products of his business, which shows definite vertical and horizontal integration, were the building of a *fondaco* in the Crimea, a short-lived control of Puerto Santa Maria (the seaport of Seville), and the first recorded voyage through the Strait of Gibraltar to England. Zaccaria died in his palace in 1307, when he was about to sail on another business venture in spite of his old age. Four years later Empress Margaret, the wife of Henry VII, spent the last days of her life in the palace of Zaccaria's heirs. Her presence could not make more 'imperial' the house that had sheltered a true empire builder.

Francesco Datini requires fewer words than the less well known Zaccaria. Datini was born in 1335, the son of a taverner of Prato, a small but lively town near Florence. At thirteen he was an orphan and a shop-boy of a Florentine merchant. Shortly thereafter he left what appeared to be a hopeless future and settled in Avignon, working as a business employee (*fattore*). At twenty-eight he founded a company with a capital of 800 florins, one half of which he contributed. At forty-seven he was back in Florence, a rich man, but still eager to increase his wealth. He died at seventy-five and bequeathed nearly all of his 70,000-florin estate to charity in spite of the fact that he had a numerous family: after all, his children were illegitimate, and he had created a trust fund for his legal wife. His public generosity shows his religious sentiments, but a sceptical man might think that his conscience disturbed him. Datini's first business had been the armament industry, which was undoubtedly the most profitable in Avignon during the Hundred Years War. But he was as eclectic as Zaccaria. We see him engaged in banking, international commerce, cloth manufacturing and dyeing, in the silk industry and still other activities—all this through a large number of small companies totally or chiefly financed by him. He had permanent *fondachi* (branches) in Avignon, Genoa, Barcelona, Valencia and Majorca and correspondents scattered throughout Western Europe and the Levant. His account books show the entire evolution from the single to the double entry method of book-keeping. The pious foundation to which he left his estate still exists, and conserves all the papers of his firms. The books number 500, and there are more than 300,000 letters exchanged between Datini and his correspondents and employees. Some of the letters show Datini's close friendship with many outstanding literati and scholars of his time. Datini, however, carefully kept out of politics, which had caused so much trouble to so many merchants, including at times Zaccaria.

Zaccaria lived in the most glorious time of medieval trade, but Datini made his fortune after the best days had gone. We have told his story only because his methods were similar to those of many merchants of the early fourteenth century. But the calamity which had made him an orphan—the Black Death—ushered in far more serious crises than the difficulties which had given rise to sedentary merchants like him.

(3) DEPRESSION AND RECOVERY

The last century of the Middle Ages (1348–1453) witnessed hard times. Several quakes opened tremendous cracks in the edifice of prosperity erected in almost four centuries of successful economic expansion. They left Southern Europe an impoverished country in spite of the superficial brilliancy of courts and upper classes, and brought closer the moment when Northern Europe would assume the dominant role in world economy. Between crises, however, business men and workers struggled hard to maintain and, if possible, to increase their prosperity. In the process, gains were made in various directions. Furthermore, some cities and regions, affected less by the depression, surpassed others which had been harder hit. Other cities and regions successfully used the accumulated wealth and experience of prosperous years to keep above water level. The interplay of regressive and progressive phenomena forms a pattern so complicated that the true significance of the last century of the Middle Ages remains much more obscure than that of the period between the mid-tenth and the mid-fourteenth century. Only by disregarding details and by encompassing the whole panorama with one glance can we realise that the general trend in trade was downward.[1]

One of the greatest tragedies in history, the Black Death of 1348, burst open the doors to the depression which had already been foretold by other ominous tokens. No less than 35% and perhaps as much as 65% of the crowded urban population succumbed to the plague. The rate of mortality was less high in the country, but it was the fate of

[1] Henri Pirenne, who was first in pointing out the importance of the economic crisis of the mid-fourteenth century, called it a 'crisis of saturation'. The writer thinks that the term 'saturation' very appropriately describes the difficulties in growth that gave rise to the sedentary merchant in the early fourteenth century. 'Depression' seems to be a better term to indicate the crisis of the mid-fourteenth century.

cities that mattered most, since cities were the leaders of economic expansion. The toll was heaviest where urbanisation was the most intensive and where the agrarian population had grown the thickest— which means that the cream of the economic world was skimmed. Nor was the Black Death the only calamity of that kind. Comparatively smaller, but still dreadful, epidemics swept Europe again and again in the late fourteenth and early fifteenth centuries. Wars also were more protracted and more destructive than they had been since the time of the last wave of barbarian invasions in the ninth and early tenth centuries. The Hundred Years War in France, civil wars in Castile and in Southern Italy, the ravages of the *condottieri* and innumerable local campaigns in Northern Italy and Southern Germany completed the work of disease and prepared that of famine. Other imponderable reasons, among which we must probably include birth control, prevented any prompt recovery. In the larger part of Europe the prosperous level of 1300 was not reached again before the sixteenth or the seventeenth century. The population of Florence, for instance, fell from about 110,000 inhabitants in 1338 to 45–50,000 in 1351; it increased only to 70–75,000 in 1380 and was still about 70,000 in 1526. Modena, a minor city in Northern Italy, fell from about 22,000 inhabitants in 1306 to 8–9000 in 1482 (Doren). Zürich, of which we have no data prior to the Black Death, had 12,375 inhabitants in 1350 and 4713 in 1468 (Keller-Escher). Montpellier had 22,500 inhabitants in 1367 and 5000 in 1379 (Germain). In France, war was perhaps an even worse calamity than the Black Death and the later epidemics. Furthermore, the definitive expulsion from the kingdom of the Jews, who were accused of spreading the plague, entirely wiped out a useful if small commercial group. As for Germany, it will be enough to recall that fourteen major epidemics after that of 1348–50 are recorded for the second half of the fourteenth century. Catalonia alone owed a temporary recovery to the fact that its commercial development reached its peak after the middle of the fourteenth century. Homesteads rose from 86,895 to 95,258 between 1359 and 1369. But the figure fell to 77,973 in 1378 and it went below the 60,000 mark in 1497 (Vandellós).

A contemporary writer ascribed the spread of the Black Death to the 'microbic' war unleashed by the Mongolian Khan of Kipchak against the Genoese colony of Caffa in the Crimea. The Khan, he says, endeavoured to break the resistance of the besieged inhabitants by catapulting into the walls bodies of men who had died with the plague. The city held out, but returning colonists carried the disease to Western Europe. Be that as it may, the siege of Caffa, which was preceded by a pogrom of Italian merchants in Tana (Azov), was very bad news in itself. It was an instance of the sudden deterioration of the situation throughout the Mongolian states. The Khan of Kipchak made peace with Caffa, but a few years later his death was followed by prolonged anarchy. The Italians suffered still heavier blows in the Khanate of Persia, where their interests had grown in a few decades almost as large as those they had acquired in the Byzantine Empire in the course of several centuries. The death of Khan Abū Sa'īd in 1338 marked the collapse of a state which had been most friendly to the foreigners. Tabriz, the most important city, was seized by a tyrant who slaughtered or robbed those merchants who had trusted in his promises. Similar disasters occurred in the Khanate of Turkestan, beginning with a massacre of Europeans in its capital, Almaligh (1339), and ending with the total collapse of the state. So long as a friendly Mongolian Khanate remained in China, some Italian merchants continued their attempts to reach that country by devious routes. We still hear of a Genoese caravan bound for Cathay in 1343. But even the Khanate of China was undermined by internal disorders which ended in its overthrow by the national dynasty of the Ming in 1368. The new rulers had neither the power nor the wish to maintain relations with Europe through the immense distances of the Asiatic continent or the Indian Ocean. It is true that China entered upon an age of unprecedented expansion by sea in the fifteenth century, when Chinese warships and merchant junks sailed as far west as the Arabian coast, but these vessels did not reach shores frequented by European merchants.

The limitless possibilities open to the westerners by the Mongolian unification of Asia were lost. It was again necessary to use the Egyptian bottle-neck and to depend upon Muslim intermediaries to obtain the goods of the Farther East. Venice, which had sent no convoys to Egypt from 1323 to 1345, now entreated the Pope to cancel the embargo and the Sultan to conclude a new commercial treaty. The Pope granted only individual licences upon payment of exorbitant fees. The Sultan gladly resumed the exploitation of the Christian merchant in a manner much more drastic than hitherto. The bitter struggle for the last bastions of the Holy Land and the subsequent European desertion of Egypt for the Mongolian markets had withered the sprouting seeds of toleration. Furthermore, Egypt itself had been impoverished by maladministration and by the strain of a double battle of survival against both Mongolians and Christians. Its ships no longer sailed further than Aden. To this harbour the goods of the Farther East came, no doubt at an increased cost to the Egyptians, in Indian ships and, during the fifteenth century, even in Chinese junks. It was imperative for the Egyptians to seek a compensation for their financial and commercial decadence in the thorough exploitation of the monopoly of trade with Europe.

As the financial crisis of Egypt grew worse, European merchants in Alexandria traded on even harder terms. Already in the late fourteenth century they had to pay duties amounting in all to around 100% of the value of the goods. In 1428 the Sultan took over the monopoly of the export of pepper, which had been sold hitherto by private Egyptian merchants, and raised its price in Alexandria from 80 to 130 *dīnār*. He acted similarly in regard to cotton at Beyrouth. Still worse was to come. In 1480, when the Venetians refused to pay 110 ducats for a *sporta* (about 480 pounds) of pepper which sold in the market for 50 ducats, the Sultan confined them two days and three nights in their *fondaci*, then dragged them to the custom-house and did not permit them to go until they had paid 70 ducats for the pepper. If this could happen to the Venetians, who were backed by the strongest navy in the world and enjoyed the exceptional distinction of owning two extra-territorial *fondaci* in Alexandria, the other merchant communities must have fared even worse. Only mutual dependence and fear prevented a very tense situation from reaching a breaking point. The Sultan needed Christians to buy his commodities and knew from experience that he could not outrage Venice without facing severe military reprisals. Venice and the other merchant communities needed Muslims to supply eastern wares and knew from experience that Egypt could be beaten but not conquered. Hence, in spite of constant friction, European commerce in Alexandria mounted to new heights.

Much more ominous clouds were gathering further north. From the early fourteenth century the Ottoman Turks had been gnawing at the Byzantine possessions in Asia. In 1352 they gained a foothold in Europe with the help of the Genoese, who needed allies against the Venetians. Before the end of the century they had conquered nearly all of the Balkan peninsula without having to break their alliance with Genoa or to cross swords with the Venetians. Although they were not necessarily hostile to foreign commerce and merchants, they certainly did not care to maintain the extraordinary privileges that the westerners had extorted from the weakness of the Byzantines. Here, as in Egypt, the merchants tried appeasement as a remedy less costly than war. Some colonies even bought immunity from attack by paying tribute. Europe, however, had to fight back when the Turks began to blockade Constantinople. At this point Tamerlane emerged from the depth of Asia, defeated the Turks and was courted by the westerners, including even the king of distant Castile, who sent him ambassadors. In spite of cruelty inflicted upon Italian colonies reached by his troops, Tamerlane seemed to many a new Chinghis Khan who would restore peace through destruction and commerce through peace in the immense territories he had subdued. But the conqueror died in 1405, and the Turks resumed their advance. The repercussions of these events upon the commerce of Constantinople can be judged from the returns of taxes levied on maritime trade in the Genoese suburb of Pera. These fell from £1,648,630 Gen. in 1334 to £1,199,046 in 1391 and to £234,000 in 1423. The decline will appear still greater if we consider the constant diminution of the weight and purchasing power of the Genoese pound.

Thus contraction of eastern markets and shrinking of home markets reversed the trend which had made the Commercial Revolution possible. Nor were conditions more favourable to the expansion of Southern European merchants into Northern Europe, since Northern Europe had also been scourged by epidemics and frequent wars. Furthermore, the Commercial Revolution of the previous period had brought distant regions more closely together and thus made them interdependent. The fluctuations of the international money market, of which the fall of the Genoese pound is an instance, had wide repercussions because most credit and commercial operations involved transactions in foreign exchange. To be sure, bankers and merchants tried to forecast the trends: in 1265, for instance, a Sienese merchant warned from Troyes one of his fellow-citizens in Lombardy to be on the alert for a probable fall in the quotations of the French currency in Italy as a result of an expedition then being prepared by Charles of Anjou. At a latter period, however, as the margin of commercial profit and interest kept shrinking, unpredictable variations in the exchange rates could doom to failure an otherwise successful business operation.

It was not 'one world' as yet, but there was a sensitive world market, and it reacted quickly to crises in distant countries. Local difficulties, for instance, cannot entirely explain why the Florentine cloth industry declined so precipitously that in 1378 the revolting weavers demanded that industrialists should pledge a minimum yearly output of 24,000 pieces—which still was less than one-third of the production of 1338. Among the causes, we must mention the loss of the Persian market to which Venetians and Genoese had exported Florentine cloth before the collapse of the Mongolian Khanate; the impoverishment of the French nobility who were great consumers of luxury cloth before the Hundred Years War; the curtailment of exports of English wool which was the basic raw material before the war; and the bankruptcy of the Bardi and Peruzzi, Florence's greatest companies of merchant-bankers, which was connected with the war. Probably other distant events, of which we fail to see the connection with Florentine industry, also contributed to its decline. World-wide difficulties also must have formed the background of the social revolts which agitated all of Europe from London to Salonika and from Majorca to Flanders in the second half of the fourteenth century, although if we observe any one of these revolts too closely we discern only local causes and local peculiarities.

We are in the presence of an all-European depression. We must explain it chiefly by all-European causes. Though the last century of the Middle Ages has not yet been fully studied, it is not impossible to perceive a leading thread through the maze of its evidence.

Perhaps the most misleading factor, more misleading to the men of the fourteenth century than to us, is that the first disasters were followed by a wave of apparent prosperity. Terrible as the catastrophies were, they had struck a strong body which reacted vigorously. After the Black Death, the opening stages of the Hundred Years War, the Genoese-Venetian-Catalan clash of 1350–55 and other smaller conflicts there was a sharp increase of the demand for goods. Mortality had automatically increased the amount of money per capita and provoked a shortage of manpower. Wage-earners were able to demand higher salaries—in money terms if not in purchasing power—and debtors and tenants found it easier to pay their dues. While a stream of new immigrants from the country answered the demand for labourers in the cities, peasants who had not as yet been able to gain liberty now bought it. Their payments enabled the landlords to increase their purchases from the merchants and industrialists. The latter were able to pay larger salaries because they sold more—not only to the landlords, but also to the labourers and to the rest of the population which had abundant money to spend owing to the inflation. The increase of mass consumption lightened competition, which had heavily restricted commercial profits in the last few years before the Black Death.

Unfortunately this prosperity, born of inflation and of the diminished productive power of the population, did not last long. Even if its bases had been sounder than they were, the recurrence of the epidemics and the continuation or the recurrence of the wars would have brought it to an early end. As soon as the ranks of labour were filled sufficiently to ensure adequate production for the slowly but steadily shrinking market, both landlords and industrialists 'cracked down' on wages. The desperate revolts of workmen, petty artisans and peasants failed to turn the tide. The peasants at least did not lose their personal liberty, but the lower classes in the cities saw their condition become much worse than it had been before the Black Death. It was they who bore the main burden of the measures by which the industrialists endeavoured to compensate their diminished sales through reducing costs and increasing efficiency of production, especially in the textile industry. By supervising workers very closely and by imposing fines for technical errors, by hiring more women and fostering immigration of unskilled labourers from the country, by adopting the putting-out system for the initial stages of manufacturing, and by inviting artisans driven from Flanders on account of economic crisis and political disorders, the

Italian clothiers were able to ride through the hard times. But over-production became a danger for the first time since the beginning of the commercial revolution. Gilds all over Europe gradually restricted the number of new masters who now shared only limited opportunities.

In commerce, also, the process of 'rationalisation' begun before the Black Death made gigantic strides. With so many markets in the Levant closing to European merchants and with the growing dullness of European markets, the *leit-motif* became to offer for sale 'only as much as one can sell in the place of destination', to quote the words of a fifteenth-century manual of business. Nor was it always possible to buy as much as was desired. The age of rapid fortunes won in daring oversea and overland ventures was over. Only the sedentary merchant who could make long-range plans to be executed with the help of numerous employees and commission agents and who could patiently wait for his investments to bring hard-won profits still had a fighting chance. In Italy, 5 to 8 % was now regarded as a fair interest rate in commercial loans. No wonder that commerce lost both capital and men to other forms of activity. Although banks increased their size and improved their methods, they used a larger part of their capital for loans to the idle upper class and more frequently to belligerent states. Genoa's funded debt, for instance, increased more than tenfold in thirty years. Moreover, a growing number of merchants retired from business, invested in real estate, lavished huge sums in magnificence, and became members of the new 'bourgeois nobility', whose high standards are described in Castiglione's *Courtier*. To be sure, this was not a new trend, but it was more stressed than ever before. It left durable gaps in the merchant class because, outside of war profiteering, there were few chances for new men to make fortunes and to take the place of old merchants becoming gentlemen. Meanwhile the Communes, the highest expression of the power of the Italian merchant class, were being overthrown by tyrants, ruled by elfish oligarchies or torn by civil wars.

These conditions dangerously increased the distance between the very rich and the very poor, and strengthened the tendency of merchants and manufacturers to cater mainly for a small group of wealthy customers. The surge of silk industry in those very centres where cloth production declined is a significant manifestation of the trend toward the growth of luxury industries. Other entrancing but alarming symptoms are the progress of industrial arts and the building of palaces of unprecedented splendour. In Florence, notwithstanding the decline of the textile industry and the shrinking of the population, the Medici family in the fifteenth century had a fortune of half a million ducats—more than three times as large as the fortune of the Peruzzi, who were the richest Florentine family one century earlier. Besides the small number of extremely wealthy families were the more than two-thirds of the taxpayers who in 1399 paid taxes of less than one florin, or the 3000 *miserabili* whose income in 1428 was too small to tax. Adverse economic trends and the hostility of the ruling oligarchy made the lot of these proletarians much harder than it was during the opening stages of the Commercial Revolution. Nor was the outlook any brighter for the lower classes in towns where capitalism had made slower progress. In Bâle 25·5% of the citizens in 1424 did not have the minimum taxable capital of 10 florins; the proportion rose to 32% in 1453. In contrast to this, 3 to 5% of the population owned more than half the wealth of the city. Inequality grew deeper even within the upper class. In Venice, which was the wealthiest city in Europe towards the end of the Middle Ages, seven opulent merchant noblemen in 1379 made a tax declaration disclosing a fortune of 140,000 to 240,000 ducats each and almost 400 noblemen disclosed fortunes of more than 12,000. But 800 members of the nobility lived on the margin of decent poverty with 1200 to 12,000 ducats, and many hundred who had still less were definitely poor. Good connections and assistance from the government enabled a few poor nobles to recoup their fortunes, but the majority sank lower and lower. In France the Hundred Years War brought greater inequality along with the general misery. If the court often displayed extravagant pomp and if a Jacques Cœur amassed about one million gold *écus*, there were 'great noblemen' who could spend no more than 20 crowns a year. The condition of most peasants and artisans was appalling.

If, however, these facts warn us against regarding the late fourteenth and the early fifteenth centuries simply as a prolongation of the economic expansion begun in the late tenth century, we must be careful not to overstress the dark side of the picture. A combination of adverse conditions had braked the wheels of commerce, but the spirit of the merchant remained substantially unchanged. The amazing progress accomplished during the commercial revolution in business methods was not lost. Indeed, depressions of necessity were times of greater improvements and rationalisation. Even if the merchants lost an entire continent in Asia, they opened new territories southwards in Africa and northwards and north-eastwards in Europe. Furthermore, some Southern European countries which had formerly been backward now felt the full impact of the Commercial Revolution. Finally, even the greatest disasters were sources of profit for some men.

War, for instance, stimulated the arms trade. We have seen how the foundation of Datini's fortune was laid in the commerce of weapons in

Avignon. Milan found in the metallurgic industries a compensation for the decline of its woollen production, even before it developed silk production. We hear that in 1427 two Milanese armourers alone were able to supply, in an emergency, arms for 4000 horsemen and 200 infantrymen in a few days. Plain suits of armour made by the famous Missaglia arms-makers cost £200 Mil. a piece wholesale.

In France the turmoil which swept away the modest welfare of the common man piled up unprecedented fortunes in the coffers of the few. Jacques Cœur—a merchant from Bourges, but one who made Montpellier his second home and Mediterranean trade one of his main activities—climbed higher and fell faster than all of the others. Many less famous men found war profiteering an easier way to accumulate capital than peacetime trade. Jean Amici of Toulouse associated with an army officer to trade in booty taken from the English; Jean Marcel of Rouen amassed a fortune through all sorts of illegal speculations and through open collaboration with the English; Guillaume de Saint-Yon made fabulous profits selling meat at inflation prices to the Parisian rich. Other business men got rich by supplying the court or by assisting the French king in fleecing the king's flock. Some of them knew how to withdraw from trade as soon as they felt rich enough to identify themselves with the feudal aristocracy. A typical case is that of the Ysalguier family of Toulouse, who, though possibly of peasant origin, had made their fortune by administering the confiscated possessions of Jews and by serving the king in other ways. After a while they felt it below their dignity to continue their profession of money-changers and traders in hay and other humble staples. They purchased land, became courtiers and entirely associated themselves with the local nobility. This attitude was very common in the French business class as late as the eighteenth century, and it is not exceptional even today. But it must also be noted that throughout the Hundred Years' War the state of the kingdom held little promise for any one endeavouring to practise commerce on a large scale. Wealth was lost more rapidly than acquired. The economy of France remained disrupted even during the intermissions between different phases of the war and during the military recovery under Charles V. Even in the most important industrial centres the working class was so depleted that it was often necessary to override gild restrictions and to encourage immigration of both skilled and unskilled craftsmen. The fairs of Champagne had lost their importance before the beginning of the war; those of St Denis, which went back to the early Middle Ages, were discontinued for very long periods; those of Lyons, which were instituted shortly before the end of the war, did not become important until the late fifteenth century. The Mediterranean seaports were in profound decadence. Narbonne in 1378 had no more than 1000 inhabitants.

No other European country, with the exception of the Byzantine territory, was as thoroughly ruined by wars as was France. In fact, both the Iberian peninsula and Southern Germany knew more intensive trade in the last century of the Middle Ages than ever before. The internecine war that weakened both Genoa and Venice helped the Catalan trade to reach its greatest splendour roughly between 1330 and 1390; but it is hard to evaluate the size of this trade, because its rich documentary material has not yet been fully studied. For a few years the Catalans were able to exclude practically all other Europeans from North-west African commerce, and they became serious competitors of the Italians in the Levant. At first their methods and their spirit were markedly behind the times. Their greatest historian, Muntaner, who was also a 'colony builder', spoke with contempt of the bourgeoisie of the communes 'who do not know what honour means'. Sailors and settlers oversea had much of the rude, savage lawlessness of the early Crusaders without their deep religious faith. The laws of Catalonia still punished by death the money-changer who was unable to pay his creditors; an unfortunate changer was beheaded in front of his *taula* (bank) as late as 1360. Narrow protectionistic legislation hindered the progress of Barcelona up to the end of the Middle Ages. But the technique of the merchants made rapid progress and in some directions more than caught up with Italian business methods. A scholar has found in a Barcelonese contract of 1332 closer resemblance to the modern *société en accomandite* than can be noticed in the *commenda* and *compagnia* contracts most commonly used in Italy at the same period. The Catalan banking system was backed by comparatively small capital, but it was well developed: the public bank of Barcelona probably antedated all other public banks of the world. Jewish-Majorcan cartographers in the mid-fourteenth century drew maps as accurate as the slightly earlier *carte da navegar* of the great Genoese and Venetian cartographers. Textile and ceramic production were fairly well developed.

Nevertheless, none of the Catalan seaports even remotely approached the importance of Venice and Genoa, and their decline was already pronounced in the first half of the fifteenth century. In 1387 they had lost to the Florentine Acciaioli family their main base in the Levant, the duchy of Athens. Soon thereafter they lost their quasi-monopoly of North-west African trade to the Italian cities. Their weakness may be ascribed partly to lingering indiscipline, but it was above all a consequence of the smallness of their population. Barcelona in the fourteenth century does not seem to have surpassed 30–35,000 inhabitants, the larger part of whom were petty craftsmen and other non-merchants. Valencia and Palma (Majorca) were still smaller, and Jews, Tuscans and Genoese maintained a prominent position in their trade. Behind these cities was not a region bustling with the activity of commercial and industrial towns, as was the hinterland of Venice, Genoa and Pisa, but a poorly developed kingdom of noblemen and peasants. In the fourteenth century—and to some extent even to-day—the Catalan coast was like the gilt façade of a building of mud and straw.

The golden age of Catalonia was already on the wane when both Portugal and Castile, often under the guidance of Genoese admirals and pilots, were opening those Southern and Western Atlantic routes that were to win for them a great place in the history of civilisation. Up to the late fourteenth century most of the scant long-distance trade of Portugal had been directed northwards, especially to Flanders, England and Normandy—therefore beyond the scope of the present chapter. But in the fifteenth century Prince Henry the Navigator promoted those famous voyages along the West African coast, which enabled a group of Portuguese seamen and merchants to amass modest capital by purchasing the gold dust of Palola from Arab merchants and by buying or capturing negro slaves. The little island of Arguin near the Mauretanian coast became the main fortified outpost of these officially sponsored expeditions, which faced the competition of more advanced but more isolated Genoese and Venetian merchants. The Portuguese also landed in the Azores and Madeira. Norman adventurers established themselves in some of the Canaries, which had already been visited in the fourteenth century by the Genoese and the Portuguese, and ruled the islands in the name of the Castilian king.

These and other successes were certainly landmarks in the history of geographic exploration, but how much did they matter in the actual development of Portuguese and Castilian trade before the mid-fifteenth century? Again, as in the case of Catalonia, the lack of adequate research into the extant commercial documents stands in the way of a positive evaluation. What little we know conveys the impression of two comparatively backward countries which depended on agriculture much more heavily than did Italy, Germany or France. Portugal exported some oil, some cork and a larger quantity of wine. Fishing supported a fairly large group of seamen, and the technique of maritime insurance was comparatively well developed. Castile was larger but less open to the influence of sea trade than was Portugal. It had a greater variety of surplus vegetable and mineral products, but lately it had concentrated its efforts upon developing the export of fine wool, even if that involved a diminution of land under cultivation. The most powerful company of sheep men, the *Mesta*, in 1477 owned 2,694,032 sheep, or roughly a sheep for every second inhabitant of Castile. Since England no longer exported very large quantities of wool, there was a great opportunity for Castile to conquer the Italian market. But the Castilians, just because of this, failed to take the other opportunity that the English were taking; they failed to create textile industries capable of supplying their own local needs, let alone the foreign market. Apart from Italian settlers and Jews, the business class was very small. Some kings of Castile and many kings of Portugal endeavoured to promote private initiative by such measures as the wisdom of their times suggested. Even if that wisdom had always been right, they could hardly have conjured up a business class by decree. When we see how great remained the influence of Italian, German and other foreign capitalists in the trade of Castile and Portugal after Columbus and Vasco da Gama, we can hardly assume that native merchants had fully exploited the opportunities created by the earlier explorations.

In the fifteenth century the most rapidly advancing region lay in the heart of Europe. Commerce and industry were booming in the towns of Southern Germany and Switzerland—Nuremberg above all, but also Augsburg, Ulm, Bâle, Zürich, St Gall, Geneva and many others. The 'great merchant company' of tiny Ravensburg, founded around 1380, had *fattori* in 21 foreign centres including Bilbao, Pest, Venice and Bruges. Ratisbon alone seems to have been on the decline after reaching its zenith around 1380; Vienna, rapidly growing up under the protection of the powerful Habsburgs, captured part of its trade, and fustian of Augsburg and Ulm eclipsed the 'Milanese' fustians made in Ratisbon. The golden age of Upper Germany came after the middle of the fifteenth century, but already in 1447 there were such men as the uncle and nephew Mundprat of Constance who amassed a taxable income of £132,424 in trade with Milan, Genoa and Spain.

Let us stop a moment to consider the rapid development of Nuremberg. If we may judge from the account books of one of its most prominent merchant companies, the Holzschuher firm, in the early fourteenth century the town did not yet have any particular importance. The firm's customers were residents of Nuremberg or lived within a thirty-mile circle. They were mostly noblemen and bourgeois who bought Flemish cloth, or Jews who borrowed money at the frightful average rate of 94%. One wonders what interest the Jews in turn had to charge on those who borrowed from them. Certainly they took more than Nuremberg's legal rate of 43%, which was the same as that generally allowed in Flanders, but was two to four times as high as the legal rate allowed in most Lombard towns. Nuremberg at that time (1304–7) produced linen and iron ware, but was not a great exporting centre. In 1332, however, we hear that its citizens enjoyed customs reductions in 69 cities, and a little later arms made in Nuremberg are mentioned in Spain, Italy and Flanders. Textile production also stepped up. In Venice the merchants from Nuremberg gradually overtook those of all the other German cities. In the early fifteenth century Nuremberg business men established connections with commission agents in Lübeck and in many cases went themselves to live in that great Hanseatic seaport. They imported Baltic herrings to Salzburg and Polish oxen to Frankfurt-on-Main. Before the middle of the century they extended their business to East Prussia and, a little later, to Livonia. Thus they were competing with the Hanseatic merchants in the Hansa's own preserve. They distributed eastern spices and western textiles in many centres of the interior where few Italian big business men went. Nuremberg had become the central hub of a network of overland communications between eastern Central Europe and the Rhineland and between the Mediterranean and the northern seas.

The surge of the Southern German cities has been explained as a result of many local causes and of the alleged mental superiority of the merchants. The former certainly had their importance, but cannot entirely explain international developments of trade. The latter is harder to evaluate in economic terms, but if the South Germans really had any intellectual superiority over the Mediterranean business men they concealed it perfectly. Up to the end of the fifteenth century the business methods of the Germans remained more primitive than those of the Italians and the Catalans. Even later, though the great Augsburg bankers employed larger capitals than did the Florentine companies at an earlier period, they hardly used more advanced methods; moreover, they were much more narrowly attached to the tradition of excluding from key positions in their business any one who did not belong to their families. The general international situation was probably the largest factor in the rise of South German capitalism. Wars and the continued unfavourable balance of trade with the Levant increased the need for both non-precious and precious metals, of which South Germany and Austria were the main sources. Furthermore, the spread of the Commercial Revolution to eastern Central Europe, from Poland to Hungary, placed South Germany at the gates of an expanding frontier. Finally, the chaos of France and the troubles in Italy and Flanders hampered traffic across the continent via the Rhone valley or the western Alps, leaving the routes across the eastern Alps as the best available alternative. The progress of cities on the Italian side of the Brenner Pass—Verona, Trento, Bolzano, Merano—is a further indication of the same trend. The fact that before the fourteenth century few Italian big business men thought it worth while to penetrate the German market had permitted the growth of a comparatively modest group of long-distance merchants in every city from the upper Rhine to the upper Danube and the upper Adige. When the new opportunities matured, these men were ready.

It would be a great mistake to assume that Italy in the last century of the Middle Ages had lost its primacy in trade. In spite of the increased difficulties we have described, the Italian cities dazzled all foreign visitors with their magnificence, and merchants and bankers from Italy still towered above the business men of the rest of the world. Continued progress of commercial techniques and increasing concentration of capital had caused the superiority of Italian big business men to increase rather than to diminish. The economic condition of Italy during the Renaissance has been rightly compared with that of England after 1870. The progress of other peoples took away from Italy its almost absolute monopoly of long-distance trade, but it also created new fields where the accumulated capital and experience of that people of commercial pioneers could be profitably employed. If all this implied decadence, neither the Italians nor their new competitors fully realised it.

Banking, maritime trade, industry and agriculture all alike were thriving in the country that had been the cradle of the commercial revolution. The Medici bank was by far the greatest financial organisation in Europe, roughly between 1430 and 1480. Its activities reached every region of Europe, the Levant and North Africa; they included not only banking operations but also trade in luxury articles and staple products, control of a few units of textile industry and monopolistic exploitation of alum mines. Many other banks in Florence and in other Central and Northern Italian cities had huge capital and world-wide business relations. On the other hand, Venice, having definitely outdistanced Genoa as a commercial centre, was undoubtedly the first seaport in the world. Substantially accurate statistics, quoted in an official report of 1423 by Doge Tommaso Mocenigo, valued the Venetian sea trade outside the Adriatic at 10 million ducats yearly for exports and as much for imports. More than one fourth of the exports represented trade with the Duchy of Milan. The capital and the other cities of the duchy—among which Como held the first place in this respect—exported through Venice 48,000 pieces of cloth. Cheaper fustians, once the great speciality of most Lombard towns, were now an important industry only in Cremona; but that little town alone exported 40,000 pieces. Even granting that the figures may have been slightly exaggerated, it still was a large production considering that much cloth also was exported via Genoa or the Alpine passes and that German merchants often purchased it directly in the Lombard cities. Silk, however, was becoming a more important industry than woollen production. The diminished inflow of raw material from Turkestan and China did not discourage the Italians, who developed sericulture at home. Upper Italy, which today is the largest raw-silk producer in Europe, had not yet won its dominant position, though its agriculture was at that period far in advance of that of the other European countries. Most silk came to the manufacturers of Northern and Central Italy from Sicily and Calabria through the seaport of Messina. The same regions also produced some cotton and a little sugar, thus turning to their own profit what originally had been a disadvantage, that is, the increasing difficulties in supply from the Levant. Saffron, once a staple of the Levant but in the thirteenth century cultivated also in Aragon and in Eastern Tuscany, now was obtained almost exclusively in Italy, the mountainous province of Abruzzi being the greatest producer. Thanks to that trade, the little town of Aquila suddenly became a great commercial centre frequented by North Italians, Germans and Dalmatians.

The Italians, not content with developing home resources, continued to expand abroad. Many had established residences in every important city of Western Europe, from Lisbon and Cadiz to London and Bruges (or, later, Antwerp) as agents of home firms or as promoters of 'commercialisation' in less advanced countries. They also extended their influence to countries they had seldom visited in the earlier period. In Germany and Austria they used their superior organisation and business methods to compete with local business men in banking and in export-import trade. In the kingdoms of Poland, Bohemia, Hungary, Serbia and Bulgaria, now for the first time entering fully into the circle of commercial economy, they introduced the luxuries of refined clothing and foodstuffs long familiar to the western gentlemen and bourgeois. They leased salt mines, mints and custom duties. Even when they became citizens of a foreign country, they usually kept very close relations with their fatherland, to which many of them retired to spend their last days. In the Levant and Africa, the oldest fields of their expansion, they adapted their methods to the changed situation. Since the colonies no longer were springboards for direct trade with the Farther East, the Italians intensified the exploitation of local resources and partly shifted their commercial activity from trade in luxuries to trade in cheap staple goods. In Africa and in the Caucasus, they had to learn how to trade with primitive peoples, who had no use for the finer products of European manufacture. It was a profitable experience, although it entailed some disappointments. In 1447 a Genoese brought a lot of quality cloth to the oasis of Tuat, very deep into the Sahara. He hoped to sell the cloth for some gold dust of Palola. But Palola lay still far away, and the negroes of Tuat were all but naked ! The unfortunate pioneer had to prepare his creditors for very bad news by writing a letter where he described his mischance. But a few years later a Florentine merchant, wiser than he, was able to sell cheap Lombard cloth in Timbuktu, on the Niger, where lived more 'progressive' negro tribes. He could not, however, reach mysterious Palola.

On the Black Sea the Italians had been familiar for a longer time with the practices of the untamed tribes of the Caucasus, and hence their business rested on a firm basis. They carried with them salt and coarse shirts, which served as money. In exchange, they obtained caviare and purchased at bargain price slaves, who were more precious than gold in trading with Egypt. The larger part of the Black Sea trade, however, was not with primitive tribes but mostly with young, coming countries of Eastern Europe. Caffa, the thriving capital of the Genoese semi-independent dominions in the Crimea, had lost its function as terminus of Pegolotti's 'quite safe' route to Peking, but it had become the greatest commercial centre of South-eastern Europe, frequented by Tatars of the Kipchak, Russians, Poles, Rumanians, Bulgarians, Turks, Armenians and Greeks. Its cosmopolitan population approached 100,000. Further south-west in the Black Sea was the coast of the Balkan peninsula, where Genoese colonists of Licostomo (Chilia?) and Maurocastro (Akkerman?) competed with the Venetian settlers in Greece and with the merchants from Ragusa and Zara for the growing trade of Walachia, Moldavia, Serbia and Bulgaria. Greece itself and the islands of the Aegean had acquired a new value for the Venetians, and offered an opportunity to develop the export of Cyprus, Cretan and Malmsey wines to new heights. Italy, one would have said, could still look forward to a bright future in the Levant as well as in continental Europe.

In 1453, however, the Turks conquered Constantinople, thus isolating the Italian colonies of the Black Sea and undermining those of the Aegean Sea. In the same year, France victoriously concluded the Hundred Years' War, thus removing the main obstacle to its own economic expansion at home and abroad. Nevertheless, the Italians preserved a large share of Western European trade, and they found ways to do business with the Turks. The beginning of foreign invasions in Italy and the great discoveries of Columbus and Vasco da Gama dealt new blows to the Mediterranean trade; still, Genoese capitalists secured a prominent part in the first ventures to America, and Indian spices during many years of the sixteenth century were cheaper and more abundant in Venice than in Lisbon. The final disasters were the Turkish conquest of Egypt, which ruined commerce through the old route to the Indies, and the Price Revolution, which devalued the capital of the old financiers and caused wages to go up in Spain and Italy faster than in the northern countries. Obviously the primacy of the Mediterranean peoples could not survive so many adversities. Yet the passing of commercial leadership away from the Italians was not like a sudden eclipse. It was a long and glorious twilight, which was still radiant after some of the new stars had sunk back into obscurity. Venice clung to the remnants of her empire in the Levant long after the Portuguese had lost theirs in the Indian Ocean. Genoese bankers tightened their grip on Spanish economy when the great Augsburg companies collapsed. Individual Italians made fortunes abroad when their country lay prostrate under foreign domination. Furthermore, the general progress of trade was such that Mediterranean commerce continued to grow absolutely even though its comparative importance steadily diminished.

There are no sudden changes in economic history, but we must stop somewhere. 1453 is a good terminal point. After that year, the golden age of Mediterranean commerce was definitely over.

CHAPTER VI
The Woollen Industry

EUROPE was as renowned for its textiles in the Middle Ages as today. Many and various fabrics were produced, whether from indigenous fibres such as wool, flax and hemp, from fibres primarily imported such as silk and cotton, or from mixtures of both such as that of cotton with wool or flax. But of all its textiles woollens may well take pride of place. Not only were they manufactured in all parts of the continent, and worn by all classes of the community, from the humblest rustic in his coarse burel to the man of rank and fashion dressed in cloth so fine that it was almost like silk. But they were one of the chief articles of exchange within Europe itself, and they were Europe's principal export to the continents of Asia, Africa and, for a short space, America. The Vikings, venturing westwards across the Atlantic in the eleventh century, carried cloth to barter with the North Americans for furs; so too the Italians, traversing Asia to the court of the Great Khan in the thirteenth century, took with them presents of cloth, and to the end of the Middle Ages Europe's woollens were marketed in bulk at the Mediterranean gateways of Asia and Africa. Widely dispersed as the industry was, three regions became pre-eminent above all others for the large-scale manufacture of woollens—Italy, England, and what may best be described by the Latin term Belgica, that is to say the land between the Somme and the Moselle. In these three regions the development of a great export industry may be studied through a thousand years of medieval history, dimly at first, then more distinctly as the centuries pass, until there can be discerned shifts in its location and changes in its technique not unlike those of more recent centuries, and an industrial organisation as complex and a social structure as unstable as any known today. The problems of an industrial society, with its many thousands of workers dependent upon distant markets and distant sources of raw materials, were all too familiar to Flanders in the thirteenth century, to Italy in the fourteenth, and to England in the fifteenth century.

I. *The Roman World*

Already in Roman days clothmaking was firmly established in these regions as an export industry producing for distant markets. Though no specimens of its work have survived to incite the speculations of the archaeologist, yet there can be no doubt that it developed as rapidly under the Empire as did the pottery and metal industries, showing not less marked, if less easily detected, changes in volume, location and organisation. Demand was expanding with the increase of wealth and the growing needs of city-dwellers and the army, and the *pax Romana*, bringing with it free trade, improved communications, a stable currency, and a reduction of risk in river, road and sea transport, created new possibilities for the long-distance exchange of raw materials and finished products; a high degree of local specialisation was thus facilitated. Moreover, the woollen industry was an ideal one for a newly developing province. For woollen cloth was in almost universal demand throughout the Empire; being neither fragile nor perishable it was admirably suited to long-distance traffic; and its production could be developed from an already existing domestic industry with comparatively little expenditure of capital. Thus while in every sheep-rearing land clothmaking flourished, in some it acquired an international reputation, and its importance in the trade of the Empire is amply attested by the sections devoted to it in Diocletian's famous edict fixing maximum wages and prices throughout his realms.

Doubtless the primitive household industry, making cloth to be worn by the family which produced it, survived to a considerable extent throughout the Empire, as it still does in some places even today. But it was increasingly giving way to commercial production. Augustus, mindful of the old Roman virtues and shocked at the extravagant garments worn by the Romans of his day, attempted to stem the tide of fashion, setting a royal example of simple living by wearing only clothes spun and woven at home by his sister, his wife and his daughter. And many great Roman ladies of the early Empire, who themselves spurned such manual labour, supervised the making of cloth by their own household slaves, like those spinners, weavers and fullers commemorated in the family vault of the consul Statilius Taurus at Rome. But in the city itself 'homespun' was fast disappearing as rich and poor took their choice from the ever-increasing range of commercially produced fabrics with which the shops were filled. In country districts it lingered longer, both among the peasants and in great households which grew their own wool. Slave women skilled in spinning and weaving were legally regarded as part of the equipment of an estate, and on cold and rainy days when farm work in the open was impossible they were set to their tasks, with wool combed and prepared for them beforehand. Even so the allurements of speciality fabrics were great. Wives, lamented Columella, disdained stuffs made at home, and with perverse desire took a fancy to clothing that cost large sums, perhaps as much as a whole year's income. Giving way to luxury and idleness they 'deigned not to carry the burden of manufacturing wool', so that stewardesses had to be appointed to supervise the work in their place. And just as luxury clothing was being purchased on the market by the rich, so cheap mass-produced clothing was coming into vogue for the poor. Homespun was too good for the ordinary slaves on a great estate. It might be used with advantage to the owner's purse, says Columella, for stewards, overseers and the better class of slaves; for the rest it was cheaper to buy.

In the main, then, the Romans of the early Empire, rich and poor, supplied their need for cloth from a specialised industry. In part this was what may be described as a handcraft industry, if we may use this term for an industry of independent, isolated artisans, living by the produce of their craft and working usually on commission direct for their customers, often making up the customer's own material. But to a much greater extent it was a large-scale industry, located often in regions far from Rome, operating under the direction of capitalist entrepreneurs, and organised for export to distant markets. It is with this *grande industrie* that we are here concerned.

In lands of the Middle East, with civilisations much older than that of Rome, such a 'great industry' had long existed. New impetus was no doubt given to it by the growth of imperial trade, and fine woollens from Greece and Phrygia found their way to the Roman market. But there was no marked development or intensification, no startling change in organisation or technique, and it was for other textiles that the region became especially famous. Egypt, most highly industrialised of all, grew rich not by woollens but by linens, mass-produced for the natives of Somaliland and shipped also to India, and by cloths woven from Indian cottons and Chinese silks, sent westwards to Rome to compete with the old-fashioned woollens of which the toga had always been made.

The really striking advance was in the West. First to develop a large-scale woollen industry here was Southern Italy. Her rapid industrialisation in the first century of the Empire was doubtless due as much to close contacts with Alexandria and the more highly developed regions of the Middle East as to the growing demands of the Roman market. From time immemorial the Romans had clothed themselves in the wool of their own sheep, and in Southern Italy sheep were to be found on every farm; they flourished particularly on the slopes of the Apennines, especially in Apulia and Calabria. There, in the little market towns at the foot of the mountains, the wool was sold to discriminating buyers, quick to appreciate differences of quality and texture; the wool of Canusium, for instance, was known to be softer than that of Tarentum, but not so glossy. There, as at Telesia, *lanariae* were built by the town officials for the sale or perhaps the preparation of the wool, while

Beneventum had its 'clerk of the wool accounts'. There too, as at Cannae, Corfinium and Amiternum, congregated the *lanipendiae* who most probably organised the putting out of the wool for spinning. For spinning then, as indeed until power was applied to it in the eighteenth century, was a process commonly entrusted to women working in their own homes. It was a stage in the making of cloth in which use could profitably be made of part-time as well as whole-time labour, in the countryside as well as in the towns, provided there were adequate arrangements for the distribution of the wool and for the collection and scrutiny of the finished yarn, to ensure that this was of full weight and of even quality. These little market towns throve on the traffic in wool and yarn. Sometimes, too, they became manufacturing towns, making up the yarn into cloth, particularly of the cheaper sorts. Such was Canusium, whose serviceable russets, 'like in colour to turbid mead', were sold in vast quantities at Rome in the first century for slaves like those Syrians of Martial's epigram who, 'dressed in Canusian wool, sweated beneath their litter poles'.

But much of the wool went down to the coast, in the form of raw wool, of yarn, or of unfinished webs, there to be fulled, dyed, finished and marketed as high-priced cloth. At Pompeii, for instance, the fullers took it in hand, as is vividly depicted in the frescoes of the House of the Vettii and on the walls of a *fullonica* there. First the raw webs were pounded under foot in a trough, with water, soap and fullers' earth. This served to cleanse them and free them from grease and also to shrink and to felt them, thus producing a firm, compact, unshrinkable cloth some two thirds the length, perhaps, of the original web. Then they were stretched on a frame so that they would dry to precisely the right size. Finally, while still damp, the nap was raised with a hedgehog skin or an instrument set with the *spina fullonia* (predecessor of the medieval teasel), and, when dry, cut with shears to a level surface, giving the cloth a smooth and even silky face after it had been pressed. Fulling was a process which demanded not only skill and a certain amount of equipment but also a considerable space of open ground for drying and a plentiful supply of clear, fresh water. From this it followed that fulleries were often set up along a watercourse in close proximity to each other and that there was need for regulating the use of the water. This may well have been one of the reasons for the frequent formation of gilds among the fullers, in Roman as in medieval times. At any rate it is clear that at Pompeii the owners of the fulleries were associated together and also that they were men of substance, concerned not merely with fulling the cloth but with selling it, and possibly acting as entrepreneurs organising its production. The great hall built at Pompeii for the fullers by the lady Eumachia is scarcely suited to a fullery, but, with its large court and colonnaded corridor, it is admirably designed for an exchange. Chance has preserved for us these tangible evidences of the fuller's trade in what was probably one of Italy's smaller industrial centres. Elsewhere in Southern Italy the fullers may have been equally, if not more, important, but little record of them has survived beyond the fact that at Arpinium there were fulleries built by the town, while there and at Spoletium, Falerium and Rome there were fullers' gilds.

Further south, Tarentum was noted for its fine wool and for its russets in the first century, and it became yet more famous for its dyeworks as the purple fisheries of the Mediterranean were developed to meet the rising demand for luxury cloths; only the wealthiest could go clothed in such purple, for the cost of dyeing a garment in this exotic medium was nearly one hundred times the cost of the wool required for weaving it. And when in the later days of the Empire private enterprise gave way more and more to state enterprise and the state itself engaged in industry on a large scale, then imperial dyeworks (*bafia*) were established at Tarentum, as imperial weaving shops also (*gynaecia*) were set up in South Italy at Venusia and Canusium.

Northern Italy, too, produced fine wool on the slopes of the Alps and the Apennines, and in the first century of the Christian era there was a woollen industry in the Po basin, whence Patavium sent quantities of clothing of all sorts to Rome. In the second and third centuries this industry continued to flourish and, stimulated no doubt by the development of the Danube provinces and the proximity of the Danube armies, it developed yet further until it quite outstripped the industry of the South, whose decline became apparent. In the great industrial towns of the North, such as Parma, Mutina or Altinum, standardised fabrics were mass-produced on a scale which implied considerable specialisation of labour and a high degree of organisation. There was a woolcombers' gild at Brixia and a woolcarders' gild at Brixellum. Verona was known for its blankets; Patavium for its stout frieze called *gausapa*; Pollentia, like Canusium, sold coarse cloth for slaves. Here too the state set up its factories when state enterprise became the fashion under the later Empire. Mediolanum and Aquileia had imperial *gynaecia*, weaving perhaps for the frontier armies, and the needs of these legions may also have been met by the *gynaecium* close to the Danube at Sirmium and by that on the Adriatic at Salona. There was also a *gynaecium* in Rome.

So actively did the cloth industry of Italy develop that her own wool, on which it at first depended, was soon insufficient to feed her looms, and from the first century of the Empire she was importing supplies from other regions, particularly from Asia Minor, Sicily, Spain and

Gaul. Most important as a source of raw materials was Spain. Once Spanish cloth had been much in request in Rome. Spanish cloaks had been taken as tribute from the conquered Celtiberi, and much cloth had come from Baetica. But now it was wool rather than cloth which was in demand. Cheaper varieties came from the North and a very fine quality from the South. Finest of all was the surpassingly beautiful black wool from the pastures of Baetica, where sheep were scientifically reared by Roman farmers such as Columella's uncle, who sent to Africa for breeding rams. From this was made a much admired dark cloth which could compete on the market even with that made of Tarentine wool dyed in Tyrian purple, boasting of itself:

> Non est lana mihi mendax nec mutor aheno;
> Sic placeant Tyriae: me mea tinxit ovis.

In South Spain the Romans also developed the production of dyes, procuring thence red dyes such as cinnabar, Sinopean earth and, more especially, large quantities of kermes. Kermes was made from the dried body of an insect (*coccus ilicis*) which feeds on a species of oak found in Mediterranean lands. It was imported from Asia Minor as well as from Spain and yielded a scarlet dye of exceptional brilliance and permanence, vying in excellence with Tyrian purple, which in time it came wholly to supersede in the West. Though costly as compared with vegetable dyes it was cheap as compared with those from the purple fisheries. To dye 1 lb. of wool with Nicene kermes, according to Diocletian's edict, might cost as much as 1500 *denarii*, as compared with 600 *denarii* for orchil purple and 16,000 *denarii* for Tyrian purple.

Thus Spain, though continuing to make some cloth of her own, became primarily a supplier of raw materials to the Italian industry. So too it was with Mediterranean Gaul. Sheep were reared on the slopes of the Cevennes and the Pyrenees, where still they may be seen depicted on the funereal monuments of the Roman period, and wool was shipped thence to Italy through the port of Narbo. At Narbo also, and at Telo, imperial dye-works were established, completing a chain of such state factories round the Western Mediterranean, for in addition to those in the gulf of Tarentum there were a number in the province of Africa and in the Balearic Isles. But apart from an imperial *gynaecium* at Arelate and another higher up the Rhone at Lugdunum, there is no trace of any large-scale woollen manufacture in Southern Gaul. In Western Gaul there seems to have been some development of the industry on the lower Garonne, for cloaks of the Bituriges were listed at a high price in the edict of Diocletian.

The most remarkable development of the industry was in Nor-thern Gaul, which witnessed an advance even more striking than that of North Italy, and one typical of the decentralisation of industry in imperial times as the centre declined in importance and economic activity on the periphery increased. In part no doubt this indicated a transference of production to the region of consumption. But it was more than this. For Northern Gaul, like Northern Italy, became an exporter on a considerable scale. The extent of her industrialisation is shown by the profusion of sepulchral monuments to workers in the woollen industry; only in Italy is there any comparable number. The manufacturing region stretched right across the country of the Belgae, from the Somme to the Moselle, through the modern Picardy, Artois, Western Belgium, Champagne and Lorraine, then occupied by the tribes of the Ambiani, Atrebates, Nervii, Remi, Treveri and Mediomatrici, with their Romanised cities of Ambiani (Amiens), Atrebates (Arras), Turnacum (Tournai), Remi (Rheims), Augusta Treverorum (Trèves), and Augustoduno (Metz).

Gallic cloaks (*saga*) and Gallic wool were finding a market in Rome in the first century of the Empire, but the wool was then rough and flocky and the fabrics woven from it coarse. Hence Gallic garments were at first the dress of the common folk, bearing the same relation, remarked Martial, to purple dyed garments made in Rome as did Arretine pottery to the finest crystal. Nevertheless they became increasingly popular, if only for the warmth and protection afforded by the stout cloaks with their capacious hoods. The development of the industry was therefore a profitable field for investment, and before long Roman sheep-farmers had succeeded in producing a much improved fleece, with the result that in due course Belgica was exporting to Italy both high-grade wool and also high-grade cloth, fetching as good a price as any. The quantity of wool produced was as notable as its quality, particularly in the region of the Atrebates. It is related by Orosius that one year real wool, mixed with rain, here fell from the clouds, and whatever the origin of his tale there can be no doubt that in the fourth century the wool of this district was peculiarly abundant and excellent. In the price edict of Diocletian it was rated more highly than any other wool, even that of Tarentum. Garments made from it were no longer scoffed at by fashionable Romans, but competed with the finest Italian clothing. Not only were they worn by Romans living in Gaul, but in Italy too they became the rage; an Atrebatic *sagum* was as indispensable in the fourth century for a well-to-do Roman as linen from Egypt. Equally famous for cloaks of high value, according to Diocletian's edict, were the immediate neighbours of the Atrebates—the Ambiani, the Treveri and the Nervii; indeed Nervian cloaks were so popular that they were being imitated in Asia Minor. It is scarcely surprising that in a region so amply provided with fine wool and skilled craftsmanship, four imperial *gynaecia* were set up—at Turnacum, Remi, Augusta Treverorum and Augustoduno.

Apart from the existence of these state workshops little can be said with certainty as to the organisation of the industry in Belgica. We do not even know to what extent it was concentrated in the towns. Some of the clothing was probably exported in a semi-finished state, for there is mention in Diocletian's edict of the price for fulling new Nervian cloaks (*birri*). But that some fulling and finishing was carried out in Gaul would seem to be indicated by the tomb at Sens which shows the fuller trampling cloth in a trough and, above, his three foot long shears. Much dyeing was certainly done, though here the Gauls could not hope to compete with Mediterranean lands since, much as they loved gaudy colours, they had neither the Tyrian purple nor the scarlet *kermes*. Vegetable dyes, however, they cultivated extensively, and with these, relates Pliny, they imitated all the colours, even producing a substitute, if not a fast, Tyrian purple, 'without running the risk of drowning by seeking the mollusc on the sea bottom; without exploiting the deep to multiply the attractions of courtesans'. The sepulchral monuments at Arlon in the heart of the cloth country, depicting men at work stirring a deep vat, have puzzled the archaeologists, but there can be little doubt that in fact they represent dyers. From the monuments, indeed, it would seem as though fullers and dyers were in a position of special importance and were men of substance as compared with the other workers. This is to be expected in view of the capital equipment they required and the fact that they were concerned with the finishing processes of clothmaking. Even more important were the cloth merchants with their expert knowledge of the foreign markets on which the very life of the industry depended. Such were the Secundini, commemorated by the sumptuous monument at Igel near Trèves, whereon may be seen their bales of precious cloth in course of transport, first by barge along a river, then on mule-back over a lofty mountain range, doubtless up the Rhine, over the Alps and into Italy itself.

In Britain, last of all the western provinces to be developed, we hear nothing of the production of cloth for export until the fourth century. But by the time of Diocletian's edict a Britannic *birrus* was on the market, fetching a good price, above that of the Canusian if below that of the Nervian *birrus*. There was also one imperial *gynaecium*, at Winchester. Beyond this we know nothing for certain of the British woollen industry in Roman times. All else is conjecture. The remains of troughs very similar in form to those depicted in the *fullonica* at Pompeii have been found in three villas—at Titsey and Darenth in Kent and at Chedworth in Gloucestershire—and since in each case they are in close proximity to beds of fullers' earth it may plausibly be argued that there were fulleries there. Traces of what may perhaps have been dye-works have also been found at Silchester. All that can be said with confidence is that a British export industry in high quality cloths existed, though it was slower to develop than that of Belgica, and never reached comparable proportions in Roman times.

II. *The Northern Industry in Transition*

What then became of this flourishing industry, with its trading connections throughout Europe and perhaps beyond, when the Empire disintegrated? Most probably it never wholly disappeared, but of its fate in the first few centuries after the collapse of Roman rule little can be known for lack of records. Certainly sheep were still reared, even if on a diminished scale; some tradition of manufacturing techniques persisted, and clothmaking continued, not merely as a domestic craft for supplying the needs of the family, but as an industry of expert artisans, working at least for a local if not for an international market. In the glimpses that we have of sixth-century Gaul the independent artisan working on commission appears in the pages of Gregory of Tours, who tells of an *artifex lanariae* called in to manufacture the royal stock of wool and of the manager of a corn mill who also '*pectinibus insedit lanasque conposuit*'. In England, when at the end of the seventh century the first clear picture of Anglo-Saxon life emerges in the pages of Bede, sheep-flocks are part of the scene; it was while Cuthbert lay awake on the mountains one night tending a flock entrusted to his care as his companions slept, that he saw the vision which tempted him to enter a monastery. And early in the following century woollen cloaks and tunics such as Anglo-Saxon clerics were accustomed to wear in England ('*sicut mos est apud nos habendi*') were sent overseas to the English missionaries on the continent, where they proved most acceptable presents to those faced with the unaccustomed rigours of a winter in the heart of Germany. Boniface, though he bought some of his clothing near the scene of his missionary labours in Frisia, looked out none the less eagerly for woollens from England. 'If it would not be too much trouble', he wrote to the Abbot of Wearmouth, 'pray send us a cloak, for this would be a great comfort on our journeys.' To the Abbess of Thanet he spoke of the comfort of the garments with which she had relieved his distress, while King Ethelbert of Kent included two woollen cloaks in the gift parcel he sent him. In a century when English people were to be found throughout Western Europe and the Levant as missionaries, merchants, pilgrims, scholars, bishops, monks or nuns, it is, indeed, not surprising that English woollens should have been found there too.

There seems no reason to suppose that clothing such as was sent to the English missionaries abroad was manufactured by the religious communities themselves, rather than by lay artisans. All the evidence points to the contrary. Nuns, indeed, sometimes occupied themselves with weaving, like those nuns of St Andrew at Florence who wove five pieces of solid stuff for the chief of their order from the wool which he sent them. But in general they seem to have been concerned with weaving as an art, for the production of small luxury articles such as altar cloths, rather than as an industry for the production of everyday clothing, and so it continued as a pleasant occupation for ladies of leisure, lay or religious, throughout the Middle Ages. The seventh-century nuns of Coldingham were censured because they spent their leisure in the weaving of fine garments with which to adorn themselves as brides, instead of in the care of their souls. Ordinary clothing was from earliest times purchased at markets often far distant from the monasteries themselves, as is made abundantly clear by monastic charters. A seventh-century charter, for instance, exempted the members of the religious houses of Corbie and St Denis from tolls when they travelled to buy clothing, and the same was doubtless true of similar houses in England and Italy. The real importance of the religious communities, as of the great lay households, in this connection lies in the fact that they provided a steady market for commercially produced cloth.

There can thus be no doubt that a considerable woollen industry existed in Western Europe in the seventh and early eighth centuries, and that much cloth was bought and sold on the open market. But of the size, structure and location of the industry little can at present be said, except that in England at least it catered for exports. Clearly it would be a mistake to measure the importance of the industry by the extent of the available evidence, for historical sources of the kind familiar to students of industrial history in the later Middle Ages scarcely exist for this period.

By the end of the eighth century the picture becomes somewhat more distinct, and we can discern what may be described as a North Sea centre of the industry, comprising the English kingdoms and the north-east part of the Carolingian Empire (as it was at Charlemagne's accession). Here, as in Roman days, there was firmly established an export industry in fine quality cloaks highly valued for their wool and for their colour; an industry fostered by wise rulers such as Offa and Charlemagne and second to none in Europe.

Important as it was, the scope of this industry must not be exaggerated, for not everyone depended upon it as in the world of to-day. Some at least of the great households then, as in Roman days, made up their own wool on the spot, setting their domain serfs to card, spin, full,

weave and dye. In this way, as Columella had pointed out, the good
estate manager could profitably employ much labour in the winter or
during bad weather when work in the open was impossible. Thus in
the royal capitularies of Charlemagne the *villici* of his rural estates were
instructed to see that the women's workshops (*gynaecia*) were well
furnished with wool, linen, woad, madder, vermilion, wool-combs,
teasels, soap, oil, and other necessaries. To what extent the products of
these workshops were marketed, in accordance with the instructions to
the *villici* to strive to improve the income of the estates, it is impossible
to say. Charlemagne, like Augustus, believed in the virtues of homespun, though only, according to Einhard, as a means of keeping his
daughters out of mischief. More important was his encouragement of
native woollens by his preference for them over the exotic silks and
other stuffs of Byzantium suited to the dignity of an Emperor. With
his hatred of foreign garments, however beautiful, and his refusal to
wear them except when in Rome, and then only at the request of the
Pope, he set a vogue for Frankish clothes which must have stimulated
sales at home as much as his presents to far-distant monarchs like
Haroun al Raschid must have stimulated them abroad.

Much discussion has raged around the precise origin of those Frisian
cloaks (*pallia fresonica*) which Charlemagne himself wore and which
played so important a part in the international commerce of his day.
Were they in fact the produce of Frisia, or were they made elsewhere,
in Flanders or in England, and called Frisian because the Frisian traders
marketed them? Probably Pirenne was right in seeing in them evidence
of an exporting industry either in the Low Countries or in their immediate vicinity. At any rate they assuredly indicate the production
somewhere in that region of fine quality cloth, dyed and finished,
and much in demand over a wide area. *Pallia fresonica* fetched a high
price, according to a capitulary of 808, and though Louis the Pious
himself disdained his father's preference for native wear and still on
great feasts gave silk to the highest dignitaries at his court, yet *pallia
fresonica* were considered sufficiently good for officers of the second rank
and were evidently very superior to the common stuffs given to simple
domestics. If such cloth found its way by ancient routes to the Levant
and on to Baghdad with Charlemagne's embassy, there perhaps to
excite a demand among the Caliph's subjects, it seems also to have gone
to newly developing markets among the Vikings of the far North
where, in the ninth century, cloth of 'Valland' was in use in Norway.
Nearer home it gave rise to a vigorous traffic, for the Frisians carried it
not only by sea along the coasts of the North Sea, but also inland up the
Rhine, where it provided a good exchange for more southerly products. Ernold le Noir, in exile in Strasbourg in the reign of Louis the

Pious, remarked that the people of the Vosges were receiving from the Frisians cloaks of diverse colours such as they had not known hitherto, in exchange for the corn and wine which they exported down the Rhine to the sea.

The acceptance of Pirenne's conclusions need not involve the rejection of the idea of an English exporting industry. Nor is such a rejection possible. For, as we have seen, English cloaks were going to the continent in considerable numbers during the first half of the eighth century. And in the second half of the century they were the subject of diplomatic exchanges between the Carolingian empire and Mercia, paramount power in England. Charlemagne's letter to Offa saying that his subjects were complaining of the 'prolixity' of the cloaks (*saga*) sent from England, and asking that they should be made 'as of old', suggests that the traffic was a regular one of long standing, and that the industry was one producing standardised articles and susceptible to some measure of state regulation. Whether such cloaks were sold for consumption in Charlemagne's realm or despatched yet further afield by Frankish merchants we have no means of knowing, but Offa, who struck coins in imitation of those of Haroun al Raschid, may at least have dreamed that English, like Frisian, woollens should reach the court of Baghdad.

Thus when at the opening of the ninth century the Vikings began to raid the shores of the North Sea on both sides of the English Channel they descended on a region prosperous industrially as well as agriculturally. Its cloth excited their cupidity as much as its corn and its wine. For they had few sheep in their own country and coveted the comfort of good woollens without as much as that of good wines within. As pirates they captured ships laden with cloth; as peaceful traders they bargained for it, exchanging fish, skins and furs from the North. In the ninth century cloth of 'Valland' was known in Norway; and by the end of the tenth and on into the eleventh century there is abundant evidence of woollens from the North Sea region being sold there. So Egil's saga relates how Thorolf sent his large sea-going ship to England 'to buy woollen cloth and other goods he needed'. So too King Sverrir thanked all those Englishmen who brought to his land 'wheat and honey, flour and cloth'.

If some of the cloth imported by Norway was English and some Frankish, some may also have been Irish. The *saga* brought by Irish merchants to Cambridge in 975 may, or may not, have been of Irish manufacture. But there is evidence of cloth being sent from Ireland to Brittany in pre-Carolingian days, and the Irish were certainly highly skilled in weaving wool as well as linen, as also in dyeing and embroidering it. Fine work was done by the women of the great houses, some of which, like Charlemagne's villas, grew their own dyestuffs; in many a cottage weaving was carried on as a bye-industry, as in the home of the poor widow of Fingal who, when visited by St Brigid, sacrificed the new beam of her loom in order that she might make a fire and cook upon it her only calf; and the important part played by the industry in the economy of the country is shown by the Book of Rights (*circa* 900) which speaks of tribute being paid in thread and wool, in cloaks and in napped cloaks. Such cloaks, often finely embroidered, must have been eagerly sought after by Norse traders as well as by Norse settlers in Ireland.

Thus the Vikings provided themselves with fine woollens from the West as with fine silks and satins from the East, and the splendour of their brightly coloured clothing was the envy of all beholders. And when they ventured forth across the Atlantic it was red cloth that they took to barter with the North Americans for furs. For a good skin, relates the Flatey Book, the natives received a span of cloth, and when the supply began to run out the Norsemen cut the cloth into smaller and smaller pieces, till the fragments measured not more than a finger's breadth.

There can be no doubt of the immense impetus given to the woollen industry in the North Sea region by the expansion of the Viking peoples, whose wealth and prosperity created a new demand, and whose far-flung trade routes facilitated the exchange of fine cloth over a wide area and the development of specialised manufacturing centres importing raw materials and marketing their cloth in distant lands. By the end of the eleventh and the beginning of the twelfth century we can discern not merely small groups of craftsmen gathered around monastery, cathedral or castle as fullers had been gathered at St Riquier in the ninth century, but large congregations of weavers and other cloth workers, contributing not a little to the growth of the cities, to the development of their free institutions, and to the whole urban renaissance of the time.

If the rapid growth of the northern industry in the eleventh century was in part due to the external stimulus of widening markets, it was in part also due to the internal development of the area, to its rising population, and to an intensified exploitation of its natural resources. Such a development was in turn dependent upon a politically stable regime, and it was probably for this reason that the district which at this time leapt most rapidly ahead, outdistancing all its rivals, was that which came under the enlightened rule of the Counts of Flanders.

In the County of Flanders, stretching from Arras to the Scheldt, there were unmistakable signs in the eleventh century of a surplus population which could no longer support itself upon the land. Many

Flemings joined the Crusades, or enrolled themselves in the armies of the Normans setting out for the conquest of Sicily or of a distracted England. Others flocked to the towns, swelling the number of landless artisans and providing the labour supply for the great urban industry, which lived by the exchange of its manufactures for food. Others again assisted in bringing new lands under cultivation by dyking, draining and clearing the wastes along the coast, and the new pastures there created sustained many thousands of sheep whose wool fed the looms of the growing industrial towns. More and more Flanders industrialised herself. New towns rose; ancient ones revived and expanded, with suburbs full of cloth workers—weavers, fullers, dyers and others— sprawling over what had once been countryside. Virtually every town in Flanders was a textile town, living by its export trade. Markets grew up, therefore, for the purchase of food and raw materials and for the sale of the finished cloth. Ghent had an active market at the opening of the century, when Adelard of Tournai arrived there with his boat laden with wool and other goods. Wool, dyestuffs and teasels were amongst the goods for which tolls were charged at Arras and St Omer in 1024 and in 1043. At fairs, such as that of Thourout, cloth was bought and sold. Merchant gilds, such as that at Valenciennes with its own cloth hall, concerned themselves both with the import of food and raw materials and with the marketing of the finished products. The reputation of Flemish cloth in the latter part of the eleventh century is shown by the poem in praise of wool by Winric of Trèves—*Conflictus Ovis et Lini*. Here Flanders is described as the centre of manufacture for cloth of fine quality, producing a fabric of exquisite finish far superior to that of her neighbours, and exporting it to England, France and Germany.

In the clothing towns of Flanders we begin gradually to discern not only associations of merchants, such as that of Valenciennes, but also associations of artisans, drawn together by common interests, common problems, and common needs in this world and the next. The origins of these associations are still obscure and will probably always remain a matter of conjecture. Yet certain factors in their early development may clearly be discerned. Almost every town possessed its Street of the Fullers and its Street of the Dyers, each on a watercourse. This suggests a specifically industrial factor. Both fullers and dyers required ample supplies of clear water. It was therefore essential that agreements should be reached among themselves to regulate the use of the streams and to prevent their pollution or interruption. Moreover, it was often equally necessary for common action to be taken in securing from the owners the right to use the streams, and in maintaining that right against other claimants; for many disputes arose about these rights, such as that at Douai in 1220 when the canons of St Amé claimed

£20 damages on the ground that the working of their corn mill was interrupted by the waste matter thrown into the stream up above it by the dyers. And just as workers living together in close proximity united to protect and regulate their trade, so too they joined together for mutual succour in distress, forming their own philanthropic fraternities; many such fraternities would seem to have been in existence in the twelfth century, though their surviving statutes do not go back beyond the thirteenth. Religion played as important a part as social security in the creation of the craft associations, for it prompted the foundation of societies to promote the welfare of their members in the world to come by the erection of a chapel or at least a permanent altar in their parish church, dedicated to a particular saint whom they took as their patron, and provided with a priest to say mass there regularly; such was the society of fullers and shearmen of St Trond.

In England, as in Flanders, the expansion of the woollen industry went forward with remarkable rapidity in the twelfth century, though in the previous century it had somewhat lagged behind. The strong rule of the Norman kings, the privileges granted by them to merchants and to towns on royal demesne, and the gradual emergence of a stable system of national government, all favoured its growth. So also did the influx of Flemish artisans in the wake of the conquest. In natural resources England was potentially quite as rich as Flanders. She too had fine pastures on which at the time of the Domesday survey there grazed flocks of many thousands of sheep. Her soil also was rich in fullers' earth and suited to the cultivation of teasels and of dyestuffs such as madder, weld and woad; the instructions in the eleventh-century *Gerefa* for the planting of madder and woad show that their production was common on many estates. Yet in the late twelfth century England's own dyestuffs were insufficient for her needs. Nowhere is the progress of her industry more clearly shown than by the fact that in the reign of Richard I she was importing large quantities of woad. Clothmaking was clearly England's premier industry, and though primarily she was still an agricultural land her manufactures were by no means negligible. Her cloth was taking its place on the European markets, and by the end of the century was the subject of national legislation. The Assize of Measures (1197) decreed that the production of dyed cloth for the market should be carried on only in the towns; it also fixed a uniform standard of width, proclaiming that cloth, wherever made, should be two ells wide within the lists, and of the same quality in the middle as at the sides.

Inevitably there grew up in England, as in Flanders, gilds of merchants concerned, amongst other matters, with securing the provision of raw materials for the textile industry as well as with the marketing of its finished wares. In cities where such gilds existed all dealing in cloth, as well as the dyeing and finishing of cloth for the market, was strictly confined to their members, and it may well have been they who inspired the Assize of Measures. At the same time many of the artisans congregated in the towns were forming gilds of their own, seeking royal sanction for them, as did the merchants, when they were in towns on royal demesne. In the earliest extant account of the royal exchequer (1130–31) there is record of payments made for such gilds by the weavers of London, Winchester, Lincoln, Oxford, Nottingham and Huntingdon, and by the fullers of Winchester. A few years later the York weavers' gild appears, paying £10. From the size of the sums paid for their privileges it is clear that these gilds were greater in numbers and importance than those of any other artisans.

Thus by the twelfth century the woollen industry of the North Sea region, whose roots stretched far back into the past, had developed afresh with astonishing speed, reaching the stage of large-scale urban manufacture of standardised fabrics for sale to distant markets. On the busy Scandinavian routes along the Baltic and the North Sea, from the Slav lands of the East to Ireland in the West, a lively interchange was carried on. Flemish cloth was well known not only in Germany but as far east as Novgorod, where each year the Fraternity of Merchants of Saint John the Baptist gave a whole cloth of Ypres to the Bishop when he said mass for them on the feast of their patron saint. English cloth was known on the Rhine and was much in demand in all Scandinavian lands; when Sweyn Olaf's son, cruising off Dublin in 1171, captured two ships out from England laden with English cloth, he returned in triumph to the Orkneys, displaying his booty by sewing the cloth to his sails, and ever after his voyage was known as 'the broadcloth cruise' (*skrúð víking*).

But already this northern traffic was beginning to be eclipsed by another, surpassing it in volume and importance. Italian merchants, journeying over the Alpine passes, had by the opening of the twelfth century penetrated to Flanders and crossed over to do business in England. By the middle of the century they were regularly visiting the fairs of Champagne at which much cloth was marketed. Flemish merchants too were making their way to Italy, and a steady stream of northern textiles was moving south towards the Mediterranean ports, some of them to be sold in Italy but most destined ultimately for Africa and the Levant. Trade with the East was transformed. Cloth now more and more took the place of the specie that had once gone East to pay for the spices, silk, gold, ivory and precious stones imported thence. Not only was the balance of trade to some extent redressed, but a great expansion of imports followed. Together with the luxuries which from time immemorial had formed the staple of the trade came raw materials for the cloth industry, particularly dyestuffs. Indeed the volume of raw materials despatched north across the Alps was perhaps as great as that of luxuries. The expansion of the Mediterranean trade and the expansion of the northern textile industry, acting and reacting upon each other, had built up in Africa and the Near East an immense new market for Europe's quantity-produced textiles, and immeasurably increased Europe's buying power, creating new demands for oriental luxuries.

No longer content with the native herbs, such as woad and madder, used by their Frankish and Saxon forebears, the northern dyers vastly extended the range and variety of their colours with more exotic products from Asia as well as from the Mediterranean. Kermes, now commonly called grain (*granum*), from Asia Minor, Spain and Portugal was now used in the North as it had been in the South in Roman days; with it was dyed the costly scarlet worn by kings. Other red dyes were undoubtedly of Eastern origin. Brasil, now used in large quantities in England and Flanders, was prepared from the wood of an East Indian tree (*Caesalpina Sappau*); the finest quality came from Ceylon, according to Marco Polo who brought seeds of it to set and sow in Venice. Brasil wood was frequently a return cargo in ships from the Levant, as also was vermilion—a mineral dye made from a crystalline substance said to have been found on the shores of the Red Sea, and gumlac, the resinous material exuded by an insect (*Coccus Lacca*) on the bark of certain trees in Southern Asia. Saffron, the bright yellow derived from the stamens of the autumn crocus, was also procured in the Levant, though much was produced in Europe itself. Even more important were the large shipments of alum, one of the principal mordants used in fixing the dyes. The alum of Northern Europe was very inferior to that of the South, and the principal sources of supply were now in Asia Minor and the Black Sea, particularly in the mines of Phocæa, exploited for over a millennium by the Greeks and now in the possession of the Genoese.

Thus by the end of the twelfth century the northern industry had come to depend in large measure upon far-distant Mediterranean markets both for its raw materials and for the marketing of its finished products. This fact is of cardinal importance for the understanding of its history. For it vitally affected both the progress of the industry and, as we shall see later, its organisation. It is assuredly no coincidence that the period when the Mediterranean trade was at its height, from the late twelfth to the late thirteenth century, was a period of great prosperity for the northern industry, and a period also of stability, when demand was increasing and industry developing, but along lines already well established, with no sharp break in continuity. It is a period which

ends with widespread labour troubles and industrial depression in many
old centres of the industry, and at the same time with the restriction of
the Mediterranean market, as Acre was lost to the Christians and trade
with Egypt prohibited, and as the Asiatic markets became more and
more uncertain and the direct routes to the Far East, though continuing,
more and more curtailed.

III. The Zenith of Flanders: Thirteenth-Century Capitalism

While no quantitative estimates are possible of the amounts of cloth
marketed in the Levant, yet from the records of Mediterranean ports
such as Venice, Genoa, Marseilles and Barcelona it is possible to assess
with some confidence the relative importance of the different centres
of production concerned in this export trade. All such records emphasise
the primary importance of the northern producing region, both for
quality and for quantity, and, within that region, the paramount
position held by the industry of Flanders and its immediate neighbourhood, with the English industry contributing cloth comparable in
quality though less in quantity. Moreover for the first time the
abundance of documents enables us clearly to define the chief production areas.

Densest of all was the concentration of industry in the County of
Flanders, one of the wealthiest, if also one of the most troublesome,
fiefs of the crown of France. Here, between the Canche and the Zwin,
in a region bounded eastwards by the Scheldt, almost every town, great
and small, was busy with the manufacture of woollens, and there were
at least a dozen centres whose cloth had won so distinctive a reputation
as to be marketed under its own name in France, Spain, Italy and beyond. In the South, French Flanders was again renowned for its cloth
as in the days of the Atrebates and the Nervii. Here pride of place was
taken by five great clothing towns: Arras and St Omer in Artois—rich
prize of war severed from the County of Flanders at the end of the
twelfth century by Philip Augustus; Douai, Lille, and Tournai. Lesser
centres with an active export trade in their own distinctive lines included Hesdin, Aire-sur-Lys and Béthune in Artois, Orchies and Bail-
leul. Northwards, in Flemish Flanders, whose industrial fame stretched
back into no such remote antiquity, there were three pre-eminent
centres—Ypres, Ghent and Bruges, and many subsidiary ones such
as Poperinghe, Dixmude, Wervicq, Courtrai and Oudenarde. Cloths
of Ypres, well known throughout Northern Europe in the early twelfth
century, surpassed all others on the southern markets towards the end

of the century, both in number and variety. And though cloths of Ghent also were then appearing on the Mediterranean market, it was not until the turn of the century that they, with cloths of Bruges, were coming to rival the products of more southerly towns such as Ypres.

While Flanders reigned supreme, there were nevertheless important extensions of the textile region southwards into the adjacent French provinces of Ponthieu and Vermandois and eastwards across the frontiers of the Empire into Brabant, Hainault and the Bishopric of Cambrai. In Vermandois, Amiens and St Quentin on the Somme, and Beauvais further south, were of primary importance, while Corbie was a considerable secondary centre. Lower down the Somme in Ponthieu lay Abbéville, with Montreuil-sur-Mer to the north, both primary centres. Even more important were Cambrai and its near neighbour Valenciennes in Hainault, both of which exported large quantities of cloths of many colours, while in Hainault there were also other noted centres such as Maubeuge and Chimay. Brabant, whose industrial development lagged far behind that of Flanders, assumed a steadily growing importance in the course of the thirteenth century, when Brussels cloth, not known on the markets of Genoa in the late twelfth century, was frequently seen in Italy, and was marketed in Paris as was that of Louvain. Malines, geographically though not politically a Brabantine town, was probably earlier in the field; its merchants had their halls in the fairs of Champagne at the end of the twelfth century, and by the mid-thirteenth century its cloth had penetrated to Persia.

Yet further, beyond these provinces, lay other outlying textile towns. In particular, some cloth was exported from the valley of the Meuse—from Liége, Namur, Huy and Maestricht; while Rheims and Champagne cities such as Châlons-sur-Marne, Provins and Aubenton were all centres of production as well as of exchange. There can be no doubt, however, that first place on the export markets was taken by the cities of Flanders—French and Flemish, with the cities of Brabant a good second by the end of the thirteenth century. It is these which the author of the *Dit de Lendit* singles out, in his long enumeration of clothmaking towns exhibiting their wares at the fair of St Denis, as producing the finest merchandise of all:

> En mon dit, vous amenteuvrai
> Gant et Ypres et puis Douay
> Et Maalines et Broiselles;
> Je les dois bien nommer com celes
> Qui plus belles son a veoir.

The whole of this great manufacturing region, stretching across modern Belgium and North-east France, may be regarded as an economic as well as a geographical unity. For its chief clothmaking towns, though divided politically among a number of different feudal principalities, owing fealty some to the Emperor and some to the King of France, were yet closely linked one with another for the furtherance of their business. Already by the end of the twelfth century they were associated in a commercial gild or *hanse* known throughout the thirteenth century by the name of 'The Seventeen Towns', though by then its membership had grown to some two dozen and more with the admission of towns later to develop such as Ghent and Bruges. Primarily these towns were concerned with regulating their relations with the fairs of Champagne, premier mart throughout this period for the textiles of the North. Together they determined which fairs should be attended; together they negotiated with the officials of the fairs; together they enforced a common discipline on their merchants. Thus the powerful merchant gilds which in each city governed the trade on which that city's life depended were now themselves linked in an intercity gild so that they might frame and execute a common export policy.

The stream of northern textiles flowing East and South was augmented, as we have seen, by cloth from England. This was then in high repute on all the markets with which European traders dealt, as it had been in Roman, Merovingian and Carolingian times. But England was much less industrialised than Flanders, and was herself importing considerable quantities from Flanders. There were indeed organised groups of professional weavers, fullers and dyers in almost every part of the country, from the Lake District and Northumberland down to the South-west, all concerned in the making of cloth for sale. Many towns too were doing business in buying up raw cloth woven in the countryside, dyeing and finishing it for sale; Shrewsbury's charter, for instance, restricted to burgesses the right to purchase '*pannum crudum*', just as the burgesses of Newcastle acquired from Henry I the sole right to purchase '*telas ad tingendam*'. But the fine quality cloths famous in the Spanish and Mediterranean trade in the thirteenth century would seem to have come wholly from that part of the lowland eastern plain which drains into the Humber and the Wash, chiefly from the towns of Lincoln, Stamford, York, Beverley, Louth, Northampton and Leicester. It is here that we can detect Europe's second most important cloth-producing region at this time, a region comparable in extent to Flanders with Artois, though much less densely industrialised. Most noted were the cities of Lincoln (*Nichole*) and Stamford. Their high-priced cloths, dyed often in the scarlet kermes ('in grain'), were much in demand for the royal wardrobe and for presents to overseas sovereigns, and they were constantly exported. Lincoln cloths were singled out for special mention in foreign tariffs, as in the Venetian tariff of 1265. Whether Stamford gave its name to the *stamforts* so popular on the continent, or whether this name was derived from *stamen forte* ('strong warp') will probably never be determined, but there is no doubt that much cloth was exported from Stamford even if all the *stamfortes de Anglia*, more numerous than the *stamforts* of Arras, Ypres and elsewhere, were not made there. Further South of this region lay a number of other industrial towns producing cheaper cloths such as russets and burels, mainly for distribution on the home market among the poorer classes of the community and thus comparable to cloths of Canusium in the ancient world. Chief among these were Colchester, London, Oxford and Winchester, but there was also a considerable internal trade in russets from small centres such as Marlborough, Bedwyn and Totnes.

Nothing could more clearly show the advance of the 'great industry' in the twelfth and thirteenth centuries and the growing interdependence of all parts of Europe upon one another than the extent to which the cloth industry in Flanders and, to a lesser degree, in England was based upon raw materials brought from other lands.

The primary raw material, wool, was, as we have seen, produced both in Flanders and England. But by the thirteenth century England was the principal supplier for the industries of both countries. Flanders was importing not only because her own wool was proving insufficient in quantity with the rapid expansion of industrial output, but also because it was less satisfactory in quality than English wool. Already early in the twelfth century many Flemings had come to England purchasing wool for cash. Such were the merchants who travelled over with the canons of Laon; threatened by pirates, they vowed all their money to Our Lady of Laon, but once safe on land, regardless of their vow, they journeyed 'almost all over the country' spending all they had upon wool. So important was this English wool trade that the merchants of the Flemish towns concerned in it united together in England at that time in the association known as the Flemish Hanse of London. And throughout the thirteenth century Flemish cloth manufacturers were contracting for large supplies, purchased either through agents or direct from the growers. It was Lincolnshire wool, especially from the Lindsey region, which was most in demand for fine quality cloth in Flanders as in the Lincolnshire towns themselves; its excellence may indeed have had much to do with the excellence of Lincolnshire cloth. But considerable quantities were bought by the Flemings in other parts of England and also in Scotland, Wales and Ireland.

Spain also was supplying the northern industry with a certain amount of wool from her rapidly developing sheep-farms, at any rate by the mid-thirteenth century. In England, Spanish wool was used in London and Winchester and doubtless in other parts of the south-eastern manufacturing region. Different in character both from the local downland wool and from the finer Lincolnshire wool, it could not be mixed with either, and regulations prohibiting such mixing still survive in some of the oldest weavers' ordinances of London, dating from the close of the thirteenth century. German wool was also reaching England and Flanders, though in much smaller quantities.

Dyestuffs were drawn from all parts of Europe and from further afield. As we have already seen, the Mediterranean regions yielded the most brilliant and costly red, in the scarlet kermes not to be found in Northern Europe, together with most of the alum used in fixing the dyes, while from tropical regions came other reds—vermilion, lake, and above all brasil. North-west Europe yielded madder, woad and weld. Madder and woad, commonest dyes of all, gave those shades of blue and red, light or dark, which predominate in the backgrounds of medieval tapestries, while woad was used also to produce black. In combination they gave various shades of purple such as violet, sanguine, and burnet (a deep almost black shade), while woad with weld gave greens such as 'Lincoln green'. Yellow, from weld alone, was in little demand. Choicest of all blues was perse, a rich deep shade dyed in woad; cloths of this colour sometimes nearly reached the price of scarlet, whereas the lighter blues such as 'clear blue' and 'azure blue' were cheapest of all the coloured cloths. Some of the purples— 'poenac', for instance, and murrey—could be dyed 'in grain', that is with woad and kermes rather than woad and any other red.

Woad and madder continued to be cultivated in the clothmaking districts of Flanders and England throughout the Middle Ages, as they had been in Saxon and Carolingian times and doubtless in Roman times also, and as they continued to be until recently. To some extent, therefore, the industries of both countries drew on local supplies; woad mills and madder mills, for crushing woad leaves and madder roots, were a feature of the clothing districts in the thirteenth century. But there was already a considerable degree of specialisation, more particularly in woad, the dye most in request since it was used not only for blues but as a foundation for so many other colours. As Lincolnshire developed its sheep rather than its woad, acquiring thereby a European reputation for its wool, so Picardy became par excellence not a wool- but a woad-producing region, supplying both England and Flanders. All along the Somme and its tributaries the woad plant was grown and harvested; there its leaves were crushed into pulp in the mills, rolled into balls and sold on the local markets, particularly at Amiens, Corbie and Nesle. The merchants of these towns united to push its sale abroad, shipping it overseas from the estuary of the Somme. Together they secured in 1237, for instance, a convention with the city of London allowing them

PLATE II

(*a*) Combing, carding and spinning with distaff.

(*b*) Spinning with spinning wheel.

(*c*) Carding and spinning with wheel.

(*See p.* 379.)

PLATE III

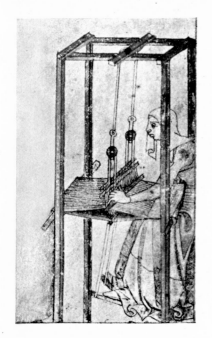

(a) Weaving on single loom.

(b) Fulling by foot.

(c) Tentering and mending.

(d) Dyeing in the piece.

(See p. 379.)

PLATE IV

(*a*) Raising with teasels.

Three of the lights in the clothmakers' window at Semur-en-Auxois, early sixteenth century (not late fourteenth century as stated in de Lasteyrie, *Histoire de la Peinture sur Verre*), showing finishing processes. Other lights show previous processes, including washing, carding, weaving (double loom) and fulling. (*See p.* 379.)

(*b*) Shearing.

(*c*) Brushing.

to warehouse within the city, to sell there to strangers and citizens and, a still more unusual privilege, to take their woad themselves into any part of the country they wished. That their business was very considerable is shown by the fact that they were prepared to pay £50 a year for these privileges and a sum of £100 down towards the cost of a new water supply for the city. Very similar privileges were granted to them elsewhere, as at Norwich and Bristol. The greatness of Amiens was indeed built upon woad. This it was which founded the fortunes of its leading families, who kept for themselves a monopoly of the trade. This too it was which led to the enrichment of Amiens cathedral, where several of the windows were presented by the *waidiers* who are still commemorated there by the life-like statue of two woadmen standing with a bulging sack of woad balls between them.

Though woad was exported mainly from Picardy at this time, it was also reaching the clothing towns from Central Germany, as for example from the Altmark, and from South-western France, and both these latter sources of supply became steadily more important. England in particular became increasingly dependent upon the woad farms of Languedoc, where enormous quantities were produced for export in the region of Toulouse, Albi and Montauban. Woad became, next to wine, the principal commodity shipped down the Garonne from Bordeaux, and England, secure as she hoped in her possession of Gascony, tended to abandon the cultivation of woad as she did that of the vine, while South-west France, on the other hand, devoted herself more and more to these crops, looking to Northern Europe for much of her food supply. 'Picardy woad' and 'Toulouse woad' were the two varieties most commonly used by English cloth-makers in the fourteenth century. It was scarcely surprising that England clung to Gascony and coveted Ponthieu, since through these two duchies, by the outlets of the Garonne and the Somme, came the principal dyestuff on which her industry depended.

The far north of Europe yielded lichens such as orchil (*roccella tinctoria*), which was imported from Norway and gave a purplish red colour, and from the Baltic forests came potash. Potash was even more in demand as a mordant than alum, for it was universally used with woad, as all medieval dyeing regulations, English or Flemish, show; hence it was needed for dyeing not only in blue but in the many colours whose foundation was woad. Thus it was decreed, for instance, that the finest dark blue, perse, must be dyed in woad alone, on white wool, mordanted with ashes, without any attempt to darken it by putting it into madder or alum or by using black or grey wool. Far greater quantities were therefore required than could be secured locally in England or Flanders from wood fires or the burning of whole trees, and ashes were imported in increasing quantities in ships from North Germany and the Baltic. They figure constantly from the mid-thirteenth century in lists of goods on which tolls were paid, both at ports and at inland cloth-making towns such as Northampton (1251) or Winchester, where they are described as ashes '*ke afferte a weide*'; they formed part of the stock in trade of almost every dyer, and special ordinances were passed for their sale and measurement, as at Douai (1250).

The remaining raw materials most commonly required for the finishing processes were mainly supplied locally. Beds of fullers' earth (*terra fullonis*) were to be found on both sides of the Channel. The diggings were controlled and turned to the profit of the urban or seigneurial authority in whose domain they lay, and ample supplies appear to have been available. Teasels (*cardones*) for the raising of the nap were also obtained locally and were evidently cultivated as a cash crop on a considerable scale. Tithes of teasels had been paid in England in the twelfth century, and in the same century at Amiens tolls were paid on them, by the thousand. Attempts were made from time to time to substitute iron instruments for the natural teasel, especially when the supply was not equal to the demand as at the opening of the fourteenth century. But such attempts were resisted. Ordinances were passed both in English and Flemish towns forbidding the use of iron implements such as *skrattes* and in England such ordinances were reiterated by Parliament at the close of the Middle Ages. The medieval preference for the teasel was no irrational prejudice. It is shared today by West of England cloth manufacturers, for the teasel, they maintain, has greater elasticity than any metal hook and is less liable to damage the delicate fibres of the wool.

Thus the 'great industry' of England and Flanders in the thirteenth century drew its supplies not only from the fields and pastures of Western Europe (thereby stimulating considerably its agrarian development) but also from the forests of the Indies and the Baltic, the mines of the Middle East, and the oak groves of the Mediterranean, just as it marketed its textiles in all these regions. It was therefore an industry peculiarly sensitive to changes in the international situation as well as to changes in the yields of certain primary products, and one subject to many fluctuations, short-term and long-term, often only to be explained by political or economic developments in lands remote from the centres of manufacture.

It will already be apparent that the completion of a piece of fine broadcloth, such as was put on the market by Lincoln, Douai and many other towns, was an operation involving many different craftsmen, each with his own specialised skill. Before turning to a consideration of the organisation of the industry and the position of these craftsmen it may be as well to make clear their various functions by a brief review of the processes involved (cf. Plates II–IV).

Dyeing might take place at almost any stage in the manufacture of the cloth; the wool might be dyed in the wool, in the yarn or in the piece. In the whole process of clothmaking it was the most intricate operation and the one demanding most skill. The dyer must be thoroughly acquainted with the properties of the various materials he used—wools, dyes and mordants, with the effects to be obtained from different quantities or combinations of them and from different methods of preparation or use. He must be able to judge good alum from bad, fresh madder from old; he must know how to set woad or cut brasil, and he must understand the different treatment required for different qualities of wool. Because of these complexities dyeing was often separated into two distinct crafts—that of the dyers in woad and the dyers in other colours. In either case it was carried out in a large circular vat, round which moved the dyer or his assistants turning over the wool or cloth as they went with long poles. This was heavy work, almost invariably done by men.

Least skill was required for the preliminary operations of sorting, beating and washing the wool, each of which was usually in charge of specialised if humble workers. Then came the preparation of the wool for spinning, by carding if it was short staple and combing if it was long staple wool; this was most frequently done by women and it was effected by means of a pair of wooden instruments, set either with short metal hooks (for carding) or with long metal teeth (for combing). The wool, duly oiled, was then spun into yarn. This was almost invariably done by women, either with the age-old distaff and spindle, in which case it could be a peripatetic occupation carried on when watching the pot or watching the sheep, or with the newly invented spinning wheel. The introduction of the spinning wheel, probably in the thirteenth century though possibly earlier, was one of the major innovations in the textile industry, but one about which little is at present known.

From the spinners the yarn went on to the weavers, unless it was to be dyed. It was prepared for weaving by workers who were often distinct from the weavers themselves—the warpers, who sized and wound the warp thread, arranging it in the requisite number of threads of the requisite length; and the spoolers, who wound the woof thread on to the bobbin for insertion in the shuttle: warp thread and woof thread were differently spun, since the warp must be the stronger. Warping was no simple task, since the full-size broadcloth which had now replaced the small *pallia* as the staple of the export trade contained some 2000 to 3000 warp threads, each thirty or more yards long before fulling. Weaving, in the case of these broadcloths some two yards wide, was done by two workers, men or women, seated side by side at a double horizontal loom—a loom which had been much developed since the eleventh century, if only to allow for the winding of the immensely long warp upon the beam. Narrow cloths were woven on a single loom. In some places the two crafts of broad and narrow loom weaving were kept entirely distinct, as at Winchester; elsewhere a weaver might possess both a broad and a narrow loom.

Fulling was one of the most arduous, if one of the comparatively less skilled, operations. Through most of the thirteenth century it was generally carried out in the clothing towns by the wearisome old Roman method of trampling in a trough (pp. 358, 362). Hence fullers were usually men and were required to be 'strong', and three were needed on a single cloth, according to an Arras ruling. Even so they were apt to demand a rise of wages on the ground that the weight of the cloth had been increased so that they could not work it '*sans trop grant grief et exil de corps et de membres*'. When the cloth had been thus washed and felted in the trough it was hung out to dry on a tenter; this was an upright wooden frame to which the lists of the cloth were fastened by innumerable tenterhooks placed along parallel bars which could be adjusted to the width of the cloth. By this means the cloth could be stretched to precisely the right length and breadth, neither more nor less. Several workers were needed on this job because of the great weight of a full broadcloth, especially when wet. Frequently they were women. Indeed the proportion of women employed in the cloth industry must have been as high then as now, from women entrepreneurs such as the *grandes drapières* of the Béguinage at Bergues St Winoc down to humble spinners and sorters.

After tentering, the fine quality broadcloths were subjected to the finishing processes of raising and shearing, so vividly depicted in the lower lights of the clothworkers' window at Semur. The raising of the nap was done by teasels set in rows on a wooden frame like an ace of spades. This was drawn down the cloth, when damp, as it hung from a wooden bar. Raising was a process often repeated many times, and sometimes carried out first at the fuller's and then at special finishing shops. Finally the cloth was shorn. This was done when the cloth was dry, with shears distinguished from sheep shears both by their size and shape; they were at least three to four feet long, and they were flat, not pointed, at the ends. Much skill must have been required of the shear-grinder to give them a cutting edge of some 18 inches, even enough and sharp enough to crop the surface of a fine cloth. Faulty grinding was often the subject of a claim for damages, and good shears were so valuable a possession that they were frequently left by will. The finest cloth was shorn and reshorn a number of times, in each case after re-damping, teasling and drying. After shearing the cloth was brushed, pressed and folded. Various subsidiary operations were performed at different stages of manufacture, such as mending to make good any faults in the weaving and burling to remove knots and impurities; these were specialised crafts, often practised by women.

All the circumstances under which the cloth industry was working —wide and elastic markets, dependence upon imported raw materials (especially in Flanders), and considerable subdivision of labour—dictated an organisation which cannot but be described as capitalist whether the Marxian or any other criterion be used. Clearly it was most unlikely that the artisans actually carrying out the various processes of manufacture would be in direct relation with the consumer, and in any case not all of them could be. The combination of the many processes alone demanded an entrepreneur; so too did the importation of the raw materials and the marketing of the cloth. In each sphere of operations entrepreneurs appeared; sometimes a single individual or a great company combined all three functions, purchasing materials direct from the producers, putting them out to the various craftsmen (some of whom were themselves entrepreneurs on a small scale), and selling the finished cloth. Whatever the precise form of the organisation—and it varied much even in a single centre—everywhere the artisan in the 'great industry' was subject to the entrepreneur, at least in so far as he was working for the export market.

One such captain of industry was Jean Boine Broke, draper (*drapier*) of Douai, who flourished in the second half of the thirteenth century. A man of property and substance, he himself owned all the raw materials and some of the implements of his business. Some wool was produced on his own estates or bought locally, but much more was imported, especially from England, where Boine Broke purchased on his own account from abbeys such as Newbo in Lincolnshire, Holmcultram in Cumberland, and Newminster in Northumberland. A little madder was also grown, but more was bought, with woad and alum and perhaps other dyestuffs too. Boine Broke's house combined the functions of home, office, warehouse, and general headquarters of the whole concern. In it were stored raw materials and also the finished cloths—murrey, violet, or white—which he marketed abroad through his agents, some of whom were members of his own family like the Boine Broke who once took merchandise for him to Scotland. Behind his house, down by the river, he possessed a dye-house and not far off a tenter-ground equipped with his own tenter-frames. In these two establishments artisans were much in the position of factory workers of today, directly dependent upon their employer, contracted to him for a definite time, and working for specified wages. Some remained in his service over long periods; one was a washer of wools for a year, another served in the dye-house for three years, and 'Sarah of the Tenters' worked at the tenters for twelve years or more. Cloth was also most probably dressed and shorn in his house, for we know that he owed money to a shear-grinder, and it seems likely that some of the preliminary processes of sorting and beating were done there too. There was thus to a certain extent a concentration of work on the premises of the entrepreneur. For the rest the work was put out to independent craftsmen who fetched the raw material from Boine Broke's house and delivered back the finished product. Sometimes dyeing also was put out in this way. These craftsmen worked in their own homes, owned the implements of their trade, and often themselves had workers under them. Here and there they were more closely bound to the entrepreneur by living in one of his houses, which they occupied on terms which assured them sufficient raw material to enable them at least to earn their rent. Since this work was done outside the entrepreneur's own premises it was inevitably paid for at piece-work rates, while to check any embezzlement of raw material the worker was regarded as having purchased the quantity received, even if only on paper, so that he could be held responsible for its full value should it not all be returned.

A similar pattern of organisation is discernible in England, where the industry was not less highly, if less extensively, developed. Here too there had emerged a class of entrepreneurs owning the raw materials, controlling the whole production of the cloth, and selling it at the fairs, where the English *draparii* rivalled the English *lanarii*. Thus for instance Henry Houhil, burgess of Leicester and contemporary of Boine Broke, dyed wool on his own premises, had it made up into cloth, put it out to be fulled, and took it himself to Boston fair, where he had his own stall in a row with the other Leicester drapers, opposite the row of the wool merchants. Similarly the London burellers 'caused cloth to be made', employing the weavers and paying them at piece-work rates, and it was from them that the king bought burel for his alms to the poor. The legend of a medieval world of independent craftsmen, owning both the raw materials and the instruments of their trade and selling direct to the consumer, dies hard. In the principal industry of the time it is far from the truth. All contemporary records, both in Flanders and England, point to a large class of wage-earning craftsmen—weavers, fullers, and others, subservient to the capitalist draper.

The position of the entrepreneurs was the stronger in that they wielded not only economic but also political power. For they were patricians, leading members of their city governments (Boine Broke was *échevin* nine times) and members too of those merchants gilds

which controlled the trade and industry of their cities, and which had
become more and more aristocratic, excluding altogether the wage-
earning artisans of the 'great industry'. Neither in Flanders nor in England might weavers, fullers, or dyers who soiled their own hands at the
work, so that they were dubbed 'blue-nails', be members of these gilds.
Nicholas the Chaloner, admitted to the merchant gild of Leicester on
condition that he put weaver's work out of his house, was later expelled
from the gild on the ground that he had not done so. The famous
laws of the weavers and fullers of Beverley (*circa* 1200) enacted that any
weaver or fuller who grew rich and wished to join the ranks of the
burgesses must forswear his craft, turning all the instruments of it out
of his house; very similar laws are extant for Winchester, Oxford, and
Marlborough. All dealing in raw materials and in the finished cloth
was strictly reserved to members of the merchant gilds. Hence the
artisan was wholly dependent upon the entrepreneur for his livelihood,
and found every detail of his life regulated by his employers through
their all-powerful position in their city's government.

Possessed of full power, the merchant gilds watched over the interests of trade and controlled the 'great industry' often in minute detail,
as from time to time seemed to them desirable. An immense mass of
industrial legislation has survived from this most regulated economy of
the thirteenth century, some of it going back to the very early years of
the century. Much of it deals with the technique of the industry.
Precise standards of length, breadth and weight were laid down,
methods defined, and the use of certain materials prescribed or forbidden. Though more regulations have survived for Flanders and the
Flemish industry was doubtless more thoroughly regimented than the
English, the character of the legislation is markedly similar in both
countries and many of the technical provisions are identical. The use of
flocks, for instance, was forbidden in many industrial towns on both
sides of the Channel, as was the mixing of different types of wool in the
same piece of yarn or cloth. Teasels might only be used on the cloth
when it was damp, shears only when it was dry. Perse might only be
dyed with woad and ashes. Such statutory provision for good workmanship and specific standards was in part a corollary of the dispersal
of production. The entrepreneur's task of supervising work done on
the worker's own premises was thereby simplified in that the penalties
for breach of such rules were sufficiently severe to act as a considerable
deterrent. In addition it assisted in maintaining the reputation of the
town's wares on the foreign market by ensuring a certain uniformity
of size and quality for the various types of cloth.

To ensure the observance of the regulations, rigid systems of scrutiny
were devised. Inspectors were appointed to cover every branch of the

trade, investigating workshops, markets and fairs. With rare exceptions they were nominated by the civic authorities, though in part at least there might be a certain representative element, and in almost every case there were merchants among them. The official list of inspectors at Douai in 1250 includes inspectors of dyestuffs, such as the seven inspectors of brasil, three of whom were to act at the fairs and four at Douai, inspectors of crafts such as weaving and shearing, and inspectors 'of England' and 'of Burgundy', i.e. of the principal market outlets. Such inspectors had the right of entry at any time to any premises where production or trade was being carried on, even into the homes of those who spun wool. It was their duty not only to see that rules were enforced and no trickery practised and to present offenders to the city authorities, but also to prevent discord and strife and to intervene in all disputes between the entrepreneurs and the masters or the masters and their servants.

Amongst the most important functions of the inspectors was that of taking part in wage negotiations and enforcing the observance of wage regulations. Almost all wages were fixed, and where this was so no deviation from the standard rates was allowed, nor could the rates be altered unilaterally or jointly by either employers or employed, but only by the civic authorities. The idea that wages should be left to find their own level and that everyone should be free to strike his own bargain, however hard, was abhorrent to the men and women of the thirteenth century. It was generally thought that wages should be 'reasonable' and this, when interpreted, meant that some variation should be allowed in accordance both with changes in supply and demand and, still more, with changes in money values. When money was cheap, and prices consequently high, wages were raised; when money was dear, and prices fell, wages were reduced. Wages in fact were related to the cost of living. The application of this principle can be observed most clearly in the records of St Omer in the first half of the fourteenth century; here the constant fluctuations of official wage rates for weavers, fullers, tenterers and shearmen were directly, and admittedly, related to the monetary changes of Philip the Fair and Charles IV. But there is no doubt that both principles were operative elsewhere and a century earlier. At Douai in 1229, for instance, it was decreed that if demand rose and the shearmen wished to improve their pay then they might appeal to the inspectors who, with two of the shearmen themselves, would put the matter before the *échevins* for their decision. If, on the contrary, work diminished or money became less abundant and the price of the precious metals rose so that the entrepreneurs sought to lower wages and the workers refused to agree, then again appeal was to be made to the *échevins*. Truck payments were

strictly forbidden, though from the frequent reiteration of the prohibition it would seem as though it was not always obeyed.

It is evident that wages were often fixed only as the result of conflict
between employers and employed, often ending in strikes, when the
city authorities stepped in to settle the matter. When, for instance, the
sliding scale principle was laid down at Douai in 1229 the shearmen
were specifically forbidden to stop work to force a rise; prohibitions
against combining to raise wages were frequent in both Flanders and
England; and the detailed schedule of rates for fulling drawn up at
Brussels in 1282 followed a strike. Certainly employers had the last
word through their position of influence on the city's government, but
machinery for negotiation at least existed and the craftsmen might at
any rate get a hearing for their case. Worst off must have been the
humbler craftsmen—beaters, carders, combers, spinners and the like,
often working on the entrepreneur's premises, who were neither
organised in their own fraternities nor grouped together under separate
inspectors. Less in a position to bargain, they must have been compelled
to accept whatever wages the city authorities chose to fix. Yet it is unlikely that these wages were wholly unreasonable. At Brussels those
working on the preparation of wool at the Béguinage petitioned in
1296 that the rates established for the town workers might apply to
them, 'to their profit'. This was agreed by the city authorities on
condition that when the townsmen's wages went down theirs should
too, and they were accordingly awarded day rates of $2\frac{1}{2}d.$ in winter,
$3d.$ in spring and autumn, and $4d.$ in summer.

Piece-work rates were paid for weaving, fulling, tentering, shearing
and dyeing (when done on the dyer's premises). They varied much,
according to the type of material. Weavers were paid by the yard;
fullers by the cloth, reckoning according to the number of days fulling
required by different types of cloth. Dyeing rates varied according to the
dyestuffs used and the dyer was obliged to display in his shop a standard
sample showing the standard colours with the statutory prices for each.

In addition to fixing the rates to be given by the entrepreneurs to the
master craftsmen the city authorities fixed the rates to be given by the
masters to their valets or journeymen. Here payment was sometimes
by the day and sometimes by the piece. Thus at Brussels in 1282 it was
decreed that of the price paid by the entrepreneur for fulling each cloth,
one third should go to the master and two thirds to the journeyman.

The length of the working day was fixed as rigidly as wages in this
regulated economy of the thirteenth century, though more rigidly, it
would seem, in the denser industrial region of Flanders than in England.
No one might work either more or less than the statutory hours. The
principle on which these hours were determined was a simple one—

that work should continue as long as there was daylight, except for a midday break of one and a half hours. Though 'night' work, that is work by artificial light, was occasionally allowed, it was universally disliked, not so much for reasons of economy as because of the danger of fire and for the avoidance of bad work. Hence not only hours but also precise times were fixed. Work began at dawn and ended at dusk. And lest there should be any doubt about it a bell was rung four times in the day, often in a belfry specially erected for the purpose, such as the belfry over the cloth hall at Bruges; first came the morning bell as day broke, then the 'dinner bell', then the 'resumption bell' and finally the evening bell. Thus great clothing towns such as Douai, Ypres or Brussels were in effect like one vast factory. In the early morning many thousands of workers might be seen flocking to the workshops of the entrepreneurs or of the weavers, fullers, dyers or shearmen, and the streets would empty as the bell rang out and they 'clocked in' to their labours. The working day therefore varied from some 8 hours in the winter to some 13 hours in the summer, and wages, where they were day wages, varied similarly (see supra p. 385). There may, however, have been some such merciful provision as at Brussels in the early sixteenth century, when during the long summer hours the workers were allowed a further break both in the morning and in the afternoon. There is certainly no trace of the harsh provisions in force in certain French towns in the late fourteenth century when a king, ignorant of the economic value of rest pauses, compelled the weavers to work without stopping from dawn till dusk, taking with them their bread for the day, and 'if they wished for soup their wives must bring it to the looms where they worked so that they should in no way be interrupted in their work'.

No work was allowed on Sundays or on Saturday afternoons, so that the normal working week varied from 60 hours or more in summer to some 44 hours in winter, though the authorities might stop all work in case of extreme cold or frost. But holidays were frequent, since all Holy Days were usually appointed as obligatory days of rest; even when only the Apostles' days were observed the total annual holiday would be longer than now, particularly since work commonly stopped at the midday dinner bell on the vigil of each feast, as laid down for instance in the weavers' ordinances of Douai and St Omer. The ordinances of the shearmen of Arras early in the thirteenth century decreed that there should be no work for four days at Christmas, eight at Easter and eight at Pentecost, but the decision of the London weavers at the end of the century to forbid work between Epiphany (January 6) and Candlemas (February 2) was challenged by the employers, and the city authorities decreed that each person might 'boldly' work during that season as well as at any other time of the year. It is impossible now to say whether these longer holiday periods reflected a shortage of work and an attempt to spread it, or an attempt to raise the price of labour by restricting its supply.

While it is permissible and indeed necessary to describe this *grande industrie* of the thirteenth century as a capitalist one, it would be a mistake to conceive of all the workers as being equally in a state of dependence. Their condition varied considerably. Lowest in the scale were the beaters, washers and others engaged in the preliminary processes, who worked usually on the entrepreneur's premises, doing humble and ill-paid tasks, owning none of their own equipment, and apparently quite unorganised among themselves. Equally unorganised were the carders, combers and spinners, but they were slightly more independent in that they worked mostly in their own homes, owned their own equipment, slight as it was, and were free to work for more than one master and, if they wished, to employ workers under them. Higher in the scale came the master weavers, fullers, dyers and shearmen. These also worked in most cases on their own premises and owned capital equipment of some value, such as the weaver's loom, the fuller's troughs and tenters, the dyer's vats, the shearman's special table and shears. They were therefore often men of property and also of necessity employers of labour, with valets or journeymen under them, for, as we have seen, in no case could their work be done alone if they were making heavy broadcloths for the export market. Combination among them to improve their condition, though frequently forbidden, was facilitated by the fact that they were grouped together by the city authorities for the purposes of control, while some of them were also associated in their own religious and social fraternities. Best off among them were probably the master dyers and shearmen, whose work was the most skilled of all. They almost always maintained a position of comparative independence, working on commission for a number of employers, while weavers and fullers at times sank almost into servitude, pledging even their implements to the entrepreneurs.

IV. *The Renaissance of the Italian Industry*

The supremacy of the northern industry remained unchallenged through the twelfth and on towards the close of the thirteenth century. All the circumstances of history and geography had favoured its growth—the long tradition of fine craftsmanship and manufacture for export, the excellence and abundance of the local wool supplies, a measure of political stability ensuring to the city magnate a happy blend of liberty and order peculiarly propitious to his business and, above all, a commanding position both on the ancient North-South route across Western Europe and on those highways of the northern seas whereon the Vikings had built up so vigorous a commerce. The whole northern world had been unified as never before. If Russians cut their suits out of Flemish cloth, Russian hats became all the fashion in norway and Iceland, while for their cloaks Norwegians and Icelanders sought the fine scarlets of Lincolnshire. On the Mediterranean markets the northern woollens quite outstripped the local stuffs in quality, quantity, and variety. A Venetian tariff of 1265 lists over thirty different kinds of cloth from England and the Flemish region and only some ten Italian varieties; almost without exception the Italian cloths are cheap; even the costliest do not approach in value those of Ypres, Douai and Cambrai, or the English stamforts.

But if in the production of cloth the Italians were at this time far behind the northerners, in its commerce they were second to none. As the flow of northern textiles southwards had increased, so it had tended more and more to concentrate on those central routes down the Rhone valley to the Ligurian coast, or over the Alps to the Lombardy plain, and thence from the ports of Italy to the shores of Africa and the Levant. Italy, in particular its northern towns, held a key position in this lucrative traffic, and it is scarcely surprising that Italian merchants became its chief intermediaries, purchasing the cloth at the fairs of Champagne and marketing it in Italy, Africa or Asia, whence they returned with those oriental dyestuffs so eagerly sought by the northern manufacturers. Thus they acquired an unrivalled knowledge of eastern and Mediterranean markets and the types of cloth in demand there, a controlling influence over the import of some of the costlier dyestuffs, and very considerable profits. These assets they turned to account by developing an industry of their own in the dyeing and finishing of northern cloths. Capital was invested in dye-works, tenter-yards and finishing shops. Kermes, brasil, orchil and alum were imported less for re-export than for use at home, and once again Italy specialised in producing those shades of scarlet, crimson and purple for which she had been famous in Roman times. Finishing techniques were elaborated and perfected; the soft, closely felted fabrics of the North were raised and shorn again and again after dyeing and were then marketed in Italy or abroad, competing keenly with those wholly manufactured in England or Flanders.

Such a cloth-finishing industry grew up during the late twelfth or early thirteenth century in most of the cities which handled the northern trade. In Genoa, for instance, the dyers were fully organised by 1222, with three *rectores de tinctoria*, and there too shearmen were at work on the northern cloths. Lucca, famous for its vermilion dye, was finishing cloths of Ypres. Best known of all is the finishing industry of Florence. By the middle of the twelfth century Florence was doing a busy traffic in northern cloths. The merchants who dealt in them had their shops in a narrow lane called, since it was a place of ill fame, the *Calimala*, and they were already associated together in the Calimala gild (*Arte di Calimala*), which took as its coat of arms an eagle bearing in his talons a corded bale of cloth. So wealthy and important was this gild that on occasion (as in 1182) its consuls were appointed to deputise for the consuls of the commune, just as they were entrusted with the care of some of the chief city buildings like the old Baptistry. By the end of the thirteenth century, if not before, the gild was as much concerned with the processing as with the import of the northern cloths, and its members had become as expert in matters of dyeing and finishing as the Flemings and Englishmen themselves.

The early fourteenth-century statutes of the Calimala gild and the books of some of its member companies such as that of Francesco Del Bene give us a vivid picture not only of what its members decreed but also of what they did. Cloths, finished and unfinished, were purchased at the fairs of Champagne or at the place of manufacture either by a member of the firm concerned or through the agency of another firm. Thence, packed together in canvas bales that could be laden on a pack-horse, they were despatched overland to the ports of Provence and thence through Pisa to Florence on a journey of some four months' duration. The gild itself maintained inns along the route for the safe-keeping of merchants and their merchandise, and organised a postal service for the despatch of letters to and from the fairs and their delivery to the merchant's place of business in the Calimala. It negotiated for the reduction or abolition of tolls along the way, and for the redress of injuries suffered by its members in a foreign land. On arrival in Florence, cloths already finished were sold locally or re-exported, while others were put out to expert dyers, menders and finishers. These craftsmen plied their trade on their own premises but were closely controlled by the gild. On no account might they themselves engage in the buying and selling of cloth, nor might cloth be even displayed to prospective buyers at the dye-works, on the tenters or in the finishing shops, unless in the presence of its owner. They might work only for members of the gild, which took security for their good behaviour, fixed their rates of pay, forbade them to combine, inspected their work, and prescribed precise technical rules very similar to those in force in Flanders, with heavy penalties for their non-observance. Particularly strict was the scrutiny of the precious scarlets. If a scarlet were found to be not wholly dyed in grain (kermes), but with some admixture of brasil, madder or orchil, the perpetrator was condemned to the crushing fine of £105 or, failing payment, to the loss of his right hand.

If the Calimala gild controlled and restricted the activities of its subordinate craftsmen, so too it did those of its own merchant entrepreneurs. The aid of the commune was invoked, not wholly perhaps with success, to ensure that all who handled any transalpine or English cloths joined the gild, so that its control could be effective, and members' shops and warehouses in Florence were subjected to close inspection, while special consuls 'for the realm of France' supervised their doings beyond the Alps. When there was a surplus of cloth on hand the gild forbade all dealings at the fairs. It laid down a schedule of length and breadth for the cloths that might be handled, and it prescribed rigid rules not only for the dyeing and finishing but also for the selling of the cloth. Credit terms were limited (at the beginning of the fourteenth century) to $3\frac{1}{2}$ months, or $2\frac{1}{2}$ months for foreigners, with one week's grace, and rates of discount and of indemnity for late payment were fixed, usually at a level of 10% per annum. That these terms were in fact observed can be seen from the Del Bene books, which show us the whole financing of the business, from the original purchase and the cost of transport, averaging some 16% of the first cost, down to the dyeing, finishing and resale. On balance, after deducting the general expenses of the firm, a Calimala company at this time might expect to make a net profit of some 12% for distribution to its shareholders.

Meanwhile Italy was not entirely without a woollen manufacture of its own. In many cities there was a wool gild (*Arte della Lana*) dealing in the whole process of cloth production from the preparation of the wool onwards. That of Florence, with a fleecy lamb of St John the Baptist as its coat of arms, goes back at least to the early thirteenth century, while in Pisa there is mention of the consuls of the *Arte della Lana* in 1188. In Northern Italy as well as in Tuscany the manufacture of woollen cloth on a commercial scale was widespread in the twelfth century, and in the following century it steadily increased. Religious communities as well as laymen engaged in it. Such were the Umiliati, originally a lay brotherhood, who in 1140 joined the Benedictine order. Like the Bogards and Béguines of Flanders they at first worked daily themselves at the actual tasks of clothmaking, differing from the secular craftsmen only in that they lived together, broke their labours for religious observances, and were subject to no control but that of their own community. Later, however, they specialised more and more on entrepreneurial functions, leaving the manual work to hired employees. Capital was obtained not only by the ploughing back of profits but by loans from lay investors and by donations from pious folk who looked for a return less in this world than the next. Their industrial activity was at its height in the mid-thirteenth century but thereafter declined rapidly, ceasing almost entirely by the end of the century. At Florence they had established themselves on an island in the Arno in 1239, but in 1277 they sold their business there and early in the following century they were exempted from all taxation because of the dire distress into which they had fallen.

Now the cloths made by the Umiliati, like almost all Italian cloths at that time, were cheap cloths of inferior quality, as we have seen from the Venetian tariff of 1265. Progress in the production of high grade cloth was impeded by the competition of textiles from the more advanced northern region, by the tendency for capital to be directed into the very profitable channel of the finishing and marketing of these cloths, and above all by the comparative poverty of the raw material which the Italian manufacturers had at their disposal in their own country. Italian woollens could not hope to equal, much less to surpass, northerns in quality as long as they were made from Italian wool. But the immense development of Italy's commercial activity, which had led the Italians to become the principal carriers of northern cloths and to perfect the technique of dyeing and finishing, led them also to deal in wool. Increasingly during the thirteenth century they were competing with English and Flemish manufacturers for the best wools of Europe. Spanish, North African, French, English and Scottish wools were imported into Italy, where the finest of them fetched three to four times the price of the native wools. Most excellent of all was the wool of England, whose superiority is shown not only by its own price but by the fact that cloth woven from it could command a price sufficiently high to cover the heavy costs of transport across Europe. Before long it had superseded all others for the making of best quality cloths. Italian merchants, profiting from their peculiar position in England as papal collectors, were travelling throughout the land buying up the clip of the great religious houses and of others besides, often for several years in advance, and transferring the proceeds of papal taxation to Italy in the form of wool. By the opening of the fourteenth century they had become the principal dealers in English wool, ousting altogether the Flemings who once had dominated the trade, and themselves supplying the Flemish market. In Italy itself imported wools had so far supplanted home-grown supplies for the manufacture of high grade cloth that, though it was still worth while to produce the finer wools of the South, in the North wool production was in many places abandoned, and in the plain of the Po lands which had once sustained large numbers of sheep were now devoted rather to the cultivation of woad.

The enterprise of the Italian merchants, which so powerfully contributed to the success of the Italian manufacturers, was assisted by a series of fortunate circumstances, more especially by the difficulties confronting the Flemish producers. From 1269 onwards trade between Flanders and England was constantly interrupted by embargoes and confiscations, so that the supply of wool to the Flemish manufacturers was intermittent and uncertain; at the same time the chief outlet for their cloths, that of the fairs of Champagne, was rendered no less precarious by their uneasy relations with the French king and by his seizures of their goods and credits. To these political difficulties were added labour troubles not less serious, culminating at the close of the century in a general revolt of the workers against the class of merchant capitalists who for so long had dominated the industry and politics of Flanders. Conflicts such as these, as we shall see later, were gravely impairing the position of the Flemish industry, threatening it from within at the very moment that the Italians, now diverting to their own country the finest of Europe's wools, were threatening it from without. And they were contributing even more directly to Italy's success. For as conditions deteriorated in Flanders more and more clothmakers emigrated, either of their own accord or banished by the state. Many went to the rising industrial towns of Italy which, with a growing demand for skilled labour, as well as for skilled direction, gave them a ready welcome. In Padua, for instance, foreigners who came into the city to make cloth were exempted by a statute of 1265 from all tolls and customs duties and later on also from personal taxes; by similar grants of privileges, reiterated in the early fourteenth century, they were allowed to import wool, dyestuffs and implements, and to export finished products, free of duty, while the whole of their profits were exempted from tax.

The inducements offered by the Italian clothing towns were designed to attract workers from neighbouring regions not less than those from across the Alps. They formed indeed in many places part of a fiscal system consciously directed towards fostering a native industry by protecting it not so much against northern manufacturers as against its own immediate rivals. For competition between city and city was more intense, if only because more readily apprehended, than competition between two geographical regions neither of which had a distinct political entity. Thus in the late thirteenth century the merchant oligarchy of Venice, while careful to do nothing that might injure the overseas traffic in northern cloth which was the lifeblood of its city, yet took measures to protect its own nascent industry against Italian competitors. Customs duties were gradually imposed not only on cloth from neighbouring cities such as Padua, Treviso and Mantua, but also on cloth from Lombardy and Tuscany; a prohibitive export duty on wool imported from Romagna and Apulia checked the drain of raw material to rival cities, while Venetian subjects were forbidden (in 1281) to go to Padua or Treviso to work in the woollen industry there.

Fed by the finest wools of Europe and by dyestuffs from the orient and the Mediterranean, amply supplied with labour from many lands and with capital from the immense wealth of the Italian merchants, and profiting from the difficulties confronting the Flemish producers, the Italian industry leapt rapidly ahead into the front rank, reaching its zenith in the first half of the fourteenth century. If the *Arte di Calimala* still held first place among Florentine gilds at the opening of the century, only a few decades later it had been outdistanced by its rival the *Arte della Lana*; for though in 1338 Florence might still be importing some 10,000 cloths each year it was then producing some 80,000.

The progress of the Italian industry was as widespread as it was rapid. Throughout the plain of the Po, in innumerable towns of Lombardy and Venetia, the manufacture of woollens had become the principal industry. Towns which had long produced coarse cloth for home consumption were now making fine cloth for the foreign market. Milan, Brescia, Verona, Padua, and Parma were as famous for their woollens as they had been in Roman days, and there was an export trade also in many other places such as Como, Monza, Bergamo, Vicenza, Treviso, Mantua and Cremona. In Venice also there had been a marked improvement in the quality of goods produced and the industry flourished exceedingly, though yielding first place to the manufacture of silk. In the Romagna there was an important centre at Bologna, and in Umbria at Perugia. If in Lombardy and Venetia, as in Belgica, such an expansion was but the renaissance of an industry reaching back a thousand years, for Tuscany there was no such ancient precedent. Its industrialisation would appear to be a wholly medieval phenomenon. Now, however, with a number of clothing towns such as Pisa, Prato, Lucca, and Florence, it was quite as important a producing region as the plain of the Po, and indeed probably more so until the close of the fourteenth century. Lucca had already won a high reputation by 1265, when it was sending to Venice not only cheap white and grey cloths and vermilion-dyed cloths of Ypres but also vermilion broadcloths of its own manufacture—the only high-priced Italian cloths specifically mentioned in the Venetian tariff of 1265. But by the early fourteenth century all other Tuscan towns had been outstripped by Florence, the brilliance of whose achievements in this as in other spheres has so attracted historians as to divert attention from achievements not less substantial, if less spectacular, elsewhere. The Florentine woollen industry, as the contemporary historian Villani proudly relates, then produced each year some 80,000 pieces of cloth and employed some 30,000 persons. Over the Ponte Vecchio in the suburb of Oltrarno, where in 1200 there had been but a few houses, there now lived many thousands of wool workers, and there too many firms of the *Arte della Lana* had their headquarters.

In all these towns the structure of the industry was highly capitalistic and essentially similar to that of Flanders. The Italian *lanaiuolo*, like the English draper and the Flemish *drapier*, was an entrepreneur, supplying capital and skilled direction, employing anything from a few only to many hundreds of craftsmen, and joining together with his fellow *lanaiuoli* in the *Arte della Lana* which controlled the production of the cloth as closely as did the merchant gilds of the North. Often he went into partnership with members of his family or others; in such a case the management was carried out by one or more of the partners or entrusted to a paid manager who sometimes participated in the profits. In Florence in 1338 there were, according to Villani, 200 such woollen manufacturing firms, employing on an average 150 operatives each, if we accept Villani's figures for the total numbers involved. In Milan at the end of the century there were 363 firms; 267 of these were individual firms and 96 were family partnerships. Almost all these Milan firms had their headquarters in a single parish near the Porta Nuova, for the cloth manufacturers here as everywhere tended to congregate together.

In one respect the organisation of the Italian industry in the four-teenth century differed markedly from that of the North in the thirteenth century. The woollen manufacturers of each city were united together in their own exclusive gild—the *Arte della Lana*, whereas in the North they were members of the more comprehensive merchant gild. Manufacturer and foreign merchant were in fact more clearly separated. The *lanaiuolo*, unlike the northern draper, seldom touched the export side of the business or indeed concerned himself in foreign trade at all, nor did he ever apparently attain such a position of wealth and influence as was occupied by the great international merchants and bankers of his day. Cloth for home consumption might be sold direct to the re-tailer, but cloth for the foreign market was almost always disposed of to export firms; only occasionally did the *lanaiuolo* export it himself, retain-ing ownership of it until it was sold abroad. In some cases he was definitely excluded from overseas trade. In Milan, for instance, where the manufacturers seem to have been controlled by the foreign merchants, as in Venice, the statutes of the commune of 1396 distinguish carefully between merchants and merchants manufacturing fine wool; these last were effectively prevented from dealing on the foreign market by being forbidden to sell cloth of more than a certain value except on short-term credit. Similarly the *lanaiuolo* seldom imported wool himself but usually purchased from large importing houses or from middlemen.

As the 'great industry' increased in intensity, there was a growing tendency towards the concentration of business in the hands of large units, whether importers, exporters or manufacturers, and towards the elimination of small capitalists, independent craftsmen and middlemen. The number of manufacturing firms in Florence contracted from some 300 to 200 in the great period of expansion between 1308 and 1338, according to Villani, though the value of their total production increased from 600 to 1200 thousand florins. In Florence also we can discern at this time the gradual extinction of the *lanivendoli*, small capitalists who bought up raw wool, had it washed and beaten, and sold it either to the public or to the *lanaiuoli*. A like fate befell the *stamaiuoli*, dealers in yarn. At first they were small entrepreneurs in their own right; they bought washed, beaten and combed wool from the *lanaiuoli*, had it spun into yarn and delivered it back to them. By the end of the fourteenth century, however, they had become merely employees of the *lanaiuoli*, charged with supervising the whole work of spinning in the countryside, including the transport of wool and yarn to and fro.

The division of labour in the 'great industry' was very similar in Italy and in Flanders, and indeed not dissimilar from that to be found in a West of England broadcloth factory today. Some two dozen specialised wool-working crafts can be discerned in fourteenth-century Florentine records. Almost all of these appear unambiguously in the records of Flanders, where there are also a few trade names which cannot with certainty be identified, and one or two more, such as *espouleresse* (spooler), which seem to have no counterpart in Italy. Then as now work was inevitably more highly specialised in the larger concerns, while in the smaller concerns more than one operation was entrusted to the same worker; only a very large finishing shop could, for instance, employ a full-time presser.

Among the workers we find, as in the North, much variety in regard to their command over capital, their economic dependence on the entrepreneur, their standard of living, and their political rights. But in general the growth of a class of industrial capitalists was everywhere accompanied by the growth of a hired proletariat of workers. If at first many of the craftsmen attached themselves spontaneously to the big industrial firms, later they were compelled to do so as they found themselves unable to acquire raw material or to dispose of the finished product and as they were brought compulsorily under the control of the *Arte della Lana*.

The condition of this proletariat may be most clearly illustrated from the history of Florence, where its numbers were undoubtedly greater than in any other city of Italy. Least independent, as in Flanders, were the workers engaged in the preliminary processes of beating, combing and carding. These possessed not even the tools of their trade; they worked mostly in the entrepreneur's central shop, and were under the immediate supervision of his foremen. Propertyless and rightless, they were forbidden to assemble together or to combine in their own fraternities, even for religious purposes, without the permission of the consuls of the gild, to whose jurisdiction they were wholly subjected but in whose election they had no voice. Threatened with mass unemployment and starvation in times of slump, in times of boom or of labour shortage their prospects might materially improve. With the scarcity of workers after the Black Death, for instance, they were in so favourable a position to bargain for higher wages that for the first time the gild intervened in the matter, abolishing freedom of contract and setting up a committee of eight *lanaiuoli* to fix wages. Paid mostly by the hour or by the day, they had no security of employment. But if it was in the employer's interest not to be burdened with superfluous hands in times of slump, it was equally necessary for him to be able in times of boom to command a body of workers which could not leave him and enter the service of a rival entrepreneur. This he often achieved by granting advances in goods or money, to be repaid later in work. Such a practice favoured the entrepreneur with considerable capital at his disposal and the attitude of the gild towards it varied according to the view that it took of the concentration of business in the hands of big firms. Early in the fourteenth century loans were forbidden, but the trend of opinion was in the opposite direction, the prohibition soon lapsed, and later on the entrepreneur's hold over the workers was tightened by an order forbidding the repayment of advances in money instead of labour.

The spinners also were by the fourteenth century wholly dependent, and tied often to a single entrepreneur whose wool alone they might spin. But their supervision was a more difficult matter, for they carried on their work in their own homes, scattered about in town and countryside, often far from the headquarters of the firm for which they worked. The *lanaiuolo* might cheat them with short weight wool and long delays in payment, despite laws passed for their protection, but they too had opportunities for trickery and bad workmanship. So the employers called to their aid the long arm of the church as well as that of the law, and pressure was brought to bear upon the Bishops of Florence and Fiesole that they should instruct their priests to preach thrice yearly from the pulpit, enjoining the spinners to obey the orders of the *stamaiuoli* on pain of excommunication.

Weaving was done mostly in the city, by a cosmopolitan throng, Italian, German and Flemish, assisted often by their wives and by other members of their households. They too became increasingly dependent, working often under the direct supervision of the *lanaiuoli*. Often they ceased even to own the tools of their trade. For in times of trouble they would pledge their looms, often at rates ruinous to themselves but so profitable to the lender that an active business grew up in this form of investment; if some investors were content with 50%, others, like the artist Giotto, took 120%.

Even the fullers and dyers tended to come increasingly under the domination of the *lanaiuoli*. For though these branches of the business required more capital and independent firms were frequently set up to carry them out, serving more than one entrepreneur, the gild itself often invested in them and acquired a controlling influence. In course of time it actually became the owner of most of the fulleries and all the tenters, letting out small parts of them—one or two stocks and a few frames—to individual fullers and stretchers, who thus became no less dependent than the weavers whose looms had fallen into the hands of their employers. The dyers, who appear to have possessed their own union in the thirteenth century, were in the fourteenth century absorbed by the *Arte della Lana*. They had more rights than other workers in that they were admitted to actual membership as *membra minora*, but since the gild was still dominated by its *membra majora* they had to submit to rates of pay fixed for them by others. Nor could they get redress against the custom of payments in instalments, with postponements even up to five years—a practice which tended to bring them also into dependence upon the entrepreneur. Twice in the fourteenth century they recovered a gild of their own, each time to lose it again, though unlike the other workers they were allowed to retain a religious fraternity, which at least gave them the right of assembly.

Only the finishers were never brought wholly under the control of the *lanaiuoli*, for they not only kept possession of their own finishing shops, and of their own tools, but continued to deal with clients as well as with masters.

As the *lanaiuoli* steadily extended their control over almost all branches of the industry, so the *Arte della Lana* in which they were all united, and of which they alone were full members, grew in power and prestige, becoming in effect very like a cartel. Not content with purely regulatory functions, the gild itself engaged in business on a considerable scale. Not only did it invest its funds in dye-works, tenter-yards and fulleries, becoming a dominant partner in, if not the owner of, many of them; it also constructed washing places along the Arno, operated a central woad store and, when supplies of this dyestuff became precarious, undertook its bulk import.

Ever zealous to stimulate sales abroad, the gild gave courteous welcome to foreign buyers, providing them not only with brokers to conduct them round the shops but also with lavish hospitality. And so that clients might be able to rely on Florentine cloth it attempted to ensure a high level of workmanship by prohibiting the use of inferior tools, methods and materials, and by fixing certain uniform standards of size and of weight. It intervened between members and their employees only when its help was urgently needed. In the case of the economically strong dyers, for instance, it elaborately controlled wages, whereas the wages of the helpless combers were left unregulated until the time of the labour shortage caused by the Black Death. But always it strove to forestall trouble from the workers by keeping them in a position of subservience and refusing to them that right of assembly, of association and of corporate action that was in large measure the secret of their own success.

The gild's powers of enforcement were formidable. A large staff of inspectors was constantly occupied in the detection of any breach of the regulations. The gild had its own police officers for the apprehension of delinquents, its own gaols for their detention, and its own court for their trial. So wide was the competence of this court that a suit brought by a *lanaiuolo* even against an outsider could be heard there. Moreover, the aid of the commune could if necessary be invoked to enforce its judgments. The penalties it was permitted to impose were of the utmost severity. Fines, often exacted in the form of a postponement of wages, were the least to be feared; more serious was deprivation of work, involving ruin or exile. Such sanctions as these were a commonplace of gild regulation throughout the clothing towns of Europe, but in Florence, where industrial capitalism may perhaps be seen in its most intense and ruthless form, they frequently gave place to more savage methods of corporal punishment, from flogging to the loss of a hand and even the loss of life. The wool-carder Cinto Brandini, for instance, accused in 1345 of holding public meetings and exhorting the workers to unite, was arrested during the night with his two sons and, despite a protest strike by all his fellow wool-combers and carders, was hanged on the gallows. And when the prosperity of the first half of the fourteenth century was threatened by increasing problems and difficulties towards its close, the industrial life of Florence became as violent and sanguinary as its political life.

V. *Crisis and Transformation in the North*

(i) *Flanders.* While the Italian industry was reaching its fullest development, the Flemish industry, first to attain maturity, was becoming increasingly conscious of the problems that torment an industrial society. That dependence upon foreign lands for its raw materials and for its markets which had dictated its capitalist organisation had also exposed it to violent fluctuations and, as a result, to widespread labour unrest. Internal and external troubles, acting and reacting upon each other, shook the industry to its foundations, and two centuries of expansion were succeeded by a period of recurrent crises, readjustments and gradual decline.

In the densely peopled clothing cities of the County of Flanders the conflict of capital and labour reached an intensity and a violence never since equalled even in the *Hochkapitalismus* of modern Europe. By the thirteenth century the cleavage between the two had become clearly pronounced. Once there had been a time when all engaged in trade and industry had united to liberate their cities from the common enemy of a feudal overlord. Thus in 1077 the weavers and fullers of Cambrai had joined forces with their fellow citizens to win freedom from the Bishop. And in the twelfth century the independent spirit of the weavers, always restless under authority, had shown itself in rebellion against the accepted tenets of the Church, when they championed what were often described both in Flanders and in England as the 'weavers' heresies'. By the thirteenth century, however, their interest in theological disputation had waned, and they were becoming increasingly absorbed in the struggle to improve their own material conditions of life. By this time the craftsman in the 'great industry' had everywhere fallen into dependence upon the entrepreneur. While the craftsman worked for wages the entrepreneur reaped the surplus profits, and as profits mounted a growing disparity of wealth became apparent. Society was sharply divided into *grands* and *petits*, *majores* and *minores*, rich and poor; the one rich in substance but few in numbers, the other poor in substance but to be counted by their tens of thousands.

The discontents of the *minores* were focussed primarily on questions of wages, not only on rates of pay but on abuses such as truck. But they went further than this, taking at times the form of vague socialist and communist aspirations, as when the weavers and fullers of Valenciennes in 1225 deposed the town government, despoiled the plutocrats and declared a commune. Such a spoliation was doubtless partly instigated by mere lust for plunder. As the chronicler Philippe Mousket put it:

> Povre gent, telier et foulon
> Estoient si privet coulon;
> Et li meliour et li plus gros
> En orent partot mauvais los.
> Et dissoient la povre gent
> Qu'il en orent or et argent.

Doubtless too the craftsmen were influenced by the mystical ideals then widely prevalent among the weavers and by the preaching of the friars who, by proclaiming the virtues of poverty and humility, unconsciously inculcated also contempt and hatred for the rich. But many of them were also convinced, and not without reason, that only by putting down the mighty from their seat could they achieve improved conditions of life. For, as we have seen, the craftsmen themselves were wholly excluded from the merchant gilds in which the employers were entrenched, and it was these gilds which dominated the town governments, fixed wages and conditions of work, controlled the import of wool and the export of cloth and, at the same time, forbade the craftsmen to combine or to hold any meetings without their permission. It was this concentration of political and economic power in the hands of the employers which the workers sought to destroy by the establishment of democratic governments, or at least by securing some share in the political life of their cities.

In the County of Flanders the popular movement came to a climax in 1280. After half a century or more of intermittent trade disputes, strikes and lock-outs, there broke out in this year a general revolution which spread in a few days to Bruges, Ypres, Douai and Tournai. The overthrow of the privileges of the communal oligarchies was the primary objective of the craftsmen, and it was this which in the first instance enabled them to ally themselves both with those lesser merchants and drapers who were excluded from the gilds, and with the Count, who was no less anxious to reduce the power of his overmighty subjects. Thus in their petition to the Count they requested the abrogation of the privileges of the merchant gilds, the abolition of the hereditary *échevinage*, the representation of the craftsmen on the city councils, and freedom for anyone to import wool, whether or no he were a member of the Hanse of London. Not for long, however, did this threefold coalition endure. Those lesser burgesses who had made common cause with the populace soon realised that if the Count wished to destroy the power of the oligarchs it was only in order that he might ultimately destroy the independence of the cities, making himself absolute sovereign in his own land. Valuing civic autonomy more than democracy they abandoned the artisans, rallying to the side of the patricians.

Issue was thus clearly joined between artisans and entrepreneurs, employers and employed. And as the artisans had appealed over the heads of their immediate masters to the Count, so the employers appealed over the head of the Count to his suzerain. Calling to their aid the King of France they admitted to their cities a 'guardian' appointed by him, renounced their allegiance to the Count, and flew from their belfries the fleur-de-lys, thus acquiring their nickname of *Leliaerts*. By so doing they jeopardised the liberty of their country. For as the Count supported the artisans in order that he might destroy the authority of

the patricians and possess himself of full power over his cities, so the
King supported the patricians only in order that he might humble the
Count, his most mighty vassal, and make himself master of Flanders.
Thus the artisans in championing the cause of democracy championed
also the freedom of Flanders, and to the cause of freedom, as to that of
democracy, they remained steadfast. The invasion and annexation of
Flanders by the King of France was the signal for a popular rising in
which the textile workers rallied the whole of the populace. At Bruges,
fullers, weavers and shearmen and indeed all the proletariat rose in
arms, led by a one-eyed weaver, Pierre de Coninc. The workers of
Ghent followed suit. Everywhere the people seized power, massacring
or putting to flight both Frenchmen and *Leliaerts*. Their victory was
sealed at the battle of Courtrai (1302) when a host of foot-soldiers,
recruited from the artisans, armed with pikes, and aided only by some
thirty horsemen, utterly routed the cavalry of France. To the astonishment of Europe, Flanders had been liberated by the heroic determination of its working people.

The cause of democracy in the cities had also triumphed at Courtrai.
The power of the merchant gilds was destroyed and thenceforward
the artisans shared in the government, just as they were permitted to
associate together in their own trade gilds. But the victory of the crafts
was illusory. The well-being of the workers depended ultimately upon
the prosperity of the industry. Absence of class strife may have been
one condition of this prosperity, but it was also a result of it. Other
conditions were ample and regular supplies of raw materials and adequate markets. Successfully as the artisans might attempt a solution of
the problem of the proletariat by limiting the power of the capitalists,
these wider problems were more intractable and less susceptible to
control. And in the discontents and miseries of the late thirteenth
century we may see not so much a cause as a symptom of the onset of
a malady to which in due course the industry was to succumb.

A dearth of wool was one of the principal troubles of the time.
Despite an increase of production, the supply of English wool, most
coveted for high-grade cloth manufacture, was insufficient to meet the
demand. England was needing more of it for the increasing quantities
of fine quality cloth of Yorkshire, Lincolnshire, and Northamptonshire
which, from the mid-thirteenth century, were being exported to the
Mediterranean, and she was herself importing wool from Spain and
from Germany. Still more serious was the competition of Italy,
whose merchants by the close of the century dominated the English
wool trade; though some of the wool they exported was sold to the
Flemings, more and more of it went south to feed the looms of Italy.
In any event, therefore, the supply of wool to Flanders was precarious.

Political developments made it yet more so. As relations between England and France became increasingly strained towards the close of the century both sides tended to use economic weapons. By threatening a cessation of wool exports England could seriously embarrass France and could also enforce the neutrality, if not the active aid, of France's most mighty fief, Flanders. France might reply by closing her markets to English wool and by seizing English wool merchants and their goods, but only at the expense of ruining Flanders and throwing her into the hands of England. From 1269 onwards trade was interrupted by a succession of embargoes and confiscations which from time to time brought industry completely to a standstill, ruining the employers and bringing misery and destitution to the artisans, who roamed the country-side in starving hordes, begging their bread. In the great wool famine of 1297 the land of Flanders was said to be well-nigh empty (*exinanitam*) 'because the people could not have the wools of England'. It was little wonder that Edward I's tactics on this occasion proved successful and that before long the Count, already turning against the French King for his support of the Flemish patricians, signed a treaty of alliance with England; England alone could secure his people's livelihood.

If wool was scarce, it was also expensive, though not only on account of its scarcity. The wool of England, declared Parliament, amounted 'to some half the value of the whole land'. Inevitably, therefore, the needs of Edward's war finance prompted a tax on wool, and in 1275 the first export duty was levied. Before long the original tax of 7s. 6d. per sack was sharply stepped up by such devices as the 'maltôte' of 5 marks per sack levied in 1294 and that of 3 marks per sack levied in 1297. A part of these duties could be passed on to the English growers in the form of lower payments, but part was necessarily transferred to the continental purchaser. And when in 1303 a yet further duty was imposed on alien exporters only, the whole of the new tax had thus to be passed on, since in dealing with the English producers the aliens were in competition with English merchants.

Prices for the foreign manufacturer thus rose steeply as a result of the English export duties. They rose yet further as a result of the weakening of Flemish money in relation to English, for the devaluation of the currency was among the principal remedies sought by the French King, Philip the Fair, against the financial embarrassments which were afflicting the French, no less than the English, monarchy. Thus the inflationary policy which so raised the cost of living as to justify the growing clamour for higher wages, at the same time so raised the price of raw materials as to make it more difficult for employers to meet these claims if their cloth was still to compete successfully on foreign markets.

If raw materials were a problem for the Flemish manufacturers so too were markets. Italian competition, as we have seen, was steadily growing. So too was that of England. In the reign of Edward I fine cloths of Stamford and Lincoln, dyed in grain, were as much in demand by the English royal family and nobility as fine cloths of Douai had once been, though still at the close of the century a considerable amount of Flemish cloth could find a sale in England. Moreover, the English market was sometimes completely closed to Flemish cloth when for diplomatic reasons trade between England and Flanders was prohibited.

At the same time the principal outlet for Flemish cloths, that to the fairs of Champagne, was frequently interrupted from the moment that Champagne became in effect part of the royal domain of France in 1285. Flanders' export trade in cloth suffered as much from the fiscal and diplomatic needs of the French King as did her import trade in wool from those of the English King. Not only were there many disputes about frontier tolls between the Flemings and the King, to whom his new territories were principally of interest for the replenishing of his exchequer, but the prohibition of all traffic across the frontier was constantly used from then on as a diplomatic weapon against the Flemings. And when in 1297 Flanders became allied to England, all the Flemish merchants throughout France were arrested, their goods and credits confiscated, and their halls seized.

Thus at the close of the thirteenth century political difficulties threatened the two life-lines of the Flemish industry, the wool route across the Channel and the cloth route across the frontier to the great fairs and so to Italy, just at the moment when the competition of English and Italian clothmakers was becoming increasingly serious. The unemployment caused by the cutting of the two life-lines, together with the rise in the cost of living resulting from the devaluation of the currency, exacerbated the discontents of the workers and stimulated their demands for higher wages, while at the same time it was less possible for the employers to meet these demands since production costs were rising, overheads had still to be met even in times of stoppage, and profits were precarious.

Such were the circumstances which made the triumph of the crafts but a Pyrrhic victory, marking indeed the beginning of the decline of the Flemish industry. The battle of Courtrai might put political power into the hands of the textile workers, but it solved none of the problems of an industrial state whose prosperity was dependent upon foreign markets, upon foreign raw materials, and upon the skill and initiative of entrepreneurs in close touch with each. These problems became more rather than less acute with the new century. Industrial conflict continued. For though the craftsmen had sought to secure economic as well as political power by destroying the monopoly of the merchant gilds and throwing open to all the trade in wool and cloth, in practice the great majority of them remained a dependent prole-tariat, working for others, since the 'great industry' demanded the capitalist entrepreneur. Their situation was fundamentally unchanged, if somewhat ameliorated. Nor was any real improvement possible in their standard of life without the re-establishment of regular imports of wool and exports of cloth. Here no recovery could be looked for along the old lines. The expanding industries of England and Italy made ever-increasing demands on English wool, and the conflict between England and France moved inexorably towards the final rupture of the Hundred Years War. Moreover, the French king still aimed at the absorption of Flanders, while the peoples of Flanders were still as passionately attached to the idea of autonomy; hence periods of peace, when trade was resumed apparently with undiminished vigour, alter-nated with open warfare and complete embargoes. Unemployment therefore continued. So too did civil war: with the disillusionment of the workers, class hatreds increased rather than diminished. A series of insurrections in the first quarter of the century culminated in that of 1324 when the weavers and fullers of Ypres and Bruges joined the peasants in revolt against the rich, proclaiming the dawn of a new era. The revolt was suppressed only by the intervention of the French, who, outside the walls of Cassel (1328), cut to pieces the armies of peasants and artisans and wreaked upon the cities a terrible vengeance.

The internal and external conflicts that drove the textile workers of Flanders again and again during the early fourteenth century to take up arms, whether against the French or the plutocrats, or among them-selves, did not wholly destroy the 'great industry', even if they gravely impaired its strength and stability. But they brought about profound changes in its location, in its organisation, and in the marketing of its products.

The significant Flemish manufacturing region had now shrunk to the maritime lands north of the Lys. Already by the mid-thirteenth century the northern centres were tending to become more important than the southern; in the early fourteenth century this tendency was intensified. For in 1312 Flanders had purchased peace for a few years by the cession to France of her Walloon districts, in which lay the clothing towns of Lille, Douai, Orchies and Béthune. In these once famous textile centres, now so often the scene of the passage of French armies, industry languished and declined, even as had that of Arras, once the industrial and commercial metropolis of the North, when Artois had been ceded to France at the close of the twelfth century. The paramount manufacturing cities were now Ypres and Bruges and

Ghent, whose vigour and vitality, not less than their greater distance from France, had preserved them, though at heavy cost, from annexation.

Within these three cities foreign had replaced native capital in two of the three branches of the trade, dominating the import of the raw material and the export of the finished product, and leaving to the Flemish capitalists only the organisation of the various processes of production. The day of the great individual entrepreneur combining all three functions, as Jean Boine Broke had done, was ended. With the suppression of the merchant gilds and the abolition of the political and economic privileges of the merchant patricians, Flemish enterprise was on a more modest scale. Just as the Flemish ships had now left the seas, so the Flemish merchants had abandoned the foreign trade; no longer did they flock to the great fairs selling their cloth, or travel through England buying up wool. The Hanse of London disappeared; the Hanse of the Seventeen Towns became in the course of the fourteenth century no more than a name. The Flemish draper still put out wool to spinners, weavers, fullers and others, but he bought his wool from foreign importers, most often Italians, and he sold his cloth, usually through the agency of native brokers, to export firms many of whom were also Italian.

If the decline of the Hanse of the Seventeen Towns was a sign of the decadence of the Flemish merchant patrician class, it was also a sign of the reorientation of the export trade. France was no longer the principal mart for Flemish textiles. The ancient landward route to the fairs of Champagne, now so frequently blocked at the frontier by new toll barriers or by the armies of France, was less and less used. In the fair towns themselves grass grew in the streets, and the halls of the Flemish merchants crumbled into ruins. The cloths of Ypres, Ghent and Bruges now found their chief outlet by sea from the port of Bruges. Bruges, yet more important for its commerce than for its industry, became the principal collecting and exporting centre for northern textiles, as Arras had been in the first phase of expansion. There the Flemish cloths were loaded on the foreign vessels that now crowded the harbour—on the long Italian galleys which since the close of the thirteenth century had opened up a direct sea route from Italy to the North; on English, French, Spanish and Portuguese ships; and, above all, on the sturdy cogs of the German Hanse, now rising to the zenith of its power, which carried Flemish cloth to the newly colonised lands on the Baltic in return for the corn and potash needed by the industrial cities of Flanders.

(ii) *Brabant*. The troubles that afflicted the textile centres of the County of Flanders in the late thirteenth and early fourteenth centuries gave to their neighbours in the Duchy of Brabant a golden opportunity. While in Flanders life for both rich and poor became less and less secure, as workshops lay silent for lack of material or for lack of markets and the land was repeatedly ravaged by sanguinary revolutions or foreign invasions, Brabant, on the contrary, achieved an astonishing measure of stability and prosperity. Fief of the Empire, she enjoyed a quasi-independence such as Flanders had known two centuries earlier. The skilful policy of a succession of able dukes ensured her autonomy while at the same time it preserved peace with her neighbours and kept open the arteries of trade. John I, his son and his grandson, were deservedly popular with the merchants and people of Brabant. Refusing to become seriously entangled either in the contest between Flanders and France or in that between France and England, now approaching its climax, they nevertheless negotiated from time to time with each of the protagonists, but only so that they might exact greater privileges as the price of their alliance or even of their neutrality. In the Anglo-French war of 1294–97, for instance, when all export of wool from England was forbidden, an exception was made in favour of the merchants of Brabant alone, for the Duke had been active in urging the Count of Flanders to ally himself with the King of England. A few years later, however, he allowed himself to be used by the French King as his agent to bring the Flemings to terms, in return for a commercial treaty giving the merchants of Brabant a privileged status above all others on the markets of France.

Thus by the astute statesmanship of her dukes Brabant's wool supply continued almost uninterrupted, and while she maintained and even strengthened her ancient commercial links with the eastern markets of the Rhineland she developed new links with the West, intensifying her trade in the markets of France at the very moment that these markets were being deserted by the Flemings.

Equally successful were the dukes in holding in check those social conflicts which, though less violent and prolonged than in Flanders, nevertheless threatened the peace of Brabant. Never once did they waver in their support of the patricians against the proletariat. The patricians on their part were undeviating in their loyalty to the dukes since in them they saw their only possible protector against the fury of the populace. Industrial unrest had given rise to sporadic, but unsuccessful, outbreaks throughout the thirteenth century. In Brabant, as in Flanders, the right of association was denied to the artisans, and they were wholly under the power of the patrician merchant gilds, from which all manual workers were excluded. The triumph of the Flemish insurgents in 1302 was the signal for a general revolt. Led by the weavers and fullers, the workers of Brussels, Louvain, Antwerp and Léau rose in arms, drove the patricians from their cities, seized the reins of power, and abolished the merchant gilds. But the Duke himself took

up arms against them, commanding in person the forces of the patricians. On the field of Vilvorde (1306) he utterly defeated the rebel
army. The revolt was suppressed with ruthless severity. Many of those
weavers and fullers who had been foremost in the fight were banished;
some, it seems likely, were even buried alive. The merchant gilds were
restored and their powers confirmed; they alone might henceforth
make regulations for the weavers, fullers, dyers, carders and spinners.
The workers were again forbidden to strike, to assemble together without permission, or to carry arms; at Brussels the death penalty was
imposed on any who were found within the walls of the city itself after
the curfew had sounded, when they should have been outside it in the
workers' suburb in which they were segregated.

If the failure of the popular movement must in part be attributed to
the firm alliance between the Duke and his patrician subjects, it must
in part also be attributed to the vigour of the merchant gilds, whose
continuing vitality in Brabant is in striking contrast to their decadence in
Flanders at this time. But this vitality is itself no doubt as much the
result as the cause of the stability of the Brabantine industry. Free to
develop their business undisturbed, the Brabantine merchants were in
a position to exploit to the full the opportunity presented by the troubles
of Flanders. Hitherto the textile industry of Brabant had lagged behind
that of Flanders. In the twelfth century, when cloths of Arras and Ypres
were being marketed throughout Europe, it had been of little importance. And though in the middle of the thirteenth century its products
were being sold on the Rhine, it was only towards the close of the
century that they appear to have reached the fairs of Champagne in any
quantity. In the most ancient list of the Hanse of the Seventeen Towns
(in the mid-thirteenth century) the cities of Brabant are wholly missing;
in a list of 1285 Louvain and Malines appear, and a few years later
Brussels, Nivelles and Diest also; all these, with Enghien, are mentioned
in a Parisian tariff of 1296-7. In the next half century, while retaining
their trade to the East, they steadily strengthened their hold in the West.

Cloths of Brussels, Malines and Louvain in particular enjoyed a
growing reputation. This may be seen, for instance, by the purchases
made between 1298 and 1328 for the household of the Countess of
Artois, whether at the fairs of Champagne or at the place of manufacture: cloths of Brussels are most numerous of all, followed closely
by those of Louvain and Malines; together purchases from these three
cities outnumber all those from Flanders. In Paris, during the early
fourteenth century, cloths of Brabant were steadily gaining on those of
Flanders; business was so brisk that Brabantine merchants were seeking
fresh space in which to display their wares, and it is significant of the
trend of the times that they hired there a part of the halls held by the

merchants of Douai since the time of St Louis. It was doubtless by these French routes that some Brabant cloths began to reach the Mediterranean in the early fourteenth century, thence penetrating to the Levant where, when Pegolotti compiled his handbook, cloths of Brussels, Louvain, Malines and Antwerp were to be found on the markets of Constantinople. But some were also going South by a more direct route, now less subject to interruption and hindrance. In the long series of Genoese notarial records beginning in the late twelfth century, to which we owe so much of our knowledge of the trade in northern cloths, the cloths of Brabant appear first in 1310. From this time on it is clear that not only Genoese agents but also Genoese ships were penetrating to Brabant, where at Antwerp they were to be found 'seeking cloths and other goods'. It was with shrewd judgment that John III bestowed upon them special privileges, encouraging them to frequent his rapidly developing port. For thus he secured a third outlet for the cloths of Brabant, and one likely to be less precarious than either the eastern or western land routes.

(iii) *England.* For the English industry, as for that of the Low Countries, the turn of the thirteenth and fourteenth centuries was a time of crisis and transformation, though of transformation which had in it the seeds of progress rather than decline. England's industrial development was as yet much behind that of Flanders. Though her production of cloth was not negligible, she was above all a supplier of raw wool to Flanders and Italy, and was herself a market for considerable quantities of foreign cloth: when Edward I needed new sources of revenue it was wool rather than cloth whose export he taxed. Hence the English clothing towns were on a very small scale compared, for example, with Ypres or Ghent. Yet here too there were signs of industrial conflict, if not of so grave a nature as in Flanders. Wage rates, restrictive practices, the right of association and the right of assembly were all matters hotly disputed between employers and employed. At Leicester the fullers were summoned (in 1275) for holding an illegal meeting not in the presence of members of the gild merchant, and the weavers (in 1264) for 'making by themselves a provision about weaving against the community of the gild merchant'. At Norwich (in 1293) the fullers were accused of having an illegal gild. The London weavers, strongly organised in their own gild with its royal charter going back at least to the early twelfth century, were in a position to defy their employers with some measure of success. Attempts to destroy their gild had proved vain. When the city government offered King John a large sum to abolish the charter, the weavers gave him a still larger sum for its restoration. By the end of the thirteenth century they were meeting the problem of rising prices by raising their own wages, demanding, if their employers the burellers are to be believed, first 2s., then 2s. 6d. and even 3s. 4d. for weaving a cloth, where formerly they had been content with 1s. 4d. or 1s. 6d., and enforcing their demands when necessary by strikes. At the same time, complained the burellers, they limited the number of looms from 380 to 80, decreed that no cloth was to be woven in less than four days, and lengthened their holidays, taking a winter break of over a month from Christmas to February 2nd.

The restrictive practices in which the London weavers were indulging at this time indicate clearly that there was not enough work to go round. Business in fact was declining, not only in London but also in many other old-established centres of the industry. At Oxford there were said to be only seven weavers left in 1290; by 1323 these seven were dead and none had taken their place. At Lincoln, once renowned for its scarlets, there were said by then to be no weavers at all; at Leicester there was but one fuller 'and he a poor man'; at Northampton by 1334 the houses where once 300 clothmakers had lived were said all to have fallen down. The Winchester weavers' gild, finding increasing difficulty in collecting its yearly payments to the crown, excused itself on the ground that large numbers of cloth-workers had left the town; the York, Lincoln and Oxford gilds were also falling into more and more serious arrears. If such complaints are too closely associated with claims for relief from taxation to be taken quite at their face value, yet they are too general and too simultaneous to be ignored.

Such a setback in the once famous clothing cities of Eastern England suggests at first sight a depression in the English industry as a whole. Its primary cause was, however, a shift in the location of the industry, due very largely to a technical revolution in one of its main branches as a result of the introduction of the water fulling mill.

The mechanising of fulling in the Middle Ages was as decisive an event as the mechanisation of spinning and weaving in the eighteenth century, but we know neither when nor where, much less by whom, the fulling mill was invented. The evidence so far available points to its having come into general use in Western Europe in the course of the twelfth century. The earliest mention of a fulling mill that has as yet come to light in England is in the survey made in 1185 of the Templars' English estates; this notes one at Newsham in Yorkshire and another at Barton in the Cotswolds. From then on references to such mills become more and more numerous. That the fulling mill was not wholly unknown in Europe before then is shown by an eleventh century charter of St Wandrille's, whose unpublished original still survives at Rouen. But two significant changes in terminology confirm the impression that from about the late twelfth century it was being widely substituted for the old-fashioned fullery. The old word 'fullery' (*fullonia*) which was common in earlier documents and clearly implies an installation little different from that in use in Roman times (cf. p. 358) now gradually disappears, giving place to 'fulling mill' (*molendinum fullericum*), and when water mills are mentioned it becomes usual to specify, as was hitherto unnecessary, whether they are for grinding corn or for some other purpose.

In the 'great industry' at least the new device had obvious advantages over the arduous old method of trampling in the trough. For in the mill the feet of men were replaced by two wooden hammers, which were alternately raised and dropped upon the cloth on the tilt hammer system, by means of a revolving drum attached to the spindle of a water wheel. Thus by a simple contrivance water power replaced human energy and a whole series of hammers could be set to work with but one man standing over them to watch the cloth and see that it was kept properly moving in the trough.

The very fact that the new process so greatly reduced the labour force required meant that its adoption was resisted by the old-established fullers in the clothing cities. Seeing in it a threat to their livelihood they strenuously opposed it, urging, like the handloom weavers of the eighteenth century, the inferiority of machine work as well as the unemployment it caused. Such was the double complaint of the Londoners in 1298, when they bewailed that cloth was being sent out to mills at Stratford 'to the grave damage of those to whom the cloth belonged and also of the men using this office in the city'.

Despite the opposition of the city fullers, however, fulling mills were by this time springing up all over England, wherever water power was available. By the opening of the fourteenth century their use was widespread. Everywhere foot-fulling was giving way to mechanical fulling; human labour was being displaced by water power; the fulling industry was being carried on at the mill rather than in the home, and it was dependent, as never before, upon considerable capital equipment. So much business was being drawn to the mills that they had become a form of investment to which much capital was attracted, capital derived from the land as well as from trade. In country districts the venture was a profitable one not only because stuffs woven in the towns were being sent out to the mills, but also because the fulling mill—like the corn mill, the oven, the winepress or the dyepan—had come to be regarded as a manorial monopoly to which the tenants owed suit. The country folk could be compelled to bring their webs to the lord's mill for fulling, instead of fulling them at home with their feet, even if they were woven only for their own use, just as they had to take their corn to the lord's windmill or watermill instead of grinding it at home with handmills. Frequently, therefore, the initiative in building the mills was taken by lords of the manor, lay and ecclesiastical, who spent large sums upon them. The Bishop of Winchester, for instance, built a fulling mill on his manor at Brightwell in 1208–9 at a cost of more than £9. Once erected, the mills were usually leased out, though occasionally they were worked by a fuller on the lord's account. The profits on them varied both according to the amount of commercial business attracted and according to the number of tenants who owed suit to the mill; thus half a share in the fulling mill of Kendal, which had once been worth 10 marks, was by 1274 worth only 8 marks, since another mill had been built higher up the river at Staveley, and to this new mill the tenants in Kentmere did suit, walking only four instead of eight miles down the Kent valley with their cloths.

The monopolistic claims of the lords of the manor, which ensured to them a substantial profit from their investments, were not unnaturally resisted by the populace. To the end of the Middle Ages the struggle against them continued, at times erupting into open revolt. When, for instance, the Abbot of St Albans, having spent no less than £100 on his corn and fulling mills, insisted that even the smallest pieces of cloth must be brought there for fulling, the people of St Albans considered this an unwarrantable usurpation and continued to full their cloth at home free of charge. And when in 1274 the Abbot sent to search their houses and distrain their cloths they resisted his servants by force, opened a fighting fund, and contested the case in the king's court, though in vain.

The rapid extension of the fulling mill affected decisively not only the technique and organisation of the English industry but also its location, spelling ruin to the old clothing centres. Some of the cities did indeed set up their own fulling mills, despite opposition to an innovation which would throw so many out of work. But the requisite space for constructing mills, with the necessary diversion of the watercourse, cannot always have been readily available. Nor were the slow-moving lower courses of the rivers on which most of the towns lay as well suited to the purpose as their swifter upper courses, where use could be made of the more efficient overshot wheel. Hence fulling came more and more to be carried on outside the cities, often in remote upland valleys. The tendency for one branch of the industry to develop in rural districts gave an immense stimulus to the development of the industry as a whole there. Groups of weavers as well as fullers and other workers began to appear round the mills, where to the advantages of water power were added the advantages of freedom from the restrictions of the urban gilds and from the high taxation to which the townsmen were subject; the industry thus became dispersed over the countryside, rather than concentrated in the ancient chartered boroughs of the plains.

Yet more important, it was in the hilly regions of England that water power could most readily be obtained. Since, therefore, water was now as decisive a factor as coal was to become in the nineteenth century, the industry tended to move outwards from the cities of the flat eastern plain between Humber and Wash to the North and West and also to the South, especially to those districts where fine wool was to be had as well as water power and clear water for dyeing. In particular it grew with startling rapidity in the West Riding of Yorkshire, the southern marches of Wales, the Cotswolds, the Mendips, and the valleys among the Wiltshire and Berkshire downs. Scarcely less remarkable was its development in the Lake District and in Devon and Cornwall, though in these parts a rougher cloth was made. In all these districts water power was being actively exploited by the early fourteenth century, though not yet nearly to its full extent, and in many places there were concentrations of industrial workers, like that at Calverley on the Aire, or that in the Stroud valley, where in the manor of Minchinhampton seven tenants, one of whom rented the manorial fulling mill, paid for leave to dig fullers' earth.

In vain the cities strove against the ever-increasing competition of the countryside. The sending out of cloth to the mills was restricted, as was also the employment of artisans outside the city walls. But such ordinances, though they might do something to prevent city manufacturers from having dealings with workers outside, could not prevent an independent industry from flourishing in the country. Some cities therefore invoked the charters which in times past had granted them the monopoly, within a certain region, of the manufacture of dyed and finished cloth. Thus, for instance, the citizens of York pleaded in 1304 that although by their charter of 1164 the making of such cloth had been restricted to York itself and the other boroughs of the county, yet now 'divers men in divers places in the county, elsewhere than in the city and in other towns, make dyed and rayed cloths'. Their petition to the king did indeed result in an official enquiry and in an order that all found plying the craft in illegal places should be compelled to refrain, but such an order could not effectively succeed in confining the industry within urban walls, much less in preventing its development in far distant parts of England.

The twelfth and thirteenth centuries, notable for so many scientific discoveries, had seen a twofold technical advance in the woollen industry with the introduction of the spinning wheel and the fulling mill. Both inventions made possible a considerable increase in production without a corresponding increase in the labour force involved. But the second—the first to substitute mechanical for human power in the textile industry—had yet more decisive results, for it brought poverty, unemployment and discontent to many of the old manufacturing centres, but wealth, opportunity and prosperity to other and more remote regions hitherto unindustrialised, but possessing in their water power a prime industrial advantage.

VI. *The Triumph of the English Industry*

The advance of the English woollen industry to that position of pre-eminence which it has since enjoyed is one of the cardinal facts of the later Middle Ages. By the close of the fifteenth century its triumph was assured; the once mighty urban industries of Flanders and Italy, having failed to solve the problem of the industrial society, were in the throes of dissolution, rent by increasing dissensions and difficulties, while England had been transformed from an exporter primarily of raw material into an exporter primarily of manufactured products.

The new possibilities inherent in the development of the fulling mill gave England, with its abundant water power, one decisive advantage over Flanders. Flanders, like Lincolnshire, is a land of windmills rather than watermills. The mechanising of fulling there on any considerable scale would have been difficult, if not impossible, even had it not been prohibited by the urban gilds, which were not less conservative than those of England, and very much more powerful. Such evidence as is at present available suggests that it was never attempted. Espinas, in his monumental study of clothmaking in French Flanders, found fulling mills only in Artois; at Ypres foot-fulling was almost exclusively used even into the sixteenth century. Italy was in this respect more favourably situated. The Arno and other streams descending from the Apennines provided sufficient power to turn a number of mills in the immediate neighbourhood of Florence, and to these mills the Florentine cloth was sent out. Unlike the Flemish cities which, each in splendid isolation, attempted to confine the industry within their walls, striving against the competition of rural neighbours and also against one another, Florence exploited the surrounding countryside, over which she herself held sway. Capital for the erection of the mills was contributed both by individual manufacturers and by the corporate *Arte della Lana*, which came gradually to acquire a controlling share in most of them.

In raw materials England had the advantage over both Italy and Flanders. From the late thirteenth century those abundant supplies of Europe's finest wools which she herself produced could be bought by her own manufacturers at prices far below those paid by the foreigner. For the purchase price abroad had now to take account, as we have seen, not only of transport charges but also of the increasingly onerous export duties imposed since 1275. Cheaper raw materials lowered the relative costs of production and enabled the English manufacturer to put his cloth on the market, at home and abroad, more cheaply than that of the foreigner. Thus the immense margin between the domestic and the foreign prices of English wool provided effective protection for an infant industry, and doubtless did more to foster its growth than did the sporadic export embargoes which could, in any event, be frequently evaded by special licence. The industry was further favoured by the comparative lightness of the export duties on cloth. Cloth, unlike wool, could be shipped from England entirely free of customs at the close of the thirteenth century. The first export duty, that of 1303, affected only alien merchants, and not until 1347 were native merchants taxed. Even then cloth paid a duty of less than 2%, as compared with one of some 33% on wool. Nor was its export restricted by any staple system. There was therefore every incentive to export cloth rather than wool.

The new and lucrative opportunities presented by technical and fiscal developments such as have been described above attracted to the English industry both capital and labour. In the country districts to which it was increasingly gravitating much use could be made of part-time workers, and many a cottar, whose time was not fully taken up on his own small holding or by the performance of the comparatively light manorial services demanded of him, took to weaving as a bye-industry, as the women had from time immemorial taken to carding, combing and spinning. Doubtless, too, many younger sons who might once have brought new lands under the plough now found careers in industry. Such rural labour tended to be cheaper than urban labour not only because it was wholly unprotected and uncontrolled, and without opportunity for collective bargaining, but also because living costs were lower in the country, where victuals, firewood and other necessaries were much more easily obtained. This was a further factor favourable to English enterprise.

Fresh impetus, too, was given to the immigration of foreign workers, particularly of skilled craftsmen from the Flemish textile centres. Such immigrations were no novelty; in the twelfth century the members of the Flemish colony settled by Henry I in Pembrokeshire were said by Giraldus Cambrensis to be well versed in the making of woollens. But from the late thirteenth century, as tension increased between England and France, their encouragement became an instrument of diplomatic policy. When export of wool and import of cloth were forbidden, to bring pressure upon the Count of Flanders or upon his suzerain the French King, such prohibitions were almost invariably accompanied by a general invitation to Flemish artisans to ply their trade in England, often on very favourable terms, and by an injunction to the English public to wear English cloth only. By such means, it was thought,

English growers might be provided with an outlet for their wool at home instead of abroad, English consumers with supplies of home-made instead of foreign cloth, and Flemish artisans with the employment of which they had been deprived in Flanders. Thus, for example, during the embargo of 1271 Henry III decreed that 'all workers of woollen cloths, male and female, as well of Flanders as of other lands, may safely come into our realm, there to make cloths', and he granted them freedom from taxation for five years. Though at first the ban on the wearing of foreign apparel did not apply to the upper income levels, as diplomatic relations became strained to breaking point it was extended to all classes of the community. Thus when in 1337 Edward III took the extreme step of claiming the crown of France, all his subjects 'of whatever degree' were bidden to wear English cloth; no import of foreign cloth or export of English wool was allowed, and 'all cloth-makers of strange lands of whatever country they be' were taken into the king's protection. Edward's agents, according to the sixteenth-century historian Fuller, were not slow to point out to the Flemings the contrast between the wretched conditions of life in the Low Countries and the rosy prospects in England. Whether or no this is true, it is not surprising that many took advantage of the invitation, abandoning a land so frequently given over to unemployment, civil tumult and foreign invasion for one enjoying an abundance of raw materials, freedom from controls, and virtual immunity from conflict. The stream of voluntary emigrants was swollen by that of political refugees. After the defeat of Cassel, for instance, some 500 weavers and 500 fullers of Ypres were banished from Flanders, and in 1344 certain weavers of Poperinghe were specifically condemned to exile in England. It is impossible now to assess the scale and pace of this migration. While individual safe-conducts were often sought by immigrants from territories with which England was, nominally at least, at war, many came over relying solely on the general offer of protection, leaving no trace in the official records of the time. The majority of the settlers would appear to have been well-to-do artisans—weavers chiefly, and also fullers and dyers—who brought with them their own journeymen and apprentices; but there were also entrepreneurs like 'John Bruyn, burgess of Ghent, now making stay in Abingdon, making woollen cloth there and trading in other wares within the realm, and his men and servants'. Some found their way to the west country, like a certain weaver at Stow-on-the-Wold, and some to the West Riding of Yorkshire, but most of them seem to have settled in the cities of Eastern and Southern England, so that they probably contributed little to the development of the new industrial districts. Their coming is of importance rather as a symptom than as a cause of the progress of English enterprise.

It is at this point in the history of the English industry that we for the first time begin to get data for some quantitative measure of its advance. With the imposition in 1347 of the duty on native as well as foreign shipments of cloth the customs accounts of the royal exchequer come year by year to record all exports of cloth as well as of wool. A remarkable transformation is thereby revealed. In the mid-fourteenth century England was still predominantly an exporter of raw materials, shipping abroad normally over 30,000 sacks of wool each year, as she had done at the close of the fourteenth century, enough to make more than 130,000 broadcloths. Cloth exports recorded for Michaelmas 1347–Michaelmas 1348 were only 4422 cloths (in terms of full-size broadcloths), though it would be dangerous to dogmatise from this one full year of cloth accounts as to the general level of exports just before the Black Death. After a marked depression in the years immediately following the Black Death exports of raw wool recovered to almost their previous level, while at the same time exports of manufactured cloth rose with great rapidity, reaching in 1366–68 an annual average of nearly 16,000 cloths, for the manufacture of which some 3700 sacks of wool were probably used. Another depression beginning in the late sixties was succeeded by a second impressive advance, and by the end of the century cloth exports were nearly tenfold the 1347–48 figure, averaging for 1392–95 some 43,000 cloths, equivalent to some 10,000 sacks of wool. Wool exports meanwhile had fallen to an average of some 19,000 sacks. It was not surprising that Chaucer, who had lived through so notable a development of England's economy and had himself been a collector of customs, included among his Canterbury pilgrims a vigorous west country clothier, the much travelled goodwife living near Bath, and wrote of her:

> Of clooth-making she hadde swiche an haunt
> She passed hem of Ypres and of Gaunt.

This spectacular rate of expansion was not maintained. Nevertheless the industry continued to progress, if more slowly, and by the mid-fifteenth century cloth exports had risen to an annual average of some 54,000 cloths, equivalent to some 12,500 sacks of wool. Since wool exports had at the same time declined to some 8000 sacks a turning point had been reached: England was now predominantly an exporter of manufactured woollens rather than of raw wool. Towards the close of the century, when the civil wars of York and Lancaster were over, the momentum of the advance again increased; by the end of Edward IV's reign woollen exports averaged 63,000 cloths, and in the time of the first two Tudors they doubled, reaching 84,000 cloths early in

Henry VIII's reign and 122,000 cloths by the middle of the sixteenth century.

The customs accounts record not only the immense increase in the export of English woollens but also the virtual cessation of the import of foreign woollens, except for certain specialities; in the course of the fourteenth century English woollens had captured the English market. Apart from this falling off of imports, however, there is no means of estimating changes in home demand; hence the trend of production, unlike that of export, cannot be satisfactorily measured. A tax was indeed imposed in England from 1353 on all cloths produced for sale, and it would at first sight appear as though we have valuable quantitative evidence of production in the accounts of the royal aulnagers who were now responsible for collecting it, as well as for measuring the cloths to ensure that they conformed to the Assize of Measures standardising length and breadth. But the returns are fragmentary and of dubious worth. Those for the late fourteenth century give us perhaps approximate figures of total production, though they can seldom be relied on for figures of individual output. Those for the fifteenth century are still less satisfactory; the majority of them prove at best to be second-hand compilations of doubtful veracity, and at worst to be pure invention; they may give a rough measure of the relative importance of different production areas at some point of time, but the figures they yield for the country as a whole towards the end of the century are certainly too low, since they would scarcely account even for the quantity exported, while the names of individual producers and the numbers of cloths so carefully allotted to each can be shown in some cases to be wholly fictitious.

By the time that the revolution had been accomplished which turned England from an exporter of raw wool into an exporter primarily of manufactured woollens, there had also been completed that revolution in the location of her industry which had been initiated by the invention of the fulling mill. No more was now heard of cloths of Lincoln, Louth, Stamford or Leicester; the industries of York and Beverley were slowly dying. First in importance among England's cloth producing regions was the West of England, which was responsible in the late fifteenth century for possibly half the whole cloth production of the country and for almost all the broadcloths. Thence came those 'Stroudwaters', 'Cotswolds', 'Castlecombes' and 'Westerns' whose reputation on the continent was now as high as that of Lincoln scarlets had once been. The manufacture of fine broadcloths, dyed and finished, was concentrated especially in the southern Cotswolds, in the Stroud valley and along the Bradford Avon and its tributaries, where were abundant supplies of fine quality wools, water power and fullers' earth. Here weaving and spinning were being carried on in almost every village and hamlet; fulling mills crowded the valleys running up into the hills, and new settlements were developing along the streams where none had been before. Thus Stroud and Chalford, for example, grew from nothing into thriving industrial centres, though the wealthy mill-owners who carried on business down in the valley lie buried in the ancient parish churches on the upland above—at Minchinhampton, Rodborough and Bisley, since there was as yet neither church nor separate parish below. Thus too at Castlecombe there lived down by the river, it is said, some seventy craftsmen—weavers, fullers and dyers—each with his servants and apprentices, and from them the lord of the manor, Sir John Fastolf, bought each year cloth to the value of £100, red and white, for the clothing of his men in the Hundred Years' War. All along the southern fringes of the Cotswolds other busy centres of the industry were emerging: Wickwar, Dursley, Wotton-under-Edge, Bath, Trowbridge, Bradford-on-Avon, Cirencester, Malmesbury and many another. South of the Avon, Somerset was famous for its 'Mendips'. Further west, through Bridgwater and Taunton and on into Devon to Barnstaple, Tiverton and Exeter, stretched a manufacturing region producing not heavily milled broadcloths but kerseys and other such cheap and light fabrics. An equally notable kersey district lay in South Wiltshire and Berkshire, particularly along the Wylie valley to Salisbury and along the Kennet valley through Marlborough and Newbury to Reading, while there was a less important extension of this kersey region through Hampshire into Surrey and Kent.

If the West of England was second to none as a producer of broadcloths, as a producer of kerseys and suchlike stuffs it had rivals both in Yorkshire and in East Anglia. Clothmaking had long been established in Essex and Suffolk. Colchester, as we have seen, had once been renowned for its cheap russets, and cloths of Maldon, Coggeshall, Sudbury and other parts of the countryside were being shipped abroad when Ipswich compiled its *Domesday Book* at the end of the thirteenth century. By the fifteenth century a remarkable concentration of industry had developed along the Stour, where was a manufacturing region comparable for the volume of its production only to that of the southern Cotswolds, and enjoying a prosperity which it has never since recaptured. Almost all the villages on both the Essex and the Suffolk banks of the Stour—from Dedham and East Bergholt through Stratford and Nayland to Sudbury, Long Melford, Glemsford, Cavendish and Clare to Haverhill—were now growing rich by clothing, as the splendour of their perpendicular churches testifies. Not less important were the clothing centres on the tributaries of the Stour, such as

Hadleigh, Kersey, Lavenham, Boxford, Great and Little Waldingfield. Beyond these were outlying centres like Bury St Edmunds, Halstead, Braintree and Coggeshall.

In Norfolk there had been established at least since the late thirteenth century the manufacture of a light stuff of high quality made of long wool, combed not carded, and requiring little milling. This was in much demand for the summer clothing of religious orders in this country and abroad—quantities were sent overseas to the Knights of St John and to the Knights Templar—and for the furnishings of churches and houses, particularly for the coverlets and testers which were an indispensable adjunct to the medieval bed. At first called serge or say, it came gradually to be described more often as worsted, most probably because it was produced chiefly at Worstead and in the immediate vicinity at other now insignificant villages like Honing, Tunstead, and Scottow; Norwich too became a centre for its manufacture as well as for its marketing. By the fifteenth century the industry appears to have been in decline, and worsteds were playing but a small part in England's export trade; though John Paston determined with true local patriotism to make his doublet 'all worsted for the honour of Norfolk', and wrote from London to his Norfolk home not five miles from Worstead asking his wife to enquire 'where William Paston bought his tippet of fine worsted which is almost like silk'.

Third in order of importance was the West Riding of Yorkshire, primarily a kersey-producing region. Here, on the rocky becks tumbling down from the Pennine moorlands which nourished a sturdy breed of mountain sheep, fulling mills (or walkmills as they were called in the North) had been springing up far and wide in the thirteenth century. In the succeeding century progress had been impeded as much by the devastations of the Scots as by those of the plague, but by the fifteenth century there was clearly discernible a thriving industry concentrating on the upper reaches of the Aire and the Calder, where today is the principal seat of England's woollen manufacture. Leeds and Bradford, Wakefield and Halifax, were then as now its leading centres; scarcely less important was Almondbury, and in almost every village, hamlet and homestead people were supplementing the meagre livelihood to be won from agriculture by the profits of industry. Elsewhere in Yorkshire a considerable quantity of cloth was being manufactured in and around Ripon and Barnsley, while the city of York was still of importance though quite outstripped by the West Riding.

Beyond these three principal regions a certain amount of cloth was being produced for export in many other parts of the country. One or two centres call for special mention. Westmorland was famous for its cheap but durable 'Kendals', made from the wool of the hardy sheep that roamed the Lakeland fells. Here there was rapid development towards the close of the Middle Ages. The industry spread far beyond Kendal and the valley of the Kent, penetrating the furthest recesses of the Rothay and the Brathay, where there was an abundance of water power and also of cheap land, barren and rocky, worthless for agriculture but suitable for the erection of tenters for stretching and drying the cloth. In the parish of Grasmere alone, in place of the one manorial fulling mill of the early fourteenth century, there were now at least twenty such mills, some in spots as remote as on the becks descending from Stickle and Easedale Tarns. Southwards in Lancashire some cloth, mostly cheap and rough, was made. Wales produced quantities of frieze, and from its southern Marches, whence came wool superior even to that of the Cotswolds and worth twice that of Yorkshire, some finer cloth was made, as at Ludlow. In Warwickshire there was an important centre at Coventry, famous for its blues, and Northampton had not yet wholly lost its ancient reputation.

While some of all these cloths were sold on local markets for home consumption, the great majority found their way to the ports by cart, pack-horse, river barge or coasting boat. If Bristol, first of provincial ports, owed much to the industrial activity of its immediate hinterland, it must in turn have greatly stimulated that activity. For with its excellent communications inland and its age-old connections along the Atlantic seaboard—from Ireland to Brittany, Gascony, Spain, Portugal and the Mediterranean, it was admirably suited to be the chief collecting centre for the whole West of England region and also for Coventry and the Marches of Wales. Exeter, too, was doing a thriving trade in Westerns, exporting about half as many cloths as Bristol. Hull, 'Key of the North' and second of the provincial ports, was the natural outlet for the Yorkshire vales, whose cloth it shipped not only eastwards to Scandinavia and the Baltic but also westwards with fleets bound for the wines of Gascony. Southampton, attracting to itself much of the trade of Wiltshire, was chiefly of importance as a collecting centre for the Italian galleys, which there took on board each winter rich cargoes of woollens from all parts of England, for despatch South to Italy, Africa and the Levant. By the close of the fifteenth century, however, it was already in decline and was handling less cloth than Hull. More and more its business, like that of the East Anglian ports, was being drawn to London, now the cloth mart *par excellence* for the whole of England. The annual fair which opened on the eve of St Bartholomew in the churchyard of the venerable priory church at Smithfield was now the most famous cloth fair in England. Thither every year journeyed cloth manufacturers from all parts of the land, there to display their wares in booths which they held on lease or as their own freehold. In addition, a weekly cloth market had been established at Blackwell Hall, purchased for the purpose by the Mayor and Commonalty in 1396; here, and here alone, between noon on Thursday and Saturday, country-men might expose and sell their cloths.

Back from the ports to the clothing centres came raw materials for England's industry: madder and teasels from Flanders, ashes from the Baltic, woad from Gascony, Picardy, Brabant, Germany and Italy, whence too came alum and saffron, grain from Spain and Portugal. From Bristol they were distributed throughout the West of England and beyond—up the Severn and so to Ludlow or Coventry, and by sea to Wales and Devon in little boats which brought back frieze and kerseys. From Southampton casks of woad and alum brought in on the Italian galleys were despatched through the whole South and West of England and much further afield; some went even as far as Kendal in the charge of those vigorous Lakeland carriers who ventured south each winter with cloth for the Italian galleys, taking home with them winter luxuries for the Westmorland housewife—oranges, nuts, wines and dried fruits—in addition to the raw materials of industry.

The structure of the 'great industry' in England at the close of the Middle Ages was inevitably capitalist, as that of the thirteenth century had been. At each stage of the industry the capitalist entrepreneur was in evidence—in the provision of the raw materials, in the combining of the various processes of manufacture, and in the marketing of the finished product. Sometimes a single individual combined all three functions, as Boine Broke had done at Douai. More often the trading and manufacturing sides of the business were separated, as in Italy.

But if neither capitalism nor the putting out system were in any sense novel phenomena, even in this country, yet in one respect the fifteenth century 'clothier' (as the English manufacturer now came to be called) differed radically from his predecessors the Flemish *drapier*, the English *draper*, and the Italian *lanaiuolo*. Not only in name was he a new and specifically English product. For he operated under what can only be described as conditions of free enterprise in contrast to the regimented control once common in England and still then customary abroad.

At the time that England's woollen industry outdistanced its rivals and won first place on the markets of Europe it was concentrated in no such vast urban agglomerations as were those of Flanders or Italy in their heyday. Nourished though it had once been in many an ancient borough behind whose walls weavers, fullers, dyers, and drapers could ply their trade in freedom and security, immune from the restraints and obligations which burdened the members of the feudal society without, the city had never gained a stranglehold upon it. For English cities had never assumed such large proportions or achieved so great a measure of autonomy as their Flemish or Italian counterparts, if only because England had been slower in developing an advanced industrial and commercial economy and quicker in developing an effective central monarchy. And when England's industry reached maturity the relative advantages and disadvantages of doing business in borough or manor were very different from what they had once been. The feudal society was in dissolution; villeinage had all but disappeared; the borough with its battlemented walls was becoming as much an anachronism as the baronial castle; its liberties had become privileges for the few, and its economy was more rigidly regimented and more heavily taxed than that of the manor had ever been. The ancient proverb 'City air maketh free' could have had little meaning for an Englishman of the late fifteenth century, least of all for an aspiring captain of industry.

The progressive manufacturer usually, though not invariably, kept away from the city and developed his business unrestricted in the countryside, making his headquarters in some small market town or village, which grew as the industry grew, in haphazard fashion, un-regulated, under the aegis of the manor rather than the borough. The pattern of the new industrial centre was strikingly different from that of the old. With no walls to confine and limit it, it was a straggling growth, integrated only by its central market place and by the stately parish church which dominated it—built originally to serve a small rural parish, but now often wholly rebuilt to meet the needs of an industrial community and to witness to its wealth. Wide open streets with low two-storey houses took the place of the narrow alleys and the tall close-packed houses with their projecting third and fourth storeys almost meeting overhead in which the city burgesses had mostly been content to live. The manor house, if such existed, was now of much less consequence than the comfortable if unpretentious homes of its clothier tenants, like that of the Paycockes at Coggeshall; indeed often its buildings were divided up and let in portions to house clothiers and craftsmen and their stuff. Moreover the new industrial township stood seldom in isolation but merged almost imperceptibly into neigh-bouring townships; a dozen such lay within a radius of seven miles in the clothing district of the West Riding which included Leeds, Bradford, Halifax and Wakefield; in Suffolk, Cavendish, Long Melford, Glemsford and Sudbury lie along a six mile stretch of the River Stour, and Dedham, Stratford and Bergholt are within a mile of each other.

Such few manorial incidents as survived did not greatly hamper industry. Here and there, especially on ecclesiastical estates, a manorial fulling mill with monopoly rights remained, but most lords of the manor were very ready to lease out not merely the manorial mill but any portion of the watercourse that could be used for additional mills. Those tenants who were still villeins were not thereby debarred from devoting themselves to business and making their fortunes. William Haynes, one of the villein clothiers of Castlecombe, had to seek permission to marry his daughters outside the manor, but at his death he held three mills and many tenements and was also possessed of wool, dyestuffs, woollen cloth, gold and silver, furniture, debts and miscellaneous chattels which were assessed by a local jury as worth 300 marks and had at first been valued by the lord's officials at 3000 marks. So considerable was his property that his widow was prepared to pay £40 for leave to enter into his holdings and another £60 for possession of his movables. Death duties might be high, but the country clothier, unlike the city clothier, had not to suffer a constant drain on his purse for local taxation, pageants, liveries, and all the burdens of public office. Nor had he to submit to the industrial controls that bound the city manufacturer. He was free to employ what workers he pleased, whether inside or outside the township; to offer whatever wages would secure them; to engage in manual labour himself if he wished, and to use any methods he chose. He had, it is true, to conform to the statutory assize fixing the length and breadth of cloth put on the market, though to this there were many exceptions, and many local specialities were permitted. But the quality of his cloth was unregulated, except for spasmodic attempts by the state to ensure certain elementary standards, as by such acts as those forbidding undue stretching of cloth and the use of waste and inferior wools—acts echoing civic ordinances and never wholly effectual since they were enforced only by occasional commissions and not by any regular system of state inspection.

Freedom to experiment had always characterised the rural industry. In an age of expanding business the progressive manufacturer was very ready to welcome new methods of mechanisation which, for a capital outlay, would enable him to reduce costs and increase production without increasing his labour force. By the early fifteenth century, if not before then, a means of mechanising the first finishing process, that of raising, had been invented, and west country clothiers were using the 'gigmill' for their fine broadcloths. Instead of the tedious process of drawing teasels by hand over the surface of the cloth, the cloth was now passed over a roller set with teasels and kept whirling by being attached to the spindle of a water wheel—a device in all essentials similar to that used today. Such a gigmill was among the possessions of William Haynes of Castlecombe at his death in 1435. That its use was becoming general, and giving rise to considerable opposition as the fulling mill had done, is shown by a petition to Parliament (4 Edward IV) asking for its prohibition—a protest as ineffective as the protests against the fulling mill, for gigmills were still in use in the sixteenth century. Experiments were also being made in the fifteenth century for mechanising shearing—one of the many problems that fascinated Leonardo da Vinci—but the long heavy hand shears remained generally in use.

Such an era of economic individualism favoured diversity of organisation as much as diversity of technique. Indeed there was so great a variety of industrial structure as almost to defy analysis. The ranks of the clothiers were recruited from all sorts and conditions of men—some from within the industry, where they had begun as weavers, fullers, dyers or shearmen; some from without, from among wool farmers, victuallers, butchers, country gentry and many others. Nor was there any sharp dividing line between clothier and artisan, as in the urban 'great industry', for there was no law compelling a man to forswear his craft if he wished to 'drape' and sell cloth. The small clothier was often himself a weaver, possessing one or two looms in his cottage and employing the members of his family and perhaps one or two others for combing, carding, spinning and weaving; fulling his webs himself, or sending them to the mill, particularly if they were heavy materials; and marketing them locally at frequent intervals. With little capital behind him he led a precarious existence, though less precarious than it might have been in a city since he relied partly on the produce of his small holding. Sometimes he combined clothmaking not only with agriculture but also with some other trade such as that of a miller or a butcher. Such a mixed economy—very like that still practised by the crofter clothiers of Skye—was characteristic of great as well as small English clothiers in the later Middle Ages. The large-scale manufacturer was often a landowner, possessed of very considerable estates and engaged in stock and arable farming. As the Frenchman pointed out in the *Heralds' Debate*: 'In England your clothiers dwell in great farms abroad in the country, where as well they make cloth and keep husbandry, as also graze and feed sheep and cattle.' On these estates they grew some of the wool they needed, though they usually bought much too, either direct from growers or through middlemen woolbrokers.

The big clothier entrepreneur, at the opposite extreme from the small clothier artisan, was occupied exclusively in management. Usually he owned considerable capital equipment. Like his predecessors in the clothing cities he favoured partly the outwork and partly the factory system. His 'head house' comprised both home and office, and here were kept his stores of wool, dyestuffs and finished cloths. The preliminary sorting and beating of the wool was usually carried out on the premises. Close to the head house there was very commonly a dye-house, the property of the clothier, where the intricate processes of dyeing the wool could be performed by his own employees under his supervision with his own carefully prepared materials. Often he also owned a fulling mill, together with tenters for drying and stretching the cloth: Thomas Spring, the noted clothier of Lavenham who died in 1486 possessed of many farms and manors, not only bequeathed his tenters in his will, as did John Hunt of Lavenham, but also remembered his tenterers. Sometimes, however, both dyeing and fulling, together with the final processes of raising and shearing to which the fine broad-cloths were subjected, were entrusted to independent firms specialising in these tasks. The dye-works and fulling and finishing establishments of the Stroud valley and Castlecombe, for instance, famous for their 'Bristol reds', were constantly employed by west country clothiers. It was also quite usual for cloths to be shorn by expert finishers in the ports to which they were sent for export: such a finishing industry flourished in collecting centres like Bristol, Exeter, Ipswich and especially London.

For the rest, carding, combing, spinning and weaving were some-times done on the clothier's own premises but were much more often put out to a host of local craftsmen working in their own homes but looking to the clothier for employment. The close and friendly re-lationship that frequently existed between employer and employed is evident from many clothiers' wills. Thomas Spring specially remem-bered his spinners and fullers as well as his tenterers; Thomas Paycocke of Coggeshall (died 1518), in addition to individual legacies to specific weavers and fullers, left 'to all my wevers, fullers and shermen 12d. apece' and willed that 'they that have wrought me verey moch wark have 3s. 4d. apece'; he also left £4 to be distributed among his combers, carders and spinners. While weaving was to a great extent concentrated in the township, spinning was dispersed all over the countryside—as in Tuscany. John Golding of Glemsford left 12d. each to his spinners 'as well out of town as in town'. For this reason alone its supervision presented as difficult a problem in England as in Italy. If unscrupulous clothiers sometimes gave out short weight, unscrupulous spinners sometimes kept back part of the wool to traffic with it, making up the weight by adding more oil and water to the remainder.

Deceits such as these, which were practised by weavers as well as by spinners, may well have encouraged some of the wealthier clothiers to bring as much of the work as possible under their immediate super-vision. A concentration of manufacture on the clothier's premises was more easily achieved for weaving than for spinning, for spinning was still to a great extent a part-time occupation combined day by day with housewifery. Moreover weaving demanded a certain capital outlay in the acquisition of a loom, and even those craftsmen who had once owned looms were sometimes compelled by dire necessity to part with them: the hiring out of looms had long been known in England, as abroad. It was not at all unusual for a fifteenth century clothier to keep a number of looms operating in his own shop, as Thomas Blanket of Bristol had done a century earlier, and the practice became still more common in the early sixteenth century, strenuously opposed though it was by the weavers, who saw in it a threat to their comparative independence. The legends that gathered round Jack Winchcombe, the wealthy clothier of Newbury who died in 1519, may or may not have been true—it was said that he had kept 1040 persons at work on his premises, in his dyehouse, fulling mill, sorting, carding, spinning, weaving and shearing rooms. But there is no reason to disbelieve the eyewitness account of Leland, who when journeying through Malmesbury shortly after the dissolution of the monasteries found the abbey lodgings converted into a factory by 'one Stumpe an exceding rich clothiar'. 'At this present tyme', he wrote, 'every corner of the vaste houses of office that belongid to thabbay be fulle of lumbes to weve clooth yn.' We know too that Stumpe planned to take over the empty buildings of Osney abbey and to employ there 2000 skilled operatives, though this scheme never materialised. In general, however, weavers as well as spinners worked in their own homes, even if it was on looms hired from the clothier and in houses built by him and rented from him.

In these young industrial townships, growing up mostly still within the framework of the manor, the throng of craftsmen with their servants and apprentices presented a novel social problem. Now and again in the manorial rolls we can glimpse measures taken to keep under control what must at times have been unruly and disturbing elements. Ordinances were passed at Castlecombe, for instance, prohibiting gambling and late hours in taverns and enjoining upon tenants the duty of restraining their servants and apprentices from poaching in the manorial fishponds. At Castlecombe, also, two wardens were appointed to supervise the dyers and fullers (*custodes et conservatores artis tintorum et fullatorum*) and two more to supervise the weavers, though how far these wardens had industrial functions we do not know. The manor courts, too, were called on to deal with cases of debt, contract, wrongful detention of goods, enticement of apprentices, and deceitful work. Here and there the running of a fulling mill on Sunday was forbidden, but beyond this there seems to have been no attempt to control hours, much less wages or industrial processes. *Laissez-faire* reigned supreme.

If the workers prospered when markets were expanding and prices rising, in times of slump their lot was an unenviable one. Wages were depressed, workers dismissed, and the new industrial communities experienced, like those of Flanders, mass unemployment and destitution. The social and religious fraternities in which many of the artisans were enrolled could do little to insure them against such wholesale calamities. The diplomatic crises which from time to time blocked the main arteries of trade in the early sixteenth century brought immediate repercussions. So too did the excessive war taxation which in 1525, for instance, threatened to cripple the woollen industry. 'For soth his name is Povertie, for he and his cosyn Necessitie hath brought us to this day', said the spokesman of the Suffolk rebels in that year, when asked who was the captain of the four thousand men who had risen in arms. 'The clothmakers', he continued, 'have put all these people and a farre greater nomber from worke.'

Just as the workfolk were helpless since, as they put it, 'we live not of ourselves but by the substanciall occupiers of this countrey', so were the clothiers, since they lived by the merchants. Few clothiers exported their own wares. Most of them sold either to the drapers, whose agents travelled up and down the country collecting cloth, or direct to merchants at the ports—to the Hanseatics, to the Italians, but above all to the Merchant Adventurers. For as the cloth trade had expanded, so in each of its principal ports the English merchants concerned in it had drawn together into fellowships of Merchant Adventurers—'adventurers' in that they were engaged not in the regular old-established traffic to and from Calais with wool, but in seeking new outlets for England's manufactures. Their wealth and influence at the close of the Middle Ages is itself eloquent witness to the growth of England's industry. In the great marts of the Low Countries where now they chiefly congregated, the Merchant Adventurers of England, who went in stately procession to their own richly furnished chapel at the opening of each mart, were then of as much consequence as once had been the merchants of the Flemish Hanse in London, for English cloth and English exporting firms were now second to none.

The steadily growing pressure of English competition on the markets of Europe was accompanied by profound disturbances in Italy and Belgica, leading gradually to a transformation of their economies. Labour unrest in the densely peopled clothing cities increased in intensity, reaching its climax in Italy in the late fourteenth century. In Florence 1378 saw the mass rising of the woolcarders, ruthlessly repressed, while in the following year the weavers of Ypres, Ghent and Bruges rose in rebellion once again, seized the reins of power, and plunged Flanders into a sanguinary civil war in which many thousands of workers were slain. To dissensions between masters and men were added dissensions between city and city, between town and country, between craft and craft. Such dissensions were both a symptom and

a cause of the decline of the industry in these once mightiest cities of
Flanders and Tuscany, a decline amply corroborated by such figures
as still exist for their industrial production at that time. Nor was
England alone in profiting by their distresses and contributing to their
troubles. In Germany too, and still more so in Holland, there was
developing at the close of the Middle Ages a woollen industry of
formidable proportions. And in Italy and Belgica, as in England,
smaller centres, where vested interests and the forces of conservatism
were less strong, were adapting themselves to new conditions by
experimenting in new methods and new materials to meet a different
clientele, challenging successfully the monopoly claimed by the old-
established centres. Thus petty Tuscan towns, of little account hitherto,
now grew rich by woollens, while cities of Lombardy and Venetia
leapt into the front rank, producing cheap stuffs abhorrent to the
Florentines. Thus, too, many a small Flemish town developed a
flourishing business in light stuffs, made almost wholly from Spanish
wool. This transfer of production from the large to the smaller centres
and from English wool to Spanish, which is so characteristic a feature
of the fifteenth century, cannot be quantitatively measured. Nor can
we hope to assess for the whole of Italy or Belgica the trend of production or even, as for England, the trend of the export trade. Yet,
despite the survival of some few of the larger centres of production
and the blossoming of many smaller ones, the impression remains of
a slow contraction in these two regions, while the English industry,
halting though the tempo of its advance was at times, moved surely
forwards until by the end of the Middle Ages it was in a position of
unchallengeable supremacy, producing cloths probably greater in
quantity and, if Erasmus is to be believed, finer in quality, than any
other region of Europe.

CHAPTER VII

Mining and Metallurgy in Medieval Civilisation[1]

Nature endowed Europe with extraordinarily varied and abundant mineral resources. The conquest of this underground wealth by the Western peoples has been inseparable from the unprecedented power obtained by men in recent centuries over the physical world.

This power has come from the solution of technical problems which earlier civilisations had never seriously faced. Many of these problems first became acute in connection with mining and metallurgy. Three examples will perhaps suffice. It was the search for adequate means of draining coal pits that led to the practical use of the force contained in jets of steam, to the invention of the steam engine. As the quantities of minerals dug out of the earth increased, their bulky character exerted increasing pressure on men's minds to discover cheaper methods of carrying them over land and water. It was the difficulty of hauling ores and coal in wagons along rough, soggy ground that led to the invention and development of the railway. The demand for larger quantities of metal for use in war as well as in peace pressed men on to discover methods of treating ores which would reduce the labour and the waste involved in separating and obtaining metals. It was the persistence of the Western Europeans in exploiting a discovery which probably had been made by many earlier peoples [2]—that iron ore actually melted when the fires were hot enough—which has produced metal in overwhelming quantities from cascades of liquid flame.

Upon this abundance the great industrial expansion of modern times partly depended. Had it not been for the blast furnace, the twentieth-century European might be giving his fiancée an iron ring as a token of their engagement, as Pliny tells us was still the custom in the rich Roman world of the first century.[3] Had it not been for the general use of coal fuel, which was no less novel than the production of large quantities of iron, the expansion of heavy industry, already striking in England as far back as the early seventeenth century, could hardly have taken place.

Fresh technical problems raised by the demand for minerals aroused

---

[1] Professors Earl J. Hamilton, Ernst Kantorowicz, Charles H. McIlwain, Otto von Simson, Cyril S. Smith, director of the Institute of Metals at the University of Chicago, and President Lynn White of Mills College, have generously read this section in typescript and have helped me by their suggestions to improve it. I am deeply grateful to them.

[2] Cf. J. Newton Friend, *Iron in Antiquity* (London, 1926), 92-3, interpreting Pliny, *Natural History*, bk. XXXIV, ch. XLI.   [3] *Natural History*, bk. XXXIII, ch. I.

the curiosity of natural scientists. Modern mining and metallurgy offered them new materials for speculative thought and experiment. Modern mining and metallurgy were among many sources which helped to lead their minds in new directions, hitherto unexplored. Again and again their general scientific discoveries have provided theoretical foundations without which many of the technical industrial achievements of the modern world, that have dazzled and also bewildered mankind, would have been impossible. Indirectly, therefore, as well as directly, the development of the mining and metallurgical industries has contributed to the triumph of industrial civilisation.

Early in the seventeenth century Bacon and Descartes dreamed of a paradise of material plenty. Without the treasures of the subsoil and the attraction they exercised on men's minds, these dreams would hardly have approached fulfilment at the beginning of the twentieth century.

The rich endowment of Asia and North America, as well as Western Europe, with mineral resources obviously presented novel challenges to human ingenuity. But such challenges come to nothing unless someone is challenged. Vast mineral resources have been present in many parts of the earth for thousands of years. But the earlier inhabitants of Europe and North America, even the highly civilised peoples of the ancient classical world and of China, showed little disposition to ransack the subsoil for these underground riches. Their existence was more a condition of the triumph of industrialism than a cause for it. How did it happen that the Western Europeans were first to respond to the challenge? Why have they been less reluctant than earlier civilised peoples to rob the earth of its treasures? A history of the efforts to exploit mineral resources in Europe during the thousand years which ended with the Reformation is a necessary prelude to any attempt to answer such questions. How far had the technical skill and economic enterprise developed among the medieval Europeans made inevitable the phenomenal progress in modern times of mining and metallurgy, which has been an essential element in the rise of industrial civilisation?

I. *The Industries in Classical Times*

At hundreds of places in Europe seams of ores containing gold and silver, copper, lead and zinc, tin and iron, as well as seams of coal, once broke through the surface, or lay hidden at such short depths below that builders uncovered them in digging foundations, if they had not been already disclosed by the plough of some husbandman.

Some of these ores had been exploited long before the Roman conquests. A growing recognition of the value of the seams, and of the course that they followed below the surface, had led miners to sink shafts and to discover further treasure at greater depths. Already in the fifth and fourth centuries B.C., thousands of work-people, mostly slaves, were employed in mining and working the famous silver-bearing lead ore on the mountain of Laurion near Athens. A few of the pits reached down three hundred feet or more into the earth. The slopes and valleys in the neighbourhood were full of men washing, breaking, and preparing the ore, or separating the silver from the lead. During the Hellenistic period of the third and second centuries mining operations were pursued with increased vigour in some of the lands surrounding the Mediterranean, so that the Romans found metallurgical enterprises in nearly all the countries they conquered.

It is not possible to determine whether the Roman conquests and the founding of the Roman Empire slowed down this progress. In any event progress continued in the sense that the production of metals went on increasing at least for several generations. Many mines were opened in Spain, Britain, Gaul, and in the Alpine regions south of the river Danube. What was lacking was the zeal, which eventually took possession of the Western Europeans, for driving on into the earth regardless of the cost. Like the Greeks, the Romans generally had little scientific knowledge of the nature of minerals. Many well-educated men thought that they grew like plants,[1] a view which persisted even among the intelligentsia in Europe into the eighteenth century. In 1709 the French *intendant* at Lyons actually consoled the *contrôleur-général* for the exhaustion of the surface coal at St Etienne by telling him that these mines had 'the happy property of reproducing themselves'![2]

In classical times mining was generally regarded as a much less desirable occupation than agriculture. A law was passed by the Roman Republic, probably towards the end of the second century B.C., prohibiting the digging of ores in Italy. Modern authorities disagree about the circumstances that led to this particular enactment. But there is agreement that it reflects the distaste felt by classical peoples for labour underground, and their preference for agrarian pursuits.

As century followed century across a millennium of highly civilised life, lived in the long, hot summers of the Mediterranean, the readily accessible surface ores were eventually largely exhausted in the more populous parts of the Roman Empire. The exhaustion of the more easily worked seams added continually to the arduous and distasteful nature of the miners' work. The difficulties of sinking shafts, draining off water and hauling ore to the surface were for ever multiplying.

[1] Maurice Besnier, 'L'interdiction du travail des mines en Italie,' *Revue archéologique*, 5th sér., x (1919), 37–8.
[2] A. M. de Boislisle, *Correspondance des contrôleurs généraux...avec les intendants* (Paris, 1897), III, no. 496.

While the classical peoples were frequently ingenious in devising machinery, they were backward about harnessing the strength of animals, of flowing streams (which were scarce and subject to drought), and even of the wind to operate their machinery. It is little wonder that labour in the mines seemed more and more intolerable. Convicts and Christians were deported to work them.[1] As a consequence of these difficulties, the costs of mining in man-power, even with slave labour, drove up the prices of the ores and the metals made from them, and discouraged their extensive use.

To a modern European or American, who has visited the coalfields of Belgium, South Wales or Pennsylvania, with the mountains of black earth beside the shafts, or who has seen the skies aflame for miles from the fires of blast furnaces in the Ruhr, the English Midlands, or North-western Indiana, the mines and forges of the Roman Empire would not have seemed impressive. Together with the quarries, they formed 'merely small islands in a sea of fields and meadows'.[2]

According to the criteria of a modern European all metals were scarce. Metal was the material of many statues, but it was never the basis for constructing ships, aqueducts, public buildings, theatres, or stadiums. It was used as sparingly as possible in making tools and machinery. Iron was almost always obtained by prolonged and patient heating in a forge fire, followed by reiterated heatings and hammerings on the anvil. Small scale operations alone were possible and much of the iron present in the ore was lost as slag and scale. The process was very costly in firewood, charcoal, and labour. Lead was preferred to iron whenever it could serve, because less fuel was needed to produce it. Bronze and brass were derived from copper, tin, zinc and their ores, all of which required less heat in smelting than iron ore. The greatest development of manufacturing in classical times occurred in regions bordering the Mediterranean, which were exceedingly poor in coal resources compared with the North of Europe or North America. Partly on that account, no attempt was made, except perhaps in Roman Britain, to substitute coal for firewood and charcoal either for domestic fuel or in industry. As the price of wood rose under the pressure of growing population and expanding industry, metallurgy and every other kind of manufacture requiring fuel was discouraged. Without the use of coal, oil, and hydroelectric power, without also the wholesale use of wood from the thick forests of Northern Europe and America, industrial changes similar to those which transformed the western world before the middle of the twentieth century were impossible.

[1] Evidence of this is to be found in the early litanies, Professor Kantorowicz tells me.
[2] M. Rostovtzeff, *The Social and Economic History of the Roman Empire* (Oxford, 1926), 296.

II. *The Course of Production c. 300–c. 1330*

A decline in the output of metal began in Europe in the third century. At first it was probably slight, but it continued for hundreds of years. From the end of the sixth century until the end of the tenth, ores were taken at much shallower depths than those that had been often reached in classical times. More primitive methods of working the mines prevailed. Gone were the long shafts such as had been occasionally sunk, for example in the neighbourhood of Cartagena in Spain, to depths of five or six hundred feet. Gone also—buried in débris—were pits forty feet or more in depth, such as had been fairly common during the second century. All the more ambitious mines of the Roman Empire in the West were eventually abandoned. They disappeared from the sight of the local villagers, to be rediscovered only during the last hundred years by modern archaeologists in the course of their excavations. With the decline in the population of Europe, which began after the third century, with the accompanying decay of towns, the shrinkage of trade, and the reduction of the acreage under cultivation, the descendants of old inhabitants, and the Germanic invaders who settled among them, contented themselves with such ores as could be won near their village huts, mostly in the remnants of old workings accessible without the sinking of shafts. Efforts to find new seams at considerable depths ceased. In many places, forests, cut down in Roman times, grew again.

The output of iron diminished less than that of other metals. Iron was still needed by woodsmen and husbandmen for axes, knives, and spades, and even for ploughshares in a few places where a knowledge of Roman methods of ploughing was preserved. Iron was wanted, above all, for weapons. As it was the most abundant of the ores dug during the Middle Ages, it could generally be had with less effort than ores containing silver, lead, copper, or tin. At many places in Gaul, the Rhineland, Saxony, Bohemia, and Tuscany, and especially in Spain and possibly on the slopes and along the valleys of the Eastern Alps,[1] iron in small quantities was produced throughout the early Middle Ages.[2]

---

[1] There is some dispute as to whether iron was worked continuously in the Eastern Alps. The principal authority on iron mining in Styria argues that when the Slavs settled this area in the sixth and seventh centuries, iron work was abandoned (L. Bittner, 'Das Eisenwesen in Innerberg-Eisenerz,' *Archiv für österreichische Geschichte*, LXXXIX (Vienna, 1901), 458–9). But a later writer, who studied the iron-making industry in Carniola, raises what seem to be weighty objections to this thesis (Alfons Müllner, *Geschichte des Eisens in Krain, Görz und Istrien* (Vienna, 1909), 112–13).

[2] Cf. Ludwig Beck, *Die Geschichte des Eisens*, 2nd ed. (Braunschweig, 1890–1903), I, 703 ff., 728–39.

An increase in iron output may have begun after the eighth century, in the Carolingian age.[1] At the end of the ninth century, at any rate, iron was an item of some prominence in the exports of Venice to the sophisticated Near East.[2] Its production probably increased considerably at this time, at least in the Eastern Alps.

There is, by contrast, little trace in historical records of mining for copper ore between the beginning of the sixth and the end of the tenth centuries. Brass, an alloy of copper and calamine, the ore of zinc, seems to have gone largely out of use until the discovery of deposits of calamine in the Alps and the North of Europe during the fifteenth century. Bronze, an alloy in which copper is the main element, is historically the oldest of the metals to be extensively used. It was used concurrently with iron, often for the same purposes. The paucity of early medieval references to copper suggests that iron may have been taking the place of bronze to a considerable extent. It would be unreasonable to suppose, however, that the demand for bronze ceased for an extended period, or that the medieval Europeans ever lost touch altogether with the copper ores needed to supply it.

According to Tacitus, one of the considerations that prompted the Claudian invasion of England in the middle of the first century was the mineral wealth. There was perhaps no part of the Empire in which mining occupied as prominent a place in industrial life as in Roman Britain. Other provinces had more impressive mines. But the relative importance of mining in Britain, not one of the most industrialised provinces, was great when compared with the Empire generally. In Britain, lead ore, some of which contained silver, seems to have been worked more extensively than any other mineral. The ancient tin mines of Cornwall were revived by the Romans in the third century; copper was worked in Shropshire and Wales; iron in many places. The rich and abundant mines of coal were dug, it seems, in a number of the fields where they poked their way close to the surface.[3]

---

[1] As Dr White suggests to me. Monsieur Georges Espinas has recently reviewed, in the *Annales: Economies, Sociétés, Civilisations*, a new French work on early iron-making, a book which was not available in the United States when this section was finished (Ed. Salin and Alt. France-Lanord, *Le Fer à l'époque mérovingienne*, Paris, 1943).

[2] H. Pirenne, *Economic and Social History of Medieval Europe* (translated by I. E. Clegg, New York, 1937), 18.

[3] The late Professor Collingwood accepted the evidence of modern archaeologists as proof that coal was rather extensively worked in Britain during the Roman period (R. G. Collingwood and J. N. L. Myres, *Roman Britain and the English Settlements* (2nd ed. Oxford, 1937), 231–2). No other scholar gives coal in Roman times so much importance (cf. M. Rostovtzeff, *The Social and Economic History of the Hellenistic World* (Oxford, 1941), III, 1615).

Neither the mining of tin nor of lead ore was abandoned altogether in Great Britain after the Saxon conquests of the fifth and sixth centuries, although these conquests were apparently followed by an eclipse of copper ore and coal mining. A more or less steady demand for lead, both in England and in most continental countries, continued after the barbarian invasions, because of the use made of it in roofing the churches which were always being built or at least repaired, during ages when the hold of Christianity tightened on all the European peoples.

In spite of the continued use of metal in small quantities, it is probable that the European production of gold, silver, copper, lead, and tin shrank to a small fraction of its former amount by the early ninth century, after the Muslim conquests. Lessees of the imperial revenues from mines in Hadrian's reign, if they could have been brought back to life seven centuries afterwards in the Carolingian period, would have been shocked to find how small was the yield of ores and metals. The mining districts which they had known in prosperous times would have seemed almost deserts. Pliny might have deplored the loss of interest in natural history, which had been associated by the classical peoples partly with mining and metallurgy, though he would perhaps have applauded the reluctance of men to raid underground treasure which in his eyes had bred mainly luxury and vice.

The growth in the output of iron, which began in the Eastern Alps towards the end of the ninth century, if not earlier, was followed in the last half of the tenth by more general progress in mining and metallurgy especially in Germany. Several new mines were discovered there. The most famous were the rich copper mines and silver-bearing lead ores of the once thickly-wooded Rammelsberg, the fine hill that rises some 1200 feet above the town of Goslar in the Harz. In German the same word was used for miner as for mountaineer. During the eleventh and twelfth centuries mining became primarily an Alpine occupation. In the Harz, the Vosges, the Jura, and especially in the Eastern Alps, the working of gold, silver, lead, copper, and iron grew in importance. After the middle of the twelfth century progress was intensified and the new interest in mining spread to other regions. The first great period in the history of mining among the western peoples began around 1170, with the discovery of the rich silver-bearing ores of Freiberg in Saxony. It continued until the fourteenth century. If statistics of output existed, they would probably show that during this period of 150 years or so there were few decades in which the production of minerals and metals in Europe failed substantially to increase.

In cultural and intellectual history this period is one of the most brilliant in the annals of Europe. Civilisation was summed up in wonderful romanesque and gothic churches. These monuments were the expression of Europe's common form of worship, at a time when the whole of life centred about religious life. The twelfth and thirteenth centuries, like the eighteenth and nineteenth, were times of extraordinary hope and extraordinary economic and social progress in which the whole of Europe shared. The directions which progress took in the earlier period were less material. The efforts of the twelfth and thirteenth century Europeans culminated in the great cathedrals with their spires, some of which, especially in the North, seemed almost to pierce the heavens. But even structures symbolising, as these churches symbolised, a transcendental conception of the destiny of man, required much concrete material to build. The walls were far thicker and firmer than those of the buildings that came afterwards.

All aspects of a civilisation are interrelated. The increase in the production of silver, gold, and less valuable metals contributed to the growth of wealth, partly by increasing the supply of money but mainly by adding to the material available for industrial purposes. A prodigious expansion of agrarian and industrial production, combined with an even more remarkable growth of trade, transformed the economic face of Western Europe between the late eleventh and the fourteenth centuries. The growth of mineral wealth helps to explain how it was possible for the people of the thirteenth century to create such magnificent and costly monuments in stone, and to embellish them with equally wonderful work in glass and metal. The growth of wealth also made possible greater leisure. This facilitated the remarkable philosophical speculations which were the chief glory of the medieval universities. But the influence of the expansion in mining apparently seemed indirect and remote to most medieval writers. Few of them mentioned it in the works they composed. Albertus Magnus, with his German background, was apparently the only famous thinker who talked much about the metallurgical development of his age. He wrote with enthusiasm of the fine quality of the silver from the great mines discovered at Freiberg shortly before his birth. The most striking progress in mining of all kinds, particularly of silver-bearing ores, took place on the margin of western civilisation, away from the chief centres of cultural and economic life. Paris and the Ile-de-France, the focus from which the culture of the thirteenth century radiated, were greatly favoured by nature. But their riches were of the soil rather than the subsoil. The progress in mining was perhaps less a cause for the economic development of medieval Europe than a result of it. Yet in the mystery of the historical process, cause and effect are so intertwined that the positive conception of them that the modern mind derived from the natural sciences is hardly of service to truth.

Among the driving forces behind the discovery and the development of mining were the increase in population and the growth in tillage, trade, and industry. Not until after 1750, not perhaps until after 1785, were the Western European races again to grow in numbers at as rapid a rate as during most of the twelfth and thirteenth centuries. The area of cultivation and pasturage was extended in every direction, especially into wooded, hilly, and mountainous country, hitherto sparsely populated. Frequently the plough of a husbandman struck against one of the outcropping seams of iron ore or coal with which the northern parts of Europe were so plentifully supplied. The location of more valuable ores was disclosed by the violence of nature in the forests, the Alpine valleys, and even on the slopes of high peaks. When the snows melted, rushing torrents overflowed their banks to strip off surface land and lay bare treasure underneath. Seams of rich ore were also revealed when a great wind uprooted trees, when lightning splintered rocks, or when an avalanche tore its path down some mountain side. As settlers and travelling traders streamed into the uplands and penetrated the woodlands, there were more eyes to watch these accidents, which encouraged prospectors to probe the earth for minerals. The increasing curiosity about the material world and the increasing agricultural, commercial, industrial, and artistic needs for gold, silver, iron, lead, copper, tin, and alloys of these metals made men eager to explore beneath the soil, to examine and to exploit the substances they found. Not until the eve of the Reformation, when fresh waves of settlers pushed into the same regions, was there another comparable movement of exploration and discovery.

This newly aroused curiosity accounts for the rapid growth of the silver mines at Freiberg in the late twelfth century. Traders carrying salt happened on some argentiferous lead ore where the spring floods had washed away the earth. They took a sample to Goslar to compare with the famous ores from the Rammelsberg. Their sample yielded a larger quantity and a finer grade of silver. As news of their discovery spread, adventurers in considerable numbers, with picks and shovels, hurried to Freiberg. They came in a spirit of adventure not altogether unlike that of the Americans who migrated to California in the gold rush of the mid-nineteenth century.

In the late twelfth and thirteenth centuries traders and colonisers everywhere were on the look-out for ores, and especially for ores containing silver or gold. Rich veins lay waiting for them near the surface, chiefly in Central Europe. Such ores as could be readily reached were especially abundant north of the Danube—in Saxony, Bohemia, Silesia, and Hungary. The lands containing them had lain for the most part beyond the borders of the Roman Empire. Partly no doubt on that account there had been relatively little mining here in Roman times. In the Middle Ages these regions—together with greater Austria, the Harz, and the Black Forest—assumed a position of dominance, like that of the Spanish peninsula in classical times, in supplying all Europe with silver, copper, and small quantities of gold. On the slopes and along the valleys of the Eastern Alps, the Carpathians, the Erzgebirge, and the Sudeten Mountains, the thick woods provided abundant lumber for building, firewood and charcoal for fuel needed in preparing ores for the smelters, in separating them from the worthless material with which they were intermingled, and in converting them to metals. The rushing brooks and streams, in which these regions abounded, were hardly less helpful than the woods. As will appear, they came to provide sources of power to drive machinery that crushed and hammered the materials or blew air upon the fires. From the beginning the abundant water courses facilitated the washing away of dirt and impurities; the ore was dressed in artfully constructed containers, made to settle the heavy minerals and to remove the lighter rocky matter.

German emigrants, some of whom were bent on mining, were pushing into regions held by Slavs and Magyars in the great colonising movement towards the East and South-east, which brought Walloons and Flemings into Saxony and Frenchmen into the Western Rhineland. It was not only in Eastern and Southern Germany, it was in almost all Central Europe that the Germans took the leading part in mining. The movements to colonise and to mine went hand in hand. One of the strongest attractions for German settlers was the glitter of precious metals.

Ores near the surface containing silver and gold were fewer and less fruitful west of the Rhine and the Alps. It was partly the accidents of nature that made Germans, rather than other western peoples, the leaders in mining and metallurgy from the twelfth to the sixteenth centuries. Travelling traders and explorers in France, England, and the Low Countries were no less eager to discover ores containing precious metal. Kings, princes, bishops, and other great landlords in the western part of Europe were not backward in encouraging prospectors. Where silver-bearing ores were discovered, as in Devon and Alsace, they were exploited as vigorously as in Central Europe.

While the search for precious metal had a special fascination for the Europeans throughout the later Middle Ages, the demand for minerals of every kind grew rapidly with the rapid growth of population, industry, and trade. The boom in mining extended to ores containing only base metals—copper, lead, tin, and iron. It extended even to coal. In the digging of coal and base ores other than copper, the Germans had no such dominance as in the digging of ores rich in silver or gold. Even in copper mining by the beginning of the fourteenth century, the mines of Stora Kopparberg in Sweden, developed under German influence, had come to rival those of the Rammelsberg. The English mines of lead ore—in Somerset, Durham, Cumberland, Shropshire, Flintshire, and above all in Derbyshire—grew increasingly prosperous during the thirteenth century, and a flourishing export trade in lead developed. Lead production in England rivalled that in Central Europe. The Continent was as dependent on Devon and Cornwall for its tin as it was on Saxony and Bohemia for its silver and gold. During the last half of the twelfth century the annual output of tin in South-western England, mostly from Devon, apparently increased nearly five-fold. The early fourteenth century was another time of rapid progress, especially in Cornwall, where the output in 1338 was more than double that in 1301. In the thirteen-thirties production in the two counties together apparently reached seven hundred tons in good years. Since the middle of the twelfth century it had increased approximately ten-fold. The figures of output for the thirteen-thirties were not regularly surpassed until the last half of the seventeenth century.[1]

As the supplies of iron ore were not localised like the supplies of scarcer minerals, there was no such concentration of population about the iron mines as about some mines of argentiferous lead ores, copper ores, and tin. But the medieval people wanted iron in much larger quantities during the great age of gothic building, which lasted from the early twelfth to the early fourteenth century. Crude iron was more needed than before for ploughshares and other farm implements, for tools, axles, chauldrons, and other accessories in the expanding industries, for anchors, keels, and nails in shipbuilding, for armour, spears, swords, and daggers to be used when the need arose in war. Iron-making prospered all over Europe. An international traffic in iron developed. Styria, Carinthia, the Basque provinces of Biscay and Guipuzcoa in Spain, and, to a lesser extent, Hungary, Sweden, and Westphalia were the principal exporting countries. Iron was carried thence on pack-horses and in carts, in river barges and in ships, especially to the most populous and civilised parts of Europe—to Italy, Northern France, and the Low Countries.

All these regions had iron ore; so the imports of iron served only to supplement the local supplies. Italy produced much of its own iron, and additional supplies came from the island of Elba across the water to the rich and populous Tuscany, where at the turn of the thirteenth and fourteenth centuries building and manufacturing were pushed further perhaps than anywhere else in Europe. Both in England and in the provinces which were to form modern France small forges

[1] G. R. Lewis, *The Stannaries* (Cambridge (Mass.), 1907), 252–5.

multiplied, especially in the wooded uplands, to supply the needs of the neighbouring towns and villages. These tiny mills required very little capital. It was not difficult for the iron-makers to pick up their equipment when they had thinned out the immediately surrounding woods for charcoal, and to move on to new clusters of trees. There were, in addition, some more important centres of production, with rather larger forges—Piedmont, the Forest of Dean, upper Champagne, Lorraine, and Dauphiné. Wrought iron was carried thence for longer distances to serve multitudes of smiths and artistic craftsmen.

In spite of the growing prosperity of the iron-making industry, iron was produced even at the beginning of the fourteenth century in quantities which seem to us, in the present great age of iron and steel, almost negligible. The annual output of all the forges in Styria, a leading iron-making centre in Europe, probably seldom exceeded two thousand tons.[1] At the beginning of the twentieth century a single great enterprise produces more in a few hours. Iron remained a valuable commodity in the Middle Ages. It was hardly less scarce than in the early Roman Empire. At a time when ever larger multitudes of town craftsmen were learning to make use in new ways of every available material which could serve in fashioning religious images and other works of art, it was natural that so rare a substance as iron, which, in its finer varieties, as prepared in charcoal fires, was not only durable but lustrous, should have been in demand hardly less for aesthetic than for utilitarian purposes. Fine iron was wanted for grills and other decorative work, especially in connection with the cathedrals, churches, abbeys, and priories which were going up everywhere in the rising cities and towns, in old villages, and in hosts of new settlements. Skilful craftsmen also used iron to fashion for laymen fine window grills, entrance keys and locks, knockers and decorations for strong boxes. As Roger Bacon explained, iron was made into charms designed to drive away evil spirits.

For the generation brought up in the early twentieth century, and accustomed to an annual output in Europe of several hundred million tons, the use of coal in the thirteenth century will seem even more insignificant than the use of iron. But the generations who lived in the most civilised parts of the classical world during the first three centuries of the Christian era would have found the use of coal, unlike the use of iron, almost entirely novel. While its burning properties were not unknown in classical times, no systematic attempt was made to dig coal out of the earth except perhaps in Roman Britain. Authentic records of its use before the last decade of the twelfth century have not been

[1] The output could hardly have been greater than it was a hundred and fifty years later, in the sixties of the fifteenth century (see below, p. 471).

discovered. For the thirteenth century such records abound. They provide further evidence of the mounting prosperity which was bringing larger quantities of metal into circulation and use. The burning of coal followed the great expansion in building and in iron working, and was in large measure caused by it. In spite of protests against the dirt and the noxious smells generated by coal fires, when wood and charcoal grew dear the lime-burner and those smiths who made the cruder iron wares turned to coal, when it could be had nearby from outcropping seams. These were found at a great many places. During the thirteenth century the local inhabitants began to dig shallow pits in nearly all the coalfields of England, Scotland, and the Low Countries, as well as in the neighbourhood of Aix-la-Chapelle, in Franche-Comté, Lyonnais, Forez, Alais, and Anjou.

The chief centres for coal mining were in the Low Countries at Liège and Mons, and in the North of England. The traditional reputation of Newcastle as the inexhaustible source of supplies dates from this age. Coal began to be sometimes loaded into ships leaving the Tyne. It served as ballast in place of the bags of sand usually carried by medieval vessels. It found a small market among smiths and lime-burners at London and, in smaller quantities, at other ports along the eastern and southern coasts of England and the northern coasts of the continent, particularly in the Low Countries. There industry throve at the end of the thirteenth century only less than in Tuscany and Northern Italy.

III. *Laws and Customs of Medieval Mining*

As the situation of mines and metallurgical works was determined by the whereabouts of accessible ores and, to a lesser extent, by the whereabouts of woodlands and swiftly moving streams, the organisation of mining and metallurgy from the twelfth to the early fourteenth century presents features which mark these industries off from the other rising medieval crafts. While cloth-making and the making of leather wares were usually the direct concern only of the towns, mining and metallurgy affected every political authority and every kind of country landholder from the emperor to the meanest serf.

The increasing need for revenue felt by almost all overlords, lay and ecclesiastical, provided them with a motive for throwing open the mines in their territories to all comers and for claiming as large a share as possible of the output. By establishing mints to coin silver and later gold, and by ordering the mining communities in the interest of their treasuries, some princes added greatly to their wealth and political power.

In feudal times, emperors, kings, popes, bishops, and numerous other lesser overlords exercised political authority in varying degrees. The origin of their claims to dispose of mines under private lands subject to their authority (the *Bergregal*) is obscure. It was certainly not Roman but feudal. Regalian rights to mines, like regalian rights to coin silver money, were not recognised in Western Europe before the tenth or even the eleventh century. The new claims probably had much to do with the remarkable growth in mining, particularly in the mining of silver-bearing ores, needed for coinage. As claims to the *regale* were frequently limited, especially until after the thirteenth century, to ores containing gold or silver, there is a temptation to assume that one source of the regalian rights may have been the idea, later set forth in favour of these rights in the English 'case of mines', in 1566, that the overlord had a special title as the most excellent person to the most excellent things within his territorial dominions.[1] As will be seen in a moment, there is solider ground for suggesting that the mining *regale* grew at least partly out of the claims of feudal overlords to dispose of waste land and 'treasure trove' or hidden treasure.[2]

During the twelfth and thirteenth centuries European overlords were claiming with much success the right to dispose of ores containing gold or silver (then won mainly from seams of argentiferous lead ore), and in some cases of tin and copper ore as well, both in their own lands and in those of their subjects. When the mines were worked, they claimed a share in the produce. This share generally included a settled portion of the ore or metal, frequently a tenth. In addition the overlords usually received coinage duties; they often had the right of pre-emption over the entire output of the best metal—i.e. a right to buy all of it at a lower price than that which it might have commanded if sold on the open market. But as it was in their interest to have the mines worked, and as they seldom cared to bear the risks of operating them, there were practical limits to their demands. They could not afford to be exorbitant. Their claims to revenue were frequently reduced to meet the increased costs which the miners had to undergo in sinking, draining, and ventilating the pits.

During the last half of the twelfth century, and possibly even earlier, when the political authority of the German emperor was theoretically very great, the emperors pressed their claims to share throughout the Empire in the revenue of all mines producing silver or gold. At Roncaglia Frederick Barbarossa (1155–89) claimed the *regale* as an

---

[1] Edmund Plowden, *The Commentaries or Reports* (1818 ed.), 310 ff. Cf. Sir John Pettus, *Fodinae Regales* (1670), 28–9.

[2] Cf. Adam Smith, *Wealth of Nations*, bk. II, chap. I.

attribute of imperial sovereignty.[1] The revival of Roman law was used as a basis for applying attributes of the Roman imperial authority to feudal conditions, for asserting that feudal overlordship everywhere belonged to the emperor. The emperors sought, not without opposition, to make the *Bergregal* a sovereign *regale*, as they tried unsuccessfully to make the *Münzregal*, or right of coinage.[2] They tried to establish the principle that the power to grant concessions for mining ores containing precious metals was exclusively imperial. As it was usually interpreted, that principle put the emperors under an obligation to set up an imperial administration for regulating the labour and the community life of the free men who came to try their luck with their picks and shovels. The emperors treated this participation in the administration of mining, along with their claim to a revenue from the mines, as attributes of sovereign authority, distinguished from those rights which went with the tenure of landed estates. According to this doctrine, no lord of the soil could have valuable minerals dug within his lands without the permission of the emperor. In case the emperor had delegated his authority to an overlord, the overlord's permission was required.

After the death of Barbarossa, the political powers of the emperors diminished throughout the Holy Roman Empire and especially in Germany. Territorial sovereign rights were increasingly split up among their chief vassals. As Charles IV made clear in his famous Golden Bull of 1356, the emperors relinquished their regalian rights to mines whenever they relinquished their sovereign authority. Regalian rights went with lordship of territories. This did not prevent a territorial prince, if he chose, from investing certain of his vassals, or even his rear vassals, with his regalian rights. He could do so while he retained the general authority which went with territorial lordship. In this way, he could rid himself of the obligation to oversee mines in many regions, at a time when mining enterprises were multiplying very rapidly. The emperors, the kings of Bohemia, the dukes of Silesia, and other princes of the Empire all took advantage of this opportunity to delegate their mining responsibilities. In consequence the number of overlords exercising regalian (or even sovereign) rights in Central Europe was continually growing. On the eve of the Reformation, the bishops, dukes, margraves, counts, and independent towns possessing these rights could be counted by dozens.

[1] P. W. Finsterwalder, 'Die Gesetze des Reichstags von Roncalia von 11 November 1158', *Zeitschrift der Savigny Stiftung für Rechtsgeschichte*, Germanistische Abteilung, XLI (1931), 43-5, 62-9, a reference called to my attention by Professor Kantorowicz. I am indebted to him and to Professor McIlwain for helping me to understand the origin of the mining *regale*. If I have not got matters right, the fault is mine.

[2] F. von Schrötter, *Wörterbüch der Munzkunde* (Berlin, 1930), 430-2.

The unwary are likely to assume that the regalian authority of the territorial princes in the Empire was more extensive than was actually the case. In the fourteenth century few holders of the *regale* had successfully put forward a claim to base ores in the lands of private owners (*Grundherren*) within their territorial dominions. Someone, however, had to assume responsibility for orderly mining and for settling disputes between groups of miners, at a time when mining was still carried on largely by small bands of work-people who claimed a share in the ownership of the ores by virtue of the technical ingenuity they exercised and the manual labour they performed. Where base ores were dug in considerable quantities in privately owned lands, the lord of the soil frequently took the place of the territorial lord. Like the territorial lord, he set up a mining administration and shared in the produce of the mines or the revenue from them.

Coal invariably and iron ore generally were treated as the property of the landlord. In the margravate of Meissen, which included the rich mines of Freiberg, the lords of the soil also retained the authority to work tin, lead, and copper ore without the permission of the margrave. In Bohemia the kings generally limited their claims to ores containing substantial quantities of gold or silver. Consequently much mining was carried on during the twelfth and thirteenth centuries outside the *regale*.

We are here frequently in the presence of a valid distinction which masks a practical reality. The territorial lord was always a private landlord as well. Within the territorial jurisdiction over which he ruled were estates that belonged to him directly. As it happened, a large part of the ores dug in Central Europe during the thirteenth century were in mountainous country, and so in waste land, in no-man's land. Territorial princes claimed such land as part of their demesne. This gave them adequate authority as private landlords to dispose of many base ores in the same way as they disposed, by virtue of their sovereign rights, of ores containing precious metal.

What was the position of a private landlord, who was not a territorial prince, when mines were worked in his soil under the authority of his overlord? His obligations were heavy, but he often had in return certain advantages. Such a landlord was obliged to allow the miners and smelters who obtained concessions from the overlord access to the ore. He was obliged, when necessary, to provide these work-people with land for their cottages, their mills, and their forges. In addition the miners and smelters were frequently given parts of his land for farming and for pasture. They were allowed to use the streams for washing their ore and driving their mills. They were generally entitled to take from his manor or lordship at least a part of the lumber that they needed for building, together with fuel for their kilns and furnaces.

The miners and smelters had to pay for these privileges. The landlords received compensation for the use of their lands and for any damage done to them. Sometimes they shared with the regalian lord in the royalty on the produce of the mines containing precious metal. There were cases, for example in Bohemia, where the landlords appointed mining officials of their own to care for their interests. Two mining administrations, those of the territorial lord and of the lord of the soil, operated concurrently.

The problems arising out of mining operations, which called for settlement by administrative, legislative, and judicial procedures, were in fact almost endless. Much of the work of mining and making metal was carried on in soil held by tenants of the landlord. These tenants were entitled to compensation when mining and metallurgical operations touched their actual holdings of arable and pasture land. There was no aspect of medieval life—economic, political, cultural, or religious— which was not affected by these expanding industries.

In the other countries of continental Europe, and in Great Britain and Scandinavia, the medieval laws and customs concerning the ownership and the working of mines resembled those in the Empire. But the division of the sovereign authority after the twelfth century, characteristic of Central Europe, was by no means the rule during the Middle Ages.

In France the process was reversed, in the sense that the supreme political authority—the French crown—was continually gaining in actual power throughout the realm. With the revival of Roman law, the legitimatisation of illegitimate children was treated as a sovereign, i.e. an imperial, right. In 1205 a decretal of Pope Innocent III declared that this power of legitimatisation belonged to the French king, Philip Augustus (1180–1223), within his dominions. Not long afterwards lawyers began to interpret the decretal as evidence that the French king was emperor in his realm—'Rex est imperator in regno suo'.[1]

During and after the reign of Philip Augustus the French kings steadily encroached upon the independent governing authorities, the principal feudal overlords. When it came to contesting the rights of such lords to dispose of minerals within their ancient jurisdictions, the French kings generally proceeded warily. Compared with the emperors, the great German princes, and the English kings, they were slow in claiming regalian rights over mines in the lands of their vassals. They were slow about insisting upon a royalty from mining operations outside the territories that formed part of their royal demesne.

Their caution resulted partly from the strength possessed by some of the greater noblemen, foremost among whom were the Dukes of

[1] J. Rivière, Le Problème de l'église et de l'état (Louvain, 1926), 424–30, another reference for which I thank Professor Kantorowicz.

Burgundy, who had already begun to exercise regalian rights over mines.[1] To take the *regale* in France from feudal overlords, who had long exercised it, involved many difficulties. It may be questioned whether such a policy could have been embarked upon as soon as it was, had silver-bearing ores been as plentiful in France as they were in Central Europe. It might even have been necessary for the French kings to decentralise the *regale* as the emperors did. In so large a kingdom as France the administrative machinery required in the form of clerks, technical experts, and judges for regulating mining in many districts would have been beyond the capacity of a medieval ruler to staff. As things were, the French kings seem to have waited until the great expansion in mining and metallurgy of the gothic age was over before acting vigorously. With the early fifteenth century, they set about to deprive French overlords of their mining authority. In 1413 a royal edict was passed making it illegal for any lord but the king to collect the royalty (*dixième*) on the produce of mines.[2] As the strength of the monarchy grew in France, and as administrative, legal, and judicial authority was more and more centralised at the end of the Middle Ages and in early modern times, the crown was able bit by bit to centralise the mining *regale*.

In England, government was centralised earlier than in any continental country, during the two centuries following the Norman conquest of 1066. Except in a few areas, like the Palatinate of Durham, the crown became the undisputed sovereign. In the thirteenth century the regalian rights which the English kings exercised in connection with mines seem hardly to have fallen short of those possessed by the emperor, or by leading princes of the Empire to whom the emperor delegated his sovereign authority. While the English kings showed no disposition to codify the customary laws of the mining communities, as some Central European princes were doing, they successfully claimed the authority to dispose of all gold- and silver-bearing ores in the lands of their subjects and to collect a royalty on the produce of gold and silver mines. While their attempts to extend their regalian rights to include base ores were sporadic and ultimately unsuccessful, they controlled the prosperous stannaries of Devon and Cornwall. In the thirteenth century the authority of the crown over the stannaries hardly fell short of that exercised over mines of silver-bearing ores by the territorial princes in Central Europe, Tuscany, and Sardinia. The privileges of prospectors for and finders of ore were at least as great as those usually allowed them

---

[1] Henri Beaune, 'Note sur le régime des mines dans le duché de Bourgogne', *Mém. de la société des antiquaires de France*, XXXI (1869), 114–15; *Inventaire sommaire des archives départementales de l'Hérault*, C. III (1887), 258.

[2] *Recueil général des anciennes lois françaises* (Paris, 1825), VII, 386–90

on the continent. Either directly, or through the Prince of Wales as Earl and later as Duke of Cornwall, the crown had the sole power to grant finders of ore and other miners concessions to tin mines in the unenclosed lands of private landlords in Cornwall and, in Devon, under the enclosed lands as well. Miners were free to search for tin in these lands without permission from the landlords.[1] The crown derived a considerable revenue from the coinage duties and from the purchase and sale of tin, which it could buy at an advantageous price by virtue of its right of pre-emption. As lord of the soil, not apparently as sovereign, the king possessed a similar control over some of the richest mines of lead ore in Derbyshire,[2] the leading centre for lead mining in the country.

In the thirteenth century the most productive mines of iron ore were probably those in the Forest of Dean.[3] The crown seems to have claimed successfully a part in the produce of all iron ore and coal mines there, apparently because much of the land belonged to the royal demesne. In other parts of England iron ore and coal were dug independently of the crown in many private lands. Coal and iron ore were then of relatively small importance.

The chief mines in England in the thirteenth century were worked mostly under royal authority. From them the king derived a revenue, either by virtue of his sovereignty or by virtue of his direct possession of soil which formed part of the royal demesne. It was not until the end of the Middle Ages, after the Hundred Years War, that important differences arose between the mineral rights attaching to overlordship on the continent and in England. In the thirteenth century the situation respecting the *regale* was much the same in all European countries. The actual authority of the English king over mineral property in his dominion was hardly inferior to that of any prince in Christendom.

While there was an extraordinary diversity in such matters as weights and measures, European civilisation in the late twelfth and thirteenth centuries had a great unity. Everywhere there was a basic similarity in the manner in which men lived and worked, as well as in the manner in which they worshipped. Conditions in mining and metallurgy were no exception. Whether the minerals were at the disposal of the emperor, a king, a prince or lord, a bishop, or a city council, by virtue of delegated as well as usurped sovereign authority, or at the disposal of the lay or

[1] Cf. Lewis, *The Stannaries*, 158–60; A. K. H. Jenkin, *The Cornish Miner* (London, 1927), 32.
[2] Cf. *Victoria County History, Derbyshire*, II, 325–7.
[3] Rhys Jenkins, 'Iron-making in the Forest of Dean', *Newcomen Society Trans.* VI (1925–6), 46.

ecclesiastical lord of some manor or vill, by virtue of his property in the land,[1] mining concessions all over Europe resembled one another. When it came to fundamentals, the relations between the miners or smelters and the officials representing the lords were everywhere much the same.

The finder of ore staked out a claim to mine by applying for a concession to the lord's principal officer, generally known in the German mining districts of Central Europe as the *Bergmeister*. This officer, or his representative, invested the miner for an indefinite term with the right to exploit a section of the seam or to extract the minerals under a given plot of land. In many districts, especially in Central Europe, it was the custom to divide up the accessible portion of the seam near the surface into a number of small sections (meers), often square and of a size prescribed by local customs. The lord's officers then granted the finder the section that he had discovered and sometimes an additional section. One or more of the other sections was usually reserved for the lord, to be worked for him directly or leased out (a practice analogous to that of treating sections of agricultural land held by tenants in common as part of their lord's demesne). Each of the remaining sections of the seam was granted to a miner, ordinarily to the first applicant. In return for promises to mine continuously, to pay the customary royalties, and to abide by the mining customs of the district as enforced by the lord's officers, the miners had full power to work their concessions.

Wherever the digging and the working of ores were sufficiently important to employ several scores of miners and smelters, little mining communities were formed. These communities were separate from those of the local peasants engaged in tillage and pasture farming. They had their own laws and customs. Such special communities multiplied rapidly in number especially in Central Europe during the late twelfth and thirteenth centuries. They were everywhere the rule in the digging and smelting of silver, gold, copper, tin, and lead ores. In the making of iron they were rather less common. In the mining of coal they were found only in the Low Countries and the Forest of Dean. As coal and

---

[1] There were districts where the power to grant concessions and to order mining operations was vested neither in a sovereign prince nor in a single lord of the soil. In the lead mines of Mendip, in Somerset, the control was in the hands of four prominent local lords, each of whom controlled an area with its own separate officers, its mining code, and its mineral courts (*Mendip Mining Laws and Forest Bounds*, ed. J. W. Gough, 1931). In the coalfield west of Mons, in Hainault, where, as in the silver-mining districts, property in mines was separated from property in the soil, concessions were granted by the local officials charged with the administration of justice—the *seigneurs haut-justiciers* (G. Arnould, *Le bassin houiller du couchant de Mons* (Mons, 1877), 22; G. Decamps, *Mémoire historique sur l'origine et les développements de l'industrie houillère...de Mons*, 58 ff.).

iron ore mining were less localised than the mining of more valuable ores, there were only a few places, such as Liège and the Erzberg in Styria, where considerable numbers of persons were engaged in either the coal-mining or the iron-making industries. Elsewhere the digging of coal for the most part, and in many cases the digging and smelting of iron ore, were undertaken more informally by a few local peasants, working either for themselves or for some lord of the soil, frequently on days when they were not engaged in husbandry. They were subject to the ordinary local laws and customs concerning labour in the fields and forests.

In Central Europe as far as the Balkans, the principal regions of German colonisation, the overlords generally threw open to all comers the rights to search for minerals, to mine, and to convert ores to metals. Elsewhere, in Western Europe generally, there were many districts in which such rights were restricted to certain local persons who formed a closed body similar to a town gild. Such exclusive groups were obviously better suited to peoples who remained in their native provinces than to colonisers who came from many different regions and settled far from the countries of their origin. Exclusive communities were fairly common in the iron-making industry, especially in France, where they were also formed in other industries dependent on abundant woods for fuel, like the making of crude glass vessels. In the wooded, hilly country about Alençon, in Perche and upper Normandy, a group of local lords, lay and ecclesiastical, known as *barons fossiers*, were alone entitled to open mines of iron ore or to build iron forges. The actual manual labour of making the charcoal fuel and the iron was in the hands of a corporation of *férons*. Admission was limited to the sons and sons-in-law of members.[1]

There were other cases in which the right to work (and indeed to own) mines was restricted to people living in a certain area. In the eastern Pyrenees no one could search for or exploit iron ore on the mountain of Rancié unless he was an inhabitant of the valley of Vicdessos.[2] Similar restrictions existed in at least one English mining district. Only persons born in the hundred of St Briavels, who had worked with their picks for a year and a day, were eligible to obtain concessions from the king's gaveller to parts in the seams of iron ore or coal within the Forest of Dean.[3]

---

[1] H. de Formeville, *Les barons fossiers et les férons de Normandie* (Caen, 1852), 1–7, and *passim*.

[2] Henri Rouzaud, *Histoire d'une mine au mineur* (Toulouse, 1908), 11–12, 23–30.

[3] *Laws and Customs of the Miners in the Forest of Dean*, ed. T. Houghton (1687); H. G. Nichols, *Iron Making in...the Forest of Dean* (1866), 71–82; Exchequer Depositions by Commission (Public Record Office, London), 13 Charles I, Mich. 42.

Whether or not the communities were exclusive, the social status of the miners and metallurgical workers was generally as high as that of the citizens in the rising towns. In the twelfth and thirteenth centuries settlement in the towns offered a means of escape from serfdom. During this age of growing population, peasants became free by taking up the profession of mining much as by taking up work as craftsmen or traders. In fact the formation of mining communities and towns may be considered as two parts of a single great movement of industrial and commercial expansion. There were cases in which these two parts converged. At Liège in the thirteenth century the coal miners were organised into a leading muncipal gild. An accident of nature at this bend in the river Meuse had placed rich coal seams under one of the most thickly settled spots in the Low Countries, so that coal mining there was actually a municipal industry. There were other cases in connection with the discovery of ores rich in precious metals where the new mining communities were large enough to form actual towns. That happened, for example, at Freiberg, at Iglau, and at Schemnitz in Hungary. In these places municipal and mining law developed concurrently.[1]

Whether the mining community formed part of a town or not, it was generally a sort of state within a state, with laws and regulations of its own, suited at least to some extent to the special needs and conditions of its members.[2] In it the actual workers possessed, to begin with, special privileges and a considerable amount of self-government. Wherever the miners or makers of metal contributed to the wealth of a sovereign prince, they were exempted from the obligation of paying the ordinary taxes. They generally had a voice in ordering their own labour. The regulations governing the manner of sinking and supporting pits, the manner of raising ore, the hours of work, and the division of profits and losses were determined by the lord's officials in company with representatives of the miners and metallurgical workers (jurés, geschwornen, jurors). Cases concerning the working of the mines and forges were tried in special courts, in which the work-people were always represented and in which they often formed the majority.

The people in these mining communities were bound to conform to the worship of the Roman Church, whose priests followed the settlers everywhere. They were subject to the general political laws and regulations of the sovereign authority within whose jurisdiction they lived. But to such authority there were invariably limits defined by traditions

[1] Cf., for Iglau, Adolf Zycha, *Das böhmische Bergrecht des Mittelalters auf Grundlage des Bergrechts von Iglau* (Berlin, 1900), I, 43–4.
[2] Cf. *Victoria County History of Cornwall*, I (1906), 523.

and customs. The customs that developed in mining, in the formation of which working miners had a share, were actually helping to circumscribe the authority of the political sovereign. When the units of labour were very small, as they were in the beginning in mining and metallurgy, the participation of work-people in political authority had a concrete and immediate reality which is less easy for workers to feel in the large industries of modern times, even when these industries are in the hands of a government which the work-people have a share in choosing. The twelfth- and thirteenth-century miners were powerless to change the overlord, but they were frequently in a strong position to influence the decisions of the local leaders he appointed to supervise and regulate the mining communities.

IV. *The Origin of Medieval Mining Laws and Customs*

In many mining communities, especially in Central Europe, the laws and customs were eventually embodied in codes written in longhand. Codes were issued by the territorial lords holding regalian rights, or by the lords of the soil when the property in the minerals went with the property in land. The first code of which we have direct evidence is for Trent in the Southern Tyrol. It was issued in 1185 by the Bishop of Trent. From that time the codification of laws and customs spread. In Central Europe and Scandinavia some codes, originally promulgated for one community, served as a model for many others. The most influential codes were apparently those enacted by the King of Bohemia for the miners of Iglau, the first of which dated from about 1249.[1] The Iglau regulations formed the basis for all the written Bohemian laws relating to the mining of silver-bearing ores during the late thirteenth and fourteenth centuries. These Iglau codes left their trace on those of several mining communities in Germany, Hungary, Transylvania, and the Venetian Republic.[2]

It would be a mistake to conclude that all medieval mining laws and customs had a common origin. The most universal customs were the product not of a single lawgiver or even of a single race. They were the product of conditions common to the whole of Europe.

Precedents can be found for them in earlier history. In Attica in the fifth and fourth centuries B.C. the principle that the right to dispose of

---

[1] Zycha, *op. cit.* I, 49.
[2] Cf. J. A. Tomaschek, *Das alte Bergrecht von Iglau* (Innsbruck, 1897), viii–ix.

valuable ores under private lands is an attribute of sovereignty, was apparently established in connection with the silver mines of Laurion.[1] While there is no evidence that this principle ever became a part of imperial Roman law, in the late Roman Empire most mines seem to have belonged to the imperial treasury or to the emperor. The emperor also levied a tax of a tenth on the produce of privately owned mines. References to this tax in the Roman codes studied by jurists in the twelfth and thirteenth centuries may possibly have encouraged medieval princes to claim a similar tax, in somewhat the same way that the emperors and later the French kings apparently used revivals of Roman law as a basis for putting forward exclusive claims to the mining *regale* as a whole.

The work of modern archaeologists has provided us with a knowledge of classical history inaccessible to medieval people. Among other things, it has proved that in the second century A.D. the Roman imperial administration issued written regulations for mining in certain imperial lands at and near Vispasca, in what is now Portugal. These regulations, set forth in the tables of Aljustrel, resemble very strikingly those embodying the customs of the medieval mining communities in the late twelfth and thirteenth centuries. There was the same division of interests between the lord and the occupiers of pits, the same kind of administrative control by the lord's officers over mining operations. There were the same little companies with transferable shares, formed by miners working together at a seam, the same special jurisdictions outside the ordinary courts for settling mining disputes. Regulations of the sort found in second-century Portugal apparently existed even earlier, as far back at least as Hellenistic times, in the countries of the Eastern Mediterranean.

A knowledge of such a mining administration could hardly have been brought to medieval Europe by the revival of Roman law in the twelfth century, for there is no trace of such regulations in the code of Justinian, in earlier compilations of imperial legislation, or in classical legal treatises. But it is possible that remnants of the system may have been preserved across many centuries in the customs of a few districts where the working of ores was never entirely abandoned. This would help to explain why in medieval England this system of mining administration is found almost exclusively in connection with lead and tin mining, the only kinds of mining which have left conspicuous traces during the Saxon period. Such laws and customs appear, moreover, at just those

---

[1] We must still regard the thesis of Henri Francotte (*L'industrie dans la Grèce ancienne* (Brussels, 1900), II, 183–91) that there were privately owned mines in Attica as unproved (G. M. Calhoun, 'Ancient Athenian Mining', in *Journal of Economic and Business History*, III (1931), 341–4).

places where the Romans are known to have encouraged mining during their occupation of Britain.

At first sight it is more difficult to understand how these mining regulations of imperial Rome could have had any influence in Saxony and Bohemia, which were the chief centres of medieval mining laws and customs. The Romans probably had not worked mines in these countries as they had in Britain. Rome may have had an indirect influence for all that. The remarkable development of mining in Bohemia at the end of the twelfth and during the thirteenth century was brought about by the immigration of German miners who are said to have come from the South German lands, especially from Tyrol and other regions of the Eastern Alps.[1] In the Eastern Alps there is more evidence of continuity between Roman and medieval mining than in any other part of Europe.[2]

We have, then, strong circumstantial evidence of a connection between a mining administration of the kind that is known to have existed in second-century Portugal and the laws and customs very widely adopted in the medieval mining communities. But why should the Western Europeans have adopted this particular form of ancient mining administration rather than another? While Montesquieu and various modern writers were wrong in thinking that classical mining was invariably the labour of slaves, slaves were perhaps the most common labourers in the mines.

For certain limited periods in classical history slave labour may have been almost universal. Somewhat less frequently mining was done by wage-earners who had no more share in ordering their work or governing themselves than the wage-earners in the European mines and factories of the eighteenth and early nineteenth centuries. The wage-earning miners of classical times were in the employ sometimes of private capitalists, sometimes of the state, sometimes of contractors acting for the state, sometimes of farmers of the public revenues. There is no reason for supposing that the different system which existed in ancient Portugal in the second century A.D. gained ground in the later Roman Empire. Professor Rostovtzeff has taught that the emperors interfered more and more with the conduct of economic enterprises of all kinds—commercial, financial, and industrial. As part of this policy, the Roman imperial administration took over many mines formerly let out in

---

[1] It was once supposed that the first German miners in Bohemia came from Western Germany, from the Harz and the Rhineland. But Zycha gives impressive evidence in favour of their Alpine origin. (Adolf Zycha, *Das bömische Bergrecht des Mittelalters* (1900), I, 17-33.)

[2] Cf. Clamor Neuburg, 'Der Zusammenhang zwischen römischem und deutschem Bergbau', in *Festgaben für Wilhelm Lexis* (Jena, 1907), 278, 298-9.

various ways to private persons. It worked them directly, sometimes employing convicts as miners, a practice for which there were a great many precedents in classical history. Nothing could be further from the spirit of medieval mining than this treatment of the work as a kind of punishment. Mining by independent associations of workmen, whose right to dig for ore rested on a grant by a superior authority representing the imperial fiscal administration, is believed to have decreased in importance after the second century. It is impossible to say whether there was a revival of it on the eve of the barbarian conquests when the imperial enterprises were apparently replaced by small mining ventures under local lords.[1] In any event the tendency of later Roman history was not in the direction of the free mining communities. These appear to have been most exceptional during the thousand years or more when mining operations were of considerable importance in the economy of classical civilisation.

Inventiveness has been characteristic of the people of Western Europe at least as far back as the eleventh century. It is a fundamental part of the process of invention to know what and how to borrow. To a greater degree than in any other age in western history, perhaps to a greater degree than in any other age in all history, the eleventh and still more the twelfth and early thirteenth centuries awoke among the humble the talent, the desire, the knowledge, and the skill indispensable for co-operating in works of genius. In late romanesque and gothic Europe the same gifts for absorbing, reconciling, and unifying divers materials were manifested in the architecture, in which many participated, as in the creative learning on which a very small proportion of the population left a visible trace.

Princes and lords, lay and ecclesiastical, were granting charters to growing towns and freedom to serfs and the sons of serfs in the country. When valuable mines were discovered, the princes and lords who claimed the authority to dispose of them had to attract hands to get them worked. In order to do this they had to offer advantages equivalent to those granted to settlers in the towns.

Work-people in the mining communities derived their privileges and their independence from other circumstances besides their bargaining power. Mining made a positive contribution of its own to the new freedom and also, though this may seem paradoxical, to the new authority exercised during and after the thirteenth century by lesser political rulers, who nominally owed allegiance to the Empire.

The conditions under which mining was generally carried on added to the prestige attaching in a small degree to many kinds of manual

[1] We have no evidence concerning the form of these ventures (cf. Neuburg, *op. cit.* 297).

labour, and especially to the artistic work in building and decorating churches and monasteries. The early miners and smelters, particularly in Saxony, the Alps, and other regions of Central Europe, were explorers and even climbers attacking forests, venturing into high valleys and scrambling up the sides of mountains. Serfdom was almost unknown among the Germans colonising these regions; so freedom was the virtually inevitable status for the miner.[1] The magic of the surroundings in which he often worked helped to class him in the hearts of men not with the slave but with the pioneer.

At the same time this connection of medieval mining and metallurgy with the highlands and woodlands helped to bring mining under the control of princes, lay and ecclesiastical, instead of under the control of private landlords. New seams were found very often in places where there had been little or no tillage and relatively few settlers before the twelfth and thirteenth centuries. In such areas the claims of strong private persons to the possession of the soil were weaker than in some thickly settled regions, where the land had been systematically exploited with little or no interruption since Roman times. The Alpine character of medieval mining, which marked it off from modern and from classical mining, facilitated the divorce, characteristic of medieval mining law, between the use of the surface and the possession of mines. As lordship of the soil was inclined to remain rather indefinite in the forests and Alpine regions, the minerals underneath could be more readily claimed by the overlords than would have been possible where the surface landlords were generally men of greater substance with traditional power over their estates.[2] Peasants who drove flocks to pasture in the Alpine regions were always moving about. They generally left during the winter. So the rights of the owners of cattle were rarely identified with any particular plots of land. If, as frequently happened, some of their animals tumbled into the miners' pits, the shepherds were outraged. They demanded compensation. But it did not occur to them to claim a share in the mines. That left the territorial princes, lay and ecclesiastical, an excellent opportunity to stake out claims to take the miners and metallurgical workers under their tutelage, at a time when they granted such working people much independence and welcomed their participation in local government.

An astonishing feature of early western history in the Pyrenees, Normandy, England, Wales, the Southern Low Countries, the Rhineland, as well as in the Alps and the Erzgebirge, was the disposition of

---

[1] Cf. Gustav Schmoller, 'Die geschichtliche Entwickelung der Unternehmung,' *Jahrbuch für Gesetzgebung, Verwaltung und Volkswirtschaft im deutschen Reich*, xv (1891), 677.

[2] Cf. Schmoller, *op. cit.* 676, 679.

overlords and lords of the soil to grant similar privileges and adopt similar regulations and similar administrative arrangements in hundreds of communities formed to exploit ores and metals. It was almost as if an invisible lawgiver inspired miners, landlords, and territorial rulers from one end of Europe to the other with a single conception of right and wrong, which could be translated into custom and positive law. For a brief spell, which in some regions hardly lasted through the thirteenth century, the western Europeans almost managed to universalise among the miners freedom and partial self-government. The conditions of industrial work in the country as well as in the town were helping to strengthen in western civilisation an allegiance, that was largely new, to the small semi-independent unit of enterprise which came with other units to form part of a local community. This allegiance came to exist concurrently with the allegiances to the authority of a centralised state and a universal church, which the Europeans had inherited from the more distant past.

Like the gothic arch and the great cathedral spires, the community of free miners was a creation of western civilisation. Like the philosophical *Summae* of Thomas Aquinas and Duns Scotus, it was indicative of a genius extensively awakened among the Europeans of the twelfth and thirteenth centuries. This genius consisted in the desire and the capacity to exploit for fresh purposes ideas, forms, and principles, including forms of industrial organisation, suggested by earlier civilised peoples, to generalise these ideas, forms, and principles in ways that made them accessible to all. The power to universalise through small units for the benefit of Western Christendom as a whole gave the age its special unity. To a degree apparently unknown in the past, the many and the one complemented and fortified without absorbing each other.

V. *The Collapse of Prosperity in the Fourteenth Century*

The balance was a delicate one. So far as mining and metallurgy are concerned, it became increasingly imperfect as the Middle Ages waned. The conditions of enterprise which prevailed during the period of expanding output at the end of the twelfth and in the thirteenth century were partly dependent upon the fortunes of nature which spread rich mineral resources out near the surface through the upland valleys, the hills and mountain sides, readily accessible to adventurers with little capital. Such resources obviously had limits.

During the fourteenth century the rapid progress in the output of minerals and metals, characteristic of most of Europe for several previous generations, came to an end. Except in a few districts, notably in eastern Franconia and perhaps in Bohemia, the miners began to encounter hard times early in the century or at least before the middle of it, when the bubonic plague swept away a substantial part of the European population. Both Franconia and Bohemia suffered relatively little from the Black Death. Their escape may have had something to do with the revival of the prosperity of the mines of silver-bearing ore in Bohemia during the third quarter of the fourteenth century. Progress was made also in the output of gold in Bohemia, Silesia, and Hungary.[1] But mining in Central Europe generally was not in a flourishing state during the fourteenth and early fifteenth centuries. The production of gold and silver in Europe as a whole actually declined. To judge from conditions at the famous copper mines on the Rammelsberg and at the equally famous tin mines in Devon and Cornwall, the production of copper and tin also diminished somewhat. In spite of frequent warfare, which kept up the demand for iron and steel, the forges in the chief iron-making districts were seldom prosperous. In many districts their number dwindled. The sea traffic in coal from England to the continent was not increasing.

What were the causes for this long slump which lasted for several generations? The prosperity of the mining and metallurgical industries was bound up with general prosperity. The depression in mining was partly a reflection of the economic and political troubles which beset most of Europe. After at least two hundred years of exceptionally rapid increase, the population was growing slowly, if at all. The peasants, who formed the great majority in every country, found it much more difficult to improve either their social status or their material welfare. In most towns there was no marked increase in the number of craftsmen or in industrial production. Except perhaps in the Low Countries under the Burgundian Duke, Philip the Good (1419–1467), there was nowhere any sustained economic boom until the last decades of the fifteenth century. Consequently there were few places where the demand for metal grew. Wars and political disputes between various European princes and between the rising national states of France and

---

[1] Cf. Kaspar Sternberg, *Umrisse einer Geschichte der böhmischen Bergwerke* (Prague, 1838), I, ii, 32–4. E. J. Hamilton, *Money, Prices and Wages in Valencia, Aragon, and Navarre*, 1351–1500 (Cambridge (Mass.), 1936), 195. But the Silesian mines generally were in a depressed state throughout the fourteenth and fifteenth centuries (Konrad Wutke, 'Die Salzerschliessungsversuche in Schlesien in vorpreussischer Zeit', *Zeitschrift des Vereins für Geschichte und Altertum Schlesiens*, XXVIII (1894), 107). Some of the gold used for the development of coinage in late fourteenth century Europe came from the Sudan, a source of supplies since at least the twelfth century (Fernand Braudel, 'Monnaies et Civilisations', *Annales: Economies, Sociétés, Civilisations*, I, no. 1 (1946), 11).

England were more frequent and more destructive than in the thirteenth century. They interfered with the growth of trade in all products, including metals. In some cases the armies attacked mines and forges, filled the pits with earth and rubbish, smashed the furnaces and bellows, and massacred some of the miners and smelters. The Hussite wars of the early fifteenth century (1415–36) left the celebrated Bohemian mining towns of Kuttenberg, Eyle, and Deutsch-Brod in ruins.

A renewal of prosperity in mining depended upon general improvement in economic and political conditions. In turn, economic progress as a whole depended on a renewal of prosperity in mining. In addition to their other ills, most of the states of Europe suffered from a shortage of gold and silver during the fourteenth and most of the fifteenth centuries, especially after about 1375. Except in those states where princes resorted to the expedient of reducing the gold or silver content of their coins, this was a period of stable or slightly falling prices. Industry and trade were stagnant partly because of the difficulties encountered in trying to sell commodities at a profit. The markets provided by the territorial princes, lay and ecclesiastical, were clogged up. One of the reasons for this sluggish demand was the unsatisfactory yield of the mines and the mints from which these princes often derived a portion of their revenues. To a degree that is difficult for modern men to grasp, orders for industrial products came from the great princes and still more from the Church—from the Pope and from the innumerable ecclesiastical foundations (large and small) spread through the whole of Europe.

In Saxony and the Harz, in Bohemia and Hungary, in Sweden, Alsace, and Devon, some of the most productive mines of silver-bearing ores were exhausted in the fourteenth century. Others were worked so deep that many miners were forced to flee before the onrush of water breaking through into the workings, if they had escaped being buried alive when the badly supported walls of underground passages caved in. Progress depended upon the discovery of new seams and better methods of draining the mines and supporting the walls. It also depended upon the invention of new and cheaper processes for extracting precious metals from the ores and for combining ores and metals.

VI. *The Progress of Industrial Technology*

Heavier capital expenditures were necessary if deeper shafts were to be dug and more machinery installed. During the earlier medieval silver rushes, mining had been generally carried on by rather primitive methods. Much has been written recently about the backwardness of the peoples of the Roman Empire in engineering skill. But archaeologists have now shown that the Romans actually used more ingenious machinery in mining than the Europeans adopted extensively during the twelfth and thirteenth centuries. If miners in the gothic age had learned of the shafts that had been sunk in Roman times to depths of some six hundred feet in Spain, if they had learned of the adits that had been driven for more than a mile to drain the workings, or of the costly drainage machinery in the forms of water-wheels and cochlea, moved apparently by human labour, their admiration for the technical skill of the ancients might have approached that felt by the schoolmen for the thought of the greatest classical philosophers. No such deep mines were to be found in medieval Europe before the end of the thirteenth century; nor were the attempts to rid the pits of water yet as enterprising as those sometimes made by ancient peoples.

Most of the coal and base ore was got either by quarrying or by digging a sort of cave, widening out at the bottom like a bell or cone, with its base only a few feet below the surface. It was only in the digging of rich silver-bearing ores in Central Europe that shaft mining had become at all general by the end of the thirteenth century. Even in silver mining the shafts seldom penetrated deeply below the surface. The normal procedure in attacking silver-bearing ores was to puncture a sloping field with dozens of very shallow pits. As soon as water interfered with the hewers' work, a pit was usually abandoned. In this way hundreds of pits were sometimes sunk in a small area in the space of a few years. Some were so close together that a man could leap the whole distance between them.[1]

The first attempts at drainage were of two kinds. Trenches open to the sky were dug for short distances from the bottom of the shafts down into the valley. Again, leather buckets filled with water were wound up from a pit by a hand-turned windlass, or passed along a chain of men stationed in an inclined shaft. In a few districts such methods of drainage went back to the beginning of the thirteenth century and probably much earlier. They seldom proved adequate for any long stretch of years, if the demand for ore grew at all rapidly. Long before medieval mining reached the depths that had been attained in the Roman Empire, such primitive drainage devices were unable to cope with the floods. The soil of the Alps and the countries to the north is much damper than that of most Mediterranean lands. At depths of from sixty to a hundred feet, flooding was likely to become a much more serious danger than it had been commonly in the mines of the Hellenistic age or of the Roman Empire.

[1] Gustav Schmoller, 'Die geschichtliche Entwickelung der Unternehmung', *Jahrbuch für Gesetzgebung, Verwaltung und Volkswirtschaft im deutschen Reich*, xv (1891), 664.

The only way to meet the difficulties was to drain off the water continuously in fairly large quantities. This called for heavy expenditures in digging drainage tunnels or installing machines. At the end of the thirteenth century or at the beginning of the fourteenth, the first experiments were apparently made with long adits in Bohemia. Some had to be driven more than a mile underground before they reached an opening in the valley below the level of the shaft bottom or sump, in which the water that had seeped into the workings was collected. But as the adits were seldom kept in repair, they were soon clogged up. Water worked its way back into the pits.

In Bohemia at the end of the thirteenth century, and a little later in Saxony, the Harz, and Southern Bavaria, water and horse-driven machines were tried for drawing water from the pits and also for raising brine water from deep salt springs. The mechanical use of water and horse power was not new. For generations water power and occasionally horse power had been employed in metallurgy and some other surface industries. But, if water and horse power were to be effective in draining deep mines, more substantial wheels, axles, and gears than those hitherto in use were indispensable. The early machines for fulling cloth, pounding rags to pulp, even those for driving the bellows and the hammers in metallurgy were not equipped with the powerful wheels needed to raise enough water out of mines to staunch a flood underground. Some thirteenth-century Europeans saw what was wanted better apparently than the Romans had seen. But the idea hardly brought important results for another two hundred years.

In the preparation and the smelting of ores and the refining of metals during the thirteenth century the methods for the most part were little more efficient mechanically than in mining. Washing, breaking, and crushing were usually done out-of-doors by hand labour. Smelters showed much resourcefulness and imagination in devising a variety of hearths, trenches, pots, ovens, and furnaces, suited to the species and the quality of the ore they had to treat. But however artful these forges and mills might be, they were not large or expensive to build and equip. Sometimes, as in the making of lead, smelting was undertaken in open-air hearths on the side of some hill where the fires were fanned by the wind. More often, as in the treatment of iron ore, the metal was produced at tiny forges equipped with hand- or foot-driven bellows. The capital invested in such forges seldom exceeded that required to set up the workshop of a smith. In the woodlands near the seams forges and hammers were almost as numerous as the pits and open works dug down to the ore. They were abandoned almost as lightly.

In metallurgy, as in mining, the first heavy capital expenditures were made in connection with silver. The extraction of this beautiful metal from argentiferous lead ore was a more complicated and expensive task than the preparation of gold or of base metals. After the ore had been raised from the shafts, it was washed, then broken and crushed, then smelted. The resulting argentiferous lead was next subjected to oxidation in a cupelling hearth to remove the lead or litharge, and the residual silver was finally refined in a separate 'test' with bellows. During the twelfth century, the hammers and stamps for breaking and crushing the ore, and the bellows used in heating it, were probably mostly driven by hand or foot labour, as had been the practice at Laurion in the halcyon days of Attic mining in the fifth and fourth centuries B.C. But primitive power-driven machinery could be more effective in many metallurgical operations than in draining mines. Western civilisation developed in many places where nature invited the use of water power. Rushing streams poured down the slopes and ran through the mountain valleys of Central Europe in a profusion unknown in the drier lands of Greece and in most of the Mediterranean basin. By the first decade of the thirteenth century, if not earlier, water-driven wheels were set up at the silver mines of Trent, in the Southern Tyrol, both for driving the hammers and the bellows. A hundred years later, in the principal silver-mining districts, water-driven machinery was frequently employed for breaking and crushing the ores as well as for blowing.

Similar water-driven wheels were introduced for operating the bellows and the hammers in the chief iron-making regions—in Styria, Carinthia, Bohemia, Lorraine, and Dauphiné. Some bellows were already more skilfully constructed than seems to have been common in classical smelting. The modern type of heart-shaped bellows with a flap-valve, never extensively used in Hellenistic or in Roman times, is said to have appeared even before the twelfth century. In the early fourteenth century there were double and fairly sophisticated bellows producing a constant, instead of a panting, blast.[1] The hotter flame from the new and longer water-driven bellows produced bigger salamanders, or masses of metal, than had been made by the older methods. Consequently larger furnaces had to be devised to hold the ore and the fuel, while power-driven tilt hammers were needed to reduce the salamanders to blooms of wrought iron at near-by mills.

Three types of furnace had begun to replace the older bloomery forges in the fourteenth century: the Catalan forge, which had an ancient origin and was adopted mainly in the Pyrenees and the adjoining parts of Spain and France; the Osmund furnace, introduced in Scandinavia; and what was called in German the *Stückofen*. The

[1] Karl Sudhoff, *Beiträge zur Geschichte der Chirurgie im Mittelalter* (Leipzig, 1914), plate xxxi, a reference which I owe to Dr White.

Stückofen, the highest and most effective of the three, was found mainly in Central Europe, Eastern France, and the Alpine districts between. Unlike the tiny woodland bloomery forges, which rose only three or four feet from the ground, the *Stückofen* was a fairly substantial structure of brick or stone, usually built close to the streams to make possible the use of water power. It was some 10 feet high, and consisted of a circular or quadrangular shaft, about 2 feet across at the top and bottom, and widening out to 5 feet or so in the middle. Such a furnace could turn out 40 or 50 tons of iron in a year, about three times the quantity ordinarily produced at the more primitive bloomery forges.

Like the long adits and the water-driven machinery for draining the silver mines, the improved methods for manufacturing iron were not widely adopted in Europe for more than a hundred years after their introduction. While more progress was made during the fourteenth and early fifteenth centuries with water-driven bellows and hammers than with water-driven drainage engines or even with adits, the less powerful methods of making iron at small bloomery forges remained the rule in all except the leading centres.

In most of Europe the miners, smelters, and refiners of metal went on digging and treating ores in the fashion to which their ancestors had become accustomed. Neither the material condition of the European peoples nor the state of learning during the fourteenth and early fifteenth centuries were as favourable to exploration and discovery as in the gothic age. In the universities, students of natural science worked the views of the schoolmen and of the classical philosophers into dogmatic systems that left little room for the kind of re-examination which some of the great men themselves would have welcomed. Scholars, whose experiences led them to distrust authority, kept their own counsel for fear of trouble with their colleagues or with the Church.

A new period of widespread prospecting for fresh seams of ore, and of remarkable technical progress in mining and metallurgy, began in the second half of the fifteenth century. It was an expression of the same forces that led to the discovery of new lands beyond the seas and to advances in natural science. The larger mines and metallurgical establishments of Central Europe became laboratories. The occasional association with them of learned men, such as Paracelsus (1493–1541) and Agricola (1494–1555), and of Biringuccio (d. 1540), a master craftsman in metal work, all of whom devoted a considerable part of their lives to science and engineering, helped to prepare the way for the destruction of the barrier which had existed during the Middle Ages between the work of the industrial craftsman and that of the speculative thinker. In the medieval hierarchy the separation of the liberal from the servile arts was perhaps as complete as the separation between two departments in some large modern university. It would be a mistake to suppose that the 'servility' of handling matter in the Middle Ages was the same sort of servility that came later to attach to the wage-earning manual labourer in mines and factories. But it was the accepted medieval convention that the manipulation of material substances was a servile art and that the more abstract labour of the intelligence belonged to a separate category. For material progress and the rise of modern science the decay of this convention was of great advantage. It persisted through the sixteenth century, but the progress of mining and metallurgy weakened it by providing a meeting ground for technical experts and some learned men.

The efforts of miners and metallurgical workers bore much fruit during the last half of the fifteenth century and the early decades of the sixteenth. New seams of rich ore were found in many districts, especially in those parts of Central Europe that had been famous for their mines already in the thirteenth century. Prospectors also came upon valuable supplies of cinnabar, the ore of mercury, and of alum stones. True brass, as distinguished from bronze, is an alloy of calamine and copper. Its production became common after centuries of neglect. The discovery of abundant calamine in the Tyrol and Carinthia, and especially at Moresnet, near Aachen, led to an extensive manufacture of brass in Germany and the Low Countries. This increased notably the demand for copper.

An invention of the mid-fifteenth century was of even greater importance than the working of calamine in the development of the copper mines. It was discovered that the separation of silver from the argentiferous copper ores, which abounded in Central Europe, could be effectively accomplished with the help of lead. The new method was apparently introduced in Saxony about 1451 by a certain Johannsen Funcken. The rich copper ores had been little exploited before this time because of the difficulty of extracting silver from them or of using them to produce brass. No other invention had so stimulating an effect as the new treatment of copper ore upon the development of the mining and metallurgical industries in Central Europe on the eve of the Reformation.

Just as this invention was helping to make profitable the working of deeper seams of copper ore, the invention of more powerful drainage engines combined with the digging of more skilfully constructed adits to make it possible to cope with the water at greater depths. Better methods of ventilating the underground passages made it possible to cope with the noxious and explosive gases.

The most ingenious of the new machines were apparently constructed in Hungary and Saxony. The most curious of all was at Schemnitz in the Carpathian mountains. There the water from the bottom of the deepest pit was pumped up in three flights before it reached a sufficient height to be carried off down an adit. Each pump was set in motion by the rotation of a large horse-driven wheel. The animals to turn these wheels were led down to their labour along inclined shafts which sloped and twisted like screws. In construction these shafts apparently resembled the ramps that enable modern automobile owners to park their cars in congested city areas. The work required ninety-six horses. They were employed in relays at each of the three wheels.[1] The peoples of antiquity had apparently never devised so powerful a drainage engine.

Less important than improvements in drainage for the progress of mining and metallurgy at the end of the Middle Ages, but far more important in its eventual consequences for the rise of modern industrial civilisation, was the invention of the blast furnace. The heavy manual labour and the great waste of metal involved in producing iron had restrained its use both in war and peace among earlier peoples than the Western Europeans. Once iron ore could be made into metal cheaply, masses of men could be outfitted with weapons based on gunpowder and other explosives, and with carriages, cars, and aeroplanes on which the weapons could be mounted. Machines and conveyances of all kinds to supply commodities intended for peaceful use and new structural materials of iron and steel for building could be produced in an equally bewildering profusion. The blast furnace was not by any means the only invention needed to bring the modern age of metal, but it was an essential one.

The discovery that led to this invention was apparently accidental. Bronze, a compound of copper and tin, melts more readily than iron ore. In the later Middle Ages, in the early twelfth century or perhaps before, a liquefied mixture of copper and tin, produced by a strong heat, was run into holes prepared in the earth where the liquid solidified in such shapes as were desired. In this way bronze was cast into the marvellous church bells of medieval Europe, as well as into statues and domestic utensils. During the great age of gothic cathedral building bells of cast bronze were hoisted into the towers of churches, where they tolled their message, summoning the faithful, across a continent. The first guns were made of bronze by a process learned from bell and statue makers. The early bronze founders contributed unintentionally to the discovery of one of man's most awful weapons.[2]

The more powerful water-driven bellows, introduced in iron-making during the thirteenth century, if not sooner, sometimes generated so fierce a flame in smelting that even the intractable ore of iron ran

[1] Cf. Georgius Agricola, *De re metallica* (Hoover edition, London, 1912), 194–5.
[2] Charles Ffoulkes, *The Gun-Founders of England* (Cambridge, 1937), 2.

before the eyes of the astonished iron-masters. As the casting of bronze was already known, it was natural that the new discovery should be exploited in the same way for casting iron. It is not certain when the first cast iron objects were made, but clearly by the beginning of the fifteenth century and probably somewhat earlier. Cannon made ot cast iron appeared before the middle of the fifteenth century in the dominion of the powerful and enterprising Dukes of Burgundy, and somewhat later in Italy. These cannon were clumsy, ineffective pieces. It was not until after the Reformation that cast iron cannon did effective execution or were turned out in any number, and then they were manufactured not on the continent but in South-eastern England. Meanwhile it was mainly cannon of wrought iron that helped to revolutionise the art of war at the turn of the fifteenth and sixteenth centuries.[1]

By this time, and possibly earlier, genuine blast furnaces, with auxiliary forges, were built in North-eastern France and Northern Italy.[2] There were few of them at the end of the Middle Ages however. An extensive development of the new process of making iron came only later in the sixteenth and during the early seventeenth centuries, in the Low Countries and Great Britain and then in Sweden.

In the few instances where larger furnaces were introduced, cast iron replaced wrought iron as the primary product. In large fires the ore was maintained for long periods in contact with carbon at high temperatures, and the carbon was absorbed by the reduced iron forming an alloy, cast iron, of much lower melting point than the pure metal. The molten metal was allowed to collect in the hearth and was run periodically through a tap hole into an open oblong mould where it solidified into pieces called 'sows'. As larger amounts were cast at one time, bars branching from the sow were added, called 'pigs'—a name suggested by their relationship to the maternal sow. The melting of the product permitted efficient recovery of the iron present in the ore and the cast iron produced was of great use in making a whole range of new products at the foundry—such as guns, shot, fire-backs, andirons, and grave slabs—but it was not in a form fit to use for wrought products— such as tools, weapons, and armour. The cast iron therefore had to be given subsequent treatment to decarbonise it. This consisted of reheating under oxidising conditions, giving an unlimited, spongy mass, that by continued forging became equivalent, and for modern industrial purposes even superior, to the old directly reduced iron. The new roundabout process not only facilitated the production of larger quantities of

---

[1] Rhys Jenkins, 'The Rise and Fall of the Sussex Iron Industry,' *Transactions of the Newcomen Society*, fifth series, I (1920-1), 17; Ernest Straker, *Wealden Iron* (London, 1931), 38–40, 141 ff.; V. Biringuccio, *Pirotechnia* (Cyril S. Smith ed., New York, 1942), 226.   [2] Straker, *op. cit.* 40–3; Biringuccio, *op. cit.* 146–8.

iron with less labour; it reduced the amount lost in the manufacture. Blast furnaces with their dependent forges were larger than the *Stückofen* of Styria, Carinthia, and other regions of Central Europe. They were equipped with more powerful bellows and hammers. Their establishment involved a heavier investment in land, buildings, machinery, and other equipment.

These inventions were only the most spectacular technical achievements of the miners and metallurgical workers in the fifteenth century and at the beginning of the sixteenth. Few years passed without some important mechanical discovery, such as mills for flattening metal or for drawing wire. Machines driven by the rush of streams came into widespread use in some metallurgical districts. Dams were built to store the water used to turn the larger and more powerful overshot wheels.

All the peoples of Europe made contributions to these technical discoveries. There was a good deal of interchange of mechanical knowledge between countries. In iron-making it was the Italians and the French, not the Germans, who led the way on the eve of the Reformation towards larger and more powerful enterprises. It is common to think of the English as backward in technique at the beginning of the sixteenth century. They were backward, but not unqualifiedly backward. Earlier in the Middle Ages they had had many things to give as well as to receive from foreigners. Even in the fifteenth century they were not without their influence on continental mining. A celebrated English master miner was brought to Saxony in 1444 by Kurfürst Friedrich II to help search for fresh seams of ore. But the stream of mechanical knowledge flowed in the opposite direction, with Central Europe as its source.

It was generally experts from Hungary, Bohemia, the Low Countries, the Tyrol, and Saxony who excelled in the technical development of mining and metallurgy. Miners and mechanics of German origin were the leaders in the discovery and the dissemination of new methods, particularly in the mining and working of ores containing silver, copper, zinc, and quicksilver, and in the manufacture of brass. New methods discovered in Central Europe spread to Scandinavia, Spain, France, and England. 'In no place of the world shalt thou finde more witty engins and excellent peeces of workemanship than in Germany,' wrote Thomas Coryate, the parson's son from Somerset, after he had travelled through much of Europe at the beginning of the seventeenth century. By this time Germany was on the point of losing this pre-eminence. She owed it mainly to the ingenuity of Germans and of some Slavs during the late fifteenth and early sixteenth centuries.

Inventions were essential to the great progress made in mining and metallurgy at the close of the Middle Ages. In the coalfields of the Low

Countries and to some extent in those of the North of England shaft mining was becoming common; depths of 150 feet or so were reached. Still deeper shafts, descending some 400 feet or so below the surface, were sunk for mining cinnabar at Idria in Carniola and at Almadén in Spain.[1] The greatest depths of all were reached in working argentiferous copper ores in Saxony, Bohemia, and Hungary, where a few pits went down 600 feet or more. At such depths the problem of drainage could be met only by driving long adits and pumping up water with powerful engines.

Remarkable though the inventions of the later Middle Ages were, they hardly revolutionised mining. Without them there would have been considerable, though less remarkable, progress in output, for new seams were still turning up at shallow depths. Only where the surface minerals were exhausted was recourse had to new methods. Horse- and water-driven drainage engines were installed almost exclusively at argentiferous copper ore mines. For the most part, the older ways of the thirteenth century prevailed. Though shaft mining was introduced for getting tin and lead ore, at the time of the Reformation most of these ores were still obtained at shallow depths of less than fifty feet, simply by surface workings. In Central Europe coal and iron ore were dug entirely from the outcropping seams, by means of open works or caves. The use of even a hand windlass for raising ore was exceptional in connection with iron.

Mining deep below the surface was actually rare even in connection with silver-bearing ores in the most advanced districts. Except perhaps on the Schneeberg in Saxony, where shafts reaching down 200 feet and more seem to have been common,[2] the usual depth in the principal copper mines in Central Europe was about 75 or 80 feet. Many productive argentiferous copper mines were worked without horse- or water-driven engines, or even long adits. In the valley of the Inn, at Schwaz, the leading mining centre in Tyrol and one of the most productive in Europe of silver and copper, men were still engaged in 1537 to pass buckets full of water up an inclined shaft. That had been the universal method at Schwaz until about 1522, when the first attempt was made to introduce an expensive water-driven pumping machine. It is not certain that the attempt succeeded, although some sort of water pump was then installed.[3]

---

[1] P. Hitzinger, *Das Quecksilber-Bergwerk Idria* (Laibach, 1860), 16; K. Häbler, *Die Geschichte der Fugger'schen Handlung in Spanien* (Weimar, 1897), 98.

[2] Oswald Hoppe, *Der Silberbergbau zu Schneeberg bis zum Jahre* 1500 (Freiberg, 1908), 158–9; cf. pp. 92–3.

[3] M. R. von Wolfstrigl-Wolfskron, *Die Tiroler Erzbergbaue*, 1301–1665 (Innsbruck, 1903), 39–41.

Folklore and superstition concerning their craft were still rife among the miners.[1] Special sight was attributed to a few experts who roamed over the hills, holding the ancient divining rod—a forked twig—straight out in front of them, until it turned and twisted as they passed over a hidden seam of ore. The mining communities still depended upon these mystery men for guidance, except when accidents of nature put them directly on the scent of new veins.

In metallurgy, as in mining, the important changes in methods were largely confined to silver and copper. At the time of the Reformation, water power had hardly begun to replace hand and foot power in the crushing, smelting, and hammering of tin or lead ore, except perhaps at a few places in Germany. Even when water power was used for driving the bellows, the forges were generally small. The making of lead and tin did not require as fierce a flame as the making of iron. While blast furnaces had been built in North-eastern France,[2] in Piedmont, along the valleys of the Rhine and the lower Meuse, and in Sussex, most iron was still made directly from the ore even in these regions. In Southern Germany and the Eastern Alps, while the blast furnace was apparently unknown, water power had become the common force both for driving the bellows and the hammers in the leading iron-making districts, such as Styria and Carinthia, where the *Stückofen* had come into widespread use. But hand- or foot-driven bellows remained the rule at the pervasive bloomery forges in less advanced districts.

It is by no means certain that the European peoples had attained in the early sixteenth century a much higher level of technical proficiency in mining and metallurgy than the classical peoples in the early Roman Empire. But they had made discoveries never exploited by the ancients, of which the blast furnace and the *Saigerhütte*[3] are outstanding examples. They were using water power for turning machinery much more extensively than the Greeks or Romans had ever used it. The respect for the miners as pioneers, the freedom and dignity which their calling had come to possess during the twelfth and thirteenth centuries, had relieved the processes of mining and metallurgy from some of the stigma frequently associated with them in earlier civilisations. Was it not partly on that account that the Western Europeans already in the later Middle Ages seem to have been less reluctant than other civilised peoples have been to exploit relentlessly the mineral riches of the earth, to devote their intellectual energies wholeheartedly to methods of cheapening the costs of mining and metallurgy?

By the period of the Reformation the study of engineering was

---

[1] Cf. Agricola, *op cit.* 37–41.
[2] Marcel Bulard, 'L'industrie du fer dans la Haute-Marne', *Ann. de géog.* XIII (1904), 232.   [3] For a description see p. 479.

beginning to claim greater attention than in classical times. Two books out of thirty-seven in Pliny's *Natural History*, written in the first century, are concerned with metals. Other Graeco-Roman works, mostly known to the moderns only at second hand, also treated the subject. But mining and metallurgy apparently never engaged the undivided attention of any classical writer[1] to the extent that they engaged men early in the sixteenth century, especially two men, a German and an Italian, Georgius Agricola and Vannoccio Biringuccio. The former devoted several treatises to it, the best known being a large book *De re metallica*. The latter was concerned with nothing else in his one long piece of writing, the *Pirotechnia*. Both treatises, and especially the *Pirotechnia*, are largely free from superstition. Neither Agricola nor Biringuccio took the divining rod seriously, and the Italian scorned the pseudo-magic of the alchemists.[2] Several of their contemporaries composed works on the same subjects, but the books have been forgotten. This novel disposition to give undivided and accurate attention to mining and metallurgy was indicative of the respect felt by Western Europeans for the occupation of the miner, which had been so distasteful to classical men that they had felt little inclination to explore with their mind the actual world underground, shunned as it was by all who could avoid the labour of mining.

VII. *The Boom in Mining and Metallurgy,* 1460-1530

The wonderful artistic achievements of the late fifteenth and early sixteenth century, when much of continental Europe was built or rebuilt in the new Renaissance style of architecture, were accompanied by a remarkable industrial development, especially striking in Northern Italy, parts of Spain, the Southern Low Countries, and in Eastern and Southern Germany. The progress of mining and metallurgy played an important part in this industrial development, above all in Central Europe. At some of the leading mines, as at Schneeberg in Saxony, the production of silver reached its zenith by the eighties of the fifteenth century. At others, as at Freiberg, the zenith was not reached until after the middle of the sixteenth century. For most mines the time of greatest prosperity was from about 1515 to 1540, when Agricola and Paracelsus reached maturity, when Dürer (1471-1528) and Holbein (1497-1543)

---

[1] Cf. M. Rostovtzeff, *The Social and Economic History of the Hellenistic World* (Oxford, 1941), II, 1212.

[2] Cyril S. Smith's introduction to *The Pirotechnia* (New York, 1942), xv. His admirable piece of editing has added substantially to knowledge of industrial history.

painted many of their incomparable masterpieces, and when the doctrines of Luther (1483–1546), Zwingli (1484–1531), and other reformers fired the German people with a new religious enthusiasm. Between 1460 and 1530 the annual output of silver in Central Europe increased several times over, perhaps more than five-fold. It probably reached a maximum during the decade 1526–35. Nearly three million ounces were then produced each year, a figure not again attained until the fifties of the nineteenth century.[1] The output of copper grew at least as rapidly as the output of silver. By the thirties of the sixteenth century, it amounted to several thousands of tons annually.

The wealth of the Germans in silver, copper, and brass had become a marvel for the rest of Europe. The most productive mines were in the Erzgebirge (at Schneeberg, Annaberg, and Joachimstal), at Schwaz, at Neusohl in Hungary, and at Mansfeld, where Luther spent part of his childhood in the mountain air after his father had moved there to earn his bread as a miner. Several thousand men were drawn to each place to work underground, in carrying materials, in preparing charcoal, and in smelting, separating, and refining the ores and metals.[2] With their families, they formed some settlements nearly as large as Leipzig and the other great towns of Southern and Eastern Germany, which were growing rich and prosperous partly through the prosperity of the mines.[3] Emperor Charles V was probably not exaggerating in 1525 when he placed at a hundred thousand the number of persons employed in mining and metallurgy in all the countries of the Empire.[4]

The rapid growth in the output from mines was not limited to Central Europe. In Sweden and Alsace the production of silver, while inferior in volume to that of Saxony, Bohemia, Hungary, the Tyrol, or even Silesia, increased at nearly as rapid a rate as in those countries. During the first half of the sixteenth century the cinnabar mines at Almadén in Spain were almost if not quite as productive as those at Idria in Carniola.[5] Italy led in the new alum-making industry. The principal enterprise was at Tolfa, near Civita Vecchia, in the Papal States. Rich deposits of alum stones were discovered there in 1461, by John de Castro, the general 'commissar' of the revenue for the Papal Chamber. He predicted that the vast works set up under his direction

[1] J. U. Nef, 'Silver Production in Central Europe', *Journal of Political Economy*, XLIX, no. 4 (1941), 584–6.

[2] Cf. Zycha, *Das böhmische Bergrecht des Mittelalters*, II, 299; Wolfstrigl-Wolfskron, *op. cit.* 45, 66–7.

[3] Cf. Ernst Kroker, 'Leipzig und die sächsischen Bergwerke', *Schriften des Vereins für die Geschichte Leipzigs*, IX (1909), 26–7, 32–3, and *passim*.

[4] Jakob Strieder, *Studien zur Geschichte kapitalistischer Organisations formen*, 2nd ed. (Munich, 1925), 3–4, 376–7.

[5] Häbler, *op. cit.* 102; Hitzinger, *op. cit. passim*.

for the popes would assure the defeat of the infidel by freeing Europe from its long dependence upon the Near East for alum. This was an essential element in the dyeing of fine cloth, at a time when textiles employed a great many more hands than any other industry. In the early sixteenth century alum-making on a considerable scale spread to other parts of Europe. The papal manufacture suffered from the new competition, which some popes sought ineffectually to curb by trying to force the faithful to buy only papal alum.

All over the continent the manufacture of iron and steel grew rapidly to meet the demands of a large number of expanding industries. Cannon, mainly of wrought iron, were coming into widespread use for the first time, as kings and princes stored up ordnance in anticipation of a coming struggle for authority and dominion, and tried out their artillery especially in Italy, where the fields were stained with the blood from frequent battles. At many places on the continent the manufacture of salt was expanding. Pumping machinery with iron parts, and iron pans the length and breadth of a fair-sized room, were installed to raise and to hold the water from the rich brine springs in Franche-Comté and Lorraine. Tools, gears, and machine parts, and various other iron wares, were wanted in larger quantities than before in mining and metallurgy, in shipbuilding, and in construction work of all kinds. In Styria the output of iron seems to have quadrupled between the sixties of the fifteenth century and the thirties of the sixteenth, when it amounted to some eight thousand tons or more a year.[1]

As the German countries were not the leaders at this time in the technical development of iron-making, it is reasonable to suppose that such an expansion in iron production was by no means exceptional. Scattered figures concerning the iron mills in the Ardennes forest and the Meuse valley indicate that the growth of the industry there at the beginning of the sixteenth century was at least as rapid as in Styria. In Carinthia, Carniola, Westphalia, and the Harz, in Lorraine, Champagne, Dauphiné, and Nivernais, in Tuscany and Piedmont, in the Eastern Pyrenees and the Basque provinces of Spain, the development characteristic of Styria and the Low Countries was repeated. The iron-masters deserted the highlands, with their woods, for the streams and rivers with their water power. They built larger mills and stayed much longer in one spot than they had done when the location of forges had been more

[1] L. Bittner, 'Das Eisenwesen in Innerberg-Eisenerz', Archiv für österreichische Geschichte, LXXXIX (Vienna, 1901), 628–9. These statistics of output are for Innerberg-Eisenerz only. There production increased from about 1300 tons in 1466 to about 5000 tons in 1536. At Vordernberg, the other iron-producing district of Styria, the annual output is said to have averaged more than 3000 tons between 1535 and 1537 (ibid. 490, n.). I have assumed that in 1466 the output at Vordernberg was more than half that at Innerberg-Eisenerz, as in 1536.

dependent upon clusters of trees, which were soon hewed down to serve the charcoal burners. Wood and charcoal were now brought from considerable distances on packhorses and in carts.

Old peasants in the valleys complained that the new furnaces, forges, and mills were converting once quiet villages into noisy bedlams. The machinery swished and creaked as the large wooden wheels, for transmitting the power, rotated in the streams or under the force of water poured from the end of an elevated wooden trough running from a newly-built reservoir. The blows of great power-driven hammers, sometimes weighing two hundred pounds and more, echoed through the forests and hills. As larger iron-works were installed, as stronger bellows were introduced, the air was often filled with such a stench and smoke as to trouble travellers as well as old inhabitants. In some places, according to the villagers, the waste products from the forges and furnaces so polluted the streams as to frighten the fish.[1]

The growth and multiplication of enterprises for mining and making metals put strains upon the forests in many parts of Europe. Lumber of various kinds was used for pit props, in making machinery, in building houses, shops, dams, and small factories needed for manufacturing metal. The demand for logs and charcoal grew almost as rapidly as the output of metal, for even the new furnaces and mills effected little saving in fuel. They caused the destruction every year of the trees and shrubbery on thousands of acres.

Increasing pressure on timber supplies aroused a fresh interest in the coal seams. In several provinces of Southern and Central France, notably in Lyonnais and Forez, where coal outcropped, and also in Germany—in Westphalia, Saxony, and Silesia—the digging of coal early in the sixteenth century began to employ larger numbers of local peasants than in the past. Some of them loaded the black stones and gravel into sacks and carried the stuff to nearby towns on pack horses, or, if river traffic was possible, in flat-bottomed boats. The dirty fuel was beginning to command a price at some distances from the pits among lime-burners and those smiths who specialised in the rougher kinds of iron work. But most of the peasants who dug and carried coal had other labour, usually in husbandry. They handled the mineral as a bye-occupation.

It was only in the principality of Liège that coal mining actually became an industry of some importance, employing considerable numbers of trained miners. The wide gently flowing Meuse, so convenient for the transport of cheap, bulky commodities, veers at almost a right angle from east to north. At Liège the production of coal had been more noteworthy during the fourteenth and fifteenth centuries

---

[1] A. Meister, 'Die Anfänge des Eisenindustrie in der Grafschaft Mark', *Beiträge zur Geschichte Dortmunds und der Grafschaft Mark*, XVII (1909), 140.

than at any other place on the continent. Charles the Bold, the fiery Duke of Burgundy, had ordered his soldiers to erase the city from the map and had vowed that even its name should not be revived. Yet in the decades that followed his death, in 1477, it became one of the great armouries for the European princes who followed him. The output of coal tripled or quadrupled to help feed with fuel the growing metal and armament manufactures in the town itself and at many places up and down the river. Liège coals were not quite carried to Newcastle! But fuel from the land of 'Luick' actually competed at Calais and other channel ports with 'seacoals' from the Tyne. At Liège the long adits which drained the coal pits were driven and interconnected in such a way as to provide the main city water supply. The mounds of black earth thrown up beside the pits were hardly less prominent a sight than the spires of the churches. They were more portentous of the future that awaited the western peoples than the city halls, the courts of justice, and the merchant palaces that were rising in profusion in a host of European towns.

VIII. *The Cleavage between Capital and Labour*

The long adits and the drainage engines, the largest of the new furnaces and mills with their horse- and water-driven machinery, were costly to construct, to maintain, and to operate. They added greatly to the capital required in mining and in extracting metals from the ores. Even when it was possible to supply the increased demand for ores and metals without fundamental changes of industrial technique, the increase in the demand often made it profitable to increase the scale of enterprise. Under the spur of technical changes and of expanding markets, a striking cleavage was taking place between capital and labour in many of the mining districts on the continent, especially in Southern and Eastern Germany, Bohemia, Hungary, and the Eastern Alps.

While mining and metallurgy had always required some capital, and had always lent themselves to enterprise on a considerable scale more readily than other important medieval industries except building, it would be a mistake to suppose that from the beginning the organisation of the workmen resembled in miniature that in a modern mine or factory. During the late twelfth and early thirteenth centuries it was common for the finders of the ore and their fellows who held adjoining meers in the same seam to band together in associations. They worked many concessions as a single undertaking much as the peasants ploughed and sowed their holdings in common. Thus companies of working miners were formed with a number of parts, in some cases as many as thirty-two. These parts could be passed from father to son. They could be sold or exchanged. In some cases they could be leased.

Working partnerships of this kind were not unknown during the thirteenth century in the preparation, the smelting, separating, and refining of ores and metals; but they were rare. Sometimes forges and hammers were provided by the miners themselves. Sometimes, especially in the production of silver, the metallurgical establishments belonged to the princes who coined money and granted mining concessions. In fourteenth-century Germany furnaces for separating silver from lead ore, and for making silver, lead, and copper, came frequently to be farmed out to a working master, generally under short-term leases with a year or so to run. In the production of iron, as we have seen, the works were frequently owned by the local lords of the soil. The iron forges themselves, or the sites on which to build them, were often leased out by these lords either to some of their chief tenants or to traders in metal from the near-by towns. In many cases the early iron forges, hammers, and mills were manorial ventures like corn mills or wine presses. The work was done for wages or under contract by local villagers, many of whom held small plots of land and were occupied in husbandry a part of their time. As it was rare before the late thirteenth century for more than four or five persons to work in one pit at a time, it was probably also rare in metallurgy for more than four or five persons to work at a single forge or stamping mill.

In many parts of Europe little manorial enterprises employing less than a dozen local villagers remained the normal type in mining and metallurgy even at the end of the Middle Ages. That was the case in the digging of coal except in the Low Countries, along the Tyne in Durham, and in Southern Nottinghamshire. It was the case with the mining of iron ore and its conversion to metal in the numerous iron-making districts where tiny bloomery forges still prevailed. It was frequently the case in tin mining and lead mining, except in those districts of Central Europe where silver was won in substantial quantities from argentiferous lead ores.

Wherever the demand for minerals and metals grew rapidly, independent partnerships of working miners or smelters were placed on the defensive. As the expenses of mining and smelting increased, the miners and smelters were obliged to borrow money. They often borrowed from the traders with whom they had been accustomed to enter into contracts for the sale of their coal, ore, or metal. It is an almost universal rule in economic history that such loans give the creditor the upper hand. During the late Middle Ages, they put him in a position to take over the enterprise when the workers were unable at a specified time to pay off the loans or the interest due on them.

Creditors who foreclosed might then work the mine on their own account. More frequently they either employed an expert to operate it for them or, if they could find someone with funds willing to assume the risks, they leased it. In any case the work-people, once independent adventurers in a small way, were turned into wage-earning employees.

In the principality of Liège by 1520 or so the independent working partnership of coal miners had given way almost entirely before small capitalistic enterprises, usually owned and managed by partnerships of town traders. Farther west in the neighbourhood of Mons, where coal had also been dug and sold for centuries, the disintegration of the working partnership under the impact of similar financial forces was already well under way. In England were a few new capitalistically organised collieries on the south bank of the Tyne opposite Newcastle, and north of the Trent near Nottingham.

On the continent in the principal iron-making districts a few of the chief ventures were staffed by scores of wage-earners, engaged in digging and carrying the ore, in preparing charcoal, and in tending the furnaces, forges, and hammers. The introduction of the roundabout process for producing iron increased the number of operations that had to be co-ordinated, and, at the same time, added to the capital equipment required in each process. The landlords generally seem to have maintained their share in the ownership of the iron-works. But they frequently leased the establishments for short terms to merchants from the nearby towns. Such merchants might form small smelting companies with transferable shares, as in the Schmalkalden district in South Hesse.

In the mining of quicksilver, copper, and all other silver-bearing ores, in the making of silver, copper, brass, and alum, the partnerships of working miners and the small manorial ventures, characteristic of mining and metallurgy in the thirteenth century, gave way almost entirely (especially in the industrial regions of Central Europe) before new forms of enterprise requiring greater resources in capital. Argentiferous copper ore mining involved especially heavy expenditures. It was almost inevitable, therefore, that the great expansion in the mining of silver-bearing copper ore at the close of the Middle Ages should help to destroy the type of mining enterprise characteristic of the thirteenth century. Under the pressure of expanding production, larger concessions were granted. It was out of the question for a single miner to work one of these alone.[1] In any case several concessions were often combined in the interest of a more efficient administration.

[1] Cf. E. Gothein, 'Beiträge zur Geschichte des Bergbaus im Schwarzwald', *Zeitschrift für die Geschichte des Oberrheins*, N.F., II (1887), 435-6.

As a consequence of the growing need for capital the old companies of working miners, common in the late twelfth and thirteenth centuries, were replaced by new companies of absentee shareholders. Parts grew more numerous. They were sold to local noblemen and landed gentry, to monasteries, merchants, sometimes to municipal governments and even to universities. By the beginning of the sixteenth century a division of mining companies into 128 parts (*Kuxen*) was usual in silver and copper mining in Saxony and Bohemia. There were companies with as many as 256, with 384, and (in at least one case) 640 parts.[1] Even these numerous parts were sometimes subdivided.

After the original capital had been raised, all the partners could be called on to meet their share in any additional expenditures. Dividends were sometimes paid in ore, the ore being separated near the mines into a number of piles of various sizes, one for each partner. When the company sold the ore, or smelted it and sold the metal, dividends were paid in cash. The actual direction of the enterprise was left increasingly to managers and foremen. They hired the hewers, barrowmen, and winders to work in the pits, paid them, and supervised their labour. As the number of partners and the partners living at some distance from the mine multiplied, it became difficult, if not impossible, for the shareholders to meet frequently to settle matters of policy. In the late fifteenth and early sixteenth centuries the weekly meeting gave way to the bi-weekly, the monthly, the quarterly, and the semi-annual meeting. There were partners who never appeared even at these infrequent meetings. They appointed local agents to manage their interests, and to represent them in dealing with the managers.

In spite of such absentee proprietorship and of the wide distribution of mining shares, the enterprises were seldom large even in the chief silver-mining districts. In each district there were commonly a number of separate competing units. At Joachimstal the chief companies had normally only from sixteen to thirty-two work-people on their payrolls. There were actually small ventures with only four or five employees.

As a result of the cleavage between capital and labour, the miners of argentiferous copper ores, together with some of the miners of tin and lead ores, lost most of the special privileges granted by the princes and overlords who had claimed regalian rights during the twelfth and thirteenth centuries. It was the owners of parts in the mining companies and the experts in the new mining technique who fell heir to such privileges, in so far as they persisted, and in so far as fresh privileges were granted in connection with newly developed mines. The exclusion of craftsmen from access to the mastership in some towns led to the

[1] Cf. Hoppe, *Der Silberbergbau zu Schneeberg*, 149–56.

organisation of journeymen's gilds. In a somewhat similar way the creation of large groups of wage-earning miners led to the formation of pitmen's associations for keeping up wages and maintaining decent working conditions. Such associations appeared at Freiberg early in the fifteenth century and at the principal mining districts in the Erzgebirge early in the sixteenth. At Joachimstal and Schneeberg dissatisfied miners struck work. The new associations and the strikes indicate how little was left of the community which the European peoples had sometimes achieved in connection with industrial labour during the first great wave of economic progress and prosperity in the twelfth and early thirteenth centuries.

To reach Strieder's conclusion that the modern struggle between capital and labour originated at the juncture of the fifteenth and six-teenth centuries would be too simple. The mining communities were split at this time not in two ways but in three. In addition to the working wage-earners and their capitalist employers, there were the holders of regalian rights. As we shall see in a moment, this third group was gaining tremendously in strength and assertiveness on the eve of the Reformation. It held the balance of power. While it can hardly be represented as a defender of the wage-earning miners against their employers, it was unwilling to have the private companies gain an ascendancy in the mining communities. That ascendancy it reserved for itself.

The regalian lords were obliged to call on wealthy merchants or financiers for help. The problems of draining pits and of ridding under-ground passages from noxious and explosive gases concerned these lords. They found it desirable not to leave such matters to the numerous groups of concessionaires, to be dealt with piecemeal by each group. It was recognised that the drainage of a mining field was actually a single task, which could be met most effectively by a single drainage system. Some of the greatest merchant-financiers of the Renaissance helped the regalian lords in meeting the costs. These wealthy men, who patronised the leading artists and lent money to kings, popes, and emperors, furnished much of the capital needed to drive long adits and to set up expensive drainage machinery. The Fuggers and Welsers and other leading mercantile families of Augsburg, Nuremberg, Leipzig, and other flourishing German towns participated in many ventures of the kind throughout Central Europe. They extended their investments into Spain and Sweden. In return they received shares in the mining companies whose pits they helped to drain.

In spite of their loss of economic independence, the working miners in Germany retained something of the dignified social status that had attached to their profession earlier in the Middle Ages. In his best

known treatise, which appeared first in 1556, when the labour struggles
at the ore mines of Central Europe had been going on for two generations, Agricola wrote that 'not even the common worker in the mines
is vile and abject'. He knew at first hand conditions in the most
populous and highly developed mining settlements of Saxony and
Western Bohemia. He had spent some years of his life as a physician
at Joachimstal, where the cleavage between the miners and their
employers was perhaps as wide as anywhere in Europe.

Carried on even more than during the thirteenth century in the
mountains and high valleys, amid some of the most charming scenery
in the world, mining retained a romance and even a certain magic
which accompanies the conquest of nature. The work of the mountain
men, as the miners were called in German, also encouraged the kind of
courage and resourcefulness that proved invaluable in the army and
that so warlike a people held in particular esteem. With the help of
their experience in driving subterranean passages, miners brought from
the silver-mining districts of the Eastern Alps in 1529 to defend Vienna
are said to have met and outwitted the Turks, who were trying to
tunnel their way under and into the city.[1]

Later, in seventeenth-century England, a customs officer, engaged in
pressing men into the navy for war with the Dutch, spurned the keel-
men who loaded coal into ships from the mines near Newcastle, saying
it 'would do more harm than good...to have such nasty creatures on
board' the men-of-war.[2] Such an attitude towards members of the
German mining settlements would have been hardly conceivable at the
time of the Reformation. In recruiting their units the German army
officers preferred miners to townsmen and even to peasants. The search
for silver-bearing ores in medieval Europe had not stained the bodies of
the workmen or made them social outcasts as coal mining later was to
do. Many miners had their Saturday night baths with an efficient
regularity that we associate with the Germans. Silver was thought of
as an excellent thing in itself. Digging for it was still widely regarded
as a more honourable way of earning a living than accumulating it in
strong boxes by sharp financial practices. The calling of the miner,
Agricola remarked, 'excels in honour and dignity that of the merchant
trading for lucre'.[3]

In France, as well as in Germany, princes frequently treated the
miners with a consideration that they did not always accord the greatest

---

[1] Wolfstrigl-Wolfskron, *op. cit.* 393; Leopold Ranke, *History of the Reformation in
Germany* (trans. by Sarah Austin, London, 1905), 582-3.

[2] Nef, *The Rise of the British Coal Industry* (London, 1932), II, 151.

[3] *De re metallica* (Hoover edition), 24. Biringuccio took the same view of the
moral superiority of the miner to the merchant.

merchants of the age. After confiscating mines of silver-bearing lead and copper ores in Lyonnais and Beaujolais belonging to Jacques Coeur, perhaps the richest French merchant of the time, Charles VII was faced with the task of reviving these enterprises. In 1454 the royal officials engaged for this purpose a large number of miners, some of the most skilful of them Germans. These work-people were sumptuously housed and lavishly nourished with varied meats, wines, and fruits, such as might have aroused the envy of the most ambitious twentieth-century trade-union leader if he had had the taste for excellent dining common among the wealthy a generation or two before.[1]

Large-scale private enterprise seems to have made its most striking progress in some branches of metallurgy, rather than in mining. The principal establishments for producing silver and copper represented a heavier concentration of buildings and labour than was apparently to be found in any single mining company. It was the discovery of the new method of separating copper and silver that led to the erection of the most impressive metallurgical works. These *Saigerhütten* were built in Saxony, Thuringia, the Tyrol, and Carinthia. Agricola described one of them in *De re metallica*. It consisted of four parallel walls, the longest more than a hundred metres long, broken by transverse walls into a series of rooms of various sizes and with diverse costly equipment. This included a great many hearths and furnaces, bellows, hammers and stamping machinery—mostly driven by water power—and a variety of tools and crucibles, all for treating the metals in different stages of manufacture.[2] At Hohenkirchen near Georgental in Thuringia, where the Fuggers built such a factory, scores of workmen were employed.[3] The same family had another equally impressive factory near Villach, at Arnoldstein.[4] Supplies of argentiferous ore were brought to both these establishments from mines at Neusohl in Hungary, hundreds of miles away.

Nowhere else in Europe, perhaps, was there a greater concentration of capital and labour in a single plant than in these *Saigerhütten*, except at the alum works of the Pope at Tolfa, at a few salt springs like those at Salins in Franche-Comté, where the houses and pans were huddled into an enclosure as large as a fair-sized medieval village, and at a few ship-

[1] S. Luce, 'De l'exploitation des mines et de la condition des ouvriers mineurs en France au XVe siècle', *Revue des questions historiques*, XXI (1877), 192–5.

[2] *De re metallica* (Hoover edition), 491–535.

[3] Ernst Koch, 'Das Hütten- und Hammerwerk der Fugger zu Hohenkirchen bei Georgenthal in Thüringen, 1495–1549', *Zeitschrift des Vereins für Thüringische Geschichte*, N.F., XXVI (1926), 296–306.

[4] F. Dobel, 'Ueber den Bergbau und Handel des Jacob und Anton Fugger in Kärnten und Tirol, 1495–1560', *Zeitschrift des historischen Vereins für Schwaben und Neuburg*, IX (1882), 194–6.

building yards such as the famous arsenal at Venice. Unlike the alum and salt works and the largest shipyards, the chief *Saigerhütten* were owned and operated by private capitalists, and not by the sovereign rulers or under their direction. The assertion of regalian authority in connection with ores was hardly possible so far away from the mines.

IX. *The Growth in the Authority of the Prince*

Nothing limited so much the power of private capitalists in the principal mining districts as the growing authority of the regalian lords. In the later Middle Ages medieval constitutionalism was breaking down. The time of Machiavelli was an age of growing despotism. The kings of France and Spain and the emperors, who were Machiavelli's contemporaries, together with scores of other princes, lay and ecclesiastical, in Italy and Central Europe, set about increasing their power at the expense of all independent authority. Mining communities were governed more and more paternally and even despotically. The capitalists, as well as the workers, were expected to obey the laws and orders of the prince and his officers.

The independence of the mining companies, and of the metallurgical enterprises which were closely dependent on the mines, was curtailed by the enactment of regulations far more comprehensive and rigid than those of the thirteenth and fourteenth centuries. During the first forty years of the sixteenth century the issue of mining laws reached a high point.[1] More mining officials were always being appointed and their authority was always being extended. Saxon mining law, as embodied in a code of 1509 issued by the Duke of Saxony for his newly developed mines of Annaberg, became the basis for mining law throughout Northern and Eastern Germany. In Southern Germany and Central Europe generally, the regulations were somewhat less comprehensive. But everywhere the new codes, notable among which were the Austrian regulations of 1517, curbed the initiative of private investors in the mines, forges, and mills.

Problems connected with the digging of long adits, which the princes often helped to finance, provided them with an excuse for increasing their supervision over all kinds of mining operations.[2] Any small scheme for draining or ventilating the pits, or for using fire to shatter the rock that was encountered in sinking shafts, had to be approved by the prince's mining officials. An *Oberberghauptmann* was given general authority by the regalian lord over the entire administration. At periodic intervals of thirteen days or so, one of the chief officers, the *Bergmeister*,

---

[1] Cf. Schmoller, *op. cit.* 979–82.   [2] Cf. *ibid.* 972, 976.

accompanied by a group of technical experts, visited each mining enterprise to see that the regulations contained in the codes and in the supplementary orders issued by the central mining administration were enforced. The wage rates and the hours of labour for the miners and the metallurgical workers were settled by this administration. Managers and foremen who worked for the mining companies and for the masters of forges could be appointed only with the approval of the prince's officials. They could be discharged without the consent of their employers, but the shareholders in the mining companies could not discharge their own managers and foremen without the approval of the prince's officers.

Officers appointed by the regalian lords had frequently participated in the working partnerships of the thirteenth and fourteenth centuries. But the new regulations forbade such officials to hold parts in the mining companies, in order to insure their loyalty to the prince. The number of these officials was continually increasing, as the work of the prince's administration was amplified. In some cases, as at Kuttenberg in Bohemia, the officials were almost as numerous as the hewers in the mines.[1] Many princes took advantage of the dissatisfaction felt by the mining companies and the buyers of ore with the private masters of the local smelting works to engross those enterprises into their own hands.[2] They provided chapels for the miners and smelters, and looked after the health as well as the religious instruction of all the workmen. Rules were passed forbidding the introduction of prostitutes into the industrial communities. Swearing was prohibited, probably because of the superstitious dread of its consequences.

In every direction the princes and other regalian lords tightened their grip on the communities of miners and smelters. The real directing unit ceased to be the individual enterprise, and became the ruler's administration. By the Reformation many of the rulers were coming to treat as their property, not only the minerals which contained precious metal but the mines.[3] Some, like those at Mansfeld and Goslar, actually became state enterprises.

This movement towards an administrative control of mining by political rulers was not confined to the German countries. It was general on the continent. The abundance of silver-bearing ores in Central Europe made the movement especially prominent there. But the French kings were proceeding in the same direction. In the late fifteenth and early sixteenth centuries they set out to gain control of mining enterprise throughout the realm. The problem of control was in some ways more

[1] Ibid. 973. [2] Cf. Schmoller, op. cit. pp. 692–3.
[3] Cf. A. Zycha, Das Recht des ältesten deutschen Bergbaues bis ins 13. Jahrhunde (Berlin, 1899), 157; Schmoller, op. cit. 1018.

difficult than in the small principalities of Central Europe. Size was a considerable handicap to effective government. Furthermore the French kings had the problem of absorbing and making their own the regalian authority exercised by territorial lords, whilst in Germany, as we have seen, it was the territorial lords who absorbed the regalian authority.

A royal mining administration was eventually created for the entire French kingdom. In general character it resembled the smaller territorial mining administrations of Central Europe. While private landlords were allowed to dig for ore in their own lands and those of their tenants, Louis XI issued an edict in 1471 requiring them to report within forty days the discovery of any minerals, and to signify their intention of working them. If they failed to comply, or if they did not wish to finance an enterprise of their own, the royal mining administration was instructed either to lease the mine or to work it directly. All mining, even that carried on by private landlords in their own lands, was placed under the supervision of the royal mining administration. The crown could send experts to search for ore in privately-owned lands without the consent of the owner. All mines which they found were at the disposal of the royal mining administration. If, in accordance with the edict, the crown worked or leased mines in privately-owned lands, the landlords were to receive compensation for damage to the soil. They were to receive also a portion of the returns, beyond the 'tenth' due to the sovereign. The holders of royal concessions and their workmen were exempted from the payment of ordinary taxes. All mining disputes, except those touching the property of the landlords, were to be settled, not by the ordinary courts, but by the king's principal mining official, the *maistre général*, or his lieutenants.[1]

While the *parlement de Paris* modified the edict of 1471 in minor respects before registering it, its main provisions were apparently upheld. During the next seventy years, the royal mining administration occasionally organised enterprises under its direct control for working silver-bearing ores. More often concessions were leased to royal favourites or capital was raised for mining by selling to merchants and traders parts in companies organised in much the same way as those in Germany.[2] Results were meagre, mainly no doubt because France was poor compared with Central Europe in silver-bearing ores, partly because of the administrative difficulties of supervising activity in remote parts of what was for the medieval European a vast realm. But practical disappointments interfered little with the assertion of the

[1] *Recueil général des anciennes lois françaises*, x, 626–7.

[2] Archives nationales, Paris, Minutier central, fonds XIX, liasse 152 (documents concerning André de Rozembourch of Bohemia and Nicholas Hermans of Brussels, masters of the French king's mines and forges of gold and silver, 1539).

principle that the king had a title to all valuable mines within his dominion.

By the middle of the sixteenth century the regalian claims of the French crown covered most of the country north and east of the Pyrenees and west of the Spanish Netherlands, Lorraine, Franche-Comté, and the Alps. Concessions were granted by royal patent to mine in almost every part of the kingdom, though not all the French nobles willingly permitted the royal concessionaires access to ores in their lands.[1] In Lorraine and Franche-Comté, which were not yet a part of France, the local rulers regulated and supervised the operations of their mining concessionaires, as in France. In Lorraine the dukes apparently threw open the mines to all comers, as had been the general practice of medieval rulers in Central Europe.[2]

With the growth of sovereign political power on the continent, efforts were made to extend regalian rights to cover base ores. In Central Europe several territorial rulers successfully brought seams of iron ore, as well as of lead and tin, into the same category with ores containing silver or gold. Iron-making enterprises in Styria, Austria, and the upper Harz were subjected by the Duke of Styria, the Emperor, and the Duke of Brunswick to taxes, regulations, and inspections similar to those which had become the rule in the silver-mining communities. The French king, François I (1515–47), also interested himself in iron production. In 1542 he levied a tax on all forges and furnaces throughout the kingdom. Its collection was confided to the royal mining administration.

The reception of Roman law in France and other continental countries in the late fifteenth and early sixteenth centuries helped rulers to stretch their regalian claims, both because a very large proportion of all mines had belonged to the state in the late Roman Empire, and because the imperial tax of a tenth on the produce of mines in privately-owned lands had been levied indiscriminately on all ores or metals,[3] at a time

---

[1] Archives nationales, X1A8624, ff. 271–4 (Ordonnance sur les mines et leur exploitation, 1560).

[2] Archives nationales, K. 876, no. 14 (Des mines de Lorraine, 1520).

[3] As we now know that Roman law did not deprive the private landlord of the ownership of mines under his land (see above, p. 452), it seems inconsistent, at first sight, to argue that the revival of Roman law helped the European princes to extend their regalian rights at the end of the Middle Ages, to cover base ores. It is true nevertheless. The use to which Roman law was put rested, to some extent, on a misinterpretation. Until the work of Achenbach was published in 1869, European jurists quite generally assumed that property in mines had been divorced from property in land under the Roman Empire. In the Middle Ages such a view was probably widely held by men learned in the law. It was encouraged by a misconstruction by Lombard commentators of passages in the Theodosian code and the code of Justinian (cf. Lewis,

when all metals were scarce. Here we have an illustration of the differences between the classical revival of the twelfth century and that of the later Middle Ages. One side of ancient experience—the administrative practices of a few districts as these practices were handed across the centuries by custom and tradition—helped the Europeans in the gothic age almost to universalise the essentially democratic community of free miners. Another side of classical experience—formal Roman law, as recorded in the codes and digests of the Empire—helped the European rulers in a later age of waxing political authority almost to universalise the claim of the state to a revenue from all mining operations.

With the increasing need for capital in mining and metallurgy in the age of the renaissance, a point had been reached, especially in the production of silver and copper, where the costs could be met only by the richest merchants, whose power came from their skill in trade and in managing money and credit, or by kings, princes, and overlords, whose power rested on their inherited position and their political rights. In mining and metallurgy, earlier than in other great industries, Europe faced a choice between the dominance of rich private capitalists and the dominance of sovereign authorities. On the continent the sovereign authorities generally prevailed.

This fact has been obscured by the conspicuous place occupied by certain enormously rich merchants, among whom the Fuggers of Augsburg have received the most attention from historical writers, at least since the time, a century ago, when Michelet wrote his chapters on 'la banque'. The cost of maintaining an elaborate mining administration strained the resources of sovereign political authorities at the end of the Middle Ages. They had recourse in this connection, as in so many others, to the money bags of merchants of great wealth—among whom these same Fuggers occupied a place of the greatest prominence. Territorial princes, who borrowed money in large doses, sometimes repaid the loan by granting their creditors, for a term of years, a portion of the revenue which they derived from their regalian rights. In extreme cases they even put the merchants in possession for a time of their entire mining administration, with all its duties and privileges, including the authority to grant mining concessions. This happened at Reichenstein, in Silesia, where the *regale* belonged to the Dukes of Münsterberg-Oels.[1] Again, the important quicksilver mines of Almadén, which had once played a

The Stannaries, 66–8). Roman law, moreover, could be legitimately invoked in favour of putting base in the same category with precious metals, for the tax that had been levied by the Roman emperors on the produce of mines had fallen on both indiscriminately (cf. Alfons Müllner, *Geschichte des Eisens in Krain, Görz und Istrien*, 195–6).

[1] E. Fink, 'Die Bergwerksunternehmungen der Fugger in Schlesien', *Zeitschrift des Vereins für Geschichte und Altertum Schlesiens*, XXVIII (1894), 308.

considerable role in the economy of the Romans, were leased for four-year periods to the Fuggers.[1]

For all this, the ultimate authority of the political rulers to control the mines was hardly questioned. If the merchant fell out of favour, it was always possible for the prince to confiscate his property. In 1453 the French king, Charles VII, acting in what nineteenth-century Europeans would have almost universally condemned as an arbitrary and despotic manner, confiscated the three mining enterprises in Lyonnais and Beaujolais belonging to Jacques Cœur of Bourges, the most glamorous merchant of the fifteenth century.[2]

Princes, lay and ecclesiastical, welcomed the participation of merchants in mining. They borrowed from them freely to get money to exercise their rights of pre-emption. They even shared control of the mining administration with them. But in continental Europe the course of history was not running in favour of mercantile domination, as it was destined to run for a time in the late eighteenth and nineteenth centuries. When it came to a show-down, the prince and not the merchant held the brute force that was decisive. In a cruel age, which was not to be the last, he was capable of exercising this force in the most ferocious ways. In the sphere of art alone was the subject left any real independence. In the last analysis, everything material was claimed by the prince, at a time when the material aspects of existence were coming into the foreground of thought, worship, and conduct to a greater extent than ever before in western history. The absolute authority that the prince exercised over the bodies as well as the economic existence of his subjects has been described in unforgettable detail by Ranke, in his chapter on Ferrara under Alphonso II. The duke had concentrated every scrap of prosperity in the court itself. The country was poverty-stricken. His control over industry extended to food, including the prime necessities of flour and bread. Even nobles were limited in their right to hunt, and one day the bodies of six men were left hanging in the market place, with dead pheasants tied to their feet, to show, it was said, that the culprits had been shot while poaching on the duke's preserves.[3] On the continent the growing strength of despots made fleeting the control exercised by mercantile capital in the mining administrations of the political rulers. At the close of the Middle Ages in most European states it was the political ruler who held the reins which guided large-scale industry.

[1] Konrad Häbler, *Die Geschichte der Fugger'schen Handlung in Spanien* (Weimar, 1897), 93–5.

[2] Cf. Pierre Clément, *Jacques Cœur et Charles VII* (Paris, 1866), 345 and *passim*.

[3] Leopold Ranke, *The Ecclesiastical and Political History of the Popes of Rome* (trans. Sarah Austin, London, 1841), bk. VI, ch. vii.

In England and Scotland no such bulwarks against the independent power of private capital in mining were built up during the later Middle Ages. Henry VIII retained the regalian rights that his predecessors had exercised during the twelfth and thirteenth centuries. He collected a revenue from mines royal and he continued to appoint officials to oversee and protect the royal rights over mineral property. But the share of the crown in the direction of mining had not been extended. No national mining administration, like that introduced in France by the Valois kings, had been established. No legislation had been passed like the French edict of 1413, making it lawful for the crown, and the crown alone, to collect a royalty on the produce of all mines worked throughout the realm. No legislation had been passed like the French edict of 1471, permitting the crown to send experts to search for ore in privately-owned land. No new codes governing mining were issued, at a time when mining legislation in Central Europe reached a peak. No apparent effort was made to regulate more minutely operations of private mining companies holding concessions from the royal authority. While the crown maintained its control over mines containing precious metals and mines under the royal demesne, while it maintained the rights of the royal family in the stannaries, elsewhere all base ores and minerals were left at the disposal of private landlords.

The resources of Great Britain in gold- and silver-bearing ores proved to be negligible. The crown was to sell a great part of the royal demesne in the late sixteenth and seventeenth centuries. The English tin mines were not again to occupy as prominent a place in European mining history as in the Middle Ages. For all three reasons the power of the sovereign in mineral matters was on the point of contracting in England, at the very time when it was expanding strikingly on the continent. Stronger than the French crown in its control over mining in the twelfth and thirteenth centuries, the English crown was potentially much weaker at the time of Henry VIII's break with Rome.

These differences between English and continental mining history in the later Middle Ages had an influence upon industrial development in modern times. They helped to make possible the regime of free economic enterprise which is associated primarily with the English-speaking countries. What are the explanations for the failure of the English kings during the late fifteenth and early sixteenth centuries to follow the course taken by so many continental rulers, and to add to their authority over mines?

The lack in Great Britain of ores which contained large quantities of precious metals and which were generally acknowledged as royal property was undoubtedly something of a stumbling block. The great abundance of such ores in Central Europe enabled the princes to establish a control over mines in many districts. When an opportunity presented itself to extend regalian rights to mines of base ores, the form of administration was ready to hand. Again England's size proved a disadvantage. While it is common today to think of Great Britain as a small island, in the sixteenth and seventeenth centuries the area covered by England and Wales was much larger than that of most of the principalities of Central Europe. The division of sovereignty within the Empire during the later Middle Ages made it easier than in England to strengthen the regalian rights which went with sovereignty. In an age when the slowness of travel and communication added to the difficulties of governing distant regions, this division often reduced to manageable dimensions the territory within which a single ruler exercised his authority over mines, and made it comparatively easy for him to maintain a staff of obedient officers sufficient to enforce his authority.

But such explanations of the divergence between the history of the mining *regale* in England and on the continent are inadequate. Neither the size of France, considerably larger than England, nor the lack of abundant supplies of ores rich in precious metals, prevented the French kings from strengthening their regalian rights. More adequate explanations of the special position occupied by England in the development of mining law in the later Middle Ages are to be found in two legal conditions. Sovereign authority was centralised earlier than in any continental country, and property claimed by the subjects, over which the crown had failed to established its control, possessed greater immunity through the greater effectiveness of the English Parliament as compared with any restraining bodies on the continent.

Sovereign authority was centralised in England during the late eleventh and twelfth centuries, at a time when medieval constitutionalism was strong. This made the medieval estates, in which mercantile interests were represented, a more essential part of the machinery of government in England than in other countries. Early centralisation also made it necessary to create a system of legal principles common to the whole realm, before imperial Roman law had been sufficiently recovered by medieval jurists to permit it to take its place as that system.[1] In imperial Roman law the sovereign political authority was much more pre-eminent than in the European practice of the eleventh and twelfth centuries.

The early authority of the English crown, which was a limited authority, fixed limits to the exercise of regalian rights. They proved less elastic than the regalian rights of most continental rulers. Partly as a result of the development of common law, the English kings were

[1] See C. H. McIlwain, 'Medieval Estates', *The Cambridge Medieval History* (Cambridge, 1932), VII, 709–14.

unable to use the revival of Roman law in the late fifteenth and early sixteenth centuries as so many continental rulers were doing, to help them to claim a royalty on the produce of mines of every description. In Europe generally the authority of great vassal landlords had been stronger in feudal times than in the later Middle Ages. The early strength of the English Parliament and of the English common law helped landlords to conserve their property rights.

The first Tudor monarchs, Henry VII and Henry VIII, might nevertheless have made an energetic bid to extend their authority over mines, as the French kings were doing, if mining and metallurgy had been growing in importance as rapidly in England as on the continent, and if they had not been confronted by a Parliament, composed of lawyers and propertied men, determined to resist encroachments upon the property rights they represented. The early Tudors showed great skill in exercising their political powers, at a time when the will of the king was still regarded by nearly all Englishmen as supreme in matters of government. According to the Spanish ambassador, Henry VII expressed the desire 'to keep his subjects low, because riches would make them haughty'.[1] It is improbable that he would have been more disposed than continental rulers to give merchants a free hand to dominate the mines if their value had been as obvious in England as it was in Central Europe. His son, Henry VIII, was out to raise all the money he could. If he bothered little with the mines it was very likely because his advisers regarded them as of trifling importance. He had a hard time, moreover, in getting his way with Parliament in matters of property, as is shown by its not ineffective opposition to the dissolution of the lesser monasteries in 1536, and by its emasculation in 1539 of the king's proposed Statute of Proclamations as finally passed.

In fact the development of mining in England during the late fifteenth and early sixteenth centuries was very slow. The searches for silver-bearing ores, conducted on the eve of the Reformation with the help of miners from Germany, gave disappointing results. The production of tin increased only some 60 or 70% between 1470 and 1540,[2] as compared with an increase of four- or five-fold in the production of metals in Central Europe. The increase little more than offset the slump in output that had occurred in England during the first half of the fifteenth century. The supremacy gained during the Middle Ages by the tin of Devon and Cornwall in continental markets was threatened by the progress of tin mining in Spain, Saxony, Bavaria, and Bohemia. English lead was also finding more competition abroad than in the past. In 1539 one of Thomas Cromwell's correspondents described the lead

[1] *Calendar of State Papers, Spanish*, 1485–1509, 177.
[2] G. R. Lewis, *The Stannaries* (Cambridge (Mass.), 1907), 253.

mines of England as 'dead'.[1] Until after the dissolution of the monasteries, mining and metallurgy were carried on mainly by tiny enterprises, which used the methods prevalent on the continent in the thirteenth and fourteenth centuries. The sluggish growth of English mining in an age of remarkable industrial expansion in many European countries, helped to keep the field open to private enterprise, unfettered by government control, at a time when the crown was strong. Later, during the late sixteenth and early seventeenth centuries, an even more remarkable industrial expansion occurred in England. But, by that time, royal authority had grown so weak that the kinds of state control over economic development which had been effectively set up in many continental countries, proved impracticable.[2]

The English crown held on to the very considerable mineral rights which it inherited from an earlier age. But a variety of conditions blocked it from extending these rights at the very time when such an extension had become the price of effective political authority in mineral matters even more in England than on the continent. Such resources as the English crown held by virtue of medieval law crumbled to dust in its hands when coal and iron ore replaced silver and gold as the main treasure of the subsoil.

X. *The Transition to Modern Times*

At the end of the Middle Ages the rapid development of continental mining and metallurgy showed signs of waning. The discovery of ores extraordinarily rich in silver in South and Central America, and particularly the opening about 1546 of the famous mines of Potosi in Bolivia, dealt a heavy blow to the European silver-mining industry. Treasure from the new world could be delivered in Europe, even by the unwieldy Spanish galleons, more cheaply than the trained miners of Saxony, Bohemia, Tyrol, Hungary, and Silesia could dig and smelt their ores and ship their metal, with the help of the most skilful German, Hungarian, and Bohemian engineers and technical experts. While a few mining communities in Silesia, and at Freiberg and Goslar in Germany, continued to prosper after the middle of the sixteenth century, a slump had begun by that time in the output of silver and gold in most parts of Central Europe, and also in Alsace and Sweden.

Fifty years later this slump in the production of precious metals had gone very far. On the eve of the Thirty Years' War (1618–48), which

[1] J. W. Gough, *The Mines of Mendip* (Oxford, 1930), 65.
[2] See Nef, *Industry and Government in France and England, 1540–1640* (Philadelphia, 1940).

was to bring mining in Central Europe temporarily almost to a standstill, the annual output of silver was perhaps less than a third as great as it had been in the twenties and thirties of the sixteenth century.[1] Even in Sweden, which unlike most of Central Europe prospered industrially during the hundred years following the Reformation, the production of silver in the best years of the mid-seventeenth century was hardly half what it had been in the fifteen-forties.[2]

At the close of the Middle Ages the progress of continental mining was bound up, almost as much as in the twelfth and thirteenth centuries, with the prosperity of mines rich in silver. The collapse of the market for European silver brought a reduction in the value of argentiferous copper and lead ores. Conditions proved almost equally unfavourable to other kinds of mining. Before the end of the sixteenth century, the rapid expansion in iron smelting[3] and coal mining on the continent came to an end. Thus the signs of industrial revolution at the end of the Middle Ages proved deceptive. The remarkable growth in the output from mining and some other heavy industries lasted only during the interval between the Hundred Years War and the beginning of the religious wars in the mid-sixteenth century. It was two hundred years more before the rate of growth in industrial output again became as rapid on the continent generally as it had been during the late fifteenth and the early sixteenth centuries

What was lacking to bring about a development of mining and metallurgy that would lead directly to the wealthy industrial civilisation destined to dominate the whole of Western Europe in the nineteenth century? Why was the new machinery for draining and ventilating mines at considerable depths, devised in connection with the mining of argentiferous copper ores, not taken over extensively in the mining of tin, lead, and above all coal on the continent, as it was in Great Britain in the late sixteenth and seventeenth centuries?

At the close of the Middle Ages warfare on the continent became more destructive and more damaging to heavy industry. The dissolution of the English monasteries and other ecclesiastical foundations played into the hands of private landlords and merchants eager to exploit mineral wealth. But in continental mining districts, the course

---

[1] Nef, 'Silver Production in Central Europe, 1450–1618', *Journal of Political Economy*, XLIX, no. 4 (1941), 589.

[2] Eli F. Heckscher, *Sveriges Ekonomiska Historia* (Stockholm, 1936), II, 439.

[3] In Styria the output of iron reached a high point during the middle decades of the sixteenth century. From 1601 to 1625 the annual production at Innerberg-Eisenerz was considerably less than from 1536 to 1560 (Bittner, *op. cit.* 490, 628–9). In Siegerland the number of forges was reduced by half in the late sixteenth century (Richard Utsch, *Die Entwicklung und volkswirtschaftliche Bedeutung des Eisenerzbergbaues und der Eisenindustrie im Siegerland* (Gorlitz, 1913), 34).

taken by the religious struggle was different and the Church retained a greater portion of the landed property. Some churchmen possessed regalian rights by virtue of their political authority. Ecclesiastical foundations were less ready than lay landlords to invest large capitals in mines and metallurgical plant. They were unwilling to lease their mines on as favourable terms as lay landlords. Again, the natural difficulties of carriage through mountainous country and the numerous tolls and taxes, which stood in the way of transporting heavy ores and coal for considerable distances, imposed handicaps upon the progress of mining on the continent. The great authority over the mines and the mining ventures, established at the end of the Middle Ages by so many continental rulers, discouraged private enterprise.

At the time of the Reformation political considerations frequently outweighed economic in the guidance of mining and metallurgy. While this helped European rulers to strengthen their authority over their subjects, it was on the whole unfavourable to the growth of industrial output, at least to the growth in the output of products like iron and coal, upon whose abundance the progress of modern industrial civilisation has been so largely based.[1] It was only in the eighteenth and nineteenth centuries, after changes in the mining laws first of France and later of Germany made conditions more favourable to the initiative of private capitalists,[2] that the output of mines again grew rapidly in either country.

In exploiting their silver resources, the Western European peoples were only following in the footsteps of their classical predecessors, who had ransacked the surface supplies of argentiferous ores in Spain and all along the shores of the Mediterranean. If the Western Europeans had turned aside from the supplies of iron and coal, as the classical peoples

[1] The late Professor Strieder made much of the collaboration between the German princes and the merchants as an element in the great expansion of mining and metallurgy in Germany and Central Europe in the late fifteenth and early sixteenth centuries (*Studien zur Geschichte kapitalistischer Organisationsformen*, 2nd ed., 362–63). To some extent, he seems to have put the cart before the horse. As Inama-Sternegg pointed out, in connection with the progress of the German salt-making industry at an earlier period, it was less that the princes' control caused the expansion, than that the expansion enabled the princes to strengthen their control. 'So ist schliesslich mehr von einer Beförderung des Regalitätsgedanken durch die Entwicklung der Salinen, als von einer Beförderung des Salinenwesens durch die Entwicklung der Regalität zu sprechen.' (K. T. von Inama-Sternegg, 'Zur Verfassungsgeschichte der deutschen Salinen im Mittelalter', *Sitzungsberichte der kaiserlichen Akademie der Wissenschaft*, CXI (1866), 578). Otto Hue found these remarks applicable to German mining. 'Dieselbe Wechselwirkung vollzog sich auch zwischen der Bergbauentwicklung und der Ausdehnung der Bergregal ansprüche' (*Die Bergarbeiter* (Stuttgart, 1910), I, 93).

[2] Marcel Rouff, *Les mines de charbon en France* (Paris, 1922), esp. part I, chaps. ii, iv, and pp. 63–4; Schmoller, *op. cit.* 1027–8.

had done, they could hardly have created the industrial world of the late nineteenth century, which seemed to offer a foretaste of the millennium for those who measured happiness primarily in material terms.

It is perhaps beyond the scope of history to enquire what would have happened if there had been no America, and no regions in the North of Europe rich in mineral resources and rich also in industrious workpeople. But it is certain that the progress of heavy industries in early modern times was not in those European countries which had been in the vanguard of civilised life during the Middle Ages. The progress occurred in Sweden, Holland, and above all in Great Britain. All of these countries were protected for various reasons from the full force of the religious struggles and the actual battles. All established, partly with the help of these favours, traditions of constitutional government. Such conditions were helpful for the realisation of the dreams of Bacon and Descartes.

Some novel inventions and discoveries, indispensable for the eventual triumph of industrial civilisation, had been made by the western peoples before the Reformation. If these inventions were actually to produce such a triumph, they had to be exploited relentlessly. Their development had to take a position of precedence in the minds of men. At the end of the Middle Ages conditions in continental Europe, where the inventions had been made, were not favourable to such precedence or to such relentless exploitation. Would the triumph of industrialism have occurred without a change of scene? An answer is impossible, but it is certain that the change of scene contributed to the triumph.

CHAPTER VIII

Building in Stone in Medieval Western Europe

IN the generation which has gone by since Werner Sombart[1] called attention to the desirability of investigating the economic history of building, relatively little has been done in that direction with regard to medieval Europe as a whole though some notable contributions have been made in regard to particular buildings and countries. A major difficulty is the scarcity, especially for the earlier Middle Ages, of the kind of record which is essential. Archaeological and literary evidences, though useful, cannot by themselves do much more than indicate the kind of question which the inquirer must ask; for the answers there are needed accounts of the expenditure on building operations. Unfortunately those relating to important buildings, such as large royal and ecclesiastical works in France during the early fourteenth century,[2] have in many cases been lost. Large numbers, relating to buildings of various kinds in different countries, have survived sporadically; but probably the fullest series in existence is that relating to works carried out for the crown in England. This is the more valuable because it includes not merely summarised accounts, from which relatively little can be learned, but particulars, in some instances even weekly statements giving the names of workmen with the amounts paid to them and similarly full detail relating to purchases. The ideal collection, which is rare, is that of which the London Bridge Accounts are a sample; these are particulars, extending from week to week or month to month over several centuries, an invaluable record of changes in wages and prices paid at the same undertaking. Other records, especially valuable in the absence of accounts, are contracts between builders and those who did the work for them, and rules laid down by lay or ecclesiastical authorities for those in their employment.

A study of the accounts for the period during which they are relatively abundant and full, that is from the later part of the thirteenth century, suggests that, however architectural styles might vary, the fundamental economic problems connected with building, and the organisation developed to deal with them, were very much the same in the chief countries of Western Europe. It is clear also that this organisation, as it existed at Caernarvon Castle in the thirteenth century, Beauvais in the fourteenth and Eton in the fifteenth, was something different in kind from that prevailing in most medieval industries, in which production was ordinarily limited by the resources and the markets of the individual

---

[1] *Der moderne Kapitalismus*, II, 2, cap. 46 (1921 edition, 772–3).
[2] Ch.-V. Langlois, in E. Lavisse, *Histoire de France*, III, ii, 417 n. (1901 edition).

country craftsman or town gild master. We shall attempt to make clear the characteristics of the industry by considering in turn (i) the impetus given to building; (ii) some technical changes of importance; (iii) the chief problems of supply; (iv) the system of administration; and (v) the conditions and organisation of master workmen and ordinary operatives in the chief building craft, that of the mason.

I. *The Demand for Building*

Feudal conditions were an important stimulus to building, both directly in themselves and indirectly through the attempt to modify or overcome them. Every man with a fief to maintain needed a place of defence, and the number of these, though it cannot be accurately known, must have run to thousands. Many could, no doubt, be fairly easily destroyed and, under strong monarchs, the number of feudal strongholds might be reduced; but they could be easily rebuilt. Moreover, their existence meant a continuing competition between the weapons of attack and the arts of defence, in the course of which ramparts had to be raised to greater heights, approaches to be complicated, lines of fortification to be multiplied and walls and towers altered in shape and made more solid. The walls of the castle of Langres, for instance, were 21 feet thick.[1] Sovereigns, in order to maintain themselves against neighbours or powerful vassals and to extend their territories, needed similar means. Hence the powerful bastions erected by the Swiss at Schaffhausen, the great Edwardian castles of North Wales and the vast works of Richard Cœur de Lion for the defence of Normandy at Les Andelys, which required more than two miles of towers and walling besides about 4000 yards of defences across the peninsula.[2] To the fortifications of kings and seigneurs, lay and ecclesiastical, must be added those of the towns. Many of these were first walled by the lords who founded them, and some, like most of the bastides of Southern France, were not very large. Neither Aigues Mortes nor Carcassonne, for instance, was more than a mile around. Rich and free cities might need much more; the fourteenth-century defences of Verona stretched for two miles and a half,[3] and Nuremberg in the same century had grown so wealthy and populous that its two chief churches had to be enlarged and new defences begun, which extended to four miles of double walling. Altogether the military needs of hundreds of towns in England, France, Spain, Italy and Germany must have required an enormous amount of mason's work.

[1] E. Viollet-le-Duc, *Military Architecture* (English translation, 1879), 185.
[2] Plans in Viollet-le-Duc, *op. cit.* 82, 85.
[3] A. M. Allen, *History of Verona*, 229.

A second great medieval stimulus to building was religion. Each parish needed its church, eventually of stone. Besides there were abbeys, with their churches, living quarters and other buildings, sometimes, as the ninth-century plan of St Gall shows, designed on an extensive scale. With the cessation of the Scandinavian and other invasions conditions were favourable to the rebuilding of destroyed churches and the extension of monastic building, at times held in check by the puritanical principles of St Bernard but eventually, even with the Cistercians, attaining to great size and splendour. Already in the eleventh century, but more frequently in the twelfth, bishops were energetically renewing or enlarging their cathedrals. Church building also provided a channel of expenditure, and opportunities to acquire spiritual merit and to show local pride, for the rising mercantile class in the towns. The contributions of the second and third Thomas Spring, clothiers, towards the building of Lavenham steeple are instances of a generosity that must have been shown to a greater or lesser degree many times before by their like in the cities of the Low Countries, the Hanseatic League and Northern Italy. In towns, as outside them, changes in architectural fashion created a good deal of work for building craftsmen. Once the gothic style had been seen in splendour it was easy for bishops and others to persuade themselves, with the help of master masons eager to be engaged on new work, that an old-fashioned church was unsafe. It could then be pulled down so that, like the thirteenth-century cathedral of Auxerre, *in elegantiorem juvenesceret speciem.*[1]

Other factors affecting the demand for building were rising population and, at any rate in towns and among the richer classes, a desire for greater comfort. Relatively little time would be required to put up a house for a peasant family, and a local carpenter and a thatcher only would be needed. Building for town dwellers might be a slower business; that is suggested by the charters of Bazas, Sauveterre (Gironde) and some other towns of bastide type which required each settler to have one third of his house finished in the first year and two thirds in the second.[2] In the larger towns, at any rate, a body of workmen would be necessary to keep pace with the growth of population and to carry out repairs; but in many towns it would be carpenters and plasterers rather than masons who would be needed. The municipal accounts of Douai make frequent mention of *plakeurs*, or daubers, who were employed not only on houses but on public buildings.[3] In Caen, the centre of a quarrying district, timber houses were being built in the

---

[1] V. Mortet and P. Deschamps, *Recueil de Textes relatifs à l'Histoire de l'Architecture etc.*, II, xv, 203.

[2] T. F. Tout, 'Medieval Town Planning' in *Collected Papers*, IV, 71.

[3] C. Enlart, *Manuel d'Archéologie Française II (Architecture Civile et Militaire)*, 186.

fifteenth and early sixteenth centuries.[1] In Hamburg *domus lapideae* were very rare before 1350 and slates were beginning to be substituted for thatch only about 1460.[2]

In the countryside not every house was purely a fortress. The Carolingian nobility had delighted in country houses and, though these were destroyed in the ninth and tenth-century invasions, the taste survived. England was rich in manor houses and in several parts of France, though conditions were less favourable, there were erected, from the twelfth century onwards, residences in which comfort and convenience were more considered than defence. By the fifteenth century these had become more numerous, and doors and windows occupied more space in their elevations; by the sixteenth, despite their moats and turrets, still preserved as ornaments and signs of nobility, they were chateaux only in name.[3] Urban houses, protected by city walls, could be designed with even less reference to security. In some French towns, it is true, there were fortified noble houses[4] and the cities of Northern Italy bristled with private fortresses—Verona is said to have had 700 at one time or another and the little town of San Gimigniano no fewer than 300—in the shape of towers, sometimes 200 feet high, built by nobles who lived in the cities and slew one another in their feuds.[5] Elsewhere nobles and prelates with town houses built for comfort, though they had an eye also for elegance. Besides walls, habitations and churches, the cities needed public buildings, especially the town hall, the bottom storey of which not uncommonly served as a market while those above were used for administrative, judicial and social purposes. A belfry was not infrequently part of the same structure. Surviving examples in the Low Countries, France, Germany and especially Italy (e.g. the town hall of Siena, built between 1289 and 1309) indicate that the municipal headquarters were often buildings of considerable pretension.

II. *Technical Capacity and Changes*

Before these various demands for building could be met a series of problems had to be solved. Those of an economic and administrative nature will be discussed later, attention being called meanwhile to certain technical matters, on some of which historical records throw

---

[1] H. Prentout, *Caen et Bayeux* (1921), 48–9.
[2] W. Möring, 'Die Wohlfahrtspolitik des Hamburger Rates im Mittelalter', *Abhandlungen z. mittl. und neuer. Geschichte*, XLV, 57–8.
[3] Enlart, *op. cit.* II, 189–95.
[4] Mortet and Deschamps, *op. cit.* I, lii.
[5] M. V. Clarke, *The Medieval City State*, 60–1.

comparatively little light. So far as is known, there was not available for medieval architects and engineers any written compendium or manual giving extensive and accurate instruction on the strength of materials and certain other matters now considered necessary parts of the professional curriculum. There is, however, no doubt that a body of technical knowledge did exist and that it was possible for intending builders to consult experts. The chapter at Gerona, for example, in 1416, when its master mason produced a plan for completing the cathedral church with a nave of one span, without the support of aisle columns, called in eleven masters from other churches to answer questions on the matter. All of them agreed that the plan was possible with safety and four of them agreed with the chapter's master mason that it was more suitable than the alternative proposed. The bishop and chapter, having discussed the replies, decided to build the one-span nave.[1] Medieval architects were familiar with the practice of driving piles to make foundations; their advice was sought in regard to the suitability of sites and the safety of structures,[2] though mistakes were made in practice, with disastrous effects at times on the central towers of churches. Masons and quarrymen possessed knowledge with regard to the 'cleaving grain' of stone and the way in which stone ought to be bedded in a building, and they understood the necessity of 'perpend' stones, going right through the thickness of a wall. Building workers were familiar with the block and pulley for lifting and with the windlass;[3] and they could, at need, construct in the scaffolding an inclined 'tramway' by means of which heavy stones could be wheeled to the top of a work.[4] The essential capacity to measure and calculate was also a fairly widespread qualification, used in the surveying and allocation of land, the laying out of sites, preparation of plans and in estimating and certifying work done. Thus Master Simon, *doctus geometricalis operis*, in charge of the preliminary works at the castle of Ardres about 1200, went about busily *cum virga sua magistrali more*, and Peter, Abbot of Andres, about 1164, took a personal part in his building work *cum ligno vel virgula geometrica lapides metiens*.[5] The construction of tracery and vaulting required geometry, in the modern sense of the term, both for designing and

---

[1] For the documents, see G. E. Street, *Gothic Architecture in Spain*, II, 319 ff.

[2] Mortet and Deschamps, *op. cit.* II, 204, 237, 269.

[3] A thirteenth-century illustration is reproduced in Knoop and Jones, 'Castle Building at Beaumaris and Caernarvon', *Ars Quatuor Coronatorum*, XLV, 17: cf., possibly, the *ingenium ad levandum lapides* included in a Carcassonne inventory of 1298 (Mortet and Deschamps, *op. cit.* II, 327 ff.).

[4] Viollet-le-Duc, *op. cit.* 112.

[5] Mortet and Deschamps, *op. cit.* I, 390; II, 190.

execution and there can be no doubt about the capacity of medieval architects to make such geometrical drawings as were required.[1] That is proved by records of payment to master masons for drawing and also entries relating to diagrams, on wooden floors, clay or slate, for the exact fitting of pieces of stonework or carpentry. Architectural drawings on parchment also, dating from the thirteenth century onwards, have survived; twenty-two of them were preserved in the cathedral of Strasbourg.

An important change in the industry occurred when building artificers turned their attention increasingly from timber to stone. The art of building in stone was not entirely lost with the collapse of the Western Empire. Workmen could still be found to erect a church of lovely design for a Visigothic king in seventh-century Spain[2] and in remote Wearmouth Benedict Biscop was able, about 675, with masons and other craftsmen from Gaul to raise a church in the Roman manner which was his delight.[3] Nevertheless, in Western Europe generally, stone was not then the chief, or even a common, building material. Timber abounded in many districts; it must have been easier to fell and work than stone was to quarry and dress; and, among the migrant Germanic peoples at least, it was a material familiar from of old and useful for many purposes which stone could not serve. Accordingly it was used for mills, bridges, defensive works, churches and baronial halls, even large ones, such as that built at Ardres about 1060.[4] For several of these purposes timber continued to be used for centuries, giving place to stone at various times in different countries. In France the substitution began on a marked scale during the last quarter of the tenth century.[5] In the eleventh, stone was being increasingly used not only in the construction of churches but also in the building of castles.[6] Developments in England kept pace with those in France but in remote Scotland the timber castle did not yield place completely to the stone keep until the fifteenth century.[7] It should be noted that despite the transition large quantities of timber were still needed, for scaffolding, centering for arches, doors, screens and partitions and, where vaulting was not used, for beams and other parts of roofs.

Another change, of which the effects were far-reaching, was an improvement in vaulting, the discovery of what the French call *la voûte*

---

[1] On medieval drawings see Enlart, *Manuel d'Archéologie Française I* (*Architecture Religieuse*), 65.
[2] B. Bevan, *History of Spanish Architecture*, 10, 11.
[3] *Bedae Venerabilis Opera Historica* (ed. Plummer), 1, 368.
[4] Mortet and Deschamps, *op. cit.* 1, 183 ff.
[5] *Ibid.* xxxiii.
[6] *Ibid.* xliii.
[7] W. M. Mackenzie, *The Mediaeval Castle in Scotland*, 4.

sur croisée d'ogives, the main structural characteristic of the gothic style. Like earlier vaulting, it had the advantage of eliminating timber for roofing and thus reducing the risk of fire and, in addition, it made possible changes amounting to a revolution in construction. The space which could be spanned was greatly increased; the centre of the vault could be carried to a very great height; and it was possible to provide with safety far more window space, so as to fill the building with light. Indeed, with skilful use of buttresses the limits of stone building were reached by French architects in the second half of the thirteenth century as in the choir of St Peter's at Beauvais, which rose to a height of 150 feet. Only in modern times and with steel, as M. Langlois[1] pointed out, could that be exceeded. The new vaulting was in use in the cathedral at Durham early in the twelfth century and at Gloucester some time between 1100 and 1120. At the same time it was known in Normandy, Picardy and the Ile de France, where, in all probability it was perfected and the gothic style really founded.[2] Between 1160 and 1180 the new style appeared in complete form at Vezelay in Burgundy and before 1220 it had reached Toulouse and also Casamari in Italy. To Germany, where it was known as *opus francigenum*, it came later, a notable instance of its use being the church of Wimpfen, near Heidelberg, begun in 1263. French influence, however, spread much further than that; it has been noted in the cathedrals of Burgos and Toledo, of Cologne, Bamberg and Naumberg, and even in Upsala and Cyprus; and, in some cases at least, the explanation is known to have been the emigration of French architects and workmen.

III. *The Supply of Materials and Labour*

In addition to making the arrangements which building work of any kind must entail, those in charge of some medieval undertakings might have to cope with special difficulties resulting from one or more of three conditions, namely remoteness, urgency and size. Monastic building, for instance, often had to be carried on in out-of-the-way places; and fortresses, such as English strongholds in Wales or Scotland, might have to be erected not only in sparsely peopled but in hostile territory. In that event it was necessary to build with speed—the vast works of Richard Cœur de Lion at Chateau Gaillard, for instance, are said to have been erected in a year[3]—and that was possible only by

---

[1] In Lavisse, *Histoire de France*, III, i, 423.
[2] On the spread of gothic, see Enlart, *op. cit.* I, 435 ff.; Ch.-V. Langlois, *op. cit.* 422; and especially G. Dehio and G. von Bezold, *Die Kirchliche Baukunst des Abendlandes*, Text, II.
[3] Viollet-le-Duc, *op. cit.* 87.

employing very large numbers of men, such as the 400 masons and 1200 other workers at Beaumaris in the late thirteenth century. In such cases the managements were faced with a problem of food supply and accommodation not unlike that with which railway contractors had to deal in the nineteenth century, and, so far as accommodation is concerned, the answer appears to have been the same, the wooden hut. An early item in the accounts relating to the building of Vale Royal Abbey in 1277 is a payment for the construction of *mansiones* for the masons and other workmen. Another feature of this temporary congregation of large and fluctuating numbers of men in places which might be far from towns is the unsuitability of the ordinary craft gild as a nexus of the organisation of craftsmen, if organisation there was to be.

1. *Supply of Materials.* In the main medieval builders used local stone, sometimes when it was not very suitable, because the cost of transport was high, and for the same reason as much as possible of the scappling and dressing was done at the quarry. Where funds permitted, however, stone might be brought from a distance: for the cathedral of Sens, for instance, stone was brought not only from Auxerre, at a distance of about 30 miles, but from Ivry, well over 100 miles away.[1] Stone was even exported by sea: the limestone of Istria, easily carried across the Adriatic, was much used in Italy, e.g. in fifth-century Ravenna and eleventh-century Venice,[2] and the oolitic limestone of Caen was widely used in England from the eleventh century onwards. The relative cheapness of water transport was an advantage to such churches as St Victor's at Xanten, to which stone was brought by way of the rivers Lippe, Ruhr and Rhine, but part of the benefit was apt to be lost through payment of tolls. In 1405 the fabric of St Victor's acquired Drachenfels and Andernach stone costing 140 gulden at the quarries; to that amount there were added 44 gulden paid in tolls, $88\frac{1}{2}$ gulden for transport to the quay at Beek, $4\frac{2}{3}$ gulden for carrying from the quay to the church, and $31\frac{1}{2}$ gulden in travelling expenses of officials in connection with the stone, so that very nearly 55% of the cost of the stone on the site was accounted for by transport, tolls and travelling. In this respect the cathedrals of Cologne and Mainz were in comparison fortunately placed.[3] Very high costs of transport were, naturally, incurred as a rule only for decorative stonework, such as the Tournai fonts found at Lincoln and elsewhere; tombs, such as that of Robert Bruce, made in Paris in 1329 for export to Scotland; and the alabaster of Chellaston, in Derbyshire, imported in

[1] On the transport of materials see Enlart, *op. cit.* I, 77 ff.
[2] Watson, *Building Stone*, 203.
[3] S. Beissel, *Die Bauführung des Mittelalters*, II, 44.

large quantities and partly in a worked state, into Normandy[1] in the fifteenth century. Timber, like stone, was mainly obtained locally; but, since medieval carpenters preferred to use only the heart of timber and wood was also needed for other uses, the supply might at times run short, and imported wood was used. Irish timber, for instance, was used at the Louvre in the fourteenth century and, in the fourteenth and fifteenth centuries, Danish timber was used in building work done for the Kings of France and the Dukes of Burgundy.[2] Bricks (*tegulae murales*), which were known in the eleventh century, were, for reasons not well understood, almost entirely given up in the centuries following, except in districts poorly supplied with good building stone, such as parts of Languedoc, Flanders, North Germany and Northern Italy. From the fifteenth century their use, either alone or in conjunction with stone, became widespread. They were, for instance, employed in large quantities for Beverley Bar, Eton College, and the fortified houses of Tattersall and Kirby Muxloe.

There were in the main two ways by which medieval builders could provide themselves with stone, namely by acquiring or leasing quarries or by buying stone from quarry owners. For England it would be possible to draw up a short list of the latter, who sold prepared stone on a fairly large scale, but, though purchases of stone by the crown and other builders were frequent, it is probable that the other method of supply was the commoner. Gifts of quarries, such as that made to the Bishop of Laon for his cathedral in 1205, were a frequent form of pious donation in France[3] and in England, and so were gifts of timber. For the transport of stone, timber and other materials the supervisors of building work either hired carts and carters—and, where necessary, boats and sailors—or had their own or, very commonly, did both. It appears, therefore, that some medieval building operations, in which quarrying, brick-making, timber felling and transport were all under one management, are to be regarded as large and more or less integrated concerns, comparable in size and the variety of operations entailed to some early firms of the Industrial Revolution.

2. *Supply of Labour.* The labour required on a large building operation included, besides the more or less skilled masons, carpenters, smiths, plumbers and glaziers, numbers of *minutii operarii*,[4] namely navvies, mortar mixers, barrowmen and other carriers. Such unskilled labour could probably be found fairly easily in most neighbourhoods. There

[1] P. le Cacheux, *Rouen au Temps de Jeanne d'Arc*, xcvi.

[2] Enlart, *op. cit.* I, 78–9.

[3] Mortet and Deschamps, *op. cit.* II, 201, n. 4.

[4] Knoop and Jones, 'Castle Building at Beaumaris and Caernarvon, etc.', *A.Q.C.* xlv, 15; cf. the contemporary French *menus ouvriers*.

was, probably, no feudal estate in Western Europe on which some building labour was not available, since building, repairing or roofing the lord's hall or the manorial mill or bakehouse were common obligations of the tenants;[1] and, in addition to unskilled or semi-skilled workers, a mason was sometimes and a carpenter often to be found on a feudal estate. Moreover, should there be a shortage of male labour, women, as some medieval examples show, could be used.

At times, at least, religious obligation, an outburst of pious fervour or a laudable local patriotism eased the problem for those in charge of building works. Thus it is provided in a French contract of 1463,[2] made with a mason repairing a parish church that *les habitans de ladite parroisse... lui feront les maneuvres que seront necesseres*. For the repair of Bodmin parish church between 1469 and 1472 the inhabitants of the town not only raised money through gilds and by rating themselves but also turned out to labour without pay. Similarly at the building of the church of St Trond, near Liége, in the second half of the eleventh century numbers of people hastened to carry stone and other materials *plaustris et curribus gratis propriisque expensis*;[3] and after the disastrous fire of 1194 at Chartres people of all classes took part in the work of reconstruction.[4] For other works, offering no opportunity to acquire merit, such enthusiasm could not be expected, but the public authority might be used. In ninth-century Germany the Roman tradition of *munera publica* is said to have been behind a decree of Louis II compelling his subjects to take their part in the work of restoring buildings,[5] and in medieval England, as will be shown later, local shortages of labour were remedied at need by means of the crown's powers of impressment and purveyance.

The supply and training of skilled labour in the quantities necessary for the building activity of the twelfth and following centuries were matters of greater difficulty. Many masons and other craftsmen learned their trades in the workshops connected with abbey and cathedral fabrics but, despite the belief of such authors as Heideloff about the importance of monastic institutions such as Kloster Hirschau under its famous abbot William (1069–91) as training schools for artisans,[6] and

---

[1] For German and other examples see Werner Sombart, *Der moderne Kapitalismus*, (ed. 1921), I, i, 81–4.

[2] G. Fagniez, *Documents relatifs à l'Histoire de l'Industrie, etc.*, II. 258–60.

[3] Mortet and Deschamps, *op. cit.* I, 158.

[4] Mortet and Deschamps, *op. cit.* II, xiv.

[5] W. Sombart, *Der moderne Kapitalismus*, I, i, 84.

[6] *Die Bauhütte des Mittelalters in Deutschland*: the basis seems to be largely the uncritical fifteenth-century writer John Trithemius. For the evidence relating to ecclesiastical and monastic architects in Catalonia and for the importance of the Abbey of Ripoll, under Abbot Oliva in the early eleventh century, as a centre for

the undoubted fact that some monks and secular clergymen are known to have had competence in architecture and even as craftsmen, there is, so far as we know, no evidence to suggest that monks or seculars played any part of importance in teaching men the practical business of using adze and saw or mallet and chisel. They did, on the other hand, take good care to provide themselves with the services of laymen skilled in the building crafts. The abbey of St Aubin d'Angers, for instance, agreed, at some date between 1082 and 1106, that a serf called Fulk should, in return for serving as painter and glazier, be made free and given land, which, however, was to return to the abbey at his death unless he should have a son capable of serving the house in the same craft.[1] Similarly the abbey of Cupar stipulated, when hiring a mason in 1497, that 'the said Thomas sal ken and informe the prentys that we or our successouris resawis al craft in masonry or any wther he can'.[2] In general the skilled craftsmen of the Middle Ages were laymen, and so also, except perhaps in the earlier centuries, were the architects. With the transition from timber to stone the number of masons and the average level of skill may be presumed to have risen. This development occurred in military as well as in ecclesiastical architecture, and there is little likelihood that the craftsmen required to erect stone strongholds owed much to monastic training. They learned their trades on the building works themselves from laymen already masters of them. One nursery of craftsmen in stone, which has so far attracted little attention but which may nevertheless have been important, is the quarry. In an early phase the callings of mason and quarryman were probably not entirely distinct; some English masons are known to have been quarrymen at one stage in their careers; and sellers of dressed and prepared stone, who are known to have existed both in England and on the continent,[3] may well have had in their employment workers who learned the mason's trade well enough to earn a living by it, as wallers if not as setters, outside the quarry.

It now remains to be seen how craftsmen were recruited by those who required their services. Where the work to be done was on a small scale, or consisted of repairs rather than new construction, masons or carpenters could be hired as need arose or a master craftsman could be found to do the work at an agreed price. Where the work was on a larger

the studies required for architecture, see J. Puig y Cadafalch, A. de Falguera and J. Goday y Casals, *L' Arquitectura Romànica a Catalunya*, II, 59 ff. One should, however, beware of taking too literally words such as *fabricavit*, *erexit*, *struxit* and the like occurring in literary sources.

[1] Mortet and Deschamps, *op. cit.* I, 264–5.

[2] C. Rogers, *Rental Book of ...Cupar-Angus*, I, 310.

[3] For purchases of stone from stone-cutters in the region of Tournai see Mortet and Deschamps, *op. cit.* II, 298–9.

scale and likely to last for a long time it was convenient to keep a staff, with a master or warden, or both, in charge in the lodge (*Bauhütte*, *chantier*) attached to every building work of importance. Such a staff could be expanded in times of special activity and reduced to a minimum at other times. On the continent unmarried journeymen were willing enough, as work finished in one place, to go elsewhere. The *tour de France* was a familiar institution, in early modern times and probably before, among building craftsmen, and German workers of the same kind were mobile in the fifteenth century; no fewer than 117 of them came to Ulm in one week when the church tower was in danger of falling in 1493.[1] Lombard masons probably travelled to Urgel in Catalonia in 1175[2] and French masons went to distant Upsala in 1287.[3] How far the movement of craftsmen was voluntary is not clear, but in most countries the civil authority would no doubt attempt to use its powers at need. Thus Raymond V, Count of Toulouse, though not specifically claiming a power to send masons away from home in time of peace, lays down the principle of compulsion in regulations of 1187,[4] requiring the master stone masons of Nîmes, if the Count should have building in progress there, to labour for one day in the week for their food only and on the other days for pay. When they joined the army they were to bring their gear, he providing transport for it and food for them as well as a stipulated sum for fortifications destroyed. In Aquitaine, earlier in the same century, there had apparently been a risk of conscription, for a charter of Duke William VIII,[5] between 1127 and 1137, expressly provided that his officers should not have power to seize workmen on one operation and send them to another. The most abundant evidence of conscription of building workers occurs in English records, which leave no doubt that the powers of the crown were being extensively used in the thirteenth century through the sheriffs and during the remainder of the Middle Ages mainly through master masons or administrative officials such as Geoffrey Chaucer, clerk of the works at St George's Chapel, Windsor, in 1390. Masons were taken sometimes by the hundred, but the system was evidently not without difficulties. There was a possibility of gathering too many men at some periods and too few at others; men could not altogether be prevented from deserting either while on the way or after arrival; and the eagerness of officials to take men for one building might hinder progress with others. Impressment was apt to interfere with ecclesiastical, municipal

[1] *Die Chroniken der deutschen Städte*, XXIII (Augsburg iv), 420.
[2] Mortet and Deschamps, *op. cit.* II, 129, 130.
[3] *Ibid.* 305–6.
[4] *Ibid.* 156.
[5] Mortet and Deschamps, *op. cit.* I, 379.

and private works, where officials were most likely to find the men they needed. Hence, in 1441, Archbishop Chicheley sought a royal order to save the workmen at All Souls' College from being pressed for work at Eton and in 1479 it was requested that the men who had finished Magdalen College should not be taken for Windsor but left to work for the University.

IV. *The Management of Large Building Operations*

The simplest arrangement known to us for the administration of a building operation is that indicated in a document of 1175 relating to the church of St Mary in Urgel, Catalonia.[1] All the funds, from rents and other sources, assigned to the fabric were to be handed over to Raymond the Lombard, apparently the master mason, who agreed to roof the church, construct a dome and raise the towers, taking seven years for the work and employing four other Lombards, to whom other masons were to be added at need. During the seven years and afterwards for his life Raymond was to have *cibum canonicale*. This provision may be compared with that in force until 1374 at St Victor's in Xanten, Germany, where the master mason held a prebend of equal status with those of the canons.[2] The system in general use, at any rate from the thirteenth century onwards, differed from that at Urgel in separating the two sides of an undertaking, the financial and administrative on the one hand and the technical or architectural on the other, and putting a different man in charge of each. Thus, at St Victor's in Xanten the *magister fabrice* or *Werkmeister* was in charge of the funds and the master mason (*magister lapicida*) in charge of the building operations. Similarly, in fourteenth- and fifteenth-century Spain, collegiate and cathedral churches entrusted the financial and administrative functions to canons or other clergymen called *canonicos fabriqueros*, *obreros* or *operarii*, leaving the management of the building work itself to the architect or master mason, the *lapicida et magister operis*.[3] In France and in England, and on ecclesiatical, royal, municipal and private buildings, a similar separation was the practice. Kings used financial officers, churches used the sacrist or another obedientiary, colleges one of the fellows and great lords their stewards to deal with accounts, inventories and the like, leaving the master mason or architect

[1] Mortet and Deschamps, ii, 129–31.
[2] S. Beissel, *Die Bauführung des Mittelalters*, i, 96, 97. On the separation in general see Dehio and von Bezold, *op. cit.* ii, 24.
[3] G. E. Street, *Gothic Architecture in Spain*, ii, 267, 321. On the administrative function of the *operarii* in an earlier period, see J. Puig y Cadafalch, A. de Falguera and J. Goday y Casals, *op. cit.* ii, 47.

free to give his whole attention to matters directly concerned with his art. The relative importance of the two chief officials varied from time to time and from one building to another, and the separation was not always complete; but the system may be presumed to have brought with it the advantages of specialisation and to have been necessary when a building operation was on a considerable scale. It was also in accord with the professional pride of the architect and master craftsman. Michelangelo was probably expressing a conviction shared by men in an earlier age when he told Cardinal Marcello: 'your office is to procure money and take care that thieves do not get the same; the designs for the building you are to leave to my care'.[1] Where the same employer had several building operations in progress, or many buildings to maintain at the same time, as was the case with the crown in England and France and, to a lesser degree, with the princes of the blood and other great nobles, some unification of control was achieved by putting a master workman in general command, with wardens or subordinate masters in charge at each work. Thus, to take one instance, Alexander de Berneval in 1421 functioned as *maistre des œuvres de machonerie du Roy* throughout the bailliage of Rouen.[2] In England from 1256 onwards there was a central office of works[3] which in the course of time had premises, including stores for materials and traceries for drawing, at Westminster and developed a large technical and administrative staff, some members of which were travelling officials.

The finance of building is outside our present scope and, accordingly, leaving on one side officials such as William of Wykeham whose functions were largely concerned with it, we have to consider their technical colleagues, the master masons, about whom some not altogether correct notions have been current. It has been held that, as craftsmen, they were less individualist than their Renaissance successors; that their work was largely anonymous; and that between the artist responsible for the design of a building and the masons and carpenters who carried it out there was no distinction.[4] By now it is known that medieval craftsmen were proud enough of their individual masterpieces; and to such well-known names as those of Erwin von Steinbach of Strasbourg and Hugues Libergier of Rheims others can be added by the dozen. It can be shown that at least as early as the thirteenth century there existed a kind of architect quite distinct in pay and status from the

[1] J. Foster, *Vasari's Lives of the most eminent Painters, etc.* (1892), v, 304.

[2] For many references to Alexander de Berneval see P. le Cacheux, *op. cit.*

[3] John H. Harvey, 'The Medieval Office of Works' in *Journal Brit. Archaeol. Assoc.* (1941).

[4] W. Sombart, *Der moderne Kapitalismus*, II, ii, 773. Similar notions are corrected in Martin S. Briggs, *The Architect in History*.

craftsmen who worked under his eye. There is, for instance, no doubting the gap between the ordinary mason working at Caernarvon Castle in the early fourteenth century for 2s. 6d. a week and the master mason, Walter of Hereford, who received 2s. a day. Such architects were called masons or carpenters, though they were commonly distinguished by the title *magister* or an adjective, *principalis* or *capitalis*. Biographical detail relating to them is difficult to gather but enough evidence remains to suggest that the more eminent of them had distinct professional qualifications. Those included the capacity to measure the quantity and assess the quality of work done and probably to estimate the quantities necessary for any given piece of work; ability in drawing and making plans; and the ability to arrange and supervise the labours of large numbers of men working at one time in one place. That was especially necessary under a system such as that prevailing in royal building in England, where a large operation was managed directly and as a unity, all the workers being hired and paid by the crown. Some operations were indeed divided into contracts or 'bargains' but with those also it was necessary that someone should be able to plan the building as a whole and to supervise the separate masters who carried out the different parts. An example of that system may be found in the erection of a college at Beauvais in 1387[1] under the general supervision of Master Raymon du Temple. He first made a schedule of the form, material, order and thickness of the edifice and had this copied by his clerk. It was then read and shown to workmen who were capable of undertaking parts of the work and, after some bargaining, contracts were made with two Paris masons for the stone work and subsequently with other artificers for the carpentry, lead work and the like. From time to time Master Raymon came to measure the quantities performed, bringing on one occasion his clerk, 'who wrote down every particular as the said Master Raymon named it'. His care for design in detail is evident from the fact that the crown of the Virgin, whose statue decorated the College, though made by Marcel the goldsmith, was *devisée par M. Raymon*.

The best known evidence of the training and interests of such architects is probably the thirteenth-century sketch book of Villard de Honnecourt.[2] He was probably a protégé of the Cistercian house of Vaucelles and travelled as far as Hungary, where the Cistercians were busily building between 1235 and 1250. Besides figure sketches and architectural drawings his book contains indications of his interest in mechanics and other aspects of thirteenth-century science, and it is clear that he knew some little Latin. Though he cannot, on the strength of

[1] G. Fagniez, *Documents etc.* II, 128 ff.
[2] For an appreciation see Ch.-V. Langlois, *op. cit.* 414–16.

buildings with which he is known to have been connected, be counted among the great architects of his day he was evidently not only professionally trained but a man of some culture, at a considerable remove from the ordinary craftsmen of his time.

V. *Masons' Contracts*

Raymon du Temple and his English contemporary, Henry Yevele, are two instances out of many which could be cited to show that the architect, in the sense not only of a designer but of a man taking charge of a whole building operation, and even several at the same time, had developed before the end of the Middle Ages. A further development, by which the architect or master mason himself contracted for the construction of a whole building or a considerable part of one, is believed to have been reached in Italy in the fifteenth century (Beltramo di Martino of Varese, active about 1450, being an example) and France in the sixteenth.[1] It may indeed be true that the contracting system became dominant only after the end of the Middle Ages, but building contracts, involving relatively large sums of money and the supply of materials by the contractor, were known before the fifteenth century. Some of Queen Eleanor's crosses were erected by such contracts in the latter part of the thirteenth century and about 1380 William Sharnhale undertook work to the value of £456—a sum equivalent to the earnings of 65 masons in a whole year—at Cowling Castle.[2]

The number of surviving building contracts of one kind or another is so large that space will permit only of general observations upon them. The simplest form of contract work was *opus ad tascam*, whereby a man or group of men received an agreed sum for scappling stone or some similar work easy to estimate quantitatively. This in effect was piece work accompanied, where several men did the work, by division of the proceeds. A common type of contract was that whereby an artificer undertook to erect a building, himself supplying the labour only; thus, for instance, in 1224 Master Nicholas of Beaumont-le-Roger agreed to build a castle for the Count of Dreux, the Count providing stone, sand, lime, timber and transport and retaining the scaffolding made by the contractor when the work had been finished.[3] Other types of agreement bind the contractor to provide, in addition to workmanship, either materials or transport or both. The contractors were sometimes ordinary working masons occasionally trying an alternative to their usual wage labour but it was by no means unknown for master masons

[1] W. Sombart, *op. cit.* II, ii, 774.
[2] On English contracts see Knoop and Jones, 'The Rise of the Mason Contractor', *Journal R.I.B.A.* 17 October, 1936.   [3] Mortet and Deschamps, *op. cit.* II, 234–5.

in charge of a building to take a contract either for work connected with it or for some quite different building. Henry Yevele,[1] for instance, while King's Master Mason and a member of the royal household as well as master mason at Westminster Abbey and Warden of London Bridge, undertook considerable contracts. Contractors who undertook to supply not only workmanship but materials were likely to be either dealers in them or owners of their own supplies. Beltramo di Martino, who has been taken as marking the advent of the new system of building, owned tileries and lime kilns in Rome; Thomas Crompe, a considerable contractor at Cowling Castle seventy years earlier, was probably a quarry master; his famous contemporary, Henry Yevele, is known to have dealt in stone and tiles in large quantities and may at one time have worked a marble quarry at Purbeck.

Building contracts, probably to an increasing extent after 1350, thus offered chances of greater gain to masons and carpenters of various grades but they were not the only way by which a craftsman might hope to attain a higher status than that of the ordinary worker in his trade. If he preferred the relative safety of a salaried position to the speculative possibilities of contracting, he might seek to become a foreman or a warden on a large works, *magister secundarius* on the fabric of a church and eventually master mason in the service of a great lord, a municipality or a cathedral chapter. In that event he would commonly be bound by a contract of appointment for a term of years or for life, generally prescribing his salary and not infrequently his entertainment,[2] limiting or prohibiting his absence to do other work without the consent of the chapter or convent, and sometimes providing him with a house and guaranteeing part of his salary or maintenance in case of continued infirmity. At least one contract contained a clause designed to offset possible fluctuations in the value of money; the bishop and canons of Lugo in Spain agreed in 1129 that their master mason should have an annual salary of 200 *sueldos*, but, if the value were to change, he should have six marks in silver and various payments in kind.[3]

VI. *Conditions of Labour*

There is no means of discovering exactly what proportion of medieval building craftsmen succeeded, by one or other of the ways described, in reaching and retaining positions which marked them off from their fellows, but it may safely be regarded as very small, and the great

---

[1] On whom see Knoop and Jones, 'Henry Yevele and his Associates' in *Journal R.I.B.A.* 25 May, 1935.

[2] This is done in detail in a French contract of 1261 printed in Mortet and Deschamps, *op. cit.* II, 288-90.   [3] G. E. Street, *op. cit.* I, 171-2.

majority of artificers in the industry remained throughout their working lives wage earners. As such they have until recently been little noticed by historians. Of the accounts, by means of which their condition can be studied, many have perished or are difficult of access or, when found, are insufficiently detailed; but enough evidence is now available to throw light not only on rates of remuneration and changes in them but also on such problems as the length of the working period, the number of holidays and, to a limited extent, on continuity of employment.

Before coming directly to those questions it will be well to indicate certain respects in which the medieval mason and, to some extent, other building craftsmen differed from their contemporaries in other industries. One was their very much greater mobility. Since, not only in the countryside but also in many towns, most houses were of timber, lath and plaster, there could have been little continuous employment, in many districts, for a large number of masons in their own villages, unless those were in a quarrying district such as Tournai where large quantities of dressed stone, pillars and part-manufactured statues were produced for export. In any event, the erection of the great castles and cathedrals of medieval Europe was possible only by gathering hundreds of craftsmen from a wide district. That was the easier to arrange because masons and carpenters were not, like the weaver, tied to a loom but could pack their instruments into a small bundle and take to the road, as they continued to do until modern times. At need the tools might even be provided by the management of the building operation which, in any case, generally paid for the sharpening and steeling of them, often employing a smith or smiths for the purpose and a *portehache* to carry them between the smithy and the work. A second difference between the mason and other workers, such as the weaver, tailor, and saddler, was that he had fewer opportunities to acquire, even in small quantities, the material in which he worked and that he was in consequence more generally in the position of a man having his labour and skill only to sell. Thirdly, unlike most medieval craftsmen, who worked in isolation or in small workshops, the mason was often employed in conditions which must have been similar to those obtaining in the industrial establishments which immediately preceded the modern mill or factory. He was thus subject to an order and discipline which, though probably less harsh in their operation, were similar in essence to those imposed upon the reluctant cotton workers of early nineteenth-century Lancashire and Alsace. Men were fined at the building of Eton College not only for fighting but for hindering their fellows by telling tales and for unpunctuality.

The mason's trade comprised two main branches, the arts practised respectively by the hewer (*cementarius, lathomus*) and the layer or setter (*positor*, *cubitor*) but the separation was not rigid and most masons were proficient to some extent in both (Pl. 1 *b*, p. 143). Hewing was considered the higher, since at its best it included sculpture, the carving of tracery and of pillar capitals and the like difficult and intricate work, but it also included the rough dressing or scappling of stone used in the core or inner part of walls, for only the outer surfaces were of smoothly dressed and squared stone. It is probable that the setting of such work as a rose window was done by the carver; on the other hand the shaping of roughly dressed stone was probably done by the men who laid it. Stones for outer surfaces, including mouldings and other carving, were commonly worked in the lodge, the mason responsible scoring his bench mark upon each one as he finished it, but sometimes the carving was done long after the stone had been laid.[1] When the hewer's work had been tried with square and mould, to see that the angles of the surfaces and the profile or pattern were accurate, it was the layer's business to set the stones truly with a plumb line in a correct bonding. The distinction between hewing and laying corresponded, though not completely, to the difference between 'freemason' and 'rough mason' or 'rowmason', the latter term being sometimes used for bricklayer.

The fact that both hewing and laying included operations requiring different degrees of skill may explain, though only in part, the puzzling variety of wage rates on some large building works. The 131 masons working at Vale Royal Abbey in 1278–80 received no fewer than eighteen different rates, and at Caernarvon and Beaumaris Castles in the early fourteenth century there were twenty-two. That this variety was not exceptional is clear from the fact that 29 masons were employed, at five different rates, on the fabric of York Minster in 1371, and ten masons, at eight different rates, at Ely in 1359–60. Whatever the causes of this multiplicity may have been, the evidence suggests that a man's wage was probably the result of an individual bargain and was not determined simply by custom or by such machinery as that of a gild. As the Middle Ages wore on, the diversity tended to diminish, in part perhaps because, during the last century and a half—say between 1350 and 1500—masons were more nearly of the same grade in skill than they had been earlier. That will not appear strange if it be borne in mind that very large numbers were employed on similar work, especially in castle building, and also that something like standardisation came in with the perpendicular style.

Of variations in wages between town and country there is little information, though enough to show that in London they were onesixth to one-third higher than in the country as a whole. There is clearer proof of the common medieval variation according to the season of the

[1] Enlart, *op. cit.* I, 14 n.

year. Thus at Verona in 1228 master masons were to be paid four *soldi* a day in summer and three in winter, because of the shorter working day.[1] The difference was less for carpenters in Dax, near Bayonne, about 1300, their wages being fixed at 12 *deniers* a day from March 1st to November 1st and ten from thence to March 1st.[2] At St Victor's in Xanten[3] the winter rate, starting on November 11th, was about two-thirds of the summer rate, starting on February 22nd; the two journey-men (*Gesellen*) who worked with the master mason there in 1356 were paid from 12 to 14 *denarii* a day in summer and 9 or 10 in winter; Herman von Offenburg and Tilman von Koeln in 1436 and 1437 drew $36\frac{1}{2}$ *denarii* a day in summer and $24\frac{1}{3}$ in winter. In London, according to regulations made between 1275 and 1296, masons were to get 5*d.* a day from Easter to Michaelmas, 4*d.* from Michaelmas to November 11th, 3*d.* from November 11th to February 2nd and 4*d.* thence to Easter.

A more important phenomenon, but one far more difficult to trace for Western Europe in general, is the secular variation. The trend of money wages in England, from 1300 onwards, is fairly clear and may be summarily stated as follows: (i) from 1300 to the Black Death the wages of masons and craftsmen of the same kind ranged about 4*d.* a day; (ii) about 1350 or 1360 they rose to 5*d.* or 6*d.* and remained, with remarkable constancy and uniformity, at about that level until the beginning of the sixteenth century; (iii) thereafter they rose steeply, to 10*d.* by 1560, 12*d.* by the end of Elizabeth's reign and 18*d.* by the Restoration. There is no reason to suppose that building craftsmen in other countries also did not share in the rise in wages which is known to have followed the Black Death. At St Victor's in Xanten,[4] for instance, the wages of a skilled mason rose from 14 *denarii* in 1350–59 to 21 *denarii* in 1360–69, 36 *denarii* in 1370–89 and 42 *denarii* in 1390–99, and the wages of other artificers on the same fabric moved in much the same way. Here the rise was a slower process than in England; moreover, after reaching a peak in 1400–9, wages in Xanten did not remain at that level but declined, more rapidly in the second half of the fifteenth century than during the first, falling from 50 *denarii* in 1400–9 to 25 *denarii* in 1510–19. The rise in the sixteenth century, like that in the fourteenth, came more slowly in Xanten than in England but it was of a similar order: the wages of a good artificer were about 54 *denarii* in 1560-69, 115 *denarii* in 1590–99 and 168 *denarii* in 1650–59. Though there are many difficulties in relating these movements to changes in the standard of living, there is little doubt that the period following the Black Death brought with it a rise

[1] A. M. Allen, *History of Verona*, 38.
[2] Mortet and Deschamps, *op. cit.* II, 336. The carpenters were partly paid in food.
[3] S. Beissel, *op. cit.* II, 150, 153, 157.
[4] On wages in Xanten see Beissel, *op. cit.* II, 149 ff.

in real wages. For England, where money wages rose approximately 42% between 1350 and 1510 and food prices may have risen by 33% in the same period, the picture is more pleasant than that which the careful researches of Beissel suggest for Xanten. Money wages there, if measured in wheat, barley and rye, tended downwards on the whole in the century and a half following 1350; the quantity purchasable by 16 days' wages in 1350–59 could be bought for an average of 13 days' wages between 1370 and 1419, but the figure rose to 16 again for the next forty years, to 19 for the period 1460–99 and to 25 for the years 1500–39. Thus, even in Xanten, though to a smaller extent than in England, the later Middle Ages were, on the surface at least, a time of relative stability and perhaps of rough plenty for artificers in the building trades; certainly there, as in England and France, they seem prosperous when compared with the catastrophic period which followed.[1]

Neither in France nor in England was the rise in wages after the Black Death allowed to take place without an attempt by the government and local authorities to prevent it. In the former country an ordinance of 1351 sought to undermine the position of journeymen not only by fixing their wages and tying them to their work but also by abolishing gild regulations limiting the number of apprentices and local restrictions on the employment of 'foreign' workmen, but the attempt was unsuccessful and further legislation was called for in 1354 and 1356. In England, where municipal regulation of masons' wages goes back as far as 1212, statutes and bye-laws dealt with the same subject repeatedly in the fourteenth, fifteenth and sixteenth centuries, aiming generally at a defined working day and a fixed maximum wage. Official views on the working day were probably much the same in all countries. The French ordinance of 1351 required journeymen to work 'loyaument du soleil levant jusques au soleil couchant', much as the English Statute of Artificers nearly two hundred years later defined the hours of work, between mid-September and mid-March, as 'from the springe of the daye in the mornynge untill the nyght', limits which probably accorded with the custom of lodges, though masons, like other craftsmen, were known to start late and finish early and to stretch the permitted breaks for meals and drinking. The second object of these regulations was only imperfectly attained even in quarters where the attempt to put the orders into practice was most to be expected. In the heart of the capital the Wardens of London Bridge in the early fifteenth century disregarded the legal obligation to keep to the maximum wage for masons, to reduce their wage in winter and to give no pay for holidays;

[1] On the fall of real wages in France see H. Sée, *Histoire Economique de la France* (1939), 93–4.

and on the King's works in the fourteenth century hundreds of men were paid at higher rates than his laws allowed.

Even if we take it that governments failed to prevent the rise in wages, we cannot be sure that medieval building craftsmen enjoyed anything like a golden age until more is known about the amount of their annual earnings. The number of days for which they were paid might be diminished by several factors; fabric funds might be exhausted so that building work would have to stop; the medieval church insisted on the observance of a considerable number of saints' days; and bad weather was a common cause of interruption. Building work was certainly slowed down, and might cease altogether, in winter: the Beauvais account of 1387 noted that *les gelees approchoient et se passoit la saison de maconner*. Many cathedral chapters and other employers probably made arrangements similar to those at Xanten in November 1399, when the staff of masons was reduced from twelve to six, who covered the stone-work with straw to protect it from cold and frost, made their wooden lodge weatherproof with turf and settled down to their winter work, cutting stone for the pillars of the choir. On some buildings laying ceased for months at a time and though other work might be found for some of the layers there must have been a good deal of seasonal unemployment. Some idea of the length of the working year may perhaps be gained from a Rochester Castle account for 1368: the majority of the masons employed there received pay for 252 days but no setter was paid for more than 180. Even when the weather was good, however, the medieval mason rarely worked a full week of six days. The number of saints' days observed, and the days themselves, varied from one building to another and from year to year but the number might work out at three or more in each month. With the Rochester account for 1368 the Xanten fabric accounts for 1356 and 1495 may be compared: the former covered 49 weeks, containing 250 working days, and the latter 53 weeks with an aggregate of 270½ working days, giving an average of 265 in a calendar year. If, as there is some evidence to suggest, the daily wage of a mason was approximately equal to three times the cost of his meat and drink, we may conclude that he would be lucky, in the climate of Northern Europe, to earn annually the equivalent of 810 days' subsistence. That would give a single man a fair margin but for a mason with a wife and child it might leave less than 27 days' earnings to meet all expenses other than the cost of food, unless, as may often have been the case, the mason's family contributed to its maintenance.

There were occasional opportunities for masons to add to their ordinary earnings by extra diligence where haste was required, and they might even work at night, as the Xanten staff did in 1399 and the London

Bridge masons were in special circumstances required to do in the fifteenth century; but systematic overtime, so far as we know, was not usual until the sixteenth century, when it helped to bridge the gap between wages and rising prices. Friendly relations between employers and employed were shown in donations on special festivals or on the completion of particular pieces of work. Thus at Beauvais in 1387, we are told, *le jour de caresme...il fust accoustume que l'on donnoit a tous les ouvriers courtoisie, c'est assavoir pour le char d'un mouton*; but the commonest form of present was drink, which, for instance, the London Bridge Wardens gave on Shrove Tuesday and the Chapter of Regensburg on June 24th. The more continuous benevolence of the canons of Xanten provided their masons with a weekly *Trinkgeld* amounting to about 2% of their earnings.

VII. *Organisation of Craftsmen*

Like other medieval workmen those in the building trades were commonly subject to some degree of organisation, which was either imposed upon them by employers or evolved by the craftsmen themselves; but, because the conditions of the industry differed from those prevailing in most others, the forms of organisation among building workers, and especially masons, were to some extent peculiar. There are, speaking generally, records of two different kinds of association among them: first, municipal gilds and secondly associations on a different basis which might be wider or narrower than the ordinary gild. Organisation in such gilds does not appear to have been either early or widespread among masons, the main reason probably being that in most towns the number of masons was too small. Of 603 craftsmen in Coventry in 1450 only seven were masons; at that date there may have been 20 in Norwich and sixty years earlier there were perhaps 23 or 24 in Oxford. It is thus not strange that in most places where municipal gilds are known to have existed the masons were joined to other craftsmen. In thirteenth-century Florence the *maestri di pietra e legname* were associated, as masons and wrights were in Edinburgh in 1475; the Quatuor Coronati gild in fifteenth-century Antwerp included with the masons tilers and paviers; that in Bruges included, besides, plasterers and brickmakers.[1] In London, indeed, there were sufficient masons to constitute a gild by themselves, formed between 1356 and 1376, and in medieval Paris, where the number of building workers

[1] Count Goblet d'Alviella, 'The Quatuor Coronati in Belgium' (*A.Q.C.*, XIII 78 ff.

was considerable,[1] the masons and carpenters were separately organised. The latter in 1268 were subject to the general supervision of Foulques du Temple, who claimed to have been appointed by the crown, and who both drew a revenue from the craftsmen and exercised jurisdiction over practically all workers in wood, each of the separate crafts having regulations of its own. The masons, together with the stone-cutters, plasterers and mortar-makers, were subject to the jurisdiction of the king's master mason, who engaged to rule the trade fairly, 'as well for the poor as the rich, for the weak as for the strong'. Though the workers in these four trades had customs and regulations of their own and were associated in a fraternity of St Blaise they do not appear to have had a monopoly, since any skilled person was free to practise the mason's trade in Paris. The objects of gilds where they existed were to regulate apprenticeship, the employment of journeymen and the examination of materials and workmanship and also to promote piety and good fellowship among the members. Tendencies towards monopoly were apt to be checked by the municipal authorities acting in the public interest. Thus the city authorities in Florence controlled the price of building materials and by an ordinance in the early fourteenth century permitted craftsmen from outside to work in the city without becoming members of the gild or even paying to it.[2] Similarly in Antwerp provision was made in 1458 for the introduction of 'foreign' workmen at need.

More widespread than such building trade gilds were the masons' lodges, of which one at least must have existed in connection with every considerable building, whether in town or country, in Western Europe and which might well contain a greater number of masons than many municipalities required. Primarily the lodge was a workshop, but it was also used for meals and for the mid-day *siesta*, and the men working within it, who no doubt discussed their pay and grievances, were conscious of some solidarity and regarded it as disloyal for a man to reveal to those outside 'the councelle of his felows in logge and in chambere.'[3] From the employer's point of view it was desirable to draw up regulations, or to sanction existing customs, for the lodge; those for the lodges at York Minster in 1352, 1370 and 1408–9, survive and similar regulations may be presumed to have existed in other places and countries. It may also be presumed that the migratory character of the mason's calling would make many craftsmen familiar with the rules of

---

[1] In 1300 there were 122 masons, 108 carpenters, 22 plasterers and 6 mortar-makers. On the Paris trades see G. Fagniez, *Etudes sur l'Industrie et la Classe Industrielle à Paris, etc.*, especially 191 ff.

[2] A. Doren, *Das Florentiner Zunftwesen*, 122.

[3] Knoop, Jones and Hamer, *The Two Earliest Masonic MSS.* 121.

lodges in different places and tend to bring about a certain uniformity in the customs of the craft. The lodge at Xanten at one time or another contained masons not only from the immediate neighbourhood but from Douai, Holland (Utrecht, Kranenberg), Antwerp, Brussels, Westphalia (Borken, Münster), the Rhineland (Dusseldorf, Cologne, Mainz, Trier) and even Nuremburg, and no doubt a similar variety existed in other lodges. This may well have made easier the development of an association to link the lodges together and to safeguard the interests of masons in general.

In Germany that stage was reached in 1459 if not before. The earliest regulations of the *Steinmetzen*[1] set forth what are claimed to be the good old customs of the craft as agreed upon by an assembly held in Regensburg in that year, and these, in a document of 1462, are said to have been accepted by masters from Magdeburg, Halberstadt, Hildesheim and other places meeting at Torgau. The regulations were confirmed by imperial authority in 1498 and 1563. English masons may have had a similar organisation in the fourteenth century, for two documents relating to the craft describe an assembly or congregation which masons were bound to attend and which had legislative and judicial functions. There is no proof that such powers were in fact regularly and systematically exercised, but the statutory prohibition of masons' congregations does suggest that assemblies of some kind had occurred. The English documents contain no indication of a regional organisation, such as the German regulations portray, with headquarters in each district. In their general tenour and spirit, however, the English and the German regulations are similar; they assume the existence of the three industrial grades of apprentice, fellow and master and lay stress on apprenticeship; they prohibit the supersession of one master by another without cause and they exhort masons to piety, morality and care of the honour of the craft. In short they attempt to reconcile the interests of the 'lord' or employer with those of the master mason, his warden and the mass of journeymen.

Whether a similar organisation existed in medieval France is doubtful, though M. Martin Saint-Léon may well be right in holding that the origins of the *compagnonnages* go back to the lodges connected with twelfth- or thirteenth-century cathedrals.[2] As we know them from later records, the *compagnonnages* were associations adapted to the needs of wandering journeymen requiring employment in the towns to which they came, or hospitality and help on their way. In Germany, no doubt, as in England and Scotland, there was a need to 'receive and

[1] For text and translation see F. Janner, *Die Bauhütten des deutschen Mittelalters*, 294 ff. and Gould, *History of Freemasonry*, I, 134 ff.
[2] E. M. Saint-Léon, *Le Compagnonnage*, 15.

cherish strange masons and set them to work' or else 'to refresh them with money to the next lodge'; and in France, Germany and Scotland there may have been a ritual and secret grips or other signs by means of which rightful claimants to this service could be distinguished from pretenders; but the French organisation, if it did indeed exist in the Middle Ages, differed from that prevailing elsewhere by excluding masters and concerning itself solely with the interests of journeymen. Associations limited to one industrial grade were common enough in other trades on the continent and not unknown in England, where the 'young men' of the carpenters had a fellowship in London in 1468. The general factors, apart from the migratory character of the craftsmen concerned, which gave rise to such associations were the increasing exclusiveness of the gilds and the decreasing chance of attaining independent status. When they formed their own organisations the journeymen adopted the model they knew, the masters' gild with its industrial, religious and convivial aspects; and they regarded themselves as being, no less than the masters, custodians of the honour and traditions of the craft. Thus the *compagnons* who were masons held themselves to be inheritors of a craft and customs in use at the building of Solomon's Temple; but, however traditional their legends might be, their organisation was based on a principle which to the constituted authorities could not but seem detestable. The *compagnonnages* nevertheless survived and were active in the nineteenth century. It may be presumed that the rise in prices and the increasing importance of the large scale building contractor, which came about after the close of the Middle Ages, did not change one of the main features of the medieval industry, its dependence on a great mass of wage-earning craftsmen.

Bibliographies

EDITORS' NOTE

In accordance with the established practice of the Cambridge series of histories, the bibliographies printed below are selective and incomplete. Their purpose is not to list all the publications bearing directly or indirectly on the subject, but to enable the readers to study some of the topics in greater detail. As a rule, books and articles superseded by later publications have not been included, and references to general treatises indirectly relevant to the subject matter of individual chapters have been reduced to the minimum. As most of the chapters are not new pieces of research, but summaries and interpretations of knowledge already available in secondary literature, references to original sources have either been left out altogether or have been confined to the principal and most essential classes of evidence.

Within the limits set by these general principles, the individual contributors were given the freedom of composing and arranging bibliographies as they thought best. The 'layout' of the bibliographical lists, therefore, varies from chapter to chapter. The editors did not even find it desirable to insist on a uniform method of abbreviating the references to learned periodicals, since the same learned periodicals may be referred to more frequently in some bibliographies than in others. The authors were asked to make their own decisions about abbreviations, and to explain them, if necessary, in prefatory notes to their bibliographies. The prefatory notes will also explain the other special features of the separate lists of authorities.

CHAPTER I

Trade and Industry in Barbarian Europe till Roman Times

I. GENERAL WORKS ON EUROPEAN PREHISTORY WITH INCIDENTAL DISCUSSIONS
ON TRADE AND INDUSTRY

CHILDE, V. G. *The Dawn of European Civilization.* London, 1950.
DÉCHELETTE, J. *Manuel d'Archéologie préhistorique, celtique et gallo-romaine.* Paris, 1908–14.
EBERT, MAX. *Reallexikon der Vorgeschichte.* Berlin, 1924–32.
HAWKES, C. F. C. *The Prehistoric Foundations of Europe.* London, 1940.

II. A. ECONOMIC HISTORY WITH INCIDENTAL REFERENCE TO PREHISTORIC EUROPE

HEICHELHEIM. *Wirtschaftsgeschichte des Altertums.* Leiden, 1938.

B. TECHNOLOGY WITH INCIDENTAL REFERENCES TO ECONOMIC
ORGANIZATION AND TRADE

BOGAYEVSKII, B. L. Техника первобытно-коммунистического общества (История Техники, i). (Indexed.) Moscow, 1936.

III. PREHISTORIES OF SPECIAL AREAS WITH IMPORTANT BUT INCIDENTAL
REFERENCES TO TRADE AND INDUSTRY

BADER, O. N., TRETYAKOV, P. I. and others. Из историй родового общества на территорий СССР. (Izvestiya GAIMK, 106.) M-L. 1934.
BRØNDSTED, J., HOUGEN, B., LINDQUIST, S. and NORDMANN, C. A. Articles in *Nordisk Kultur*, XVI. Oslo, 1934.
CHILDE, V. G. *Prehistoric Communities of the British Isles.* London, 1947.
—— *Scotland before the Scots.* London, 1946.
FILIP, JAN. *Pravěké Československo.* Prague, 1948.
FORSSANDER, J. E. *Der ostskandinavische Norden während der ältesten Metallzeit Europas.* Lund, 1936.
HENCKEN, H. O. *The Archaeology of Cornwall and Scilly.* London, 1932.
KOSTRZEWSKI, J. *Prehistoria Ziem Polskich.* Cracow, 1948.
VOUGA, P. *La Tène.* Neuchâtel, 1923.

IV. SPECIAL INDUSTRIES

1. *Mining*

ANDREE. *Bergbau in der Vorzeit.* Leipzig, 1922.
PITTIONI, R. and others. 'Untersuchungen im Bergbaugebiete Kelchalpe bei Kitzbühel, Tirol.' *Mitteilungen der prähistorischen Kommission der Akademie der Wissenschaften*, III, 1–3 and V, 2–3. Vienna, 1937 and 1947.
ZSCHOCKE, K. and PREUSCHEN, E. 'Das urzeitliche Bergbaugebiet von Mühlbach-Bischofshofen.' *Materialien zur Urgeschichte Österreichs*, VI. Vienna, 1932.
YESSEN, A. A. and DEGEN-KOVALEVSKII, B. E. Из историй древней металлургий Кавказа. (Izvestiya GAIMK, 120.) M-L. 1935.

2. *Stone Implements*

HAZZLEDINE, WARREN S. 'The Neolithic Stone Axes of Graig Lwyd.' *Archaeologia Cambrensis*, LXXVII (1922), 1–36.

3. *Metal working.* (See also § 1)

OLDEBERG, A. *Metalltechnik under Förhistorisk Tid.* Lund, 1943.

V. TRADE

1. *Mainly Neolithic*

BUTTLER, W. 'Beiträge zur Frage der jungsteinzeitlichen Handels.' *Marburger Studien*, pp. 26–33. Darmstadt, 1938.

CLARK, J. G. D. 'Objects of South Scandinavian Flint in the Northernmost Provinces of Norway, Sweden and Finland.' *Proceedings of the Prehistoric Society*, XIV (1948), 219–32.

MONTELIUS, O. 'Der Handel in der Vorzeit.' *Praehistorische Zeitschrift*, II (1910), 249–60.

SEEWALD, O. 'Ein jungsteinzeitlicher Grabfund mit Muschelschmuck.' *Wiener Prähistorische Zeitschrift*, XXIX (1942), 1–18.

2. *Mainly Bronze Age*

BECK, HORACE and STONE, J. F. 'Fayence Beads of the British Bronze Age.' *Archaeologia*, LXXXV (1935), 203–52.

BOSCH GIMPERA, P. 'Relations préhistoriques entre l'Irlande et l'ouest de la péninsule ibérique.' *Préhistoire*, II (1933), 195–250.

CLARK, J. G. D. 'Fresh Evidence for the Dating of Gold Lunulae.' *Man* (1932), 46.

DAVIES, O. 'The ancient tin sources of Western Europe.' *Proceedings of the Belfast Natural History and Philosophical Society* (1931–2), 41–50.

MEGAW, B. R. S. and HARDY, E. M. 'British decorated Axes and their Diffusion during the earlier Part of the Bronze Age.' *Proceedings of the Prehistoric Society*, IV (1938), 272–307.

DE NAVARRO, J. M. 'Prehistoric Routes between Northern Europe and Italy defined by the Amber Trade.' *Geographical Journal* (1925), 481–507.

NESTOR, I. 'Sur l'exploitation préhistorique du cuivre en Roumanie.' *Dacia*, IX–X (1941–4), 173–6.

ORIORDAIN, SEAN P. 'The Halberd in Bronze Age Europe.' *Archaeologia*, LXXXVI (1937), 195–321.

PRZEWORSKI, S. 'Znalesisko Kruchowickie: najstarsze ślady handlu wschodniego na ziemiach polskich.' *Swiatowit*, XIII (Warsaw, 1932), 3–39.

SZLANKÓWNA, A. 'Kilka importów staroitalskich i zachodnio-europejeskich z południowo-wschodniej Polski i Ukrainy.' *Swiatowit*, XVII (1938), 293–306.

WACE, A. J. B. and BLEGEN, C. 'Pottery as Evidence for Trade and Colonization in the Aegean Bronze Age.' *Klio*, XXXII (1939), 131–50.

3. *Iron Age*

FOX, C. *A Find of the Early Iron Age from Llyn Cerrig Bach, Anglesey.* Cardiff, 1946.

JACOBSTHAL, P. and LANGSDORFF, A. *Die Bronzeschnabelkanne.* Berlin, 1929.

DE NAVARRO, J. M. 'Massilia and Early Celtic Culture.' *Antiquity*, II (1928), 423–42.

VI. CURRENCY

FOX, C. 'Distribution of Currency Bars.' *Antiquity*, XIV (1940), 427–33.

HAWKES, C. F. C. 'The Double Axe in Prehistoric Europe.' *Annual of the British School at Athens*, XXXVII (1936–7), 141–59.

MILNE, J. G. 'The *Aes Grave* of Central Italy.' *Journal of Roman Studies*, XXXII (1942), 27–32.

SELTMAN, C. *Greek Coins.* Cambridge, 1933.

CHAPTER II

Trade and Industry under the Later Roman Empire in the West

The following abbreviations have been used in this bibliography:

Act. arch.	Acta archaeologica
AJP.	American Journal of Philology
BSA	Annual of the British School at Athens
CAH.	Cambridge Ancient History
Class. Phil.	Classical Philology
CMedH.	Cambridge Medieval History
JRS.	Journal of Roman Studies
Mon. ant.	Monumenti antichi pubblicati per cura della reale Accademia nazionale dei Lincei
Num. Chron.	Numismatic Chronicle and Journal of the Numismatic Society
TAPA.	Transactions and Proceedings of the American Philological Association

I. ANCIENT SOURCES

Literary. For the early empire Strabo, Pliny's *Natural History*, and Petronius's *Cena Trimalchionis* can be supplemented by scattered references in a wide selection of other authors, including Martial and Juvenal. For the second and third centuries various speeches of Aristides and Dio Chrysostom offer valuable evidence; and the *Historia Augusta*, though it probably reflects to a large extent the conditions of the fourth century (cf. N. H. Baynes, *The H.A., its date and purpose*, Oxford, 1926; A. Alföldi, *Die Kontorniaten*, Budapest, 1943), is important if used critically. For the later empire in the West the *Expositio totius mundi* (ed. Riese in *Geographici latini minores*, pp. 105–26; Sinko in *Archiv f. lateinische Lexicographie u. Grammatik*, XIII, 1904, 531–71), a work probably composed towards the end of the reign of Constantius, and the *Notitia dignitatum* (ed. O. Seeck, 1876), which dates to the early fifth century in its present form, but incorporates earlier material (cf. Piganiol, *L'empire chrétien*, p. x, for bibliography), are the two main works. The Church historians and Christian Fathers also contain much that is of value for the economic historian.

Legal codes. These are of prime importance, especially the Theodosian Code (*Theodosiani libri XVI cum constitutionibus Sirmondianis*, ed. Mommsen-Meyer, Berlin, 1905), which is invaluable for social and economic problems; also important are the various parts of Justinian's codification.

Inscriptions, papyri, etc. These comprise the most important material of all, including such revealing documents as the Mine-law of Vipasca in Portugal (Dessau, 6891) and Diocletian's Edict on Prices (see below). The papyri, though all come from the eastern part of the Empire, mainly Egypt, give information which is relevant for the West as well. Finally, there is the evidence of coins, and the results of excavation in every province of the West.

The following bibliography should be supplemented from those contained in *CAH.* X, XI and XII (especially those of Oertel in X, 944–5 and XII, 750–54), in *CMedH.* I (especially pp. 688 ff.), and in Frank's *Economic Survey of Ancient Rome*; for the coinage see the works listed by Mattingly in *Num. Chron.* 6, VI (1946), 111–20; and in general Rostovtzeff, *Social and economic history of the Roman Empire*, passim, and Piganiol, *L'empire chrétien*, pp. vii–xvi.

These works deal in particular with the *Edictum Diocletiani de pretiis*:

BÜCHER, K. *Die Diokletianische Taxordnung vom Jahre 301.* (Tübing. Beiträge z. Wirtschaftsgesch., 1922, pp. 179 ff. Originally appeared in *Zeitschr. f. die gesamte Staatswissensch.* L (1894), 188–219.)

GRASER, E. R. 'The Edict of Diocletian,' ed. and transl. in vol. V of Frank's *Economic Survey of ancient Rome*, pp. 305–421.

—— 'The significance of two new fragments of the Edict of Diocletian.' *TAPA.* LXXI (1940), 157–74.

GUARDUCCI, M. 'Il primo frammento scoperto in Italia dell' editto di Diocleziano.' *Atti della Pontificia Accademia Romana di Archaeologia: Rendiconti*, XVI (1940), 11–24.

JACOPI, G. 'Gli scavi della missione archeologica italiana ad Afrodisiade nel 1937. *Mon. ant.* XXXVIII (1939), 130–52, 159.

MICHELL, H. 'The Edict of Diocletian: a study of price fixing in the Roman Empire.' *Canadian Journ. of Econ. and Pol. Sci.* XIII (1947), 1–12.

SEECK, O. 'Die Schatzungsordnung Diokletians.' *Zeitschr. f. Sozial- u. Wirtschaftsgesch.* IV (1895), 275–342.

SEGRÈ, A. See the articles listed under § 5 below.

WEST, L. C. 'Notes on Diocletian's *Edict*.' *Class. Phil.* XXXIV (1939), 242–4.

YEO, C. A. 'Land and sea transportation in Imperial Italy.' *TAPA.* LXXVII (1946), 221–44.

2. GENERAL

AUBIN, H. *Vom Altertum zum Mittelalter*. Munich, 1949.

BARROW, R. H. *Slavery in the Roman Empire*. London, 1928.

BAYNES, N. H. 'M. Pirenne and the unity of the Mediterranean world.' *JRS.* XIX (1929), 230–35.

BESNIER, M. 'L'empire romain de l'avènement des Sévères au concile de Nicée.' *Histoire romaine*, IV, 1. Paris, 1937.

BRATIANU, G. I. *La distribution de l'or et les raisons économiques de la division de l'empire romain*. Paris, 1938.

BRÉHIER, L. 'Colonies d'orientaux en occident au commencement du moyen âge.' *Byzantinische Zeitsch.* XII (1903), 1 ff.

BURY, J. B. *History of the late Roman Empire from the death of Theodosius I to the death of Justinian* (A.D. 395–A.D. 565). 2 vols. London, 1923.

—— 'Rome and Byzantium.' *Quart. Rev.* CXCII (1900), 129–55.

CHARLESWORTH, M. P. *Trade routes and commerce of the Roman Empire*, 2nd ed. Cambridge, 1926.

DILL, S. *Roman society in the last century of the Western Empire*, 2nd ed. London, 1899.

DOPSCH, A. *Wirtschaftliche u. soziale Grundlagen der europäischen Kulturentwicklung aus der Zeit von Cäsar bis auf Karl den Grossen*. 2 vols. 2nd ed. Vienna, 1923–4.
    A condensed translation of this work appeared as *The Economic and Social Foundations of European Civilisation*. London, 1937.

—— 'Frühmittelalterliche u. spätantike Wirtschaft.' *Verfassungs- u. Wirtschaftsgeschichte des Mittelalters*, 219–34. Vienna, 1928.

FRANK, T. *Economic history of Rome*, 2nd ed. Baltimore, 1927.

—— Editor of *Economic survey of Ancient Rome*. Five volumes and index. Baltimore, 1933–40.

—— 'Notes on Roman commerce.' *JRS.* XXVII (1937), 72–9.

FRIEDLÄNDER, L. and WISSOWA, G. *Darstellungen aus der Sittengeschichte Roms*. 10th ed., 4 vols. Leipzig, 1919–23. Translated into English from Ed. 7 as *Roman Life and manners under the early Empire*. London, 1910–13.

GELZER, M. 'Das Römertum als Kulturmacht.' *Hist. Zeitsch.* CXXVI (1922), 189–206.

—— 'Altertumswissenschaft u. Spätantike.' *Hist. Zeitsch.* CXXXV (1927), 173–87.

GUMMERUS, H. *Der römische Gutsbetrieb als wirtschaftlicher Organismus nach den Werken des Cato, Varro und Columella*. Klio, Beiheft 5. Leipzig, 1906.

—— *Die Fronden der Kolonen*. (Öfversigt af Finska Vetenskaps-Societetens Förhandlingar, L, 3.) Helsinki, 1907–8.

—— 'Die römische Industrie.' *Klio*, XIV (1914), 149 ff.; XV (1918), 256 ff.

HARTMANN, L. M. *Ein Kapitel vom spätantiken und frühmittelalterlichen Staate*. Stuttgart, 1913. Translated into English with notes by H. Liebeschütz as *The early medieval state: Byzantium, Italy and the West*. London, 1949.

HAYWOOD, R. M. 'Some traces of serfdom in Cicero's day.' *AJP.* LIV (1933), 145–53.

HEICHELHEIM, F. M. *Wirtschaftsgeschichte des Altertums vom Paläolithikum bis zur Völkerwanderung der Germanen, Slaven und Araber.* 2 vols. Leiden, 1938.
—— 'Welthistorische Gesichtspunkte zu den vormittelalterlichen Wirtschaftsepochen.' *Schmollers Jahrb.* CVI (1933), 994 ff.
KÖSTER, A. *Studien zur Geschichte des antiken Seewesens. Klio,* Beih. 32. Leipzig, 1934.
KORNEMANN, E. 'Die unsichtbaren Grenzen des römischen Kaiserreichs', on pp. 96 ff. of *Staaten, Völker, Männer.* Leipzig, 1934.
—— *Weltgeschichte des Mittelmeerraumes von Philipp II von Makedonien bis Muhammad,* II. Munich, 1949.
LANDRY, A. 'Quelques aperçus concernant la dépopulation dans l'antiquité.' *Rev. hist.* CLXXVII (1936), 1–33.
LEFEBVRE DES NOËTTES. *L'attelage: le cheval de selle à travers les âges.* Paris, 1931.
—— *De la marine antique à la marine moderne.* Paris, 1935.
LOPEZ, R. S. 'Mohammed and Charlemagne: a revision.' *Speculum,* XVIII (1943), 14–38.
—— 'Silk industry in the Byzantine Empire.' *Speculum,* XX (1945), 1 ff.
LOT, F. *La fin du monde antique et le début du moyen âge.* Paris, 1927.
MICKWITZ, G. 'Der Verkehr auf dem westlichen Mittelmeer um 600 n. Chr.' *Festschrift Dopsch* (1938), pp. 74 ff.
MOMMSEN, TH. 'Die Provinzen von Caesar bis Diokletian.' *Römische Geschichte,* 4th ed., v. Berlin, 1894. Translated into English as *The provinces of the Roman Empire from Caesar to Diocletian.* London, 1909.
OERTEL, F. 'The economic unification of the Mediterranean region: industry, trade and commerce.' *CAH.* X (1934), 382–424 (bibl. 944–5).
—— 'The economic life of the Empire'. *CAH.* XII (1939), 232–281 (bibl. 750–4) (cf. pp. 724–5: note on 'Inflation in the second and third centuries').
PARKER, H. M. D. *A history of the Roman World* (A.D. 138–337). London, 1935.
PARVÂN, V. *Die Nationalität der Kaufleute im römischen Kaiserreich.* Breslau, 1909.
PASSERINI, A. *Linee di storia romana in età imperiale.* Milan, 1949.
PERSSON, A. *Staat und Manufaktur im römischen Reiche.* Lund, 1923.
PIGANIOL, A. 'L'empire chrétien (325–95).' *Histoire romaine,* IV, 2. Paris, 1947.
PIRENNE, H. *Mahomet et Charlemagne,* 3rd ed. Paris, 1937.
ROSTOVTZEFF, M. *Social and economic history of the Roman Empire.* Oxford, 1926. A third edition has appeared in Italian as *Storia economica e sociale dell' impero Romano.* Florence, 1933.
SCHAAL, H. *Vom Tauschhandel zum Welthandel.* Leipzig, 1931.
—— 'Flussschiffahrt und Flusshandel im Altertum.' *Festschrift f. die 400. Jahr-Feier des Alten Gymnasiums in Bremen,* pp. 370 ff. Bremen, 1928.
SCHMIDT, A. *Drogen und Drogenhandel im Altertum.* Leipzig, 1924.
SEECK, O. *Geschichte des Untergangs der antiken Welt,* 4th ed., 2 vols. and 2 vols. of notes. Stuttgart, 1921.
STEIN, E. *Geschichte des spätrömischen Reiches,* I. Vienna, 1928.
SÜNDWALL, J. *Weströmische Studien.* Berlin, 1915.
VAN BERCHEM, D. *Les distributions de blé et d'argent à la plèbe romaine sous l'empire.* Geneva, 1939.
VAN SICKLE, C. E. 'Diocletian and the decline of the Roman municipalities.' *JRS.* XXVIII (1938), 9 ff.
VINOGRADOFF, P. *The growth of the manor,* 2nd ed. London, 1911.
—— 'Social and economic conditions of the Roman Empire in the fourth century.' *CMedH.* I (2nd ed. 1924), 542–67 (bibl. 688 ff.).
WEBER, M. *Grundriss der Sozialökonomik: III. Abteilung: Wirtschaft und Gesellschaft,* 2nd ed. Tübingen, 1928.
WEST, L. C. 'The economic collapse of the Roman Empire.' *Class. Journ.* XXVIII (1932–3), 96 ff.
WESTERMANN, W. L. 'On inland transportation and communication in antiquity.' *Pol. Sci. Quart.* XLIII (1928), 364.

3. TECHNIQUES; SPECIAL INSTITUTIONS; GUILD ORGANIZATION

BINAGHI, R. *La metallurgia ai tempi dell' impero romano.* Rome, 1946.

BLOCH, M. 'Le moulin à eau.' *Ann. d'hist. écon.* VII (1935), 538 ff.

DAVIES, O. *Roman mines in Europe.* Oxford, 1935.

DE ROBERTIS, F. M. *Il diritto associativo romano.* (Storia delle corporazioni, I, I.) Bari, 1938.

FELDHAUS, F. *Die Technik der Antike u. des Mittelalters.* Potsdam, 1931.

GORCE, D. *Les voyages, l'hospitalité, et le port des lettres dans le monde chrétien des IVe et Ve siècles.* Paris, 1925.

GROAG, E. 'Collegien u. Zwangsgenossenschaften im III. Jahrhundert.' *Vierteljahrsch. f. Sozial- u. Wirtschaftsgesch.* II (1904), 481 ff.

HARDEN, D. B. *Roman glass from Karanis.* Ann Arbor, 1936.

HOLMBERG, E. J. *Zur Geschichte des Cursus Publicus.* (Diss.) Uppsala, 1933.

MICKWITZ, G. *Die Kartellfunktionen der Zünfte.* (Societas scientiarum Fennica: commentationes humanarum literarum, VIII, 3.) Helsinki, 1936.

PFLAUM, M. 'Essai sur le *cursus publicus* sous le Haut-Empire romain.' *Mém. présentés à l'Académie des Inscriptions et Belles-Lettres,* XIV (1940), 189–390.

SCHÖNBAUER, E. *Beiträge zur Geschichte des Bergbaurechts.* Münch. Beitr. z. Pap.-Forsch. u. ant. Rechtsgesch. XII. Munich, 1929.

STÖCKLE, A. *Spätrömische und byzantinische Zünfte.* Klio, Beih. 9. Leipzig, 1911.

TACKHOLM, U. *Studien über den Bergbau der römischen Kaiserzeit.* Uppsala, 1937.

WALTZING, J. P. *Étude historique sur les corporations professionelles chez les Romains depuis les origines jusqu'à la chute de l'Empire de l'Occident.* 4 vols. Louvain, 1895–1900.

4. PARTICULAR AREAS

AUBIN, H. 'Die wirtschaftliche Entwickelung römischen Deutschlands.' *Hist. Zeitsch.* CXLI (1930), I ff.

BENOIT, F. 'Un port fluvial de cabotage. Arles et l'ancienne marine à voile du Rhône.' *Ann. d'hist. soc.* II (1940), 199–206.

BOLIN, STURE. *Fynden av romerska mynt i det fria Germanien.* Lund, 1926.

BONNARD, L. *La navigation intérieure de la Gaule à l'époque gallo-romaine.* Paris, 1913.

BROGAN, O. 'Trade between the Roman Empire and free Germany.' *JRS.* XXVI (1936), 195–222.

CHENET, G. *Fouilles et documents d'archéol. antique en France, I. La céramique gallo-romaine d'Argonne du IVe siècle et la terre sigillée décorée à la molette.* Mâcon, 1941.

COLIN, J. *Les antiquités de la Rhénanie.* Paris, 1927.

COLLINGWOOD, R. G. *Roman Britain.* In Frank's *Economic survey of ancient Rome,* III. Baltimore, 1937.

—— (with J. N. L. MYRES). *Roman Britain and the English invasions,* 2nd ed. Oxford, 1937.

DOBSON, D. P. 'Roman influence in the North.' *Greece and Rome,* V (1936), 73 ff.

DRAGENDORFF, H. *Westdeutschland zur Römerzeit,* 2nd ed. Leipzig, 1919.

ECKHOLM, G. 'Zur Geschichte des römisch-germanischen Handels.' *Act. arch.* VI (1935), 49 ff.

FILLIOZAT, J. 'Les échanges de l'Inde et de l'empire romain aux premiers siècles de l'ère chrétienne.' *Rev. hist.* CCI (1949), 1–29.

FRANK, T. 'On the export tax of Spanish harbours.' *AJP.* LVII (1936), 87–90.

—— *Rome and Italy of the Empire,* in his *Economic survey of ancient Rome,* V. Baltimore, 1940.

GREN, E. *Kleinasien und der Ostbalkan in der wirtschaftlichen Entwicklung der römischen Kaiserzeit.* Uppsala-Leipzig, 1941.

GRENIER, A. *Manuel d'archéologie* (ed. Dechelette), V and VI: *Archéologie gallo-romaine.* Paris, 1931–4.

—— *La Gaule romaine.* In Frank's *Economic survey of ancient Rome,* III. Baltimore, 1937.

GUMMERUS, H. *Die südgallische Terrasigillata-industrie nach den Graffiti aus La Graufesenque.* (Comm. hum. lit. III.) Helsinki, 1932.

HAVERFIELD, F. and MACDONALD, G. *The Romanization of Roman Britain*, 4th ed. Oxford, 1923.

HAYWOOD, R. M. *Roman Africa*, in Frank's *Economic survey of ancient Rome*, IV. Baltimore, 1938.

HERTLEIN, F., PARET, O. and GOESSLER, P. *Die Römer in Württemberg.* 3 vols. Stuttgart, 1928–32.

JULLIAN, C. *Histoire de la Gaule*, VII and VIII. Paris, 1926.

KOEPP, F. *Die Römer in Deutschland*, 3rd ed. Bielefeld-Leipzig, 1926.

LAMBRECHTS, P. 'Le commerce des Syriens en Gaule.' *L'Antiquité classique*, VI (1937), 34–61.

—— 'Le commerce des Syriens en Gaule.' *Ant. class.* VI (1937), 34–61.

LEDROIT, J. *Die römische Schiffahrt im Stromgebiet des Rheines.* Kulturgeschichtlicher Wegweiser durch das röm.-germ. Zentralmuseum, no. 12. Mainz, 1930.

LOANE, H. J. *Industry and commerce of the city of Rome* (50 B.C.–A.D. 200). Baltimore, 1938.

PIGEONNEAU, H. 'L'annone romaine et les corps de naviculaires particulièrement en Afrique.' *Rev. de l'Afrique française*, IV (1886), 220–37.

RICKARD, T. A. 'The mining of the Romans in Spain.' *JRS*. XVIII (1928), 129–43.

SCHULZ, S. 'The Roman evacuation of Britain.' *JRS*. XXIII (1933), 36 ff.

SCHUMACHER, K. *Siedelungs- und Kulturgeschichte der Rheinlande.* Vol. II: *Die römische Periode.* Mainz, 1923.

SCRAMUZZA, V. *Roman Sicily.* In Frank's *Economic survey of ancient Rome*, III. Baltimore, 1937.

SELIGMAN, C. G. 'The Roman orient and the Far East.' *Antiquity*, XI (1937), 5–30.

SHERWIN-WHITE, A. N. 'Geographical factors in Roman Algeria.' *JRS*. XXXIV (1944), 1–10.

STAEHELIN, F. *Die Schweiz in römischer Zeit*, 3rd ed. Basle, 1948.

THOUVENOT, R. *Essai sur la province romaine de Bétique.* Paris, 1940.

VAN NOSTRAND, J. J. *Roman Spain.* In Frank's *Economic survey of ancient Rome*, III. Baltimore, 1937.

VAN SICKLE, C. E. 'The public works of Africa in the reign of Diocletian.' *Class. Phil.* XXV (1930), 173–9.

VERCAUTEREN, F. 'Notes sur la ruine des villes de la Gaule d'après quelques auteurs contemporains des invasions germaniques.' *Mélanges Bidez*, II (1934), 955–63.

WAGNER, F. *Die Römer in Bayern*, 4th ed. Munich, 1928.

WARMINGTON, E. H. *The commerce between the Roman Empire and India.* Cambridge, 1928.

WEST, L. C. *Imperial Roman Spain: the objects of trade.* Oxford, 1929.

—— *Roman Britain: the objects of trade.* Oxford, 1931.

—— *Roman Gaul: the objects of trade.* Oxford, 1935.

WILLERS, H. *Neue Untersuchungen über die römische Bronzeindustrie von Capua und von Nieder-Germanien.* Hanover-Leipzig, 1907.

WILSON, F. H. 'Studies in the social and economic history of Ostia.' *BSA*. XIII (1935), 41–68; XIV (1938), 152–62.

5 COINAGE AND FINANCE: TAXATION

BOAK, A. E. R. 'Early Byzantine tax receipts from Egypt' (on *adaeratio*). *Byzantion*, XVII (1944–5), 16–28.

BOLIN, S. 'Der solidus.' *Acta instituto Romani regni Sueciae*, ser. 2, I (1939). (Δραγμα Nilsson), 144 ff.

DÉLÉAGE, A. *La capitation du Bas-Empire.* Mâcon, 1945. (Cf. review by Piganiol, *Journ. des Savants* (1946), 128–39.)

DOPSCH, A. *Naturalwirtschaft und Geldwirtschaft in der Weltgeschichte.* Vienna, 1930.

GIESECKE, W. *Antikes Geldwesen.* Leipzig, 1938.

HEICHELHEIM, F. M. 'Zur Währungskrise des römischen Imperiums im 3. Jahrhundert n. Chr.' *Klio*, XXVI (1933), 96 ff.

—— 'New light on currency and inflation in Hellenistic and Roman times.' *Econ. Hist.* (*Suppl. to Econ. Journ.*), Feb. 1935.

KUBITSCHEK, W. 'Der Übergang von der vordiokletianischen Währung ins vierte Jahrhundert: Randbemerkungen zu Schriften von G. Mickwitz.' *Byzantinische Zeitsch.* XXXV (1935), 340 ff.

MATTINGLY, H. *Roman Coins*. London, 1928.

—— 'The monetary system of the Roman Empire to Theodosius I' (with full bibliography). *Num. Chron.* 6, VI (1946), 111–20.

MICKWITZ, G. *Geld und Wirtschaft im römischen Reich des IV. Jahrhunderts*. (Comm. hum. lit. IV, 2.) Helsinki, 1932.

—— 'Le problème de l'or dans le monde antique.' *Ann. d'hist. écon.* VI (1934), 239 ff.

—— *Die Systeme des römischen Silbergeldes im IV. Jahrhundert*. (Comm. hum. lit. VI, 2.) Helsinki, 1935.

—— 'Ueber die Kupfergeldinflationen in den Jahren der Thronkämpfe nach Diokletians Abdankung.' *Trans. Internat. Numism. Cong.* 1936 (Oxford, 1938), pp. 219 ff.

PASSERINI, A. 'Gli aumenti del soldo militare da Commodo a Massimino.' *Athenaeum*, N.S. XIV (1946), 145–59.

—— 'Sulla pretesa rivoluzione dei prezzi durante il regno di Commodo.' *Studi in onore di Gino Luzzatto* (Milan, 1949), 1–17.

PEARCE, J. W. E. 'The *vota*-legends on the Roman coinage.' *Num. Chron.* 5, XVII (1937), 112–23.

—— 'Gold coinage of the reign of Theodosius I.' *Num. Chron.* 5, XVIII (1938), 205–46.

PIGANIOL, A. 'Le problème de l'or au IVe siècle.' *Ann. d'hist. soc.* (1945), 47 ff.

—— 'La capitation de Dioclétien.' *Rev. hist.* CLXXVI (1935), 1–13.

SEDGWICK, W. B. 'The gold supply in ancient and mediaeval times, and its influence on history.' *Greece and Rome*, V (1936), 148 ff.

SEECK, O. 'Die Münzpolitik Diokletians u. seiner Nachfolger.' *Zeitsch. f. Numismatik*, XVII (1890), 63 ff.

SEGRÈ, A. *Metrologia e circolazione monetaria degli antichi*. Bologna, 1928.

—— 'Inflation and its implication in early Byzantine times.' *Byzantion*, XV (1940–1), 249–79.

—— 'The *annona civica* and the *annona militaris*.' *Byzantion*, XVI (1942–3), 393–444.

VAN BERCHEM, D. 'L'annone militaire.' *Mém. de la soc. nat. des antiq. de France*, LXXX (1937), 117–202.

WEST, L. C. 'The Roman gold standard and the ancient sources.' *AJP.* LXII (1941), 289–301.

Valuable material will be found in the following articles in the *Real-Encyclopädie der classischen Altertumswissenschaft* (ed. Pauly-Wissowa-Kroll-Ziegler): Adaeratio (Seeck), Berufsvereine (Suppl.-B. IV: Stöckle), *collatio lustralis* (Seeck), *collegium* (Kornemann), *colonatus* (Seeck), Domänen (Suppl.-B. IV: Kornemann), *fabri* (Kornemann), *fabricenses* (Seeck), *follis* (Seeck), *frumentum* (Rostovtzeff), Industrie u. Handel (Gummerus), Inflation (Suppl.-B. VI: Mickwitz), Kapitalismus (Sigwart), Monopol (Heichelheim), Münzkunde (Regling), *navicularii* (Sigwart), *siliqua* (Regling), Sklaverei (Suppl.-B. VI: Westermann).

CHAPTER III

Byzantine Trade and Industry

I. ORIGINAL SOURCES

Note. Relevant information can be obtained from all the Byzantine chroniclers and writers. See Bibliographies in the *Cambridge Medieval History*, vols. II and IV, and the *Cambridge Economic History*, vol. I, chap. V. Below are given sources particularly concerned with Byzantine trade and industry.

1. *Collections of Sources*

Corpus der Griechischen Urkunden des Mittelalters. Ed. F. Dölger. Munich/Berlin, 1924– (in progress).
Jus Graeco-Romanum. Ed. K. E. Zachariae von Lingenthal. 7 parts. Leipzig, 1856–84.
Jus Graeco-Romanum. Ed. J. and P. Zepos. 8 vols. Athens, 1931.
MIKLOSICH, F. and MULLER, J. *Acta et Diplomata Graeca Medii Aevi.* 6 vols. Vienna, 1860–90.
SATHAS, C. N. Μεσαιωνική Βιβλιοθήκη (Medieval Library). 6 vols. Venice, 1872.
TAFEL, G. L. F. and THOMAS, G. M. *Urkunden zur älteren Handels- und Staatsgeschichte der Republik Venedig mit besonderer Beziehung auf Byzanz und die Levante von 9ten bis zum Ausgang des 15ten Jahrh.* 3 parts in *Fontes Rerum Austriacarum*, 2nd sect., vols. XII–XIV. Vienna, 1856–7.

2. *Individual Sources*

BENJAMIN OF TUDELA. *Itinerary.* Ed. M. N. Adler. London, 1907.
CODINUS. *De Officialibus Palatii Constantinopolitani et de Officiis Magnae Ecclesiae.* Corpus Scriptorum Historiae Byzantinae. Bonn, 1839.
CONSTANTINE VII PORPHYROGENNETUS. *De Ceremoniis Aulae Byzantinae.* 2 vols. *De Thematibus et De Administrando Imperio.* 1 vol. Bonn, 1829–40.
COSMAS INDICOPLEUSTES. *Christian Topography.* Ed. O. Winstedt. London, 1909.
Ἐπαρχικὸν Βίβλιον: *Le Livre du Préfet.* Ed., with Latin transl., by J. Nicole. Geneva, 1893.
—— Ed. in English under title of *Roman Law in the Later Roman Empire*, by E. H. Freshfield. Cambridge, 1938.
LEO VI SAPIENS, *Les Nouvelles de Léon VI le Sage.* Ed. P. Noailles and A. Dain. Paris, 1944.
Timarion. Ed. Hase, in *Notes et Extraits*, vol. IX, 2me partie. Paris, 1813.

II. MODERN WORKS

ANDREADES, A. Ἱστορία τῆς Ἑλληνικῆς Δημοσίας Οἰκονομίας (History of Greek Political Economy). Athens, 1918.
—— 'Byzance, Paradis du Monopole et Privilège.' *Byzantion*, IX (1934), 171–81.
—— 'Deux Livres Récents sur les Finances Byzantines.' *Byzantinische Zeitschrift*, XXVIII (1928), 287–323.
BELAIEW, N. 'The Daric and the Zolotnic' (in Russian with English résumé). *Seminarium Kondakovianum*, IV (1931), 179–204.
BOISSONADE, P. *Le Travail dans l'Europe Chrétienne au Moyen Age.* Paris, 1921.
BRATIANU, G. I. *Recherches sur le Commerce Génois dans la Mer Noire au XII siècle.* Paris, 1929.
—— 'Une Expérience d'Economie Dirigée: Le Monopole du Blé à Byzance au XIe Siècle.' *Byzantion*, IX (1934), 643–62.
—— *Etudes Byzantines d'Histoire Economique et Sociale.* Paris, 1938.
—— *Privilèges et Franchises Municipales dans l'Empire Byzantin.* Paris/Bucharest, 1934.
BURY, J. B. *The Imperial Administrative System in the IXth Century.* London, 1911.

CICOTTI, E. *Il Tramonto della Schiavitù nel Mondo Antico*. Turin, 1899.

DIETERICH, K. 'Zur Kulturgeographie und Kulturgeschichte der Byzantinischen Balkanshandels.' *Byzantinische Zeitschrift*, XXXI (1931), 37–57, 334–49.

DÖLGER, F. *Beiträge zur Geschichte der byzantinischen Finanzverwaltung, Byzantinische Archiv*, IX. Leipzig/Berlin, 1927.

—— 'Das Ἀερικόν.' *Byzantinische Zeitschrift*, XXX (1929–30), 450–7.

EBERSOLT, J. *Constantinople Byzantine et les Voyageurs du Levant*. Paris, 1919.

—— *Les Arts Somptuaires de Byzance*. Paris, 1923.

HEYD, W. *Histoire du Commerce du Levant*. 2 vols. (rev. ed. in French). Leipzig, 1936.

JEANSELME, E. and OECONOMOS, L. *Les Œuvres d'Assistance et les Hopitaux Byzantins*. Antwerp, 1921.

LOMBARD, M. 'L'Or Musalman du VIIe au XIe siécle.' *Annales: Economies, Sociétés, Civilisations*, No. 2 (1947).

LOPEZ, R. S. 'Mohammed and Charlemagne, a Revision.' *Speculum*, XVIII (1943), 14–39.

—— 'Silk Industry in the Byzantine Empire.' *Speculum*, XX (1945), 1–43.

MACRI, C. M. *L'Organisation de l'Economie Urbaine dans Byzance*. Paris, 1925.

MICKWITZ, G. *Geld und Wirtschaft im römischen Reich des 4ten Jahrh.* Helsinki, 1932.

—— 'Byzance et l'Occident Mediévale.' *Annales d'Histoire Economique et Sociale*, VIII (1936).

MILLET, G. 'Sur les Sceaux des Commerciaires Byzantins.' *Mélanges G. Schlumberger*. Paris, 1924.

MONNIER, H. *Les Nouvelles de Léon le Sage*. Bordeaux, 1923.

OSTROGORSKY, G. 'Lohne und Preise in Byzanz.' *Byzantinische Zeitschrift*, XXXII (1932), 293–333.

SEGRE, A. 'Inflation and its Implication in Early Byzantine Times.' *Byzantion*, XV (1941), 249–80.

—— 'Essays on Byzantine Economic History.' *Byzantion*, XVI (1942–3), 393–445.

SOUTZO, M. 'Les Origines du Sesterce et du Miliarense et leur Continuité jusqu'au Temps Byzantins.' Académie Roumaine, *Bulletin de la Section Historique*, XIII (1927), 54–9.

SPULBER, C. A. *L'Eclogue des Isauriens*. Cernauti, 1934.

STARR, J. *The Jews in the Byzantine Empire*. Athens, 1939.

STEIN, E. *Studien zur Geschichte des byzantinischen Reiches*. Stuttgart, 1919.

STÖCKLE, A. *Spätrömische und byzantinische Zünfte*. Klio, vol. IX. Leipzig, 1911.

TAFRALI, O. *Thessalonique au Quatorzième Siècle*. Paris, 1913.

—— *Thessalonique des Origines au XIVme Siècle*. Paris, 1919.

VASILIEV, A. A. 'Economic Relations between Byzantium and Russia.' *Journal of Economic and Business History*, IV, 2 (1932), 314–34.

VASILIEVSKY, V. 'Material for the Internal History of the Byzantine Empire' (in Russian). *Journal of the Russian Ministry of Public Instruction*, CCII (1879), 160–232, 368–438; CCX (1880), 98–170, 355–440.

WALTZING, J. P. *Etude Historique sur les Corporations Professionelles chez les Romains*. 4 vols. Louvain, 1895–1900.

ZACHARIAE VON LINGENTHAL, K. E. *Geschichte des griechisch-römischen Rechts*. Berlin, 1892.

ZAKYNTHINOS, D. 'Crise Monétaire et Crise Economique à Byzance du XIIIme au XVme Siècle.' *L'Hellénisme Contemporain*, I, 2 (1947), 162–92; II, 2 (1948), 150–67.

ZOPAS, G. *Le Corporazioni Bizantini*. Rome, 1933.

CHAPTER IV

The Trade of Medieval Europe: the North

I. Printed Sources

FAGNIEZ, G. *Documents relatifs à l'histoire de l'industrie et du commerce en France (au moyen âge)*. 2 vols. Paris, 1898, 1900.

GREGORY OF TOURS. *The History of the Franks*, I and II (transl. by O. M. Dalton). Oxford, 1927.

HÖLBAUM, K., KUNZE, K. and STEIN, W. *Hansisches Urkundenbuch*. Verein für Hansische Geschichte. Halle and Leipzig, 1876–1907.

KOPPMANN, K. *Die Recesse und Andere Akten der Hansetäge, von 1236–1340*, I–VIII. Die Historische Kommission bei der Königl. Akad. der Wissenschaften. Leipzig, 1870–97.

KUNZE, K. *Hanseakten aus England, 1275 bis 1412*. *Hansische Geschichtsquellen*, VI. Verein für Hansische Geschichte. Halle, 1891.

KUSKE, B. *Quellen zur Geschichte des Kölner Handels und Verkehrs im Mittelalter*. 3 vols. Gesellschaft für Rheinische Geschichtskunde. Bonn, 1918–23.

LANGE, C. C. A., UNGER, C. R. and others. *Diplomatarium Norvegicum*, vols. I ff. Oslo, 1847, etc.

LAPPO-DANILEVSKY, N. *Recueil des documents relatifs à l'histoire de la Neva*. Petrograd, 1916. (Edition of the Imperial Academy of Sciences.)

LECHNER, G. *Die Hansischen Pfundzollisten des Jahres 1368*. Quellen z. Hansisch. Gesch., N.F. vol. X. Lübeck, 1935.

NEALE, E. W. W. *The Great Red Book of Bristol*. Text (pt. I). Bristol Record Society's Publications, vol. IV, 1937.

POELMAN, H. A. *Bronnen tot de Geschiedenis van den Oostzeehandel*, I. Rijks Geschiedenkundige Publicatiën. The Hague, 1917.

POSTHUMUS, N. W. *Bronnen tot de Geschiedenis van de Leidsche Textielnijverheid, 1333–1795*. Rijks Geschiedenkundige Publicatiën. The Hague, 1910–22.

ROPP, G. VON DER. *Hanserecesse 1431–76*. Zweite Abteilung, I–VII. Verein für Hansische Geschichte. Leipzig, 1876–92.

SEVEREN, L. GILLIODTS-VAN (ed.). *Cartulaire de l'ancienne Estaple de Bruges*. 4 vols. Société d'Emulation, Bruges, 1904–6.

SMIT, H. J. *Bronnen tot de Geschiedenis van den handel met Engeland, Schotland en Ierland, 1150–1485*. Rijks Geschiedenkundige Publicatiën. The Hague, 1928.

SNELLER, Z. W. and UNGER, W. S. *Bronnen tot de Geschiedenis van den handel met Frankrijk*, I. Rijks Geschiedenkundige Publicatiën. The Hague, 1930.

THOMAS, A. H. *Calendar of Early Mayor's Court Rolls of the City of London, 1298–1307*. Cambridge, 1924.

—— *Calendar of Plea and Memoranda Rolls of the City of London*. 2 vols., 1323–64, 1364–81. Cambridge, 1926, 1929.

—— *Calendar of Select Pleas and Memoranda of the City of London, 1381–1412*. Cambridge, 1932.

UNGER, W. S. *De Tol van Iersekeroord: documenten en rekeningen, 1321–1572*. The Hague, 1939.

—— *Bronnen tot de Geschiedenis van Meddelburg in het landsheerlijken tijd*. Rijks Geschiedenkundige Publicatiën. The Hague, 1923.

WARNER, G. (ed.). *The Libelle of Englyshe Polycye*. Oxford, 1926.

II. Secondary Authorities

ABEL, W. 'Bevölkerungsgang und Landwirtschaft im Ausgehenden Mittelalter in Lichte der Preis- und Lohnbewegung.' *Schmoller's Jahrbücher*, 58 Jahrg., 1934.

—— *Agrarkrisen und Agrarkonjunktur im Mitteleuropa*. Berlin, 1935.

—— *Die Wüstungen des ausgehenden Mittelalters*. Jena, 1943.

AGATS, A. *Der Hansische Baienhandel.* Heidelberg, 1904.

ARENS, FRANZ. 'Wilhelm Servat von Cahors zu London.' *Vierteljahrsch. für Sozial- und Wirtschaftsgesch.* 1904.

ARUP, E. *Studier i Engelsk og Tysk Handels Histoire, etc.* 1350–1850. Copenhagen, 1907.

AVENEL, G. DE. *Histoire économique de la propriété, des salaires, des denrées et de tous les prix.* 6 vols. Paris, 1886–1920.

BÄCHTOLD, H. *Der Norddeutsche Handel im 12. und beginnenden 13. Jahrhundert.* Abhandlungen zur mittleren und neuen Geschichte, hrsg. von G. v. Below, H. Finke und F. Meinecke, Heft. 21. Berlin and Leipzig, 1910.

BAHR, C. *Handel und Verkehr der deutschen Hanse in Flandern während des vierzehnten Jahrhunderts.* Leipzig, 1911.

BAKER, J. L. N. *Medieval Trade Routes.* Historical Association Pamphlet, no. 111. 1938.

BEARDWOOD, ALICE. *Alien Merchants in England 1350–1377. Their Legal and Economic Position.* Cambridge (Mass.), 1931.

BECK, L. *Die Geschichte des Eisens.* 4 vols. Brunswick, 1891–9.

BELOCH, J. 'Die Bevölkerung Europas im Mittelalter.' *Zeitschrift für Sozial- und Wirtschaftsgesch.* III, 405. Freiburg i. B., 1894.

BELOW, G. VON. *Aus Sozial- und Wirtschaftsgeschichte.* Stuttgart, 1928.

—— *Probleme der Wirtschaftsgeschichte.* Tübingen, 1920.

BENS, G. *Der deutsche Warenfernhandel im Mittelalter.* Breslau, 1926.

BEVERIDGE, W. 'Wages in the Winchester Manors.' *Econ. Hist. Rev.* (1936), VII, no. 1.

—— 'Yield and Price of Corn in the Middle Ages.' *Economic History* (Suppl. to *Econ. Journ.*), no. 2 (1927).

BIGWOOD, G. 'Les Financiers d'Arras.' *Revue Belge de Philologie et d'Histoire*, 1924.

—— 'La Politique de la Laine en France sous les règnes de Phillipe le Bel et de ses fils.' *Revue Belge de Philologie et d'Histoire*, 1936.

BLOCH, M. 'Le Problème de l'Or au Moyen Age.' *Annales d'Histoire Sociale et Economique*, 1933.

BLOCKMANS, FR. *Het Gentsche Stadspatriciaat tot Omstreeks 1302.* Antwerp, 1938.

BOUQUELOT, G. *Les foires de Champagne.* 2 vols. Mémoires d'Académie des Sciences et Belles Lettres. Paris, 1938.

BOUTRUCHE, R. *La Crise d'une Société: Seigneurs et Paysans du Bordelais pendant la Guerre de Cent Ans.* Paris, 1947.

BOUVIER, R. *Un Financier Colonial au XV Siècle. Jacques Cœur.* Paris, 1928.

BOYER, H. *Histoire de l'industrie et du commerce à Bourges.* Bourges, 1884.

BRUNS, F. (ed.). *Die Lübecker Bergenfahrer und ihre Chronistik.* Hansische Geschichtsquellen, N.F., Bd. II. Verein für Hansische Geschichte. Berlin, 1900.

BUCHER, K. *Die Entstehung der Volkswirtschaft.* 2 vols. Leipzig, 1920.

BUGGE, A. *Den Norske Traelasthandels Historie*, I. Skien, 1925.

—— 'Handelen mellem England og Norge indtil Begyndelsen af det 15de Aarhundrede.' *Historisk Tidskrift*, Raekke III, Bind 4, pp. 1–149. Oslo, 1898.

—— 'Die nordeuropäischen Verkehrswege im früheren Mittelalter.' *Vierteljahrsch. f. Sozial- u. Wirtschaftsgesch.* IV (1906).

—— 'Der Untergang der Norwegischen Seeschiffahrt.' *Vierteljahrsch. f. Sozial- u. Wirtschaftsgesch.* 1904.

CARUS-WILSON, E. M. (ed.). *The Overseas Trade of Bristol in the later Middle Ages.* Bristol Record Society's Publications, VII (1936).

CARUS-WILSON, E. M. 'Trends in the Export of English Woollens in the Fourteenth Century.' *Econ. Hist. Rev.* III, 1950.

DAENELL, E. R. *Die Blütezeit der deutschen Hanse. Hansische Geschichte von der zweiten Hälfte des XIV. bis zum letzten Viertel des XV. Jahrhunderts.* 2 vols. Berlin, 1905–6.

DEROISY, ARMAND. 'Les Routes Terrestres de laines Anglais vers la Lombardie.' *Revue du Nord*, XXV (1939).

DES MAREZ, G. *Etudes sur la Propriété Foncière dans les villes du Moyen Age et spécialement au Flandre.* Université de Gand. Recueil des travaux publiés par la Faculté de Philosophie et Lettres, 1898.

DION, R. 'Orléans et l'ancienne navigation de la Loire.' *Annales de Géographie*, XLVII, 1938.

DOPSCH, A. *Economic and Social Foundations of European Civilisation.* (Transl.) London, 1937.
—— *Die Wirtschaftsentwicklung der Karolinger Zeit.* 2 vols., 2nd ed. Weimar, 1922.
EBEL, W. 'Das Rostocker Transportgewerbe.' *Vierteljahrsch. für Sozial- und Wirtschaftsgesch.* 1938.
ECK, A. *Le Moyen Age Russe.* Paris, 1933.
ESPINAS, G. *La Vie Urbaine de Douai au Moyen-Age,* I–IV. Paris, 1914.
—— *Les Origines du Capitalisme.* 2 vols. Lille, 1933, 1936.
FEAVERYEAR, A. E. *The Pound Sterling.* Oxford, 1931.
FLOWER C. T. *Public Works in Medieval Law,* I and II. Selden Society Publications, 1923.
DE FREVILLE. *Mémoires sur la commerce maritime de Rouen.* 2 vols. Rouen and Paris, 1857.
GILLIARD, CH. 'L'Ouverture du St Gothard.' *Annales d'Histoire Economique et Sociale,* 1929.
GIRY, A. *Histoire de la Ville de Saint-Omer.* Paris, 1877.
GOETZ, L. K. *Deutsch-Russische Handelsgeschichte des Mittelalters.* Hansische Geschichtsquellen, N.F., Bd. v. Lübeck, 1922.
GRAS, N. S. B. *The English Customs System.* Cambridge (Mass.), 1918.
—— *The Evolution of the English Corn Market.* Cambridge (Mass.), 1915.
GRAY, H. L. 'The Production and Exportation of English Woollens in the Fourteenth Century.' *Eng. Hist. Rev.* XXXIX (1924), 13–35.
GRIERSON, P. 'The Relations between England and Flanders before the Norman Conquest.' *Trans. Roy. Hist. Soc.,* 4th ser., XXIII (1941).
GUIRAUD, L. *Recherches et conclusions nouvelles sur le prétendu rôle de Jacques Cœur.* Paris, 1900.
HÄNSELMAN, L. 'Braunschweig in seinen Beziehungen zu den Harz- und Seegebieten.' *Hansische Geschichtsblätter,* 1873.
HAPKE, R. *Brugges Entwicklung zum Mittelalterlichen Weltmarkt.* D. Schaffer's Abhandlungen zur Verkehrs- und Seegeschichte, no. 1. Berlin, 1908.
—— *Der Deutsche Kaufmann in Niederlanden.* Hansische Pfingsblätter, no. 7. Lübeck, 1911.
—— *Der Untergang der Hanse.* Lübeck, 1923.
HARTWICH, C. *Die menschlichen Genussmittel.* Leipzig, 1911.
HAYEM, J. *Mémoires et Documents pour servir à l'Histoire du Commerce et de l'Industrie en France.* Paris, 1922.
HENAUX, F. *Fabrique d'armes de Liège.* Liège, 1858.
HEWITT, H. J. *Medieval Cheshire.* Manchester, 1929.
HIRSCH, T. *Danzigs Handels- und Gewerbsgeschichte unter der Herrschaft des deutschen Ordens.* Leipzig, 1858.
HOOPT, C. G. 'T. *Het ontstaan van Amsterdam.* Amsterdam, 1917.
HUVELIN, P. *Essai historique sur le droit des marchés et des foires.* Paris, 1897.
IMBERTIN, F. 'Les Routes Mediévales.' *Annales d'Histoire Economique et Sociale,* 1939.
INAMA-STERNEGG, K. T. VON. *Deutsche Wirtschaftsgeschichte.* 3 vols. Leipzig, 1899.
JASTROW, IGNAZ. 'Über Welthandelstrassen in d. Geschichte d. Abendlandes.' *Volkswirtschaftliche Gesellschaft, Volkswirtschaftl. Fragen,* Jahrg. VIII. Berlin, 1887.
JENKINSON, H. 'A Money-lender's Bonds of the Twelfth Century.' Lane Poole, *Essays in History,* 1927.
JOHNSEN, O. ALBERT. *Norgesveldets Undergang, et Utsyn og et Opgjør Nedgangstiden.* Oslo, 1924.
JULLIAN, C. *Histoire de Bordeaux depuis les origines jusqu'en 1895.* Bordeaux, 1895.
KENDRICK, T. D. *A History of the Vikings.* London, 1930.
KETNER, F. *Handel en Scheepvaart van Amsterdam in de Vijftiende Eeuw.* The Hague, 1936.
KEYSER, E. 'Der bürgerliche Grundbesitz der Rechtsstadt Danzig im 14. Jahrhundert.' *Zeitschrift d. Westpreusischen Geschichtsverein,* Heft LVIII (1918).
KIESSELBACH, G. A. 'Schleswig als Vermittlerin des Handels zwischen Nordsee und Ostsee vom 9. bis in das 13. Jahrhundert.' *Zeitschrift für Schleswig-Holsteinischen Lauenburgische Gesch.* 1907.

KLETTLER, P. *Nordwesteuropas Verkehr, Handel und Gewerbe im frühen Mittelalter.* Deutsches Kultur, Historische Reihe, geleitet von A. Dopsch. Vienna, 1924.

KÖSTER, G. 'Die Entwicklung der nordostdeutschen Verkehrstrassen bis 1800.' *Forschungen zur Brandenburgischen und Preussischen Gesch.* Bd. 48 (1936).

KOSTER, A. *Schiffahrt und Handelsverkehr des Östlichen Mittelmeeres.* Leipzig, 1924.

KOWALEWSKY, M. *Die ökonomische Entwicklung Europas bis zum Beginn der kapitalistischen Wirtschaftsform.* 8 vols. Berlin, 1901–14.

KROCKER, E. *Handelsgeschichte der Stadt Leipzig. Die Entwicklung des Leipziger Handels und der Leipziger Messen.* Vol. VII of von Schulte's and Hoffmann's *Beiträge zur Stadtgeschichte.*

KULISCHER, J. *Allgemeine Wirtschaftsgeschichte.* Berlin, 1928.

—— *Russische Wirtschaftsgeschichte,* I. Jena, 1925.

LAMPRECHT, K. *Beiträge zur Geschichte des Französischen Wirtschaftslebens im XI. Jahrhundert.* Leipzig, 1878.

LAPSLEY, G. T. 'The Account Roll of a Fifteenth-Century Iron Master.' *Eng. Hist. Rev.* XIV, 1899.

LAUFFER, V. 'Danzigs Schiffs- und Waarenverkehr.' *Zeitschr. d. Westpreussischen Geschichtsvereins,* Heft XXXIII. Danzig, 1894.

LAURENT, H. *Un grand commerce d'exportation au moyen âge: La draperie des Pays Bas en France et dans les Pays Mediterranéens, XII–XVe siècle.* Paris, 1935.

—— *Choix de documents inédits pour servir à l'histoire de l'expansion commerciale des Pays-Bas en France au Moyen Age* (XIIe–XVe siècle). Brussels, 1934.

—— 'Marchands du palais et marchands d'abbayes.' *Revue Historique,* CLXXXIII, 1938.

LESTOCQUOY, J. *Les Dynasties Bourgeoises d'Arras du XIe au XVe siècle* (*Patriciens du Moyen-âge*). Arras, 1945.

—— 'Les Etapes du développement urbain d'Arras.' *Revue Belge de Philologie et d'Histoire,* 1944.

LEVASSEUR, E. *Histoire du commerce de la France,* I. Paris, 1910. *Histoire des classes ouvrières et de l'industrie en France avant 1789.* 2nd ed. Paris, 1901.

—— *Histoire de la population française avant 1789....* 3 vols. Paris, 1889–92.

LEWIS, G. R. *The Stannaries, a study of the English tin mines.* Cambridge (Mass.), 1908.

LOMBARD, M. 'L'Or Musalman du VIIe au XIe siècle.' *Annales: Economies, Sociétés, Civilisations,* no. 2 (1947).

LOT, F. *L'état des paroisses et des feux de 1328.* Paris, 1929.

LOT, F. and FAWTIER, R. *Le premier budget de la monarchie française* (1202). Paris, 1932.

LUNT, W. E. *Financial Relations of the Papacy with England to 1327.* Cambridge (Mass.), 1939.

LUZATTO, G. *Storia del Commerzio.* Florence, 1914.

MAGNUSEN, F. 'Om de Engelskes Handel og Foerd paa Island i det 15de Aarhundrede.' *Nordisk Tidskrift for Oldkyndighed,* II. Copenhagen, 1833.

MALOWIST, M. 'Le développement des rapports économiques entre la Flandre, la Pologne et les Pays Limitrophes du XIIIe au XIVe siecle.' *Revue Belge de Philologie et d'Histoire.* X, 1931.

MARQUANT, R. *La vie économique à Lille sous Philippe le Bon.* Paris, 1940.

MICKWITZ, G. *Die Kartellfunktionen der Zünfte.* Helsingfors, 1936.

MOERMAN, H. J. 'Bijdragen tot de Economische Geschiedenis van Kampen in de Middeleuwen.' *Economisch Historisch Jaarboek,* 1920.

NAUDE, W. *Getreidehandelspolitik der europäischen Staaten, XIII.–XVIII. Jahr.* Berlin, 1901.

NEF, J. U. 'Silver Production in Central Europe, 1450–1618.' *Journal of Political Econ.* XLIX, 1941.

NETTA, GHERON. *Die Handelsbeziehungen zwischen Leipzig und Ost- und Südosteuropa bis zum Verfall der Warenmessen.* Zurich, 1920.

NEUBURG, C. *Goslars Bergbau bis 1552.* Hanover, 1872.

NEUMANN, G. *Heinrich Castorp.* Lübeck, 1932.

NIERMEYER, J. F. *De Wording van onze Volkshuishouding.* The Hague, 1946.

Nöe, Albert. *De Handel van Noord-Nederland op Engeland in de XIIIe Eeuw.* Haarlem, 1918.

Ochenkowski, W. von. *Englands wirtschaftliche Entwickelung im Ausgange des Mittelalters.* Jena, 1879.

Pigeonneau, H. *Histoire du Commerce de la France.* I. Paris, 1885.

Pirenne, H. *Histoire de Belgique,* vol. I, 5th ed. Brussels, 1929 and vol. II, 3rd ed., Brussels, 1922.

—— *Medieval Cities. Their Origins and the Revival of Trade.* Princeton, 1925.

—— *Mahomet et Charlemagne.* Paris, 1937.

—— 'Un Contraste économique: Mérovingiens et Carolingiens.' *Revue Belge de Philologie et d'Histoire,* II (1923).

—— 'Les Périodes de l'histoire sociale du capitalisme.' *Bulletins d'Académie Royale de Belgique,* no. 5 (1914).

Posthumus, N. W. *De Geschiedenis van de Leidsche Lakenindustrie,* I. The Hague, 1908.

Power, E. E. 'The English Wool Trade in the reign of Edward IV.' *Camb. Hist. Journ.* II. Cambridge, 1926.

—— *The Wool Trade in English Medieval History.* Oxford, 1941.

Power, E. E. and Postan, M. M. *Studies in English Trade in the Fifteenth Century.* London, 1933.

Püschel, A. *Das Anwachsen der deutschen Städte in der Zeit der mittelalterlichen Kolonialbewegung.* Berlin, 1910.

Renouard, Yves. *Les Hommes d'Affaires Italiens du Moyen Age.* Paris, 1949.

Reyer, E. *Zinn: eine geologisch-montanistisch-historische Monographie.* Berlin, 1881.

Reynolds, R. L. 'The Market for Northern Textiles in Genoa, 1179–1200.' *Revue Belge de Philologie et d'Histoire,* VIII (1929).

—— 'Merchants of Arras and the Overland Trade with Genoa, XIIth Century,' *ibid.* IX (1930).

Rhodes, W. E. *The Italian bankers in England and their loans to Edward I and Edward II.* In Owens College Essays (eds. T. F. Tout and J. Tait). Manchester, 1902.

Rogers, J. E. Thorold. *A History of Agriculture and Prices in England.* Oxford, 1866–1902.

Rörig, F. *Hansische Beiträge zur Deutschen Wirtschaftsgeschichte.* Breslau, 1928.

—— *Der Markt von Lübeck. Topographisch-statistische Untersuchung zur deutschen Sozial- und Wirtschaftsgeschichte.* Leipzig, 1922.

—— *Mittelalterliche Weltwirtschaft.* Jena, 1933.

Ruding, R. *Annals of the Coinage of Great Britain.* London, 1840.

Ruinen, J. *De Oudste Handelsbetrekkingen van Holland en Zeeland met Engeland.* (Dissertation.) Amsterdam, 1919.

Russell, J. C. *British Medieval Population.* Albuquerque, 1948.

Rutkowski, J. *Histoire économique de la Pologne avant les partages.* Paris, 1927.

Sabbe, E. 'L'importation des tissus orientaux.' *Revue Belge de Philologie et d'Histoire,* 1935.

Salzman, L. F. *English Trade in the Middle Ages.* Oxford, 1931.

Sapori, A. *Studi di Storia Economica Medievale.* Florence, 1947.

—— *La Crisi delle Compagnie Mercantili dei Bardi e dei Peruzzi.* Florence, 1926.

Schäfer, D. *Die Hanse.* Monographien zur Weltgeschichte, no. XIX. Bielefeld and Leipzig, 1903.

—— *Das Buch des Lübeckschen Vogts auf Schonen.* Hansische Geschichtsquellen, IV. Halle, 1887.

Schanz, G. *Englische Handelspolitik gegen Ende des Mittelalters, mit besonderer Berücksichtigung des Zeitalters der beiden ersten Tudors, Heinrich VII und Heinrich VIII.* 2 vols. Leipzig, 1881.

Scheffel, P. H. *Verkehrsgeschichte der Alpen.* 2 vols. Berlin, 1908–1914.

Schreiner, J. *Pest og Prisfall i Senmiddelalderen.* Oslo, 1948.

Schulte, A. *Geschichte der grossen Ravensburger Handelsgesellschaft.* 3 vols. Stuttgart and Berlin, 1923.

SCHULZ, F. *Die Hanse und England von Edwards III bis auf Heinrichs VIII Zeit*. Abhandlungen zur Verkehrs- und Seegeschichte, v. (Ed. D. Schäfer.) Berlin, 1911.

SÉE, H. 'Peut-on évaluer la population de l'ancienne France?' *Revue d'économie politique*. Paris, 1924.

SEEGER, H.-J. *Westfalens Handel und Gewerbe*. Studien zur Geschichte der Wirtschaft und Geisteskultur. Bd. I. Berlin, 1926.

SMIT, H. J. 'De betekenis van den Noordnederlandschen in 't bijzonders van den Hollandschen en Zeeuwschen handel in de laatste helft der 14er eeuw.' *Bijdragen en Mededeelingen van het Historisch Genootschap*. Utrecht, 1930.

—— 'Handel en Scheepvaart in het Noordzeegebied gedurende de 13e eeuw.' *Bijdragen voor Vaderlandsche Geschiedenis en Oudheidkunde* (1928).

SNELLER, Z. W. 'De Hollandsche Korenhandel in het Sommegebied in de 15e eeuw.' *Bijdragen en Mededeelingen van het Historisch Genootschap*, 1925.

—— 'De entwikkeling van den handel tusschen Noord-Nederland en Frankrijk tot het midden der vijfteinden eeuw.' *Bijdragen en Mededeelingen van het Historisch Genootschap*, 1922.

—— 'Wijnvaart en wijnhandel tusschen Frankrijk en de Noordelijke Nederlanden in de tweede helft der 15e eeuw.' *Bijdragen en Mededeelingen van het Historisch Genootschap*, 1924.

SÖDERBERG, T. *Storra Kopparberget ander Medeltiden*. Stockholm, 1932.

—— 'Det Svenska Bergsbrukets uppkomst.' *Historisk Tidskrift*, 1936.

SOMBART, W. *Der moderne Kapitalismus*, 3rd ed., I. Munich and Leipzig, 1913.

STEIN, W. 'Die Hanse und England beim Ausgang des hundert-jährigen Krieges.' *Hansische Geschichtsblätter*, Bd. XXVI (1921), 27–126.

STEINHAUSEN, G. *Der Kaufmann in der deutschen Vergangenheit*. Jena, 1912.

STERCK, J. F. M. 'De opkomst van Aemstelredam godsdienstig en economik.' *Tijdschrift voor Geschiedenis*, 1926.

STIEDA, W. *Hildebrand Veckinchusen*. Leipzig, 1921.

—— 'Über die Quellen der Handelsstatistik im Mittelalter.' *Abhandlungen d. Königl. Preussischen Akad. der Wissenschaften*, 1903.

STURLER, J. DE. *Les Relations politiques et les échanges commerciaux entre le Duché de Brabant et l'Angleterre au moyen âge*. Paris, 1936.

SWANK, J. M. *History of the Manufacture of Iron in All Ages*. Philadelphia, 1892.

TYLER, J. E. *The Alpine Passes*. Oxford, 1930.

UNGER, W. S. 'De Hollandsche graanhandel en graanhandelspolitiek in de middeleeuwen.' *De Economist* (1916).

UNWIN, G. (ed.). *Finance and Trade under Edward III*. Manchester, 1918.

—— *The Gilds and Companies of London*. The Antiquary's Books, ed. J. C. Cox, 1908.

—— *Studies in Economic History* (Collected Papers), 1927.

USHER, A. P. *The History of the Grain Trade in France*. Cambridge (Mass.), 1913.

VERCAUTEREN, F. *Etude sur les Civitates de la Belgique Seconde*. Brussels, 1934.

VOGEL, W. *Geschichte der deutschen Seeschiffahrt*, I. *Von der Urzeit bis zum Ende des XV. Jahrhunderts*. Berlin, 1915.

—— 'Ein seefahrender Kaufmann um 1100.' *Hansische Geschichtsblätter*, 1912.

VOLLBEHR, F. *Die Holländer und die deutsche Hanse*. Jena, 1930.

WALSH, A. *Scandinavian Relations with Ireland during the Viking Period*. Dublin and London, 1922.

WERVEKE, H. VAN. 'Der Flandrische Eigenhandel in Mittelalter.' *Hansische Geschichtsblätter*, 1935.

—— 'Monnaie, lingots et marchandises.' *Annales d'Histoire Economique et Sociale*, 1932.

—— 'Currency Manipulation in the Middle Ages: The Case of Louis de Male, Count of Flanders.' *Trans. Roy. Hist. Soc.* ser. 4, XXXI (1949).

—— 'Essor et déclin de la Flandre.' *Studi in onore di Gino Luzzatto*. Milan, 1949.

WILLARD, J. F. *Parliamentary Taxes on personal property 1290–1334*.' Cambridge (Mass.), 1934.

—— 'Inland Transportation in England during the Fourteenth Century.' *Speculum*, I. 1926.

ZYCHA, A. *Das Recht des ältesten deutschen Bergbaues bis ins 13. Jahrhundert*. Berlin, 1899.

CHAPTER V

The Trade of Medieval Europe: the South

The following bibliography does not cover all the evidence used in the text—some details were drawn directly from the sources, both printed and unprinted—and it includes a few important works which the author has been unable to obtain. It lists only a few essays on industry and guilds, on banking, money, mining, rural economy, demography business theory and practices and other topics which are covered more fully in other chapters. Works on numismatics and on the Crusades are too numerous for quoting; special bibliographies furnish adequate information. But a large number of strictly local monographs has been included, because information on local history is particularly hard to obtain. The standards in choosing have been dictated chiefly, though not exclusively, by the amount of groundwork made so far in each region. Muslim trade is practically an unexplored field, and wide unmapped areas remain in central France and Spain; but most towns and regions in northern and central Italy, Mediterranean France, Switzerland and Danubian Germany have formed the subject of a large number of good monographs, not all of which could be listed. It must be pointed out, in addition, that the best of the general histories often illuminate trade better than do the less satisfactory of the works of commercial history.

The following abbreviations have been used:

AHDE.	Anuario de Historia del Derecho Español
AHES.	Annales d'Histoire Economique et Sociale, later Annales d'His toire Sociale, Mélanges d'Histoire Sociale, Annales (Econo-mies, Sociétés, Civilisations)
AHR.	American Historical Review
ASI.	Archivio Storico Italiano
ASLi.	Atti della Società Ligure di Storia Patria.
ASLo.	Archivio Storico Lombardo
AV.	Archivio Veneto
BSBS.	Bollettino Storico-Bibliografico Subalpino
EcHR.	Economic History Review
GSLL.	Giornale Storico e Letterario della Liguria
JEBH.	Journal of Economic and Business History.
JEH.	Journal of Economic History
JNOS.	Jahrbücher für Nationalökonomie und Statistik
NAV.	Nuovo Archivio Veneto
NRS.	Nuova Rivista Storica
RB.	Revue Belge de Philologie et d'Histoire
RDC.	Rivista di Diritto Commerciale
RH.	Revue Historique
RHES.	Revue d'Histoire Economique et Sociale
RSE.	Rivista di Storia Economica
VSWG.	Vierteljahrschrift für Sozial- und Wirtschaftsgeschichte.

The author wishes to express his indebtedness for assistance to Professors Eugene H. Byrne, Gino Luzzatto, Irving Raymond and Florence and Raymond de Roover.

I. GENERAL WORKS; SINGLE NATIONS

ANGELESCU, I. N. *Histoire économique des Roumains*, I. Geneva, 1919.

AZEVEDO, J. L. DE. *Epocas de Portugal económico*. Lisbon, 1929.

BALLESTEROS Y BERETTA, A. *Historia de España y de su influencia en la historia universal*, II and III. Barcelona, 1919–29.

BARBAGALLO, C. *Storia Universale, Il Medioevo*. 2 vols. Turin, 1935.

BOISSONNADE, P. *Life and Work in Medieval Europe.* (Engl. transl.) London, 1927.

CARLI, F. *Storia del Commercio Italiano (Il mercato nell'alto medio evo; Il mercato nell'età del Comune).* 2 vols. Padua, 1934–6.

CARO, G. *Sozial- und Wirtschaftsgeschichte der Juden.* 2 vols., 2nd ed. Frankfurt-am-Main, 1924.

COLMEIRO, M. *Historia de la economia política en España.* 2 vols. Madrid, 1863.

DIETZE, H. *Geschichte des deutschen Handels.* Leipzig, 1923.

DOMANOVSKY, A. *Geschichte Ungarns.* Munich, 1923.

DOREN, A. *Wirtschaftsgeschichte Italiens im Mittelalter.* Jena, 1934. (Ital. transl., with additional bibliogr.: Padua, 1937.)

GEERING, T. *Grundzüge einer schweizerischen Wirtschaftsgeschichte.* Berne, 1912.

GRAS, N. S. B. *Business and Capitalism, an Introduction to Business History.* New York, 1939.

HEYD, W. *Histoire du commerce du Levant au Moyen-Age.* 2 vols. Leipzig, 1885.

INAMA-STERNEGG, K. T. *Deutsche Wirtschaftsgeschichte.* 6 vols. Leipzig, 1909.

KNIGHT, M. M. *Economic History of Europe.* Boston, 1928.

KOETZSCHKE, R. *Allgemeine Wirtschaftsgeschichte des Mittelalters.* Jena, 1924.

KOVALEWSKY, M. *Die ökonomische Entwicklung Europas bis zum Beginn der kapitalistischen Wirtschaftsform.* (Germ. transl.) 7 vols. Berlin, 1901–14.

KULISCHER, J. *Allgemeine Wirtschaftsgeschichte des Mittelalters und der Neuzeit,* 1 *(Das Mittelalter).* Munich, 1928.

—— *Russische Wirtschaftsgeschichte,* 1. Jena, 1925.

LEVASSEUR, E. *Histoire du commerce de la France,* 1. Paris, 1910.

LUZZATTO, G. *Storia del Commercio,* 1 *(Medioevo).* Florence, 1915; *Storia economica, L' età moderna,* 2nd ed. Padua, 1937.

MAYER, T. *Deutsche Wirtschaftsgeschichte des Mittelalters.* Leipzig, 1928.

PIGEONNEAU, H. *Histoire du commerce de la France,* 1. Paris, 1885.

PIRENNE, H. *Economic and Social History of Medieval Europe.* (Engl. transl.) London, 1936.

SAKAZOV, I. *Bulgarische Wirtschaftsgeschichte.* Berlin, 1929.

SAPORI, A. *Il mercante italiano nel medioevo.* Milan, 1941.

SCHAUBE, A. *Handelsgeschichte der Romanischen Völker des Mittelmeergebiets bis zum Ende der Kreuzzüge.* Munich, 1906.

SÉE, H. *Histoire économique de la France,* 1. Paris, 1939.

SEGRE, A. *Storia del Commercio,* 1, 2nd ed. Turin, 1923.

SILVA, P. *Il Mediterraneo dall' unità di Roma all' impero italiano,* 2nd ed. Milan, 1939.

SOMBART, W. *Der moderne Kapitalismus.* 2 vols., 2nd ed. Munich, 1916–17.

STEINHAUSEN, G. *Der Kaufmann in der deutschen Vergangenheit.* Jena, 1912.

II. Some Special Problems; Collected Miscellaneous Papers[1]

ARCANGELI, A. *Scritti di diritto commerciale e agrario.* 3 vols. Padua, 1935.

AVENEL, G. DE. *Histoire économique de la propriété, des salaires, des denrées et de tous les prix.* 6 vols. Paris, 1886–1920.

BARON, S. W. *The Jewish Community.* 3 vols. Philadelphia, 1942.

BAUER, C. *Unternehmung und Unternehmungsformen im Spätmittelalter und in der beginnenden Neuzeit.* Jena, 1936.

BELOCH, J. 'Die Bevölkerung Europas im Mittelalter.' *Zeitschrift für Sozialwissenschaft,* III, 1900.

—— *Bevölkerungsgeschichte Italiens.* 2 vols. Berlin, 1937– (in progress ?).

BELOW, G. VON. *Probleme der Wirtschaftsgeschichte,* 2nd ed. Tübingen, 1928.

BESTA, E. *Le obbligazioni nella storia del diritto italiano.* Padua, 1937.

[1] This list includes only a few representative works on those topics which are covered more fully in the bibliography of other chapters, and essays which could not be classified under local headings.

BLOCH, M. 'Le problème de l'or au moyen-âge.' *AHES.* v, 1933.
—— 'Economie nature ou économie argent: un pseudo dilemme.' *AHES.* xi, 1939.
BOGNETTI, G. P. *Note per la storia del passaporto e del salvacondotto.* Pavia, 1933.
BRENTANO, L. *Die wirtschaftende Menschen in der Geschichte.* Leipzig, 1923.
COULTON, G. G. *The Black Death.* London, 1929.
DILLEN, J. G. VAN (ed.). *Contributions to the History of Banking.* The Hague, 1934.
DOPSCH, A. *Natural- und Geldwirtschaft in der Weltgeschichte.* Vienna, 1930.
EBERSTADT, R. *Der Ursprung des Zunftwesens und die älteren Handwerkerverbände des Mittelalters,* 2nd ed. Munich, 1915.
GOLDSCHMIDT, L. *Universalgeschichte des Handelsrechts.* Stuttgart, 1891.
HAUSER, H. *Les origines historiques des problèmes économiques actuels.* Paris, 1930.
—— 'Le sel dans l'histoire.' *Revue économique internationale,* 1927.
HECKSCHER, E. F. *Mercantilism.* (Engl. transl.) 2 vols. London, 1935.
HOUTTE, J. VAN. 'Les courtiers au moyen-âge.' *Revue Historique de droit français et étranger,* xv, 1936.
HUVELIN, P. *Le droit des marchés et des foires.* Paris, 1897.
IMBERDIS, F. 'Les routes médiévales.' *AHES.* xi, 1939.
KELLER, R. VON. *Freiheitsgarantien für Person und Eigentum im Mittelalter.* Heidelberg, 1933.
LATTES, A. 'Note per la storia del diritto commerciale.' *RDC.* xxxi and xxxiii, 1933 and 1935.
LAURENT, H. *Un grand commerce d'exportation au Moyen-Age: La draperie des Pays-Bas en France et dans les pays méditerranéens.* Paris, 1935.
LEICHT, P. S. *Corporazioni romane e arti medievali.* Turin, 1937.
LESTOCQUOY, J. 'Le commerce des œuvres d'art au moyen-âge.' *AHES.* 1943.
LIPPMANN, E. VON. *Geschichte des Zuckers,* 2nd ed. Berlin, 1929.
LIVI, R. *La schiavitù domestica nei tempi di mezzo e nei moderni.* Padua, 1928.
LOPEZ, R. (S.). *Dieci documenti sulla guerra di corsa.* Casale Monferrato, 1938.
LUCAS, H. S. 'The Great European Famine of 1315–17.' *Speculum,* v, 1930.
LUSCHIN VON EBENGREUTH, A. *Allgemeine Münzkunde und Geldgeschichte des Mittelalters und der neueren Zeit,* 2nd ed. Munich, 1926.
LUZZATTO, G. 'Sull' attendibilità di alcune statistiche economiche medievali.' *Giornale degli Economisti,* ser. 4, LXIX, 1929.
MICKWITZ, G. *Die Kartellfunktionen der Zünfte und ihre Bedeutung.* Helsingfors, 1936.
MOCHI-ONORY, S. *Studi sulle origini storiche dei diritti essenziali della persona.* Bologna, 1937.
MONTI, G. M. *Le corporazioni nell' evo antico ed nell' alto medio evo.* Bari, 1934.
NAUDÉ, W. *Getreidehandelspolitik der europäischen Staaten, XIII.–XVIII. Jahrh.* Berlin, 1901.
NEWTON, A. P. (ed.). *Travel and Travellers of the Middle Ages.* London, 1930.
PIRENNE, H. *Medieval Cities.* (Engl. transl.) Princeton, 1925.
—— 'Stages in the Social History of Capitalism.' *AHR.* xix, 1914.
POWER, E. *Medieval People.* London, 1924.
ROERIG, F. *Mittelalterliche Weltwirtschaft.* Jena, 1933.
ROOVER, R. DE. 'La formation et l'expansion de la comptabilité à partie double.' *AHES.* ix, 1937.
SAPORI, A. *Saggi di storia economica medievale,* 2nd ed. Florence, 1946.
SCHEFFEL, P. H. *Verkehrsgeschichte der Alpen.* 2 vols. Berlin, 1908–14.
SOMBART, W. *The Quintessence of Capitalism.* (Engl. transl. of *Der Bourgeois.*) London, 1915.
—— *The Jews and Modern Capitalism.* (Engl. transl.) London, 1913.
STRIEDER, J. *Studien zur Geschichte kapitalistischer Organisationsformen,* 2nd ed. Munich, 1925.
TAWNEY, R. H. *Religion and the Rise of Capitalism,* 7th ed. London, 1938.
TROELTSCH, E. *The Social Teachings of the Christian Churches.* (Engl. transl.) 2 vols. London, 1931.

TYLER, J. T. *The Alpine Passes in the Middle Ages.* Oxford, 1930.

VERLINDEN, C. 'L'origine de Sclavus = Esclave.' *Bulletin Ducange*, XVII, 1942.

WEBER, M. *Gesammelte Aufsätze zur Sozial- und Wirtschaftsgeschichte.* Tübingen, 1924. (Engl. transl. *Essays in Sociology*: New York, 1946.)

WERVEKE, H. VAN. 'Monnaie de compte et monnaie réelle.' *RB.* III, 1924.

—— 'Economie-nature et économie-argent.' *AHES.* III, 1931.

WHITE, L. T. 'Technology and Invention in the Middle Ages.' *Speculum*, XV, 1940.

III. TRADE IN THE EARLY MEDIEVAL PERIOD

(a) *Southern Catholic Europe and its Relations with the East*

BASTIAN, F. 'Legende vom Donauhandel im Frühmittelalter.' *VSWG.* XXII, 1929.

BELGRANO, L. T. 'Cartario genovese e illustrazione del Registro arcivescovile.' *ASLi.* II, 1873.

BICKEL, H. *Die Wirtschaftsverhältnisse des Kloster St. Gallen von der Gründung bis zum Ende des 13. Jahrhunderts.* Freiburg-i.-B., 1914.

BOGNETTI, G. P. 'Arimannie e Guariganghe.' *Wirtschaft und Kultur, Festschrift A. Dopsch.* Leipzig, 1938.

—— 'Il problema monetario dell' età longobarda.' *ASLo.* n.ser. IX, 1944.

BRÉHIER, L. 'Les colonies d'Orientaux en Occident au commencement du Moyen-Age.' *Byzantinische Zeitschrift*, XII, 1903.

BRUTZKUS, J. 'Trade with Eastern Europe, 800–1200'. *EcHR*, XIII, 1943.

BUCKLER, F. W. *Harunu'l-Rashid and Charles the Great.* Cambridge (Mass.), 1931.

BUECHNER, R. *Die Provence in merowingischer Zeit.* Stuttgart, 1933.

CARTA RASPI, R. *La Sardegna nell' alto medioevo.* Cagliari, 1933.

CESSI, R. *Venezia Ducale.* 2 vols. Padua, 1928–9.

—— 'Il "pactum Lotharii" dell' 840.' *Atti del R. Istituto Veneto di Scienze, Lettere e Arti*, XCIX, 1939–40.

CHIAPPELLI, L. 'Per la storia della viabilità nell' alto medioevo.' *Bullettino Storico Pistoiese*, XXVIII, 1926.

—— 'La formazione storica del comune cittadino in Italia.' *ASI.* ser. 7, VI–XIV, 1927–33.

COVILLE, A. *Recherches sur l'histoire de Lyon du Ve siècle au IXe siècle.* Paris, 1928.

DOPSCH, A. *Die Wirtschaftsentwicklung der Karolingerzeit.* 2 vols., 2nd ed. Weimar, 1921–2.

—— *Wirtschaftliche und soziale Grundlagen der Europäischen Kulturentwicklung.* 2 vols. Wien, 1918–24. (Partial Engl. transl.: London, 1937.)

DUPONT, A. *Les cités de la Narbonnaise première depuis les invasions germaniques jusqu'au Consulat.* Nîmes, 1942.

EBERSOLT, J. *Orient et Occident.* 2 vols. Paris, 1928–9.

GANSHOF, F. L. 'Note sur un passage de la vie de St Géraud.' *Mélanges N. Jorga.* Paris, 1929.

—— 'Note sur les ports de Provence du VIIIe au Xe siècle.' *RH.* CLXXXIII, 1938.

GEISS, H. *Geld- und naturalwirtschaftliche Erscheinungsformen im Aufbau Italiens während der Götenzeit.* Stuttgart, 1931.

GUALAZZINI, U. *Il 'populus' di Cremona e l'autonomia del Comune.* Bologna, 1940.

HAHN, B. *Die wirtschaftliche Tätigkeit der Juden im fränkischen und deutschen Reich bis zum Kreuzzug.* Freiburg-i.-B., 1911.

HALPHEN, L. *Etudes critiques sur l'histoire de Charlemagne.* Paris, 1921.

HARTMANN, L. M. *Zur Wirtschaftsgeschichte Italiens im frühen Mittelalter.* Gotha, 1904.

—— 'Die wirtschaftlichen Anfänge Venedigs.' *VSWG.* II, 1904.

HOLLAND, L. B. *Traffic Ways About France in the Dark Ages.* Allentown, Penna., 1919.

IMBART DE LA TOUR, H. D. 'Des immunités commerciales des églises du VIIe au IXe siècle.' *Etdeus G. Monod.* Paris, 1896.

JORDAN, L. 'Der "mercennarius" der Westgotengesetze und seine Nachkommen.' *VSWG.* XVII, 1924.

KALISCHER, E. *Beiträge zur Handelsgeschichte der Klöster zur Zeit der Grossgrundherrschaften.* Berlin, 1911.

KATZ, S. *The Jews in the Visigothic and Frankish Kingdoms.* Cambridge (Mass.), 1937.

KLOSS, F. *Geldvorrat und Geldverkehr im Merowingerreich.* Baden, 1929.

LAMBRECHTS, P. 'Le commerce des Syriens en Gaule.' *Antiquité Classique,* VI, 1937.

LAURENT, H. ' Marchands du palais et marchands d'abbayes.' *RH.* CLXXXIII, 1938.

LEVILLAIN, L. 'Essai sur les origines du Lendit.' *RH.* CLV, 1927.

—— *Recueil des actes de Pépin I et II, rois d'Aquitaine.* Paris, 1926.

LOPEZ, R. S. 'Mohammed and Charlemagne: a Revision.' *Speculum,* XVIII, 1943.

—— 'Byzantine Law in the Seventh Century and its Reception by the Germans and the Arabs.' *Byzantion,* XVI, 1942–3.

—— 'Silk Industry in the Byzantine Empire.' *Speculum,* XX, 1945.

—— 'Le problème des relations anglo-byzantines du VIIe au Xe siècle.' *Byzantion,* XVIII, 1946–7.

MENGOZZI, G. *La città italiana nell' alto medio evo,* 2nd ed. Florence, 1931.

MERORES, M. *Gaeta im frühen Mittelalter.* Gotha, 1911.

MICKWITZ, G. 'Der Verkehr auf dem westlichen Mittelmeer um 600.' *Festschrift A. Dopsch.* Leipzig, 1938.

—— 'Un problème d'influence: Byzance et l'économie de l'Occident médiéval.' *AHES.* VIII, 1936.

MONNERET DE VILLARD, U. 'L'organizzazione industriale nell' Italia longobarda.' *ASLo.* ser. 4, XLVI, 1919.

—— 'La moneta in Italia durante l' alto medio evo.' *Rivista Italiana di Numismatica,* XXXI–XXXIII, 1919–21.

PAULOVA, M. 'L'Islam et la civilisation méditerranéenne.' *Vestník Kralovské České Společnosti Nauk,* 1933.

PIRENNE, H. *Mohammed and Charlemagne.* (Engl. transl.) New York, 1939.

PIVANO, S. *Stato e Chiesa da Berengario ad Arduino.* Turin, 1908.

PROU, M. *Catalogue des monnaies mérovingiennes et carolingiennes de la Bibliothèque Nationale.* 2 vols. Paris, 1892–6.

RIETSCHEL, S. *Die 'civitas' auf deutschem Boden bis zum Ausgange der Karolingerzeit.* Leipzig, 1894.

SABBE, E. 'Quelques types de marchands des IXe et Xe siècles.' *RB.* XIII, 1934.

—— 'L'importation des tissus orientaux en Europe Occidentale aux IXe et Xe siècles.' *RB.* XIV, 1935.

SALVIOLI, G. *Storia economica d'Italia nel Medio Evo: Le nostre origini.* Bari, 1923.

SANCHEZ-ALBORNOZ, C. *Estampas de la vida en León durante el siglo X.* Madrid, 1926.

—— 'El precio de la vida en el reino asturleonés hace mil años.' *Logos,* III, 1945.

SCHIPA, M. *Il mezzogiorno d' Italia anteriormente alla monarchia.* Bari, 1923.

SERRANO, L. *El obispado de Burgos y Castilla primitiva.* 3 vols. Madrid, 1936.

SOLMI, A. *L'amministratione finanziaria del Regno Italico nell' alto medio evo.* Pavia, 1932. (Also in *Bollettino della Società Pavese di Storia Patria,* XXXI, 1931.)

THOMPSON, J. W. 'The Commerce of France in the Ninth Century.' *Journ. Polit. Econ.* XXIII, 1915.

TORRES, M. 'El estado visigótico.' *AHDE.* III, 1926.

VALDEAVELLANO, L. G. DE. 'Economia natural y monetaria en León y Castilla durante los siglos IX, X y XI.' *Moneta y Crédito,* 1944.

VERCAUTEREN, F. 'Cataplus et Catabolus.' *Bulletin Ducange,* II, 1925.

VISCONTI, A. 'Negotiatores de Mediolano; Ricerche sul diritto pubblico milanese nell' alto Medio Evo.' *Annali della R. Università di Macerata,* IV–VI, 1929–31.

VOLPE, G. 'Pisa e i Longobardi.' *Studi Storici,* X, 1901.

WERVEKE, H. VAN. 'Monnaie, lingots ou marchandises?' *AHES.* IV, 1932.

WROTH, W. *Catalogue of the Coins of the Vandals, Ostrogoths and Lombards...in the British Museum.* London, 1911.

(b) The Muslim World

ABEL, A. 'Les marchés de Baghdad.' *Bulletin de la Société Belge d'Etudes Géographiques*, IX, 1939.

AMARI, M. *Storia dei Musulmani di Sicilia*. 3 vols., 2nd ed. Catania, 1933–42.

ARIN, F. *Recherches historiques sur les opérations usuraires et aléatoires en droit musulman*. Paris, 1929.

BECKER, C. *Islamstudien*. 2 vols. Leipzig, 1924.

BUSSI, E. 'Del concetto di commercio e di commerciante nel pensiero giuridico musulmano.' *Studi A. Albertoni*, III. Padua, 1938.

COHN, E. *Der Wucher in Qor'an, Chedith und Fiqh*. Berlin, 1903.

Encyclopedia of Islam, especially articles *Tidjara* (Heffening), *Shirka* (Heffening), *Muhtasib* (Levy), *Sinf* (Massignon), *Tiraz* (Grohmann) and entries on single countries and cities.

FERRAND, J. *Relations de voyages et textes géographiques arabes, persans et turks relatifs à l'Extrême-Orient*. 2 vols. Paris, 1913–14.

FISCHEL, W. J. *Jews in the Economic and Political Life of the Medieval Islam*. London, 1937.

GABRIELI, F. 'Il valore letterario e storico di Tanuhi.' *Rivista degli Studi Orientali*, XIX, 1940.

GAUDEFROY-DEMOMBYNES, M. *La Syrie à l'époque des Mamlouks*. Paris, 1923.

GAUTIER, E. F. *Les siècles obscurs du Maghreb*. Paris, 1927.

GOEJE, M. DE. 'International Haandelsverkeer in de Middeleeuwen.' *Verslagen en Mededeelingen, Afdeeling Letterkunde* of the K. Academie van Wetenschappen of Amsterdam, ser. 4, IX, 1909.

GRASSHOFF, R. *Das Wechselrecht der Araber*. Berlin, 1899. (Published also with the title *Die suftaja und hawala der Araber*. Göttingen, 1899.)

HEFFENING, W. *Beiträge zum Rechts- und Wirtschaftsleben des Islamischen Orients*, I. Hanover, 1925 (in progress?).

HIRTH, F. and ROCKHILL, W. Introduction to Chan Ju-Kua, *Chu-fan-chi*. St Petersburg, 1911.

JACOB, G. 'Die ältesten Spuren des Wechsels.' *Mitteilungen des Seminar für Orientalistische Sprachen an d. Univ. zu Berlin, Westasiatische Studien*, XXVIII, 1925.

—— *Die nordisch-baltische Handel der Araber im Mittelalter*. Leipzig, 1887.

KAMMERER, A. *La mer Rouge, l'Abyssinie et l'Arabie depuis l'Antiquité*, I. Cairo, 1929.

KOHLER, J. *Die Commenda im islamischen Rechte*. Würzburg, 1885.

KREMER, A. VON. *Kulturgeschichte des Orients unter den Chalifen*. 2 vols. Wien, 1875–8. (Partial Engl. transl.: Calcutta, 1929.)

LAMMENS, H. 'La république marchande de la Mecque en l'an 600 de notre ère.' *Bulletin de l'Institut Egyptien*, 1910.

LANE-POOLE, S. *History of Egypt in the Middle Ages*. 4th ed. London, 1925.

LAVOIX, H. *Catalogue des monnaies musulmanes...de la Bibliothèque Nationale*. 3 vols. Paris, 1887–92.

LE STRANGE, G. *Palestine under the Moslems*. London, 1890.

—— *Baghdad during the Abbasid Caliphate*. Oxford, 1900.

—— *The Lands of the Eastern Caliphate*. Cambridge, 1905.

LEVI-PROVENÇAL, E. *L'Espagne musulmane au Xe siècle*. Paris, 1932.

LEVY, R. *A Baghdad Chronicle*. Cambridge, 1929.

LEWIS, B. 'The Islamic Guilds.' *EcHR*. VIII, 1938.

MARÇAIS, G. *La Berbérie Musulmane et l'Orient au Moyen Age*. Paris, 1946.

MASSIGNON, L. 'L'influence de l'Islam au Moyen-Age sur la fondation et l'essor des banques juives.' *Bulletin d'Etudes Orientales de l'Institut Français de Damas*, I, 1931.

MAUNIER, R. *Mélanges de sociologie nord-africaine*. Paris, 1930.

MEZ, A. *Die Renaissance des Islâms*. Heidelberg, 1922. (Very poor Engl. transl.: London, 1937.)

MINORSKII, V. F. *Hudud al 'Alam, The Regions of the World*. London, 1937.

PÉRÈS, H. *La poésie andalouse en arabe classique au XIe siècle...et sa valeur documentaire.* Paris, 1937.

RITTER, H. 'Ein arabisches Handbuch der Handelswissenschaft.' *Der Islam,* XVII, 1917.

SAUVAGET, J. 'Esquisse d'une histoire de la ville de Damas.' *Revue des Etudes Islamiques,* VIII, 1934.

—— *Alep. Essai sur le développement d'une grande ville Syrienne.* Paris, 1941.

WIET, G. *L'Egypte arabe,* 642–1517. Paris, 1937.

ZAYDÁN, G. *Umayyads and Abbasids.* Leyden, 1907.

IV. TRADE DURING THE GOLDEN AGE

(a) *The Big Four: Florence, Genoa, Milan, Venice*

ADY, C. M. *History of Milan under the Sforza.* London, 1907.

ASTUTI, G. *Rendiconti mercantili inediti del cartolare di Giovanni Scriba.* Turin, 1933.

BARBADORO, B. *Le finanze della repubblica fiorentina.* Florence, 1929.

BARBIERI, G. *Economia e politica nel ducato di Milano.* Milan, 1938.

BAUER, C. 'Venezianische Salzhandelspolitik bis zum Ende des 14. Jahrh.' *VSWG.* XXIII, 1930.

BISCARO, G. 'Gli estimi del comune di Milano.' *ASLo.* ser. 5, LV, 1928.

BONOLIS, G. *La giurisdizione della Mercanzia in Firenze.* Florence, 1901.

BOSISIO, A. *Origini del Comune di Milano.* Messina, 1933.

BROGLIO D'AJANO, R. *L'arte della seta in Venezia.* Milan, 1902.

BYRNE, E. H. 'Easterners in Genoa.' *Journal of the American Oriental Society,* XXXV, 1918.

—— *Genoese Shipping in the Twelfth and Thirteenth Century.* Cambridge (Mass.), 1930.

CAGGESE, R. *Firenze dalla decadenza di Roma al Risorgimento,* I. Florence, 1912.

CASSANDRO, G. I. *Le rappresaglie e il fallimento a Venezia nei secoli XIII–XVI.* Turin, 1938.

CASSUTO, U. *Gli Ebrei a Firenze nell' età del Rinascimento.* Florence, 1918.

CESSI, R. 'Studi sulle maone medievali.' *ASI.* ser. 6, LXXVI, 1919.

—— 'Problemi monetari e bancari veneziani del secolo XIV.' *Archivio Veneto Tridentino,* IX, 1926.

—— *Problemi monetari veneziani fino a tutto il secolo XIV.* Padua, 1937.

—— *Storia della Repubblica di Venezia,* 2 vols. Milan, 1944–6.

CESSI, R. and ALBERTI, A. *La politica mineraria veneziana.* Rome, 1924.

CHIAUDANO, M. *Contratti commerciali genovesi del secolo XII.* Turin, 1925.

CIASCA, R. *L' arte dei medici e speziali nella storia del commercio fiorentino.* Firenze, 1927.

CODARA, G. *I navigli di Milano.* Milan, 1927.

DAVIDSOHN, R. *Forschungen zur Geschichte von Florenz.* 4 vols. Berlin, 1896–1908.

DI TUCCI, R. *Studi sull' economia genovese del secolo XII.* Turin, 1923.

—— 'Le imposte sul commercio genovese.' *GSLL.* n.ser., VI, 1930.

DOREN, A. *Studien aus der florentiner Wirtschaftsgeschichte.* 2 vols. Stuttgart, 1901–8.

FANO, N. 'Ricerche sull' arte della lana a Venezia nel XIII e XIV secolo.' *AV.* n.ser., XVIII, 1936.

GRUENZWEIG, A. 'Les soi-disant statuts de la confrérie de Sainte-Barbe de Florence.' *Commission d'Histoire de l'Acad. Royale de Belgique,* XCVI, 1932.

HAZLITT, W. C. *The Venetian Republic.* 2 vols. London, 1900.

HERMES, G. 'Der Kapitalismus in der florentiner Wollenindustrie.' *Zeitschrift für die gesamte Staatswissenschaft,* LXXII, 1916.

HEYNEN, R. *Zur Entstehung des Kapitalismus in Venedig.* Stuttgart, 1905.

LANE, F. C. *Venetian Ships and Shipbuilding of the Renaissance.* Baltimore, 1934.

—— *Andrea Barbarigo Merchant of Venice,* 1418–1449. Baltimore, 1944.

LA SORSA, S. *L' organizzazione dei cambiatori fiorentini nel medio evo.* Cerignola, 1904.

LOPEZ, R. (S.). *Genova marinara nel Duecento: Benedetto Zaccaria.* Messina, 1933.

—— 'L' attività economica a Genova nel marzo 1253.' *ASLi.* LXIV, 1935.

—— *Studi sull' economia genovese nel medio evo.* Turin, 1936.

—— 'Aux origines du capitalisme génois.' *AHES.* IX, 1937.

LUZZATTO, G. 'La commenda nella vita economica dei secoli XIII e XIV (a Venezia).' *Atti del Congresso Internazionale di studi storici del diritto marittimo ad Amalfi.* Naples, 1934.
—— 'Les activités économiques du Patriciat vénitien.' *AHES.* IX, 1937.
MANNUCCI, F. L. 'Delle società genovesi d'arti e mestieri.' *GSLL.* VI, 1905.
MARENGO, E., MANFRONI, C. and PESSAGNO, G. *Il Banco di San Giorgio.* Genoa, 1911.
MASI, G. 'I banchieri fiorentini nella vita politica della città sulla fine del Dugento.' *Archivio giuridico*, ser. 4, XXI, 1931.
MELZING, O. *Das Bankhaus der Medici und seiner Vorläufer.* Jena, 1906.
MOLMENTI, P. *Venice, its Individual Growth from the Earliest Beginnings to the Fall of the Republic.* (Engl. transl.) 6 vols. London, 1906-8.
MOTTA, E. 'Per la storia dell' arte dei fustagni nel secolo XIV.' *ASLo.* ser. 2, XVII, 1890.
PADOVAN, G. (pseudonym of LUZZATTO, G.). 'Capitale e lavoro nel commercio veneziano dei secoli XI e XII.' *RSE.* VI, 1941.
—— 'L'attività commerciale di un patrizio veneziano del Quattrocento.' *RSE.* VIII, 1943.
PIERI, P. *Intorno alla storia dell' arte della seta in Firenze.* Bologna, 1927.
PITZORNO, B. 'I "consules" veneziani di Sardegna e Maiorca.' *NAV.* n.ser., XI, 1906.
RADO, A. *Maso degli Albizzi e il partito oligarchico in Firenze.* Florence, 1926.
REYNOLDS, R. L. 'The Market for Northern Textiles in Genoa; Merchants of Arras and the Overland Trade with Genoa.' *RB.* VIII-IX, 1929-30.
—— 'Genoese Trade in the Late Twelfth Century.' *JEBH.* III, 1931.
—— 'Some English Settlers in Genoa in the Late Twelfth Century.' *EcHR.* IV, 1933.
—— 'In Search of a Business Class in Thirteenth-Century Genoa.' *JEH.* suppl. V, 1945.
RODOLICO, N. *Il popolo minuto, note di storia fiorentina*, 1343-1378. Bologna, 1899.
—— *I Ciompi.* Florence, 1945.
—— 'The Struggle for the Right of Association in Fourteenth-Century Florence.' *History*, VIII, 1924.
ROOVER, R. DE. 'The Medici Bank.' *JEH.* VI-VII, 1946-7.
SALVEMINI, G. *Magnati e popolani in Firenze*, 1280-1295. Florence, 1899.
SANTORO, C. *La matricola dei mercanti di lana sottile di Milano.* Milan, 1941.
SAPORI, A. *La crisi delle compagnie mercantili dei Bardi e dei Peruzzi.* Florence, 1926.
—— *Una compagnia di Calimala ai primi del Trecento.* Florence, 1932.
SAYOUS, A. 'Un marché de valeurs au XIIIe siècle, les "Compere Salis" de Gênes.' *AHES.* IV, 1932.
—— '"Der moderne Kapitalismus" de Werner Sombart et Gênes aux XIIe et XIIIe siècles.' *RHES.* XIX, 1931.
SIEVEKING, H. *Genueser Finanzwesen.* 2 vols. Freiburg-i.-B. 1898; Tübingen, 1900.
—— 'Aus venetianischen Handlungsbüchern.' *Schmollers Jahrbuch*, XXV-XXVI, 1901-2.
—— 'Aus Genueser Rechnungs- und Steuerbüchern.' *Sitzungsberichte d. K. Akad. der Wissenschaften, Wien*, CLII, 1909.
SIMONSFELD, H. *Der Fondaco dei Tedeschi in Venedig.* 3 vols. Stuttgart, 1887.
SORBELLI, A. *La lotta tra Genova e Venezia per il predominio del Mediterraneo.* Bologna, 1921.
SOTTAS, J. *Les Messageries Maritimes de Venise aux XIVe et XVe siècles.* Paris, 1938.
STIEDA, W. *Hansisch-Venetianische Handelsbeziehungen im 15. Jahrh.* Rostock, 1894.
Storia di Genova dalle origini al tempo nostro (Formentini, Scarsella, Vitale and others), II-III. Milan, 1941 (in progress).
VALSECCHI, F. *Le corporazioni nell' organismo politico del medioevo (a Milano).* Milan, 1931.
VERGA, E. *La Camera dei Mercanti di Milano nei secoli passati.* Milan, 1931.
VILLARI, P. *The Two First Centuries of Florentine History.* (Engl. transl.) 2 vols. London, 1894-5.
VISCONTI, A. *Storia di Milano.* Milan, 1937.
ZERBI, T. *La banca nell' ordinamento finanziario visconteo.* Como, 1935.
—— *Aspetti economico-tecnici del mercato di Milano nel Trecento.* Como, 1936.

(b) *Minor centres and regions in Upper and Central Italy; Italy in general*

BARUCHELLO, M. *Livorno e il suo porto: origini e vicende dei traffici.* Leghorn, 1932.

BATTISTELLA, A. 'I Lombardi nel Friuli.' *ASLo.* ser. 4, XXXVII, 1910.'

BENSA, E. *Francesco di Marco da Prato (Datini).* Milan, 1928.

BERNINI, F. 'Note sulla politica comunale al principio dell' impero di Federico II.' *NRS.* XXVII, 1943.

BERTONI, G. 'Banchieri a Imola nel secolo XIII.' *Studi Medievali*, III, 1911.

BOGNETTI, G. P. 'I magistri Antelami e la Val d' Intelvi.' *Periodico Storico Comense*, n.ser., II, 1938.

BOZZOLA, A. 'Appunti sulla vita economica, sulle classi sociali e sull' ordinamento politico del Monferrato.' *BSBS.* XXV, 1923.

BRENNI, L. *La seteria italiana.* Milan, 1927.

BREZZI, P. 'Politica e attività economica nel comune di Chieri.' *BSBS.* n.ser., IV, 1938.

BROGLIO D'AJANO, R. *Lotte sociali in Italia nel secolo XIV.* Rome, 1911.

BRUGARO, A. 'L' artigianato pisano nel medio evo, 1000–1406.' *Studi Storici*, XVI and XX, 1907 and 1912.

BRUN, R. 'A Fourteenth-Century Merchant: Francesco Datini.' *JEBH.* II, 1930.

CAGGESE, R. *Un comune libero alle porte di Firenze: Prato.* Florence, 1905.

—— 'La repubblica di Siena e il suo contado nel secolo XIII.' *Bullettino Storico Senese*, XIII, 1906.

CASANOVA, E. and DEL VECCHIO, A. *Le rappresaglie nei comuni medievali.* Bologna, 1894.

CESSI, R. 'La corporazione dei mercanti di panni e della lana in Padova.' *Memorie del R. Istituto Veneto di scienze, lettere e arti*, XXVIII, 1908.

CHIAPPELLI, L. 'Notizie sui banchieri e sui mercanti pistoiesi nel Dugento. *Bullettino Storico Pistoiese*, XVIII, 1915.

CHIAUDANO, M. *Studi e documenti per la storia del diritto commerciale italiano nel secolo XIII.* Turin, 1930.

—— 'I Rothschild del Dugento: La Gran Tavola di Orlando Buonsignori.' *Bullettino Storico Senese*, n.ser., VI, 1935.

—— 'La costituzione di una società commerciale a Pinerolo nel 1327.' *BSBS.* XLII, 1940.

CIPOLLA, C. M. 'Il valore di alcune biblioteche nel Trecento; In tema di trasporti medievali.' *Bollettino Storico Pavese*, n.ser., V, 1944.

CISCATO, A. *Gli Ebrei in Padova.* Padua, 1901.

CUSIN, F. 'Per la storia del castello medievale (in Italia).' *Rivista Storica Italiana*, ser. 5, IV, 1939.

DIETZ, A. 'Industry in Pisa in the early Fourteenth Century.' *Quart. Journ. Econ.*, XXVIII, 1914.

DORINI, U. *L' arte della seta in Toscana.* Florence, 1928.

FAINELLI, V. *Le condizioni economiche dei primi signori scaligeri.* Verona, 1917.

FALCO, G. 'Appunti di diritto marittimo medievale dal cartulario di Giovanni di Giona di Portovenere.' *Diritto Marittimo*, 1927.

FANFANI, A. *Un mercante del Trecento* (Giubileo Carsidoni di Sansepolcro). Milan, 1935.

—— *Saggi di storia economica italiana.* Milan, 1936.

FASOLI, G. 'Un comune veneto nel Duecento: Bassano.' *NAV.* ser. 5, XV, 1934.

—— 'La legislazione antimagnatizia dei comuni dell' alta e media Italia.' *Rivista di Storia del Diritto Italiano*, XII, 1939.

FIUMI, L. *L' utilizzazione dei lagoni boraciferi della Toscana nell' industria medievale.* Florence, 1943.

FOSSATI, F. 'Appunti e note per la storia economica di Vigevano.' *Viglevanum*, III–V, 1909–11.

FRATI, L. *La vita privata a Bologna nel secolo XIII.* Bologna, 1900.

GUALAZZINI, U. *I mercanti di Cremona.* Cremona, 1928.

— *Rapporti fra capitale e lavoro nelle industrie tessili lombarde del Medio Evo.* Turin, 1932.

LATTES, A. *Il diritto commerciale nella legislazione statutaria delle città italiane.* Milan, 1884.
—— *Il diritto consuetudinario delle città lombarde.* Milan, 1899.
—— *Il diritto marittimo privato nelle carte liguri.* Vatican City, 1940.
LAZZARESCHI, E. and PARDI, F. *Lucca nella storia, nell' arte e nell' industria.* Lucca, 1941.
LEICHT, P. S. 'Note sull' economia friulana al principio del secolo XIII.' *Festschrift Alfons Dopsch.* Liepzig, 1938.
LIVI, G. 'I mercanti di seta lucchesi in Bologna nei secoli XIII–XIV.' *ASI.* ser. 4, VII, 1880.
LIZIER, A. *Note intorno al comune di Treviso.* Modena, 1901.
LUSCHIN VON EBENGREUTH, A. 'I monetieri del Sacro Romano Impero in Italia.' *Rivista Italiana di Numismatica,* XXI, 1907.
LUZZATTO, G. 'Prezzi e salarii nel secolo XIII.' *Le Marche,* n.ser., II, 1907.
—— 'Piccoli e grandi mercanti nelle città italiane.' *Studi G. Prato.* Turin, 1930.
MARONI, M. 'Patti dei Lombardi e dei Catalani col comune di Ancona.' *ASLo.* VIII, 1881.
MENGOZZI, N. *Il Monte dei Paschi di Siena.* 7 vols. Siena, 1891–1907.
MIRA, G. *Aspetti dell' economia comasca all' inizio dell' età moderna.* Como, 1939.
MONDOLFO, U. G. *Il 'populus' a Siena nella vita della città e nel governo....* Genoa, 1911.
PALMIERI, A. *La montagna bolognese nel medio evo.* Bologna, 1919.
PANCOTTI, V. *I paratici piacentini e i loro statuti.* Parma, 1923.
PATETTA, F. 'Nobili e popolani in una piccola città (Belluno).' *Annuario della R. Università di Siena,* 1901–2.
POZZA, F. 'Le corporazioni d'arti e mestieri a Vicenza.' *NAV.* n.ser., X, 1895.
ROBERTI, M. *Le corporazioni padovane d' arti e mestieri.* Venice, 1902.
ROMANO, G. 'Pavia nella storia della navigazione fluviale.' *Bollettino della Società Pavese di storia patria,* XI, 1911.
ROON-BASSERMANN, E. VON. *Sienesische Handelsgesellschaften des 13. Jahrh.* Mannheim, 1912.
ROTH, C. *The History of the Jews of Italy.* Philadelphia, 1946.
SACCO, I. M. *Professioni, arti e mestieri in Torino.* Turin, 1940.
SANDRI, G. 'I Bevilacqua e il commercio del legname tra la val di Fiemme e Verona.' *AV.* ser. 5, XXI, 1940.
Savona nella storia e nell' arte, scritti offerti a Paolo Boselli. Genoa, 1928.
SAYOUS, A. E. 'Les transformations des méthodes commerciales dans l'Italie médiévale.' *AHES.* I, 1929.
—— 'Sienne de 1221 à 1229.' *AHES.* II, 1930.
SENIGAGLIA, Q. 'Le compagnie bancarie senesi dei secoli XIII e XIV.' *Studi Senesi,* XXIV–XXV, 1907–8.
SILVA, P. 'Intorno all' industria e al commercio della lana in Pisa.' *Studi Storici,* XIX, 1910.
SIMEONI, L. *Gli antichi statuti delle arti Veronesi.* Venice, 1914.
SITTA, P. 'Le università delle arti a Ferrara.' *Atti della Deputazione Ferrarese di Storia Patria,* VIII, 1896.
SORBELLI, A. *La Signoria di Giovanni Visconti a Bologna.* Bologna, 1901.
SORIGA, R. 'Sulle corporazioni artigiane di Pavia nell' età comunale.' *Bollettino della Società Pavese di storia patria,* XV, 1915.
TAMASSIA, G. (N.). *La famiglia italiana nei secoli XV e XVI.* Palermo, 1910.
TORELLI, P. *Un comune cittadino in territorio a economia agricola* (Mantova). Mantua, 1930.
TRASSELLI, C. *Veneziani e fiorentini a Merano nel secolo XIV.* Bolzano, 1941.
VERGANO, L. 'Il mercante astigiano nel medio evo.' *Rivista di Storia, Arte e Archeologia per la provincia di Alessandria,* XLVII, 1938.
VERGOTTINI, G. DE. 'Il popolo nella costituzione del Comune di Modena sino alla metà del XIII secolo.' *Miscellanea Pietro Rossi,* Siena, 1931.
VOLPE, G. *Medio Evo Italiano,* 2nd ed. Florence, 1928.
—— *Movimenti religiosi e sette ereticali nella società medievale italiana,* 2nd ed. Florence, 1926.

VOLPE, G. 'Montieri...una terra mineraria toscana.' *VSWG.* VI, 1908.
—— 'Lambardi e Romani nelle campagne e in città.' *Studi Storici,* XIII, 1904.
VOLTELINI, H. VON. *Die ältesten Pfandleihbanken und Lombarden-Privilegien Tirols.* Innsbruck, 1904.
ZANAZZO, G. B. 'L' arte della lana in Vicenza.' *Miscellanea di storia veneta,* ser. 3, VI, 1914.
ZANONI, L. *Gli Umiliati nei loro rapporti con l' eresia, l' industria e i Comuni.* Milan, 1911.
ZDEKAUER, L. *Il mercante senese nel Dugento.* Siena, 1901.
—— *Fiera e mercato in Italia sulla fine del medio evo.* Macerata, 1920.
ZIMOLO, G. C. 'Cremona nella storia della navigazione interna.' *Atti e memorie del III Congresso Storico Lombardo.* Milan, 1939.

(c) Papal States and Finances; Kingdom of Sicily; Sardinia, Corsica

AMAT DI SAN FILIPPO, P. 'Indagini e studi sulla storia economica della Sardegna.' *Miscellanea di storia italiana,* ser. 3, VIII, 1903.
BAUDI DI VESME, C. *Dell' industria delle miniere nel territorio di Villa di Chiesa.* Turin, 1870.
BESTA, E. *La Sardegna medievale.* 2 vols. Palermo, 1909.
BORLANDI, F. *Per la storia della popolazione della Corsica.* Milan, 1942.
BOÜARD, M. DE. 'Problèmes des subsistances dans un état médiéval: le marché et le prix des céréales au royaume angevin de Sicile.' *AHES.* X, 1938.
CAFARO, A. G. 'Dell' attività commerciale e marittima dei Benedettini di Cava.' *Rivista storica benedettina,* XII, 1921.
GAGGESE, R. *Roberto d'Angiò e i suoi tempi.* 2 vols. Florence, 1922–31.
CALASSO, F. *La legislazione statutaria dell' Italia Meridionale.* Rome, 1929.
CAMERA, M. *Memorie storico-diplomatiche dell' antica città e ducato di Amalfi.* 2 vols. Salerno, 1876–8.
CARABELLESE, F. *Saggio di storia del commercio delle Puglie.* Trani, 1900.
—— *La Puglia nel secolo XV.* Bari, 1901.
—— *Carlo d'Angiò nei rapporti politici e commerciali con Venezia e l' Oriente.* Bari, 1911.
CHONE, H. *Die Handelsbeziehungen Kaiser Friedrichs II zu den Seestädten Venedig, Pisa und Genua.* Berlin, 1902.
CICCAGLIONE, F. 'La vita economica siciliana nel periodo normanno-svevo.' *Archivio Storico della Sicilia Orientale,* X, 1913.
COHN, W. *Das Zeitalter der Normannen in Sizilien; Das Zeitalter der Hohenstaufen in Sizilien.* 2 vols. Bonn and Breslau, 1920–5.
CUSUMANO, V. *Storia dei banchi della Sicilia.* 2 vols. Rome, 1892.
CUTOLO, A. *Re Ladislao di Angiò Durazzo.* 2 vols. Milan, 1936.
DELIPERI, A. 'Aspetti della vita economica della Sardegna nel secolo XII.' *Mediterranea,* 1935.
—— 'Notizie storiche sul movimento commerciale della Sardegna nel secolo XIII.' *Archivio Storico Sardo,* XXXIII, 1937.
DI TUCCI, R. 'Le condizioni dei mercanti stranieri in Sardegna durante la dominazione aragonese.' *Archivio Storico Sardo,* VII, 1911.
—— 'Le corporazioni artigiane della Sardegna.' *Archivio Storico Sardo,* XVI, 1920.
DORIA, G. *Storia di una capitale* (Napoli). Naples, 1936.
DRINKWATER, G. 'The Origin of the Town of Subiaco.' *Essays in Honor of J. W. Thompson.* Chicago, 1938.
FARAGLIA, N. *Storia dei prezzi a Napoli,* 1131–1860. Naples, 1878.
FEDELE, P. 'Contributo alla storia economica di Roma.' *Scritti storici in onore di G. Romano.* Pavia, 1907.
FERORELLI, N. *Gli ebrei nell' Italia meridionale,* 2nd ed. Turin, 1915.
GARUFI, C. A. 'Sulla curia stratigoziale di Messina.' *Archivio Storico Messinese,* V, 1905.
GENUARDI, L. 'Commercio e diritto marittimo in Napoli nei secoli XIII, XIV e XV.' *Studi di storia napoletana in onore di M. Schipa.* Naples, 1926.

LOPEZ, R. (S.). 'Contributo alla storia delle miniere argentifere della Sardegna.' *Studi economico-giuridici della R. Università di Cagliari*, XXIV, 1936.

—— 'Risse tra Pisani e Genovesi nella Napoli di Federico II.' *Rassegna Storica Napoletana*, III, 1935.

LUNT, W. E. *Papal Revenues in the Middle Ages.* 2 vols. New York, 1934.

MONTI, G. M. *Nuovi studi angioini.* Trani, 1937.

MUSSONI, G. 'L' antico commercio dello zafferano nell' Aquila.' *Bollettino della Società di Storia Patria Antinori negli Abruzzi*, XVIII, 1906.

ARDONE, P. *Genova e Pisa nei rapporti commerciali col Mezzogiorno d' Italia.* Prato, 1923.

NINA, L. *Le finanze pontificie nel medioevo.* 3 vols. Milan, 1930.

PARDI, G. 'Storia demografica della città di Palermo; Napoli attraverso i secoli.' *NRS.* III and VIII, 1919 and 1924.

PONTIERI, E. *Ricerche sulla crisi della monarchia meridionale nel secolo XIII.* Naples, 1943.

RENOUARD, Y. *Les relations des papes d'Avignon et des compagnies commerciales et bancaires de 1316 à 1378.* Paris, 1941.

RODOCANACHI, E. *Les corporations ouvrières à Rome depuis la chute de l'Empire Romain.* 2 vols. Paris, 1894.

SAVINI, F. *Il Comune Teramano nella sua vita intima e pubblica.* Rome, 1895.

SCHIPA, M. 'Contese sociali napoletane nel Medio Evo.' *Archivio Storico per le Province Napoletane*, XXXI–XXXIII, 1906–8.

TRIFONE, R. *La legislazione angioina.* Naples, 1921.

VITALE, V. A. *Trani dagli Angioini agli Spagnuoli.* Bari, 1912.

—— 'Le relazioni commerciali di Genova col regno normanno-svevo.' *GSLL.* n.ser., III, 1927.

YVER, G. *Le commerce et les marchands dans l'Italie méridionale au XIIIe et au XIVe siècle.* Paris, 1903.

ZENO, R. *Documenti per la storia del diritto marittimo nei secoli XIII e XIV* (in Sicilia). Turin, 1936.

ZIPPEL, G. 'L' allume di Tolfa e il suo commercio.' *Archivio della Società Romana di Storia Patria*, XXX, 1907.

(d) Catholic Spain

ALZOLA Y MIÑONDO, P. DE. *Regimen económico, administrativo, antiguo y moderno de Vizcaya y Guipúzcoa.* Bilbao, 1910.

BAER, F. *Die Juden im Christlichen Spanien: Aragonien und Navarra.* Berlin, 1929.

BALARÍ Y JOVANI, J. *Origenes históricos de Cataluña.* Barcelona, 1899.

BALLESTEROS Y BERETTA, A. DE. *Sevilla en el siglo XIII.* Madrid, 1913.

CAPMANY Y MONTPALAU, A. DE. *Memorias históricas sobre la marina, comercio y artes de la antigua ciudad de Barcelona.* 4 vols. Madrid, 1779–92.

CARANDE, R. 'Sevilla, fortaleza y mercado.' *AHDE.* II, 1925.

CASTRO, A. 'Unos aranceles de aduanas del siglo XIII.' *Revista de Filologia Española*, VIII–X, 1921–3.

ESPEJO, C. and PAZ, J. *Las antiguas ferias de Medina del Campo.* Madrid, 1912.

FAJARNÉS, E. 'Associaciones gremiales en Mallorca durante la Edad Media; Los Judíos en Mallorca.' *Boletín de la Societat Arqueológica Lul-liana*, VII, 1897.

FERNANDEZ Y GONZALEZ, F. *Estado social y político de los Mudejares de Castilla.* Madrid, 1866.

FINOT, J. *Etude historique sur les relations commerciales entre la Flandre et l'Espagne au Moyen-Age.* Paris, 1899.

FONT RIUS, J. M. 'Origines del régimen municipal de Cataluña.' *AHDE.* XVI, 1945.

GUIARD Y LAURRARI, T. *Historia del consulado y casa de contratación de Bilbao.* 2 vols. Bilbao, 1913–14.

HAEBLER, K. 'Das Zollbruch der Deutschen in Barcelona und der deutschen Handel in Catalonien.' *Würtembergische Vierteljahrschrift für Landesgeschichte*, X–XI, 1901–2.

HAMILTON, E. J. *Money, Prices and Wages in Valencia, Aragon and Navarre, 1351–1500.* Cambridge (Mass.), 1936.

HINOJOSA, E. DE. *Estudios sobre la historia del derecho español.* Madrid, 1903.

KLEIN, J. *The Mesta, a Study in Spanish Economic History.* Cambridge (Mass.), 1920.

LACARRA, J. M. 'Para el estudio del municipio navarro medieval.' *Revista Principe de Viana,* II, 1941.

LATTES, A. 'Barcellona nei suoi istituti commerciali.' *RDC.* XXX, 1932.

LEONHARD, R. 'Ueber Handwerkergilden und Verbrüderungen in Spanien.' *JNOS.* III, 1909.

LEVI, E. 'I fiorentini nel Maestrazgo al tramonto del medioevo.' *Boletín de la sociedad Castellonense de Cultura,* 1929.

MAYER, E. *Historia de las instituciones sociales y políticas de España y Portugal durante los siglos V a XIV.* 2 vols. Madrid, 1925.

MENENDEZ PIDAL, R. *La España del Cid.* 2 vols. Madrid, 1929. (Partial Engl. transl.: London, 1934.)

MERRIMAN, R. B. *The Rise of the Spanish Empire,* I. New York, 1918.

MIRET I SANS, J. 'Les represálies a Catalunya en l'edat mitjana.' *Revista jurídica de Cataluña,* XXXI, 1925.

MOTTA, E. 'Mercanti milanesi in Spagna nel Quattrocento.' *ASLo.* ser. 4, XIII, 1910.

MURGUÍA, M. *Historia de Galicia,* I, 2nd ed. Coruna, 1902.

QUADRADO, J. M. *Forenses y ciudadanos, historia de las disensiones civiles de Mallorca en el siglo XV,* 2nd ed. Palma, 1895.

RAU, V. *Subsidios para o estudio das feiras medievais partuguesas.* Lisbon, 1943.

SAYOUS, A. E. 'Les méthodes commerciales de Barcelone.' *Estudis Universitaris Catalans,* XVI and XVIII, 1931 and 1933.

—— 'La technique des affaires: Un contrat de société à Barcelone; La Table des Changes de Valence.' *AHES.* VI, 1934.

SILVA, P. 'Sulle relazioni commerciali tra Pisa e l' Aragona.' *Bollettino Pisano d' Arte e di Storia,* I, 1913.

SIMONET, F. J. *Historia de los Mozárabes de España.* Madrid, 1903.

SMITH, R. S. *The Spanish Guild Merchant,* 1250–1700. Durham, N.C., 1940.

SOUZA SOARES, T. B. DE. *Apontamentos para o estudio da origem das instituções municipais portuguesas.* Lisbon, 1931.

TORRES, M. *Lecciones de historia del derecho español.* 2 vols. Salamanca, 1933.

TRAMOYERES BLASCO, L. *Instituciones gremiales: su origen y organización en Valencia.* Valencia, 1889.

—— 'Letras de cambio valencianas.' *Revista de Archivos, Bibliotecas y Museos,* IV, 1900.

UÑA Y SARTHOU, J. *Las asociaciones obreras en España.* Madrid, 1901.

USHER, A. P. *The Early History of Deposit Banking in Mediterranean Europe,* I. Cambridge (Mass.), 1943.

VALDEAVELLANO, L. G. DE. 'El mercado. Apuntes para su estudio en León y Castilla durante la Edad Media.' *AHDE.* VIII, 1931.

VALLS I TABERNER, F. *Estudis d'Historia jurídica catalana.* Barcelona, 1929.

VANDELLÓS, J. A. *Catalunya, poble decadent.* Barcelona, 1935.

VENTALLO VINTRÓ, J. *Historia de la Industria Lanera Catalana; Monografia de sus antiguos gremios.* Tarrasa, 1904.

VERLINDEN, C. 'L'esclavage dans le monde ibérique médiéval.' *AHDE.* XI–XII, 1934–5.

—— 'L'histoire urbaine dans la péninsule ibérique.' *RB.* XV, 1936.

—— 'Contribution à l'étude de l'expansion commerciale de la draperie flamande dans la péninsule ibérique au XIIIe siècle.' *Revue du Nord,* XXII, 1936.

—— 'La grande peste du 1348 en Espagne...conséquences économiques et sociales.' *RB.* XVII, 1938.

—— 'The Rise of Spanish Trade in the Middle Ages.' *EcHR.* X, 1939–40.

(e) *France south of the Loire and of the great bend of the Rhone*

AHRENS, F. 'Analekten zur Geschichte des spätmittelalterlichen Geldhandels in der Dauphiné.' *VSWG.* XXI, 1928.

AUBENAS, R. 'La famille dans l'ancienne Provence.' *AHES.* VIII, 1936.

BADEY, L. 'Les premières routes des vins de France...au long de la Saône et du Rhône.' *Annales de Bourgogne*, VII, 1935.

BALASQUE, J. and DALAURENS, E. *Etudes historiques sur la ville de Bayonne*. 3 vols. Bayonne, 1862–75.

BIGWOOD, G. 'La politique de la laine en France sous les règnes de Philippe le Bel et de ses fils.' *RB.* XVI, 1936.

BILLIOUD, J. 'Le roi des merciers du comté de Provence aux XIVe et XVe siècles.' *Bulletin philologique et historique*, 1922–3.

—— 'De la confrérie à la corporation: Les classes industrielles en Provence.' *Mémoires de l'Institut Historique de Provence*, IV, 1929.

BLANC, A. 'Le livre des comptes de Jacme Olivier, marchand narbonnais du XIVe siècle.' *Bulletin de la Commission Archéologique de Narbonne*, IV, 1896.

BLOCH, M. 'Sur le passé de la noblesse française.' *AHES.* VIII, 1936.

BOISSONNADE, P. 'La renaissance et l'essor de la vie maritime en Poitou, Aunis et Saintonge, Xe–XVe siècles.' *RHES.* XII, 1924.

BOSSEBŒUF, L. A. *Histoire de la soierie à Tours du XIe au XVIIIe siècle*. Tours, 1900.

BOUDET, M. 'Les Gayte et les Chauchat: étude sur les sociétés marchandes et financières du moyen-âge.' *Revue d'Auvergne*, 1911–16.

BOUDET, M. et GRAND, R. *Étude historique sur les épidémies en Haute Auvergne*. Paris, 1902

BOURGEOIS, A. *Les métiers de Blois*. Blois, 1892.

BOUTRUCHE, R. 'Aux origines d'une crise nobiliaire...en Bordelais.' *AHES.* XI, 1939.

BOUVIER, R. *Un financier colonial au XVe siècle, Jacques Cœur*. Paris, 1928.

BOYER, H. *Histoire de l'industrie et du commerce à Bourges*. Bourges, 1884.

BRÉSARD, M. *Les foires de Lyon au XVe et XVIe siècles*. Paris, 1914.

BUSQUET, R. *Etudes sur l'ancienne Provence*. Paris, 1930.

CAILLET, L. 'Lyon et les Lucquois au XVe siècle.' *Revue d'histoire de Lyon*, IV, 1909.

CHARLES-ROUX, J. *Saint-Gilles, sa légende, son abbaye, ses coutumes*. Paris, 1911.

CLAVEL, M. 'La mévente du vin à Tarascon.' *Mémoires de l'Académie de Nîmes*, ser. 7, XXXI, 1901.

COORNAERT, E. *Les corporations de France avant 1789*. Paris, 1941.

CURIE-SEIMBRES, A. *Essai sur les villes fondées dans le sud-ouest de la France...sous le nom de bastides*. Toulouse, 1880.

DEJEAN, P. 'L'évolution à travers les âges de la metallurgie dans le sud-ouest de la France.' Technique moderne, 1927.

DELISLE, L. 'Les opérations financières des Templiers.' *Mémoires de l'Institut National des Inscriptions et Belles Lettres*, LXXXIII, 1889.

DENHOLM-YOUNG, N. 'The Merchants of Cahors.' *Medievalia et Humanistica*, 1946.

DENIFLE, H. *La désolation...en France vers le milieu du XVe siècle*. Mâcon, 1897.

DION, R. 'Orléans et l'ancienne navigation de la Loire.' *Annales de Géographie*, XLVII, 1938.

DUPONT, A. *Les relations commerciales entre les cités maritimes de Languedoc et les cités méditerranéennes d'Espagne et d'Italie du Xe au XIIIe siècle*. Nîmes, 1942.

Encyclopédie Départementale des Bouches du Rhône, II, XIV and XV. Marseilles, 1924–37.

EVANS, J. *Life in Medieval France*. Oxford, 1925.

FAGNIEZ, G. *Documents relatifs à l'histoire de l'industrie et du commerce en France*. 2 vols. Paris, 1898–1900.

FORESTIÉ, E. *Les livres de comptes des Frères Bonis, marchands montalbanais du XIVe siècle*. 3 vols. Auch, 1890–4.

GAUTHIER, L. *Les Lombards dans les Deux Bourgognes*. Paris, 1907.

GAUTHIER-ZIEGLER, G. *Histoire de Grasse au moyen-âge*. Paris, 1935.

GERMAIN, A. *Histoire du commerce de Montpellier au moyen-âge*. 2 vols. Montpellier, 1861.

GOURCY, C. DE. *La foire de Beaucaire*. Poitiers, 1911.

GOURON, M. 'Note sur l'ancienne navigation dans la Petite Camargue.' *Bulletin de la Société d'Histoire et Archéologie de Nîmes et du Gard*, 1938–9.

GUIBERT, L. *Les anciennes corporations de métiers du Limousin*. Limoges, 1883.

GUIRAUD, L. *Recherches et conclusions nouvelles sur le prétendu rôle de Jacques Cœur.* Paris, 1900.

HÉRUBEL, M. A. *Les origines des ports de la Gironde et de la Garonne maritime.* Paris, 1934.

JEULIN, F. *L'évolution du port de Nantes.* Paris, 1929.

JOLY, A. 'Etablissements de Jacques Cœur dans le Lyonnais.' *Bibliothèque de l'Ecole des Chartes,* LXXXIX and XCIII, 1928 and 1932.

JOUBERT, A. *La vie privée en Anjou au XVe siècle.* Angers, 1884.

KLEINCLAUSZ, A. (ed.). *Histoire de Lyon,* I (Déniau, Poozet and others). Lyon, 1939.

LANGLOIS, C. V. *La vie en France au moyen-âge.* 4 vols., 2nd ed. Paris, 1925–38.

LEMPEREUR, L. *Les chevaliers merciers du Rouergue.* Rodez, 1928.

LEVASSEUR, E. *Histoire des classes ouvrières et de l'industrie en France avant 1789.* 2nd ed. Paris, 1901.

LEWIS, A. R. 'The Development of Town Government in Montpellier.' *Speculum,* XXII, 1947.

LIMOUZIN-LAMOTHE, R. *La commune de Toulouse et les sources de son histoire.* Toulouse, 1932.

LODGE, E. *Gascony under English Rule.* London, 1926.

LOPEZ, R. S. 'Le relazioni commerciali tra Genova e la Francia nel medio evo.' *Cooperazione Intellettuale,* VI, 1938.

LORBER, P. 'Le village et le château de Pau depuis leurs origines jusqu'à la fin du XIVe siècle.' *Bulletin de la Société des Sciences, Lettres et Arts de Pau,* 1914–17.

LOT, F. *L'état des paroisses et des feux de 1328.* Paris, 1929.

LOT, F. et FAWTIER, R. *Le premier budget de la monarchie française (1202).* Paris, 1932.

LUCE, S. *La France pendant la guerre de Cent Ans.* Paris, 1890–3.

LUCHAIRE, A. *La société française à l'époque de Philippe-Auguste.* Paris, 1909.

—— *Les communes françaises à l'époque des Capétiens directs,* 2nd ed. Paris, 1911.

MALVEZIN, T. *Histoire du commerce de Bordeaux,* I. Bordeaux, 1892.

MARSH, F. B. *English Rule in Gascony, with Special Reference to the Towns.* Ann Arbor, 1912.

MARTIN DE SAINT LÉON, E. *Histoire des corporations de métiers depuis leurs origines…,* 4th ed. Paris, 1941.

MAYER, G. *Essai sur les origines du crédit en France du XIIIe au XIVe siècle.* Paris, 1902.

MOREL, P. 'Les troubles populaires à Solignac au XIIIe siècle.' *Bulletin de la Société Archéologique et Historique du Limousin,* LXXVII, 1938.

MORIZE, J. 'Aigues-Mortes au XIIIe siècle.' *Annales du Midi,* XXVI, 1914.

MOSSÉ, A. *Histoire des Juifs d'Avignon et du Comtat-Venaissin.* Paris, 1934.

MULHOLLAND, M. A. *Early Gild Records of Toulouse.* New York, 1941.

PERNOUD, R. *Essai sur l'histoire du port de Marseille.* Marseilles, 1935.

PIRENNE, H. 'Un grand commerce d'exportation au moyen-âge, les vins de France.' *AHES.* V, 1933.

PORT, C. *Essai sur l'histoire du commerce maritime de Narbonne.* Paris, 1852.

POUX, J. *La cité de Carcassonne, histoire et description,* I–II. Toulouse, 1922–38.

RIBBE, C. *La société provençale à la fin du moyen-âge.* Paris, 1898.

ROYER, J. *Libourne: Etude d'évolution de ville.* Libourne, 1929.

SAYOUS, A. E. 'L'activité de deux capitalistes-commerçants marseillais.' *RHES.* XVII, 1929.

—— 'Le commerce terrestre de Marseille au XIIIe siècle.' *RH.* CLXIII, 1930.

—— 'Le commerce de Nice avec l'intérieur.' *AHES.* XI, 1939.

SAYOUS, A. E. and COMBES, J. 'Les commerçants et les capitalistes de Montpellier aux XIIIe et XIVe siècles.' *RH.* CLXXXXVIII–IX, 1940.

SCLAFERT, T. *Le Haut Dauphiné au moyen-âge.* Paris, 1926.

—— 'Les routes du Dauphiné et de la Provence sous l'influence du séjour des papes à Avignon.' *AHES.* I, 1929.

THOMAS, L. J. *Montpellier, ville marchande, histoire économique et sociale.* Montpellier, 1936.

TOURNAFOND, A. *Les Marchés et les foires de Limoges.* Limoges, 1941.

USHER, A. P. *The History of the Grain Trade in France*, 1400–1710. Cambridge (Mass.), 1913.

—— 'The General Course of Wheat Prices in France, 1350–1388.' *Rev. Econ. Statistics*, 1930.

VAILLANT, P. 'Grenoble et ses libertés; Gap et les libertés gapençaises.' *Annales de l'Université de Grenoble*, XII, XIV, XVIII, 1935–7, 1942.

VIGNE, M. *La banque à Lyon du XVe au XVIIIe siècle*. Lyon, 1903.

VILLARD, J. 'Jean Casse, armateur et marchand marseillais du XIVe siècle.' *Annales de la Société d'études provençales*, IV, 1907.

VIVIER, R. 'Une crise économique au milieu du XIVe siècle; la première intervention de la royauté dans le domaine économique.' *RHES*. VII, 1920.

WOLFF, P. 'Une famille du XIIIe siècle au XVIe: les Ysalguier de Toulouse.' *AHES*. 1942.

—— 'Registres d'impôts et vie économique à Toulouse sous Charles VI.' *Annales du Midi*, LVI–LVIII, 1944–6.

(f) Switzerland, Austria, Danubian Germany

AEBISCHER, P. 'Banquiers, commerçants, diplomates et voyageurs à Fribourg avant 1500.' *Zeitschrift für Schweizerische Geschichte*, VII, 1927.

AMMANN, H. *Freiburg und Bern und die Genfer Messen*. Langensalza, 1921.

—— 'Die wirtschaftliche Bedeutung der Schweiz im Mittelalter.' *Festschrift A. Schulte*, Düsseldorf, 1927.

—— *Neue Beiträge zur Geschichte der Zurzacher Messen*. Aarau, 1930.

APELBAUM, J. *Basler Handelsgesellschaften im 15. Jahrhundert*. Berne, 1915.

BAECHTOLD, H. *Die schweizerische Volkswirtschaft in ihren Beziehungen zu Deutschland*. Frauenfeld, 1927.

BASTIAN, F. 'Zur österreichische Handelsgeschichte.' *VSWG*. IX, 1911.

—— 'Das wahre Gesicht des "vorkapitalistischen" Kaufmanns.' *VSWG*. XXIV, 1931.

—— *Das Runtingerbuch 1383–1407 und verwandtes Material*, I. Regensburg, 1944.

BECHTEL, H. *Der Wirtschaftsstil des deutschen Spätmittelalters*. Munich, 1930.

BELOW, G. VON. *Der Ursprung der deutschen Stadtverfassung*. Düsseldorf, 1892.

—— *Territorium und Stadt*. Munich, 1900.

BIRKNER, E. *Die Behandlung der Nürnberger im Ostseegebiet*. Kiel, 1927.

BOREL, F. *Les foires de Genève au XVe siècle*. Geneva, 1892.

CARO, G. *Beiträge zur Deutschen Wirtschafts- und Verfassungsgeschichte*. 2 vols. Leipzig, 1905–11.

CHROUST, A. and PROESLER, H. *Das Handlungsbuch der Holzschuher in Nürnberg von 1304–7*. Erlangen, 1934.

DEROISY, A. 'Les routes terrestres des laines anglaises vers la Lombardie.' *Revue du Nord*, XXV, 1939.

DURRER, R. 'Studien zur ältesten Geschichte Luzerns und des Gotthardweges.' *Geschichtsfreund*, LXXXIV, 1930.

ECKERT, E. *Die Krämer in süddeutschen Städten bis zum Ausgang des Mittelalters*. Freiburg-i.-B., 1913.

EHRENZELLER, W. *Kloster und Stadt St Gallen im Spätmittelalter*. St Gall, 1931.

EVÉQUOZ, H. *Essai sur l'histoire de l'organisation communale et des franchises de la ville de Sion*. Berne, 1925.

GEERING, T. *Handel und Industrie der Stadt Basel*. Basle, 1886.

GIERKE, O. F. *Das deutsche Genossenschaftrecht*. 4 vols. Berlin, 1868–1913.

GOTHEIN, E. *Wirtschaftsgeschichte des Schwarzwaldes und der angrenzenden Landschaften*. Strasbourg, 1892.

GROSS, L. *Beiträge zur städtische Vermögenstatistik in Oesterreich*. Innsbruck, 1913.

HEIMPEL, H. *Das Gewerbe der Stadt Regensburg im Mittelalter*. Stuttgart, 1926.

—— 'Zur Handelspolitik Kaiser Sigismunds.' *VSWG*. XXIII, 1930.

HOFFMANN, M. *Der Geldhandel der deutschen Juden während des Mittelalters*. Leipzig, 1910.

HOPPE, O. *Silberbergbau zu Schneeberg bis* 1500. Freiberg, 1908.

JANSEN, M. *Studien zur Geschichte der Fugger*, I. Leipzig, 1907.

KELLER-ESCHER, C. *Das Steuerwesen der Stadt Zürich im XIII.–XV. Jahrh.* Zürich, 1904.

KEUTGEN, F. 'Der Grosshandel im Mittelalter.' *Hansische Geschichtsblätter*, X, 1901.

—— *Aemter und Zünfte*. Jena, 1903.

KLAIBER, L. *Beiträge zur Wirtschaftspolitik oberschwäbischer Reichsstädte im ausgehende Mittelalter.* Stuttgart, 1927.

KOEHLER, E. *Einzelhandel im Mittelalter.* Stuttgart, 1938.

KOGLER, F. *Recht und Verfassung der Stadt Rattenberg im Mittelalter.* Munich, 1929.

LUSCHIN VON EBENGREUTH, A. *Wiens Münzwesen, Handel und Verkehr im späteren Mittelalter.* Vienna, 1902. (Also in *Geschichte der Stadt Wien*, II. Vienna, 1902.)

MAYER, T. *Der auswärtige Handel des Herzogtums Oesterreich im Mittelalter.* Innsbruck, 1909.

—— 'Zwei Passauer Mautbücher aus den Jahren 1400–1402.' *Verhandlungen des historischen Vereins für Niederbayern*, XL, XLIV–XLV, 1908–9.

—— 'Zur Frage der Städtegründungen im Mittelalter.' *Mitteilungen des Oesterreichischen Instituts für Geschichtsforschung*, XLIII, 1929.

MOOSER, F. *Das Strassen- und Schiffahrtswesen der Nordostschweiz im Mittelalter.* Thurgau, 1931.

MUELLER, J. 'Der Umfang und die Hauptrouten des Nürnberger Handelsgebiets im Mittelalter.' *VSWG.* VI, 1908.

—— 'Die Handelspolitik Nürnbergs im Spätmittelalter.' *JNOS.* XXXVIII, 1908.

NORDMANN, C. *Nürnberger Grosshändler im spätmittelalterlichen Lübeck.* Nürnberg, 1933.

—— *Oberdeutschland und die deutsche Hanse.* Weimar, 1939.

NUEBLING, E. *Ulms Handel und Gewerbe im Mittelalter.* 2 vols. Ulm, 1899–1900.

PENNDORF, B. *Geschichte der Buchhaltung in Deutschland.* Leipzig, 1913.

PLANITZ, H. 'Forschungen zur Stadtverfassungsgeschichte.' *Zeitschrift der Savigny-Stiftung*, Germ. Abt., LX, LXIII, LXIV, 1940–4.

REUTHER, O. *Die Entwicklung der Augsburger Textilindustrie.* Diessen, 1915.

RIETSCHEL, S. *Markt und Stadt in ihrem rechtlichen Verhältnis.* Leipzig, 1897.

RUNDSTEDT, H. G. VON. *Die Regelung des Getreidehandels in den Städten Südwestdeutschlands und der deutschen Schweiz....* Stuttgart, 1930.

SCHEITLIN, O. *Das Sanket Gallische Zunftwesen von den Anfängen bis zum Ende des 16. Jahrh.* St Gall, 1937.

SCHIB, K. *Geschichte der Stadt Schaffhausen.* Schaffhausen, 1945.

SCHLEESE, K. *Die Handelsbeziehungen Oberdeutschland zu Posen im Ausgange des Mittelalters.* Greifswald, 1915.

SCHMOLLER, G. *Deutsches Städtewesen in älterer Zeit.* Bonn, 1922.

SCHNYDER, W. *Die Bevölkerung der Stadt und Landschaft Zürich vom 14. bis zum 17. Jahrh.* Zürich, 1925.

SCHUENEMANN, K. *Die Entstehung des Städtewesens in Südosteuropa.* (Gran) Breslau, 1929.

SCHULTE, A. *Geschichte der grossen Ravensburger Handelsgesellschaft.* 3 vols. Stuttgart, 1923.

—— *Geschichte des mittelalterlichen Handels und Verkehrs zwischen Westdeutschland und Italien mit Ausschluss von Venedig.* 2 vols. Leipzig, 1900.

—— 'Wer war um 1430 der reichste Bürger in Schwaben und der Schweiz?' *Deutsche Geschichtsblätter*, I, 1900.

—— 'Mercanti lombardi a Lucerna e nel Vallese.' *Bollettino Storico della Svizzera Italiana*, XXX, 1908.

SPANGENBERG, H. *Territorialwirtschaft und Stadtwirtschaft.* Munich, 1932.

SPIESS, W. *Das Marktprivileg.* Heidelberg, 1916.

SRBIK, H. VON. *Studien zur Geschichte des österreichischen Salzwesens.* Innsbruck, 1917.

STOEVEN, M. *Der Gewandschnitt in den deutschen Städten des Mittelalters.* Berlin, 1915.

STRAMPF, I. VON. *Die Entstehung und mittelalterliche Entwicklung der Stadt Nürnberg in geographischer Betrachtung.* Erlangen, 1929.

STRIEDER, J. *Zur Genesis des modernen Kapitalismus* (Augsburg). Leipzig, 1904.

THOMPSON, J. W. *Feudal Germany*. Chicago, 1928.

VINCENT, J. M. *Costume and Conduct in the Laws of Basel, Bern and Zürich*. Baltimore, 1935.

VOLTELINI, H. VON. 'Anfänge der Stadt Wien.' *Mitteilungen des Vereins für Geschichte der Stadt Wien*, I, 1920.

WEISS, L. 'Beiträge zur Geschichte der mittelalterlichen Stadtwirtschaft in Ungarn.' *VSWG*. XII, 1914.

WILD, E. *Die eidgenössischen Handelsprivilegien in Frankreich 1444–1635*. St Gall, 1909.

(g) *Istria and Dalmatia*

BENUSSI, B. *Nel medio evo, pagine di storia istriana*. Parenzo, 1897.

BRUNELLI, V. 'Il comune di Zara in sul finire dei tempi di mezzo.' *Archivio storico per la Dalmazia*, IX, 1934.

DE FRANCESCHI, C. 'Esuli fiorentini della compagnia di Dante Mercanti e prestatori a Trieste e in Istria.' *AV*. ser. 5, LXVIII, 1939.

GELCICH, G. *Delle istituzioni marittime e sanitarie della Repubblica di Ragusa*. Trieste, 1882.

JIRECEK, C. 'Die Bedeutung von Ragusa in der Handelsgeschichte des Mittelalters.' *Die Feierliche Sitzung der K. Akademie der Wissenschaften*. Vienna, 1897.

KREKICH, A. 'La "curia consulum et maris" del comune medievale zaratino.' *Atti e memorie della Società Dalmata di storia patria*, I, 1926.

LEJERER, C. 'Aus den ältesten Handlungsbüchern der Republik Ragusa.' *Zeitschrift für Betriebswirtschaft*, VI, 1929.

SOLOVIEV, A. 'Le patriciat de Raguse au XVe siècle.' *Resetarov Zbornik iz dubrovacke Proslosti*. Dubrovnik (Ragusa), 1931.

ГEJA, A. *Aspetti della vita economica di Zara*, I. Zara, 1936; II, in *Rivista Dalmatica*, 1941.

(h) *Expansion of the Mediterranean Peoples beyond Southern Europe*[1]

AMARI, M. *I diplomi arabi del R. Archivio Fiorentino*. Florence, 1863.

ANDRÉADÈS, A. M. 'L'administration financière et économique de Venise dans ses possessions du Levant.' *Acropole*, 1926.

BAUTIER, R. 'Marchands siennois et draps d'Outremonts aux foires de Champagne.' *Annuaire-Bulletin de la Société de l'Histoire de France*, 1945.

BERZA, M. 'La colonia fiorentina di Costantinopoli nei secoli XV–XVI.' *Revue historique du Sud-Est européen*, XXI, 1944.

BIGWOOD, G. 'Les Tolomei en France au XIVe siècle.' *RB*. VIII, 1929.

BORLANDI, F. Introduction to *El libro di mercatantie et usanze de' paesi*. Turin, 1936.

BRANDT, W. 'Pierre Dubois: Mediaeval or Modern?' *AHR*. XLI, 1930.

BRATIANU, G. I. *Recherches sur le commerce génois dans la Mer Noire au XIIIe siècle*. Paris, 1929.

—— *Recherches sur Vicina et Cetatea Alba*. Bucarest, 1935.

—— 'Les Vénitiens dans la Mer Noire...après la deuxième guerre des Détroits.' *Echos d'Orient*, XXXIII, 1934.

—— *Les Vénitiens dans la Mer Noire au XIVe siècle*. Bucarest, 1939.

BROWN, H. 'The Venetians and the Venetian Quarter in Constantinople.' *Journ. Hellenic Studies*, XL, 1920.

BYRNE, E. H. 'Genoese Trade with Syria in the Twelfth Century.' *AHR*. XXV, 1920.

---

[1] Works dealing with the expansion of Mediterranean peoples into other countries of Southern Europe are listed with works dealing with the trade of these countries. All titles dealing with expansion into England have been omitted, because the bibliography of the special chapter on England has a full list. Only a few representative works dealing with expansion into the Mediterranean Levant have been included.

BYRNE, E. H. 'The Genoese Colonies in Syria.' *Historical Essays presented to D. C. Munro*. New York, 1928.

CADDEO, R. Introduction to A. Ca' Da Mosto, *Le navigazioni atlantiche*, 2nd ed. Milan, 1929.

CERONE, F. 'La politica orientale di Alfonso d' Aragona.' *Archivio Storico per le province Napoletane*, XXVII–XXVIII, 1902–3.

CESSI, R. 'Venezia e l' acquisto di Nauplia ed Argo.' *NAV*. n.ser., XXX, 1915.

—— *Le colonie medievali italiane in Oriente*, I. Padua, 1942.

CIASCA, R. 'Un centro marocchino del traffico genovese nel medioevo.' *Rivista Internazionale di Scienze Sociali*, ser. 3, VI, 1935.

COLOMER, L. *Le rôle de Marseille dans les relations de la France avec les pays d'Orient*. Toulouse, 1929.

DELAVILLE LE ROULX, J. *Les Hospitaliers en Terre Sainte et à Chypre*. Paris, 1904.

DESIMONI, C. 'Actes passés à l'Ayas, Beyrouth et Famagouste par devant des notaires génois.' *Archives de l'Orient Latin*, I–II, 1881–2 and *Revue de l'Orient Latin*, I, 1893.

—— 'I conti dell' ambasciata al Khan di Persia.' *ASLi*. XIII, 1879.

—— 'I genovesi ed i loro quartieri a Costantinopoli....' *Giornale Ligustico*, I and III, 1874–6.

DIEHL, C. 'La colonie vénitienne à Constantinople à la fin du XIVe siècle.' *Mélanges d'archéologie et d'histoire*, III, 1883.

DI TUCCI, R. *Il genovese Antonio Malfante*. Bologna, 1935.

—— 'Documenti inediti sulla spedizione di Ceuta.' *ASLi*. LXIV, 1935.

DOEHAERD, R. *Les relations commerciales entre Gênes, la Belgique et l'Outremont*, I. Brussels, 1941.

DUDAN, B. *Il dominio veneziano nel Levante*. Bologna, 1938.

DURO, C. F. *La marina de Castilla*. Madrid, 1894.

EVANS, A. Introduction to F. Balducci Pegolotti, *La pratica della mercatura*. Cambridge (Mass.), 1936.

FOTHERINGHAM, F. K. *Marco Sanudo, Conqueror of the Archipelago*. Oxford, 1915.

GEROLA, G. *Monumenti Veneti nell' isola di Creta*. 5 vols. Venice, 1905–31.

GRUENZWEIG, A. *Correspondance de la filiale de Bruges des Medici*, I. Brussells, 1931 (in progress?).

HÓMAN, V. 'La circolazione delle monete d'oro in Ungheria dal X al XIV secolo e la crisi europea dell' oro.' *Rivista Italiana di Numismatica*, XXXIV, 1922.

HOPF, K. 'Griechenland.' *Ersch und Grüber Enzyklopädia*.

JONA, C. 'Genova e Rodi agli albori del Rinascimento.' *ASLi*. LXIV, 1935.

JORGA, N. *Notes et extraits pour servir à l'histoire des Croisades au XVe siècle*. 4 vols. Bucarest, 1900–15.

KOCH, S. *Italienische Pfandleiher im nördlichen und östlichen Frankreich*. Breslau, 1904.

KRUEGER, H. 'The Routine of Commerce between Genoa and Northwest Africa.' *Mariner's Mirror*, XIX, 1933.

—— 'Genoese Trade with Northwest Africa; Wares of Exchange in Twelfth-Century Genoese-African Trade.' *Speculum*, VIII and XII, 1933 and 1937.

LAENEN, J. 'Les Lombards à Malines.' *Bulletin du cercle archéologique, littéraire et artistique de Malines*, XV, 1906.

LA RONCIÈRE, C. DE. *Histoire de la marine française*, I–II, 3rd ed. Paris, 1909.

—— *La découverte de l'Afrique au moyen-âge*. 3 vols. Cairo, 1925–7.

LEVI, C. A. *Venezia e il Montenegro*, 1443–1494. Venice, 1896.

LOPEZ, R. S. *Storia delle colonie genovesi nel Mediterraneo*. Bologna, 1938.

—— 'European Merchants in the Medieval Indies, the Evidence of Commercial Documents.' *JEH*. III, 1943.

—— 'Le facteur économique dans la politique africaine des Papes.' *RH*. CXCVIII, 1947.

LYBYER, A. H. 'The Ottoman Turks and the Routes of Oriental Trade.' *Eng. Hist. Rev*. XXX, 1915.

MAGNAGHI, A. *Precursori di Colombo? Il tentativo di viaggio transoceanico dei fratelli Vivaldi*. Roma, 1936.

MANFRONI, C. 'Le relazioni tra Genova, l' Impero Bizantino e i Turchi.' *ASLi*. XXVIII, 1898.
—— *Storia della marina italiana*. 2 vols. Leghorn, 1899–1902.
—— *Il Genio Italiano all' Estero: I Colonizzatori*. 2 vols. Rome, 1933.
MARENGO, E. 'Genova e Tunisi, 1388–1515.' *ASLi*. XXXII, 1901.
MAS LATRIE, M. L. DE. *Histoire de l'île de Chypre*. 3 vols. Paris, 1860.
MILLER, W. *The Latins in the Levant, a History of Frankish Greece*. London, 1908.
—— *Essays on the Latin Orient*. Cambridge, 1921.
MIROT, L. 'Etudes Lucquoises.' *Bibliothèque de l'Ecole des Chartes*, LXXXVI–CI, 1925–40.
MONTI, G. M. *L'espansione mediterranea del Mezzogiorno d'Italia e della Sicilia*. Bologna, 1942.
MOREL, P. *Les Lombards dans la Flandre française et le Hainaut*. Lille, 1908.
NALDINI, L. 'La politica coloniale di Pisa nel medio evo.' *Bollettino storico pisano*, 1939.
NICOLAU D'OLWER, L. *L'expansió de Catalunya en la Mediterrània oriental*. Barcelona, 1926.
NISTOR, J. *Handel und Wandel in der Moldau bis zum Ende des 16. Jahrh*. Czernowitz, 1912.
NOIRET, H. *Documents inédits pour servir à l'histoire de la domination vénitienne en Crète*, 1380–1435. Rome, 1892.
OLSCHKI, L. *Marco Polo's Precursors*. Baltimore, 1943.
PELLIOT, P. *Mongoles et Papes aux XIIIe et XIVe siècles*. Paris, 1922.
PITON, C. *Les Lombards en France et à Paris*. Paris, 1892.
PTASNIK, S. *Gli Italiani in Polonia*. (Ital. summary by SAPORI, A.) *ASI*. ser. 7, III, 1925.
REPARAZ, G. DE. *Catalunya a les mars*. Barcelona, 1930.
ROSSI-SABATINI, E. *L' espansione di Pisa nel Mediterraneo*. Florence, 1935.
RUBIÓ I LLUCH, A. *Catalunya a Grècia*. Barcelona, 1906.
—— *Los Catalanes en Grècia*. Madrid, 1927.
—— 'La població de la Grècia Catalana.' *Memòries del Institut de Estudis Catalans*, 1933.
SAUVAGET, J. 'Notes sur la colonie génoise de Pera.' *Syria*, XV, 1934.
SAYOUS, A. E. *Le commerce des Européens à Tunis depuis le XIIe siècle*. Paris, 1929.
—— 'Les mandats de St Louis sur son trésor et le mouvement international des capitaux.' *RH*. CLXVII, 1931.
SETTON, K. M. 'The Avignonese Papacy and the Catalan Duchy of Athens.' *Byzantion*, XVII, 1944–5.
SILBERSCHMIDT, M. *Das orientalische Problem zur Zeit der Entstehung des türkischen Reiches*, 1381–1400. Leipzig, 1925.
SKRZINSKA, E. 'Les inscriptions latines des colonies génoises en Crimée.' *ASLi*. LVI, 1928.
SORANZO, G. *Il Papato, l' Europa Cristiana e i Tartari*. Milan, 1930.
STARR, J. 'Jewish Life in Crete under the Rule of Venice.' *Proceedings of the American Academy for Jewish Research*, XII, 1942.
STEVENSON, E. L. *The Portolan Charts, their Origin and Characteristics*. New York, 1911.
TADINI, O. 'I marinai italiani in Francia, Spagna e Inghilterra.' *Rivista marittima*, 1887, 1892 and 1898.
TERROINE, A. 'Gandoufle d'Arcelles et les compagnies placentines à Paris.' *AHES*. 1945.
VITALE, A. V. 'Statuti e ordinamenti…del Banco di San Giorgio a Famagosta.' *ASLi*. LXIV, 1935.
VOJNOVIĆ, L. *Dubrovnik i Osmansko carstvo*, 1365–1482. Belgrade, 1898.
XANTHOUDIDÉS, S. A. Ἡ Ἐνετοκρατία ἐν Κρήτῃ (The Venetian Rule in Crete). Athens, 1939.
YULE, H. *Cathay and the Way Thither*. 4 vols., 2nd ed. London, 1913–16.

CHAPTER VI
The Woollen Industry

The following bibliography takes no account of original sources, except in the case of two major printed collections devoted exclusively to the woollen industry. Nor does it attempt to acknowledge either unpublished theses or discussions with scholars, though to these, as to the source material, published and unpublished, the chapter is much indebted. Only works relating to the regions more specially dealt with in the chapter are included, and, with few exceptions, only those primarily concerned with cloth or its raw materials.

It will at once be apparent that the field of study is at present very unevenly covered by modern works. For the Low Countries, for instance, there is a detailed survey of the industry in French Flanders, but as yet no comparable study for Flanders as a whole (despite the magnificent collection of documents published by Espinas and Pirenne), much less for the entire Low Countries region. Similarly for Italy much remains to be done; there has as yet been no such thorough investigation of the northern manufacturing centres as of Florence, while the history of the Florentine industry, hitherto written largely from gild statutes—like many older industrial histories, has only recently begun to be studied in the light of actual business records. For England even less has as yet been done and a great quantity of source material remains not only unused but also unprinted, while many even of the best of those secondary works that do exist are vitiated by an uncritical use of the ulnage accounts.

I. GENERAL: TECHNIQUE AND RAW MATERIALS

BARDENHEWER, L. *Der Safranhandel im Mittelalter.* Bonn, 1914.

BORLANDI, F. 'Note per la storia della produzione e del commercio di una materia prima. Il guado nel medio evo.' *Studi in onore di Gino Luzzatto.* Milan, 1949.

DAVIDSOHN, R. 'Garbowolle und Garbotuch.' *Historische Vierteljahrschrift*, VII. Leipzig, 1904.

HEYD, W. *Histoire du commerce du Levant au moyen âge.* 2 vols., édit. fr. Leipzig, 1923.

HURRY, J. B. *The Woad Plant and its Dye.* London, 1930.

KLEIN, J. *The Mesta; a study in Spanish economic history*, 1273–1836. Harvard Economic Studies, vol. XXI. Cambridge (Mass.), 1920.

POWER, E. *The Wool Trade in English Medieval History.* London, 1941.

SAVARY DES BRUSLONS, J. *Dictionnaire universel de commerce.* 3 vols., n.éd. Geneva, 1742.

SCHULTE, A. 'Garbo und Florenz. Zur Geschichte der Wollproduktion im Mittelalter.' *Zeitschrift für die gesamte Staatswissenschaft*, LVIII. Tübingen, 1901.

WECKERLIN, J. B. *Le drap 'escarlate' du moyen âge. Essai sur l'étymologie et la signification du mot écarlate, et notes techniques sur la fabrication de ce drap de laine au moyen âge.* Lyons, 1905.

II. THE ROMAN EMPIRE

Cambridge Ancient History. 12 vols. Cambridge, 1928–39.

CHARLESWORTH, M. P. *Trade Routes and Commerce of the Roman Empire*, 2nd ed. Cambridge, 1926.

ESPÉRANDIEU, E. *Recueil général des Bas-reliefs, statues et bustes de la Gaule romaine.* 10 vols. Paris, 1907–28.

FOX, G. E. 'Notes on some probable traces of Roman Fulling in Britain.' *Archaeologia*, LIX (Society of Antiquaries). London, 1904.

FRANK, T. and others (eds.). *An Economic Survey of ancient Rome.* 5 vols. Baltimore, 1933–40.

MAU, A. *Pompeji in Leben und Kunst*, 2nd ed. Leipzig, 1908.

ROSTOVTZEFF, M. I. *The Social and Economic History of the Roman Empire.* Oxford, 1926.

VERCAUTEREN, F. *Etude sur les civitates de la Belgique Seconde.* Mémoires de l'Académie royale de Belgique, Classe des Lettres et des Sciences morales et politiques. Brussels, 1934.

WALTZING, J. P. *Etude historique sur les corporations professionelles chez les Romains.* Mémoires couronnés de l'Académie royale des Sciences, des Lettres et des Beaux-Arts de Belgique, L. 4 vols. Brussels, 1895–1900.

WEST, L. C. *Roman Britain: the Objects of Trade.* Oxford, 1931.
—— *Roman Gaul: the Objects of Trade.* Oxford, 1935.

III. THE LOW COUNTRIES

COORNAERT, E. *L'industrie de la laine à Bergues-Saint-Winoc.* Paris, 1930.
—— *La draperie-sayetterie d'Hondschoote* (XIVe–XVIIIe siècles). Paris, 1930.

DE SAGHER, H. E. 'L'industrie drapière à Bruges.' *Revue de l'instruction publique en Belgique,* LIII. Brussels, 1910.

DES MAREZ, G. *L'organisation du travail à Bruxelles au XVe siècle.* Mémoires couronnés de l'Académie royale des Sciences, des Lettres et des Beaux-Arts de Belgique, LXV. Brussels, 1904.
—— 'Les Bogards dans l'industrie drapière à Bruxelles.' *Mélanges Paul Fredericq.* Société pour le progrès des études philologiques et historiques. Brussels, 1904.
—— 'La première étape de la formation corporative.' *Bulletin de l'Académie royale de Belgique, Classe des Lettres et des Sciences morales et politiques.* Brussels, 1921.

DOEHAERD, R. *Les Relations commerciales entre Gênes, la Belgique et l'Outremont d'après les archives notariales génoises aux XIIIe et XIVe siècles.* Institut historique belge de Rome; Etudes d'histoire économique et sociale. 4 vols. Brussels, 1941.

ESPINAS, G. 'Essai sur la technique de l'industrie textile à Douai aux XIIIe et XIVe siècles (1229–1403).' *Mémoires de la Société nationale des antiquaires de France,* LXVII. Paris, 1909.
—— *La vie urbaine de Douai au moyen âge.* 4 vols. Paris, 1913.
—— *La draperie dans la Flandre française au moyen âge.* 2 vols. Paris, 1923.
—— 'La draperie rurale d'Estaire (1428–1434).' *Revue d'histoire économique et sociale.* Paris, 1923.
—— 'Une petite correspondance de drapiers de Douai et de Paris en 1313.' *Mélanges d'histoire offerts à Henri Pirenne.* 2 vols. Brussels, 1926.
—— 'La confrérie des tisserands de draps de Valenciennes (1337).' *Annales d'histoire économique et sociale,* II. Paris, 1930.
—— 'L'organisation corporative des métiers de la draperie à Valenciennes, 1362–1403.' *Annales de la Société scientifique de Bruxelles,* LII. Brussels, 1932.
—— *Les origines du capitalisme.* I. *Sire Jehan Boinebroke, patricien et drapier Douaisien.* Bibliothèque de la Société d'histoire du droit des pays flamands, picards et wallons, VII. Lille, 1933.

ESPINAS, G. and PIRENNE, H. *Recueil de documents relatifs à l'histoire de l'industrie drapière en Flandre.* 4 vols. (Additions in *Bulletins de la Commission royale d'histoire,* XCIII, 1929.) Brussels, 1906–23.

LAURENT, H. *Un grand commerce d'exportation au moyen âge: La draperie des Pays-Bas en France et dans les pays méditerranéens* (XIIe–XVe siècle). Paris, 1935.

MALOWIST, M. 'Le développement des rapports économiques entre la Flandre, la Pologne et les Pays Limitrophes du XIIIe au XIVe siècle.' *Revue belge de philologie et d'histoire,* X. Brussels, 1931.

MARQUANT, R. *La vie économique à Lille sous Philippe le Bon.* Paris, 1940.

PIRENNE, H. 'Draps de Frise ou draps de Flandre? Un petit problème d'histoire économique à l'époque carolingienne.' *Vierteljahrschrift für Sozial- und Wirtschaftsgeschichte,* VII. Berlin, 1909.
—— 'Draps d'Ypres à Novgorod au commencement du XIIe siècle.' *Revue belge de philologie et d'histoire,* IX. Brussels, 1930.

PIRENNE, H. *Histoire de Belgique*. I. *Des origines au XIVe siècle*, 5th ed. Brussels, 1929.
—— II. *Du commencement du XIVe siècle à la mort de Charles le Téméraire*, 4th ed. Brussels, 1947.
—— III. *De la mort de Charles le Téméraire à l'arrivée du duc d'Albe dans les Pays-Bas*, 4th ed. Brussels, 1950.
See also under ESPINAS *and* PIRENNE.
POSTHUMUS, N. W. *De Geschiedenis van de Leidsche lakenindustrie*. I. *De Middeleeuwen*. The Hague, 1908.
—— *Bronnen tot de Geschiedenis van de Leidsche textielnijverheid*. Rijks Geschiedkundige Publicatiën 8. 6 vols. The Hague, 1910–22.
REYNOLDS, R. L. 'The Market for Northern Textiles in Genoa, 1179–1200.' *Revue belge de philologie et d'histoire*, VIII. Brussels, 1929.
—— 'Merchants of Arras and the Overland Trade with Genoa.' *Revue belge de philologie et d'histoire*, IX. Brussels, 1930.
—— 'Genoese Trade in the late Twelfth Century.' *Journal of Economic and Business History*, III. Cambridge (Mass.), 1931.
VAN WERVEKE, H. 'De koopman-ondernemer en de ondernemer in de Vlaamsche lakennijverheid van de middeleeuwen.' *Mededelingen van de Koninklijke Vlaamse Academie voor Wetenschappen, Letterenen Schone Kunsten van België, Klasse der Letteren*, VIII. Antwerp, 1946.
—— 'De Omvang van de Ieperse Lakenproductie in de veertiende eeuw.' *Mededelingen van de Koninklijke Vlaamse Academie voor Wetenschappen, Letteren en Schone Kunsten van België, Klasse der Letteren*, IX, 2. Antwerp, 1947.
VERLINDEN, C. 'L'expansion commerciale de la draperie flamande dans la péninsule ibérique au XIIIe siècle.' *Revue du Nord*, XXI. Lille, 1935.
—— 'Draps des Pays-Bas et du Nord de la France en Espagne au XIVe siècle.' *Le Moyen Age*, ser. 3, VII. Brussels, 1937.
—— 'Brabantsch en Vlaamsch laken te Krakau op het einde der XIVe eeuw.' *Kon. Vlaamse Academie voor Wetenschappen, Letteren en Schone Kunsten van België, Klasse der Letteren*, V, 2. Antwerp, 1943.

IV. ITALY

BENSA, E. *Francesco di Marco da Prato. Notizie e documenti sulla mercatura italiana del sec. XIV*. Milan, 1928.
BINI, T. *I Lucchesi a Venezia. Alcuni studi sopra i secoli XIII e XIV*. Lucca, 1853–6.
BRUN, R. 'A Fourteenth Century Merchant of Italy: Francesco Datini of Prato.' *Journal of Economic and Business History*, II. Cambridge (Mass.), 1930.
BYRNE, E. H. 'Commercial Contracts of the Genoese in the Syrian Trade of the Twelfth Century.' *Quarterly Journal of Economics*, XXXI. Boston (Mass.), 1916–17.
CESSI, R. 'Le Corporazioni dei mercanti di panni e della lana in Padova fino a tutto il secolo XIV.' *Memorie del R. Istituto Veneto di Scienze, Lettere ed Arti*, XXVIII, no. 2. Venice, 1908.
DAVIDSOHN, R. *Geschichte von Florenz*. Vol. IV, *Die Frühzeit der Florentiner Kultur*, pt. II, *Gewerbe, Zünfte, Welthandel und Bankwesen*. Berlin, 1925.
—— 'Blüte und Niedergang der Florentiner Tuchindustrie.' *Zeitschrift für die gesamte Staatswissenschaft*, Bd. 85. Tübingen, 1928.
DE ROOVER, R. 'A Florentine firm of cloth manufacturers; management and organisation of a sixteenth century business.' *Speculum*, XVI. The Medieval Academy of America. Cambridge (Mass.), 1941.
DOEHAERD, R. *See under* LOW COUNTRIES.
DOREN, A. *Studien aus der Florentiner Wirtschaftsgeschichte*, I. *Die Florentiner Wollentuchindustrie vom XIV. bis zum XVI. Jahrhundert*. Stuttgart, 1901.
—— *Italienische Wirtschaftsgeschichte*, I. Jena, 1934.
EDLER, F. *Glossary of Medieval Terms of Business, Italian Series 1200–1600*. The Medieval Academy of America. Cambridge (Mass.), 1934.

FANO, N. 'Ricerche sull' arte della lana a Venezia nel XIII e XIV secolo.' *Archivio Veneto*, ser. v, nos. 35–36. Venice, 1936.

GRUNZWEIG, A. 'Les soi-disants status de la Confrérie de Sainte-Barbe.' *Bulletin de la commission royale d'histoire*, XCVI. Brussels, 1932.

HERMES, G. 'Der Kapitalismus in der Florentiner Wollenindustrie.' *Zeitschrift für die gesamte Staatswissenschaft*, LXXII. Tübingen, 1916.

LOPEZ, R. *Studi sull' economia genovese nel medio evo*: II. *Le origini dell' arte della lana*. Turin, 1936.

LUZZATTO, G. *Enciclopedia Italiana di Scienze, Lettere ed Arti, Istituto della Enciclopedia Italiana fondata da Giovanni Treccani*, sub. voc. 'Lana'. Rome, 1933.

RENARD, G. *Histoire du Travail à Florence*. 2 vols. Paris, 1913.

REYNOLDS, R. L. *See under* LOW COUNTRIES.

RODOLICO, N. 'The Struggle for the Right of Association in Fourteenth Century Florence.' *History*, the Quarterly Journal of the Historical Association, VII. London, 1922.

—— 'Proletariato operaio in Firenze del secolo XIV.' *Archivio storico italiano*, I. Florence, 1943.

—— *I Ciompi. Una pagina di storia del proletariato operaio*. Florence, 1945.

SAPORI, A. 'Una compagnia di Calimala ai primi del Trecento.' *Biblioteca storica toscana*, VIII. Florence, 1932.

SCHULTE, A. *Geschichte des mittelalterlichen Handels und Verkehrs zwischen Westdeutschland und Italien*. 2 vols. Leipzig, 1900.

SILVA, P. 'Intorno all' industria e al commercio della lana in Pisa.' *Studi Storici*, XIX. Pisa, 1911.

ZANAZZO, G. B. 'L'arte della lana in Vicenza.' *Miscellanea di storia Veneta*, ser. 3, VI. Venice, 1914.

ZANONI, L. *Gli Umiliati nei loro rapporti con l' eresia, l' industria della lana ed i comuni nei secoli XII e XIII, sulla scorta di documenti inediti*. Milan, 1911.

ZERBI, T. *Aspetti economico tecnici del mercato di Milano nel trecento*. Como, 1936.

V. ENGLAND

ARMITT, M. L. 'Fullers and Freeholders of the Parish of Grasmere.' *Transactions of the Cumberland and Westmorland Antiquarian and Archaeological Society*, n.ser., VIII. Kendal, 1908.

ASHLEY, W. *The Early History of the English Woollen Industry*. Publications of the American Economic Association, II, no. 4. Baltimore, 1887.

—— *An Introduction to English Economic History and Theory*, vol. I, pt. I, *The Middle Ages*, 3rd ed. London, 1894; pt. II, *The End of the Middle Ages*, 4th ed. London, 1906.

CARUS-WILSON, E. M. 'The Aulnage Accounts: a Criticism.' *Economic History Review*, II, no. I. London, 1929.

—— 'The Trade of Bristol.' *Studies in English Trade in the Fifteenth Century*. Ed. E. Power and M. Postan. London, 1933.

—— 'An Industrial Revolution of the Thirteenth Century.' *Economic History Review*, XI. London, 1941.

—— 'The English Cloth Industry in the late Twelfth and Early Thirteenth Centuries.' *Economic History Review*, XIV. London, 1944.

—— 'The Origins and Early Development of the Merchant Adventurers' Organisation in London.' *Economic History Review*, IV, no. 2. London, 1933.

—— 'Trends in the Export of English Woollens in the Fourteenth Century.' *Economic History Review*, 2nd series, III, no. 2, 1950.

CHOPE, R. PEARSE. 'The Aulnager in Devon.' *Devon Association for the Advancement of Science, Literature and Art*, XLIV. Plymouth, 1912.

CONSITT, F. *The London Weavers Company*. Vol. I, *From the Twelfth Century to the close of the Sixteenth Century*. Oxford, 1933.

DE SAGHER, H. 'L'immigration des tisserands flamands et brabançons en Angleterre sous Edward III.' *Mélanges d'histoire offerts à Henri Pirenne.* 2 vols. Brussels, 1926.

GRAY, H. L. 'The Production and Exportation of English Woollens in the Fourteenth Century.' *English Historical Review,* XXXIX. London, 1924.

HEATON, H. *The Yorkshire Woollen and Worsted Industries.* Oxford Historical and Literary Studies, X. Oxford, 1920.

LIPSON, E. *The History of the English Woollen and Worsted Industries.* London, 1921 (see below).

—— *The Economic History of England.* I. *The Middle Ages,* 7th ed. (revising much that is in previous editions and in *The History of the English Woollen and Worsted Industries* above). London, 1937.

McCLENAGHAN, B. *The Springs of Lavenham and the Suffolk Cloth Trade in the XV and XVI Centuries.* Ipswich, 1924.

POWER, E. *The Paycockes of Coggeshall.* London, 1920.

RAMSAY, G. D. *The Wiltshire Woollen Industry in the Sixteenth and Seventeenth Centuries.* Oxford Historical Studies. Oxford, 1943.

ROGERS, J. E. THOROLD. *History of Agriculture and Prices in England.* 7 vols. Oxford, 1866–1902.

SALZMAN, L. F. *English Industries of the Middle Ages,* new ed., Oxford, 1923.

SELLERS, M. 'The Textile Industries.' *The Victoria History of the Counties of England, Yorkshire,* II. London, 1912.

THORNTON, G. A. *A History of Clare, Suffolk.* Cambridge, 1930.

UNWIN, G. 'Woollen Cloth—the Old Draperies.' *The Victoria History of the Counties of England, Suffolk,* II. London, 1907.

—— *The Gilds and Companies of London,* 3rd ed. London, 1938.

WATSON, C. E. 'The Minchinhampton Custumal and its place in the story of the Manor.' *Bristol and Glouc. Archaeological Society Transactions,* LIV. Bristol, 1932.

CHAPTER VII

Mining and Metallurgy in Medieval Civilisation

I. SOURCES

AGRICOLA, GEORGIUS. *De Re Metallica.* Translated from the Latin edition of 1556 by H. C. and L. H. Hoover. London, 1912.

BIRINGUCCIO, VANNOCCIO. *De la Pirotechnia.* Transl. from the Italian edition of 1540. and edited by Cyril S. Smith and M. T. Gnudi. New York, 1942.

ERMISCH, HUBERT. *Das sächsische Bergrecht des Mittelalters.* Leipzig, 1887.

Laws and Customs of the Miners in the Forest of Dean. Ed. T. Houghton, 1689.

LOUVREX, M. G. DE. *Recueil contenant les édits et règlements faits pour le pais de Liège et comté de Looz.* 4 vols. Liége, 1749–52.

MATHESIUS, JOHANN. *Sarepta Darinnen allerlei Bergwerck und Metallen.* Munich, 1571.

Mendip Mining Laws and Forest Bounds (ed. J. W. Gough). Somerset Record Society Publications, XLV (1931).

PARACELSUS (THEOPHRASTUS BOMBASTUS VON HOHENHEIM). *Von der Bergsucht und anderen Bergkrankheiten* (1533–34?). Dillingen, 1567. (Engl. transl. in *Four Treatises of Paracelsus.* Ed. Henry E. Sigerist. Baltimore, 1941.)

PLOWDEN, EDMUND. *The Commentaries or Reports.* 1818 ed.

Recueil général des anciennes lois françaises. Par MM. Jourdan, Decrusy, Isambert. 28 vols. Paris, 1822–33.

WUTKE, KONRAD. *Schlesiens Bergbau und Hüttenwesen—Urkunden und Akten* (1529–1740). *Codex Diplomaticus Silesiae,* XX and XXI. Breslau, 1900–1.

ZIVIER, E. *Akten und Urkunden zur Geschichte des Schlesischen Bergwesens.* Kattowitz, 1900.

ZYCHA, ADOLF. *Das böhmische Bergrecht des Mittelalters auf Grundlage des Bergrechts von Iglau.* 2 vols. Berlin, 1900.

II. MODERN WORKS

A. *Genera*

ALLEMAGNE, HENRY RENÉ D'. *Ferronnerie ancienne.* 2 vols. Paris, 1924.

ARNDT, ADOLF. *Bergbau und Bergbaupolitik.* Leipzig, 1894.

BAUERMAN, H. *A Treatise on the Metallurgy of Iron,* 5th ed. London, 1882.

BECK, LUDWIG. *Die Geschichte des Eisens in technischer und kulturgeschichtlicher Beziehung.* 5 vols., 2nd ed. Brunswick, 1890–1903.

BECKMANN, JOHANN. *A History of Inventions, Discoveries and Origins.* (Transl. by Wm. Johnston. 2 vols., 4th ed. London, 1846.)

BENNETT, RICHARD and ELTON, JOHN. *History of Corn Milling.* London, 1898–1904.

BRAUDEL, FERNAND. 'Monnaies et Civilisations: de l'or du Soudan à l'argent d'Amérique.' *Annales: Economies, Sociétés, Civilisations,* I, no. 1, pp. 10–21. Paris, 1946.

CLÉMENT, PIERRE. *Jacques Cœur et Charles VII.* Paris, 1866.

EHRENBERG, RICHARD. *Das Zeitalter der Fugger, Geldkapital und Creditverkehr im 16. Jahrhundert.* Jena, 1896. (Transl. in part as *Capital and Finance in the Age of the Renaissance* by H. M. Lucas. London, 1928.)

FELDHAUS, FRANZ M. *Die Technik der Antike und des Mittelalters.* Potsdam, 1931.

HECKSCHER, ELI F. *Sveriges Ekonomiska Historia från Gustav Vasa.* 2 vols. Stockholm, 1935–6.

JARS, G. *Voyages métallurgiques ou recherches et observations sur les mines...en Allemagne, Suède, Norvège, Angleterre et Ecosse.* 3 vols. Lyons, 1774–81.

LEXIS, W. 'Beiträge zur Statistik der Edelmetalle.' *Jahrbücher für Nationalökonomie und Statistik,* XXXIV (1879), 361–417.

McILWAIN, C. H. 'Medieval Estates.' *Cambridge Med. History,* VII, 664–715.

NEF, J. U. 'A Comparison of Industrial Growth in France and England from 1540–1640.' *Journ. Polit. Econ.* XLIV (1936).

—— 'Industrial Europe on the Eve of the Reformation.' *Journ. Polit. Econ.* XLIX (1941).

—— *Industry and Government in France and England.* Memoirs of the American Philosophical Society. Philadelphia, 1940.

PERCY, JOHN. *Metallurgy,* II. London, 1880.

PIRENNE, HENRI. *Economic and Social History of Medieval Europe.* New York, 1937. (Transl. by I. E. Clegg. London, 1936.)

—— *Histoire de Belgique,* I–III, 3rd ed. Brussels, 1909, 1922, 1923.

POWER, EILEEN E. 'Peasant Life and Rural Conditions.' *Cambridge Med. History,* VII (1932).

SMITH, J. RUSSELL. *The Story of Iron and Steel.* New York, 1908.

SOETBEER, ADOLF. *Edelmetall-Produktion und Werthverhältnis zwischen Gold und Silber seit der Entdeckung Amerikas bis zur Gegenwart.* Gotha, 1879.

SOMBART, WERNER. *Der moderne Kapitalismus.* 4th ed., 4 vols. Munich and Leipzig, 1916.

STRIEDER, JACOB. 'Werden und Wachsen des europäischen Frühkapitalismus.' *Propyläen Weltgeschichte,* IV. Ed. Walter Goetz. Berlin, 1932.

—— *Zur Genesis des modernen Kapitalismus.* Leipzig, 1904.

SWANK, JAMES M. *History of the Manufacture of Iron in All Ages,* 2nd ed. Philadelphia, 1892.

USHER, ABBOTT PAYSON. *The Early History of Deposit Banking in Mediterranean Europe.* Cambridge (Mass.), 1943.

—— *A History of Mechanical Inventions.* New York, 1929.

WEBER, MAX. *General Economic History.* (Transl. by F. H. Knight.) London, 1927.

B. *On Mining and Metallurgy in Antiquity*

ARDAILLON, EDOUARD. *Les mines du Laurion dans l'antiquité.* Paris, 1897.

BESNIER, MAURICE. 'L'interdiction du travail des mines en Italie sous la république.' *Revue archéologique,* ser. 5, X (1919), 31–50.

—— 'Le commerce de plomb à l'époque romaine.' *Revue archéologique,* ser. 5, XII (1920), 211–44; XIII, 36–76; XIV, 98–121.

CALHOUN, G. M. 'Ancient Athenian Mining.' *Journ. Econ. and Business History*, III (1931), 333–61.

COLLINGWOOD, R. G. and MYERS, J. N. L. *Roman Britain and the English Settlements*, 2nd ed. Oxford, 1937.

DAVIES, OLIVER. *Roman Mines in Europe*. Oxford, 1935.

FRANCOTTE, HENRI. *L'industrie dans la Grèce ancienne*. 2 vols. Brussels, 1900–1.

FRANK, TENNEY. *An Economic History of Rome*, 2nd ed. Baltimore, 1927.

FRIEND, J. NEWTON. *Iron in Antiquity*. London, 1926.

MISPOULET, JEAN-BAPTISTE. *Le régime des mines à l'époque romaine et au moyen âge d'après les tables d'Aljustrel*. Paris, 1908.

NEUBURG, CLAMOR. 'Untersuchungen zur Geschichte des römischen Bergbaus.' *Zeitschrift für die gesamte Staatswissenschaft*, LVI (1900).

NEUBURGER, ALBERT. *Die Technik des Altertums*. Transl. by Henry L. Brose, *The Technical Arts and Sciences of the Ancients*. London, 1930.

ROSSIGNOL, JEAN PIERRE. *Les métaux dans l'antiquité*. Paris, 1863.

ROSTOVTZEFF, M. 'Geschichte der Staatspacht in der römischen Kaiserzeit bis Diokletian.' *Philologus*, Suppl., IX (1904).

—— *Studien zur Geschichte des römischen Kolonates*. Leipzig, 1910.

—— *The Social and Economic History of the Hellenistic World*. 3 vols. Oxford, 1941.

—— *The Social and Economic History of the Roman Empire*. Oxford, 1926.

C. *Central Europe and Italy*

ACHENBACH, H. *Das französische Bergrecht und die Fortbildung desselben durch das preussische allgemeine Berggesetz*. Bonn, 1869.

—— *Das gemeine deutsche Bergrecht*. Bonn, 1871.

—— 'Geschichte der Cleve-Märkischen Berggesetzgebung und Bergverwaltung bis zum Jahre 1815.' *Zeitschrift für Bergrecht*, XXXIII (1887).

AMRHEIN, AUGUST. 'Der Bergbau im Spessart unter der Regierung der Churfürsten von Mainz.' *Archiv des historischen Vereins von Unterfranken und Aschaffenburg*, XXXVII (1895).

ARNDT, AD. *Zur Geschichte und Theorie des Bergregals und der Bergbaufreiheit*. Halle, 1878.

—— 'Noch einmal der Sachsenspiegel und das Bergregal.' *Zeitschrift der Savigny-Stiftung für Rechtsgeschichte*, Germanische Abt., XXIII (1902).

—— 'Einige Bemerkungen zur Geschichte des Bergregals.' *Zeitschrift der Savigny-Stiftung für Rechtsgeschichte*, Germanische Abt., XXIV (1903).

BERNHARD, LUDWIG. 'Die Entstehung und Entwicklung der Gedingeordnungen im deutschen Bergrecht.' *Staats- und sozialwissenschaftliche Forschungen*. Ed. G. Schmöller, vol. XX, no. 7. Leipzig, 1902.

BITTNER, L. 'Das Eisenwesen in Innerberg-Eisenerz.' *Archiv für österreichische Geschichte*, LXXXIX (ii). Vienna, 1901.

BOYCE, HELEN. *The Mines of the Upper Harz from 1514 to 1589*. Menasha, Wisconsin, 1920.

BRUCHMÜLLER, W. *Der Kobaltbergbau und die Blaufarbenwerke in Sachsen bis zum Jahre 1653*. Crossen a. O., 1897.

CSALLNER, ROBERT. 'Alte deutsche Bergwerkskolonien im Norden Siebenbürgens.' In *Studium Lipsiense*, by Karl Lamprecht. Berlin, 1909.

DOBEL, FRIEDRICH. 'Ueber den Bergbau und Handel des Jacob und Anton Fugger in Kärnten und Tirol, 1495–1560.' *Zeitschrift des historischen Vereins für Schwaben und Neuburg*, IX (1882), 193–213.

FINK, E. 'Die Bergwerksunternehmungen der Fugger in Schlesien.' *Zeitschrift des Vereins für Geschichte und Altertum Schlesiens*, XXVIII (1894).

FÖHRENBACH, OTTO. *Der badische Bergbau in seiner wirtschaftlichen Bedeutung vom Ausgang des Mittelalters bis zur Gegenwart*. Zell im Wiesenthal, 1910.

GOTHEIN, EBERHARD. 'Beiträge zur Geschichte des Bergbaus im Schwarzwald.' *Zeitschrift für die Geschichte des Oberrheins*, N.F. II (1887), 385–448.

GOTHEIN, EBERHARD. *Wirtschaftsgeschichte des Schwarzwaldes und der angrenzenden Landschaften.* Strasbourg, 1892.

GRÉAU, E. *Le fer en Lorraine.* Nancy, 1908.

HASSLACHER, A. 'Geschichtliche Entwicklung des Steinkohlenbergbaues im Saargebiete.' *Zeitschrift für Bergbau, Hütten und Salinenwesen im preussischen Staate,* XXXII (1884).

HASSLER, FRIED. 'German Miners in Foreign Lands in the Sixteenth Century.' *Research and Progress,* March/April, 1939.

HITZINGER, PETER. *Das Quecksilber-Bergwerk Idria.* Laibach, 1860.

HOPPE, OSWALD. *Der Silberbergbau zu Schneeberg bis zum Jahre 1500.* Freiberg, 1908.

HUE, OTTO. *Die Bergarbeiter. Historische Darstellung der Bergarbeiterverhältnisse von der ältesten bis in die neueste Zeit.* 2 vols. Stuttgart, 1910, 1913.

HÜLLMAN, KARL D. *Geschichte des Ursprungs der Stände in Deutschland.* Frankfurt an der Oder, 1806.

INAMA-STERNEGG, K. T. VON. *Deutsche Wirtschaftsgeschichte des 10. bis 12. Jahrhunderts.* Leipzig, 1891.

JACQUOT, E. 'Notice sur la fabrication de la fonte, du fer et de l'acier dans le Thüringerwald et le Frankenwald.' *Annales des mines,* ser. 4, II (1842).

ÄGER, ALBERT. 'Beiträge zur Tirolisch-Salzburgischen Bergwerks-Geschichte.' *Archiv für österreichische Geschichte,* LIII (1875), 337–456.

JANSEN, MAX. *Jakob Fugger der Reiche. Studien zur Fugger-Geschichte,* 3. Heft. Leipzig, 1910.

KOCH, ERNST. 'Das Hütten- und Hammerwerk der Fugger zu Hohenkirchen bei Georgenthal in Thüringen, 1495–1549.' *Zeitschrift des Vereins für Thüringische Geschichte,* N.F., XXVI (1926).

KROKER, ERNST. 'Leipzig und die sächsischen Bergwerke.' *Schriften des Vereins für die Geschichte Leipzigs,* IX (1909).

LANGER, JOHANNES. 'Der ostelbische Bergbau im und am Gebiet der Dresdner Heide und der sächs. Schweiz.' *Neues Archiv für sächsische Geschichte und Altertumskunde,* I (1929), 1–66.

MANNEL, GOTTFRIED. *Die Eisenhütten und Hämmer des Fürstentums Waldeck.* Leipzig, 1908.

MEISTER, A. 'Die Anfänge des Eisenindustrie in der Grafschaft Mark.' *Beiträge zur Geschichte Dortmunds und der Grafschaft Mark,* XVII (1909).

MÜCK, WALTER. *Der Mansfelder Kupferschieferbergbau in seiner rechtsgeschichtlichen Entwicklung.* 2 vols. Eisleben, 1910.

MÜLLNER, ALFONS. *Geschichte des Eisens.* Erste Abteilung. In *Krain, Görz und Istrien.* Vienna, 1909.

NEF, J. U. 'Silver Production in Central Europe, 1450–1618.' *Journ. Polit. Econ.* XLIX (1941), no. 4.

NEUBURG, CLAMOR. *Goslars Bergbau bis 1552.* Hanover, 1892.

—— 'Der Zusammenhang zwischen römischem und deutschem Bergbau.' *Festgaben für Wilhelm Lexis.* Jena, 1907.

OPET, OTTO. 'Das Gewerbschaftsrecht nach den deutschen Bergrechtsquellen des Mittelalters.' *Zeitschrift für Bergrecht,* XXXIV (1893).

PETER, KARL. 'Die Goldbergwerke bei Zuckmantel und Freiwaldau.' *Zeitschrift des Vereins für Geschichte und Altertum Schlesiens,* XIX (1885).

PFLUG, KARL. 'Zur Geschichte des Bergbaues im Waldenburger Berglande.' *Zeitschrift des Vereins für Geschichte und Altertum Schlesiens,* XLIII (1909).

SCHMÖLLER, GUSTAV. 'Die geschichtliche Entwicklung der Unternehmung.' *Jahrbuch für Gesetzgebung, Verwaltung und Volkswirtschaft im deutschen Reich,* XV (1891).

SCHNÜRLEN, MATHILDE. *Geschichte des Württembergischen Kupfer- und Silbererzbergbaus.* Berlin, 1921.

SIMONIN, L. 'De l'exploitation des mines et de la métallurgie en Toscane pendant l'antiquité et le moyen âge.' *Annales des mines,* ser. 5, XIV (1858), 557–615.

STEINBECK, AEMIL. *Geschichte des schlesischen Bergbaues.* Breslau, 1857.

STERNBERG, KASPAR. *Umrisse einer Geschichte der böhmischen Bergwerke.* 2 vols. Prague, 1836, 1838.

STODDART, ANNA M. *The Life of Paracelsus.* Philadelphia, 1911.

STRIEDER, JAKOB. *Studien zur Geschichte kapitalistischer Organisationsformen,* 2nd ed. Munich, 1925.

TOMASCHEK EDLER VON STRADOWA, J. A., *Das alte Bergrecht von Iglau.* Innsbruck, 1897.

UTSCH, RICHARD. *Die Entwicklung und volkswirtschaftliche Bedeutung des Eisenerzbergbaues und der Eisenindustrie im Siegerland.* Görlitz, 1913.

WEYHMANN, ALFRED. *Geschichte der älteren Lothringischen Eisenindustrie.* Metz, 1905.

WICK, WILHELM. *Die landesherrlichen Eisenhütten und Hämmer im ehemaligen Kurhessen bis zum Ende des XVII. Jahrhunderts.* Cassel, 1910.

WOLFSTRIGL-WOLFSKRON, M. R. VON. *Die Tiroler Erzbergbaue,* 1301–1665. Innsbruck, 1903. (This is the only comprehensive work on mining in the Tyrol during the Middle Ages, but it has not been well received by scholars. It is rather unintelligently and clumsily put together, and it is said by Stephan Worms to contain many errors of fact and of interpretation.)

WORMS, STEPHAN. *Schwazer Bergbau im fünfzehnten Jahrhundert.* Vienna, 1904.

ZYCHA, ADOLF. *Das Recht des ältesten deutschen Bergbaues bis ins 13. Jahrhundert.* Berlin, 1899.

—— 'Zur neuesten Literatur über die Wirtschafts- und Rechtsgeschichte des deutschen Bergbaus.' *Vierteljahrschrift für Soz. und Wirtschaftsgeschichte,* V (1907); VI (1908).

D. *France, Spain, and the Low Countries*

ARNOULD, G. *Le bassin houiller du couchant de Mons.* Mons, 1877.

BARDON, ACHILLE. *L'exploitation du bassin houiller d'Alais sous l'ancien régime.* Nîmes, 1898.

BEAUNE, HENRI. 'Note sur le régime des mines dans le duché de Bourgogne.' *Mém. de la société des antiquaires de France,* XXXI (1869).

BORLASE, W. C. *Tin Mining in Spain, Past and Present.* London, 1898.

BOUZY, ALF. 'Essai hist. sur l'ancien mandement d'Allevard.' *Bull. de la soc. de statistique de l'Isère,* I (1839).

BULARD, MARCEL. 'L'industrie du fer dans la Haute-Marne.' *Annales de géog.,* XIII (1904), 223–42, 310–21.

CHABRAND, ERNEST. *Essai historique sur la métallurgie du fer et de l'acier en Dauphiné et en Savoie.* Grenoble, 1898.

CHAZAUD, A. M. 'Les mines de houille de Charbonnier (Puy-de-Dome) au XVe siècle.' *Bulletin de la soc. d'émulation du dépt. de l'Allier,* X (1868).

CORBIER. 'Notice sur les forges impériales de la Chaussade.' *Bull. de la soc. nivernaise des lettres, sciences et arts,* ser. 2, IV (1869).

COUFFON, OLIVIER. *Les mines de charbon en Anjou.* Angers, 1911.

DÉCAMPS, G. 'Mémoire historique sur l'origine et les développements de l'industrie houillère dans le bassin du couchant de Mons.' *Société des arts et des lettres du Hainant, publications,* ser. 4, V (1880); ser. 5, I (1889).

DESTRAY, P. 'Note sur les anciennes forges du prieuré de la Charité.' *Mém. de la soc. acad. du Nivernais,* XVII (1913).

—— 'Les houillères de la Machine (Nivernais) au 16e siècle.' *Mémoires et documents pour servir à l'histoire du commerce et de l'industrie en France* (ed. Julien Hayem). Ser. 4. Paris, 1916.

FEBVRE, LUCIEN. *Philippe II et la Franche-Comté.* Paris, 1912.

FINOT, J. 'La seigneurerie de Ronchamp et l'origine de l'exploitation des houillères de cette localité, 1220–1789.' *Rev. d'hist. nobilliaire et d'archéol. héraldique,* 1882.

FORMEVILLE, A. DE. *Les barons fossiers et les férons de Normandie.* Caen, 1852.

GÉRIN, RICARD, H. DE. 'Mines et mineurs autrefois et aujourd'hui. Etude économique sur les charbonnages de Provence du 15 au 19 siècle.' *Soc. stat. de Marseille,* XLVII (1906–7).

GIRAUD, J.-B. *Documents pour servir à l'histoire de l'armement au moyen âge*, I. Lyons, 1895.

—— *Documents pour l'histoire de l'armement au moyen âge et à la renaissance*, II. Lyons, 1904.

GORIS, J. A. *Étude sur les colonies marchandes méridionales à Anvers de 1488 à 1567.* Louvain, 1925.

GRAS, L. J. *Essai sur l'histoire de la quincaillerie et petite métallurgie à Saint-Etienne et dans la région stéphanoise comparée aux régions concurrentes.* Saint-Etienne, 1904.

—— *Histoire économique générale des mines de la Loire.* Saint-Etienne, 1922.

HÄBLER, KONRAD. *Die Geschichte der Fugger'schen Handlung in Spanien.* Weimar, 1897.

HAMILTON, EARL J. *American Treasure and the Price Revolution in Spain, 1501–1650.* Cambridge (Mass.), 1934.

—— *Money, Prices and Wages in Valencia, Aragon, and Navarre, 1351–1500.* Cambridge (Mass.), 1936.

HAUSER, HENRI. *Ouvriers du temps passé.* Paris, 1899.

HENAUX, F. *Fabrique d'armes de Liège.* Liège, 1858.

LAMÉ-FLEURY. *De la législation minérale sous l'ancienne monarchie.* Paris, 1857.

LECORNU, L. 'Sur le métallurgie du fer en Basse-Normandie.' *Mém. de l'acad. nat. des sciences, arts, et belles-lettres de Caen*, 1884.

LEJEUNE, JEAN. *La formation du capitalisme moderne dans la principauté de Liège au 16ᵉ Siècle.* Paris, 1939.

LEROUX, MAURICE. *L'industrie du fer dans le Perche.* Paris, 1916.

LEVAINVILLE, J. *L'industrie du fer en France.* Paris, 1922.

LOPEZ, ROBERTO. *Contributo alla storia delle miniere argentifere di Sardegna.* Milan, 1936.

LUCE, SIMÉON. 'De l'exploitation des mines et de la condition des ouvriers mineurs en France au XVe siècle.' *Revue des questions historiques*, XXI (1877).

MALHERBE, RENIER. 'Historique de l'exploitation de la houille dans le pays de Liège jusqu'à nos jours.' *Mémoire de la société libre d'émulation de Liège*, n.sér., II. Liège, 1862.

MASSÉ, ALFRED. *Monographies nivernaises.* Nevers, 1913.

MIGNERON, M. 'The Mining Laws of France.' *Trans. Roy. Geog. Soc. Cornwall*, VI, 239–58.

NIMAL, H. DE. 'La métallurgie à l'exposition de Charleroi en 1911 avec des notes historiques sur la forgerie.' *Livre d'or de l'exposition de Charleroi.* Charleroi, 1913.

PAGÉ, CAMILLE. *La coutellerie depuis l'origine jusqu'à nos jours.* 6 vols. Chatellerault, 1896–1904.

PIRENNE, HENRI. *Histoire de Belgique*, I–III. Brussels, 1900–32.

ROUZAUD, HENRI. *Histoire d'une mine au mineur. La mine de Rancié depuis le moyen âge jusqu'à la Révolution.* Toulouse, 1908.

SAINT SAUD, COMTE DE. 'Privilèges concernant les maîtres de forges.' *Bulletin de la société archéologique du Périgord*, XXVII (1900).

SCLAFERT, THÉRÈSE. *L'industrie du fer dans la région d'Allevard au moyen âge.* Grenoble, 1926.

VERNEILH, BARON DE. 'Notes sur les anciennes forges du Périgord et du Limousin.' *Revue des sociétés savantes*, ser. 6, IV (1876).

VILLEFOSSE, HÉRON DE. *De la richesse minérale.* 3 vols. Paris, 1810, 1819.

E. *Great Britain and Scandinavia*

ABRAHAMS, ISRAEL. 'Joachim Gaunse: a mining incident in the reign of Queen Elizabeth.' *Jewish Hist. Soc. Trans.*, IV. London, 1899–1901.

ASHTON, T. S. *Iron and Steel in the Industrial Revolution.* Manchester, 1924.

ATKINSON, STEPHEN. *The Discoverie and Historie of the Gold Mynes in Scotland, written in 1619.* Edinburgh (Bannatyne Club), 1825.

CUNNINGHAM, A. S. *Mining in the Kingdom of Fife.* Edinburgh, 1913.

FFOULKES, CHARLES. *The Gun-Founders of England.* Cambridge, 1937.

GALLOWAY, ROBERT L. *A History of Coal Mining in Great Britain.* London, 1882.

GALLOWAY, ROBERT L. *Annals of Coal Mining and the Coal Trade.* London, 1898.
GOUGH, JOHN W. *The Mines of Mendip.* Oxford, 1930.
HAMILTON, HENRY. *The English Brass and Copper Industries to 1800.* London, 1926.
HECKSCHER, ELI F. *Sveriges Ekonomiska Historia från Gustav Vasa.* 2 vols. Stockholm, 1935–6.
—— 'Un grand chapitre de l'histoire du fer: le monopole suédois.' *Annales d'histoire économique et sociale,* IV (1932), 127–39, 225–41.
HOUGHTON, THOMAS. *The Compleat Miner; or a Collection of the Laws, Liberties, ancient Customs...and Privileges of the several Mines and Miners in the Counties of Derby, Gloucester and Somerset.* 3 pts. London, 1687–88.
JENKIN, A. K. HAMILTON. *The Cornish Miner.* London, 1927.
JENKINS, RHYS. 'Iron-Making in the Forest of Dean.' *Newcomen Soc. Trans.,* VI (1925–6).
—— 'The Rise and Fall of the Sussex Iron Industry.' *Newcomen Soc. Trans.,* I (1920–1).
LAPSLEY, G. T. 'The Account Roll of a Fifteenth-Century Iron Master.' *Engl. Hist. Rev.* XIV (1899).
LARSON, HENRIETTA M. 'Notes and Documents: A Medieval Swedish Mining Company.' *Journal of Economic and Business History,* II, 545–59. Cambridge (Mass.), 1930.
LEADER, R. E. *History of the Company of Cutlers of Hallamshire,* I. Sheffield, 1905.
LEWIS, E. A. 'The Development of Industry and Commerce in Wales during the Middle Ages.' *Roy. Hist. Soc. Trans.,* n.ser., XVII (1903), 121–73.
LEWIS, G. R. *The Stannaries.* Cambridge (Mass.), 1907.
LLOYD, G. I. H. *The Cutlery Trades.* London, 1913.
LOWER, MARK ANTONY. 'Historical and Archaeological Notices of the Iron Works of the County of Sussex.' *Sussex Arch. Collections,* II (1849), 169–220.
MACADAM, I. 'Notes on the Ancient Iron Industry of Scotland.' *Proc. Soc. Antiq. Scot.* XXI, (1886–87).
NEF, J. U. *The Rise of the British Coal Industry.* 2 vols. London, 1932.
—— 'Note on the Progress of Iron Production in England, 1540–1640.' *Journ. Polit. Econ.,* XLIV (1936), 398–403.
NICHOLL, JOHN. *Some Account of the Worshipful Company of Ironmongers,* 2nd ed. London, 1866.
NICHOLLS, HENRY GEORGE. *Iron-Making in the Olden Times as instanced in the Ancient Mines, Forges, and Furnaces of the Forest of Dean.* London, 1866.
PATRICK, ROBERT W. C. *Early Records Relating to Mining in Scotland.* Edinburgh, 1878.
SALZMAN, LOUIS FRANCIS. *English Industries of the Middle Ages,* 2nd ed. Oxford, 1923.
SOPWITH, THOS. *An Account of the Mining Districts of Alston Moor, Weardale and Teesdale in Cumberland and Durham.* Alnwick, 1833.
STRAKER, ERNEST. *Wealden Iron.* London, 1931.
Victoria History of the Counties of: Cornwall, Derby, Durham, Gloucester, Lancaster, Nottingham, Shropshire, Warwick, York.

CHAPTER VIII

Building in Stone in Medieval Western Europe

(i) A short general sketch, with some indication of the sources of information, will be found in Werner Sombart, *Der Moderne Kapitalismus* (Munich and Leipzig, 1921), especially vol. II, pt. 2, pp. 772–79. There is a more recent treatment in G. G. Coulton, *Art and the Reformation* (1928). Particular aspects of the subject are treated with reference to several countries in the following:

BRIGGS, MARTIN S. *A Short History of the Building Crafts.* Oxford, 1925.
—— *The Architect in History.* Oxford, 1927.
TOUT, T. F. *Mediaeval Town Planning.* Manchester, 1934.
VIOLLET-LE-DUC, E. *Military Architecture.* (Engl. transl., 2nd ed.) Oxford and London, 1879.

(ii) *Great Britain.* A list of the more important manuscript and printed sources and of secondary authorities is given in D. Knoop and G. P. Jones, *The Mediaeval Mason* (Manchester, 1933). The following have appeared since that date:

BROOKS, F. W. 'A Medieval Brick-yard at Hull.' *Journ. Brit. Archaeol. Assoc.*, ser. 3, IV, 1939.

HARVEY, JOHN H. 'The Medieval Office of Works.' *Journ. Brit. Archaeol. Assoc.*, ser. 3, VI, 1941.

KNOOP, D. and JONES, G. P. 'London Bridge and its Builders.' *Ars Quatuor Coronatorum*, XLVII, 1934.

—— —— 'Henry Yevele and his Associates.' *Journ. Roy. Inst. Brit. Architects*, XLII (1935), ser. 3, No. 14.

—— —— 'The Rise of the Mason-Contractor.' *Journ. Roy. Inst. Brit. Architects.* XLIII (1936), ser. 3, no. 20.

—— —— 'The Impressment of Masons for Windsor Castle.' *Economic History* (Suppl. to *Econ. Journ.*), 1937.

—— —— 'The Decline of the Mason-Architect in England. *Journ. Roy. Inst. Brit. Architects.* XLIV (1937), ser. 3, no. 19.

—— —— 'The Impressment of Masons in the Middle Ages. *Econ. Hist. Rev.* Nov. 1937.

—— —— 'Overtime in the Age of Henry VIII.' *Economic History* (Suppl. to *Econ. Journ.*), 1938.

—— —— 'The Medieval English Quarry.' *Econ. Hist. Rev.* Nov. 1938.

—— —— *The Scottish Mason and the Mason Word.* Manchester, 1939.

The following, though included in the bibliography to *The Mediaeval Mason*, may be separately noted here as especially important :

THOMPSON, A. H. 'Mediaeval Building Documents and what we learn from them.' *Somerset Archaeol. Soc. Trans.* LXVI.

(iii) *France.* An account of building materials and technique and of medieval architects will be found in the first chapter of C. Enlart, *Manuel d'Archéologie Française*: vol. I, *Architecture Religieuse* (Paris, 1902); vol. II, *Architecture Civile et Militaire* (Paris, 1904). Most of the chapters have separate bibliographies appended.

LE CACHEUX, P. *Le Livre de Comptes de Thomas du Marest.* Rouen, 1905.

FAGNIEZ, G. *Études sur l'Industrie et la Classe Industrielle à Paris au XIIIe et au XIVe Siècle.* Paris, 1877.

—— *Documents relatifs à l'Histoire de l'Industrie et du Commerce en France.* Paris, 1898–1900.

MORTET, V. (vols. I and II) and DESCHAMPS, P. (vol. II). *Recueil de Textes relatifs à l'Histoire de l'Architecture et à la Condition des Architectes en France au Moyen Age.* Paris, 1911, 1929.

STEIN, H. *Les Architectes des Cathédrales Gothiques.* Paris, 1929.

(iv) *Germany.*

BEISSEL, S. *Die Bauführung des Mittelalters.* Freiburg im Breisgau, 1889.

JANNER, F. *Die Bauhütten des deutschen Mittelalters.* Leipzig, 1876.

(v) *Spain.*

PUIG Y CADAFALCH, J., DE FALGUERA, A. and GODAY Y CASALS, J. *L'Arquitectura Romànica a Catalunya,* 2 vols. Barcelona, 1919–1921.

STREET, G. E. *Some Account of Gothic Architecture in Spain* (ed. King, Georgiana K.). 2 vols. London and Toronto, 1914.

(vi) *Italy*

FOSTER, J. *Vasari's Lives of the most eminent Painters, Sculptors and Architects.* London, 1884–94.

(vii) On the organisation of craftsmen, besides most of the books and articles noted above, the following may be cited:

DOREN, A. *Das Florentiner Zunftwesen*. Stuttgart and Berlin, 1908.

GOBLET D'ALVIELLA, COUNT. 'The Quatuor Coronati in Belgium.' *Ars Quatuor Coronatorum*, XIII, 1900.

KNOOP, D. and JONES, G. P. 'The London Masons' Company.' *Economic History* (Suppl. to *Econ. Journ.*). Feb. 1939.

—— —— *The Genesis of Freemasonry*. Manchester, 1947, chapter III.

KNOOP, D., JONES, G. P. and HAMER, D. *The Two Earliest Masonic MSS*. Manchester, 1938.

SAINT-LÉON, E. M. *Le Compagnonnage*. Paris, 1901.

(vii) On the organisation of sentiment, besides most of the books just enumerated above, the following may be cited:

Dorgan, A. *Les Organismes Fantômes*. Sentiment and Reason, 1918.
Gaultier, P. *A notice*. *Choses*. *The Quinary German in Belgium*. *The Quinary Volitionum*, XII, 1917.
Kimball, D. and Ramsey, P. *The Frontier Artisan Company*. *Notes on Programme*, 10–12 in. Jointy, Feb. 1919.
—— *The Country of Programme*. *Manchester*, 1919, chapter II.
Nadier, D. Jones, G. P. and Hanson, P. *The Lancashire Cotton Industry*. Manchester, 1934.
Saint et Cox. *Technics and Companionate*. Paris, 1921.

INDEX